# American
## mashUP

## A Popular Culture Reader

### Aaron Michael Morales
Indiana State University

PEARSON

Boston   Columbus   Indianapolis   New York   San Francisco   Upper Saddle River
Amsterdam   Cape Town   Dubai   London   Madrid   Milan   Munich   Paris   Montreal   Toronto
Delhi   Mexico City   São Paulo   Sydney   Hong Kong   Seoul   Singapore   Taipei   Tokyo

Senior Editor: Brad Potthoff
Senior Development Editor: David Kear
Senior Marketing Manager: Sandra McGuire
Senior Supplements Editor: Donna Campion
Production Manager: Denise Phillip
Project Coordination, Editorial Services, and Text Design: Electronic Publishing Services Inc., NYC

Art Rendering and Electronic Page Makeup: TexTech
Senior Cover Design Manager/Cover Designer: Nancy Danahy
Cover Image: Nancy Danahy
Senior Manufacturing Buyer: Roy Pickering
Printer/Binder: R. R. Donnelley/Crawfordsville
Cover Printer: Lehigh-Phoenix Color/ Hagerstown

Credits and acknowledgments borrowed from other sources and reproduced, with permission, in this textbook appear on the appropriate page within text [and on page 604].

---

**Library of Congress Cataloging-in-Publication Data**
Morales, Aaron Michael.
    American mashup : a popular culture reader / Aaron Michael Morales.
        p. cm.
    Includes index.
    ISBN 978-0-205-82372-7
1. Readers—Popular culture.   2. Academic writing—Study and teaching—United States.
3. Popular culture—United States—Problems, exercises, etc.   4. Report writing—Study and teaching—United States.   5. Critical thinking—Problems, exercises, etc.   6. English language—Rhetoric—Problems, exercises, etc.   I. Title.
    PE1417.M6184 2011
    808'.0427—dc23

                                                                                2011032869

10 9 8 7 6 5 4 3 2 1—DOC—14 13 12 11

ISBN 10: 0-205-82372-6
ISBN 13: 978-0-205-82372-7

# Contents

## Chapter 3    Identity Construction    63

## Chapter 4    Social Media    133

## Chapter 5   Mass Media   193

## Chapter 6   Sexuality and Relationships   244

# Chapter 7    Violence    299

# Chapter 8    Alcohol and Drugs    362

## Chapter 9   Advertising and Shopping   424

# Chapter 10    Heroes and Celebrities    482

# Chapter 11    Work and Careers    543

# Preface

What separates current college students from previous generations—and significantly so—is that they write more on a daily basis than any generation to come before them. All day long students log into Facebook and update their statuses. They write notes and they send emails. They tweet and text. They comment on each other's online pictures, statuses, news stories, and comments, and then they comment on their comments' comments, and on and on. They easily and effortlessly write hundreds, often thousands of words a day without giving it a second thought. But when it comes time to write an essay for a class, they sometimes lock up, unable to construct a couple of sentences about a topic, straining to push onward to the minimum page requirement. They think they cannot write.

Students can become unengaged when they are met with a series of essay options that do not pique their interest. A student may pick her favorite topic of the lot, but imagine if she could approach various selections within the chapter (or other chapters) and combine them to answer a larger question. Imagine that the student wants to incorporate other pop culture texts, such as iPhone apps or Facebook groups, or some new form of technology or social networking that has emerged since the publication of this book. We professors speak constantly about the importance of critical thinking, and then we sometimes pass up opportunities to allow our students a meaningful way to critically think about many layers of text at once. Sometimes, we do not offer them the opportunity to do this because we worry more about ensuring that they finally get what an argumentative essay or a compare-contrast essay *is*. In reality, many of these writing strategies can be combined easily to allow for a more sophisticated approach to student writing. This book teaches students to critically and thoughtfully read texts (both traditional and multimedia), and then it sets them free to make complex connections on their own. We build on the textual readings they do on a daily basis, unaware of the fact that they are judging, critiquing, and evaluating texts without consciously thinking about the process.

Students simply cannot care about something they deem irrelevant to their lives. The example I often use is of a fatal car crash. If you drive by a wreck that obviously resulted in a fatality, you are certainly disturbed and saddened by this knowledge. But think of how much the tragedy would multiply if you realized that same car crash had claimed the life of someone you know. *Then* you are invested in that moment. You care because it is someone you know, and that directly affects your life. Now it is a much more meaningful moment. It's the difference between an ad in a textbook that students *might* have encountered in their childhood (Pepsi's "Generation Next" campaign, for instance), versus one that most likely had an impact on their actual spending habits in very recent years (the iPhone ads by Apple, Google's catchy Android phone ads, or even the much-lauded Nike 2010 World Cup advertisement would be more relevant examples). If nothing else, the students can be led in a discussion about these iPhone versus Android ads (which nearly all students have seen) and it would take no time at all to divide the class into pro-iPhone and pro-Android groups. They have an investment in a product that they might not even be aware they had. They have a reason for their preference, some of which undoubtedly can be linked to the differences in marketing for the two phones and each brand's identity. The students know this. They've just most likely never articulated it openly.

In short, *American Mashup* appeals to your students in the same way an iPhone might appeal to them over an Android. We include much more than academic journals about popular culture, and we move beyond the usual authors chosen for pop culture readers. Instead, we have gone to the sources that help create and influence popular culture. We go to the blogs, the magazines, the advertisers, and yes, even the esteemed pop culture gurus. We incorporate the current trends in music, fashion, advertising, entertainment, and technology to provide students with fodder for essay assignments and in-class discussions.

Today's students inherently understand the concept of semiotics. They read texts around themselves all day long, every single day. They "digg" and "like" and "stumbleupon" and "tag" articles and pictures and videos all the time. They review everything from movies to apartment complexes. They rate their professors and employers. They interact with various media nonstop. The concept of "multitasking" is foreign to them. Constantly dividing their attention between messages is the norm.

What *American Mashup* sets out to do is to give credit to students for what they already do, while simultaneously teaching them how to harness these skills and learn the rhetorical strategies that will allow them to write about the culture around them. Rather than imply that they do not interact with texts or read into them, the textbook points out the ways in which they already accomplish this bit of work. Once students are aware of the manner in which they already engage in contextualizing messages that bombard them, they will understand that this is a task they are quite capable of doing in a more sophisticated and meaningful fashion.

As a concept, the Mashup approach is embedded in the text. It encourages reading on multiple levels, just as it encourages reading and writing across topics and strategies. Students will become aware of how these topics are all interrelated in one way or another, and they will benefit from the level of comfort they feel with the text. It is, after all, a text that strives to engage students on the issues closest to them. And, if students are in constant contact with a variety of media throughout the course of a day, enabling them to synthesize these texts and topics is not nearly as difficult to accomplish as one might think.

Most importantly, *American Mashup* is valuable to college students because of how the text simultaneously prepares them for college writing across a wide variety of disciplines and exposes them to writing styles and practices that they will both encounter and create beyond their college experience. It teaches them to think and to write critically for college, and it prepares them to engage and to interact with the outside world even after they have graduated.

## Mashing It Up

*American Mashup* introduces an entirely new writing strategy—the Mashup essay. The Mashup essay is a hybrid form of the ten most commonly taught essay-writing strategies. It calls for students to synthesize multiple selections within a chapter, or even across the various chapters. It also allows for students to incorporate other texts with which they interact on a regular basis into their essays. In short, *American Mashup* puts theory into practice. It doesn't just talk about pop culture; it encourages students to become active participants in popular culture. It gives them an opportunity to read, critique, and interact with popular culture in a meaningful and lively way.

The **"MashItUp"** discussion and writing prompts featured in each chapter will enable students and instructors to respond to multiple selections within the chapter, enabling a more critical, comparative, and textual analysis approach, without explicitly stating so. The idea is that each chapter will lend itself to all ten commonly taught writing strategies: Descriptive Essays, Narrative Essays, Illustrative Essays, Process-Analysis Essays, Compare-Contrast Essays, Classification Essays, Definition-Informative Essays, Cause-Effect Essays, Argumentative Essays, and Research Essays. Furthermore, in the "MashItUp" sections of each chapter, students will be given the opportunity to write from multiple strategic approaches, thereby elevating their critical thinking/arguing skills beyond the simpler single-strategy approach. These prompts will also encourage students' creativity, allowing for them to put the idea of different texts into practice themselves by potentially incorporating media beyond just the ink and page of a traditional college composition essay.

Each chapter contains one **"Mashup essay,"** which is given a more detailed introduction and dissection than the other selections within the chapter. Each Mashup essay provides a model for students to use when writing their own Mashup essays. Before students read the selections, the Mashup essay introductions thoroughly break down the ways in which each Mashup essay author employs various writing techniques, as well as how the authors incorporate a wide variety of texts and media into the essay. To further illustrate this concept, each Mashup essay is accompanied by a flowchart that shows the different writing methods used, as well as the various traditional and multimedia texts. Finally, each Mashup essay is also annotated so that students can see specifically how the different texts and writing styles are used within the essay itself.

For the students' convenience, each of the writing strategies is briefly defined and explained in the introductory chapters, prior to the explanation of the Mashup essay and the sample student essay.

## Features

Students and faculty will be able to find a common ground on which to build discussions, essay topics, classroom projects, group work, and even projects that involve engagement with the outside world. The possibilities for its applications are limitless. Students can engage their campus community, the community in which their college or university is situated, online communities, or virtually any location deemed interesting to them.

In an effort to facilitate discussion and purposeful essay topics, *American Mashup* provides ample essay topic suggestions in each chapter, as well as a number of other apparatuses to expand the text's usefulness in the classroom. Following are some of the text's features:

- The **chapter introduction.** Each chapter begins with a brief introduction that situates the subsequent selections within the context of the chapter's topic. It allows students to look at our popular obsessions as Americans and find meaning where there might not appear to be any. What the introductions don't do is prod students in one direction or another. This is not a right- or left-leaning textbook. There are no "right" or "wrong" readings of a text, provided students can back up their readings with some sort of textual evidence.

- The **"Let's Start Here"** section prefacing each selection is meant to give students a lens with which to view the piece that follows. The intent is not to manipulate the students' viewpoints on the text, but rather to give them an entry point into reading the text. The goal is also to situate the text in terms of the chapter topic and how it can be read in order to find meaning in the text.

- The **"Let's Pause Here"** section functions as a means of enabling the beginnings of classroom discussion. By working off of students' immediate reactions, we hope to focus their thoughts on various important elements of each selection. These are to be seen as "thinking points," which, when considered, will form a springboard for in-depth classroom discussion.

- The **"Let's Take It Further"** notes following each selection strive to generate discussion beyond the classroom, whether in the form of an essay or a continued dialogue in groups or online. These notes primarily focus on the main points of the text, allowing for yet another method of dissecting the text's meaning while encouraging students to synthesize chapter selections with outside sources. Additionally, these notes can easily be used as writing prompts that will directly address the text, as well as the most common writing strategies used in college composition classrooms.

- The **"Let's Connect"** feature of the textbook will encourage students to "like" *American Mashup* on Facebook where they will be presented with newer, more current readings that have come into print since the textbook's production. This alleviates the dilemma of having a pop culture textbook be out of date as soon as it is in print. It will also bridge the gap between editions, so that students will have access to the most up-to-date information until the newest edition comes into print. *American Mashup* is on Facebook at www.facebook.com/americanmashup.

- The **"Pop-out"** glossary. Rather than add a glossary to the end of the book, or place words at the beginning or end of a selection or chapter, as is often done, we define the word in question (such as "ameliorate" in the "Picture Imperfect" article) in the margin of the page where the word is used.

## For the Instructor

The Instructor's Manual provides a chapter-by-chapter breakdown of the selections and themes within the textbook, in order to facilitate further potential connections across chapters or to aid in the process of creating an entirely different thematic Mashup course. Each selection is briefly summarized in terms of content and theme, as well as cross-listed with other selections within the text with which a logical pairing could be made. The discussion and writing prompts are identified for instructors and coded to the various writing strategies being suggested with each prompt or question. The Instructor's Manual also includes sample syllabi for semester and quarter-based courses, as well as syllabi arranged by theme, writing strategy, and genre of selections. It also includes teaching tips, potential group work, first-day classroom exercises, and many more helpful tips and ideas for instructors.

## Acknowledgments

The author would like to thank the following people for their support and assistance: the entire Morales clan for supporting and believing in me during this project—particularly Elizabeth, without whom this book's concept would never have seen the light of day; Dr. Robert Perrin, for being a wonderfully professional role model and leader, as well as a good friend; Suzanne Phelps-Chambers, for your excitement and enthusiasm for the Mashup project; Molly Riggs, for suggesting that I pitch the idea to Pearson in the very beginning; and David Kear, for being a wonderful, honest, humorous, and brutal editor—all of which are the qualities of the best editors.

I am grateful for the honest feedback and criticism of the following people who reviewed the text in its various stages:

Joyce Miller Bean, DePaul University; Darcy Brandel, Marygrove College; Meghan Brewer, Temple University; Gina Claywell, Murray State University; Linsey Cuti, Kankakee Community College; Elizabeth Whitmore Funk, Marymount College; Carole Ganim, Miami University Middletown; Rachel Groner, Temple University; Katherine D. Harris, San Jose State University; Brooke Hughes, California State University–Bakersfield; Glenn Hutchinson, Johnson C. Smith University; Parmita Kapadia, Northern Kentucky University; Leslie Lim, Central Oregon Community College; Nicholas Mansito III, Broward College; Jamie O'Connor, American Academy of Art; John Prince, North Carolina Central University; John Ribar, Palm Beach State College; Rebecca Rudd, Citrus College; Sharon Samuels, Miami-Dade College North; Lisa Shaw, Miami-Dade College North; Tara Timberman, Community College of Philadelphia; Stephanie Tingley, Youngstown State University; and Alina Vanciu, Cerritos College.

And a very special thanks to Leslie J. Brown for her research and writing, featured throughout this text.

## About the Author

*Rachel Wedding McLelland*

Aaron Michael Morales is a teacher, fiction writer, essayist, book reviewer, and performance artist from Tucson, Arizona. He is a graduate of Purdue University's M.F.A. program. Currently, he is an associate professor of English and Gender Studies at Indiana State University, where he teaches composition, creative writing, contemporary American and Latino literature, and masculinity studies. His first novel, *Drowning Tucson*, was released by Coffee House Press in 2010, and he recently completed his second novel, *Eat Your Children*. Morales is a regular contributor to *MultiCultural Review, Latino Poetry Review,* and *Terre Haute Living,* as well as the fiction editor for *Grasslands Review.*

# Reading Popular Culture

## The College Composition Course

For many students, a college composition course is the place where your writing will become more sophisticated and where you will learn to employ critical thinking skills that will serve you for the entirety of your college careers and the rest of your lives. This is important because, regardless of your major, mastering the skill of writing will dramatically affect your academic success, as well as your success after graduation. After all, when you graduate and apply for a job, you will undoubtedly be required to submit a cover letter and a résumé, and how well (or poorly) you write will factor heavily into whether you are granted an interview. Graduates who have the skills to articulate their thoughts in writing will stand out from those who do not. This is an easy way for potential employers to thin the applicant pool. Ultimately, in your college composition class you will build on your previous writing foundations and develop new and long-lasting writing skills and habits.

The purpose of taking a popular culture approach to a composition course is equally simple. Studies have found that students produce more lively and engaged writing when they are given the opportunity to discuss topics relevant to their lives, many of which can be found in our popular culture. Today's incoming college freshmen know popular culture—they are positively steeped in and invested in popular culture more than any generation that has come before them. This statement will only become more accurate with each passing year, as technology and global consciousness marry cultures throughout the world, and as we become more connected to each other as a society.

Take a moment to ponder your daily activities. The things that take up large portions of your leisure time—fashion, TV shows, websites, apps, networking tools, and other technologies—are powerful texts that carry meanings within them far beyond their surface implications. All of the elements of daily life with which you interact have messages that can be interpreted, have goals they strive to achieve, and affect the decisions we make, sometimes without our even knowing. When a course is taught with a focus on popular culture and all of its facets, you will find, by virtue of engaging in and reading the culture that surrounds you, that you leave the course a better critical thinker and observer of the world, and you have a better understanding of your role in it.

A popular culture reader—and a composition course designed around the theme of popular culture—gives you the opportunity to rein in all of this information that surrounds you, and it allows you the opportunity to find meaning in the relentless bombardment of information we are subjected to in our daily lives. A writing course that focuses on popular culture helps you to dissect the signs, trends, and movements that exist everywhere in our world. Most importantly, this approach to a composition course gives you the opportunity to put this concept of examining texts on a deeper level into practice by allowing you to write about your observations and incorporate them into essays, as well as applying these techniques to your entire academic experience. You will become a more observant member of society, and you will be able to better articulate your observations to others.

So how will all of this be accomplished? First, we have included timely selections of topics ranging from violence in our culture to our obsession with heroes and celebrities. There are chapters on sexuality and relationships, and chapters on the role of drugs and alcohol in our culture. You will be reading essays that address these (and other) topics, as well as bringing in various forms of media—the sort with which you interact on a daily basis. These sources will include blog posts, YouTube clips, excerpts from novels, works of art, and even advertisements. You will be encouraged not only to see the value of all these types of media and the meaning buried within each, but you will also learn how to incorporate different forms of media into your own writing as well as learn how to write *about* texts other than traditional print essays and articles. In effect, rather than simply stating that *The Wire* is one of your favorite TV shows, you will be able to write about what makes it a good show, and potentially go even further by outlining the way urban, drug-infested environments are portrayed in the series.

Another element to this popular culture reader, and the design of this course, is that you will be given the opportunity to write essays using more than one writing strategy. We call it the Mashup essay. Put simply, a Mashup essay utilizes more than one writing strategy, which will enable you to take a multifaceted (or mashed up) approach to any given topic. For example, you will be able to incorporate argumentation into a narrative essay, or bring research into an informative essay in which you compare and contrast a company and a website. The possibilities and benefits of mashing up various writing strategies, as well as various types of media sources, make this approach to writing unlike that used in any other type of composition textbook. These days, when people regularly remix and mashup songs, videos, and newscasts online and place them on YouTube as parodies, it makes perfect sense to bring this approach into the classroom to breathe new life into the writing process.

In short, by using the idea of popular culture and our mashup approach to produce sophisticated college-level essays, you will equip yourself with the tools to apply the critical thinking and analytical skills acquired here to your academic studies elsewhere. You will be able to incorporate numerous writing strategies into essays of any subject, in virtually any course, with more confidence and skill. And you might even enjoy the process of picking apart the world around you and commenting on it in a meaningful way.

## Defining Popular Culture

In its simplest definition, popular culture is all around us. It is the stuff with which we surround ourselves: our TV shows, our celebrity obsessions, our iPhones, and our laptops. Popular culture is also the brand of our clothing and the summer's biggest blockbuster film. It is the millions of blog posts and the tens of millions of Tweets produced every month. Our Facebook profiles, our tattoos and piercings, and our favorite music all comprise popular culture, as do the popular fashion trends in America and the ways in which Americans, in general, define ourselves in contrast to the rest of the world. These are the elements of popular culture about which most people are aware.

Yet, on a more critical level, popular culture is a somewhat complicated concept. It is indeed that which is popular in our culture, in the now, but it is also an accumulation of our cultural elements that have remained constant over the years. For example, cars and American culture go hand in hand. Yes, drive-in movie theaters might be a thing of the past, but all teenagers still look forward to turning 16. It is a pivotal and meaningful age within our culture. Why? Put simply, every American teenager inherently understands the significance of getting a driver's license and a first car. A first car means hitting the road. It means independence and freedom. It means getting out of the house and not having to depend on someone else for a ride. The act of learning to drive is one of the classic American rites of passage. This has been a cultural constant since the birth of the very first Model-T Ford, and so it has become thoroughly engrained in the popular culture of our country.

Try making a list of very American institutions or traits. One brief list of the most popular American experiences might include the following: the McDonald's Happy Meal, apple pie, frozen pizza, french fries, chili-dogs, drive-thru dining, or even Coke. Notice these are all food-related items. The same sort of list could be compiled just as quickly when thinking of bands, sports, movies, actors, books, clothing, vehicles, or any other element of our culture.

Of course, there is much more to the American identity than just our popular culture. Although you may not have heard the term "high culture" before, it is probably a familiar concept as well. When people think of art galleries, attending the opera, or having a vacation home, we realize that this is indeed a part of culture, but it is usually not what the general public takes part in regularly. After all, opera performances aren't available in all locations of our country; they tend to be in our largest cities, and tickets are usually expensive enough that most people consider them to be unaffordable. Some people who do not regularly attend art gallery openings and receptions find the idea boring. So, while high culture is a *part* of American culture as a whole, it is not thought of as popular culture because the general population doesn't take an interest in it. It is a slice of our culture accessible to a limited number of participants. Popular culture, on the other hand, is accessible to everyone, regardless of background, which is precisely what makes it popular.

Americans have our own popular culture obsessions as a society. We have our particular famous bands, actors, politicians, and even writers. Regardless of the part of the country in which you were raised or your economic or cultural background, many of these elements of our culture will be familiar to you. This is where the real distinction between popular culture and other cultures in America is made. While we are a country of many cultures (ethnic, racial, religious, economic, political, sexual, etc.), it is the things that bubble to the top, the shared cultural experiences such as those mentioned above, that come to be known as popular culture. Consider the fact that you, or maybe even your parents, might not care about Tiger Woods as an athletic or cultural icon. Despite that fact, you know who he is and that he's famous for his accomplishments in golf, even if you don't watch the sport. More interestingly, it would be nearly impossible for anyone living in the United States to not have heard about Tiger Woods's extramarital affairs and ensuing divorce. These are the popular culture elements of Tiger Woods about which most people have a general awareness.

Our American culture—both high and popular—is very particular to our country and its people. There are elements of our culture—our language, our lifestyle, our political system, our bodily gestures, even our style of dress—that set us apart from many countries in the world. However, as the world becomes increasingly connected, we are finding that American popular culture is seeping into other cultures while others seep into our own, in what is turning out to be a reciprocal relationship of cultural sharing and blending.

Perhaps you've seen a television advertisement soliciting donations to feed the poor in another country. Maybe, if you looked close enough, you might have noticed a child in one of these TV ads wearing a Mickey Mouse shirt. Did that strike you as odd or out of place, or did you even notice? For better or for worse, American popular culture seems to be invading other cultures more and more quickly, and because of this it is important to consider further implications of American culture as they move from popularity in our country alone to the larger world. Is it a bad thing or a good thing when another culture adopts elements of our own? There are some intriguing arguments for both sides of this debate.

Rap music, which has always been considered a completely American genre of music because it was invented here 40 years ago, can now be heard being performed in virtually every language on the planet. Try Googling the terms "French rapper," "Swahili rapper," or even "Tagalog rapper," and see how many results you get. You will be surprised. More importantly, the results you find will illustrate two things that make this textbook even more significant as you make your way through this course. First, our American culture is potent and fascinating enough to be emulated around the world, even though there are certainly cultures that frown upon ours. The second, perhaps more intriguing idea is that the example of foreign rappers taking our very-American rap music and putting their spin on it is precisely the mashup concept this book will be teaching you to use throughout the entirety of the course. A Filipino rapper might take the beats and rhyme schemes prevalent in American rap to use in his music, but it still has his own cultural flavor—the language, the instruments, and the sounds particular to his part of the world. This is the beauty of the mashup concept. It is a fluid concept. It is open to innovation. The potential connections that can be made between writing strategies, topics, and elements of our culture are virtually unlimited. Just like our world.

## Why Popular Culture Matters

On the surface, it might seem that popular culture is an irrelevant topic in a college composition course. However, over the years it has become generally accepted by researchers and college instructors that students of writing find that they can make a connection with their subject matter much more easily if the topics about which they write actually matter to them. Who wouldn't rather discuss the importance of *America's Got Talent* or the strange national addiction to *Jersey Shore*, instead of writing about a congressional debate on CSPAN? More importantly, scholars have been writing on popular culture for several decades now, and they realize that the study of popular culture allows us to take the temperature of our nation at any given moment. Each generation has its own concerns, its own language, its own mark that it leaves on our culture, and who better understands this than the generation making its mark on America's popular culture now?

This is where you come in. You are both a creator of and a consumer of America's next wave of culture, whether or not you realize it. From you and your fellow students in class will come our next business leaders, our politicians, our entertainers, our entrepreneurs, our athletes, even our clergy. In short, popular culture matters because we are all contributors to it in one way or another, and we are all affected by it.

## How We Think About Popular Culture

Truthfully, most of us do not *actively* think about popular culture very often. Instead, we interact with it on a daily basis in a variety of ways. We update our Facebook statuses. We read celebrity Tweets. We download apps to our smartphones, and we read Perez Hilton's scandalous blog to see what's new with our favorite (or least favorite) celebrities. On a subconscious level, however, we regularly engage with popular culture in more ways than even the most astute consumer can imagine. When you're trying to decide between Hollister skinny jeans or the much more expensive distressed jeans from True Religion, you are making a choice based on several factors. Cost plays a role in your decision, as does the latest fashion trend. But then you have to decide what a label that reads True Religion will *say* about you. Maybe you never articulate what that statement is, but there is no doubt that something significant is being said when you buy jeans for $200 instead of $60. It's all in the label. And the manufacturers of these clothing brands know this.

As consumers, we interact with popular culture every day, in meaningful ways. Your ringtone—when it blares out in a Starbucks unexpectedly—speaks volumes about your sense of humor, the type of music you like, even who you are. It speaks volumes about you because you took the time to download the ringtone to your phone, making the purposeful decision to have this ringtone represent you in some way. So, even when we think we are not thinking about popular culture, we are. When you choose the restaurant where you want to eat dinner, when you choose which grocery store chain to shop for food, when you slap a bumper sticker on your car, you are making a cultural decision that will tell others about who you are.

For some people, there is a certain societal stigma to shopping at Wal-Mart, just as for others there is an inherent understanding that comes with shopping at Whole Foods. These differences might go unspoken in the moment when you are actually shopping at one of these supermarkets, but in the back of your mind a choice was made, knowing the implications that come with shopping at one store versus the other. What this textbook will do is allow you the opportunity to pause for a moment and consider the *meaning* behind your actions on a daily basis. You will be given the opportunity to finally articulate the difference between Wal-Mart and Whole Foods, for example, and to discuss the pros and cons of one over the other, based on our cultural perceptions of each store.

## How We "Read" Cultural Texts and Media

Whether or not we realize it, we regularly interpret and read cultural texts around us. This is a process that has become commonplace for us, both as consumers and as citizens in a media-saturated culture. The people who are among the most influential creators of popular culture—for better or for worse—are the men and women who produce advertisements. They are the people who actively try to create trends and sell us products that we weren't aware we needed or wanted until they were brought to our attention. Of course, having grown up being bombarded with television and Internet ads, we would like to think that we are immune to the powers of advertising and that we cannot be swayed by some fancy, multimillion dollar ad campaign. Unfortunately, that is not so.

We are, however, astute readers of the ads that are created for us, even if we do not actively try to read them. Consider the wildly popular "I'm a Mac. I'm a PC." advertising campaign run by Apple in 2008. Apple, in a series of very brief TV commercials, managed to pull a major coup in the personal computing industry: they made a significant dent in Microsoft's market share with a relatively simple concept.

So what was the message that Apple was attempting to convey? On the surface, it was an innocent concept. Apple wanted to do what all advertisers want to do: to show the superiority of their product over their competitors' product. Apple wanted you to buy their Macbook laptops and their iMac desktops. But the methods they used to show the superiority of their products were decidedly clever. In fact, no computers are actually seen in the advertisements until the final seconds. Instead, human actors are used to stand in for products. The result was immediate and profound.

It is no accident that the actor playing the Mac was a young, hip man with messy hair, jeans, a rumpled t-shirt, and an air of disinterest in the man standing next to him. It's as if he knew he was so cool that he did not need to stoop to the level of talking to the other actor. Likewise, it is no mistake that the actor who played the PC was a middle-aged man wearing thick-rimmed glasses and the clothing typically associated with computer geeks. By purposely choosing to have their product represented by a disinterested young man, Apple aligned their brand identity with coolness. In achieving this goal, they managed to make PCs look old, outdated, and as uncool as hanging out with your parents at the mall when you're a teenager.

Perhaps you did not realize that this was Apple's intention. But it is quite easy to find proof of the success brought on by their "I'm a Mac. I'm a PC." ad campaign. Simply go to the commons of your school, or any coffee shop or library where students gather, and observe the number of Macs, iPods, iPhones, and iPads being used by students versus the number of PCs, Zunes, Droids, or Kindles. To own an Apple is to have the newest, coolest product on the market. Apple is such a powerful force in our culture that the annual unveiling of new products by Apple each year is a worldwide event, viewed by millions of Apple fans and Apple haters alike. This is no accident.

So how can an ad be read to determine the advertiser's true intention? If Apple never explicitly stated that people who use PCs are out-of-touch geeks, then how were they able to get their message across? Well, quite simply, consumers "read" the message that Apple was trying to convey, and they bought into it. They agreed with Apple's message and they responded by snapping up Apple's products by the millions. This trend continues to this day. In fact, each time Apple releases a new version of the iPhone, or a new product such as the iPad, we regularly see images on the news of people waiting in lines for hours—sometimes even camping out overnight—to get their hands on Apple's newest releases.

Though it might seem too much is being read into the "I'm a Mac. I'm a PC." ad campaign, there are methods that can be used to read the texts around us, regardless of whether it is an actual text—an article, a story, a print ad—or a "printless" text, such as a line of clothing, a type of food, or a type of car. This textbook will encourage you to read the texts around you, and to make sense of the messages we are being shown all day long, every single day. It will also show you concrete ways to take this knowledge and incorporate it into your own writing and analysis for your college courses and beyond by giving concrete professional examples in each chapter. There is also a distinct discussion about incorporating multimedia texts in your writing.

# Reading Strategies

Let's take a few moments to observe the process of reading texts and how we read signs and other alternative texts to gain an understanding of what they are saying. For example, if you wanted to read a television ad the same way we just read the Apple ads, you can do so by employing the steps outlined in this section. If you apply these techniques while reading, regardless of the type of text, you will then be taking a systematic approach to every step of the reading and analyzing process. Each of these steps—pre-reading, reading, rereading, and verifying source credibility—allows you to decipher the text's meaning by giving you the tools to break down a text, unpack its message, and write about it in your essays.

When it comes to reading, most people conceive of the process as the act of encountering letters, words, sentences, and paragraphs. We compile information as we move from the first word of a text to its last. This is the traditional meaning behind the act of reading. And yet, there are other things that we read besides words, often subconsciously.

## Understanding Signs, Signals, and Symbols

Think, for example, of taking a written driver's test at your local license branch. One of the elements of the test is that they quiz you on the shape of road signs. Why would they quiz you on the shape of a sign if you can read the words written on it? Because each sign's shape has a corresponding meaning so that, say, if you see an upside-down triangle but you can't read the writing on it because it's too dark out, you still know that it is a yield sign. The same holds true for a stop sign's octagonal shape. You have been taught to read not only the sign's words, but also its shape, and the sign's shape has just as much meaning as its words. In the United States, these are universal signs. All drivers on the road, if they have taken and passed the written driver's test, understand that the shapes of road signs carry meaning.

We understand countless other signs, signals, and symbols without ever being tested. Consider for a moment the symbols of male and female. How do you know which bathroom to use if the doors are only marked with figures instead of the words *Men* and *Women*? Women look for the figure of a person wearing a skirt, and men look for the figure not wearing a skirt. At what point were you taught that these symbols carry these meanings? Surely you know that some women don't wear skirts or dresses. And surely you know that men don't necessarily always wear pants. Yet we have all agreed, as a society, that these are the symbols of men and women—on bathroom doors at least—and so we read these symbols when determining which door we are supposed to enter.

In the world of texts around us, signs and symbols carry meanings not explicitly stated but understood by most of us. We all know what it means when someone flips us off, or when a person is puckering his face after tasting a piece of food that was undesirable to him. We know what it means when someone holds his hand out to us, palm facing out. It means stop. If the palm is facing up, he is asking for money or some other form of assistance.

We can look to the world around us and interpret what we see using signs, signals, and symbols, as well as words. Not only can we read into a series of words, but we can also read into the placement of symbols and the particular image choices made, say, by an advertiser who is trying to sell us a beauty product. Take a moment to look around the room you are in, and see what sorts of signs and symbols you encounter that have meaning but are not accompanied by words. Now, take a look at the images here

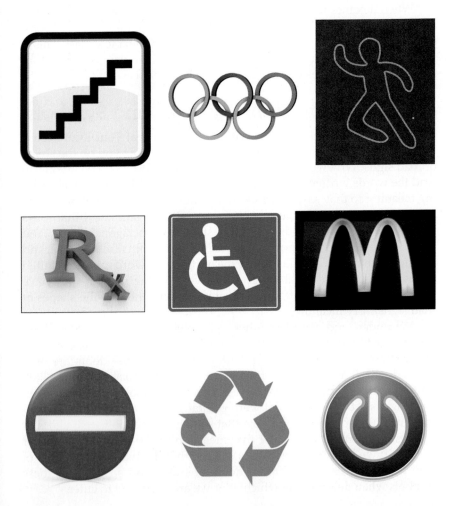

and see the various signs, signals, and symbols that are represented. How many of them do you immediately recognize? What do they mean?

These images illustrate the power of symbols and their importance to our everyday lives. Symbols and signs have the power to convey both simple and complex messages very quickly. We often read them without realizing it. And we have internalized the meanings of thousands of signs, signals, and symbols and draw on them when we come across them.

Let's take this idea of reading signs one step further, into a more sophisticated form of reading. Consider the car manufacturing company Hummer. As we entered the 21st century, the Hummer grew in popularity for several reasons. Gas was much cheaper than it is now. The vehicles themselves were previously made for use exclusively by the military, so they carried with them an inherent symbol of strength, masculinity, and even invincibility. Most common cars, for example, would not stand a chance in a wreck with a Hummer because of their massive and sturdy construction. Celebrities began buying the vehicles as status symbols, due to their enormity and high price tags. It was a way to set oneself apart from those who could not afford such an expensive vehicle. And yet, as the Hummer grew in popularity, the manufacturer saw a larger potential market available to them, so they subsequently released the H2 and H3 models, which were more affordable (though still expensive) and made to look sleeker, more stylized, and slightly smaller than their military-style predecessor.

Then a recession hit in mid-2008. In a complete turnabout for Hummer, the vehicles were no longer associated with wealth and celebrity. Instead, they became—along with many other large SUVs—identified with foolish excess and brazen consumption. To drive a Hummer in public meant to be insensitive to the millions of people who could barely afford to drive their cars because of skyrocketing gas prices and dismal unemployment rates. It became a symbol for the waste (since it only got roughly 8 to 10 miles per gallon) and frivolous spending that many saw as the cause of our deep recession. Because of this perception, sales of Hummers dropped off dramatically, and the company all but stopped producing vehicles for public consumption. Hummer dealers shuttered their businesses, and a trend died before our eyes as quickly as it had emerged.

Messages are conveyed by objects as common as the cars we drive and the clothes we wear. All of these things tell a story about the people who consume them. A person who owns a Mac, or one of the other many Apple products, knows that they are part of a hip consumer group who "gets it" when it comes to which electronic products are superior. A person who owned a Hummer around the time that gas prices hit $4 a gallon and higher looked foolish in the eyes of someone who could barely afford to put gasoline in his compact car. These are the messages we can read into products and the consumers who buy them. As you navigate through the course and this textbook, keep an open mind and remember that you have a wealth of options, an endless stream of media—whether street signs, advertising images, newspaper articles, or material objects—that can be read in both conventional and nonconventional ways. More importantly, realize that we can write about the objects around us, we can deconstruct their meanings and the stories they tell, in much the same way we did in the above example of the Hummer. Most anything can be read as a text, and you can apply the readings of these various texts to your own writing.

Next we will take a moment to discuss specific reading strategies, and then we will apply your observations to examples of writing.

## Pre-Reading

When reading a text for the first time, you must first determine the *type* of text you are about to read because it changes the way something can be read. For example, when most of us go to the movies, we know there are certain messages that are going to emerge. The first is that we will be tempted into spending money at the concession stand by the smells, posters, bright lights, and the sounds of popcorn popping. All of this is intentional on the part of the theater owners. We know this, and so we brace ourselves for this experience. We are pre-reading the situation by making ourselves aware of what we are going to be met with as we enter the movie theater itself. Then, we wander down the hall, and we find a seat, and we sit through splashy car ads, exciting previews, and another reminder that there are snacks available for sale at the concession stand. We like to think that we are above the advertising. But even so, we think about it. We cannot help it. In those moments before the movie starts, we think about buying the food, the drinks, and maybe going to see some of the movies advertised in the previews.

We can easily take this same approach when we are confronted by other texts. For example, when you first opened this book, you might have braced yourself for reading an English composition textbook. Maybe you rolled your eyes. Maybe you were intrigued. Regardless of how you reacted to this textbook, you *prepared yourself* by looking at the book, identifying it as a textbook, feeling its weight, and then eventually diving in to read these very words. You, then, are in the habit of pre-reading.

Now, you need only become more aware of this habit that we all have and take control over it. The first step in pre-reading is to **identify** what you are about to read. Pre-read by noting the text and what you see as its intention. If we stick with the example of this very textbook, you should have (and probably already have) identified a number of important factors prior to opening the book. You identified the **type of media**, which is a physical textbook meant to be referenced and used in your classroom as well as outside of the class. You also identified the **purpose** of the book, which is to teach, at the college level, how to read and write about popular culture. In all likelihood, you also brought a number of **assumptions** to the textbook before ever cracking the cover open. Perhaps you expected some of the same writing techniques you used throughout your pre-college education, or maybe you had a different definition for popular culture in your mind than how it has been defined here. This, too, is pre-reading. Finally, you should identify **what you hope to accomplish** by interacting with the text you're pre-reading. So, maybe you hope to determine, once and for all, what a narrative essay is. Maybe you look forward to reading and writing about the world in which you are engaged. Either way, identifying the previously mentioned elements of your reading experience will make your reading of the text more meaningful and manageable. These techniques will help you situate yourself with the text as its audience. Already, you are interacting with the text before you even begin to read it in the conventional sense of the word.

Now let's apply this concept to some of the texts from our daily lives. When you turn on your laptop and pull up your Facebook page, you have clearly identified the text with which you are about to interact. You know there will be updates from your friends that vary wildly from items such as new pictures they have added to some random TV show they have decided to "like." But you have identified Facebook itself as the website where you go to get updates on your friends and their lives. Naturally, because it is a website (which is a type of media), you understand the capabilities and the limitations of the site in your life. It is not the same as writing a letter to your aunt, or picking up the phone to call your friend. However, for those of us who would rather keep up with someone's life in a less time-consuming manner than writing a letter, Facebook's ability to give tiny insights into the lives of many people at once is the perfect tool for keeping tabs on someone without requiring large portions of our personal time. The purpose of Facebook, like so many other social networking sites, is to connect people. We "friend" the people with whom we have connections—family, schoolmates, fellow fans of a band, citizens of the same city—and build an online identity and community. While the particular assumptions we might have about the website and its capabilities vary from person to person, all Facebook users are aware of the site's ability to let us search and find people, become their virtual friends, and then keep track of their lives, depending on how much information they make available to us. If you were to log on to the site and there were no updates from your friends, you would probably be quite surprised, since that is what we have come to expect from Facebook. So you can pre-read a website in much the same way you can pre-read an advertisement, a textbook, or an experience such as attending a movie.

Let's take a few moments to apply these techniques to a selection from the textbook itself. Take a look at the poem below, "The Body as Weapon, as Inspiration," by Paul Martínez Pompa, which appears in the "Violence" chapter of this textbook.

### THE BODY AS WEAPON, AS INSPIRATION

The body as weapon, as inspiration
when she walks into a Jerusalem market
and explodes herself. Not so much
the explosive force, but the shrapnel

a year ago that tore through her
mother's chest and maimed her
brother's legs. Her father was spared
unnecessary pain—instantly dead under

the collapse of ceiling joists & plywood.
Somehow she survived. Now only a scar
on her forehead and an unofficial apology
from the State. Soon men will fall

to the ground with ringing in their ears.
There will be tiny fragments of glass
& bone caught in the skin of the undead.
There will be retaliation strikes,

missile bombardments, another round
of bulldozers. And there will be a poet
thousands of miles away, excited
by the burden of writing this thing.

After a quick glance, what were your impressions of the poem? There's a good chance, if you do not regularly read contemporary poetry, you were surprised by the accessibility of the language. It is written in the language we currently use, rather than employing the sometimes-confusing language and symbolism of classic poems. Maybe you thought the title, which refers to the body as a weapon, was an odd concept, and you were drawn into the poem to find out what the author meant by the title. Perhaps this is because we rarely think of the body as a weapon that can cause harm, especially because we spend so much time and energy trying to protect our fragile bodies from the harmful elements of life. As a symbol, the body is usually meant as a way to identify ourselves. We use our bodies to identify ourselves based on our height, our weight, our skin color, and the attributes of our gender. It is strange, then, to see a poem in which the body is introduced as something foreign to us: a weapon.

When pre-reading this poem, perhaps you were surprised in some other ways. If you stop to consider what you normally expect when reading a poem, maybe you realized that you usually come to poetry expecting it to be about love, or to be written as a sonnet or haiku. If that is the case, then you may have been surprised to note that there was no rhyme scheme to this poem. In that way, this poem might very well have defied your expectations of what a poem *is*.

Furthermore, people often consider poetry to be a romantic form of writing that utilizes beautiful and flowery language. This poem does the exact opposite. If you skimmed over the poem to get a general impression, you most likely observed the language Pompa uses to describe the suicide bomber's loss of her family in a previous event that led to her retaliation. He uses brutally honest language—"the shrapnel . . . that tore through her / mother's chest and maimed / her brother's legs"—to convey the atrocities of war on both sides. Why do you think Pompa would resort to this sort of language to make his point? Were you shocked to see words describing death, desperation, and destruction, rather than words of love and happiness? It is quite likely that he knew he was writing about a controversial subject, and so he decided to be as vivid as possible to paint a picture we rarely, if ever, see in the media: the story behind a suicide bomber's action. Were his language choices not shocking, he would have had more difficulty making his point. Symbolically, the words we use to define ideas, events, and even people carry a lot of weight. So, when we think of poetry as being beautiful and romantic—if that is our expectation when we pre-read a poem—in all likelihood Pompa's poem defies everything we expect a poem to be.

## Reading and Commenting

The next step is to read the text itself. On the most basic and obvious level, this requires you to shut out all other distractions and focus on the words, images, and symbols being conveyed. But, more importantly, it is a vital step in the reading process that readers *interact* with a text by commenting on it. This, too, is something you already do in your everyday life. When you log into your Facebook account and comment on someone's photos, or when you update your status by commenting on your life in general, you are interacting with the website by putting your own commentary on something that is otherwise static (a photo, a homepage that features a picture of you and a list of information about yourself).

Obviously, reading proper—the act of finding meaning in a string of letters, words, and phrases—is a talent that all of us have to varying degrees. However, reading and commenting together is not something we commonly do as readers. We are sometimes taught not to write in books, and so it can be difficult to get into this habit. There are many benefits to interacting with a text by writing on it, or in a nearby journal, as you read. Some people find that writing directly on the text is more helpful because you can underline or highlight a particular word or phrase and then jot a note down right next to it. This makes it easy to locate information when you return to write about it for an essay assignment. Other people prefer to write notes in a journal or notebook. This, too, is a good method, as it enables you to process your thoughts and then articulate them on paper. No matter which method you use, you should most certainly make note—as you read articles and stories, poems and novel excerpts, websites and clothing choices—of the ways the text is influencing you. Just be sure to point out why and how the text made you feel whatever emotion you felt while reading it. You can also point out whether you agree or disagree with a text, or ask questions about passages that don't make sense. These are habits that will make interpreting and writing about texts much easier in the long run.

Take a moment to read the poem "The Body as Weapon, as Inspiration." Consider the poem's subject matter as you read it. Everyone knows what a suicide bomber is. We hear about them on the news with tragic regularity. Maybe you've even seen a picture or two of a suicide bombing's aftermath. Still, what makes this poem so dramatically different than so many other poems is that the subject of the poem—a female suicide bomber—is not usually linked with the idea of poetry in general. Symbolically, most people's idea of suicide bombers is that they represent a threat to the very core of our American existence. We cannot help but remember the attacks of 9/11 when we hear about suicide bombers because 9/11 has become a national symbol of the most extreme horrors we can imagine as Americans when it comes to terrorism.

If we consider the fact that Pompa is actually describing a *female* suicide bomber, then this poem becomes an even more complex issue. After all, we have a sort of generic image of what a suicide bomber looks like. Most people do not conjure up the image of a woman when envisioning a suicide bomber. If you were to make a list of female traits, most likely you would not have the words "violent" or "terrorist" anywhere on the list. So this is another example of how this poem defies our expectations as readers.

But Pompa's poem takes this notion even further. The author asks the reader to consider the reasons behind a suicide bomber's actions. He does not in any way advocate or endorse suicide bombing, but instead ponders the cause behind someone willing to kill herself along with other innocent people. When the author takes a step back from the emotional reaction to the horror of a suicide bombing and contemplates the meaning behind it—when he *reads* into this sort of event beyond the normal reading—he unearths a very disturbing, but highly likely scenario. He puts forth the idea that maybe not *all* suicide bombers are the radical extremists hell-bent on murdering people for kicks and shock value that the media often portrays them to be. Some of them might be desperate or helpless enough, having lost all sense of a normal life, that the notion of killing oneself to make a political point might not be such a far-fetched idea.

Whether or not you agree with Paul Martínez Pompa's line of thinking, to read this poem is to undergo some sort of emotional reaction, and you should make note of your reactions alongside the text, or perhaps in a journal, as you experience them. Maybe you felt angered at the nerve of a poet to write about a suicide bomber. Maybe you do not think suicide bombers deserve to have their version of events considered. Or, maybe you thought for the first time about what might trigger someone to knowingly give their own life to make a point, regardless of how foolish their actions or their message might be. In the end, to commit the act of suicide bombing—whether for retaliation or merely to strike terror and uncertainty into the hearts of your enemy—is to display a striking, albeit horrifying message for others to read.

Note on the poem, or in your journal, some specific passages that bother you, entertain you, or even frighten you. The important thing is to interact with the poem *as you read it*, while the ideas and impressions you have about the poem are still fresh in your mind. The very act of commenting on something as you read it will help you to understand the text in the moments when you are reading it, as well as when you return to the text later. Think of it as commenting much in the same way you would on a friend's picture on Facebook. Does the poem give you something to say? If so, say it. No matter how intellectual or silly. This will help you articulate your thoughts better in the long run, in the event you decide to write an essay and incorporate this poem into one of your writing assignments.

## Rereading

When you pre-read and then read a text for the first time, you have a limited idea of what the text will contain. You have a series of impressions the text made on you prior to reading it. You might know that "The Body as Weapon, as Inspiration" is a poem, and you might even know that it is a poem about a suicide bomber. But now that you have finished the poem, there is much more to consider. For example, how do you feel now that you have finished the poem and you realize that Mr. Pompa has written the poem from the perspective of the suicide bomber? Does it anger you? Or does it make you consider something you may have never considered before, such as what might cause someone to strap explosives to herself? Maybe you find yourself wondering what she might be thinking in the moments leading up to her final act. It is certainly a different perspective than we are used to hearing on the news when we hear about suicide bombings. We usually get the location, the number killed, and maybe a picture or two of the aftermath. We never, ever get the story of the suicide bomber. After all, we cannot help but think of them as a weapon. And who wants to hear the story of a weapon? Especially when its target is innocent civilians or our own American servicemen and servicewomen.

When you reread the poem, you come to it with an entirely new perspective. That is to say, now you know what the poem is *about*. Now you know what the subject matter of the poem is and so the poem's title makes much more sense. When you first read the title, you might have thought something along the lines of "how can the body be a weapon?" But now, when you revisit the poem, the possible confusion of its title no longer exists. And so you get a better, more thorough read the second time around because you are seeing the poem more clearly now that the task of determining what the poem is literally about can be set aside.

When you reread, try to identify elements of the poem that were not apparent the first time you read it. Look at the author's use of language, and the way he portrays the suicide bomber. Observe the way he literally describes the woman. What types of words is he using? Violent, dark words? Beautiful, kindly words? See if you can identify what the author thinks of this particular person about whom he is writing. Is he judging her? Is he merely trying to paint a portrait of someone who it is difficult for us to see as human? Do you feel that he has succeeded in any of this? After all, the very thought of killing oneself is taboo in our culture, but the idea of killing yourself *and* other people is horrific beyond words. Yet this is the very thing the poem is illustrating. So, after the initial shock of the poem's subject wears off, and after the strangeness of reading a poem that is not a typical love poem subsides, you will be able to glean more information from the poem itself, as well as the author's intentions in writing the poem in the first place.

Now take a moment to consider rereading another text we've previously mentioned. Perhaps you have seen a Hummer on the road and thought the vehicle was ridiculously large. Maybe you liked how it looked and wanted one for yourself. But, now that we have "read" the Hummer as a text and what it stands for in many people's minds, to reread the Hummer might give you a different impression. We know, for example, that gas prices regularly fluctuate, so people will not always view the Hummer as a symbol of wastefulness. We also have enough distance from the beginnings of our country's recession that some of the anger of the housing crisis, large numbers of unemployment, and the excesses of a few people have eased a little. This is what the Hummer used to represent in many people's minds. Either way, it still stands to reason that a person driving a Hummer is giving off a different message than someone who is driving a Toyota Prius, whether or not that is his intention.

One car, the Prius, is known for getting up to 50 miles per gallon on the highway. The Hummer, however, is known for getting very low gas mileage. In popular culture, the Prius, as with most hybrid cars, has become aligned with the types of people who wish to conserve energy and make a less dramatic impact on the environment by driving a hybrid vehicle. The Hummer, however, has done little to become a more fuel-efficient car and therefore likely retains its status as a wasteful vehicle.

These are just a few examples of the benefits of rereading a text. What is to be gained is a more thorough understanding. You can read more deeply into any text when you have already read it once and answered the initial questions raised by the text, its presentation, and what you perceive to be its purpose. These skills can be utilized regardless of what type of text you are reading. Whether you are reading an article in an academic journal, or reading the cereal box in front of you as you sit down for breakfast, these reading strategies will help you to glean more information from the texts you encounter.

## Credibility and Reliability in Sources

Thus far, we have been focusing on the act of reading various texts and finding meaning in them. But it is also important to take the time to determine the *source* of a text. If you are watching an advertisement, you understand that the same company whose product is being sold to you has created the advertisement in question, and this changes how you understand the message. You inherently understand, as an American consumer, that companies will only show the positive elements of a good or a service, so you must seek out potential problems with the company. When we read sources—regardless of whether they are traditional or nontraditional texts—it is important to ask some questions about them to determine their authenticity, reliability, and credibility. This is especially important when it comes time to make a decision about whether a source is reliable or credible enough to cite in your own writing.

When you approach a professional journal or publication, for example, you might be aware that in order to publish in such a venue, authors submit their research to the people who run the journal, often experts themselves in that particular field. In that case, you can assume that what you are reading has been written by a reliable professional who works daily within the field being represented. Some of the texts you will encounter fall under this umbrella of reputable sources that have some organization or body of professionals who are giving them their blessing. However, as you venture out to find other "texts" in the world around you, you will find that many are not so easily identified as being backed by a particular professional organization. There are some questions you can easily ask to determine the authenticity and reliability of any source, regardless of whether it is a print essay or a comment on a Web article coming from some anonymous source.

The first question you should always ask yourself is who has authored the text you are reading. What is the author's relationship to the area of study he is representing? Is he a renowned professional in his field? Or is he simply a person with a point-of-view on a subject that interests him? There are several ways to determine an author's credibility. Often, in online articles or blogs, there is a name and a brief biography attached to the text you are reading (this has also been done for each selection included in this textbook). You should take a few moments to research the text's author to see what sort of work she has done in the discipline she is representing. If she is commenting on a new immigration law, for example, it would be wise to ask whether the person is a lawyer, a lawmaker, or in some other role that requires her to have in-depth knowledge about law. Perhaps she is commenting on the law as a regular citizen who simply has an opinion about whether she agrees or disagrees with a new piece of legislation. The key is to know *who* is writing the text you are about to read so that you can read it with a more critical eye.

Secondly, you should also consider the source. Is this text being published on a person's blog, or has it been published in a legitimate source with the backing of a nationally or regionally recognized group of professionals in the field? It is important to determine the credibility or authenticity of the source of the article so that we can determine whether the author of the essay has been fact-checked and vouched for by the experts in his field. That's not to say that someone's opinion on her blog is not legitimate. However, there is a large difference between an opinion and a fact-based text that uses verifiable data to back the claims made.

There is nothing wrong with reading texts from nonacademic sources, but you should take care to read such texts with caution and a slight bit of skepticism. A writer of any background doesn't necessarily need to be an expert on a particular subject to have an opinion, but in order to lend an opinion credibility, the best nonexpert writers know to incorporate expert research and data into their opinions. This is what you should strive to do in your own writing, since doing so will make your opinions and statements more credible as well.

However, do not assume that just because a study has been conducted, there is no wiggle room for the reader. If, for example, you are reading an essay on why marijuana should be legalized for medicinal use, and it is written by a doctor and published in a medical journal, it does not mean that you have to agree with the author's statements or findings. Part of reading, as we have already discussed, is to interact with the text. If you find that you disagree with the doctor's findings about the benefits of medicinal marijuana, you are free to do so. But, if you are going to do that, it is important that you locate research and other information to back your dissenting point of view. That is the best part about texts of all sorts. They are meant to be engaged, and they are meant to be commented on.

In terms of the kinds of sources available, there is a wealth of information on any given subject at your fingertips online. While Google should not be the only source to which you turn for research or information about a subject, it is still a good tool to practice questioning a source's credibility and its authenticity. Just because an article is posted online does not mean that it is fact- or research-based. As readers, we should question the author's intentions and his credentials. If it is hard to determine whether the author is an expert in her field after researching her validity and credibility, then you should keep this in mind when reading what she has to say.

Finally, understand that there are texts that exist for which the agenda is quite clear. An advertisement wants to sell you something, whether it is selling you a computer or a political candidate. In addition to questioning a text's author and source, you should question what the agenda, or purpose, of the text might be. It goes without saying that an advertisement of any sort seeks to make its product or service superior to that of its competition. That was the angle Apple took with its "I'm a Mac. I'm a PC." ads. Like any good consumer of texts, knowing the purpose of the text and its source will help you more clearly read it.

## Reading Other Texts

In our daily lives we are surrounded by texts that go beyond the standard understanding we have of a text as a series of words that are meant to be read. Despite the fact that we will be focusing on a variety of media that contain words, there will also be many opportunities to read into other types of media.

## Visual Media

One of the most common types of media we encounter on a daily basis is print ads. We see billboards when driving down the road. We see posters in the hallways of malls. Ads are scattered throughout our favorite magazines. There are even cars that are advertisements on wheels.

Much thought goes into each and every ad we encounter. This has been the driving creative force behind the hit TV series *Mad Men*, which shows the great lengths advertisers go to in order to manipulate their audiences into buying whatever product they are selling. Behind every ad we see is an undeniable message. Sometimes there are several messages. Some are more subtle than others. Take a look at the advertisement on page 22, for example.

**Nothing. Zero. That's what's added to our burgers.**

They're simply 100% beef, seasoned with a touch of salt and pepper after cooking.
And we only ever use whole cuts of beef, from British and Irish farms.

**That's what makes McDonald's."**

© 2006 McDonald's. All references marked with a TM or an ® are trade marks of McDonald's Corporation and its affiliates.

The first thing that probably stood out most was a series of O-shaped pictures, which might have made you wonder what the advertisement was trying to say. Next, your eye was probably drawn to the universally famous Golden Arches that represent McDonald's, one of the world's most successful fast food chains. Finally, you probably scrutinized the writing at the bottom of the ad, which explains the presence of all the O-shaped pictures. On the most basic level, McDonald's is telling us that their hamburgers are 100% real beef. This is why they have produced an ad featuring creative images that all make the shape of a zero—that is, that their burgers are zero percent additives of any sort.

However, if you look at the advertisement again—if you reread it— you will see the other messages implied. For example, why would McDonald's need to reiterate the fact that their hamburgers have no added ingredients or fillers by showing six "zeroes" and then stating "Nothing. Zero. That's what's added to our burgers."? Why state this a total of eight times in a one-page ad? What does it say about the company that they are advertising about the "purity" of their burgers? Are they rebutting a common argument or belief? Are they merely telling us that their meat is better than their competitors? If you revisit the images themselves, you'll note that there are children in five of the six photographs. Why do you think McDonald's chose to include only children in each photo that features a person? It is probably no coincidence that people often equate childhood and children with the concept of innocence and purity, so if you put all of the visual and textual elements of the advertisement together and read them as a whole, the overall message that McDonald's is making becomes clear. Their burgers are pure and innocent, like the children making zeroes. Their burgers aren't made up of filler and impurities. They're both good for your children, and as unthreatening as a child. This is what the "spoken" and "unspoken" elements of the advertisement combine to get across to the viewer.

This is how we read print media that sometimes have words but rely heavily on images to send more messages to their readers. Most print advertisements use images to send messages, and nearly all of them can be read for meaning in much the same way a traditional text would be. When you read into texts such as these, be aware of the different messages being portrayed in addition to the literal words on the page. Note how we picked apart the advertisement to find its different messages. In advertising, nearly every single element of the ad has undergone extensive thought and purposeful placement of messages. Be aware of these messages as you encounter them, and be sure to note them so that you can give examples of these messages in your own writing.

## Film and Television

In much the same way print ads may be read, so too can television and film be read by seeking out imagery that carries meaning within it (though when it comes to writing about television and film, there are particular issues we will address in the next chapter). Consider the commercials for Axe men's hygiene products that came onto the market a few years ago. In most of their television ads, young men are shown spraying Axe cologne on their bodies and then venturing out into the larger world (often a college campus or a mall) where young women are so overwhelmed by the smell of Axe that they tackle the men because they just cannot help themselves.

So what is Axe trying to say? They are trying to convince young men that Axe is not the kind of cologne their fathers would wear. It is a young, desirable man's cologne that leaves women beside themselves. The underlying message is that young men who have trouble getting dates or getting noticed by attractive young women will achieve this goal easily with the application of Axe cologne before leaving the house.

Or consider the television ads for most liquors. Nearly every one of them features a club scene, with pounding DJ beats and beautiful, well-dressed people who are dancing and happy. No one is sweating or too drunk. Everyone is having a great time and getting along. Everyone looks great dancing. No one is stumbling around or getting sick, and there are no fights. The advertisers for an expensive brand of vodka, for example, are purposely aligning themselves with a classy clientele. They are saying that their vodka is exactly what you need to throw a good party, or what you should order when you go to a bar to show you are a responsible and trendy drinker. Their liquor, according to their ad, is for the beautiful people, not for the town drunk who drives a scooter because he has gotten so many DUIs.

Films do much the same thing, but for extended periods of time. While they are not necessarily trying to sell products, they are still usually trying to push a message. For example, in the movie *Avatar*, the film's producers never explicitly state that they are trying to get the viewer to become more environmentally conscious, and yet the whole reason the human characters in the movie embark on a voyage to the planet Pandora is because we humans have basically trashed our own environment and are seeking either another planet that might sustain human life, or the much-needed resource, "unobtainium," that will allow us to repair some of the damage back on earth.

One comment frequently seen on blogs and online forums about the film was that people wished there really were a planet like Pandora because it was such a pure and beautiful place. The unstated message of *Avatar* is that the earth *is* our Pandora, but we have mistreated it with pollution and carelessness. We can presume, then, that the earth still can be our Pandora, as long as we recognize how we are harming it and take some sort of action to restore it to its natural beauty. So, in essence, it is an environmentalist film disguised as a sci-fi movie.

The important thing to remember through all of these examples is that there is almost always a message that can be read from TV shows, from films, and most certainly from advertisements. Though we as viewers might not be aware of the message a movie or a TV show is trying to convey, we do know through pre-reading these texts that we are going to be sold something during the commercial breaks, and we prepare ourselves for these experiences accordingly.

## Websites

The sheer number of websites now in existence makes this form of media one of the most common texts people encounter on a daily basis. From our iGoogle homepages to the main page of a site like Amazon, we are constantly being bombarded with information, much of it advertising. Perhaps you remember one of the many times Facebook changed their privacy policy to allow their website to take your personal information and sell it to advertisers. Initially, there was always a backlash to this invasion of privacy, as users saw it. Facebook groups popped up overnight bashing the website for overstepping its bounds. The user revolts always caused Facebook to take a step back, but only so far. And now, the very practice that early Facebook users revolted against is a commonplace occurrence on the website. Users have simply succumbed to the reality that their personal information online is no longer personal. We have allowed advertisers and websites unlimited access to us, for free. To see how you have represented yourself online, it is an interesting exercise to actually pay attention to the ads being sent your way by Google and Facebook. Do an experiment sometime to see how accurately these sites have "read" you based on your online activities.

Besides the ever-popular social networking sites that are used by nearly a billion people all over the globe, websites exist to make information accessible to anyone with an Internet connection. To this end, there are countless websites where information is readily available to computer users. But, aside from the actual text—the literal words on any given website—there are a number of other texts with which users are interacting. Whether or not you use MySpace, which has fallen out of favor as the primary social networking tool for most people, you can still go to the MySpace website, where you will be greeted with movie advertisements, ads for upcoming TV shows, or splashy banner ads enticing you to buy the newest Eminem album.

What might at first seem like a mere distraction is actually an advertising tool that generates tens of billions of dollars' worth of income for the companies who pay to place ads on websites. These sites can be read as advertisements with which we interact, or they can be read in an entirely different way.

Nearly every website that publishes news stories, information feeds, videos, or photos allows readers to interact with the information and even pass it along to friends by "sharing it" via Facebook or Twitter. This is a relatively new phenomenon, but it wonderfully illustrates the point this textbook is trying to make about websites being texts. When you comment at the bottom of a CNN news article, or on a YouTube video, or even on a friend's Facebook picture, you are interacting with these things as texts. You are responding to something that amuses you, offends you, or simply intrigues you.

This approach can be utilized not only when encountering websites, but also when writing about them. It is a common practice now for people to rate things—movies, professors, song clips—and the very act of rating or commenting is the type of interaction and "reading" of popular culture that this textbook seeks to use when illustrating how one can write about our culture around us.

# Apps

In a strange turn of events, websites themselves have recently begun to fall out of favor. Sure, people still check their email and log on to IMDB.com to read about their favorite actor's film career, but more and more people are utilizing apps on their smartphones and other app-friendly devices. This has become such a powerful movement that services such as Twitter rarely even bother updating their actual website. Instead, they simply update their app because more people use it than visit the official Twitter site.

While it might not appear to be so, these apps are also texts, but they are texts tailored to very specific interests. At last count, Apple.com featured well over 200,000 apps for the iPhone and iPad. Some of the apps are simply games or GPS devices, but others are designed to send information—news stories, friend updates—without the need to seek out the information on any given website. Now information comes directly to users without the need to log on to a website to view updates.

The ramifications of such a technological advance are quite impressive when you stop to think about it. For one, it means that users are taking the power of the Web into their own hands and dictating what they want to see. Instead of going to the *New York Times* website and sifting through ads for cars and banks to get to a news article, we can have the news sent directly to us. It means that we are changing the way we interact with online texts by choosing ahead of time what we want to know and only getting relevant information sent to us.

What does this mean in terms of this textbook? It means that apps are yet another text that can be read in order to find what is popular in our culture around us. In the same way that some previously popular social networking sites (e.g., Friendster, Wayn, and MySpace) have been made irrelevant by the powerhouse services of Facebook and Twitter, there will also be apps that become wildly popular, and they will then become a part of our larger culture. Some will be games. Some will be networking tools. But there will most certainly emerge a preferred method of receiving news and information that will bubble to the top of the app heap.

# Reading People

Despite the focus of this textbook on media such as film, television, websites, apps, and traditional texts, there are additional—quite powerful—texts we encounter even when we are offline or not watching TV. One very common example of this is the way we read other people. We read each other's body language to tell if someone to whom we are talking is disinterested in our conversation (arms crossed, looking in another direction). We read people's facial expressions to determine their mood. We even go so far as to read other people based on the manner in which they dress.

Perhaps this, too, is subconscious, but it is certainly one of the ways we try to get a read on another person. If you ever want to test this theory, wear a casual outfit—such as jeans and a t-shirt—and go into an expensive clothing store. Note the manner in which you are treated. Were you greeted by a store employee? If so, how did he or she address you? Did you feel as though you were being watched, or not being taken seriously? Were you ignored? Now try the reverse. Go into that same store dressed in your nicest clothing and see how you are treated differently. Was the difference noticeable? Were you addressed directly or taken more seriously than before? What is at work in this situation is that you are being "read" based on your clothing, your looks, and the way in which you carry yourself. We all do this to each other, whether or not we realize what we are doing.

No matter what our preference in clothing, all of us are acutely aware of what our clothing says about us. We know what people will think if we wear baggy jeans. We know what they think about us if we wear revealing clothing. The ways in which we dress help people to get a read on us. We are walking texts.

By this point it should be apparent that whether it is an online ad or a stranger approaching us to say hello, we read things and people constantly using a series of techniques and methods of dissecting social cues to determine the message behind simple things such as a person's outfit or the unstated meaning behind a magazine advertisement.

The next step is to gather all this information and make sense of it so that you can begin to write articulately about the many themes and subjects of this book, which we address in the next chapter. Within our chapter on writing about popular culture we will apply these reading techniques—of both traditional and nontraditional multimedia texts—and explain how to utilize the Mashup approach to reading within your writing assignments generated by the subsequent thematic chapters. Furthermore, we will speak to how all of these skills—reading and writing about popular culture—will benefit you in the composition classroom, as well as in other college courses and life beyond the classroom.

# Chapter 2

# Writing About Popular Culture

The following chapter puts the first chapter's theory into practice by providing concrete examples of ways you can apply our approach to "reading" the popular culture around us—in all of its many guises—to your actual college writing assignments. We will discuss methods of constructing an essay, from generating a basic starting idea all the way through to a final product. This chapter also incorporates both traditional and nontraditional texts into many of the stages laid out within its pages.

Furthermore, we will also discuss the value and application of this approach to writing so that you can get a sense of how it will serve you both in and beyond your entire college writing experience.

## Planning Your Essay

Many of the essays, articles, and other media within this textbook will undoubtedly cause you to have an instinctual or gut reaction to the topics that are being presented. This is precisely the textbook's intention because the things that cause the strongest reaction or spark the greatest interest often generate the best discussion and writing.

When you are deciding which topics or prompts to respond to, it is best to choose those discussion or essay questions about which you have the strongest opinions. This will enable you to generate ideas more quickly than if you were to respond to a question about which you have little interest or opinion. As you consider the various types of responses each selection will potentially allow you to write, and as you consider the wide variety of traditional and nontraditional texts available to you, it is helpful to use as many of the following writing strategies as you find necessary.

These common writing strategies will help you begin the process of constructing an idea, and then carrying it through to the final product: an engaging, thought-provoking, and sophisticated essay that utilizes the many texts that make up our American popular culture and employs multiple writing strategies within one essay.

## Invention Strategies

One common problem that many of us frequently confront when we begin to plan an essay is that we are not entirely sure which element of any given selection we want to write about for an extended period of time. And for most of us, over the course of our secondary education, we were given a variety of methods to use in generating possible paper topics. This textbook will give several writing prompts for each selection in every chapter. Your job, as a writer, will be to determine what your topic and approach to any given selection might be and apply the methods of interpreting texts that were showcased in Chapter 1 to your own writing. Then, you will need to begin constructing an essay that shows the results of your interpretation and understanding in a logical and formal manner. But first you must get your essay "off the ground," so to speak. To aid in this process, here are several invention strategies to get help you through the various steps of your essay, from start to finish.

### Brainstorming

The most basic technique is often called brainstorming and consists of writing down simple words or phrases that can act as a starting point for an essay. You can determine what you do and do not know about any given topic by quickly writing down a list of words or phrases to help focus your ideas. Once again, consider the poem discussed in the previous chapter, "The Body as Weapon, as Inspiration." Here is a list of potential topics generated by a student, Leslie Brown, in response to the poem:

Effects of war/terrorism on citizens

Suicide bombers

Reasons behind suicide bombings

*The human cost of war*

*Violence as a political tool*

*The other side of terrorism*

*The psychological impact of terrorism*

By brainstorming for a few moments on the themes of the poem "The Body as Weapon, as Inspiration," Ms. Brown was able to generate a list of potential topics for her essays. Then, to reduce the number of potential topics, she eliminated several of the ones that seemed less appealing to her, and narrowed the list down to two: "Effects of war/terrorism on citizens" and "The human cost of war." Ms. Brown was able to determine that it would be too involved and too complicated to write about the psychological impact of terrorism in a few pages, so she opted for the choices that showed the most promise for an interesting and engaging short topic.

## Clustering

Another common method of pre-writing is called clustering. Clustering allows you to explore the relationships between ideas and topics by starting off with a central idea, and branching out into related themes or topics. The method is similar to brainstorming, but rather than listing several different topics, you move from a central idea or theme to a more specific theme or main idea for a paper.

Observe the cluster where Ms. Brown started from the idea of "terrorism" and ended up finding several distinct relationships within that very broad topic. The result of the cluster is that the student came up with five distinct lines of thinking. One of them—the idea of political poetry—provided her with such a broad array of writers that she had difficulty narrowing the topic. As it turned out, there were far more poets who could be classified as political than she first imagined, so she would have needed a much more specific topic than merely "political poetry." Additionally, the student realized that she had heard plenty about the two conflicts in the Middle East in which the United States is engaged, but she did not find that line of thinking to be that appealing as a topic. She was somewhat interested in the idea of suicide bombing as an act of revenge (as hinted at in Mr. Pompa's poem), as well as the intriguing idea of female suicide bombers (since we frequently think of them as men). However, Ms. Brown ultimately decided that she was most interested in exploring the concept of images of violence in the media, especially in relation to another selection in the chapter on violence, titled "Picture Imperfect."

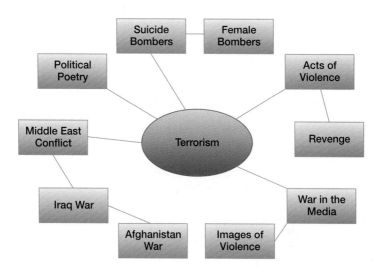

## Freewriting

One of the most helpful of all techniques to generate essay topics is to simply write for a few minutes, without any concern for grammar, punctuation, or spelling. **Freewriting** keeps you from worrying about the formalities of writing, allowing you to think about ideas and write them down as they come into your mind. Instead of writing down lists of potential topics, you will try to get fully formed ideas onto the page. Here is an example of freewriting from Ms. Brown's developing essay on Mr. Pompa's poem and the article titled "Picture Imperfect."

> Picture Imperfect – showing pictures will spur violence. It captures only an image and fails to tell any of the background story, surrounding events leading up to the action taking place in an image.

> A picture showing an American soldier beating a seemingly helpless Iraqi will incense the people of Iraq as well as some Americans, but story what about the story behind it? Perhaps the person had struck the soldier or another one. Perhaps right before the picture, the American was being attacked or perhaps it was correct and the soldier was just being brutal without provocation.

> Tabloid magazines capture images of celebrities hugging another person and turn it into a scandal. With a picture, any caption can go with it and change the story to something completely different.

It is the same for war images but worse because they're not just an interesting bit of trash and gossip. They're about things people actually care about enough to stand up for and resort to violence to defend.

Pictures taken of a woman suicide bombing or the aftermath will cause more violence, bombing, fighting etc. It looks like she was acting solely out of hatred and cold-blooded opposition to the U.S. not out of love and grief from the loss of her family and way of life. Without making her story more humane, relating it to others, to ourselves, and going only on the image of a woman killing herself and as many others as possible makes it easy to continue violence and get revenge as though all the people over there are lowly savages with feelings not nearly as acute as our own, and makes it easier to rationalize killing them.

If you read the above paragraphs closely, you will find grammatical errors, as well as spelling errors and gaps in logic. Some ideas overlap. Some ideas never get completed. Nevertheless, what emerges from nearly all of her freewriting is the idea of pictures—specifically violent pictures—and the power they wield over the people who view them. Slowly but surely, an idea is beginning to take shape. That is precisely the point behind freewriting. When you get ideas down onto the page, a more specific topic that has the potential to be a strong thesis will become apparent.

## Constructing a Thesis

By now the idea of a thesis—or an essay's main idea—is familiar to most students, and we will not stray far from your current understanding of what a thesis is. What we will do, instead, is learn to move from a broad and undeveloped topic to a more specific and thorough one.

Let's revisit Ms. Brown's cluster to see this theory in action. Beginning with the broad idea of terrorism, and prompted by her brainstorming on the topics of Mr. Pompa's poem and the "Picture Imperfect" article, she was able to specifically narrow her topic to depictions of war in the media, and then narrow it even further to the topic of violent images related to war. Through her freewriting exercise, Ms. Brown discovered that she could discuss the power of violent images and the danger of taking these images out of context. This is where a more sophisticated thesis emerged. The temptation was there for her to simply write about violent images being bad, but that is a familiar concept that has been discussed for many years by psychologists, sociologists, and politicians alike. Instead,

Ms. Brown took it one step further and decided to explore *why* violent images are bad, the negative impact they can have, and how appropriate context should be given to any picture published by the media, regardless of whether the images are violent. This is the thesis she came up with for her essay:

> With any photo, a caption, positive or negative, may be attached to it, causing the audience to have skewed assumptions of the actions taking place.

While this thesis will undergo further revision, the main idea that Ms. Brown will be working with is present in this version. Her basic point—that pictures can be manipulated with language to distort the event being depicted—is a good place to begin generating a larger essay.

## Outlining

Once you have identified an intriguing thesis for your essay, the next logical step is to create an outline. You can create outlines for a paper in two ways. The first is to make an outline beginning with the paper's main idea, or thesis, followed by each of the main idea's supporting topics, and ending with a conclusion. The second, less common method is to make an additional outline of your essay after its completion to see the patterns that emerge, as well as to search for gaps in logic or flow of ideas. Then you should compare the two outlines to determine whether you have achieved the goals in your paper that you put forward within your initial outline.

For her topic—the power of pictures to influence viewers—Ms. Brown created the following outline to begin to construct a fuller and more specific examination of her main idea:

### Outline

I. Introduction—Photos in tabloid magazines
    a. Celebrities are subject to any story that will sell magazines
        i. Gerard Butler and Jennifer Aniston
        ii. Brad Pitt and Angelina Jolie
    b. Any caption can be attached to a photo and skew the audience's view
II. Photos of war have a more dramatic effect on viewers
    a. Picture Imperfect Supports Obama and Bush administrations
    b. Beneficial to censor war photos from public

    c. Photos of American soldiers' brutality toward Iraqi prisoners

        i. Only capture split second, no background information

        ii. Only people present can know what happened

III. "Body as Weapon, as Inspiration" as example of other side

    a. Destruction of woman's family

    b. Reason she did it not apparent to rest of the world

    c. Without understanding woman's reasons, it is easier to rationalize killings and war

IV. Past presidential administrations were right to censor photos

    a. Curbs violent reactions about war

    b. Public reactions to marine wedding photo were varied

    c. Monitoring footage reduces tension

V. Conclusion—Power of Images

    a. Consider consequences of publishing photos

    b. Media's responsibility to accurately portray photos

    c. Images should not be taken out of context

You can see from her outline that she has chosen to expand on her initial idea of violent images in the media by incorporating another essay from the violence chapter, as well as outside media examples in pop culture, to make a more detailed and narrowed point about the effects of wartime photography and the power of taking photographs out of their true contexts. Though her outline is still a bit disconnected, it allows her to find a starting point and an ending point so she can begin the work of expanding on her thesis.

# Writing Your Essay

Once you have generated a list of potential topics and narrowed them down to a single idea—your thesis—on which to build your essay, you will need to begin thinking about an entry point into your essay and its topic. The best way to do this is to consider ways to engage your reader on your topic, while systematically writing the stages of an essay that take us from your paper's beginning to its end. The idea is that you will want to engage your readers early and quickly, and make them interested in and intrigued by your essay's topic. The opening paragraphs of an essay serve this purpose. The body of an essay is the space where you will elaborate on your topic by bringing your thesis into each paragraph and breaking it down to support it, one main idea at a time. Finally, the conclusion is where you will wrap up your discussion by reiterating the message that you hope readers will take away from your paper.

Before we discuss the most effective methods of writing successful, engaging introductory and concluding paragraphs, we will take a moment to revisit some of the writing strategies you may have used in previous composition classes. We will also introduce you to a new writing strategy that incorporates and builds on your knowledge of common writing strategies: the Mashup essay.

## Writing Strategies: The Mashup Essay

The exciting thing about this textbook is that, along with building on previous habits learned prior to your college education, we also introduce a new strategy of writing that allows you to put into practice the act of reading and commenting on many types of texts. Although you will most certainly revisit the types of essays with which you are already familiar, you will be given the opportunity to write hybrid essays that not only incorporate more than one writing strategy, but also incorporate outside popular culture texts. In addition to utilizing the selections included in each chapter, you will be encouraged to bring to your essays some of the many different types of texts we have identified in our earlier discussion of alternative texts. We call these types of multimedia and multitextual essays "Mashup essays." However, before giving a more thorough explanation of what a Mashup essay is, and before we discuss how to write about multimedia texts, it would be good to refresh your memory on some of the other types of essays you will be writing in this and other college classes. A great number of these approaches to writing, if not all, will be familiar to you.

There are ten common writing strategies that are used in nearly all of your writing experiences while in college and beyond. What follows is a brief outline of these ten types of essays and a description of what each writing strategy entails.

- **Descriptive Essays**
  Descriptive essays are usually shorter essays (a few paragraphs or a couple of pages) that tend to have a relatively simple subject. For example, you might be asked to describe your first car, your childhood home, or the city where you grew up. Usually these essays are assigned to familiarize students with the process of accurately and clearly describing using one or more of the five senses (sight, smell, sound, touch, taste). The process of description is often used as one part of a larger writing strategy, but it is a very important building block for writing strong, vivid papers.

- **Narrative Essays**

  A narrative essay is an essay in which you tell a story. However, a narrative essay is not fiction. Instead it is an essay based on true events. What writers seek to do using this writing strategy is to tell an intriguing story about a person or an event with the hope of informing or entertaining readers. Unlike journalists, who must simply give the facts, use quotes from people who were present at the event, and avoid incorporating their opinions into their articles, you are free to give your own impression of the story you are telling. This is the most natural form of writing, since we regularly tell stories to our friends or families about our weekend or something funny we witnessed on the drive to school. The important thing to remember about this approach to writing is that you must be sure to present the story in chronological order so that your readers can follow along.

- **Illustrative Essays**

  Like descriptive essays, illustrative essays seek to describe something or someone, but usually the subject being described is a little more abstract or complicated than a simple description of a house or a car. One example of this would be describing a visit to a war-torn country. You could simply describe the bombed-out buildings, the streets in disarray, or the children wearing tattered clothing, but that would only be scratching the surface of what it would mean to properly *illustrate* the various elements of a war-torn nation. Other elements you might want to describe would be the political situation, whether people are living in poverty, and how they are coping with the devastation and bloodshed. You might also want to illustrate the reasons for the war, the war's outcome, as well as where and how the country might move forward from this point to rebuild.

- **Process-Analysis Essays**

  Process-analysis essays are often referred to as "how-to" essays. This is because you are describing a process (such as how to change the oil in a car) while analyzing the steps along the way and explaining their purpose. Instead of a simple list of instructions, such as those that might accompany a build-it-yourself bookshelf or dresser, you should explain the rationale behind each step of the process to make sense of the entire procedure for someone who is not knowledgeable about the activity you are describing. You are not only describing how something is done and what the necessary steps are, but also what the end result will be. A good process-analysis essay also points out the reason a person might want to learn a specific process or skill in the first place. It seeks to show the benefits of a process, to teach how to do something, and to explain why it should be done.

- **Compare-Contrast Essays**

  Compare-contrast essays require a minimum of two things to be placed against one another to show their similarities and their differences. This form of thinking is used many times daily, so it is nearly as natural a form of writing as narrative essays are. We are constantly comparing and contrasting things—sports teams, types of cars, potential mates, restaurants—in our lives in order to choose what will best suit us. We make judgments about things in order to make sense of the world around us. When we compare and contrast objects, services, or even people, we naturally come to a definite conclusion. Sometimes we find the two things to be equal, and sometimes we find one is better or more preferable than the other. In a compare-contrast essay, you document the process of judging and describe your findings.

- **Classification Essays**

  In this form of essay writing, you usually take three or more groups and classify them. The purpose of this writing strategy is to show the ways these groups of objects, people, places, or ideas are different from one another. For example, you might talk about military personnel and their role in a war. There are two ways to go about classifying them. One way would be to classify these military personnel by the branch in which they serve—Army, Navy, Air Force, or Marines—which are qualities imposed on them by the definition of their military branch of service. There is a built-in difference in each of these branches by nature of the different purposes they serve in the larger military. Once you have these separate classes, you could then divide the military servicemen and servicewomen further according to their roles within each branch. They might be cooks, medical personnel, soldiers, officers, and so on.

- **Definition-Informative Essays**

  Occasionally the purpose of an essay is merely to inform. For example, when a new trend in music emerges (such as screamo), or a new disease is identified (such as swine flu or H1N1), many articles are produced in order to inform the general public about what these things are. The rationale behind a definition or informative essay, then, is to make an audience who is unfamiliar with a concept aware of its meaning, its origin, and its purpose. Think of encyclopedia or even Wikipedia entries. The purpose behind each of these is to inform people on subjects about which they have little or no knowledge.

- **Cause and Effect Essays**

  In this form of writing you are usually asked to present some sort of problem or event, and then illustrate some sort of outcome (whether it is a solution or another unresolved problem). If you were asked to describe the problem of the 2010 BP oil spill in the Gulf of Mexico, you might show the effect of the spill on the entire Gulf Coast community. Another approach would be to show the problem and then present a potential solution. Most essays using this approach follow this basic logical construction: "If [one particular event occurs (the cause)], then [another event may occur (the effect)]."

- **Argumentative Essays**
Argumentative essays are also often called persuasive essays. The purpose of these essays is quite simply to get your reader to agree with you on a particular topic. For example, if you feel that American cars are superior to Korean cars, you could make the case (citing facts, figures, or even experiences) to support your stance in the argument. Try not to confuse an argumentative essay with an argument you have with someone when you are angry. Instead, think of it as a systematic, rational approach to convince someone to see your side of a particular issue. The more logical and rational you are in your argument, and the better your supporting data, the more likely you will be to have your audience agree with you.

- **Research Essays**
A research essay is often a lengthier essay than any of the previously mentioned writing strategies because you are expected to do a very thorough examination of a given topic. The length of any particular research essay, as well as the number of sources needed to be successful, are dictated by the topic chosen and by how thorough you need to be. In theory, a research essay should not be constrained by page limits or minimums, nor should it be constrained or limited by a required number of sources. Realistically, this is rarely possible, and so most instructors give general topics from which you can begin your research, as well as page requirements and a specified number of sources. The key word in this approach to writing is *research*. You should allow yourself ample time to sift through a variety of sources, with the understanding that the first few sources you unearth during your search might not be the perfect match for your essay. When conducting research, remember to apply the previously discussed methods of determining source credibility.

These ten writing strategies are the most likely forms of writing you have used when generating formal assignments for classes. These are undoubtedly the most important forms of writing a student needs to master before graduating from college because after college you will regularly find yourself in a scenario (or scenarios) that will require you to call on these methods to make your case on a specific topic in all types of situations. Maybe you will need to describe what your daily activities at the office entail in order to justify a raise. Perhaps you will figure out a way to improve productivity at your office and will need to write up the process in a formal manner to present to company administrators. Regardless of which field of work you enter after graduation, you will inevitably find yourself recalling the writing strategies listed here to aid in your "real-life" writing.

However, one thing that makes the Mashup approach to incorporating multiple writing strategies a unique and valuable tool for college writing outside the composition classroom is that writing assignments in many different college settings often demand—by their very nature—that you utilize more than one writing strategy. For example, if you are a biology major and you are asked to give a presentation or construct a lab report on the research you conducted pertaining to cancer cells and the process by which they divide and replicate, the descriptive writing strategy would be the most logical place to begin. But, when you want to make a more sophisticated presentation, merely describing your work is not enough. You may begin by describing your research, but further explaining the process the cells undergo, in turn, shows your level of understanding in terms of the larger picture. You would also do well to provide media alongside your research that shows the real-world relevancy of your research (e.g., a YouTube video of cancer cells replicating or a photo collage of precancerous and postcancerous organs). Your writing on a topic would become still more impressive if you discussed the outcome of your research and its implications on the field of cancer research (the cause-effect strategy). The possibilities and combinations of writing strategies, as well as traditional and nontraditional texts, at your disposal in your writing are many, regardless of the specific college class you are attending. This is what you should remember as you generate essays for this and other college classes.

Additionally, you can use the Mashup approach when writing for your life beyond college. In the real world—regardless of your line of work—common writing situations often demand that you utilize more than one writing strategy. Take, for example, a person in the business field. If you were to graduate with a business major and find yourself employed in the type of environment where you needed to pitch a project to upper management, you would need to write more than a simple definition-informative essay or presentation. Your pitch would almost certainly require elements of research to prove the value of the project to the business as a whole. The proposal would also benefit greatly from the presence of a solid argument throughout because that would show you have considered the pros and the cons of the project (using, no less, comparison-contrast and cause-effect lines of thinking) and have prepared arguments in favor of your particular idea.

Now, take a moment to consider the recurring theme throughout the first two chapters of this textbook, which has been the theme of creating more sophisticated writing, learning critical thinking skills (the ability to read texts around you), and using the tendency for writing that you utilize every day when you text, tweet, or comment. All of these combined skills lay the groundwork for the concept of a Mashup essay.

So, what is a Mashup essay? One way to think of it is as an essay that combines one or more of the writing strategies listed previously. Think, for example, of how much better an illustrative essay about your visit to a war-torn country would be if you were to research the history of the war as well as the financial, political, or religious beliefs at the root of the conflict. You would then have an illustrative research essay. Or, consider the power of an argumentative essay in which you are attempting to persuade your reader to start a company in a foreign country. How much more powerful would your argument be if, besides quoting facts and figures, you were to include a narrative of the life of an average citizen in the impoverished country you are proposing as a great business location? Combining two or more of these writing strategies makes for more intriguing, more complex, and more meaningful essays than a standard single line of thinking or a single approach to any given topic.

There is another way this textbook envisions the Mashup essay, which is to include a variety of texts that go beyond the traditional concept of a printed article. We have spent a great deal of time preparing you for selections and themes in this textbook by illustrating the many texts around us that are often not seen as texts. And so, a Mashup essay would—and should—include more than just standard, traditional texts (essays, articles, the printed word). A Mashup essay could include video, the logo of a tennis ball, a "How I See It" story from a Starbucks cup, the shape of a car, an online video or music clip, or practically any other object that you believe to be a text. As long as you can justify its significance as a text, as long as you can "read" it and interpret it for your audience, then you can and should consider including these alternative texts in a Mashup essay.

The theory behind the Mashup writing strategy (using both traditional and nontraditional texts, as well as incorporating multiple writing strategies), beyond attaining a more sophisticated level of engagement and talent as a writer, is that we, as Americans, live in a society where the concept of a mashup prevails. We create parodies of parodies on YouTube. We mix and match hip-hop dressing styles with hipster styles. Nearly every element of our popular culture is made up of a variety of factors that, at first glance, might seem to be unrelated. Consider, for a moment, the recent trend in music where emo bands cover hip-hop songs. Or where hip-hop artists cover country songs. Or where R&B ballads are played acoustically in coffee shops. Our culture is so much a mashup—ethnically, racially, economically, artistically—that to find one element that is not being influenced by another is nearly impossible.

If we are to study and write about popular culture, in which the idea of a mashup is ever-present, then why not mirror culture itself by allowing ourselves this method of writing?

Though we have taken the time to define what a Mashup essay is and how it fits into the college classroom, the true Mashup essay and its capabilities are only limited by your imagination and your technological capabilities. Video essays in the middle of a text essay? Why not? A research essay that includes an online poll produced and conducted by you? Definitely. Posting your essay to a blog, sharing it with your friends, and recording their feedback or comments? Well, that would make an essay that is an active document, a living organism of sorts, with which people can interact.

Let's return once more to Ms. Brown's essay about images in the media. Observe the ways in which she makes it a Mashup essay. Not only does she include more than one selection from the chapter on violence, she turns to outside texts (photographs, Facebook groups, and even an Iraqi comment board) on the Web, and incorporates them into the overall picture. She does not need to speculate on how people might respond to a particular photograph because she sought out their reactions online. She makes no claim of being an expert. Instead, she lets the pictures speak for themselves, just as she lets the reactions in the viewers' comments speak for themselves. This is just one example of the potential of this form of essay writing.

Besides bringing a variety of texts and media to her essay, Ms. Brown also employs three different writing strategies in one essay, which is another form of Mashup essay. She combines descriptive writing with argumentation, as well as comparing and contrasting several different sources and people's reactions to them online. The end result is an essay that dissects her topic—the power of pictures and the danger of misconstruing their

**A Sample Mashup Essay Flowchart**

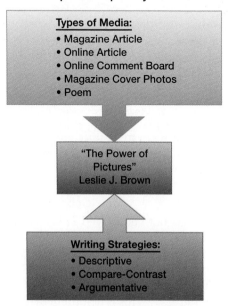

Types of Media:
• Magazine Article
• Online Article
• Online Comment Board
• Magazine Cover Photos
• Poem

"The Power of Pictures"
Leslie J. Brown

Writing Strategies:
• Descriptive
• Compare-Contrast
• Argumentative

messages—more elaborately than if she were to have employed only one of the three writing strategies.

Examine the illustration of the Mashup concept at work. The blue box contains the first approach, which is to include several types of texts and media. The red box contains the multiple writing strategies she employs to make her essay more engaging. You can choose to take either of these approaches, or both, in your own writing.

If the Mashup essay is anything, it should be writing that reflects the multitude of texts around us. We encourage you to read the texts in the world around you and incorporate them into your own writing.

Once you are ready to begin writing about your observations of popular culture and its many texts, and after you have generated an idea and potential outline for your paper, you will need to quickly and effectively engage your reader with your essay's opening paragraphs.

## Opening and Supporting Paragraphs

In the introductory paragraph of an essay, the idea is to move from a general topic to a more specific thesis statement so that your reader can follow along with your logic. This will allow your reader to accompany your thought process as you go from a broad subject to a more specific one. Observe the manner in which Ms. Brown accomplishes this with her opening paragraph:

> In tabloid magazines, pictures are published of Hollywood celebrities going about their daily lives. Gossip gets started when a celebrity is spotted communicating with another person, and the photos taken are subject to whatever story will sell. A picture of Gerard Butler and Jennifer Aniston laughing and talking gets the headline "Jennifer Aniston and Gerard Butler: It's For Real!" (STAR Magazine). A picture of Brad Pitt looking away from Angelina Jolie at an awards show results in a headline flashing "Brad and Angelina: Headed for Breakup" (AccessHollywood.com). It is never assumed that Butler and Aniston are just friends working on the set of their new movie, or that Pitt was simply not paying attention to the cameraman. With any photo, a caption, positive or negative, may be attached to it, causing the audience to have skewed assumptions of the actions taking place.

While Ms. Brown has not yet arrived at her final thesis, in this first paragraph she takes the reader from a general topic (celebrity photos in tabloids) to a more specific topic (without appropriate context, photos can be misconstrued in countless ways).

Most of us are in the habit of making the thesis of our essays known in the first paragraph of the essay. This is helpful in many contexts, but in the college context, it is perfectly acceptable to work toward your idea in one or more paragraphs. Ms. Brown decided to use this approach in her essay, and so the idea of her thesis emerges over the course of two paragraphs. Observe how her idea becomes more refined in the second paragraph:

> Photos of celebrities with headlines concerning who is dating whom and which couples are splitting up offer a bit of meaningless reading while waiting in the grocery store line. However, images of dying American soldiers scattered in the sand after a suicide bombing in Afghanistan, or a battered, burnt, disfigured marine on his wedding day have more dramatic effects on the viewers. Photos concerning powerful, controversial subjects cause viewers to take action and stand up for their beliefs. This phenomenon is addressed in the essay "Picture Imperfect: What the Torture Photos Can't Tell Us" by Jed Perl, which discusses how releasing photos of Americans fighting and dying in Iraq or Afghanistan could spur violent actions. The article also supports the decision of the Obama and Bush administrations to censor war photos released to the general population. Photos released portraying unnecessary brutality of American soldiers toward Iraqi prisoners have negative effects on rallying public support and makes the citizens of Iraq less inclined to work alongside America in its nation-building efforts. Any image captured only conveys what is happening in that split second and cannot accurately portray the preceding or subsequent action. Without a substantial narrative background, the photo's story can be twisted in different directions, telling a tale sometimes far from the truth. Perhaps in a photo of a soldier striking a prisoner, the soldier was retaliating to the prisoner's initial violent outburst, or perhaps the soldier was simply being brutally inhumane. The only people who know what actually happened were the individuals present. Everyone else can simply speculate and apply what he sees as a plausible story.

In the second paragraph the student built on her earlier idea while being more specific about the types of images she sees as problematic—specifically, wartime images that have been censored by the government. She adds to her previous thesis by showing her concern over the potential result of negative images coming out of wartime media coverage. Additionally, Ms. Brown specifically alludes to Jed Perl's article, "Picture Imperfect," by addressing its topic of bans on certain types of war photographs from appearing in print. Though not directly stated, she clearly agrees with the censorship of some wartime photography because, as she sees it, the potential negative outcomes of such a publication far outweigh the possible positive outcomes.

This is but one illustration of a thesis and introductory paragraphs. What you will find, as you read the selections in this textbook, is that there are many variants of introductory paragraphs at your disposal. In fact, it would be good practice to observe the ways in which the various authors get their essays off the ground throughout the many texts presented in the following chapters. Try to identify the ways these writers engage their readers while moving from a general topic to a more exact and sophisticated thesis.

There is one final point to consider when writing engaging introductory paragraphs to an essay. A good introduction to any topic will answer the following questions for a reader: "What is the author writing about?" "What does the author have to say about this particular topic?" "Why has the author chosen to write about this particular topic?" "What does the author hope for the reader to take away from the essay?" If your beginning paragraphs answer these questions, you will have achieved a clear and concise introduction to whatever topic you have chosen to explore within the pages of your essay.

## Conclusions

A strong conclusion should leave the reader with some final point to consider about the topic, rather than only restating points that have already been made. One helpful approach would be to make it clear why you wrote about the particular topic you chose. What engaged you about the topic? What did you hope to accomplish by writing about it? What do you want the reader to take away from your essay? Why should we care? If you can write a conclusion that addresses these questions, you will have achieved a confident and concise conclusion to your paper.

Here is Ms. Brown's conclusion:

> Clearly, the power of images to affect a viewer's opinion is stronger than most people initially think. Because of this, it is important that we consider the ramifications of printing photographs, as well as the stories that accompany them. Published photographs—whether they are slamming the marital shortcomings of a celebrity, or showing the aftermath of a bloody suicide bombing—should be honestly and accurately portrayed. It is the responsibility of the media who publish these photographs to regulate their publications so that they do not paint an inaccurate picture of what is being represented in the photographs. After all, even though a picture might be worth a thousand words, these thousand words could be very damaging, even devastating, if they are taken out of context.

Rather than restate her main ideas, Ms. Brown took the approach outlined above, answering the questions often posed by readers when they reach the end of an article or essay. A question-by-question dissection of the concluding paragraph will illustrate the manner in which she accomplished this.

*What engaged her about this topic?* Ms. Brown realized, over the course of reading the poem and the article mentioned in her essay, "that the power of images to affect a reader's opinion is stronger than most people initially think." Note the confident tone implied by beginning her concluding paragraph with the word "clearly." This implies that she feels she has made her point and does not need to restate all of her main ideas.

*What did she hope to accomplish by writing about this topic?* She hoped to illustrate the "ramifications of printing photographs, as well as the stories that accompany them," which include harm to a person's personal life (in the example of celebrity photographs) or even the potential violence being sparked by the posting of the disfigured marine's picture online.

*What did she want the reader to take away from her essay?* She calls for media who publish photographs to take responsibility for the potential harm they can do by demanding that published pictures "be honestly and accurately portrayed" and by calling on the media to "regulate their publications."

*Why should we care?* This is the strongest and most important point that Ms. Brown makes, and it is apt that it is her last line in the essay. She warns us that pictures can be "very damaging, even devastating, if they are taken out of context."

## Refining Your Essay

Chances are you have heard the term "revision" before, but odds are that you might have never paused to consider the meaning of the word. Often, when we think of revision as a concept, the first thought that comes to mind is editing. Editing, or proofreading, and revision are not the same, though many writers confuse the two. Proofreading will be addressed and explained in a moment, but first, observe the explanation and definition of revision as a concept and a writing tool.

## Revision

On the most basic level, the word "revision" has at its root the word "vision," which is the act of seeing. So, the word "revision" means to "see again." To that end, one of the most important and valuable approaches you can take when it comes to revision is getting some distance from your work. If you have written your paper ahead of time, you can put it away and forget about it for a couple of days. When you return to your essay and read it after you have been away from the writing, you will literally be seeing the manuscript with different eyes—a different point of view— than you would had you typed out the paper, printed it, reread it at that instant, and tried to find places where significant changes could be made.

One very helpful method of revising is to return to the concept of outlining mentioned earlier. When you make two outlines—one before writing the paper and one after—you can compare the two outlines and see how closely your paper actually came to the outline you created before writing the paper. You can see where you left out information that you intended to write. Conversely, you can also identify information you added while writing the essay that you did not initially intend to include. The idea is that you will then be able to seamlessly include the points you left out of your essay that were included in the original outline, or you can integrate the points you added to the essay that were not originally included in the first outline.

Another good revision technique is to have a classmate read your paper while asking a series of questions about the topic. Do not have him or her merely check for spelling or grammar. Instead, try to generate a list of "bigger picture" questions that will enable the reader to critique the *content* of your paper, rather than simply editing for mistakes.

The reason peer reviewing is such a powerful tool is that most writers, when we reread our papers during the revision process, self-correct the paper's errors in logic or reasoning while we read. It is hard for us to realize when we have made a leap in logic because we correct it in our minds during a rereading of the essay. This is not as likely to happen when another person reads your paper. He or she will not know where you intended to go with your topic and so will be much more likely to notice a faulty argument or a flaw in your paper's logic or order.

Think of revision not only as "seeing the paper again," but also as the step in the writing process where you will sometimes need to make drastic changes, such as cutting or adding entire paragraphs, finding additional sources, or sometimes even altering your opinion on a topic. As writers, the goal of revision is to improve the content of our papers, not just to clear up deficiencies in spelling and grammar.

## Proofreading

Proofreading is what most people envision when we think of the word "revision," but it is in this step that writers are actually editing. It is here that you should be on the lookout for grammatical errors, spelling errors, and strange word choices.

A number of wonderful proofreading techniques are available to you, among them the spellcheck tool. However, be sure to keep in mind that spellcheck is simply a program. It does not always understand context. In fact, most of us are in the habit of trusting spellcheck's decisions without taking a longer look at our own writing. One example of how spellcheck is not foolproof is that it will allow you to spell the wrong word correctly. If you spelled "their" and you meant "there," spellcheck might not be able to discern the fact that you correctly spelled the wrong word. The program mostly looks for incorrectly spelled words.

One of the best proofreading techniques—other than having a classmate proofread your paper—is to keep a running log of the types of mistakes you are prone to making in your writing. You probably already know whether you have a tendency for writing run-on sentences. Or maybe your teachers over the years have consistently pointed out your frequent sentence fragments, trouble with spelling, or some other grammatical issue. No matter what your personal writing issues are, if you keep a running log (think of it as a journal) documenting the types of mistakes you frequently make, you can go back over your paper during the proofreading process to seek out your common writing errors.

Writing labs are also helpful because they are staffed with people who are knowledgeable about the various processes involved in creating, revising, and proofreading papers. If your school does not have a writing lab, there are many online writing labs that have exercises to help you identify and correct whatever grammatical or structural issues you may notice in your writing. One of the best of these online writing labs is the Purdue University Online Writing Lab (Purdue OWL), which has a variety of exercises, PowerPoint presentations, and downloadable handouts to supplement your classroom instruction.

## Finding and Citing Your Sources

The format followed by most college English classes is a documentation style whose rules are standardized and regularly updated by the Modern Language Association (MLA). MLA style shows how to cite sources within the text each time you quote or describe them, as well as how to document all the sources you used in your essay in what is called a "Works Cited" page at the end of your paper. This is an additional page added to the end of your essay, separate from the body of the essay itself.

The purpose of using MLA citation style is to allow you to briefly identify your sources within the text so that the reader can refer to your Works Cited page for a complete citation. In-text citation is designed to be minimally disruptive, yet still provide credit to your source. In the Works Cited, you will be giving the information necessary to (a) credit the sources you've used in your writing and (b) allow your reader ample information so that she may locate the sources herself if she is interested in reading the complete document.

The purpose behind citation is three-fold, and it is important to understand this before bringing outside sources—whether traditional or multimedia—into your own work. Whether it is a printed essay, an advertisement in a magazine or on a billboard, or the body design of the

2012 Volkswagon Beetle, all of these texts are the result of someone else's hard work and vision, and the person should be credited for his role in creating the text that you are using in your essay.

First, the act of citation gives credit for another's work that you have included in your own. Whether you are using someone's research to support your own, or you are using another person's idea (for example, her reasoning and argument for why medicinal marijuana should be legalized), it is necessary to give appropriate credit to the idea and its original source. This can be thought of, in a sense, as a form of royalties—much like a musician might receive for every copy of an album sold. However, instead of paying people, your "royalty" is ensuring that people know who did the original work on which you are building.

The second reason behind the concept and practice of citation is that it lends credibility to your own research or argument. By deferring to the original person's work, all of his expertise and credentials give validity to the work from which you are citing, which, by extension, lends part of that credibility to your own argument, thereby strengthening it.

The third reason citation is required when using another person's work is to avoid *not* giving credit, which is referred to as plagiarism. To protect yourself against plagiarism (taking another person's work without giving her credit and passing it off as your own), you cite the source. This includes whether you are paraphrasing a person's work (restating an idea that isn't your own, but in your own words) or quoting directly.

On another note, keep in mind that if you are correctly using the Mashup approach outlined in this textbook, there is a fairly good chance you will occasionally run across a source type that is not listed in the following discussion. Should that occur, there are several free online resources at your disposal. Online documentation websites such as easybib.com or Purdue University's OWL website are convenient tools for finding citation methods for less commonly cited sources.

## In-Text Citations

The appropriate method of using an in-text citation is to use the author's name and page number in the same sentence where you quote, paraphrase, or summarize his ideas or words. Information not explicitly stated in the sentence should come at the end of the sentence between parentheses. There is no need to repeat the information.

If you were to cite Nick Redding's *Methland*, and you've already mentioned his name in the sentence, your sentence would look like this:

Nick Redding captures the lucrative appeal to meth dealing by pointing out how Lori Arnold, a famous Iowan meth dealer, "bought fourteen houses" in a short period of time (65).

If you do not mention the author's name in the sentence, then your sentence should read as follows:

> In a very short period of time, the powerhouse Iowan meth dealer, Lori Arnold, had "bought a car dealership," as well as "fourteen houses" (Redding 65).

Note that the parenthetical note falls within the sentence itself. The end punctuation comes last.

Here are some sample sentences using the most likely situations you will encounter when citing sources written by people.

### Source with One Author

> It became clear for many unemployed Iowans that Lori Arnold, who had recently "bought a car dealership" from her drug money, was up to something (Redding 65).

### Source with Two Authors

> The trick to locating a good poem is to "find the moments in our lives that man can relate to" (Knorr and Schell 5).

### Source Quoted Within Another Source (such as a person being quoted in an article from which you are quoting)

> Even Mildred Binstock sees corruption everywhere, which she illustrates when she makes the statement, "police are canoodling with the bad elements of this burg" (qtd. in Redding 95).

For other circumstances, such as a source with three or more authors, with no attributed author, with a corporate author (such as the American Medical Association), or from a multivolume work, search online for the phrase "MLA citation" to find valuable and exhaustive citation websites.

## Constructing a Works Cited

This list, which is compiled on a separate page at the end of your essay, should include every source you referred to using an in-text citation within your essay. The list should be alphabetized by each author's last name, in ascending order. In other words, list the last names beginning at A and ending at Z. Should you have a source with no author, you then alphabetize it by the title of the source. Furthermore, note that the first line of each citation is aligned all the way to the left, and, if the entry is longer than one line of text, the subsequent lines will be indented five spaces (or one tab). The entire document, including the entries themselves, should be double-spaced. Listed below are some common examples of types of sources you are most likely to encounter and use in your writing. Should you encounter a type of media or source not mentioned here, you can refer to online citation guides.

## Nonelectronic Sources

Note that all nonelectronic sources, or print publications, end with the word "Print." Because of the rise of professional and amateur electronic publishing (websites, ebooks, etc.), it has become necessary to indicate whether you are citing a source that appears in physical print on paper. Below are some of the most common nonelectronic types of sources you will encounter.

### Book by One Author

Brown, Larry. *Fay*. London: Black Swan, 2001. Print.

### Book by Two or More Authors

Shapard, Robert, and James Thomas. *New Sudden Fiction: Short-Stories from America and Beyond*. New York: W.W. Norton, 2007. Print.

### Work in an Anthology (including short stories, poetry, and essays in a collection)

Lee, Li-Young. "The Gift." *The Language of Life: A Festival of Poets*. Ed. Bill Moyers. New York: Doubleday, 1995. 228-29. Print.

### Article in a Newspaper

Glanton, Dahleen. "'Transformers 3' Work Wraps Early After Accident." *Chicago Tribune* 4 Sept. 2010, natl. ed.: A4. Print.

### Article in a Weekly Magazine

Adams, Rebecca. "Health Policy by Comparison." *CQ Weekly* 16 Aug. 2010: 1968+. Print.

### Article in a Monthly Magazine

Reynolds, Glenn Harlan. "Photo Phobia." *Popular Mechanics* Aug. 2010: 52–53. Print.

### Article in a Journal

Edgecombe, Rodney Stenning. "Emblems and Ecphrases in *Dombey and Son.*" *Dickens Quarterly* 27.2 (2010): 102–18. Print.

### Personal Interview

Sluder, Daniel. Personal interview. 23 August 2007.

### Published Interview

Carr, Judy. "Interview with Judy Carr." By Noah Eli Gordon. *Denver Quarterly* 44.3 (2010): 39–54. Print.

### Print Advertisement

Dickies. Advertisement. *Spin* Oct. 2008: 12. Print.

## Electronic Sources

Note that all references to websites, or to content found or retrieved using an Internet connection, end in a date. This is not necessarily the date the piece was published to the Web because most sites frequently edit, remove, or add content at irregular intervals. Because of this trait surrounding information accessed from or posted online, it is necessary that you end your citation entry with the date on which you accessed whatever information it is that you are citing. Secondly, because of the ever-changing nature of online publications, it sometimes becomes difficult to know who authored a piece, when it was first published, and whether it has been altered since its original publication. Because of this volatile nature of Internet publications and other forms of online texts, follow the bulleted list, step by step, and include any information you can locate for each step.

We will give an example using a source with all the information provided, and then apply this list to common online sources to show how these steps can be used to document virtually any online or electronic text.

The following citation is from a *Huffington Post* online news article.

Hindman, Nathaniel Cahners. "The Most (And Least) Stressed Counties in the U.S." *Huffingtonpost.com*. HuffingtonPost.com, Inc., 8 Sept. 2010. Web. 10 Sept. 2010.

### Online Publication Citation Checklist

- Name of author, creator, artist, editor, composer, director, translator, compiler, founder, or owner.

- Title of work.
- Title of overall website.
- Publisher or sponsor of the site; if not available, use N. pag.
- Date of publication (day, month, and year, if available); if nothing is available, use n.d.
- Medium of publication.
- Date of access (day, month, and year).

### Professional Website

Pareene, Alex. "Insurers Blame Rate Rises on Obamacare." *Salon.com*.
    Salon Media Group, 8 Sept. 2010. Web. 20 Sept. 2010.

### Personal Website

Saenz, Benjamin Alire. Benjaminaliresaenz.com. Web. 4 May 2009.

### Blog

Ciabattari, Jane. "Still Thinking About New Orleans." *Bookcritics.org*.
    National Book Critics Circle, 29 Aug. 2010. Web. 30 Aug. 2010.

### Online Book

Nabokov, Vladimir. *Lolita*. *Books.google.com*. Google, Inc., n.d. Web.
    19 Jan. 2009.

### Online Poem, Story, or Essay

Zatorski, Charlene. "Once." *Wordriot.org*. Word Riot, NFP., 15 Apr. 2010.
    Web. 30 June 2010.

### Online Newspaper Article

Savage, Charlie. "Court Sides with C.I.A. on Seizure of Terror Suspects."
    *Nytimes.com*. The New York Times Company, 8 Sept. 2010. Web.
    12 Sept. 2010.

### Online Magazine Article

Schwartz, Judith. "How to Save the Grasslands: Bring in More Cattle."
    *Time.com*. Time Warner, 7 Sept. 2010. Web. 8 Sept. 2010.

## Online Reference Source

"Hubert H. Humphrey. (Vice-president of the United States)" *Britannica.
com*. Encyclopedia Brittanica, Inc., 2010. Web. 8 Sept. 2010.

## Online Journal

Giles, Molly. "Ghost Dog." *Blackbird.vcu.edu*. Virginia Commonwealth
University, 2008. Web. 16 Dec. 2009.

## Online Scholarly Project

Thompson, Christen. "Information Illiterate or Lazy: How College Students
Use the Web for Research." *Muse.jhu.edu*. The Johns Hopkins
University, n.d. Web. 8 July 2009.

## Application

"Bejeweled." *Apple.com/iPhone*. PopCap Games, 2008. Web. 4 Jan. 2009.

## Videogame

Chichoski, Ben. *Call of Duty*. Activision, 2003. CD-ROM.

## Film or DVD

*Fight Club*. Dir. David Fincher. Perf. Edward Norton, Brad Pitt, Helena Bonham
Carter, Jared Leto, and Meatloaf. Fox 2000 Pictures, 1999. DVD.

## Compact Disc

To list one song from an album, simply place the title in quotes before the
album title. Place the songwriter credit (if different from the artist)
immediately after the album title.

Apple, Fiona. *Tidal*. Epic Records, 1996.

## E-mail

Plouffe, David E. "Re: State of the Union." Message to Ginger Hollibaugh.
25 Jan. 2010.

## Facebook Profile

Flores, Lucia. "Facebook: Lucia Flores." *Facebook.com*. Facebook, Inc.,
n.d. Web. 13 Feb. 2008.

### Twitter Feed

To list an individual Tweet, simply place the date of the Tweet before "Web." (using the day, month, and year format), followed by a period. Because a Tweet itself cannot be titled, the next best thing when referencing one is to use the date of the Tweet, which will enable a person to locate all the Tweets for that particular user on that particular day.

Spears, Britney. "Britney Spears on Twitter." *Twitter.com/britneyspears*
Twitter, Inc, 20 Feb. 2011. Web. 8 Sept. 2011.

## Sample Student Essay

Following you will find the complete student essay by Leslie Brown. You should read through the essay and the accompanying notes to see how Ms. Brown puts into practice the various elements of reading texts and writing about texts as discussed throughout the introductory chapters. Not only does Ms. Brown include a variety of texts and media, but also she uses multiple writing strategies to make her essay more engaging. Feel free to revisit this essay as often as needed to see a concrete example of a Mashup essay, which utilizes multiple writing strategies and a variety of different media as texts. In addition, to further illustrate the Mashup concept of writing at work, each of the following thematic chapters includes a professional essay that utilizes the Mashup approach—both in employing multiple writing strategies and in using traditional and nontraditional texts. For your convenience, each chapter's professional Mashup essay is accompanied by a flowchart like the one featured in this chapter, and each essay is also annotated to showcase the particular ways each author employs a variety of standard and multimedia texts. The complete student essay has also been annotated.

Outline

I. Introduction—Photos in tabloid magazines
   a. Celebrities are subject to any story that will sell magazines
      i. Gerard Butler and Jennifer Aniston
      ii. Brad Pitt and Angelina Jolie
   b. Any caption can be attached to a photo and skew the audience's view

II. Photos of war have a more dramatic effect on viewers
   a. "Picture Imperfect" supports Obama and Bush administrations
   b. Beneficial to censor war photos from public
   c. Photos of American soldiers' brutality toward Iraqi prisoners
      i. Only capture split second, no background information
      ii. Only people present can know what happened

III. "Body as Weapon, as Inspiration" shows different view of suicide bombing
   a. Destruction of woman's family
   b. Reason she did it not apparent to rest of the world
   c. Without understanding woman's reasons, it is easier to rationalize killings and war

IV. Past presidential administrations were right to censor photos
   a. Curbs violent reactions about war
   b. Public reactions to marine wedding photo
      i. Pro-American reactions
      ii. Anti-American reactions
   c. Monitoring footage reduces tension

V. Conclusion—Power of Images
   a. Consider consequences of publishing photos
   b. Media's responsibility to accurately portray photos
   c. Images should not be taken out of context

Leslie J. Brown

Prof. Aaron Morales

English 108

07/07/2010

The Power of Pictures

In tabloid magazines, pictures are published of Hollywood celebrities going about their daily lives. Gossip gets started when a celebrity is spotted communicating with another person, and the photos taken are subject to whatever story will sell. A picture of Gerard Butler and Jennifer Aniston laughing and talking to each other gets a headline that reads "Jennifer Aniston and Gerard Butler: It's For Real!" A photograph of Brad Pitt looking away from Angelina Jolie at an awards show is accompanied by a headline that flashes "Brad and Angelina: Headed for Breakup." It is never assumed that Butler and Aniston are just friends working on the set of their new movie, or that Pitt was simply not paying attention to the cameraman. With any photo, a caption, positive or negative, may be attached to it, causing the audience to have skewed assumptions of the actions taking place.

Photos of celebrities with headlines concerning who is dating whom and which couples are splitting up offer a bit of meaningless reading while waiting in the grocery store line. However, images of dying American soldiers scattered in the sand after a suicide bombing in Afghanistan or a disfigured marine on his wedding day have more dramatic effects on the viewers, which is why their publication should not be taken lightly. Photos concerning powerful, controversial subjects cause viewers to take action and stand up for their beliefs through a variety of means, such as starting Facebook groups like "I Support the War on Terrorism!" or, on the opposite end of the spectrum, terrorist organizations using these pictures to recruit new members.

---

**Throughout the essay, the student employs multiple writing strategies. However, the primary strategy to which she frequently returns is the strategy of argumentation.**

**The student begins her essay by looking to photographs on magazine covers (an outside source) as texts and reading the images as well as the photographs.**

**This entire introductory paragraph sets up the general concept of the paper's thesis: "pictures can be misconstrued by text or misread out of context."**

**This is the basic thesis of the paper, which she then expands further in the next paragraph.**

**In this paragraph, she refines her thesis to be more specific about the *types* of dangers these photographs might pose.**

Brown 2

This phenomenon is addressed in the essay "Picture Imperfect: What the Torture Photos Can't Tell Us," by Jed Perl. In his essay, Perl discusses how releasing additional photos of Americans soldiers torturing or mistreating prisoners of war could spur violent actions. The essay also supports the decision of the Obama and Bush administrations to censor other torture photos, and war photos in general, to keep them from reaching a wider audience. Perl summarizes his opinion on the matter in the following articulate fashion:

> Photographic truth is a particular kind of truth, and that is the case even when the photograph has not been doctored or edited. In going back to the courts to urge that these pictures not be released, the Obama administration is acknowledging this very fact. The argument against releasing them is not that they are not truthful, but, rather, that they represent an aspect of the truth about U.S. behavior in Iraq that Islamic militants will be able to use to create lies about the United States. (13)

Here the student summarizes and responds to the selection "Picture Imperfect," from our violence chapter.

Photos released that portray the unnecessary brutality of American soldiers toward Iraqi prisoners have negative effects on rallying public support, and they make the citizens of Iraq less inclined to work alongside America in its nation-building efforts. They also give fodder to groups such as Al Qaeda to use for war propaganda.

It is essential that publishers of these pictures, as well as the general public, understand that any image captured only conveys what is happening in that split second and cannot accurately portray the preceding or subsequent action. Without a substantial narrative background, the photo's story can be twisted in different directions, telling a tale sometimes far from the truth due to individual interpretations from both the author and the audience.

Brown 3

The danger of improperly interpreting images is that viewers' responses may be both unnecessary and based on untruths. Perhaps in a photo of a soldier striking a prisoner, the soldier was retaliating to the prisoner's initial violent outburst, or perhaps the soldier was simply being inhumane. The only people who know what actually happened are the individuals who were present. Everyone else can simply speculate and apply what they see as a plausible story. This can be dangerous to public morale and our soldiers' safety because differing opinions over controversial subjects can lead to undue tension among citizens during crucial times such as wartime. At a time when the country should be standing strong and united for both the soldiers and the world's perception of us, our fractured country risks seeming as though we are a disjointed, petulant group.

One wonderful example of how an event or a photograph of an event has more than one side to the story would be the poem "The Body as Weapon, as Inspiration," by Paul Martínez Pompa. In his emotional poem, Pompa considers another view of suicide bombings than what our media usually depicts. Rather than just condemning the bomber and dismissing her as yet another radical terrorist, Pompa provides a plausible reason for how a human being could be willing to cause such devastation. The poem describes the destruction of a young woman's family, the death of her father, and permanent disfiguring injury to her mother and brother from Israeli bombings of Palestinians. With strong, violent imagery, Pompa shows his readers "the shrapnel / a year ago that tore through / her mother's chest and maimed her / brother's legs," and we understand how her grief leads her to

Here she illustrates the concept of how there is more than one interpretation to any given moment caught on film.

This quote allows the two main sources from our text to back each other's message because of how she uses them to show the other side of the "photo" she imagines. Note that she also uses the compare-contrast strategy by looking at a particular incident from two different sides.

strap on a bomb, and walk into a Jerusalem market, exploding herself and as many of the people and surrounding buildings as possible (37). A picture taken of the woman as she detonates the bomb strapped to herself in the middle of a crowd of innocent bystanders could never capture the reason why she did it. It allows viewers from the rest of the world to immediately believe that she is simply acting out of loathsome hatred and cold-blooded opposition, instead of considering that she may be reacting because of an overwhelming sense of love, a painful need for justice, and the suffocating grief felt from the loss of her family and way of life.

Without making her story more humane by showing the public the real reasons she might have resorted to suicide bombing, it is easy for militaries to continue with bombings and wars, rationalizing the destruction caused by making the opposition appear as lowly savages with feelings not half as acute as our own, instead of the multi-facetted individuals they very well may be. When we look at a photo of a suicide bombing, it is too easy to dismiss a bomber who we see as too different from ourselves. Without her story we cannot imagine that she might experience the same chest-aching national pride when she sees her flag flapping in the wind as we do, or that she loves her family with as much fervor as we love ours and experiences the same tug of obligation to protect their unique existence. When the humanistic side of the opposition is lost in a sea of our own outrage and pain, it becomes easier to continue killing, bombing, and obliterating the enemy and their way of life.

Like Perl, I believe that the Obama and Bush administrations were right to censor the photographs shown to the general public in order to prevent misconceptions and unnecessary hostility from the general public, or world citizens offended by our war. Both presidential administrations understood that seeing the images in question

Brown 5

without knowing the individual circumstances in that split second allows for inaccurate speculation by viewers. In wartime, when opinions tend to be staunchly for or against military action, censoring photos protects the soldiers, the countries involved, and the general public. It helps curb violent reactions from people opposed to the war, acting out against our country, or from people supporting the war, becoming incensed by the horrors occurring from the opposing side and discriminating against all people from the Middle East.

Here is an example of this phenomenon of misreading pictures played out in an online forum. Photojournalist Nina Berman won the 2006 World Press Photo competition for a wedding photo of a twenty-four-year-old Marine war veteran who had been disfigured beyond recognition, with his ears, eyes, nose, mouth, and chin melted away from the destruction of a suicide bomber. In an interview by Lindsay Beyerstein at Salon.com, Berman was asked about public reactions from the photo (Beyerstein). She says after she took the photo and posted it online, over one hundred thousand people viewed it in one day through Fark and it got linked to sites ranging from pro-war and anti-war to Valentine's Day sites. Some saw the Marine's disfigurement as a painful reminder of the damage to American soldiers and their families, and as another reason to end the wars. Others were incensed, feeling America should fight harder, and get revenge on the "savage terrorists." However, there were others who felt American soldiers were getting what they deserved. In a repost of the article on www.iraq-war.ru, a comment was posted that stated, "hopefully more invaders will suffer similar pain" ("News from Iraq").

> Here the student brings in a photo published online and the comments posted in response. She goes another step further, later on, and seeks out opposing views, which strengthens her thesis.

Brown 6

With one image, many strong and differing opinions were felt, causing tension and acting as a catalyst for violence. These reactions could be avoided if we continue monitoring and censoring the footage unveiled to the public.

Clearly, the power of images to affect a viewer's opinion is stronger than most people initially think. Because of this, it is important that we consider the ramifications of printing photographs, as well as the stories that accompany them. Published photographs—whether they are slamming the marital shortcomings of a celebrity, or showing the aftermath of a bloody suicide bombing—should be honestly and accurately portrayed. It is the responsibility of the media who publish these photographs to regulate their publications so that they do not paint an inaccurate picture of what is being represented in the photographs. After all, even though a picture might be worth a thousand words, these thousand words could be very damaging, even devastating, if they are taken out of context.

Brown 7

Works Cited

Beyerstein, Lindsay. "The Face of War." *Salon.com.*
Salon, Inc., 2007. Web. 4 Jul 2010.

"Brad and Angelina: Headed for Breakup?"
*Accesshollywood.com.* NBC Universal Television
Group, 2010. Web. 4 Jul 2010.

"Jen Aniston & Gerard Butler: They're On."
*Starmagazine.com.* The American Media, Inc.,
9 Sept 2009. Web. 4 Jul 2010.

"News from Iraq: War, Politics, Economy." *Iraq-war.ru.*
N. pag. n.d. Web. 6 July 2010.

Perl, Jed. "Picture Imperfect: What the Torture Photos
Can't Tell Us." *The New Republic.* 17 June 2009:
12–14. Print.

Pompa, Paul Martínez. "The Body as Weapon, as
Inspiration." *My Kill Adore Him.* Notre Dame:
U of Notre Dame P, 2009. 37. Print.

# Identity
# Construction

**Chapter 3**

## Making the Cultural Connection

It is not easy to pin one definition on a culture as diverse and complicated as ours. We Americans have varying perspectives of ourselves, as well as stereotypes that we both despise and believe in. For example, some people believe that Americans are steadily becoming more ignorant, more overweight, more unhealthy, and more closed-minded, while others believe that we are rapidly evolving as a country that has become a beacon of hope to other countries who strive for equality, justice, and the acceptance of difference. So which of these two is a correct assessment of American identity, and is there a way to sort out all of these contradictions? Is there a place, or places, where we can turn to find out how we define ourselves as a country of people?

Regardless of whether there is a simple unifying definition of what it means to be American, the undeniable fact is that America is a country made up of many different

63

cultural, religious, ethnic, racial, economic, geographic, and sexual identities, to name just a few. Although all of these complex and sometimes overlapping identities are too numerous to address in one chapter of a textbook, we will nevertheless attempt to uncover what it means to be American and how each of these variants in our identities comes together to define us as a nation. There most certainly are elements of our society that will go unmentioned, but throughout this chapter and each subsequent thematic chapter in the textbook, the groundwork will be laid for you to explore many other facets of American identity within your own writing.

One interesting exercise in contemplating American identity is to observe the ways in which other countries view us. We need not look far to realize that our relationship with the rest of the world is complicated, and because of that, other countries' opinions of us are forever shifting. To those who oppose our ideals and lifestyle, we appear to be a nation composed of citizens with loose moral values. To others, we are a nation of overeating, gun-toting drug addicts who have no manners. After all, we are home to the world's largest illicit drug market. We are also home to companies like Taco Bell, who cleverly came up with the concept of the "Fourth Meal," which encourages people to eat more than is physically necessary. And, yes, our nation is currently suffering from an obesity epidemic. So the images here are not exactly incorrect.

However, the opposite point of view, from those countries that admire ours, is that we are a land of great wealth, where people from all walks of life have the opportunity to further themselves. We are a country with countless success stories of people who started with nothing, with the clichéd "clothes on their backs and a few dollars in their pockets," only to make a comfortable life for themselves and their families. We are a nation whose Constitution is one of the oldest in the world. Through revisions and

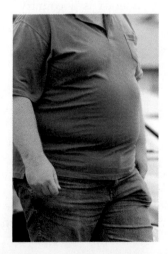

amendments, we have addressed our country's faults, and we continue to do so to this day. So, to our nation's admirers, America surely has its flaws, but we have the amazing capacity to reinvent ourselves, to right our wrongs, and to set a positive example for the rest of the world. These are the positive elements of American identity.

When it comes to the idea of a national identity, it is worth noting that nearly everyone in America has heard of the "American Dream," which many of us see as our birthright. But what exactly does this concept mean? It is the unspoken promise made to all Americans that those who do hard and honest work will see their lives improve. It is the unspoken promise that regardless of one's personal identity, everyone will have a fair chance to carve out a comfortable existence, and some of us might even become enormously wealthy. On the surface of things, this is mostly true. But on a personal level, the definition of this American Dream shifts according to what we hope to achieve in our lives. For some of us, it is as simple as finding a good enough job to pay our bills and cover our basic needs, to pull ourselves up out of poverty. Others dream of becoming millionaires, living in sprawling estates, and traveling all over the world. For most of us, however, our dreams lie somewhere in between these two examples.

Still, the question is, how do we form our identity as Americans, especially within our own particular groups with which we identify? To where do we turn to understand who we are as individuals within the greater landscape of American identity? Many people turn to the media. For example, young men and women might turn to men's and women's magazines for advice on defining themselves in regard to their gender. We look to TV shows to see how other people like us act on screen. We watch movies, visit websites, and scour online profiles, all in an effort to glean from a variety of sources those traits that we feel best suit how we identify ourselves. When it comes to the media's representation of Americans, we mostly understand that not everyone is represented in the mainstream outlets. However, the media plays a pivotal role in how we shape our identities, if for no other reason than they illuminate for us what is acceptable or unacceptable in our society. For example, until Ellen DeGeneres came out publicly in the Nineties, very few public figures would have dared to speak openly about their sexual orientation for fear of losing their careers and fan bases. Of course, as we now know, Ellen's gamble paid off, and she paved the way for countless other men and women who have since realized that a person can be open about his sexual orientation and not fear reprisals. In the wake of Ellen's coming out, we have had a wide variety of TV shows, movies, and popular songs that show society has become more accepting of various sexual orientations than it was even a few decades ago. This, then, is the role the media and popular culture often play in the complicated process of identity construction.

In addition to popular culture and the media, many of us also turn to our parents to see what traditions we have in our own particular ethnic and racial backgrounds. We may turn to them in order to observe them as role models for the men and women we hope to become. We also associate ourselves with peers who believe as we do, and we align ourselves with those with whom we feel a sense of community. In a nutshell, this is how we find a community of people with similar identities.

America continues to become more diverse and more complex as it mirrors the people who inhabit the country. Because of this, our culture undergoes a significant shift with each generation, and more identities emerge. For example, what was once merely referred to as the "homosexual community" now frequently goes by the initials "LGBTQ," which stands for lesbian, gay, bisexual, transgendered, and questioning (those who are still questioning their sexual orientation). In terms of race, one need only look to the 2010 U.S. Census form to see the wide variety of racial backgrounds represented in our country. To see how our culture has shifted, you could easily locate earlier census questionnaires online and observe how the categories have multiplied over the years.

Regardless of whether a person chooses to identify with a particular race, ethnicity, gender, religion, political party, geographic region, or sexual orientation, each American citizen's identity is made up of some combination of these groups, and subgroups within these groups. Although the potential identities are as numerous as our country's inhabitants, this chapter will address some of the more predominant identity issues in our culture, with the understanding that it is not meant to be all-inclusive. However, many discussion and writing prompts in this chapter and throughout the entire textbook will enable you to do a much more thorough dissection and study of identity. In this chapter we will, for example, explore the impressions that people from other countries have of Americans, as well as the different impressions we have of ourselves based on our geographic locations. After all, those who live in a rural area are not likely to understand the subtleties of urban existence, and vice versa. We will also discuss race relations in our country, as well as how and why people identify with a particular race.

The important thing to keep in mind as you proceed through this chapter is that we live in a country whose stated mission is justice and equality for all. The essays in this section address this concept from various angles in an attempt to let specific groups speak for themselves, or at least to observe the way these groups are portrayed in the media and whether the portrayals are accurate. We will discuss what it means to be a man, and what it means to be a woman, as well as where our definitions of masculinity and femininity come from. Do we turn only to our parents, or are there other cultural messages from which we learn gender roles and definitions? Are we as a country divided between rural and urban populations, or do we tend to divide ourselves more by race? Are younger people more tolerant than their elders, and if so, why? These, among other topics, are what we will address as we explore what it means to be American, as well as what our personal identities say about us. This discussion of American identity will reoccur throughout the entire text as we examine American identity and culture from a variety of different angles and perspectives.

## Citizenship
### David Fitzsimmons

David Fitzsimmons is a political cartoonist and columnist for the *Arizona Daily Star*, based out of Tucson, Arizona. He is also a nationally syndicated cartoonist with Cagle Cartoons. This cartoon first appeared in the *Arizona Daily Star* on July 21, 2009.

## Thinking About American Identity

Take a moment to look at the accompanying cartoon. Like most political cartoons, this drawing is attempting to make a statement about a topic that is popular in our culture. This cartoon's subject matter, which can be discerned at a glance, is American identity, or, more specifically, the way in which we Americans identify ourselves in terms of what it means to be a citizen in the United States. Note that the cartoon is titled "Citizenship," which also implies it is addressing the recent political debates on potentially repealing the 14th Amendment to the U.S. Constitution (the amendment that declares anyone born on U.S. soil is automatically a citizen). If, indeed, the artist is addressing the issue of citizenship, then it would appear he is also alluding to the concept of a "citizenship test," which is a requirement for all people who apply for U.S. citizenship. These citizenship tests ask applicants questions about U.S. history, politics, leaders, culture, and our country's Constitution.

Citizenship—a person's legal status of citizen in a particular country—is, of course, a concept about which many people have very strong feelings. Some Americans feel that all those who apply for citizenship to our country should be granted this status if they have something to contribute to our society, while others feel that our borders should be locked down and no one further should be let into the States. Regardless of your feelings on the subject, it is worth noting that at the root of American citizenship is the idea of what it means to be American. This is the purpose of asking potential citizens questions about American culture and history. In theory, anyone who wants to be a citizen of our country should have some general knowledge about its history, its government, its ideals, and its traditions. At least, that is the logic behind the existence of a citizenship test.

Even if you are not familiar with the actual test that people applying for citizenship must pass, you may have heard the criticism of the test that states most Americans could not answer the majority of the test's questions. This is the allusion being made by the words above the cartoon that read "7 out of 10 Americans," which implies that seven of ten current U.S. citizens would not be able to pass our own citizenship test. Part of the message of this cartoon is that Americans are just as ignorant, if not more so, about our own country and its history as a foreign-born person might be. Naturally, there are Americans who know a great deal about our culture and history, just as there are people who know very little about either. Some American critics who believe our country is slowly being overrun with ignorance might even argue that our ability to ignore—or to show very little interest in—our culture and history is a very American attribute in itself. Which of these two points of view do you believe that Fitzsimmons holds, based on his depiction of Americans in the cartoon?

Aside from the question of citizenship and Americans' knowledge about our own culture, the other idea raised by Fitzsimmons's cartoon is the question of what it means to be an American citizen. Notice the various American stereotypes he addresses in his cartoon. Which of these, if any, do you agree with? Which of them, if any, do you find offensive? Which American stereotypes did he leave out?

Now, take a closer look at Fitzsimmons's cartoon. Notice some of the finer details. How many of the questions addressed in each frame would you be able to correctly answer? How many of the depictions of "average" Americans do you think are accurate? What does it say about our society that so many of us might not be able to answer such basic questions about our own country and its history? What do you think Fitzsimmons is saying about our obsession with immigration and citizenship? For example, how much do you believe a potential citizen should be required to know about our country? Conversely, how much should an American citizen know about her country?

Finally, and perhaps most importantly, reconsider the words written at the top of the cartoon: "7 out of 10 Americans." If this figure is even remotely accurate, what does it say about our country that we expect those applying for citizenship to know more than the majority of our own citizens do? Do you see this lack of cultural and historical knowledge about one's own country as problematic? Why or why not? If you were to ignore the stereotype being addressed in this cartoon—that Americans are ignorant—how might you define what it means to be American? How might race or economic background factor into your definition? If you were to draw a cartoon of a stereotypical American, what might the "text" of the person say about him? What sorts of traits are considered to be "American" in general? How might a person from another country depict a stereotypical American?

# Objectif Lune                                   Charles Dantzig

**Let's Start Here••• ▶**    As Americans, we undoubtedly have a vision of ourselves that differs from the opinions an outsider might hold of us. After all, it is easy to both criticize and glorify ourselves and our fellow countrymen. We enjoy doing both through our television and radio shows, websites, magazines, and newspapers. However, like most countries, we reserve the right to be our own biggest critics. We do not appreciate people from other countries criticizing us, which is what makes the following selection of interest in a chapter in which we attempt to define what it means to be American.

In the following piece, writer Charles Dantzig—a French citizen—creates an encyclopedia entry on what he sees as the defining traits of American citizens. In true encyclopedic form, what Dantzig gives his readers is a general overview of Americans, as he perceives us. He also gives specific descriptions about stereotypical American habits. Some of these descriptions are more meaningful and relevant than others, but a general sense of Dantzig's opinion of American people becomes quite clear over the course of his essay.

As you read the following essay, try to determine which descriptions you believe he gets correct, as well as those that he gets wrong.

---

Charles Dantzig is a French novelist, essayist, poet, and publisher. This selection is excerpted from Dantzig's "Liste des Américains," in his *Encyclopédie capricieuse du tout et du rien*, published in France in the winter of 2009 by Grasset & Fasquelle. The encyclopedia explains the world in a series of 800 lists. Translated from the French by Lorin Stein.

---

Americans consider themselves polite, but they stick their hands in their pockets, drink from the bottle, speak in raised voices. Someone ought to train them how to behave in museums. Not only do they converse as if they were in their own houses; they do so in order to give educational lectures. With all their terrible goodwill, they wish to learn and to make all things serve this purpose. It is an American vice to believe that a work of art must teach something. In the same way, they were persuaded to drink red wine because they were told that wine was good for them, without consideration of pleasure. Their passion for learning is naïve and honorable.

One thing about Americans that I always forget and that always strikes me when I arrive in their country—or, rather, step onto the airplane—is the bad cut of their jeans. And also their taste for muscle. Whether this is one practical manifestation of a taste for brute force I cannot say. Also the soft drinks, which come in bottles twice as big as anywhere else, and the power lines, which instead of being buried underground encumber the edges of the sky. And that it's a country of blonds. And their obsession with the weather, forever plastered on the screen by NY1 and printed at the bottom of the back page of the *New York Times* along with the temperature, humidity level, and wind speed. In the end, what we forget about countries is everything banal that we want to call characteristic. Isn't this what goes by the name of sociology?

**banal:**
Uninteresting.

They are overly fond of brown.

They eat all the time. What anguish must be theirs!

Charles Olson—or was it Melville?—said that America has replaced history with geography. What makes for boredom, which in America can be so violent, is the unfilled urban space. In contrast to Europe or Asia, which are stuffed to overflowing, in the United States the population density per square kilometer is very low. Whence those depressing suburbs, depressing because one can always find a parking place. In America one feels not solitude but isolations.

They are a people without balconies. Yet they cannot help interfering in other people's business, according to the Protestant custom. And on courthouse steps one sees people brandishing signs that say, as if they knew, GOD HATES ABORTIONISTS. It is a country fascinated by lust.

Americans spend less time arguing over things than over the right to speak about those things.

It is also one of the only countries where rights count. Everyone has the right to question whatever he chooses, starting with things laid down by law. In most other countries, rights are, by comparison, a laughing matter. And there are not many places on earth where people spend their lives fighting injustices committed against the weak.

They go to court over everything. This is a way of making money, of course, and of causing trouble for one's neighbor, but more deeply it points to the fact that, for them, nothing follows from itself. One good quality of the United States is that here common sense is never taken for an established thing. These litigious people believe more in reason than in fatalism.

Thanks to their lamentable admiration for brute force, they are described as fascist, but they lack one essential trait that makes a fascist: the admiration for death.

It is the only country in the world where no one remains a foreigner. A person can go by the name of Zgrabenalidongsteinloff and no one will raise an eyebrow. "In New York there are no impossible names," as I was told by a novelist whose name raised the eyebrows of elegant racists in Paris. This is what makes everything possible. They walked on the moon because they are the moon. One admires their courtesy.

**litigious:**
Frequently involved in lawsuits.

**fatalism:**
A belief in the idea that humans are powerless to change their circumstances because everything is predetermined for us.

**fascist:**
Political belief that values the nation (and sometimes a race) above the individual and uses physical force or violence to subdue the opposition.

---

**Let's Pause Here••• ▶** What are your initial reactions to Charles Dantzig's list of American traits? Do you think his essay is more pro-American or anti-American, and why? Do you think he is joking or serious in his criticisms of Americans? What leads you to believe that he is being sarcastic or serious, depending on which you believe him to be doing? What—if anything—is the effect of reading this encyclopedia entry on your opinion of Americans in general? Which of the two are more serious and carry more weight, his criticisms or his praises of Americans?

---

**Let's Take It Further••• ▼**

1. What do you believe to be the point, or the message, behind Dantzig's encyclopedia entry about Americans? Based on his language and usage of vocabulary, who do you think his intended audience is, and why? How might this "entry" differ if he were to address it to Americans?

2. Regardless of whether you believe Dantzig is joking or serious, which of his many descriptions of American traits do you believe are his most accurate and why (even if they might be sensitive topics)?

3. Of Dantzig's criticisms of American "rudeness," which of them do you actually consider to be rude behavior, if any? How might someone outside of America perceive these same actions to be rude? What types of "rudeness" do you witness with enough frequency that it might be attributed to Americans in general?

4. What do you think about Dantzig's reference to our "terrible goodwill"? What do you think he means by this phrase? Do you agree with his usage of the phrase? What type of goodwill can be perceived as an "American" type of goodwill? How might our particular style of goodwill be perceived by others as terrible, and why?

5. Generate a list of pros and cons about American people and compare it to the list in Dantzig's piece. How are your depictions of the positive elements of American citizens similar to and different from Dantzig's depictions of Americans? How are your negative traits of Americans similar to or different from Dantzig's criticisms of American people? How can you account for the ways in which your list differs from his? What about the manner in which your list is similar?

6. Do you agree or disagree with Dantzig's assertions that our American landscape is "depressing"? Whether or not you agree with him, describe the American landscape as you are familiar with it by illustrating the elements of our country that are aesthetically pleasing as well as the elements of our landscape that are less attractive. In your opinion, what is the most beautiful part of our country that you have seen? What is the most unattractive part of the country you have seen? Compare and contrast the two. What locations in our country would you most recommend that a visitor to America should see, and why?

7. Using references to American popular culture (particularly our mass media, as defined in the next chapter's introduction), argue for or against Dantzig's claim that we Americans have a "taste for muscle," and indicate whether you agree that we also have "a taste for brute force," as he suggests.

8. Research popular cultural trends by looking to our most popular mass media outlets (TV channels, websites, magazines, and newspapers) and illustrate our country's obsessions according to trends that emerge. With what do Americans most concern ourselves, judging from our mass media? If an outsider turned to our popular media to define Americans, what effect might it have on how that person might think of our country? How might the person get the wrong or the right impression of who we really are as a nation?

9. Choose a foreign country and make an encyclopedia entry about the people who live there. From where did you get your impressions of the people whose country you chose? Is your entry attempting to be humorous or critical? Explain your decision to define the country in either a humorous or critical way. How is your entry meant to be similar to or different from Dantzig's entry on Americans? What do you hope the impression of your entry would be if someone from the country you wrote about were to read your essay?

10. Create a video essay/collage (post on YouTube, a website, or within a PowerPoint presentation) that answers the question, "What is an American?" Accompany the video with an essay that explains the imagery used throughout your visual essay, as well as the definitions you have come up with for what an American is.

# America: The Multinational Society
**Ishmael Reed**

In the time since the devastating 9/11 attacks on the World Trade Center, Americans have discovered new ways to band together as a nation. Despite the fact that we regularly discuss and debate our differences, there is a distinctly American trait that many believe to be the reason for our nation's rise and strength in the two hundred plus years since our founding: we are a nation composed of many cultures whose brightest minds flock to our country to pursue the "American Dream."

The following essay by American literary icon Ishmael Reed is, in many ways, a simultaneous discussion of the value of our multicultural society and an attempt to define America from an American's perspective. Although the essay is two decades old, it is every bit as relevant now as it was when Reed first published it. In fact, the general topic of the essay is one that might be even *more* relevant to our time, as we publicly debate the issue of immigration reform and discuss the value of the various cultures that are woven into our country's fabric of identity.

As you read the essay, see whether you agree with Reed's opinion of what America means as a place as well as an idea. Furthermore, note the examples he gives to prove his point about what makes America such a unique country.

---

Ishmael Reed is a poet, essayist, novelist, editor, and critic whose often-controversial writing frequently deals with race relations in America. Widely regarded as one of the most influential modern-day African American literary icons, Reed also spent 35 years as a lecturer at the University of California, Berkeley. This essay appeared in Reed's 1988 book, *Writin' Is Fightin': Thrity-Seven Years of Boxing on Paper.*

> At the annual Lower East Side Jewish Festival yesterday, a Chinese woman ate a pizza slice in front of Ty Thuan Duc's Vietnamese grocery store. Beside her a Spanish-speaking family patronized a cart with two signs: "Italian Ices" and "Kosher by Rabbi Alper." And after the pastrami ran out, every–body ate knishes.
>
> —*New York Times* 23 June, 1983

On the day before Memorial Day, 1983, a poet called me to describe a city he had just visited. He said that one section included mosques, built by the Islamic people who dwelled there. Attending his reading, he said, were large numbers of Hispanic people, forty thousand of whom lived in the same city. He was not talking about a fabled city located in some mysterious region of the world. The city he'd visited was Detroit.

A few months before, as I was leaving Houston, Texas, I heard it announced on the radio that Texas's largest minority was Mexican-American, and though a foundation recently issued a report critical of bilingual education, the taped voice used to guide the passengers on the air trams connecting terminals in Dallas Airport is in both Spanish and English. If the trend continues, a day will come when it will be difficult to travel through some sections of the country without hearing commands in both English and Spanish; after all, for some western states, Spanish was the first written language and the Spanish style lives on in the western way of life.

Shortly after my Texas trip, I sat in an auditorium located on the campus of the University of Wisconsin at Milwaukee as a Yale professor—whose original work on the influence of African cultures upon those of the Americas has led to his ostracism from some monocultural intellectual circles—walked up and down the aisle, like an old-time southern evangelist, dancing and drumming the top of the lectern, illustrating his points before some serious Afro-American intellectuals and artists who cheered and applauded his performance and his mastery of information. The professor was "white." After his lecture, he joined a group of Milwaukeeans in a conversation. All of the participants spoke Yoruban, though only the professor had ever traveled to Africa.

**ostracism:**
Exclusion or symbolic exile by general consent of a group of people.

**monocultural:**
Dominated or concerned with one culture above all others.

One of the artists told me that his paintings, which included African and Afro-American mythological symbols and imagery, were hanging in the local McDonald's restaurant. The next day I went to McDonald's and snapped pictures of smiling youngsters eating hamburgers below paintings that could grace the walls of any of the country's leading museums. The manager of the local McDonald's said, "I don't know what you boys are doing, but I like it," as he commissioned the local painters to exhibit in his restaurant.

Such blurring of cultural styles occurs in everyday life in the United States to a greater extent than anyone can imagine and is probably more prevalent than the sensational conflict between people of different backgrounds that is played up and often encouraged by the media. The result is what the Yale professor, Robert Thompson, referred to as a cultural bouillabaisse, yet members of the nation's present educational and cultural Elect still cling to the notion that the United States belongs to some vaguely defined entity they refer to as "Western civilization," by which they mean, presumably, a civilization created by the people of Europe, as if Europe can be viewed in monolithic terms. Is Beethoven's Ninth Symphony, which includes Turkish marches, a part of Western civilization, or the late nineteenth- and twentieth-century French paintings, whose creators were influenced by Japanese art? And what of

**bouillabaisse:**
Stew of many ingredients.

**monolithic:**
Made up of a single unchanging or unvaried culture.

the cubists, through whom the influence of African art changed modern painting, or the surrealists, who were so impressed with the art of the Pacific Northwest Indians that, in their map of North America, Alaska dwarfs the lower forty-eight in size?

Are the Russians, who are often criticized for their adoption of "Western" ways by Tsarist dissidents in exile, members of Western civilization? And what of the millions of Europeans who have black African and Asian ancestry, black Africans having occupied several countries for hundreds of years? Are these "Europeans" members of Western civilization, or the Hungarians, who originated across the Urals in a place called Greater Hungary, or the Irish, who came from the Iberian Peninsula?

> **dissidents:**
> People who oppose a system of beliefs, religion, or politics.

Even the notion that North America is part of Western civilization because our "system of government" is derived from Europe is being challenged by native American historians who say that the founding fathers, Benjamin Franklin especially, were actually influenced by the system of government that had been adopted by the Iroquois hundreds of years prior to the arrival of large numbers of Europeans.

Western civilization, then, becomes another confusing category like Third World, or Judeo-Christian culture, as man attempts to impose his small-screen view of political and cultural reality upon a complex world. Our most publicized novelist recently said that Western civilization was the greatest achievement of mankind, an attitude that flourishes on the street level as scribbles in public restrooms: "White Power," "Niggers and Spics Suck," or "Hitler was a prophet," the later being the most telling, for wasn't Adolph Hitler the archetypal monoculturalist who, in his pigheaded arrogance, believed that one way and one blood was so pure that it had to be protected from alien strains at all costs? Where did such an attitude, which has caused so much misery and depression in our national life, which has tainted even our noblest achievements, begin? An attitude that caused the incarceration of Japanese-American citizens during World War II, the persecution of Chicanos and Chinese-Americans, the near-extermination of the Indians, and the murder and lynchings of thousands of Afro-Americans.

Virtuous, hardworking, pious, even though they occasionally would wander off after some fancy clothes, or rendezvous in the woods with the town prostitute, the Puritans are idealized in our school-books as "a hardy band" of no-nonsense patriarchs whose discipline razed the forest and brought order to the New World (a term that annoys Native American historians). Industrious, responsible, it was their "Yankee ingenuity" and practicality that created the work ethic. They were simple folk who produced a number of good poets, and they set the tone for the American writing style, of lean and spare lines, long before Hemingway.

> **patriarchs:**
> Male founders.
>
> **razed:**
> Destroyed.

They worshipped in churches whose colors blended in with the New England snow, churches with simple structures and ornate lecterns.

The Puritans were a daring lot, but they had a mean streak. They hated the theater and banned Christmas. They punished people in a cruel and inhuman manner. They killed children who disobeyed their parents. When they came in contact with those whom they considered heathens or aliens, they behaved in such a bizarre and irrational manner that this chapter in the American history comes down to us as a late-movie horror film. They exterminated the Indians, who taught them how to survive in a world unknown to them, and their encounter with the calypso culture of Barbados resulted in what the tourist guide in Salem's Witches' house refers to as the Witchcraft Hysteria.

The Puritan legacy of hard work and meticulous accounting led to the establishment of a great industrial society; it is no wonder that the American industrial revolution began in Lowell, Massachusetts, but there was the other side, the strange and paranoid attitudes toward those different from the Elect.

The cultural attitudes of that early Elect continue to be voiced in everyday life in the United States: the president of a distinguished university, writing a letter to the *Times*, belittling the study of African civilizations; the television network that promoted its show on the Vatican art with the boast that this art represented "the finest achievements of the human spirit." A modern up-tempo state of complex rhythms that depends upon contacts with an international community can no longer behave as if it dwelled in a "Zion Wilderness" surrounded by beasts and pagans.

When I heard a schoolteacher warn the other night about the invasion of the American educational system by foreign curriculums, I wanted to yell at the television set, "Lady, they're already here." It has already begun because the world is here. The world has been arriving at these shores for at least ten thousand years from Europe, Africa, and Asia. In the late nineteenth and early twentieth centuries, large numbers of Europeans arrived, adding their cultures to those of the European, African, and Asian settlers who were already here, and recently millions have been entering the country from South America and the Caribbean, making Yale Professor Bob Thompson's bouillabaisse richer and thicker.

One of our most visionary politicians said that he envisioned a time when the United States could become the brain of the world, by which he meant the repository of all of the latest advanced information systems. I thought of that remark when an enterprising poet friend of mine called to say that he had just sold a poem to a computer magazine and that the editors were delighted to get it because they didn't carry fiction or poetry. Is that the kind of world we desire? A humdrum homogeneous world of all brains and no heart, no fiction, no poetry; a world of robots with human attendants bereft of imagination, of culture? Or does North America deserve a more exciting destiny? To become a place where the cultures of the world crisscross. This is possible because the United States is unique in the world: The world is here.

**Let's Pause Here•••▶**  Do you agree with Reed's overall view about what makes America a unique country? What other countries can make a similar claim, if any? How does our country differ from theirs? How relevant is this essay, which originally appeared in 1988, to our time? Or does it seem to be dated?

**Let's Take It Further•••▼**

1. What language choices and rhetorical techniques do Reed use that prove his intended audience is American people? What specific group or groups of Americans might Reed be speaking to in his essay? How might Reed have differed in his language choices or specific examples of multinationalism if he were speaking to people outside America?

2. What is the effect of Reed opening his essay with a quote from the *New York Times*? How does that set the stage and the tone for the rest of his essay?

3. Why does Reed begin his essay by describing a variety of different nationalities and then making the statement, "The city he'd visited was Detroit"? Were you surprised by that statement? If so, what was surprising about the fact that Reed was describing Detroit? If not, why was it no surprise?

4. One of the most prophetic points that Reed makes is when he states: "a day will come when it will be difficult to travel through some sections of the country without hearing commands in both Spanish and English." How accurate was his prediction? How has the "trend" that he was describing surpassed even his own predictions? What predictions might be made for the future if this essay were written today?

5. Why do you think that Reed is so amazed by the fact that a McDonald's in Milwaukee would exhibit African and African American artwork? How does this represent the very point that Reed is attempting to make throughout the entirety of his essay?

6. Locate and identify examples of what Reed calls the "blurring of cultural styles" within your own community. Describe each element (the generically "American" and the outside influence) and how they interact with one another, as well as how they stand out from one another. How do the two styles work together to complement one another? How is this representative of America's multinational culture?

7. Describe an artists' movement (or a specific artist) whose work was obviously influenced by an outside culture. For the purposes of this assignment, artists may include writers, filmmakers, musicians, and those who work in media beyond the traditional artist's realm. Define/describe the movement or artist and explain how his or her style is made up of at least one outside (foreign cultural) influence. In what specific ways has the artist/movement taken this outside inspiration and made it his or her own?

8. Reed refers to "scribbles in public," or graffiti, as a way of understanding the current mood in the public sphere in relation to our nation's multinationalism. Research/locate graffiti in your own community and describe the nature of the graffiti you encounter. How does it reflect the person's attitude toward our nation as a whole, as well as the person's attitude toward our nation's ever-growing multinational population? Use descriptions of the graffiti to back your opinion.

9. Reed repeatedly explains how he fears that monoculturalism will lead America to become a "humdrum homogenous world of all brains and no heart." How has America managed to avoid becoming the place Reed feared it might become? In other words, research a culture whose impact on an American community has had profound effects. One consideration that should be made is that most major cities have neighborhoods largely represented by a dominant cultural group (e.g., "Chinatown" or "Little Italy"). Locate one such neighborhood in your community or a nearby city, and describe the dominant culture, as well as how it interacts with the larger community (or city) in which it is located.

10. Create a video or pictoral collage, accompanied by an essay, that illustrates your own community. Which multinational cultures are represented and what role do they play in the community? Describe the history of the dominant cultural group and how it has shifted (grown or shrank) over time. Do you see the demographic shift (if your community has had one) as a positive or negative development, and why?

# *Friday Night Lights*: Rural Mojo on TV
### David Masciotra

**Let's Start Here•••▶**   There is, of course, more to American identity than a person's ethnicity, gender, or even sexual orientation. For many, the place where they are raised is just as much a part of their identity as their race or gender. There are two distinct types of geographic identity that most Americans use to differentiate themselves: rural and urban. If you identify yourself as someone from rural America, then there are certain shared experiences that you and most other people from rural parts of the country will have in common.

Although there are many variants on the idea of what rural and urban America mean, rural life as a whole is often ignored by mainstream media. Our movies are most often set in big cities, as are our TV shows, our large businesses, and even our "cultural" activities.

It is because of this lack of popularity of rural areas as a setting that David Masciotra, in the following essay, feels that the significance of the television show *Friday Night Lights* should not go unnoticed. In his essay, he outlines why he feels the show is important, as well as how successfully he believes the show captures small-town, rural existence. As you read the essay, observe the elements of the show that Masciotra focuses on, and decide whether you agree with him in terms of their level of importance as he discusses the realities of rural life and the ways in which they are depicted on TV.

David Masciotra is a writer and cultural critic whose work has appeared in several Chicago area newspapers and *Z Magazine*. On the Web, he has written features for *PopMatters* and occasional or single columns for *Nerve, Common Dreams New Center, Pop and Politics,* and *PopPolitics.* This essay was originally published by the rural cultural website, Daily Yonder, on May 14, 2010.

Stanley Crouch writes that whenever people pretentiously and proudly announce, "I don't watch television," they should follow it up with "I don't look at America either."

**pretentiously:** With excessive or unnecessary value placed on their claim.

Between cartoonish reality shows and grotesque game shows, there isn't much dramatic television giving big, clear windows into America.

However, on the rare occasion that TV does get it right, it is often the stuff of pure emotive and intellectual brilliance. In the 21st century, American television is a home run hitter with a very low batting average.

One of its most beautiful and powerful homeruns was David Simon's *The Wire.* From 2002 to 2008, the HBO series moved a magnifying glass over the underbelly of urban America. From crime and poverty to police incompetence and political corruption, *The Wire* gave viewers a rare, and brutally honest, insight into the afflictions of American cities.

Although not as comprehensive in scope, *Friday Night Lights,* which just started its fourth season on NBC, put viewers through the looking glass of rural America, allowing them to explore family, faith, and of course, football with sociological savvy and emotional maturity.

Working class struggles, educational difficulty, and communal solidarity loom large in the background in this program that, on paper, is about a high school football coach named Eric Taylor, his family, his players, and their families.

**solidarity:** Group unity based on shared values and beliefs.

As the *FNL* characters have progressed through triumph and tragedy, the series has come to represent much more than one coach's fight to take his team of dedicated upperclassmen to the Texas High School State Football Championship. It is about small towns in modern America, and what their families do to maintain communal strength, familial love, and individual excellence under unfriendly economic conditions, intense social divisions, and limited local opportunity.

Set in Dillon, Texas—a fictional East Texas town—it also gives viewers something that is unfortunately unique: A presentation of complex Americans, who do not live in a big city or a wealthy suburb connected to a big city.

*FNL*'s small town setting is hardly glamorous, but it is often beautiful. It can be ugly too, because it presents reality—a rural reality, communal reality, and sociopolitical reality.

**sociopolitical:** Relating to both social and political factors.

Success and failure stand side by side in Dillon. The Taylors—Coach Eric, high school principal Tami, and daughter Julie—do very well. Julie is college bound, Tami is a smart and strong leader, and

Eric is respected as one of the best high school football coaches in the state after taking the Dillon Panthers to the State Championship two of the last three seasons, winning one of them.

"Smash" Williams, a lighting fast running back is off to a local college, having lost his scholarship to a prestigious Texas university after suffering a severe injury. Coach Taylor trained Smash hard and worked a connection with the local school to get him a spot on their roster. Lila, the beautiful daughter of Buddy Garrity—the owner of a car dealership and a dedicated booster of Panther football—has gone to Vanderbilt University.

Lila's ex-boyfriend Tim Riggins, however, has not done as well. The town sex symbol and former football star could be a fourth verse in Bruce Springsteen's "Glory Days." He lives with his brother, has no viable career track, and entertains himself with women he doesn't like half as much as Lila, let alone love.

His best friend, Jason Street was on the road to football glory before he took a devastating hit in a senior year football game, which left him not only out for the season but in a wheel chair for the rest of his life.

Riggins accompanied Street to New York to help him get a job and win back the mother of his child. Leaning against the side of a cab, as Riggins watches Street enter the house at the invitation of a very happy woman, he smiles, realizes it is goodbye, and begins to cry. It is the most moving scene of two young friends parting ways since the conclusion of Larry McMurtry's *The Last Picture Show*.

On paper, this sequence doesn't sound like much nor does Smash's long battle to get into college, which ends with his single mother screaming, crying, and hugging him. Matt Saracen—the graduated quarterback who took the Panthers to State in the first season—caring for his grandmother, who suffers from dementia, wouldn't captivate anyone if explained in an essay either.

*Friday Night Lights* doesn't have the artsy guts of *The Sopranos*, the suspense of *24*, or the political relevancy of *The Wire*, yet it still belongs in the company of those innovators.

It has more heart than the three of them, and tells its seemingly ordinary stories so well that viewers will have no choice but to give into the powerful urge that all art seeks to inculcate: the urge to care—to care about the characters of the fictional drama and then channel that concern into real life struggles in which the consequences impact actual human beings.

The targets of concern in Dillon are working class families of diverse racial and ethnic backgrounds who fight for everything they have. They are people who live far outside the rich territories of glamour, and seek individual sustenance and communal strength in familial sacrifice, working towards a

**inculcate:**
To teach something by use of repetition.

**sustenance:**
The basic means of support or nourishment for living or surviving.

shared purpose, and spiritual hope. Religion is depicted as a powerful and stabilizing force in the lives of Dillon residents.

*Friday Night Lights* is as close to a reality show as one can get without falling into that genre, perhaps even closer. Its rural setting and small town stories give it a unique appeal in not only a television market, but also a culture that too often overlooks the value, pain, and pleasure of small town communities.

The fourth season begins with Coach Taylor touring the raccoon infested, trash decorated football facilities of East Dillon High—a reopened high school on the poor side of town where he has been named head coach after being forced out by the Dillon school board. (Board members had been paid off by some rich families with grudges against the Taylors.)

The school building is dilapidated, faculty morale is dangerously low, and the behavior of the football players is discouraging, to put it mildly—borderline disgraceful. Nearly half of the team quits after the second practice because they don't want to take orders or work hard.

Taylor's only assistant for most of the first few weeks is a manager at Sears who begs for the job. The first game ends in a forfeit at the half when East Dillon is down 45-0 and a handful of their players are injured.

If there is anything more emblematic of America on television, it is certainly the country's best-kept secret. The empire is wobbling, the economy is wavering, and the United States is a gigantic East Dillon.

> **emblematic:** A symbol or representation of something.

*Friday Night Lights*, through its portrayal of commitment to community, hard won hope, and ferocious faith, gives American families a simple, yet applicable message in the dark hour of Dillon and a million Dillons scattered throughout the country:

"Clear eyes, full hearts: Can't lose."

**Let's Pause Here•••▶**     Whether or not you have ever seen the television show in question, do you agree with Masciotra about why he feels that a show like *Friday Night Lights* is important to American culture? Do you think it is necessary for rural life to be portrayed on television just as frequently and accurately as urban life? If so, why? If not, why not? How is the show (as the author defines it) different from or similar to your own upbringing? Also, do you agree with Masciotra's assertion that East Dillon is a symbol of America? Why or why not?

**Let's Take It Further•••▼**

1. Considering the fact that the original audience of this particular essay was a website called the Daily Yonder (a website devoted to rural living and the rural American lifestyle), why do you think Masciotra chooses the language that he does to make the case for the

value of *Friday Night Lights*? How can you tell who his audience is, based on his word choices and writing strategies? How might his writing strategy shift were his audience an urban one?

2. Why do you think Masciotra believes it is so important to show the rest of America how small towns "maintain communal strength, familial love, and individual excellence under unfriendly economic conditions, intense social divisions, and limited local opportunity" by producing shows such as *Friday Night Lights*? What can "the rest of America" gain by seeing how these smaller communities cope with hardship?

3. Do you think it is a trait particular to rural culture that a young person's success might be measured according to whether she is accepted into college? If so, why is college more important to those from rural regions of the country than it might be to those from urban centers? If not, then what accounts for Masciotra's constant mentioning of how various characters are "college-bound," and others are not?

4. Why might sports be more meaningful to a rural community as a means of growth and interaction between those who live there than they would be to an urban community? How does the general purpose of *Friday Night Lights* (as outlined by Masciotra) prove this to be true?

5. Masciotra points out that in *Friday Night Lights*, "religion is depicted as a powerful and stabilizing force" in rural life. Do you think that this is an actual trait of rural life, or does religion play an equally important role in stabilizing the lives of people in urban centers? In which of the locales might religion play a more important role, and why?

6. If you are familiar with rural culture, how accurately do you feel the TV show in question depicts rural existence? Research the portrayal of rural existence on TV by watching one or more episodes of *Friday Night Lights*, and describe specific scenes and scenarios wherein they accurately capture rural existence. Also, describe which elements, if any, the show gets wrong. Argue whether you agree or disagree with Masciotra's assessment that this particular show "gets it right" in its representation of rural life.

7. Can you locate other TV shows that use rural life as the central focus of their plotlines? Do they do a better or worse job of illustrating rural life than *Friday Night Lights*? Which show or shows would you recommend to someone who wanted to see what it would be like to live in small-town America, and why? Make your case by explaining the show's importance in a manner similar to that used by Masciotra. What would you hope the person would gain from viewing the show or shows in question?

8. Using a television show about rural America and a show about urban America, describe the difference in how the two aspects of American existence are portrayed. Which of the two lifestyles seems to be preferred by American television producers? In what specific ways are urban and rural life compared and contrasted, and which do you believe to be a more fair representation? Which one is painted as the better of two existences? Which is illustrated as having more downsides than the other? How might this negatively affect a person's opinion of one geographic location/lifestyle over the other?

9. Masciotra states that one of the greatest attributes of *Friday Night Lights* is its ability to make its viewers "care about the characters of the fictional drama and then channel that

concern into real life struggles in which the consequences impact actual human beings." Are there other shows on television that you feel fit the same definition that Masciotra applies to *Friday Night Lights*? If so, describe such a show and argue the ways in which it accomplishes this same goal among its viewers. Be sure to include specific scenes from the show, as Masciotra does throughout his essay. How does the show make you care about its characters and their dilemmas, and how does it affect your impression of the world around you?

**10.** Visit the Daily Yonder website to see what issues seem to be of greatest importance to the people who read the website, as well as those whose work gets published there. Create a video or photo collage (utilizing YouTube, a website, or PowerPoint) that shows your community and the particular traits that you feel best represent the people who live there. Explain why these traits are representative of your community and its identity.

# Stirring the Nation's Melting Pot
### Sean Alfano

**Let's Start Here•••▶** Regardless of a person's ethnic or racial background, most people have heard the refrain implied in Alfano's essay: "You're not a *real* [insert race/ethnicity/gender/ sexual orientation here]." While the heart of his essay focuses on what many people in the Latino community see as a loss of identity among its younger people and how that is both a potentially positive and negative thing, his essay still pertains to anyone who has ever been on the receiving end of this question about authenticity.

Naturally, every ethnic culture has its own traditions that it seeks to pass down through each generation, regardless of whether or not the younger generation understands the importance of these traditions. For some groups, such as Latinos, these traditions not only include food, history, and geographical knowledge, but also language. As evidenced in Alfano's essay, it is clear that people within his own ethnic community see some—if not all—of these traditions dwindling more and more with each successive generation as they become "Americanized." Some celebrate this trend, and others worry about its negative effects.

As you read the following essay, observe the manner in which Alfano not only attempts to address the issue of what it means to be Latino, but also the ways in which Latinos authenticate themselves in both American and Latino culture. Also, note the differing viewpoints on the issue of becoming American.

---

Sean Alfano is a journalist based out of New York City who writes regularly for CBS News and the *New York Daily News*. This essay originally appeared on the CBS News website on November 12, 2009.

By the year 2040, there will be 60 million Latinos in the United States.

All they had to do was take to the streets, together, this spring to force the question, yet again, in our immigrant history: is it different this time? Is this invasion a threat? Will we become them or will they become us, asks CBS *Sunday Morning* contributor Martha Teichner.

The Barajas family, gathered at their house in East Los Angeles for a birthday party, offered a glimpse into Latino assimilation in America.

**assimilation:**
The act of assimilating, or absorbing into a culture or system of beliefs.

"Happy Birthday" was sung in English and the name on the cake read "Bobby" not Roberto.

Louis Barajas, Bobby's brother, says everyone he knows comes from an immigrant family. "There isn't a friend that I have that doesn't have parents that came from Mexico," he says.

The Barajas' are the living, breathing embodiment of a statistic immigration analysts consider proof that Latinos are assimilating into American life—from Louis's parents to his 13-year-old daughter, Aubrey.

**embodiment:**
Concrete example.

"I talk to my parents in English. I talk to my grandpa in Spanish," Aubrey says.

By the third generation, the vast majority of Latinos, nearly 80 percent, speak English. Many speak no Spanish at all.

So the good news is that if you look at those numbers, it's clear that Latinos are no different from the immigrant groups who preceded them to this country, but depending on your viewpoint, that's also the bad news, because anxiety over Latino immigration is all about numbers and their impact on American culture.

There are 40 million Latinos in the United States, more than 13 percent of the population.

Just turn on the television: Spanish language broadcasting is a multi-billion dollar growth industry. Look around at the nation's construction workers, janitors, lawn crews and restaurant staff—Latino faces everywhere.

"People always emphasize the Latinization of America, and they don't look at what's happening to the Americanization of Latinos," says Harry Pachon.

Pachon is president of the Tomas Rivera Policy Institute at the University of Southern California.

"You can look at where do the loyalties lie. Forty Latinos are Medal of Honor winners. Fourteen percent of the marines are of Hispanic origin. So what is this Latinization going on? It's not a one-way street, it's a two-way street," Pachon says.

A White House photo-op last week said it all. The three soldiers, wounded in Iraq, that the president swore in as U.S. citizens: two Mexicans and a Dominican.

"I live among immigrants. These folks had to rip themselves up from another culture, from their families and work in order to achieve a better life. They have voted with their feet and had the faith of the convert," claims Henry Cisneros, the former Secretary of Housing and Urban Development in the Clinton administration.

It's in the nation's interest to help them, according to Cisneros, a third generation Mexican-American, who was also mayor of San Antonio, Texas.

"We need to create institutions at our churches, at our neighborhood groups, at our community development corporations and yes, sometimes, government, i.e. the schools that offer an Americanizing curriculum that says, this is the way you become an American," Cisneros says.

Louis Barajas thinks Latinos ought to be doing the teaching.

He went to UCLA on scholarship, got an MBA and went to work doing financial planning for Anglo millionaires.

A genuine American success story, with books and a lecture series to prove it, Barajas decided the rich didn't need him, immigrants did.

"What I learned was that to become successful in America you had to have a specific mindset, a different mindset. I thought I pretty much had mastered that and I wanted to teach that to the Latinos. Not just financial. But changing the way they think," Barajas says.

Maria Cruz is his client—one of nine children, she grew up in Mexico.

"We were very, very poor, you know. We didn't have enough food to eat," Cruz remembers.

She came to the United States at the age of 18. At 38, she owns three WIC stores in the Los Angeles area, depots where low-income women cash in vouchers for food. There are more than a million and a half Latino-owned businesses in the United States, injecting well over $200 billion a year into the economy.

"Working hard and always trying to have a—what I should say—attitude of 'I wanna be better.' Always better. You never say, 'I'm fine, this is good enough,'" Cruz says.

Now a U.S. citizen, Cruz was an illegal immigrant.

Until after World War I, there really wasn't such a thing as illegal immigration in the United States. Millions of immigrants just showed up in great waves, mainly Europeans escaping poverty and politics.

The United States has always been schizophrenic about Latinos, especially Mexicans, over and over again, inviting them in to fill labor shortages and then when times got tough, throwing them out.

For more than 20 years, there was even a guest worker program. It ended in 1964, but the migrants came anyway—illegally—their numbers multiplying exponentially ever since.

Today, an estimated 12 million are here illegally.

A CBS News/*New York Times* poll found that nearly 9 out of 10 Americans consider illegal immigration either a serious or very serious problem.

"You just have to say, 'Hey folks, let's go. Let's be practical. Get over it. Let's think it through in a practical way.' First of all, they're really not going anywhere," Cisneros says.

Born in Mexico, Alex Vega has been in the United States, undocumented, under the radar more than half his life. But in April he defiantly showed himself. He marched through downtown Los Angeles for immigrant rights, one of millions nationwide who understood what it meant to be seen and counted for the first time.

"I'm a ghost. I'm a ghost. I don't—I'm 45 years old, I got 10 children, I have a business, I own a house, but nothing is in my name," Vega says.

Within five years, all 10 of Vega's children, born here, U.S. citizens, will have reached voting age.

"In 20 years then we gonna run the country. Right now we running the cities. So little by little, we are running the show. Little by little—so the sleeping giant, it's already awakened," Vega says.

Last year, Los Angeles elected Antonio Villaraigosa as its first Latino mayor in more than a century. He joins three U.S. senators and something like 6,000 other Latino officeholders at all levels of government.

If that scares some people, it reassures others.

> **credo:**
> Set of fundamental beliefs.

"Yes, it will change the country, but I believe, fundamentally, it adds to the richness of the country and more importantly, this is a population that understands the basic credo, the basic core of the American idea," Cisneros says.

"They want to be part of the American dream."

---

**Let's Pause Here•••▶** As you read Sean Alfano's essay, were there any complaints with which you are familiar, even though you might be from a different ethnic background than him? How are the members in his community similar to or different from the members of your community? Were you surprised by any of the similarities? How about the differences?

---

**Let's Take It Further•••▼**

1. Why might some people be bothered by the idea of the Latino population rising so dramatically in such a short period of time? What might be a potentially negative outcome?

2. Have you, or someone you know, ever been subjected to the statement, "You're not a *real* ___"? What were the circumstances surrounding the statement, which at its

core implies a person who has assimilated into a larger culture has lost some of his authenticity? What was the reaction of the person to whom the statement was addressed?

**3.** Do you agree or disagree with Louis Barajas's assertion that becoming American is a good thing for immigrants? Does this really make the American Dream more accessible? Why or why not?

**4.** What do you believe is Alfano's purpose in discussing the issue of language in his essay? Does this prove or disprove the larger point he is trying to make about the positives and negatives of assimilation? Based on his discussion of Americanization, how might a Latino audience respond to his writing? How might a non-Latino audience respond to this writing strategy? Do you see this particular technique as a positive or negative strategy? In other words, does it help or harm Alfano in making his point?

**5.** Consider the following statement that Alfano makes in his essay about America's "schizophrenic" relationship with Latino immigrants: "[Americans invite immigrants] to fill labor shortages and then when times got tough, throw them out." Do you believe he is correct in his assessment of America's relationship with immigrants? How does the statement fit into his larger argument about the positives and negatives of immigrants' loss of identity? How might the treatment of immigrants play a role in their cultural identity and cause them to want to assimilate?

**6.** Define and describe what you see as *your* culture. What sets it apart from the larger popular American culture? How does your culture differentiate itself from other cultures in America, and what traditions, beliefs, and cultural peculiarities define your own background? Which elements of your culture do you see as important to learn and pass on to other generations, and why? Which elements are not as important, and why? How have people from your culture succeeded or failed at assimilating into American culture?

**7.** This essay continually addresses the notion of what it means to be "real," both as an American and as a member of a particular ethnic culture Define the idea of what it means to be real, as well as how people within your own culture exhibit proof of their "realness." Describe how a person might act, dress, or speak in order to prove their authenticity. What positive or negative outcomes might result from someone attempting to be "real" within your particular culture, as you see it?

**8.** Alfano repeatedly discusses the concept of being "Americanized." Define what this term means to you. Are there ways in which you have noticed how you are different, or more "American," than older people from your culture? If so, in what ways are you more American? Explain whether this is a good or a bad thing. Do you believe, as Alfano implies that some elders in the Latino community believe, that Americanization risks a loss of cultural identity? Why or why not? Define and support your opinion on the matter by using examples from your own community to illustrate how older people differ from younger generations.

**9.** Alfano repeatedly illustrates within his essay how Louis Barajas believes strongly in the concept of assimilation. However, despite Barajas's advocacy for Latinos to become

Americanized, there are people who feel the exact opposite of how Barajas does, often lamenting the fact that to assimilate means to lose a portion of one's identity. Does (or did) your family have a cultural trait or tradition that they have purposely attempted to lose so that they could be taken more seriously as citizens and succeed at achieving the American Dream? If so, what was that trait? Was your family successful in losing that particular trait, or does it still linger? If they were successful, is there a movement among your family or culture to regain the lost trait in an effort to retain some form of cultural identity? What has the result been?

10. Create a video or pictorial collage that illustrates your own culture to someone who might be from a different culture. What specific traits do you find in your own culture that differ from those of other cultures? Why did you choose the traits that you did? Also, illustrate how your own culture is changing from one generation to the next, and how it compares to the larger concept of American popular culture in general.

# mash**UP** essay

The following essay is this chapter's Mashup selection. Keeping in mind our definition of a Mashup essay from Chapter 2 (an essay that includes multimedia texts, as well as multiple writing strategies), observe the way the speech's author, Barack Obama, utilizes multimedia texts. For example, the central concept to which his essay refers is America's history of racial inequality, which he illustrates by alluding to the now-defunct Jim Crow segregation laws that the Civil Rights movement of the 1960s sought to battle. Obama also refers to a couple other well-known historical events from recent years—the O. J. Simpson murder trial and the Hurricane Katrina disaster—evoking the infamous media images that accompanied both events. Additionally, Obama begins his essay by referring to the U.S. Constitution, and then repeatedly circles back to our Constitution's core principles of equality and justice to build his case for racial equality in America. Rather than simply critiquing American culture at large, Obama also refers to his own particular upbringing by using passages from his first book, *Dreams from My Father*, to show his relationship to the Trinity United Church that was the focus of so much criticism during his 2008 presidential campaign. He also discusses the various YouTube videos of his minister, Reverend Wright, giving sermons that were the cause of national uproar, as well as frequently referring to the subsequent news reports and national outrage that Reverend Wright's remarks incited. But Obama makes a concerted effort to repeatedly, and frequently, turn back to our nation's founding document to make the case for how inequalities still linger, while pointing out the many ways America's race relations have indeed improved in the years since the document's founding. The result is a well-rounded speech that allows all Americans to consider our nation's current race relations, as well as other ways in which we might address lingering inequalities between genders, races, and sexual orientations.

The strength of Obama's speech is bolstered by his willingness to seek out a wide variety of sources to back his argument that America—though we have come a long way—still has much work to do in creating a landscape of true equality for all of its citizens. Instead of simply pointing out that inequalities still exist among different races, genders, and sexual preferences, Obama patiently patches together his argument by using many sources that also prove how far America has come since its founding in providing opportunities for its people. This makes for a more engaging and thought-provoking argument, a more sophisticated and important oral essay, because it is hard to argue with the sources he uses to prove that conditions have improved for all Americans, though they certainly could be improved further. And so Obama simultaneously praises America's progress toward equality, while pointing out ways in which we can improve.

One of the most intriguing elements of the essay is that Obama employs more than just a straightforward argumentative approach in his writing. The major thrust of the essay is, indeed, that Obama wants to persuade his readers and listeners to see how race relations can be further improved among Americans, but this is couched in several other writing strategies that he employs. In addition to the argumentation writing strategy, Obama simultaneously uses many strategies to show the wide-reaching effects of racial inequality on many different generations and many different races. One such strategy Obama employs is the illustrative writing method, which allows him to paint a vivid picture of the state of race relations in the United States at the time he gave his speech. By stringing together many examples of how equality has improved in the United States, Obama is able to show why many Americans believe that race relations are good—or at least better. This allows us to see that Obama's speech does not complain, but rather it seeks to give credit for the accomplishments we have made over the years in improving racial equality. However, Obama also employs the compare–contrast strategy to show how there are still lingering inequalities that he compares to the many strides we have taken toward equality as a country, which he gives as the reason for resentment on the part of older generations of citizens who grew up with fewer opportunities than modern-day citizens. Obama also uses the descriptive writing strategy to illustrate several different examples of exisiting inequalities, as well as describing the political landscape of the time in which his speech was set. By using this technique he is able to allow his readers to see specific ways in which people perceive inequalities to still exist, as well as the ways in which they actually do and do not exist.

In terms of using research in his writing (the research writing strategy), Obama not only continually mines the U.S. Constitution for passages to include in his speech that will strengthen his position, he also refers to the words of one of America's most famous southern authors—William Faulkner—to reinforce the stance he is taking within his oration. He also chooses to include his own book, news reports, YouTube videos, voting exit polls, and even the Civil Rights movement of the 1960s to show the changes in equality within our country over the years. In doing his research, Obama also employs the definition–informative writing strategy as he discusses the U.S. Constitution's intentions with regard to justice and equality, as well as how the Constitution fits into our modern American existence. He also employs the cause–effect writing strategy by showing the outcomes of Jim Crow legislation on subsequent generations of African Americans, which Obama makes a point of addressing as one of the root causes of Rev. Wright's inflammatory comments.

Ultimately, the essay as a whole is both illustrative and argumentative in that it argues the author's main point—inequalities (both real and perceived) still exist in modern-day America—in a variety of intriguing and effective ways. For example, we are shown how the media's portrayal of the O. J. Simpson trial and the slow government response to Hurricane Katrina's devastation of New Orleans led many people to believe that African Americans were still viewed as second-class citizens, even so many years after the Civil Rights movement. Obama further cements both sides of his argument by employing the narrative technique, which he uses to show how his very candidacy for president proves that many inequalities have fallen by the wayside, as well as how his own white grandmother was petrified of black men and saw them as a threat. But the most intriguing aspect of Obama's essay is that he avoids being preachy and instead allows our Constitution to make his case for him, while still giving credit to the many injustices we have alleviated as a country.

When you begin writing a Mashup essay of your own in response to the selections in this chapter, revisit Obama's essay to generate ideas for multimedia texts and multiple writing strategies. Use the flowchart to see the ways in which Obama employs the various writing strategies and multimedia texts he utilizes in his writing.

**Mashup Essay Flowchart**

<u>Types of Media:</u>
- The United States Constitution
- News Reports on Wright Scandal
- YouTube Videos of Rev. Wright's Sermons
- Quotes from *Dreams from My Father*
- Quote from William Faulkner
- Jim Crow Segregation Laws
- O. J. Simpson Trial
- Hurricane Katrina Images/Aftermath

"A More Perfect Union"
Barack Obama

<u>Writing Strategies:</u>
- Illustrative
- Narrative
- Definition-Informative
- Cause-Effect
- Argumentation
- Compare-Contrast
- Descriptive
- Research

# A More Perfect Union

**Barack Obama**

**Let's Start Here••• ▶** It would be an understatement to point out that America has a tumultuous history with the issue of race relations in our country. Because of the makeup of our
nation and its quest to be a "melting pot" of ethnicities, cultures, and religions, the inevitable
clashes that occur between these various groups who differ from one another have played a
major role in our nation's history—just as surely as they have in other nations.

For those who thought that our nation's racial troubles ended with the Civil Rights movement of the 1960s, the presidential election of 2008 proved this notion to be quite inaccurate. As
it turned out, the problem of race relations in America is far from resolved, despite the many great
strides we have made toward racial equality in our country.

The following essay is a speech given by then-presidential candidate Barack Obama in response to the outcry over his church's minister, Jeremiah Wright, and comments Rev. Wright
made during a notorious sermon that went viral on YouTube.

Instead of merely defending his minister's actions, Obama decided to use the opportunity
provided by the Rev. Wright scandal to address our nation's still-problematic race relations. What
follows, then, is an eloquent argument that reopened the national dialogue about the role of race
in American society, as well as the lingering inequalities that still exist.

As you read the speech, observe the manner in which Obama breaks down the issue of
race relations in our time, as well as the way in which he both criticizes and defends Rev. Wright.
Also, note the fact that this speech was given in Philadelphia, across the street from where the
U.S. Constitution was signed in 1787 at the Constitutional Convention, and consider the reason
why Obama chose this location to give this speech.

---

Barack Obama is the 44th president of the United States of America. This speech was given on March
18, 2008, during his campaign to seal the nomination for the 2008 Democratic Party presidential nomination. The speech was delivered at the National Constitution Center in Philadelphia,
Pennsylvania, as a response to the controversial remarks given by his former minister,
Reverend Jeremiah Wright, in sermons that circulated widely on YouTube and became an issue of national debate.

> Obama quotes
> directly from the
> opening (Preamble) of
> the U.S. Constitution
> in an effort to situate
> his entire argument in
> terms of the nation's
> founding document.

**improbable:**
Unlikely, and yet
very real.

"We the people, in order to form a more perfect union."

Two hundred and twenty one years ago, in a hall that
still stands across the street, a group of men gathered and,
with these simple words, launched America's improbable
experiment in democracy. Farmers and scholars; statesmen
and patriots who had traveled across an ocean to escape

tyranny and persecution finally made real their declaration of independence at a Philadelphia convention that lasted through the spring of 1787.

The document they produced was eventually signed but ultimately unfinished. It was stained by this nation's original sin of slavery, a question that divided the colonies and brought the convention to a stalemate until the founders chose to allow the slave trade to continue for at least twenty more years, and to leave any final resolution to future generations.

Of course, the answer to the slavery question was already embedded within our Constitution—a Constitution that had at is very core the ideal of equal citizenship under the law; a Constitution that promised its people liberty, and justice, and a union that could be and should be perfected over time.

And yet words on a parchment would not be enough to deliver slaves from bondage, or provide men and women of every color and creed their full rights and obligations as citizens of the United States. What would be needed were Americans in successive generations who were willing to do their part—through protests and struggle, on the streets and in the courts, through a civil war and civil disobedience and always at great risk—to narrow that gap between the promise of our ideals and the reality of their time.

This was one of the tasks we set forth at the beginning of this campaign—to continue the long march of those who came before us, a march for a more just, more equal, more free, more caring and more prosperous America. I chose to run for the presidency at this moment in history because I believe deeply that we cannot solve the challenges of our time unless we solve them together—unless we perfect our union by understanding that we may have different stories, but we hold common hopes; that we may not look the same and we may not have come from the same place, but we all want to move in the same direction—towards a better future for of children and our grandchildren.

This belief comes from my unyielding faith in the decency and generosity of the American people. But it also comes from my own American story.

I am the son of a black man from Kenya and a white woman from Kansas. I was raised with the help of a white grandfather who survived a Depression to serve in Patton's Army during World War II and a white grandmother who

---

*Obama uses the description strategy to paint a vivid picture of the people who attended the original signing of the Declaration of Independence, within shouting distance of the same room where he delivered his speech.*

*Obama repeatedly sites the "document," which is in reference to the Constitution. He uses this as a supporting text throughout the entirety of his speech.*

*This idea is what will be at the core of Obama's central argument.*

*Obama employs the compare-contrast writing technique to illustrate how American citizens have more similarities than we do differences.*

*Obama utilizes the narrative (or storytelling) writing strategy to give his brief life story, which he uses as evidence to support his central argument.*

worked on a bomber assembly line at Fort Leavenworth while he was overseas. I've gone to some of the best schools in America and lived in one of the world's poorest nations. I am married to a black American who carries within her the blood of slaves and slaveowners—an inheritance we pass on to our two precious daughters. I have brothers, sisters, nieces, nephews, uncles and cousins, of every race and every hue, scattered across three continents, and for as long as I live, I will never forget that in no other country on Earth is my story even possible.

It's a story that hasn't made me the most conventional candidate. But it is a story that has seared into my genetic makeup the idea that this nation is more than the sum of its parts—that out of many, we are truly one.

**Again, Obama employs the compare-contrast writing strategy to contrast the actual results of his campaign to the opposite expectations people had predicted.**

Throughout the first year of this campaign, against all predictions to the contrary, we saw how hungry the American people were for this message of unity. Despite the temptation to view my candidacy through a purely racial lens, we won commanding victories in states with some of the whitest populations in the country. In South Carolina, where the Confederate Flag still flies, we built a powerful coalition of African Americans and white Americans.

This is not to say that race has not been an issue in the campaign. At various stages in the campaign, some commentators have deemed me either "too black" or "not black enough." We saw racial tensions bubble to the surface during the week before the South Carolina primary. The press has scoured every exit poll for the latest evidence of racial polarization, not just in terms of white and black, but black and brown as well.

**polarization:** Dividing into two opposing sides.

And yet, it has only been in the last couple of weeks that the discussion of race in this campaign has taken a particularly divisive turn.

On one end of the spectrum, we've heard the implication that my candidacy is somehow an exercise in affirmative action; that it's based solely on the desire of wide-eyed liberals to purchase racial reconciliation on the cheap. On the other end, we've heard my former pastor, Reverend Jeremiah Wright, use incendiary language to express views that have the potential not only to widen the racial divide, but views that denigrate both the greatness and the goodness of our nation; that rightly offend white and black alike.

**reconciliation:** The act of reestablishing harmony or friendship.

**Obama uses the cause-effect writing strategy to illustrate the outcome, or effect, of Reverend Wright's remarks.**

I have already condemned, in unequivocal terms, the statements of Reverend Wright that have caused such controversy. For some, nagging questions remain. Did I know him to be an occasionally fierce critic of American domestic and foreign policy? Of course. Did I ever hear him make remarks that could be considered controversial while I sat in church? Yes. Did I strongly disagree with many of his political views? Absolutely—just as I'm sure many of you have heard remarks from your pastors, priests, or rabbis with which you strongly disagreed.

But the remarks that have caused this recent firestorm weren't simply controversial. They weren't simply a religious leader's effort to speak out against perceived injustice. Instead, they expressed a profoundly distorted view of this country— a view that sees white racism as endemic, and that elevates what is wrong with America above all that we know is right with America; a view that sees the conflicts in the Middle East as rooted primarily in the actions of stalwart allies like Israel, instead of emanating from the perverse and hateful ideologies of radical Islam.

As such, Reverend Wright's comments were not only wrong but divisive, divisive at a time when we need unity; racially charged at a time when we need to come together to solve a set of monumental problems—two wars, a terrorist threat, a falling economy, a chronic health care crisis and potentially devastating climate change; problems that are neither black or white or Latino or Asian, but rather problems that confront us all.

Given my background, my politics, and my professed values and ideals, there will no doubt be those for whom my statements of condemnation are not enough. Why associate myself with Reverend Wright in the first place, they may ask? Why not join another church? And I confess that if all that I knew of Reverend Wright were the snippets of those sermons that have run in an endless loop on the television and YouTube, or if Trinity United Church of Christ conformed to the caricatures being peddled by some commentators, there is no doubt that I would react in much the same way.

But the truth is, that isn't all that I know of the man. The man I met more than twenty years ago is a man who helped introduce me to my Christian faith, a man who spoke to me about our obligations to love one another; to care for the sick and lift up the poor. He is a man who served his country as a U.S. Marine; who has studied and lectured at some of the finest universities and seminaries in the country, and who for over thirty years led a church that serves the community by doing God's work here on Earth—by housing the homeless, ministering to the needy, providing day care services and scholarships and prison ministries, and reaching out to those suffering from HIV/AIDS.

---

*Obama again employs the argumentation strategy to show how a central element of his essay consists of his rejection of Wright's statements.*

**endemic:** Characteristic or prevalent.

**emanating:** Stemming from a particular source.

*This entire paragraph is an example of Obama using the illustrative writing strategy to partially explain Reverend Wright's point of view.*

*Obama references YouTube videos as texts directly.*

*Here Obama employs the definition-information approach to define and describe the type of man Reverend Wright is outside of the statements made during the controversial sermons in question.*

Obama quotes from another source, this time his own book, to narrate his first experience at Trinity.

In my first book, *Dreams from My Father*, I described the experience of my first service at Trinity:

> People began to shout, to rise from their seats and clap and cry out, a forceful wind carrying the reverend's voice up into the rafters. . . . And in that single note—hope!—I heard something else; at the foot of that cross, inside the thousands of churches across the city, I imagined the stories of ordinary black people merging with the stories of David and Goliath, Moses and Pharaoh, the Christians in the lion's den, Ezekiel's field of dry bones. Those stories—of survival, and freedom, and hope—became our story, my story; the blood that had spilled was our blood, the tears our tears; until this black church, on this bright day, seemed once more a vessel carrying the story of a people into future generations and into a larger world. Our trials and triumphs became at once unique and universal, black and more than black; in chronicling our journey, the stories and songs gave us a means to reclaim memories that we didn't need to feel shame about . . . memories that all people might study and cherish—and with which we could start to rebuild.

That has been my experience at Trinity. Like other predominantly black churches across the country, Trinity embodies the black community in its entirety—the doctor and the welfare mom, the model student and the former gang-banger. Like other black churches, Trinity's services are full of raucous laughter and sometimes bawdy humor. They are full of dancing, clapping, screaming and shouting that may seem jarring to the untrained ear. The church contains in full the kindness and cruelty, the fierce intelligence and the shocking ignorance, the struggles and successes, the love and yes, the bitterness and bias that make up the black experience in America.

**bawdy:** Humorously indecent or irreverent.

And this helps explain, perhaps, my relationship with Reverend Wright. As imperfect as he may be, he has been like family to me. He strengthened my faith, officiated my wedding, and baptized my children. Not once in my conversations with him have I heard him talk about any ethnic group in derogatory terms, or treat whites with whom he interacted with anything but courtesy and respect. He contains within him the contradiction—the good and the bad—of the community that he has served diligently for so many years.

I can no more disown him than I can disown the black community. I can no more disown him than I can my white grandmother—a woman who helped raise me, a woman who sacrificed again and again for me, a woman who loves me as much as she loves anything in this world, but a woman who once confessed her fear of black men who passed by her on the street, and who on more than one occasion has uttered racial or ethnic stereotypes that made me cringe.

These people are a part of me. And they are a part of America, this country that I love.

Some will see this as an attempt to justify or excuse comments that are simply inexcusable. I can assure you it is not. I suppose the politically safe thing would be to move on from this episode and just hope that it fades into the woodwork. We can dismiss Reverend Wright as a crank or a demagogue, just as some have dismissed Geraldine Ferraro, in the aftermath of her recent statements, as harboring some deep-seated racial bias.

**demagogue:**
A person in a role of leadership who uses prejudices, as well as false claims and promises, to gain a position of power.

Obama refers to another politician's reaction to the Wright scandal as yet another source in the construction of his argument.

But race is an issue that I believe this nation cannot afford to ignore right now. We would be making the same mistake that Reverend Wright made in his offending sermons about America—to simplify and stereotype and amplify the negative to the point that it distorts reality.

The fact is that the comments that have been made and the issues that have surfaced over the last few weeks reflect the complexities of race in this country that we've never really worked through—a part of our union that we have yet to perfect. And if we walk away now, if we simply retreat into our respective corners, we will never be able to come together and solve challenges like health care, or education, or the need to find good jobs for every American.

Obama cites one of America's most beloved southern writers as another text to incorporate into his own essay.

Understanding this reality requires a reminder of how we arrived at this point. As William Faulkner once wrote, "The past isn't dead and buried. In fact, it isn't even past." We do not need to recite here the history of racial injustice in this country. But we do need to remind ourselves that so many of the disparities that exist in the African-American community today can be directly traced to inequalities passed on from an earlier generation that suffered under the brutal legacy of slavery and Jim Crow.

Obama uses historical events as texts whose very mention carry with them heavy connotations and historical reminders.

Segregated schools were, and are, inferior schools; we still haven't fixed them, fifty years after Brown v. Board of Education, and the inferior education they provided, then and now, helps explain the pervasive achievement gap between today's black and white students.

**pervasive:**
Present or spreading through every part of something.

Legalized discrimination—where blacks were prevented, often through violence, from owning property, or loans were not granted to African-American business owners, or black homeowners could not access FHA mortgages, or blacks were excluded from unions, or the police force, or fire departments—meant that

These five paragraphs are another example of Obama employing the illustrative writing strategy to describe the situations that play a major role in people's viewpoints on matters of race.

black families could not amass any meaningful wealth to bequeath to future generations. That history helps explain the wealth and income gap between black and white, and the concentrated pockets of poverty that persists in so many of today's urban and rural communities.

A lack of economic opportunity among black men, and the shame and frustration that came from not being able to provide for one's family, contributed to the erosion of black families—a problem that welfare policies for many years may have worsened. And the lack of basic services in so many urban black neighborhoods—parks for kids to play in, police walking the beat, regular garbage pick-up and building code enforcement—all helped create a cycle of violence, blight and neglect that continue to haunt us.

Obama makes another part of his argument explaining the reasoning behind Reverend Wright's viewpoints toward race relations in America.

This is the reality in which Reverend Wright and other African-Americans of his generation grew up. They came of age in the late fifties and early sixties, a time when segregation was still the law of the land and opportunity was systematically constricted. What's remarkable is not how many failed in the face of discrimination, but rather how many men and women overcame the odds; how many were able to make a way out of no way for those like me who would come after them.

But for all those who scratched and clawed their way to get a piece of the American Dream, there were many who didn't make it—those who were ultimately defeated, in one way or another, by discrimination. That legacy of defeat was passed on to future generations—those young men and increasingly young women who we see standing on street corners or languishing in our prisons, without hope or prospects for the future. Even for those blacks who did make it, questions of race, and racism, continue to define their worldview in fundamental ways. For the men and women of Reverend Wright's generation, the memories of humiliation and doubt and fear have not gone away; nor has the anger and the bitterness of those years. That anger may not get expressed in public, in front of white co-workers or white friends. But it does find voice in the barbershop or around the kitchen table. At times, that anger is exploited by politicians, to gin up votes along racial lines, or to make up for a politician's own failings.

And occasionally it finds voice in the church on Sunday morning, in the pulpit and in the pews. The fact that so many people are surprised to hear that anger in some of Reverend Wright's sermons simply reminds us of the old truism that the most segregated hour in American life occurs on Sunday morning. That anger is not always productive; indeed, all too often it distracts attention from solving real problems; it keeps us from squarely facing our own complicity in our condition, and prevents the African-American community from forging the alliances it needs to bring about real change. But the anger is real; it is powerful; and to simply wish it away, to condemn it without understanding its roots, only serves to widen the chasm of misunderstanding that exists between the races.

In fact, a similar anger exists within segments of the white community. Most working- and middle-class white Americans don't feel that they have been particularly privileged by their race. Their experience is the immigrant experience—as far as they're concerned, no one's handed them anything, they've built it from scratch. They've worked hard all their lives, many times only to see their jobs shipped overseas or their pension dumped after a lifetime of labor. They are anxious about their futures, and feel their dreams slipping away; in an era of stagnant wages and global competition, opportunity comes to be seen as a zero sum game, in which your dreams come at my expense. So when they are told to bus their children to a school across town; when they hear that an African American is getting an advantage in landing a good job or a spot in a good college because of an injustice that they themselves never committed; when they're told that their fears about crime in urban neighborhoods are some-how prejudiced, resentment builds over time.

> Here is where Obama most critically uses the compare-contrast strategy to show how these viewpoints are shared by both black and white Americans who feel wronged or ignored.

Like the anger within the black community, these resent-ments aren't always expressed in polite company. But they have helped shape the political landscape for at least a generation. Anger over welfare and affirmative action helped forge the Reagan Coalition. Politicians routinely exploited fears of crime for their own electoral ends. Talk show hosts and conservative commentators built entire careers unmasking bogus claims of racism while dismissing legitimate discussions of racial injustice and inequality as mere political correctness or reverse racism.

Just as black anger often proved counterproductive, so have these white resentments distracted attention from the real culprits of the middle class squeeze—a corporate culture rife with inside dealing, questionable accounting practices, and short-term greed; a Washington dominated by lobbyists and special interests; economic policies that favor the few over the many. And yet, to wish away the resentments of white Americans, to label them as mis-guided or even racist, without recognizing they are grounded in legitimate concerns—this too widens the racial divide, and blocks the path to understanding.

This is where we are right now. It's a racial stalemate we've been stuck in for years. Contrary to the claims of some of my critics, black and white, I have never been so naïve as to believe that we can get beyond our racial divisions in a single election cycle, or with a single candidacy—particularly a candidacy as imperfect as my own.

But I have asserted a firm conviction—a conviction rooted in my faith in God and my faith in the American people—that working together we can move beyond some of our old racial wounds, and that in fact we have no choice if we are to continue on the path of a more perfect union.

For the African-American community, that path means embracing the burdens of our past without becoming victims of our past. It means continuing to insist on a full measure of justice in every aspect of American life. But it also means binding our particular grievances—for better health care, and better schools, and better jobs—to the larger aspirations of all Americans—the white woman struggling to break the glass ceiling, the white man whose been laid off, the immigrant trying to feed his family. And it means taking full responsibility for own lives—by demanding more from our fathers, and spending more time with our children, and reading to them, and teaching them that while they may face challenges and discrimination in their own lives, they must never succumb to despair or cynicism; they must always believe that they can write their own destiny.

Ironically, this quintessentially American—and yes, conservative—notion of self-help found frequent expression in Reverend Wright's sermons. But what my former pastor too often failed to understand is that embarking on a program of self-help also requires a belief that society can change.

**quintessentially:** Purest and most representative.

The profound mistake of Reverend Wright's sermons is not that he spoke about racism in our society. It's that he spoke as if our society was static; as if no progress has been made; as if this country—a country that has made it possible for one of his own members to run for the highest office in the land and build a coalition of white and black; Latino and Asian, rich and poor, young and old—is still irrevocably bound to a tragic past. But what we know—what we have seen—is that America can change. That is true genius of this nation. What we have already achieved gives us hope—the audacity to hope—for what we can and must achieve tomorrow.

**irrevocably:** Impossible to take back or change.

**audacity:** Boldness or daring.

In the white community, the path to a more perfect union means acknowledging that what ails the African-American community does not just exist in the minds of black people; that the legacy of discrimination—and current incidents of discrimination, while less overt than in the past—are real and must be addressed. Not just with words, but with deeds—by investing in our schools and our communities; by enforcing our civil rights laws and ensuring fairness in our criminal justice system; by providing this generation with ladders of opportunity that were unavailable for previous generations. It requires all Americans to realize that your dreams do not have to come at the expense of my dreams; that investing in the health, welfare, and education of black and brown and white children will ultimately help all of America prosper.

In the end, then, what is called for is nothing more, and nothing less, than what all the world's great religions demand—that we do unto others as we would have them do unto us. Let us be our brother's keeper, Scripture tells us. Let us be our sister's keeper. Let us find that common stake we all have in one another, and let our politics reflect that spirit as well.

Obama refers to the Bible as another text to support his argument.

For we have a choice in this country. We can accept a politics that breeds division, and conflict, and cynicism. We can tackle race only as spectacle—as we did in the OJ trial—or in the wake of tragedy, as we did in the aftermath of Katrina—or as fodder for the nightly news. We can play Reverend Wright's sermons on every channel, every day and talk about them from now until the election, and make the only question in this campaign whether or not the American people think that I somehow believe or sympathize with his most offensive words. We can pounce on some gaffe by a Hillary supporter as evidence that she's playing the race card, or we can speculate on whether white men will all flock to John McCain in the general election regardless of his policies.

Obama refers to these famous cultural events as texts to provide evidence for his argument.

We can do that.

But if we do, I can tell you that in the next election, we'll be talking about some other distraction. And then another one. And then another one. And nothing will change.

That is one option. Or, at this moment, in this election, we can come together and say, "Not this time." This time we want to talk about the crumbling schools that are stealing the future of black children and white children and Asian children and Hispanic children and Native American children. This time we want to reject the cynicism that tells us that these kids can't learn; that those kids who don't look like us are somebody else's problem. The children of America are not those kids, they are our kids, and we will not let them fall behind in a 21st century economy. Not this time.

This time we want to talk about how the lines in the Emergency Room are filled with whites and blacks and Hispanics who do not have health care; who don't have the power on their own to overcome the special interests in Washington, but who can take them on if we do it together.

This time we want to talk about the shuttered mills that once provided a decent life for men and women of every race, and the homes for sale that once belonged to Americans from every religion, every region, every walk of life. This time we want to talk about the fact that the real problem is not that someone who doesn't look like you might take your job; it's that the corporation you work for will ship it overseas for nothing more than a profit.

This time we want to talk about the men and women of every color and creed who serve together, and fight together, and bleed together under the same proud flag. We want to talk about how to bring them home from a war that never should've been authorized and never should've been waged, and we want to talk about how we'll show our patriotism by caring for them, and their families, and giving them the benefits they have earned.

I would not be running for President if I didn't believe with all my heart that this is what the vast majority of Americans want for this country. This union may never be perfect, but generation after generation has shown that it can always be perfected. And today, whenever I find myself feeling doubtful or cynical about this possibility, what gives me the most hope is the next generation—the young people whose attitudes and beliefs and openness to change have already made history in this election.

This is where we start. It is where our union grows stronger. And as so many generations have come to realize over the course of the two-hundred-and-twenty-one years since a band of patriots signed that document in Philadelphia, that is where the perfection begins.

**Let's Pause Here•••▶** What was your overall impression of Obama's speech? Do you feel this was more of the usual campaign rhetoric, or was there something else occurring within this speech that made it more relevant and meaningful to our time? What, if anything, about the speech moved you emotionally? What was your emotional response to it, and what in particular did you have an emotional response to? Does it change your opinion of race relations in our country in any way? About what in particular did the speech raise your awareness, if there were elements of the speech's content that you were unfamiliar with prior to reading it?

## Let's Take It Further••• ▼

1. Why do you believe Obama chose Philadelphia as the location to give this speech? What impact might it have had on its listeners and readers as a strategy to situate his argument? How is the symbolism of the location working for or against the speech and its intentions?

2. How does Obama's tone, as well as his use of language and textual (multimedia as well as actual texts) evidence, show who his audience is and how he seeks to appeal to their sense of reason? Do you feel this particular strategy was successful?

3. Obama states that the U.S. Constitution was "ultimately unfinished. It was stained by this nation's original sin of slavery." What does he mean when he says the document was both unfinished and stained? And what, in particular, was our "original sin" to which he refers? Do you agree that our "original sin" actually did leave the Constitution unfinished?

4. What do you believe Obama is trying to accomplish with the following quote: "We perfect our union by understanding that we may have different stories, but we hold common hopes; that we may not look the same and we may not come from the same place, but we all want to move in the same direction—towards a better future for our children and our grandchildren." Do you feel he accomplishes what he sets out to do with this quote? How does or doesn't he accomplish his goal?

5. What does Obama mean when he says, "For as long as I live, I will never forget that in no other country on Earth is my story even possible"? Do you agree with his statement?

6. How does Obama's quote from his book, *Dreams from My Father*, explain the way in which Trinity United Church reflects the diversity of the African American people in the United States?

7. Locate the Reverend Wright sermon(s) on YouTube that initially caused the public outcry during the 2008 presidential election. What, in particular, about Wright's remarks was cause for offense on the part of viewers, which was the effect of his remarks (based on your own opinion as well as comments made beneath the videos themselves)? How does Obama's speech help to put those remarks in perspective? Ultimately, do you agree or disagree with the assessment that Obama makes of Wright's remarks? Make your case for whether you agree with his explanation, and describe how you came to your conclusion.

8. Note the way that Obama paints a portrait of Trinity United Church as a representative of the wide spectrum of black experiences in the United States. If you attend a church yourself, detail the ways in which your church is representative of a particular slice of American culture by classifying the type of church and its churchgoers in relation to other churches. Be sure to give detailed descriptions of the people who attend your church, as well as the backgrounds from which they come, in order to illustrate the particulars of your congregation. What would someone who visited your church learn about your particular community by attending a service? Make the case for how it is representative of your particular community, and why.

9. Obama states in his speech that "if we walk away now, if we simply retreat into our respective corners, we will never be able to come together and solve [our nation's]

challenges." In your opinion, have we "walked away" from our challenges as a nation, or have we come together to address them as Americans? Be sure to research and to cite media sources and political events since Obama's election to back your opinion. How, for example, is our country any different now than it was before his election? How is it still the same? Do you feel that race relations and inequalities have been addressed? Why or why not?

10. Obama states that "most working- and middle-class white Americans don't feel that they have been particularly privileged by their race." Conduct a video interview of a working- or middle-class white person to test Obama's theory. In an accompanying essay, explain whether Obama is correct in his assessment of this particular group of Americans. How does he get it right or wrong? How might a white working- or middle-class person feel as though being white hasn't necessarily made her existence any better than that of someone of another race?

11. Give examples of what Obama refers to as "Americans in successive generations who were willing to do their part—through protests and struggle, on the streets and in the courts . . . and always at great risk—to narrow that gap between the promise of our ideals and the reality of their time." Choose and research a specific historical event (which can even be from recent years) of a group of people fighting for equality in one way or another. Describe the process (or event) in which they attempted to achieve equality, what their fight was for, and whether it was a success or if it continues to this day.

# mash it UP

Here is a series of essay and discussion topics that draw connections between multiple selections within the chapter. They also suggest outside texts to include in your essay or discussion. Feel free to bring in further outside texts, remembering the variety of texts (beyond articles) available to you.

1. Compare and contrast Reed's version of America (as outlined in his essay "America: The Multinational Society") to Dantzig's list of American traits in his essay "Objectif Lune." In which ways do the two essays agree on what it means to be American? In which ways do they differ? Which do you feel is more accurate, and why?

2. If you had to choose one television show that you feel most accurately portrays American life as you know it, what would that show be? How does it better encapsulate what it means to be American over other TV shows? What impression might it give of America to an outsider? What, if anything, does it neglect to include in its depiction of American life?

3. The concept of being racially or ethnically genuine, or "real," is one underlying message behind Sean Alfano's essay "Stirring the Nation's Melting Pot." Dave Chapelle, the famous comedian behind the wildly successful Comedy Central program *Chapelle's Show*, addresses this same issue in his own way. In his "keeping it real" skits that he featured throughout each of the show's seasons, Chapelle has his own answer to the social dilemma of what it means to be "real," and what the potential negative outcomes might be. Compare one such Chapelle skit to Alfano's discussion of the issue of ethnic authenticity. Which of the two assessments do you agree with, and why? How are their two approaches different?

4. What elements of American identity have not been addressed in this chapter? In other words, if you had to make a list of traits for which Americans are known outside of America (in the spirit of Charles Dantzig's "Objectif Lune"), what might these traits be? Identify one important American trait that you believe warrants a discussion much like the other elements of American identity addressed in the first half of this chapter, then locate an essay, website, or TV show that features this trait as its main interest. Construct an argument detailing why this particular American trait should be more thoroughly discussed alongside issues of race, geography, education, and other ways in which Americans identify themselves.

5. In his essay "*Friday Night Lights*: Rural Mojo on TV," David Masciotra explains how one of the show's characters—Tim Riggens—could easily "be a fourth verse in Bruce Springsteen's 'Glory Days.'" Locate another popular song that you believe illuminates a particular aspect of American life, and explain which particular demographic of America the song portrays and specifically how the song accomplishes this.

6. Locate other media venues or shows that regularly concern themselves with race relations in the United States (for example, *The Tavis Smiley Show*) and describe how their opinion on the current state of race relations differs from or is similar to Obama's perspective (as outlined in his speech "A More Perfect Union"). On which issues, specifically, do the various parties agree? On which issues do they disagree?

7. Create a video or pictorial collage that defines the "American Dream" as you see it. Revisit the essays of Reed, Masciotra, Alfano, and Obama for various definitions of the "American Dream." Then define the "American Dream," as you understand it, and, in an accompanying essay, illustrate what the dream means to you within the context of visual images that you have chosen to represent your definition of the "American Dream."

# Runaway Bride
Mike Lester

Mike Lester, who has been a political cartoonist for over 25 years, is also a children's writer, an editor, and a book illustrator. He lives in Rome, Georgia, where he is a cartoonist for the *Rome News-Tribune*. His cartoons are nationally syndicated with Cagle Cartoons. This cartoon first appeared in the *Rome News-Tribune* on May 2, 2005.

# Thinking About Gender and Sexual Identity

Take a moment to look at the accompanying cartoon. It is apparent that the artist, Mike Lester, is giving a nod to yet another facet of identity in America: a person's gender identity. While we have focused on geographic, economic, and racial identity in the first half of this chapter, the second half will discuss the ways in which we identify ourselves as men and women, as well as touching on the issue of sexual identity.

In terms of gender identity, there exists a discrepancy in our culture between how men and women are treated and how they are expected to behave publicly, which is the topic of Lester's cartoon. For those students who are familiar with the details of Bill Clinton's presidency, most likely you are aware of the notorious sex scandal between he and his White House intern, Monica Lewinsky. Of course, it goes without saying there were many other details of his presidency that Americans should remember, but the Lewinsky sex scandal has been a long-running joke, even though so many years have passed since Clinton endured an impeachment hearing for his marital shortcomings.

The other aspect of Lester's cartoon is the notion of a runaway bride, which is the term used for a woman who decides at the last minute that she no longer wants to marry the person to whom she is engaged. However, "Runaway Bride" also refers to a specific case of a young woman, Jennifer Carol Wilbanks, who ran away from home on April 26, 2005, to avoid marrying her fiancé. What followed was a media storm, likened to a "circus" by many media critics of the time. Despite abundant speculation that her fiancé had murdered her, Wilbanks emerged safely in Albuquerque, New Mexico, several days later, claiming that she had been abducted and sexually assaulted—a claim that was later proven to be false and resulted in criminal proceedings against Wilbanks. However, the claims made by both people—Clinton and Wilbanks—though not word-for-word excuses, were quite similar.

So, if these two images are being contrasted with one another, what do you think Lester is attempting to say about the differences between the treatment of men and women in American culture? How is Lester using the image of President Clinton (and all the connotations of power and masculinity that come with it), and how is he contrasting this with the image of the Runaway Bride? What is the difference in the posture and details of each person? Who shows more shame, and why do you think this is?

As a society, we have expectations of what it means to be a man and what it means to be a woman. To be sure, these expectations and definitions of masculinity and femininity are constantly shifting, but most people would argue that there is still a large discrepancy between the way men and women are treated, especially when it comes to fidelity, promiscuity, sexuality, and the various concessions men and women are given when it comes to these issues. Still, we understand that to be a man in America and to be a woman in America requires a different set of skills. We are trained from a very young age which roles accompany our gender, and we spend our lives either adhering to these roles or fighting against them, depending on whether we agree with our gender's particular culturally established guidelines. If this is what it means to be a man or a woman in America, what do you believe the artist's feelings are on the issue? With whom does he side on the issue of gender equality (or inequality), and what in the cartoon specifically leads you to believe this?

Do you agree with Lester's assessment of gender roles in America, or do you think he is either oversimplifying or exaggerating them?

Now, revisit the cartoon for a moment to see how Lester blends the images of Bill Clinton and the Runaway Bride. What do you think about the two different "off-camera" statements that accompany each frame of the cartoon? Do you believe these words to be exaggerations, or do you find them to be accurate representations of the current societal differences between how men and women are treated on similar issues? How about the fact that this is more or less the same excuse given by each person? Why do you believe he has chosen to use the same dialogue as an explanation for both characters in the cartoon? How does the meaning or effect of the words change based on who is saying them? Why wasn't it enough to simply poke fun at Clinton for his infidelity, as so many other political commentators have done in the past? Why include the other side of the coin, which is to say the female perspective, the Runaway Bride? How does this change the message of the cartoon? How would it have been different if Lester had only used the image of the Runaway Bride? What is the effect of using the two together?

Finally, it is worth noting that most Americans probably do not need to be reminded that we view men and women as distinctly different, despite political and societal movements that seek to do just the opposite. Still, one interesting dissection of modern gender identity is to see which definitions of masculinity and femininity have shifted in the past few decades and which remain the same. If you were to create a cartoon about the ways in which men and women's lives differ in modern America, what might you include in your drawing? Do you think that the two genders are more equal than they have been in the past, or have we simply shifted our understanding of what gender expectations are for men and women in modern America? How might you illustrate this yourself if you wanted to comment on current gender roles and stereotypes?

# The Problem with Boys    Tom Chiarella

**Let's Start Here•••▶**    Men, both young and old alike, have often wrestled with how to define what it means to be a man. This has been the subject of countless stories, essays, novels, movies, songs, and conversations. While on the surface it might seem as though the answer to this question is both simple and self-evident, the truth is that what it means to be a man in America is dramatically different than what it means to be a man in other parts of the world, especially for modern men. Over time, of course, the definitions and expectations of masculinity shift and change as men's roles in society, family, and relationships also shift and change.

Enter Tom Chiarella, who, in the following essay, attempts to answer this ever-nagging question of how a person can succinctly and meaningfully define what a man *is*. By attempting to identify what ails modern men, Chiarella primarily uses the compare-contrast writing strategy to differentiate between *men* and *boys*. In the course of defining the difference between the two, Chiarella unearths a number of problems that plague modern boys *and* men, as well as proposing several solutions to the dilemmas that plague them.

While you read Chiarella's essay, make note of the definitions of masculinity that come as a surprise to you. Also, see whether you agree with the problems he identifies that are keeping modern boys from fully maturing into men. Finally, determine if the solutions he proposes seem logical or confusing. Are there suggestions that show a bias on his part toward a certain kind of man? On whom (or what) is Chiarella placing the blame?

---

Tom Chiarella is a fiction writer, sports writer, essayist, writer-at-large for *Esquire*, and visiting professor at DePauw University in Greencastle, Indiana. Besides hundreds of articles in *Esquire* since 1996, his magazine work has appeared in *The New Yorker, Golf Digest,* Forbes.com, *Links, O: The Oprah Magazine, Washington Golf Monthly, Indianapolis Monthly, The London Observer,* and *Men's Style* (Australia) and has been syndicated internationally in 19 different countries. He is the recipient of a National Magazine Award. Chiarella has also twice appeared in the *Best American Magazine Writing* anthologies (2004 and 2009). This essay first appeared in *Esquire* magazine in the July 2006 issue as part of a special "State of the American Man" issue.

I have two sons. One is sixteen, the other thirteen. Like any boys, they are a little too muscular in their expectations from life. In a single evening, they can be sullen, sweet, hurtful, gentle, distant, funny, and full of grit. Tonight I dropped the younger one at soccer practice dressed all in yellow. Yellow sweatshirt, yellow jersey, yellow shorts, yellow kneesocks. "I just wish I had yellow shoes," he told me when he got out. "That would be the topper."

Both spend hours watching reruns of *Jackass*. One likes shooting baskets; the other likes watching anime. One goes to summer camp; the other doesn't. Lately, they both have begun to talk about bands that I have never heard of. They murmur to each other so that I am just out of earshot.

They want their laundry done for them. They never clear their dishes or make their beds. They love their grandparents, but they never send them thank-you notes. They both still expect me to kiss them goodnight. They are boys.

They know I am writing this article. I've been wanting to write it for years. Here's what I tell them: I'm a little worried about boys.

I've taught at the same midwestern liberal-arts college for the past seventeen years. I was chair of one of the largest departments on campus for five years. I like working there. It has a distinguished faculty and an excellent academic program; it's a fine little school. I say this because I want to be clear that I am not a malcontent, that I am not some tenured jackass dying to bite the hand that feeds me. I'm just a little worried about boys.

About ten years ago, university GPA statistics started crossing my desk, because I was department chair, and I wondered aloud why men at our college generally received lower grades than women. The pattern was consistent, almost lockstep. Women's average GPA was as much as a quarter of a point higher than men's some semesters. Were women just smarter? Did they just work harder?

It made a certain amount of sense. Female students have always seemed more focused to me, more comfortable with interpretation, more fluid in their ability to enter discussion. When it came to boys, I could often see their disengagement in the classroom. They fidgeted. They slouched. They sat in the back of the room, hidden behind the brims of their baseball caps.

About this same time, I began to notice something else. The enrollment of men at our university was slipping. It is a fact of life at colleges today that women outnumber men. It certainly is at my school, where last year's freshman class was 42 percent male. In any given year, I would call this small potatoes. In 1979, when women surpassed men in college enrollment, I would have called it a triumph. More than twenty years later, as the numbers pile up, it begins to feel as if something, somewhere, is out of balance. I'm often told that there's a perfectly reasonable explanation for this, that the larger share of women in colleges today reflects, in part, the imbalance in the larger population.

I looked that one up. There are indeed more women around than men, but it turns out males make up 51.5 percent of the population of eighteen- to twenty-four-year-olds—the college-going age. They just die faster.

The shift I noticed reinforced itself in subtler ways. I watched as my colleagues expressed an increasing disdain for men in the classroom. I listened as they moaned about seminars that happened to be made up mostly of men. I went to faculty lunches dealing with disruptive students, only to realize that what we were talking about was primarily male behavior, that men themselves were in some fashion perceived to be the disruption. Men who seemed to have an answer for every question. Men who didn't listen. Men who radiated indifference. Men who griped about reading lists sometimes dominated by women authors. Men who resisted the authority of the teacher.

In the middle of one of these lunches, I leaned over and told a friend, "What we're talking about here is boys." I meant the students weren't men yet, that they hadn't yet figured out what mattered. My friend shook her head. "Not really," she said. "Some of these are girls who act like boys."

I watched as nearly every significant social problem was laid at the feet of the male student population: sexual violence, binge drinking, hazing, anti-intellectualism, homophobia, bullying. I have to say it didn't seem unfair to talk about the role of boys in these issues. High time, actually. I was on board. On the whole, boys do seem unfocused to me, a whole lot dimmer in their sense of their path in the world. Everything about them that is male—their physicality, their hunger for stimulation, their propensity to argue—seemed clipped by the academic world I lived in. I was not waiting for the birth of a men's movement so much as I was looking for a little discussion, a chance to engage boys in the same way women engaged girls forty years ago.

> **propensity:**
> An intense, often "natural," inclination to do something.

What did my university do in the face of these problems? It formed a task force on the status of women. Its finding? That the university needed a women's center to augment its twenty-year-old women's-studies program.

There is something odd and forbidden about the word *boy*. Typing it feels a little creepy, almost pornographic. *Boy*. A little word, naked and weak, an iconic expression of smallness, of vulnerability. The boy alone. Scraggled hair, upward glance, the smear of ketchup on his chin. Cute maybe, but defenseless, naive, insulated, and unaware. A boy doesn't have a clue.

There's something equally forbidden about arguing the ongoing boys crisis. It's a loser. It doesn't sell. It doesn't translate as much more than a hobbyhorse for conservative think tanks.

But here's the deal if you are a boy in this country right now:

You're twice as likely as a girl to be diagnosed with an attention-deficit or learning disorder. You're more likely to score worse on standardized reading and writing tests. You're more likely to be held back in school. You're more likely to drop out of school. If you do graduate, you're less likely to go to college. If you do go to college, you will get lower grades and, once again, you will be less likely to graduate. You'll be twice as likely to abuse alcohol, and until you are twenty-four, you are five times as likely to kill yourself. You are more than sixteen times as likely to go to prison.

"As long as ten years ago, we started seeing the data that showed boys were slipping behind," says Kati Haycock, director of the Education Trust, an advocacy group for low-income and minority students. "People were still arguing: We don't have a boys problem, we have a girls problem. It just didn't match what these data say. There's still a lot of resistance among rank-and-file educators."

The growing achievement gap between boys and girls has landed in our laps. Fueled by slim percentages in some cases, the numbers are stacking up over time. We're faced with the accrual of a significant population of boys who aren't well prepared for either school or work. "The problem," says Haycock, "is what this will add up to in twenty years."

Before junior high, I always liked school. It felt like a place that belonged to me, was set up for me, a place that I owned in some fashion. Sitting in a classroom now with Joel Klein, the chancellor of New York City schools, it occurs to me that he must really feel that way. The room sits in the Tweed Courthouse in lower Manhattan, his office two floors above. Classes from around the city rotate in and out every two weeks. Klein, a former antitrust lawyer for the Clinton administration who took over the city's schools in 2002, visits often.

"People try to separate out how much of this is a general boy-girl thing versus how much resides in subgroups," Klein says. "In New York City, it's quite clearly a boy-girl thing. Eleven percent more women graduate than men, consistent across the major racial and ethnic groups. It's a huge number. That's a lot of kids."

He's ready to show me charts reflecting different achievement rates at different grade levels. We run through them, one column to the next, but it feels rote to me. The numbers are enervating. A couple percentage points here, a couple there. I stop him. I want to take a look at the classroom library, so we walk. Once I'm turning the pages of a book on Lewis and Clark, I hook a finger back toward the pile of charts. "What does it all add up to?" I ask.

**enervating:**
Causing a reduction in mental or moral strength.

Klein picks up a book on Peter the Great and tilts his head. "What you see is a story about problems with literacy, with reading, that develop into a consistent increase in dropouts and lower graduation rates." The numbers, he says, show a literacy gap between boys and girls from fourth grade through twelfth. "We need to find things they will read."

Klein sighs: "I remember how I read. It was very powerful. I read all of John R. Tunis's books about baseball. I went forward with that. I took it to *Jude the Obscure* and Dostoyevsky. That's the kind of connection you cannot predict. Sports led me to literature." He speaks of the way he pictured himself as a boy, then a man. "I thought of myself as a ballplayer. Then as a ballplayer/lawyer. Then, finally, just a lawyer. That was the way I went. We have to find paths."

"When I was a kid," Klein says, "we had this view of education that the teacher stood up there, taught, and tried to keep each kid in the same place. Boys and girls. All the same. Each grade was a sort of franchise, with the same product. We've learned that we have to tailor to the individual student. Boys are different. We have to get comfortable with that difference. Quickly."

It occurs to me that it must be odd for Klein to have come from the world of intellectual property rights, a world where meetings were surely overpopulated by men, to parent meetings like the one he describes to me: "A school auditorium. A room of forty people. Two men. Very typical. I told both men, You have to go out and find two more men to come to the next meeting, then they tell two more. I give people an assignment. It's how I work. Two more men. I just start with two more men."

There's a boy named Gerald who's twenty-two who lives in West Lafayette, Indiana, with my girlfriend's daughter. He's had his own set of grim struggles: drugs, alcohol, an absent father. In some ways, he's like most boys at first—withdrawn, a little sullen, his eyes on the horizon. When he can separate his anger from the gist of what he's feeling, I've known him to be witty, intelligent, kind.

But how long can that last? He did not return to high school after being expelled his junior year and now scrambles from one gig to the next. Sometimes he makes panels for car doors or takes a job roofing for a few weeks or hangs drywall. Every time he gets hired, they lay him off before he gets benefits, or he fails a drug test, or he just gets fired. I worry. If he doesn't have a car, he can't get to work. If he can't get to work, he can't keep a car. He can't do any better than a job where they hire him for a week or two, tease him with belonging, then toss him out. This gives him no chance to advance, no chance to supervise, no chance to grow in any sort of trade.

He's got no way to grab on to the culture of work. Nowhere to go, except Iraq maybe. They keep raising the bonus for enlistment; they keep tempting him to put himself in the mix. I always think he's a bag of flesh to them, a bullet stopper. But it must cross his mind. He's got to be mad. He's got to be hurting. I'm always afraid to ask. I'm always afraid of what my own advice would be.

I am in Kansas City, Missouri, on my way to see the commanding general of the U. S. Army Combined Arms Center. I'm staying at the airport Radisson, eating room service during a tornado warning, watching *Kundun*, the story of the Dalai Lama's childhood in Tibet. It's like that these days. Everywhere I look, there's another boy staring back at me.

The Dalai Lama was a wildly curious boy—about cars, movies, machines, traveling. He laughs, he fidgets, he stares off into the distance. I imagine he farts for pleasure. He hungers for other places. And I'm thinking about how much the monks seemed to like him, to tolerate him as a boy. They were both his followers and his leaders. And how being a boy, just being allowed to prosper as a boy, made him the greatest man—gentle and smart, kind and ballsy. I can still see the boy inside the man I know now. Then the electricity goes out.

The next morning I drive to Fort Leavenworth, where Lieutenant General David Petraeus waits for me. I've never been to a military base in my life, although I took military-history courses in college, only because

I wanted to squeeze money out of ROTC. I'm not sure what I was expecting. Dust, I guess. Huge lots where men and women march in formation. But the base looks more like a turn-of-the-last-century college campus, replete with cottages and dormitories. There is an order to the comings and goings that one might expect but an inclusiveness I find surprising. Men shake hands. People wave. Guys in camouflage push strollers.

"There's a kind of embrace to the military," General Petraeus says after hearing what I felt coming in. "Done right, the connections are similar to a family."

This man has six pages of handwritten notes and twenty pages of research, all balanced on his knee. He reads through his comments precisely but fields my questions as they come. He's an academic, too, having taught international relations at West Point for two years. He had a meeting on this subject with several staff members before I arrived. "I wanted to do a little thinking before we talked. It's urgent, but I can't say I have a simple answer."

I tell him about the boys I know, about how I'm concerned that the Army may be the only option for a kid like Gerald. "That's the problem," he says. "It may not *be* an option for him. We have a profile we're looking for; we need high school graduates who are physically fit and driven by the desire for self-improvement. We need men who are prepared to be better soldiers.

"I see the same things you do. The numbers are declining among boys," he says, clearing his throat. "I always call them men.

"I'm concerned in three respects: as a citizen, as an educator, as a military officer. As a citizen, there's a keen recognition that our competitiveness is defined by the education of our workforce. Beyond that, as a teacher, I can see that it's not just economic growth we're talking about; it's overall quality of life, the balance of the society itself. I always keep in mind that quality of political discourse depends on an educated electorate.

**electorate:**
A group or body of people with the right to vote.

"You have to try to construct a culture with great care. That's what we do in the military. There is the sense here that every individual can be the decisive person in a key point, in a key situation. It's a sense of ownership and connection that isn't provided elsewhere."

I ask him about a solution, about a direction for boys. He corrects me: "It's men." I think for a moment that he means using the term to refer to boys, but he doesn't. The answer, he means, is men.

"What boys need," he says, "are role models, parental supervision, encouragement to pursue excellence in all that they do, especially in education, where we must do whatever is necessary to keep them in school. They need direction to stay on the straight and narrow, a push to participate in athletics and extracurricular activities, help to pursue a healthy lifestyle, recognition that they must be accountable for their actions, and reinforcement of good performance."

But how do we do that? The adults. The men. What's our end?

"We have to embrace mentoring," he says, "and we have to be conscious role models. Parents, teachers, coaches, bosses all have to do what leaders do—give energy and encouragement to those who soldier for them. And young men undoubtedly need that more than any other group in America. Indeed, if we can get them through the years during which they're particularly vulnerable, they often will flourish."

I shrug. I'm a little skeptical. Mentoring seems more like a buzzword than a real practice. "It has to be very conscious," he says. "I have dozens of young officers I mentor. I typically call several each month on Saturday mornings and e-mail the others. We actually schedule the Saturday-morning calls."

When I ask if he has role models of his own, in this embrace he speaks of, he snaps off a list of ten names. Generals, teachers, coaches. There is not one among them I recognize, but he clearly knows each one for a different reason, for a different aspect of his own need. "I have to trust people who've been there before me," he says. "It's not a hard thing to learn because of its inherent value. But it's not a part of the larger culture of boys. They don't ask for help enough to know that it's there."

I'm a little worried about boys, so lately I've been thinking a lot about what can be done to help them. I've been griping, to my friends mostly, for a decade about something I've felt in my gut. Every time an article on a perceived boys crisis appears, there is a backlash, a rehashing of the numbers, a recasting of the crisis. Get this much straight: Things are much worse for black boys, for Latino boys, than they are for white ones. And for poor boys as well. I see that clearly.

But why such great resistance to the idea that the problem may be that boys—*all* boys—have lost their foothold, their sense of a linear future, a path in the world? Why does maleness even matter if all we do is resist and undermine it in our schools?

"The masculine impulse is limits testing, even self-destructive. We don't want to extinguish it," Camille Paglia, feminist critic and cultural provocateur, told me when I called. "In the age of terrorism, who will defend us? Young jihadists sure aren't tempering their masculinity. Americans are in unilateral gender disarmament."

**unilateral:**
One-sided.

**disarmament:**
Taking away a means of attack or defense.

I don't think there is a gender war. I don't think there is any war on boys really. It's not that conscious. It's more like a great forgetting. The women's movement was about making room for women, and the numbers show, in schools at least and in the workplace to some extent, that we have.

The gains of girls, Kati Haycock points out, are "the result of a couple of generations of advocacy on the part of women, and girls getting the message that anything is possible. It's a result of women constantly being reminded that they have to watch out for their financial well-being, and they could do this through schools. Women got that message. They are still getting it. That's what's owed the boys. It's a matter of generational focus. We have no goals asking educators to pay attention to boys, nothing really concrete. The record shows that when we really concentrate on something like this, we tend to have progress."

We don't have to feel threatened by the gains girls have made. We need to study them, to use them as a model for boys. The solution may be to grab on to that which is male and use it as a means to fix the problem rather than as a symptom of it. In the classroom, there's ample evidence that certain changes could help boys prosper. They like to do their work in bite-sized chunks. They need differing levels of activity, often tied to some element of competition or short-term goal. They tend to gravitate toward nonfiction in their reading—more facts, shorter pieces. They need physical activity, too, up to four recesses a day, to stay focused.

We also have to think about the way boys put the world together outside the classroom. In England, gaps in achievement have been attributed, in part, to what is known as laddishness. Since boys tend to run in packs, their values are defined by the boys who lead them. There's a sort of antiestablishment disaffection passed from boy to boy, a sense that school doesn't matter. Educators there used that pattern as a means to reinvent it. They used intensely focused mentorship, aimed at the pack leaders, to break down these attitudes, cracking into the structures that keep boys distant from school.

**disaffection:**
Filled with discontent or unrest.

Women forced the issue with girls. Men have to do the same with boys. As it is now, men don't even have the language to discuss what it means to be male. Forget the Right and the Left. I am as skeptical of character training, championed by conservatives as the answer to the crisis, as I am scornful of sensitivity training, which put our classrooms in their current posture. We don't need a new orthodoxy. We need a deeper sense of involvement.

**orthodoxy:**
Conventional set of beliefs.

Men have to be willing to care about the way boys are being treated, taught, and cared for in this country and advocate for them. Find the books that boys read—they are out there—and make sure they are in the libraries and under the Christmas trees. If the classrooms don't work, men must be in the schools—at the PTA meetings, at parent-teacher conferences, in front of school boards, in classes teaching or just talking about their jobs. Young men, men without children, must take a stake and volunteer to coach, to counsel, to read to kids. You can't wait for fatherhood to hit you in the face. Men whose children are grown must mentor a new generation of children. Select two boys, the ones who need it, the ones you know are hurting. Take a lesson from Joel Klein and convince two more men to do the same. Two more men: That's your assignment.

Go talk to boys. You don't have to use baby talk with them or buy them things. You just have to listen to them. Ask them who they are. The answers they give may not always make sense, but talk to enough of them and you will surely realize that boys themselves are not the problem. And it sure as hell isn't women or girls.

The problem is men.

**Let's Pause Here•••▶** What was your overall impression of Tom Chiarella's essay? Were you surprised by the problems that he has identified as stunting young men's maturation? Were you aware of any of the figures that he cites in terms of falling numbers of graduates and college-bound young men? Do you mostly agree or disagree with how he defines the difference between boys and men? Do you think his essay is a serious contemplation of the essay's title, or is it simply giving excuses that allow for boys to take more time in becoming men than their predecessors did?

**Let's Take It Further•••▼**

1. Why do you think Chiarella opens the essay by discussing his sons and defining them as boys? How does this situate the argument that he makes throughout the rest of the essay? Is it an effective use of a definition of "boys," or is it problematic?

2. Based on Chiarella's definitions of men and boys, and the language and examples he uses to prove his point, who would you say his audience is? What, specifically, in his essay proves that the target audience is who you have identified? How might his tone or vocabulary change if he were addressing a different audience—for example, young women?

3. Chiarella states that in the course of discussions with his colleagues at the school where he teaches, a female colleague of his leaned over and said that the figures about males' classroom behavior might be misleading because "some of these [students] are girls who act like boys." How does a "boy" act? What does it mean to "act like a boy," especially if a person making that statement is talking about a girl? What sorts of behaviors are acceptable or expected from one sex but not from the other? From where do these definitions come?

4. Chiarella mentions in his essay that he has not been "waiting for the birth of a men's movement"; instead he has been "looking for a little discussion." If there were such a thing as a "men's movement," what might that look like? What sorts of things might a men's movement seek to address, especially in light of this essay?

5. One other interesting point that Chiarella makes within his essay is the idea that there is something "forbidden about arguing the ongoing boy crisis. It's a loser. It doesn't sell." Do you agree with this statement? Why do you think that a men's movement, or arguing

to resolve the problems that face modern young men, is something that people are likely to ignore or even possibly become offended by?

**6.** Research the statistics cited throughout Chiarella's essay (as well as the statistics located at the end of the online version of this article, which can be found by searching the essay's title on Esquire.com) and compare them to more up-to-date statistics from the same sources (e.g., the Department of Education website). How, if at all, have these numbers changed in the years since this essay's original publication? Has the outlook for young men, or "boys," as Chiarella describes them, changed for the better or for the worse? What accounts for these shifts? In your opinion, are things looking more bleak for young American men, or have their prospects gotten better? Back your opinion with sources found during your research.

**7.** Using the same approach and methodology as Chiarella does in his essay, compile your own list of the differences between men and boys (regardless of whether you are a man or a woman). List at least ten traits for each and describe how these traits define or illustrate the difference between men and boys. Also, explain the importance of these traits in differentiating between a man and a boy.

**8.** In his essay, Chiarella cites the findings of Education Trust, an advocacy group for low-income and minority students that tracks data on young men and their progression in relation to schooling. Research and locate another advocacy group that directly deals with the issue of young men and the obstacles that they face that prevent them from becoming productive "men," as defined by both Chiarella and General Petraeus. What is this advocacy group, what do they do, and how are they working to alleviate some of the problems that Chiarella has identified in this essay? What strides have been made toward improving the status of young men in our society, if any?

**9.** Conduct a video interview of a young man and question him about the potential obstacles he feels are standing in the way of his achievement. Then, in an accompanying essay, compare these to the various problems Chiarella has identified. How are the obstacles cited by the interviewee and Chiarella different or similar? What reasons are given by the interviewee to explain why the problems he has identified are viable obstacles in his path to success? How might Chiarella's proposed solutions actually help the situation of "real" young men?

**10.** The key to Chiarella's essay is not only understanding the difference between boys and men, but also understanding that Chiarella sees men as both the problem *and* the solution when it comes to boys becoming men. In what ways might a man be the problem in a younger man's life? In what ways might older men be a solution to the types of problems that face young men? Identify a solution that directly includes men, and explain how men might be able to help the next generation of young men become more successful in the face of the various obstacles defined throughout the essay.

**11.** Whether you are a man or a woman, volunteer for a mentoring program like one described in this essay (e.g., the Boys & Girls Club of America) and describe the story of your experience. What sort of younger person did you mentor? What problems (if any) did the younger person have, and how did you provide a solution? Overall, would you say the experience was a positive or a negative one, and why? Give specific examples from your experience to back your claim.

# I Won. I'm Sorry.
### Mariah Burton Nelson

**Let's Start Here••• ▶** As men attempt to define what it means to be a man, so too do women frequently seek out the definition of what it means to be a woman. The messages for modern women are as contradictory and confusing as they are for modern men. There are hundreds of magazines, films, television and radio shows, as well as websites that give varying definitions of what a woman is. Women in American culture have a difficult set of traits to navigate. On the one hand, women are told that they should strive to be independent and self-reliant. On the other hand, they are encouraged to be "lady-like" and to retain elements of femininity no matter how self-sufficient they are.

This is the central issue in the following essay by Mariah Burton Nelson. In her essay, Nelson dissects what it means to be a woman in America by primarily focusing on the dilemma of female athletes who strive to achieve greatness in their respective sports while still adhering to society's expectations of how women should act and present themselves publicly. While the dilemma of a female athlete most certainly differs from a nonathlete, the root issues of feminine identity are the same and apply to all women in America. Though Nelson does not profess to have all the answers, she still raises some important questions about what a woman is, and how a woman can navigate the complex territory of female identity in American culture.

As you read her essay, observe the manner in which Nelson dissects gender stereotypes and expectations, and what she offers up as potential solutions to the dilemma of modern female identity in America. Also, pay attention to the way Nelson turns to our popular media as the place where our culture displays what she sees as both the pros and cons of modern femininity.

---

Mariah Burton Nelson is an award-winning athlete, author, journalist, speechwriter, and speaker. For years Nelson has played a leading role in redefining what it means to be a female athlete. She has written books, articles, and speeches on a variety of subjects, mostly related to sports and success—plus one on forgiveness—and she now serves as executive director of the American Association for Physical Activity and Recreation. This essay first appeared in the March 1998 issue of *Self* magazine.

When Sylvia Plath's husband, Ted Hughes, published his first book of poems, Sylvia wrote to her mother: "I am so happy that HIS book is accepted FIRST. It will make it so much easier for me when mine is accepted. . . ."

After Sylvia killed herself, her mother published a collection of Sylvia's letters. In her explanatory notes, Aurelia Plath commented that from the time she was very young, Sylvia "catered to the male of any age so as to

**bolster:**
To support or prop up.

**collude:**
To plot or conspire together.

bolster his sense of superiority." In seventh grade, Aurelia Plath noted, Sylvia was pleased to finish second in a spelling contest. "It was nicer, she felt, to have a boy first."

How many women still collude in the myth of male superiority, believing it's "nicer" when boys and men finish first? How many of us achieve but only in a lesser, smaller, feminine way, a manner consciously or unconsciously designed to be as nonthreatening as possible?

Since I'm tall, women often talk to me about height. Short women tell me, "I've always wanted to be tall—but not as tall as you!" I find this amusing, but also curious. Why not? Why not be six-two?

Tall women tell me that they won't wear heels because they don't want to appear taller than their husbands or boyfriends, even by an inch. What are these women telling me—and their male companions? Why do women regulate their height in relation to men's height? Why is it still rare to see a woman who is taller than her husband?

Women want to be tall enough to feel elegant and attractive, like models. They want to feel respected and looked up to. But they don't want to be so tall that their height threatens men. They want to win—to achieve, to reach new heights—but without exceeding male heights.

How can you win, if you're female? Can you just do it? No. You have to play the femininity game. Femininity by definition is not large, not imposing, not competitive. Feminine women are not ruthless, not aggressive, not victorious. It's not feminine to have a killer instinct, to want with all your heart and soul to win—neither tennis matches nor elected office nor feminist victories such as abortion rights. It's not feminine to know exactly what you want, then go for it.

Femininity is about appearing beautiful and vulnerable and small. It's about winning male approval.

One downhill skier who asked not to be identified told me the following story: "I love male approval. Most women skiers do. We talk about it often. There's only one thing more satisfying than one of the top male skiers saying, 'Wow, you are a great skier. You rip. You're awesome.'

"But it's so fun leaving 99 percent of the world's guys in the dust—oops," she laughs. "I try not to gloat. I've learned something: If I kick guys' butts and lord it over them, they don't like me. If, however, I kick guys' butts then act 'like a girl,' there is no problem. And I do mean girl, not woman. Nonthreatening."

Femininity is also about accommodating men, allowing them to feel bigger than and stronger than and superior to women; not emasculated by them.

Femininity is unhealthy, obviously. It would be unhealthy for men to act passive, dainty, obsessed with their physical appearance, and dedicated to bolstering the sense of superiority in the other gender, so it's unhealthy for women too. These days, some women are redefining femininity as strong, as athletic, as however a female happens to be, so that "feminine" becomes synonymous with "female." Other women reject both feminine and masculine terms and stereotypes, selecting from the entire range of human behaviors instead of limiting themselves to the "gender-appropriate" ones. These women smile only when they're happy, act angry when they're angry, dress how they want to. They cling to their self-respect and dignity like a life raft.

> **synonymous:** Having the same meaning or implication as something.

But most female winners play the femininity game to some extent, using femininity as a defense, a shield against accusations such as bitch, man-hater, lesbian. Feminine behavior and attire mitigate against the affront of female victory, soften the hard edges of winning. Women who want to win without losing male approval temper their victories with beauty, with softness, with smallness, with smiles.

> **mitigate:** To make less painful or unpleasant.

In the fifties, at each of the Amateur Athletic Union's women's basketball championships, one of the players was crowned a Beauty Queen. (This still happens at Russian women's ice hockey tournaments.) Athletes in the All-American Girls Baseball League of the forties and fifties slid into base wearing skirts. In 1979, professional basketball players with the California Dreams were sent to John Robert Powers' charm school. Ed Temple, the legendary coach of the Tennessee State Tigerbelles, the team that produced Wilma Rudolph, Wyomia Tyus, Willye White, Madeline Manning, and countless other champions, enforced a dress code and stressed that his athletes should be "young ladies first, track girls second."

Makeup, jewelry, dress, and demeanor were often dictated by the male coaches and owners in these leagues, but to some extent the players played along, understanding the tradeoff: in order to be "allowed" to compete, they had to demonstrate that they were, despite their "masculine" strivings, real ("feminine") women.

Today, both men and women wear earrings, notes Felshin, "but the media is still selling heterosexism and 'feminine' beauty. And if you listen carefully, in almost every interview" female athletes still express apologetic behavior through feminine dress, behavior, and values.

Florence-Griffith Joyner, Gail Devers, and other track stars of this modern era dedicate considerable attention to portraying a feminine appearance. Basketball star Lisa Leslie has received more attention for being a model than for leading the Americans to Olympic victory. Steffi Graf posed in bikinis for the 1997 *Sports Illustrated* swimsuit issue. In a Sears commercial, Olympic basketball players apply lipstick, paint their toenails, rock babies, lounge in bed, and pose and dance in their underwear. Lisa Leslie, says "Everybody's allowed to be themselves. Me, for example, I'm very feminine."

In an Avon commercial, Jackie Joyner Kersee is shown running on a beach while the camera lingers on her buttocks and breasts. She tells us that she can bench-press 150 pounds and brags that she can jump farther than "all but 128 men." Then she says: "And I have red toenails." Words flash on the screen: "Just another Avon lady."

Graf, Mary Pierce, Monica Seles, and Mary Jo Fernandez have all played in dresses. They are "so much more comfortable" than skirts, Fernandez explained. "You don't have to worry about the shirt coming up or the skirt being too tight. It's cooler, and it's so feminine."

"When I put on a dress I feel different—more feminine, more elegant, more ladylike—and that's nice," added Australia's Nicole Bradtke: "We're in a sport where we're throwing ourselves around, so it's a real asset to the game to be able to look pretty at the same time."

Athletes have become gorgeous, flirtatious, elegant, angelic, darling—and the skating commentators' favorite term: "vulnerable." Some think this is good news: proof that femininity and sports are compatible. "There doesn't have to be such a complete division between "You're beautiful and sexy" and "you're athletic and strong," says Linda Hanley, a pro beach volleyball player who also appeared in a bikini in the 1997 *Sports Illustrated* swimsuit issue.

Athletes and advertisers reassure viewers that women who compete are still willing to play the femininity game, to be Cheerleaders. Don't worry about us, the commercials imply. We're winners but we'll still look pretty for you. We're acting in ways that only men used to act but we'll still act how you want women to act. We're not threatening. We're not lesbians. We're not ugly, not bad marriage material. We're strong but feminine. Linguists note that the word "but" negates the part of the sentence that precedes it.

There are some recent examples of the media emphasizing female power in an unambiguous way. "Women Muscle In," the *New York Times Magazine* proclaimed in a headline. The *Washington Post* wrote, "At Olympics, Women Show Their Strength." And a new genre of commercials protests that female athletes are NOT cheerleaders, and don't have to be. Olympic and pro basketball star Dawn Staley says in a Nike commercial that she plays basketball "for the competitiveness" of it. "I need some place to release it. It just builds up, and sports is a great outlet for it. I started out playing with the guys. I wasn't always accepted. You get criticized, like: 'You need to be in the kitchen. Go put on a skirt.' I just got mad and angry and went out to show them that I belong here as much as they do."

Other commercials tell us that women can compete like conquerors. A Nike ad called "Wolves" shows girls leaping and spiking volleyballs while a voice says, "They are not sisters. They are not classmates. They are not friends. They are not even the girls' team. They are a pack of wolves. Tend to your sheep." Though the athletes look serious, the message sounds absurd. When I show this commercial to audiences, they laugh. Still, the images do depict the power of the volleyball players: their intensity, their ability to pound the ball almost through the floor. The script gives the players (and viewers) permission not to be ladylike, not to worry about whether their toenails are red.

But in an American Basketball League commercial, the Philadelphia Rage's female basketball players are playing rough; their bodies collide. Maurice Chevalier sings, "Thank heaven for little girls." The tag line: "Thank heaven, they're on our side."

Doesn't all this talk about girls and ladies simply focus our attention on femaleness, femininity, and ladylike behavior? The lady issue is always there in the equation: something to redefine, to rebel against. It's always present, like sneakers, so every time you hear the word athlete you also hear the word lady—or feminine, or unfeminine. It reminds me of a beer magazine ad from the eighties that featured a photo of Olympic track star Valerie Brisco-Hooks. "Funny, she doesn't look like the weaker sex," said the print. You could see her impressive muscles. Clearly the intent of the ad was to contrast an old stereotype with the reality of female strength and ability. But Brisco-Hooks was seated, her legs twisted pretzel style, arms covering her chest. But in that position, Brisco-Hooks didn't look very strong or able. In the line, "Funny, she doesn't look like the weaker sex," the most eye-catching words are funny, look, weaker, and sex. Looking at the pretzel that is Valerie, you begin to think that she looks funny. You think about weakness. And you think about sex.

When she was young, Nancy Kerrigan wanted to play ice hockey with her older brothers. Her mother told her, "You're a girl. Do girl things."

Figure skating is a girl thing. Athletes in sequins and "sheer illusion sleeves" glide and dance, their tiny skirts flapping in the breeze. They achieve, but without touching or pushing anyone else. They win, but without visible signs of sweat. They compete, but not directly. Their success is measured not by confrontation with an opponent, nor even by a clock or a scoreboard. Rather, they are judged as beauty contestants are judged: by a panel of people who interpret the success of the routines. Prettiness is mandatory. Petite and groomed and gracious, figure skaters—like cheerleaders, gymnasts, and aerobic dancers—camouflage their competitiveness with niceness and prettiness until it no longer seems male or aggressive or unseemly.

The most popular sport for high school and college women is basketball. More than a million fans shelled out an average of $15 per ticket in 1997, the inaugural summer of the Women's National Basketball Association. But the most televised women's sport is figure skating. In 1995 revenue from skating shows and competitions topped six hundred million dollars. In the seven months between October 1996 and March 1997, ABC, CBS, NBC, Fox, ESPN, TBS, and USA dedicated 162.5 hours of programming to figure skating, half of it in prime time. Kerrigan earns up to three hundred thousand dollars for a single performance.

Nearly 75 percent of the viewers of televised skating are women. The average age is between twenty-five and forty-five years old, with a household income of more than fifty thousand dollars. What are these women watching? What are they seeing? What's the appeal?

Like golf, tennis, and gymnastics, figure skating is an individual sport favored by white people from the upper classes. The skaters wear cosmetics, frozen smiles, and revealing dresses. Behind the scenes they lift weights and sweat like any serious athlete but figure skating seems more dance than sport, more grace than guts, more art than athleticism. Figure skating allows women to compete like Champions while dressed like Cheerleaders.

In women's figure skating, smiling is part of "artistic expression." In the final round, if the competitors are of equal merit, artistry weighs more heavily than technique. Midori Ito, the best jumper in the history of women's skating, explained a weak showing at the 1995 world championships this way: "I wasn't 100 percent satisfied. . . I probably wasn't smiling enough."

The media portray female figure skaters as "little girl dancers" or "fairy tale princesses" (NBC commentator John Tesh); as "elegant" (Dick Button), as "little angels" (Peggy Fleming); as "ice beauties" and "ladies who lutz" (*People Magazine*). Commentators frame skaters as small, young, and decorative creatures, not superwomen but fairy-tale figments of someone's imagination.

After Kerrigan was assaulted by a member of Tonya Harding's entourage, she was featured on a *Sports Illustrated* cover crying "Why me?" When she recovered to win a silver medal at the Olympics that year, she became "America's sweetheart" and rich to boot. But the princess turned pumpkin shortly after midnight, as soon as the ball was over and she stopped smiling and started speaking. Growing impatient during the Olympic medal ceremony while everyone waited for Baiul, Kerrigan grumbled, "Oh, give me a break, she's just going to cry out there again. What's the difference?"

What were Kerrigan's crimes? She felt too old to cavort with cartoon characters. Isn't she? She expressed anger and disappointment—even bitterness and bad sportsmanship—about losing the gold. But wasn't she supposed to want to win? What happens to baseball players who, disappointed about a loss, hit each other or spit on umpires? What happens to basketball players and football players and hockey players who fight? Men can't tumble from a princess palace because we don't expect them to be princesses in the first place, only athletes.

Americans fell out of love with Kerrigan not because they couldn't adore an athlete who lacked grace in defeat, but because they couldn't adore a female athlete who lacked grace in defeat.

Female politicians, lawyers, and businesswomen of all ethnic groups also play the femininity game. Like tennis players in short dresses, working women seem to believe it's an asset to look pretty (but not too pretty) while throwing themselves around. The female apologetic is alive and well in corporate board rooms, where women say "I'm sorry, maybe someone else already stated this idea, but . . . " and smile while they say it.

When Newt Gingrich's mother revealed on television that Newt had referred to Hillary Clinton as a bitch, how did Hillary respond? She donned a pink suit and met with female reporters to ask how she could "soften her image." She seemed to think that her competitiveness was the problem and femininity the solution.

So if you want to be a winner and you're female, you'll feel pressured to play by special, female rules. Like men, you'll have to be smart and industrious, but in addition you'll have to be "like women": kind, nurturing, accommodating, nonthreatening, placating, pretty, and small. You'll have to smile. And not act angry. And wear skirts. Nail polish and makeup help, too.

**Let's Pause Here•••▶** How well do you think that Mariah Burton Nelson captures the double-bind of what it means to be a woman in America today? Does her usage of female athletes strengthen her argument about the complexities of women's identity, or is there a better group of women she could have chosen to address the issue? Overall, do you agree with her assessment of modern women's dilemma, or do you think she could have made her point differently?

**Let's Take It Further•••▼**

1. Why do you think that Nelson begins her essay by using the example of a famous female poet, Sylvia Plath, and describing Plath's gratitude that her husband was published before she was? How does this set the tone for the rest of Nelson's article? Based on this opening to her essay, as well as the word usage and examples employed throughout, to whom do you believe Nelson is trying to appeal? What, specifically, leads you to identify who her audience is based on her writing strategies? Why do you think Nelson chose to title her essay, "I Won. I'm Sorry."? What effect does this have on the reader from the very start, if any?

2. Nelson alludes to the "myth of male superiority" in the beginning of her essay as well. What are some of the common myths of male superiority in our present American society? From where do these myths emerge, and how are women to know which are myths and which are truths?

3. Nelson also discusses the fact that many women are not fond of the idea of being as tall as, or taller than, their male counterparts. Besides height, what other physical attributes or features do women usually avoid in an effort not to be perceived as a threat to men? How might these attributes be seen as threatening to men by men? How might they be

seen as a threat to men by women? Are these attributes actual threats, or are they engrained in women to be considered threats?

**4.** Are you surprised by the fact that, despite their athletic prowess, many of the female athletes whom Nelson interviewed for her essay stated that they want to beat men but know that they need to "act like girls," even after they have proven their athletic superiority? What, if anything, is surprising about that statement, and what does it mean to "act like a girl"?

**5.** One of the most basic dilemmas for modern women that Nelson outlines in her article is that a large portion of one's identity as a woman is "about winning male approval." Explain what you believe Nelson means by this statement, and give specific examples and descriptions of the ways in which modern women attempt to win male approval (as depicted in popular culture and our mass media). Show the process by which a woman might seek to accomplish this. Also, explain whether you think this is a positive or a negative trait of femininity, and why.

**6.** Explain the phenomenon that Nelson describes as "the femininity game." Illustrate what the "femininity game" consists of, and how modern women attempt to navigate this "game." Argue whether you see this "game" as a good thing or a bad thing, and why. Regardless of whether you are a man or a woman, discuss where you believe women learn what the "game" is, and how they go about attempting to "play" it. What is the outcome for women who "play the game" correctly, versus those who do not? Locate a real life example of each type in popular culture to back your opinion.

**7.** Find an example of a female athlete who does not subscribe to the definition of "feminine" that plagues so many of the athletes Nelson interviews in her essay. Who is the particular athlete that you've chosen, what is her sport, and how does she rebel against society's demands that so many other female athletes (at least in Nelson's essay) seem to succumb to so that they still might be considered feminine?

**8.** Nelson quotes notable feminist sports scholar J. Felshin as saying "the media is still selling heterosexism and 'feminine' beauty" when it comes to women in sports. Locate media sources that deal with female athletes and use these sources to either agree or disagree with Felshin's assessment of the media's role in complicating the gender identity of women in sports. Does the media still sell feminine beauty and heterosexism alongside female athleticism, or has there been a shift in recent years? How is media treatment different from or similar to the examples Nelson gives in her article? Do you see this as a good or a bad thing, and why?

**9.** How are women depicted in modern advertisements—and not just ones that deal with female athletes? Has society's depiction of women gotten better, worse, or stayed the same in the years since Nelson's article was first published (1998)? If young women were to turn to modern advertisements in search of a definition of female identity, what messages would they receive about what it means to be a woman? What is negative or positive about the definitions of femininity given by our popular media today?

**10.** Create a video or photo collage that shows famous women (athletes or otherwise) who break the mold in which Nelson fears some women might easily fall. In an accompanying essay, explain the ways in which these women defy the dilemma that Nelson predicts for them. Conversely, create a video montage of famous women who—despite their talents—still feel as though they must "act like girls" in order not to be a threat. In an accompanying essay, explain the process of how they "act like girls" and what might be at risk for the women in question if they weren't to play the "femininity game," as defined by Nelson in her essay.

**11.** Interview a female athlete at your school and discuss the concept of the "femininity game" with her. Using your questions and her responses, determine whether the issues raised in Nelson's essay are still relevant to women in today's culture. If so, how are things still similar to the ways in which Nelson described them? How have expectations changed or improved in the years since Nelson's essay was first published? Do you see this as a good or a bad development, and why?

# What Is The It Gets Better Project?

ItGetsBetter.org

**Let's Start Here••• ▷** One final aspect of how we forge our identities in modern America that this chapter will address is the issue of sexual identity. While some Americans might not give much thought to a person's sexual identity, there are still many of us for whom the issue of sexual identity is both a pivotal and complex one. Although, arguably, we live in an era in which society is more tolerant of sexual difference, the following essay and accompanying video testimonies prove that, for many Americans, the issue of one's sexual identity is still front-and-center in terms of how people define themselves. It also proves that there remains some misunderstanding and confusion about this issue—as well as tragedies that regularly occur because of these misunderstandings.

The following essay is an explanation of the founding of the advocacy website ItGetsBetter. org, which was created in response to a sudden spike in suicides by teenagers who were bullied because of their sexual preferences. In the essay, Dan Savage explains why he felt compelled to create the advocacy group, as well as the goals the It Gets Better Project hopes to achieve.

As you read the essay, observe the way Savage makes the case for the It Gets Better Project's existence, as well as the way in which he tries to appeal to all people, regardless of their sexual preferences or identities. Try to determine what the website and organization are advocating based on their stated rationale, as well as the "pledge" they ask all the website visitors to sign. Also, when you have finished reading the following essay, visit the website www.itgetsbetter. org and watch some of the testimonials that have been uploaded to the site. If you want to view a specific video (such as one by any of the celebrities listed in the following essay), you can easily search YouTube for the phrase "It Gets Better" and the name of the person or company you are interested in viewing.

Dan Savage is an American author, media pundit, journalist, and newspaper editor. Savage writes the internationally syndicated relationship and sex advice column, "Savage Love." Its tone is frank in its discussion of sexuality and often humorous. Savage, who is openly gay, has often been the subject of controversy regarding some of his opinions that pointedly clash with cultural conservatives and those put forth by what Savage has been known to call the "gay establishment." He and his partner, Terry, created the It Gets Better Project in response to a rash of nationally noted suicides in 2010 by gay teenagers who suffered from bullying.

## About the It Gets Better Project

Growing up isn't easy. Many young people face daily tormenting and bullying, leading them to feel like they have nowhere to turn. This is especially true for LGBT kids and teens, who often hide their sexuality for fear of bullying. Without other openly gay adults and mentors in their lives, they can't imagine what their future may hold. In many instances, gay and lesbian adolescents are taunted—even tortured—simply for being themselves.

Justin Aaberg. Billy Lucas. Cody Barker. Asher Brown. Seth Walsh. Raymond Chase. Tyler Clementi. They were tragic examples of youth who could not believe that it does actually get better.

It Gets Better: Dan and Terry
by itgetsbetterproject

While many of these teens couldn't see a positive future for themselves, we can. The It Gets Better Project was created to show young LGBT people the levels of happiness, potential, and positivity their lives will reach—if they can just get through their teen years. The It Gets Better Project wants to remind teenagers in the LGBT community that they are not alone—and it WILL get better.

## What Is the It Gets Better Project?

In September 2010, syndicated columnist and author Dan Savage created a YouTube video with his partner Terry to inspire hope for young people facing harassment. In response to a number of students taking their own lives after being bullied in school, they wanted to create a personal way for supporters everywhere to tell LGBT youth that, yes, it does indeed get better.

Two months later, the It Gets Better Project (TM) has turned into a worldwide movement, inspiring nearly 10,000 user-created videos and over 30 million views. To date, the project has received submissions from celebrities, organizations, activists, politicians and media personalities, including President Barack Obama, Secretary of State Hillary Clinton, Rep. Nancy Pelosi, Adam Lambert, Anne Hathaway, Colin Farrell, Matthew Morrison of "Glee," Joe Jonas, Joel Madden, Ke$ha, Sarah Silverman, Tim Gunn, Ellen DeGeneres, Suze Orman, the staffs of The Gap, Google, Facebook, Pixar, the Broadway community, and many more. For us, every video changes a life. It doesn't matter who makes it.

The website www.itgetsbetter.org is a place where young people who are lesbian, gay, bi, or trans can see how love and happiness can be a reality in their future. It's a place where our straight allies can visit and support their friends and family members. It's a place where people can share their stories, take the It Gets Better Project pledge, watch videos of love and support, and seek help through the Trevor Project and GLSEN.

## Who Is Dan Savage?

Dan Savage is author of the internationally syndicated relationship and sex column Savage Love and the weekly podcast Savage Lovecast. He is editorial director of the Seattle weekly *The Stranger*, where he was formerly Editor-in-Chief. He is a regular contributor to PRI's "This American Life" and has been featured as a Real Time Reporter on HBO's "Real Time with Bill Maher."

Dan heard about the suicides of Justin Aaberg and Billy Lucas and had a reaction so many LGBT adults had. "I wish I could've talked to that kid for five minutes before he killed himself," Dan recently said. "I'd tell him that however bad it was in high school or middle school . . . it gets better." The It Gets Better Project was born.

Watch the videos at www.itgetsbetter.org.

**Let's Pause Here•••▶** What is your initial reaction to the need for a project such as It Gets Better to exist? Do you believe the website might actually be helpful to a teenager who is in distress? How might witnessing the testimonial of Dan Savage and his partner Terry dissuade young people from taking their lives? What, if anything, about the rationale for the project's existence seems problematic?

**Let's Take It Further•••▼**

1. Based on the content of the essay, as well as the video posted by Dan and Terry on the website's main page, who do you think the target audience for this website is? Who else should the website include? How do other videos posted by celebrities and everyday citizens address the site's shortcomings, if at all?

2. Critics of the It Gets Better Project have often cited the fact that the site does nothing to address the problem of bullying, instead noting that the project aims to tell young people to wait out the rough times, so to speak, by saying "if [gay teens] can just get through their teen years." Do you agree with this criticism of the It Gets Better Project? Why or why not?

3. What do you think are the benefits of the It Gets Better Project? What specifically about the website, the pledge, and the videos do you think might actually positively impact a young person's life?

4. Have you personally witnessed any instances of taunting or bullying of a person based on his or her sexuality? If so, how did others respond? How did the person being bullied respond? What impact did the event have on your perception of bullying, if any?

5. Locate teen suicide statistics before and after the creation of the website to determine whether teen suicides directly related to bullying have decreased. Do you think the website has had any impact since its creation? Explain why or how you believe the website may or may not have had an impact on teens with alternative sexual lifestyles.

6. Research the story of any of the young people listed in the "About the It Gets Better Project" portion of the essay. What was the story of the particular person you chose? How might his situation have been different had the It Gets Better Project existed? Do you know anyone with a similar story? If so, how did he or she come to terms with the issue of his or her sexuality in light of the struggle he or she may have had with bullying peers?

7. One long-standing debate on the question of sexual identity is the issue of whether homosexuality is a choice or a part of a person's identity about which the person has no say. Research this issue using academic and medical sources to determine where you stand on the issue. Use your research to support your stance.

8. Either by yourself or with a group of friends or classmates, create and post your own "It Gets Better" video to YouTube (following the guidelines listed on the It Gets Better website). Then write an essay that describes the process of making the video, as well as what overall message you hope to get across with the contents of your video. Also, outline the points you specifically hope to make, and explain who your intended target audience is.

9. Choose two celebrities' (or companies') It Gets Better videos and compare the message behind each. Which of the two do you think is more likely to make an impact in someone's life, and why? How would you improve either or both of the videos? Next, compare two videos by everyday people and explain which you think the better of the two is and why. Overall, assess the potential success of this campaign based on the videos that you watched. How do you think it will make a difference? In what ways could the videos or the larger project be improved?

# mash it UP

Following is a series of essay and discussion topics that draw connections between multiple selections within the chapter. They also suggest outside texts to include in your essay or discussion. Feel free to bring in further outside texts, remembering the variety of texts (beyond articles) available to you.

1. Using a similar approach to Chiarella's in his "The Problem with Boys" essay, construct an essay that defines the difference between "girls" and "women" in modern American society. Be sure to give specific examples of how older women impact younger women and their perceptions of female identity gender roles.

2. Draw a comparison to the ways in which men are depicted in sports versus the ways women are depicted. How are men treated differently than women? What expectations does our culture appear to have for both our male and female athletes? Which of these expectations do you believe to be realistic, and which do you see as problematic?

3. What other dilemmas do men and women face in terms of how we define ourselves in relation to our gender? To where do we turn to learn what it means to be a man or a woman in America? Which of these sources provide positive definitions for men and women, and which of these provide negative definitions about how we define our gender roles?

4. How have gender roles in America shifted in recent decades (especially in light of the way femininity is depicted in the essay "I Won. I'm Sorry.")? One place that students can turn to for a comparison between older gender definitions and modern ones would be the smash television hit *Mad Men* on AMC. How are men and women depicted in this show, which is set in the late Fifties and early Sixties?

Or, students can research shows that actually ran during the Fifties and Sixties. Conversely, how are men and women depicted in television shows set in our current era? Are there any significant differences between the two time periods? If so, what are they?

5. Using modern popular media (such as movies or TV shows), explain the level of acceptance (or lack thereof) in our society for sexual difference. How do these media outlets deal with sexual difference, and in what ways do they help to establish what is or is not acceptable in our larger culture?

6. Research YouTube videos that give advice to men and women about how to define themselves in terms of gender. Which of the videos, in your opinion, are more realistic and helpful in their approach and why? Describe the videos that you find helpful, as well as the videos that you believe to be of no help, to people genuinely seeking definitions of masculinity and femininity. How can the advice realistically be applied to a person's life?

7. Locate the article "The End of Men" by Hanna Rosin online (www. theatlantic.com) and the accompanying article "Are Father's Necessary?" by Pamela Paul. Which of the two articles in this chapter ("The Problem with Boys" or "I Won. I'm Sorry.") do you feel these two articles most support? How do these two *Atlantic* articles support whichever article you have chosen, and in what ways do they show how the gender roles in America have shifted from the year in which the article in this chapter was first published?

8. Create a video interview or a video/photo collage that shows where modern men and/or women get their definitions of masculinity and femininity in popular culture. In an accompanying essay, explain what these popular culture sources are, as well as how they impact a person's gender identity. Do you see these sources as positive or negative role models for masculinity and femininity, and why?

**Let's Connect •••▶** 🄵 "Like" our Facebook page for free, up-to-date, additional readings, discussions, and writing ideas on the topic of identity. Join other students and teachers across the country sharing in an online discussion of popular culture events. *American Mashup* is on Facebook at www.facebook.com/americanmashup.

# Social Media

# Chapter 4

## Making the Cultural Connection

If there is anything we Americans—and people all over the world—cannot seem to live without, it is our technology and the social media connections that technology affords us. Our lives are absolutely steeped in and dependent on both social media and technology, in ways we sometimes don't even realize. These days, virtually everyone has a cell phone, an MP3 player, and a laptop, all of which we use to access our various social networking tools and to interact with one another, and none of which we could imagine being without for a single day. However, there are countless other forms of technology with which we interact on a daily basis, often without considering the roles they play in our lives. The GPS devices in our cars and on our phones were the stuff of science

### SELECTIONS IN THIS CHAPTER

fiction a few years ago, as was the idea that we would be able to read books, watch movies, and video conference on a device the size of a deck of cards. Computer chips in our pets? The ability to make money selling virtual products to someone playing a video game half a world away? These concepts were unthinkable not so long ago. But today, all of these examples are as commonplace as plumbing. After all, how silly would it be to discuss plumbing when we have simply incorporated it into our lives as a given? In fact, most people probably wouldn't consider plumbing to be a form of technology, but it is. Just over one hundred years ago, the technology of plumbing helped to eradicate diseases like cholera that plagued major cities all over the world due to an explosion in population and the public health issues that stemmed from so many people concentrated in one place.

We have a special relationship with technology and innovation in our country. Our scientists, engineers, inventors, and businesspeople regularly lead the rest of the world with entrepreneurial ideas that dramatically change our everyday lives. The phrase "Silicon Valley," which refers to the area of California that is home to many of our nation's leading technology firms, has become synonymous with technological daring and greatness. From this area of America, some of the greatest gifts of technology—and especially social networking and media—have been given to the larger world. Think of the following services and how often you use them in your life, and you'll begin to see the sort of impact technology has on our daily lives: Google, Amazon, eBay, PayPal, Apple, Yahoo!, Adobe, Intel, Netflix, Electronic Arts, Microsoft, YouTube, Facebook, and Twitter. This list includes only a fraction of the technology and social media companies started in America that have had a great impact on our culture and the rest of the world.

So why does this matter? Consider the fact that during the sweeping political protests throughout the Middle East that began in early 2011 (Bahrain, Tunisia, Egypt, Iraq, and Libya, to name just a few of the larger uprisings), the world was frequently given two different versions of each story. First, there was the position of the various government regimes, which tried to downplay the violence and unrest unfolding in the streets. Then, there were the hundreds of thousands of Twitter updates, cell phone videos, and photographs (such as those pictured here) that told an entirely different story. Without these technologies and social media outlets, it is unlikely that the outside world would have been able to witness the events as they occurred. In fact, had the same events occurred a mere five years earlier, only one narrative would have been likely to emerge: the official version of events given to the larger world by the governments in power seeking to control the images and news reports going out to the rest of the world.

By now, it is no secret to most people who follow international news that social media outlets have been at the heart of many political uprisings. From the post presidential election protests that broke out in Iran in 2009, to the many protests throughout the Middle East in 2011, Facebook and Twitter were frequently cited as the virtual spaces and communities that gave rise to organized public unrest. Whether this is a positive or negative development for world politics remains to be seen, but it is undeniable that social media has had an irrevocable impact on international politics.

Of course, there are many other ways that social media changes our lives daily. From the ability to find long-lost friends or relatives, to the ability to make vast sums of money by developing third-party applications for social media outlets, we have reached a point where life *without* social media is unimaginable for nearly everyone in America who has access to the Internet, cell phones, and computers. Relationships begin and end online. Struggling artists find millions of online fans without the aid of major corporations. Wars are waged and politics are debated. And all of this would have been unthinkable even at the turn of the century.

The important thing to consider, however, isn't just how convenient and wonderful these products and services are to us. Instead, it is necessary that we contemplate the way these various technologies and social media have become a part of our popular culture and even our personal identities. This chapter will do just that. Rather than only point out the convenient and fascinating technological advances we have made as a society—from YouTube celebrities born overnight to the ability to download an entire e-book in a matter of seconds—the selections that follow will ask you to think about how we interact with one another both virtually and physically in light of the technological products and social networking services we use every day.

You will be asked to consider, for example, why Facebook has become the go-to source for keeping up with friends and family, as well as how it affects the modern concept of "friendship." You will read about the rise of Facebook's popularity and the many ways in which we incorporate it into our lives. There are selections that will ask you to consider the way both social media and technology have impacted our religious institutions, our relationships, and even our ability to experience emotions. If there has ever been a time when the things we own and use give people a way to read us, it is now, and this chapter will give you the opportunity to read into how our electronic devices and our virtual selves define who we are, both individually and as a larger culture.

We will even consider the notion of privacy and how dramatically it has shifted in the last few years. In many scholars' opinions, our society, and most certainly our popular culture, has become one where the concept of privacy is nearly extinct. A person's Facebook page is a portal into his personality, his interests, even his intimate relationships. Many of us post pictures without thinking of the long-term implications, such as being denied employment because of questionable activities being publicized online. These shifting notions of privacy—where we post personal details of our lives online but then expect people not to use those details in our real lives—as well as the benefits of social media's approach to friendship will be frequently addressed throughout this chapter.

How valuable are technology and the social media it provides in our lives? How has social networking affected real-life relationships for better or worse? What might the "next big thing" in either technology or social media be? This chapter will engage these questions and more and afford you the opportunity to consider technology and social media in our everyday lives, as well as in our larger culture in America and throughout the world.

# Social Media                                         Bob Englehart

A native of Indiana, Bob Englehart studied at the American Academy of Art in Chicago before joining the staff of *Chicago Today* in 1966 as a cartoonist and illustrator. In 1972, Englehart returned to Fort Wayne, Indiana, as a freelance artist for the *Journal-Gazette*. He became a full-time cartoonist in 1975 when he joined the staff of the *Journal Herald* (Dayton, Ohio). In 1980, Englehart was hired as the first full-time editorial cartoonist for the *Hartford Courant* (Hartford, Connecticut). Englehart's cartoons are now syndicated, and he has published several collections of his editorial cartoons in addition to illustrating a children's book and providing television cartoon commentary. The following cartoon, "Social Media," was first published on November 23, 2010, by the *Hartford Courant.*

## Thinking About Social Media

Take a moment to look at the cartoon above. Like most political cartoons, this drawing is attempting to make a statement about a topic that is relevant to our popular culture. The topic, which can be discerned at a glance, is the common notion that there is a disconnect between older and younger generations when it comes to the value of social media. Despite the fact that there are more than 500 million Facebook users on the planet, that is still less than ten percent of the world's population. This begs the question, who is using Facebook and what do they use the website for? Even though it seems as if "everybody" has a Facebook page, with more than 70 percent of Facebook users located outside the United States (according to Facebook's own statistics page), it might not be the ever-present and all-consuming website in American popular culture after all. Or maybe there is some truth in our country to the notion that Facebook *is* ever-present within some age groups and not used as widely by others.

Of course, there is the common misconception that the older a person is, the less likely he is to engage social media to build relationships and network in a virtual way, which is why the stereotypical grumpy old man sitting on a park bench declares to the young men standing beside him that the novel he has in his hands is "*anti*-social media." This misconception stems from the earliest days of online social networking—Friendster, MySpace, and even GeoCities—when the most avid users tended to be young, technically savvy people. In fact, young people used to consider it "creepy" when someone in their thirties or older used these early websites—as if they were understood to be the domain of the young. However, that notion fizzled very quickly in late 2005 when Facebook, with its simplicity and openness, invited anyone in the world to join. When that occurred, social media reached a tipping point, and people of all ages and backgrounds flocked to Facebook, LinkedIn, and many other less popular but equally engaging social media websites.

To understand the full impact of what this cartoon is trying to address, however, you will need to look beyond the surface question of whether young people "own" social media and older people are "out of the loop." In the era of iPads, Nooks, Kindles, and other e-readers, to hold up a book and declare it to be the *anti*-social media" is to raise an interesting point. After all, the very products just mentioned were originally designed to allow consumers to carry vast digital libraries with them, though dissenters hailed these e-readers as the impending death of the printed word. Instead, what has happened since the debut of these products (in addition to people buying millions of books for their e-readers) is that they have been updated to incorporate social media in one form or another. On the Kindle, for instance, a consumer can share libraries with other users, check email, browse the Web, and upload reviews to Amazon (which is a social media tool of its own now, with online profiles; ranking; the ability to "like," share, and comment on content, as well as many other common features of other social media). But there is also the fact that a physical book *is* a form of anti social media. There is, after all, no way to access anything virtual with it, and to read a physical book is a solitary experience. So the grumpy old man raises a valid point. The question is, will books and their solitary nature continue to be important? And to whom does the death of physical books really matter? Older people? Librarians? Authors? Book lovers? How would you feel if there were no longer bookstores, libraries, or even printed books in your daily life? Would it matter? If so, why? If not, why not?

One final point to consider when viewing Englehart's cartoon is the common complaint about younger people that older generations of people have: while one boy is talking to the old man, the other stands a couple feet away and texts away on his cell phone—communicating virtually while the other two people next to him communicate physically. People regularly complain that young people—with their obsession for virtual friendship, as well as their constant "connection" with virtual media—are actually missing out on genuine human relationships and interaction. This particular debate continues to this day, with psychologists, talk show hosts, sociologists, parents, clergy, and other experts and non experts trying to determine the impact of social media and technology on the generations of young people who have never known another world. This will be addressed in a few different ways throughout the chapter. Nevertheless, based on Englehart's depiction of the three characters interacting in his cartoon, what would you say his opinion on this debate is? What in the cartoon leads you to believe this?

Now, take a moment to consider how other types of technologies and social media could render some aspect of our lives obsolete (in the same way e-readers might threaten physical books and online profiles might threaten physical interaction between people). Is there an emerging technology or social media that you can imagine capable of changing our lives in a similar fashion? If so, how might you illustrate this in a cartoon of your own?

## The End of a Social Media Era?     Emily Long

**Let's Start Here•••▶**   With over half a billion users who visit the website every day, Facebook has become one of the world's most successful websites. Chances are slim that you know someone who does not have a profile on the social networking website. Social networking, as a popular culture phenomenon, is at an all-time high, which begs the question, where and when will social networking end? Theories abound about the purpose these sites serve in our lives, but there is no question that the very idea of having an online presence in the form of a profile has become the norm.

While many websites have waxed and waned in popularity (Friendster, MySpace, LinkedIn, and Gather come to mind as once-popular examples), the social networking website as a concept has remained steady in our culture for the last decade. In the following essay, Emily Long turns to recent data that suggest the era of social media may finally have reached its peak. Observe her argument and decide for yourself whether the data she presents make the case for this era of social interaction online drawing to a close. If we are indeed reaching the end of a social media era, what might be the reason for it? Are we finally becoming so saturated with networking websites and apps that we might want to disconnect? Or have the researchers gotten it wrong?

Emily Long is a contributing writer to the "Tech Insider" feature of the U.S. government website Next.gov. Next.gov is a website devoted to the posting of documents, articles, and discussions of "technology and the business of government." Emily Long's essay first appeared on the Next.gov website on June 18, 2010.

Are we facing the end of the social media era?

Justin Kistner, an analyst at Webtrends, reports that the social media phase of the Web will peak in 2012, with the next big thing coming right on its heels in 2015. Kistner says we're in the Era of Social Media, the third era of the Web (after new media and Web 2.0). Facebook is a huge driver of online traffic and sends more hits to news sites than Google, he reports. In addition, social media has surpassed porn as the number one Internet activity.

However, based on Internet trends and the life cycle of Web 2.0 technologies like blogs and wikis, the social craze may soon decline, he says, though he does acknowledge that it actually may peak later than 2012. And it's possible that Facebook and Twitter may continue to evolve to meet users' changing needs in unexpected ways. So what would the decline of social media mean for federal agencies, who are just now starting to use these tools regularly and for broad purposes? Government isn't the quickest to pick up on new trends, so how will quick turnover impact communication strategies?

During a Thursday hearing of the House Oversight Information Policy, Census and National Archives Subcommittee, Rep. Eleanor Holmes Norton, D-D.C., joked about social media's popularity and the challenges it poses for federal record-keeping:

"God help us if Twitter becomes a primary form of communication," she said.

**Let's Pause Here•••▶** First of all, do you agree or disagree that we are reaching the end of a social media era? Which data that Ms. Long presents bring you to this conclusion? How do you feel about the fact that we are told the "next big thing" will arise by 2015, yet we are given no alternative? Why do you think social media is so important to our culture?

**Let's Take It Further•••▼**

1. What problems arise—if any—from the limited sources Emily Long cites to back her claim? Is there merit to her argument?

2. What is the effect of Long asking so many questions throughout her short essay? What is it that she seeks to accomplish with this writing strategy, and do you feel it is an effective one? Why or why not?

3. Why do you think Long ends her brief article with the quote, "God help us if Twitter becomes a primary form of communication," which she attributes to Representative Norton?

4. Why do you think Long chooses to point out that social media now "surpass[es] porn as the number one Internet activity"?

5. In what ways, if any, have you shared news stories with your friends online, which Long suggests is the primary way people now get their news? How did you get your news before the days of friends recommending news stories on their profile feeds?

6. The author quotes Justin Kistner as saying that we are now in the "third era of the Web." Research and define what the first two Web eras were. If social media defines this particular era that we're in now, what were the defining traits of the first two eras? Describe popular examples that represent both eras.

7. What role did pornography play in building the Internet? Why is it even worth noting that something other than porn is now the number one Internet activity? Research and compare earlier Web traffic to present-day Web traffic and describe how it has changed over the years. For example, how did the pornography industry shape the Internet, and what role does it play in the online world now?

8. Consider the implications of social media in your life. How often, and for how long, do you spend every day on your Facebook page? What do you do? What other ways do you communicate with friends and family? In your opinion, do you see the era of social media as a positive or negative development in how people interact with one another? Describe how you communicated before the era of social media, and compare it to how you communicate with friends and family now.

9. What might the next era of the Web look like? If social networking goes the way of the personal website, what might replace it in popularity? Describe what you think the "next big thing" could be, and explain the process of how this next thing might actually work.

10. Track your online activity for one day, noting the sites you visit and for what purpose. Describe how much of your day you spent on Facebook, for example, and how you spent your time on the website. What sorts of trends emerged? What activities did you engage in most often? How long were you on the site?

11. Create a potential "next wave" website or application mock-up, using images, a website, or a PowerPoint presentation to describe and define it. Explain its purpose, its audience, how it might work, and what the benefit to society might be.

# mash**UP** essay

The following essay is this chapter's Mashup selection. Keeping in mind our definition of a Mashup essay in Chapter 2 (an essay that includes multimedia texts, as well as multiple writing strategies), observe the way the author, Christine Rosen, utilizes multimedia texts. For example, she refers to some of the more popular (and a couple now defunct) social networking websites, and she reads these websites as texts. Indeed, much of Rosen's article is focused on the idea that the very purpose of social networking—to some extent—is to create virtual texts of ourselves to be read by others. In addition to the virtual texts of online profiles, Rosen compares these types of self-portraits to the concept of painted portraits commissioned by upper-class people as status symbols. Rosen also incorporates a variety of different scholarly studies into her discussion of social networking, not only to bring more credibility to her own article, but also to show the academic response to this phenomenon and where experts believe it might lead. There are many other outside, multimedia texts Rosen uses to give her writing a many-layered approach. See if you can identify some of them.

Rosen also employs multiple writing strategies within the pages of this article. For example, she uses a definition-illustration approach to writing in order to describe what social networking sites are (for the very few people left who might not know) and how they work. But Rosen also regularly brings in other people's personal stories of social networking by using the narrative strategy. This allows her to bring to life, in a sense, the events she is attempting to convey, such as the social anxiety that a person might undergo when deciding whether to accept or reject a friend request. You should also note the way Rosen employs an "if . . . then" technique in pondering the possible ramifications of social networking on the current generation of kids who grew up with an online presence (the cause-effect strategy). Finally, you should also note how Rosen includes extensive outside sources (the research writing strategy) dating back to the first versions of online communities and traces them to the present day (the process-analysis strategy).

When you begin writing a Mashup essay of your own in response to the selections in this chapter, revisit Rosen's essay to generate ideas for multimedia texts and multiple writing strategies. Use the flowchart to see the ways in which Rosen employs the various writing strategies and multimedia texts she utilizes in her writing.

**Mashup Essay Flowchart**

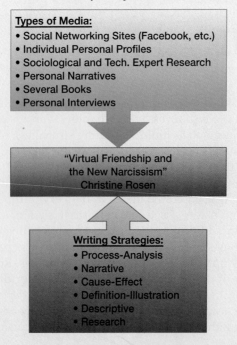

<u>Types of Media:</u>
- Social Networking Sites (Facebook, etc.)
- Individual Personal Profiles
- Sociological and Tech. Expert Research
- Personal Narratives
- Several Books
- Personal Interviews

"Virtual Friendship and
the New Narcissism"
Christine Rosen

<u>Writing Strategies:</u>
- Process-Analysis
- Narrative
- Cause-Effect
- Definition-Illustration
- Descriptive
- Research

# Virtual Friendship and the New Narcissism

**Christine Rosen**

**Let's Start Here••• ▶**     If we are surrounded by texts that can be read, including the way we represent ourselves as texts, then it is oddly appropriate that the most popular place where people conduct this sort of activity (reading each other and writing ourselves) is named Facebook—as though the site itself is aware of the act of reading frequently practiced by its customers. This idea of how we choose to represent ourselves online, as texts made up of pictures, collections of friends, and shared interests, is one that Rosen explores in the following article. As you read it, notice how quickly trends change. Which websites that she mentions are no longer popular to use? Which features of Facebook or MySpace no longer exist as she describes them? Finally, as she discusses the potential outcomes of a generation raised on online social networking, try to identify whether any of the predictions made by Rosen or the experts she cites have come true. Are there outcomes she is describing that now seem humorous or unbelievable because of how social networking has changed in the years since this article was first published?

---

Christine Rosen is senior editor of the *New Atlantis: A Journal of Technology & Society,* where she writes about the social impact of technology, bioethics, and the history of genetics. Rosen is the author of *Preaching Eugenics: Religious Leaders and the American Eugenics Movement* (2004), a history of the ethical and religious debates surrounding the eugenics movement in the United States. Her most recent book is *My Fundamentalist Education,* which tells the story of the Christian fundamentalist school she attended as a child in St. Petersburg, Florida. Since 1999, Rosen has also been an adjunct scholar at the American Enterprise Institute for Public Policy Research, where she has written about women and the economy, feminism, and women's studies. Rosen's opinion pieces and essays have appeared in many publications, including the *New York Times Magazine,* the *Wall Street Journal, The New Republic,* and the *Washington Post.* The following essay first appeared in the summer 2007 issue of the *New Atlantis.*

For centuries, the rich and the powerful documented their existence and their status through painted portraits. A marker of wealth and a bid for immortality, portraits offer intriguing hints about the daily life of their subjects—professions, ambitions, attitudes, and, most importantly, social standing. Such portraits, as German art historian Hans Belting has argued, can be understood as "painted anthropology," with much to teach us, both intentionally and unintentionally, about the culture in which they were created.

> This is one of the many examples of the extensive research Rosen has done in constructing her essay.

Self-portraits can be especially instructive. By showing the artist both as he sees his true self and as he wishes to be seen, self-portraits can at once expose and obscure, clarify and distort. They offer opportunities for both self-expression and self-seeking. They can display egotism and modesty, self-aggrandizement and self-mockery.

> **self-aggrandizement:** To make oneself seem greater or more important.

Today, our self-portraits are democratic and digital; they are crafted from pixels rather than paints. On social networking websites like MySpace and Facebook, our modern self-portraits feature background music, carefully manipulated photographs, stream-of-consciousness musings, and lists of our hobbies and friends. They are interactive, inviting viewers not merely to look at, but also to respond to, the life portrayed online. We create them to find friendship, love, and that ambiguous modern thing called connection. Like painters constantly retouching their work, we alter, update, and tweak our online self-portraits; but as digital objects they are far more ephemeral than oil on canvas. Vital statistics, glimpses of bare flesh, lists of favorite bands and favorite poems all clamor for our attention—and it is the timeless human desire for attention that emerges as the dominant theme of these vast virtual galleries.

> Rosen uses profiles on MySpace and Facebook as texts that can be read to define people based on how they represent themselves online.

> **ephemeral:** Something that is fleeting or lasts for a very short time.

Although social networking sites are in their infancy, we are seeing their impact culturally: in language (where *to friend* is now a verb), in politics (where it is *de rigueur* for presidential aspirants to catalogue their virtues on MySpace), and on college campuses (where *not* using Facebook can be a social handicap). But we are only beginning to come to grips with the consequences of our use of these sites: for friendship, and for our notions of privacy, authenticity, community, and identity. As with any new technological advance, we must consider what type of behavior online social networking encourages.

> **de rigueur:** Proper etiquette, or required by custom.

Does this technology, with its constant demands to collect (friends and status), and perform (by marketing ourselves), in some ways undermine our ability to attain what it promises—a surer sense of who we are and where we belong? The Delphic oracle's guidance was *know thyself*. Today, in the world of online social networks, the oracle's advice might be *show thyself*.

> In this section, Rosen employs the definition-informative writing strategy by explaining how social networking websites work, as well as the narrative writing strategy by telling social media's evolutionary story.

## Making Connections

The earliest online social networks were arguably the Bulletin Board Systems of the 1980s that let users post public messages, send and receive private messages, play games, and exchange software. Some of those BBSs, like The WELL (Whole Earth 'Lectronic Link) that technologist Larry Brilliant and futurist Stewart Brand started in 1985, made the transition to the World Wide Web in the mid-1990s. (Now owned by Salon.com, The WELL boasts that it was "the primordial ooze where the online community movement was born.") Other websites for community and connection emerged in the 1990s, including Classmates.com (1995), where users register by high school and year of graduation; Company of Friends, a business-oriented site founded in 1997; and Epinions, founded in 1999 to allow users to give their opinions about various consumer products.

Rosen uses The WELL as a text in the same way she reads MySpace and Facebook.

**primordial:**
The earliest form of something that later evolved into a more sophisticated object or thing.

A new generation of social networking websites appeared in 2002 with the launch of Friendster, whose founder, Jonathan Abrams, admitted that his main motivation for creating the site was to meet attractive women. Unlike previous online communities, which brought together anonymous strangers with shared interests, Friendster uses a model of social networking known as the "Circle of Friends" (developed by British computer scientist Jonathan Bishop), in which users invite friends and acquaintances—that is, people they already know and like—to join their network.

Rosen employs the process-analysis strategy to show how Friendster works compared to earlier social media, as well as each time other social media platforms are mentioned.

Friendster was an immediate success, with millions of registered users by mid-2003. But technological glitches and poor management at the company allowed a new social networking site, MySpace, launched in 2003, quickly to surpass it. Originally started by musicians, MySpace has become a major venue for sharing music as well as videos and photos. It is now the behemoth of online social networking, with over 100 million registered users. Connection has become big business: In 2005, Rupert Murdoch's News Corporation bought MySpace for $580 million.

**behemoth:**
A thing of monstrous size or power.

Besides MySpace and Friendster, the best-known social networking site is Facebook, launched in 2004. Originally restricted to college students, Facebook—which takes its name from the small photo albums that colleges once gave to incoming freshmen and faculty to help them cope with meeting so many new people—soon extended membership to high schoolers and is now open to anyone. Still, it is most popular among college students and recent college graduates, many of whom use the site as their primary method of communicating with one another. Millions of college students check their Facebook pages several times every day and spend hours sending and receiving messages, making appointments, getting updates on their friends' activities, and learning about people they might recently have met or heard about.

There are dozens of other social networking sites, including Orkut, Bebo, and Yahoo 360°. Microsoft recently announced its own plans for a social networking site called Wallop; the company boasts that the site will offer "an entirely new way for consumers to express their individuality online." (It is noteworthy that Microsoft refers to social networkers as "consumers" rather than merely "users" or, say, "people.") Niche social networking sites are also flourishing: there are sites offering forums and fellowship for photographers, music lovers, and sports fans. There are professional networking sites, such as LinkedIn, that keep people connected with present and former colleagues and other business acquaintances. There are sites specifically for younger children, such as Club Penguin, which lets kids pretend to be chubby, colored penguins who waddle around chatting, playing games, earning virtual money, and buying virtual clothes. Other niche social networking sites connect like-minded self-improvers; the site 43things.com encourages people to share their personal goals. Click on "watch less TV," one of the goals listed on the site, and you can see the profiles of the 1,300 other people in the network who want to do the same thing. And for people who want to join a social network but don't know which niche site is right for them, there are sites that help users locate the proper online social networking community for their particular (or peculiar) interests.

Social networking sites are also fertile ground for those who make it their lives' work to get your attention—namely, spammers, marketers, and politicians. Incidents of spamming and spyware on MySpace and other social networking sites are legion. Legitimate advertisers such as record labels and film studios have also set up pages for their products. In some cases, fictional characters from books and movies are given their own official MySpace pages. Some sports mascots and brand icons have them, too. Procter & Gamble has a Crest toothpaste page on MySpace featuring a sultry-looking model called "Miss Irresistible." As of this summer, she had about 50,000 users linked as friends, whom she urged to "spice it up by sending a naughty (or nice) e-card." The e-cards are

> Here is another example of Rosen using outside research to strengthen her argument.

emblazoned with Crest or Scope logos, of course, and include messages such as "I wanna get fresh with you" or "Pucker up baby—I'm getting fresh." A P&G marketing officer recently told the *Wall Street Journal* that from a business perspective, social networking sites are "going to be one giant living dynamic learning experience about consumers."

As for politicians, with the presidential primary season now underway, candidates have embraced a no-website-left-behind policy. Senator Hillary Clinton has official pages on social networking sites MySpace, Flickr, LiveJournal, Facebook, Friendster, and Orkut. As of July 1, 2007, she had a mere 52,472 friends on MySpace (a bit more than Miss Irresistible); her Democratic rival Senator Barack Obama had an impressive 128,859. Former Senator John Edwards has profiles on twenty-three different sites. Republican contenders for the White House are poorer social networkers than their Democratic counterparts; as of this writing, none of the GOP candidates has as many MySpace friends as Hillary, and some of the leading Republican candidates have no social networking presence at all.

Despite the increasingly diverse range of social networking sites, the most popular sites share certain features. On MySpace and Facebook, for example, the process of setting up one's online identity is relatively simple: Provide your name, address, e-mail address, and a few other pieces of information and you're up and running and ready to create your online persona. MySpace includes a section, "About Me," where you can post your name, age, where you live, and other personal details such as your zodiac sign, religion, sexual orientation, and relationship status. There is also a "Who I'd Like to Meet" section, which on most MySpace profiles is filled with images of celebrities. Users can also list their favorite music, movies, and television shows, as well as their personal heroes; MySpace users can also blog on their pages. A user "friends" people—that is, invites them by e-mail to appear on the user's "Friend Space," where they are listed, linked, and ranked. Below the Friends space is a Comments section where friends can post notes. MySpace allows users to personalize their pages by uploading images and music and videos; indeed, one of the defining features of most MySpace pages is the ubiquity of visual and audio clutter. With silly, hyper flashing graphics in neon colors and clip-art style images of kittens and cartoons, MySpace pages often resemble an overdecorated high school yearbook.

By contrast, Facebook limits what its users can do to their profiles. Besides general personal information, Facebook users have a "Wall" where people can leave them brief notes, as well as a Messages feature that functions like an in-house Facebook e-mail account. You list your friends on Facebook as well, but in general, unlike MySpace friends, which are often complete strangers (or spammers) Facebook friends tend to be part of one's offline social circle. (This might change, however, now that Facebook has opened its site to anyone rather than restricting it to college and high school students.) Facebook (and MySpace) allow users to form groups based on mutual interests. Facebook users can also send "pokes" to friends; these little digital nudges are meant to let someone know you are thinking about him or her. But they can also be interpreted as not-so-subtle come-ons; one Facebook group with over 200,000 members is called "Enough with the Poking, Let's Just Have Sex."

### Degrees of Separation

It is worth pausing for a moment to reflect on the curious use of the word *networking* to describe this new form of human interaction. Social networking websites "connect" users with a network— literally, a computer network. But the verb *to network* has long been used to describe an act of intentional social connecting, especially for professionals seeking career-boosting contacts. When the word first came into circulation in the 1970s, computer networks were rare and mysterious. Back then, "network" usually referred to television. But social scientists were already using the notion of networks and nodes to map out human relations and calculate just how closely we are connected.

In 1967, Harvard sociologist and psychologist Stanley Milgram, best known for his earlier Yale experiments on obedience to authority, published the results of a study about social connection that he called the "small world experiment." "Given any two people in the world, person X and person Z," he asked, "how many intermediate acquaintance links are needed before X and Z are connected?" Milgram's research, which involved sending out a kind of chain letter and tracing its journey to a particular target person, yielded an average number of 5.5 connections. The idea that we are all connected by "six degrees of separation" (a phrase later popularized by playwright John Guare) is now conventional wisdom.

But is it true? Duncan J. Watts, a professor at Columbia University and author of *Six Degrees: The Science of a Connected Age*, has embarked on a new small world project to test Milgram's theory. Similar in spirit to Milgram's work, it relies on e-mail to determine whether "any two people in the world can be connected via 'six degrees of separation.'" Unlike Milgram's experiment, which was restricted to the United States, Watts's project is global; as he and his colleagues reported in *Science*, "Targets included a professor at an Ivy League university, an archival inspector in Estonia, a technology consultant in India, a policeman in Australia, and a veterinarian in the Norwegian army." Their early results suggest that Milgram might have been right: messages reached their targets in five to seven steps, on average. Other social networking theorists are equally optimistic about the smallness of our wireless world. In *Linked: The New Science of Networks*, Albert-László Barabási enthuses, "The world is shrinking because social links that would have died out a hundred years ago are kept alive and can be easily activated. The number of social links an individual can actively maintain has increased dramatically, bringing down the degrees of separation. Milgram estimated six," Barabási writes. "We could be much closer these days to three."

What kind of "links" are these? In a 1973 essay, "TheStrength of Weak Ties," sociologist Mark Granovetter argued that weaker relationships, such as those we form with colleagues at work or minor acquaintances, were more useful in spreading certain kinds of information than networks of close friends and family. Watts found a similar phenomenon in his online small world experiment: weak ties (largely professional ones) were more useful than strong ties for locating far-flung individuals, for example.

Today's online social networks are congeries of mostly weak ties—no one who lists thousands of "friends" on MySpace thinks of those people in the same way as he does his flesh-and-blood acquaintances, for example. It is surely no coincidence, then, that the activities social networking sites promote are precisely the ones weak ties foster, like rumor-mongering, gossip, finding people, and tracking the ever-shifting movements of popular culture and fad. If this is our small world, it is one that gives its greatest attention to small things.

**congeries:** Collections.

Rosen employs the cause-effect writing strategy.

Even more intriguing than the actual results of Milgram's small world experiment—our supposed closeness to each other—was the swiftness and credulity of the public in embracing those results. But as psychologist Judith Kleinfeld found when she delved into Milgram's research (much of which was methodologically flawed and never adequately replicated), entrenched barriers of race and social class undermine the idea that we live in a small world. Computer networks have not removed those barriers. As Watts and his colleagues conceded in describing their own digital small world experiment, "more than half of all participants resided in North America and were middle class, professional, college educated, and Christian."

Nevertheless, our need to believe in the possibility of a small world and in the power of connection is strong, as evidenced by the popularity and proliferation of contemporary online social networks. Perhaps the question we should be asking isn't how closely are we connected, but rather what kinds of communities and friendships are we creating?

**proliferation:** Rapidly increasing or growing in number.

### Won't You Be My Digital Neighbor?

According to a survey recently conducted by the Pew Internet and American Life Project, more than half of all Americans between the ages of twelve and seventeen use some online social networking site. Indeed, media coverage of social networking sites usually describes them as vast teenage playgrounds—or wastelands, depending on one's perspective. Central to this narrative is a nearly unbridgeable generational divide, with tech-savvy youngsters redefining friendship while their doddering elders look on with bafflement and increasing anxiety. This seems anecdotally correct; I can't count how many times I have mentioned social networking websites to someone over the age of forty and received the reply, "Oh yes, I've heard about that MyFace! All the kids are doing that these days. Very interesting!"

**anecdotally:** Consisting of stories or non-professional observations.

Numerous articles have chronicled adults' attempts to navigate the world of social networking, such as the recent *New York Times* essay in which columnist Michelle Slatalla described the incredible embarrassment she caused her teenage daughter when she joined Facebook: "everyone in the whole world thinks its super creepy when adults have facebooks," her daughter instant-messaged her. "unfriend paige right now. im serious . . . . i will be soo mad if you dont unfriend paige right now. actually." In fact, social networking sites are not only for the young. More than half of the visitors to MySpace claim to be over the age of 35. And now that the first generation of college Facebook users have graduated, and the site is open to all, more than half of Facebook users are no longer students. What's more, the proliferation of niche social networking sites, including those aimed at adults, suggests that it is not only teenagers who will nurture relationships in virtual space for the foreseeable future.

Rosen uses text messages as texts themselves.

What characterizes these online communities in which an increasing number of us are spending our time? Social networking sites have a peculiar psychogeography. As researchers at the Pew project have noted, the proto-social networking sites of a decade ago used metaphors of *place* to organize their members: people were linked through virtual cities, communities, and homepages. In 1997, GeoCities boasted thirty virtual "neighborhoods" in which "homesteaders" or "GeoCitizens" could gather—"Heartland" for family and parenting tips, "SouthBeach" for socializing, "Vienna" for classical music aficionados, "Broadway" for theater buffs, and

**psychogeography:** The study of how geographic upbringing or environment affects a person's emotions or behaviors.

so on. By contrast, today's social networking sites organize themselves around metaphors of the *person*, with individual profiles that list hobbies and interests. As a result, one's entrée into this world generally isn't through a virtual neighborhood or community but through the revelation of personal information. And unlike a neighborhood, where one usually has a general knowledge of others who live in the area, social networking sites are gatherings of deracinated individuals, none of whose personal boastings and musings are necessarily trustworthy. Here, the old arbiters of community—geographic location, family, role, or occupation—have little effect on relationships.

Also, in the offline world, communities typically are responsible for enforcing norms of privacy and general etiquette. In the online world, which is unfettered by the boundaries of real-world communities, new etiquette challenges abound. For example, what do you do with a "friend" who posts inappropriate comments on your Wall? What recourse do you have if someone posts an embarrassing picture of you on his MySpace page? What happens when a friend breaks up with someone—do you defriend the ex? If someone "friends" you and you don't accept the overture, how serious a rejection is it? Some of these scenarios can be resolved with split-second snap judgments; others can provoke days of agonizing.

Enthusiasts of social networking argue that these sites are not merely entertaining; they also edify by teaching users about the rules of social space. As Danah Boyd, a graduate student studying social networks at the University of California, Berkeley, told the authors of *MySpace Unraveled*, social networking promotes "informal learning . . . .It's where you learn social norms, rules, how to interact with others, narrative, personal and group history, and media literacy." This is more a hopeful assertion than a proven fact, however. The question that isn't asked is how the technology itself—the way it encourages us to present ourselves and interact—limits or imposes on that process of informal learning. All communities expect their members to internalize certain norms. Even individuals in the transient communities that form in public spaces obey these rules, for the most part; for example, patrons of libraries are expected to keep noise to a minimum. New technologies are challenging such norms—cell phones ring during church sermons; blaring televisions in doctors' waiting rooms make it difficult to talk quietly—and new norms must develop to replace

**deracinated:**
To be uprooted or removed from a group of people or one's native environment.

**arbiters:**
Persons or ideas with the power to pass judgment or whose opinions are considered to have great authority.

**unfettered:**
Freed or unrestrained.

This is another example of how Rosen employs the cause-effect writing strategy to discuss the potential downsides of social media.

**assertion:**
Declaration.

**transient:**
Short-lived or quickly passing.

the old. What cues are young, avid social networkers learning about social space? What unspoken rules and communal norms have the millions of participants in these online social networks internalized, and how have these new norms influenced their behavior in the offline world?

Social rules and norms are not merely the strait-laced conceits of a bygone era; they serve a protective function. I know a young woman—attractive, intelligent, and well-spoken—who, like many other people in their twenties, joined Facebook as a college student when it launched. When she and her boyfriend got engaged, they both updated their relationship status to "Engaged" on their profiles and friends posted congratulatory messages on her Wall.

> These two paragraphs are an example of Rosen employing the narrative strategy to tell the story of a friend whose experience with social media illustrates Rosen's overall point.

But then they broke off the engagement. And a funny thing happened. Although she had already told a few friends and family members that the relationship was over, her ex decided to make it official in a very twenty-first century way: he changed his status on his profile from "Engaged" to "Single." Facebook immediately sent out a feed to every one of their mutual "friends" announcing the news, "Mr. X and Ms. Y are no longer in a relationship," complete with an icon of a broken heart. When I asked the young woman how she felt about this, she said that although she assumed her friends and acquaintances would eventually hear the news, there was something disconcerting about the fact that everyone found out about it instantaneously; and since the message came from Facebook, rather than in a face-to-face exchange initiated by her, it was devoid of context—save for a helpful notation of the time and that tacky little heart.

## Indecent Exposure

Enthusiasts praise social networking for presenting chances for identity-play; they see opportunities for all of us to be little Van Goghs and Warhols, rendering quixotic and ever-changing versions of ourselves for others to enjoy. Instead of a palette of oils, we can employ services such as PimpMySpace.org, which offers "layouts, graphics, background, and more!" to gussy up an online presentation of self, albeit in a decidedly raunchy fashion: Among the most popular graphics used by PimpMySpace clients on a given day in June 2007 were short video clips of two women kissing and another of a man and an obese woman having sex; a picture of a gleaming pink handgun; and an image of the cartoon character SpongeBob SquarePants, looking alarmed and uttering a profanity.

> **quixotic:** Unpredictable and even inaccurate.

> Rosen employs the descriptive writing strategy to paint a vivid picture of the types of graphics people placed on their MySpace profiles.

This kind of coarseness and vulgarity is commonplace on social networking sites for a reason: it's an easy way to set oneself apart. Pharaohs and kings once celebrated themselves by erecting towering statues or, like the emperor Augustus, placing their own visages on coins. But now, as the insightful technology observer Jaron Lanier has written, "Since there are only a few archetypes, ideals, or icons to strive for in comparison to the vastness of instances of everything online, quirks and idiosyncrasies stand out better than grandeur in this new domain. I imagine Augustus' MySpace page would have pictured him picking his nose." And he wouldn't be alone. Indeed, this is one of the characteristics of MySpace most striking to anyone who spends a few hours trolling its millions of pages: it is an overwhelmingly dull sea of monotonous uniqueness, of conventional individuality, of distinctive sameness.

The world of online social networking is practically homogenous in one other sense, however diverse it might at first appear: its users are committed to self-exposure. The creation and conspicuous consumption of intimate details and images of one's own and others' lives is the main activity in the online social networking world. There is no room for reticence; there is only revelation. Quickly peruse a profile and you know more about a potential acquaintance in a moment than you might have learned about a flesh-and-blood friend in a month. As one college student recently described to the *New York Times Magazine*: "You might run into someone at a party, and then you Facebook them: what are their interests? Are they crazy-religious, is their favorite quote from the Bible? Everyone takes great pains over presenting themselves. It's like an embodiment of your personality."

> **homogenous:** The same or similar in nature.

> **reticence:** Being reluctant or reserved.

It seems that in our headlong rush to join social networking sites, many of us give up one of the Internet's supposed charms: the promise of anonymity. As Michael Kinsley noted in *Slate*, in order to "stake their claims as unique individuals," users enumerate personal information: "Here is a list of my friends. Here are all the CDs in my collection. Here is a picture of my dog." Kinsley is not impressed; he judges these sites "vast celebrations of solipsism."

Social networkers, particularly younger users, are often naïve or ill-informed about the amount of information they are making publicly available. "One cannot help but marvel at the amount, detail, and nature of the personal information some users provide, and ponder how informed this information sharing can be," Carnegie Mellon researchers Alessandro Acquisti and Ralph Gross wrote in 2006. In a survey of Facebook users at their university, Acquisti and

> Here is yet another example of the wide variety of sources that Rosen uses throughout her essay to back her opinion.

Gross "detected little or no relation between participants' reported privacy attitudes and their likelihood" of publishing personal information online. Even among the students in the survey who claimed to be most concerned about their privacy—the ones who worried about "the scenario in which a stranger knew their schedule of classes and where they lived"—about 40 percent provided their class schedule on Facebook, about 22 percent put their address on Facebook, and almost 16 percent published both.

This kind of carelessness has provided fodder for many sensationalist news stories. To cite just one: In 2006, NBC's *Dateline* featured a police officer posing as a 19-year-old boy who was new in town. Although not grounded in any particular local community, the imposter quickly gathered more than 100 friends for his MySpace profile and began corresponding with several teenage girls. Although the girls claimed to be careful about the kind of information they posted online, when *Dateline* revealed that their new friend was actually an adult male who had figured out their names and where they lived, they were surprised. The danger posed by strangers who use social networking sites to prey on children is real; there have been several such cases. This danger was highlighted in July 2007 when MySpace booted from its system 29,000 sex offenders who had signed up for memberships using their real names. There is no way of knowing how many sex offenders have MySpace accounts registered under fake names.

There are also professional risks to putting too much information on social networking sites, just as for several years there have been career risks associated with personal homepages and blogs. A survey conducted in 2006 by researchers at the University of Dayton found that "40 percent of employers say they would consider the Facebook profile of a potential employee as part of their hiring decision, and several reported rescinding offers after checking out Facebook." Yet college students' reaction to this fact suggests that they have a different understanding of privacy than potential employers: 42 percent thought it was a violation of privacy for employers to peruse their profiles, and "64 percent of students said employers should not consider Facebook profiles during the hiring process."

**compartmentalize:**
To separate into smaller categories or groups.

This is a quaintly Victorian notion of privacy, embracing the idea that individuals should be able to compartmentalize and parcel out parts of their personalities in different settings.

It suggests that even behavior of a decidedly questionable or hypocritical bent (the Victorian patriarch who also cavorts with prostitutes, for example, or the straight-A business major who posts picture of himself funneling beer on his MySpace page) should be tolerated if appropriately segregated. But when one's darker side finds expression in a virtual space, privacy becomes more difficult and true compartmentalization nearly impossible; on the Internet, private misbehavior becomes public exhibitionism.

In many ways, the manners and mores that have already developed in the world of online social networking suggest that these sites promote gatherings of what psychiatrist Robert Jay Lifton has called "protean selves." Named after Proteus, the Greek sea god of many forms, the protean self evinces "mockery and self-mockery, irony, absurdity, and humor." (Indeed, the University of Dayton survey found that "23 percent [[of students]] said they intentionally misrepresented themselves [[on Facebook]] to be funny or as a joke.") Also, Lifton argues, "the emotions of the protean self tend to be free-floating, not clearly tied to cause or target." So, too, with protean communities: "Not just individual emotions but communities as well may be free-floating," Lifton writes, "removed geographically and embraced temporarily and selectively, with no promise of permanence." This is precisely the appeal of online social networking. These sites make certain kinds of connections easier, but because they are governed not by geography or community mores but by personal whim, they free users from the responsibilities that tend to come with membership in a community. This fundamentally changes the tenor of the relationships that form there, something best observed in the way social networks treat friendship.

> **mores:**
> Societal norms or customs.

> **tenor:**
> Concept and meaning.

## The New Taxonomy of Friendship

> **taxonomy:**
> The study of how something is classified.

There is a Spanish proverb that warns, "Life without a friend is death without a witness." In the world of online social networking, the warning might be simpler: "Life without hundreds of online 'friends' is virtual death." On these sites, friendship is the stated *raison d'être*. "A place for friends," is the slogan of MySpace. Facebook is a "social utility that connects people with friends." Orkut describes itself as "an online community that connects people through a network of trusted friends." Friendster's name speaks for itself.

> ***raison d'être:***
> The reason for its existence.

But "friendship" in these virtual spaces is thoroughly different from real-world friendship. In its traditional sense, friendship is a relationship which, broadly speaking, involves the sharing of

**reciprocity:**
A mutual exchange of interests or actions.

mutual interests, reciprocity, trust, and the revelation of intimate details over time and within specific social (and cultural) contexts. Because friendship depends on mutual revelations that are concealed from the rest of the world, it can only flourish within the boundaries of privacy; the idea of public friendship is an oxymoron.

The hypertext link called "friendship" on social networking sites is very different: public, fluid, and promiscuous, yet oddly bureaucratized. Friendship on these sites focuses a great deal on collecting, managing, and ranking the people you know. Everything about MySpace, for example, is designed to encourage users to gather as many friends as possible, as though friendship were

**philately:**
Stamp collecting.

philately. If you are so unfortunate as to have but one MySpace friend, for example, your page reads: "You have 1 friends," along with a stretch of sad empty space where dozens of thumbnail photos of your acquaintances should appear.

This promotes a form of frantic friend procurement. As one young Facebook user with 800 friends told John Cassidy in *The New Yorker*, "I always find the competitive spirit in me wanting to up the number." An associate dean at Purdue University recently boasted to the *Christian Science Monitor* that since establishing a Facebook profile, he had collected more than 700 friends. The phrase universally found on MySpace is, "Thanks for the add!"—an acknowledgment by one user that another has added you to his list of friends. There are even services like FriendFlood.com that act as social networking pimps: for a fee, they will post messages on your page from an attractive person posing as your "friend." As the founder of one such service told the *New York Times* in February 2007, he wanted to "turn cyberlosers into social-networking magnets."

The structure of social networking sites also encourages the bureaucratization of friendship. Each site has its own terminology, but among the words that users employ most often is "managing." The Pew survey mentioned earlier found that "teens say social networking sites help them manage their friendships." There is something Orwellian about the management-speak on social networking sites: "Change My Top Friends," "View All of My Friends" and, for those times when our inner Stalins sense the need for a virtual purge, "Edit Friends." With a few mouse clicks one can elevate or downgrade (or entirely eliminate) a relationship.

To be sure, we all rank our friends, albeit in unspoken and intuitive ways. One friend might be a good companion for outings to movies or concerts; another might be someone with whom you socialize in professional settings; another might be the kind of person for whom you would drop everything if he needed help. But social networking sites allow us to rank our friends publicly. And not only can we publicize our own preferences in people, but we can also peruse the favorites among our other acquaintances. We can learn all about the friends of our friends—often without having ever met them in person.

## Status-Seekers

Of course, it would be foolish to suggest that people are incapable of making distinctions between social networking "friends" and friends they see in the flesh. The use of the word "friend" on social networking sites is a dilution and a debasement, and surely no one with hundreds of MySpace or Facebook "friends" is so confused as to believe those are all real friendships. The impulse to collect as many "friends" as possible on a MySpace page is not an expression of the human need for companionship, but of a different need no less profound and pressing: the need for status. Unlike the painted portraits that members of the middle class in a bygone era would commission to signal their elite status once they rose in society, social networking websites allow us to *create* status—not merely to commemorate the achievement of it. There is a reason that most of the MySpace profiles of famous people are fakes, often created by fans: Celebrities don't need legions of MySpace friends to prove their importance. It's the rest of the population, seeking a form of parochial celebrity, that does.

> **debasement:** Lowering or cheapening of status or meaning.

> **parochial:** Limited in range or reach, or being located within a small community.

But status-seeking has an ever-present partner: anxiety. Unlike a portrait, which, once finished and framed, hung tamely on the wall signaling one's status, maintaining status on MySpace or Facebook requires constant vigilance. As one 24-year-old wrote in a *New York Times* essay, "I am obsessed with testimonials and solicit them incessantly. They are the ultimate social currency, public declarations of the intimacy status of a relationship . . . . Every profile is a carefully planned media campaign."

The sites themselves were designed to encourage this. Describing the work of B.J. Fogg of Stanford University, who studies "persuasion strategies" used by social networking sites to increase participation, *The New Scientist* noted, "The secret is to tie the acquisition of friends, compliments and status—spoils that humans will work hard for—to activities that enhance the site." As Fogg told the magazine, "You offer someone a context for gaining status, and they are going to work for that status." Network theorist

Albert-László Barabási notes that online connection follows the rule of "preferential attachment"—that is, "when choosing between two pages, one with twice as many links as the other, about twice as many people link to the more connected page." As a result, "while our individual choices are highly unpredictable, as a group we follow strict patterns." Our lemming-like pursuit of online status via the collection of hundreds of "friends" clearly follows this rule.

What, in the end, does this pursuit of virtual status mean for community and friendship? Writing in the 1980s in *Habits of the Heart*, sociologist Robert Bellah and his colleagues documented the movement away from close-knit, traditional communities, to "lifestyle enclaves" which were defined largely by "leisure and consumption." Perhaps today we have moved beyond lifestyle enclaves and into "personality enclaves" or "identity enclaves"—discrete virtual places in which we can be different (and sometimes contradictory) people, with different groups of like-minded, though ever-shifting, friends.

## Beyond Networking

This past spring, Len Harmon, the director of the Fischer Policy and Cultural Institute at Nichols College in Dudley, Massachusetts, offered a new course about social networking. Nichols is a small school whose students come largely from Connecticut and Massachusetts; many of them are the first members of their families to attend college. "I noticed a lot of issues involved with social networking sites," Harmon told me when I asked him why he created the class. How have these sites been useful to Nichols students? "It has relieved some of the stress of transitions for them," he said. "When abrupt departures occur—their family moves or they have to leave friends behind—they can cope by keeping in touch more easily."

So perhaps we should praise social networking websites for streamlining friendship the way e-mail streamlined correspondence. In the nineteenth century, Emerson observed that "friendship requires more time than poor busy men can usually command." Now, technology has given us the freedom to tap into our network of friends when it is convenient for us. "It's a way of maintaining a friendship without having to make any effort whatsoever," as a recent graduate of Harvard explained to *The New Yorker*. And that ease admittedly makes it possible to stay in contact with a wider circle of offline acquaintances than might have been possible in the era before Facebook. Friends you haven't heard from in years, old buddies from elementary school, people you might have (should have?)

fallen out of touch with—it is now easier than ever to reconnect to those people.

But what kind of connections are these? In his excellent book *Friendship: An Exposé*, Joseph Epstein praises the telephone and e-mail as technologies that have greatly facilitated friendship. He writes, "Proust once said he didn't much care for the analogy of a book to a friend. He thought a book was better than a friend, because you could shut it—and be shut of it—when you wished, which one can't always do with a friend." With e-mail and caller ID, Epstein enthuses, you can. But social networking sites (which Epstein says "speak to the vast loneliness in the world") have a different effect: they discourage "being shut of" people. On the contrary, they encourage users to check in frequently, "poke" friends, and post comments on others' pages. They favor interaction of greater quantity but less quality.

This constant connectivity concerns Len Harmon. "There is a sense of, 'if I'm not online or constantly texting or posting, then I'm missing something,'" he said of his students. "This is where I find the generational impact the greatest—not the use of the technology, but the *overuse* of the technology." It is unclear how the regular use of these sites will affect behavior over the long run—especially the behavior of children and young adults who are growing up with these tools. Almost no research has explored how virtual socializing affects children's development. What does a child weaned on Club Penguin learn about social interaction? How is an adolescent who spends her evenings managing her MySpace page different from a teenager who spends her night gossiping on the telephone to friends? Given that "people want to live their lives online," as the founder of one social networking site recently told *Fast Company* magazine, and they are beginning to do so at ever-younger ages, these questions are worth exploring.

The few studies that have emerged do not inspire confidence. Researcher Rob Nyland at Brigham Young University recently surveyed 184 users of social networking sites and found that heavy users "feel less socially involved with the community around them." He also found that "as individuals use social networking more for entertainment, their level of social involvement decreases." Another recent study conducted by communications professor Qingwen Dong and colleagues at the University of the Pacific found that "those who engaged in romantic communication over MySpace tend to have low levels of both emotional intelligence and self-esteem."

**narcissistic:**
The character trait of loving oneself.

**exhibitionistic:**
The character trait of performing publicly for others.

The implications of the narcissistic and exhibitionistic tendencies of social networkers also cry out for further consideration. There are opportunity costs when we spend so much time carefully grooming ourselves online. Given how much time we already devote to entertaining ourselves with technology, it is at least worth asking if the time we spend on social networking sites is well spent. In investing so much energy into improving how we *present* ourselves online, are we missing chances to genuinely *improve* ourselves?

We should also take note of the trend toward giving up face-to-face for virtual contact—and, in some cases, a preference for the latter. Today, many of our cultural, social, and political interactions take place through eminently convenient technological surrogates—Why go to the bank if you can use the ATM? Why browse in a bookstore when you can simply peruse the personalized selections Amazon.com has made for you? In the same vein, social networking sites are often convenient surrogates for offline friendship and community. In this context it is worth considering an observation that Stanley Milgram made in 1974, regarding his experiments with obedience: "The social psychology of this century reveals a major lesson," he wrote. "Often it is not so much the kind of person a man is as the kind of situation in which he finds himself that determines how he will act." To an increasing degree, we find and form our friendships and communities in the virtual world as well as the real world. These virtual networks greatly expand our opportunities to meet others, but they might also result in our valuing less the capacity for genuine connection. As the young woman writing in the *Times* admitted, "I consistently trade actual human contact for the more reliable high of smiles on MySpace, winks on Match.com, and pokes on Facebook." That she finds these online relationships more *reliable* is telling: it shows a desire to avoid the vulnerability and uncertainty that true friendship entails. Real intimacy requires risk—the risk of disapproval, of heartache, of being thought a fool. Social networking websites may make relationships more reliable, but whether those relationships can be humanly satisfying remains to be seen.

**Let's Pause Here•••▶** Do you agree with the idea put forth by Christine Rosen that people who use social networks are driven to collect friends for status? If so, what sort of status does a person gain from this activity? What sort of status might a person lose if she doesn't have enough online friends? Has there been any change to this activity online since the article's publication? If narcissism (the love of oneself) is the driving force behind people creating online profiles, how might this account for the way you think about your own online presence? Is there another reason you are online?

## Let's Take It Further•••▼

1. Consider the outcome of one or more of Ms. Rosen's hypothetical situations. How many of the situations she describes (e.g., the way real-life interaction might be diminished by online interaction) have actually come to pass? Can you give any examples of this?

2. How familiar are you with the examples of websites and social media tools Rosen mentions that are now unpopular to use? If you ever did use them, why don't you anymore? What makes one site better than another?

3. Based on Rosen's definition-informative approach throughout most of her essay (as well as the examples she gives and the language she uses to explain social networking), who is Rosen's audience supposed to be? If she were trying to reach a different age group or a group of people more savvy with social media, how might her essay have been different? Do you think her approach is an effective one for reaching her target audience? Why or why not?

4. Note that Rosen talks about a mother whose child was mortified when she joined Facebook. How have things changed in terms of who is "permitted" to use Facebook, now that the site is open to virtually everyone?

5. Rosen briefly mentions the idea of people learning social cues from networking with other people. We learn how to act in certain social situations such as libraries by going to them and seeing that people are generally quiet to allow others to concentrate on reading, studying, and so on. What habits have become more socially acceptable in the wake of online social networking that might have been considered "bad taste" in the days before pokes, comments, tagging, and the many other features these websites afford their users?

6. If you've ever found yourself in a situation where you suffered anxiety because of an online activity (e.g., to friend or not to friend someone, a relationship ending publicly, unwanted photos of you being posted online), describe the situation and tell the story of how you responded to it. What process did you take to address the problem? How have you prepared yourself to deal with future situations of the sort?

7. Discuss the evolution of the social networking site that you most prefer. Why did you join the site, and when? How has it changed compared to the earlier times when you first became a member? How has this caused a change in your real life as a result of your virtual profile, if anything has changed? Describe how much time you spend on the site, and explain the activities you take part in while you are there.

8. Take the time to "read" the online profile of someone whom you know well in real life. What "text" emerges about that person based on the information he or she has chosen to make public? Construct a video or image collage of elements of the person's online profile to illustrate who he or she wants himself or herself to be online. Use these images (and write an accompanying essay) to dissect the person's online representation of themselves and contrast the virtual representation to the real person. How is that person different than the online

persona he or she has created? Read and interpret both the "real" and the "virtual" texts being portrayed by the person, and compare the two. What might account for the differences between one text and the other?

9. Pretend, for a moment, that social networking websites suddenly disappeared. How might that affect your life? Can you name activities you currently do online that you would be unable to do in person? Or, more importantly, if the Internet simply crashed and we were reduced to face-to-face interaction, what would you replace Facebook with? Conversely, you might discuss what you did in the days before Facebook to interact with friends and family.

10. Much has been said about the potential downfalls of engaging with social networking websites, many of which are outlined in Rosen's article. Yet there must be positives that outweigh the potential negatives, or how else can we account for the wild, worldwide success of social networking sites? Describe and discuss the benefits to an online presence and how it has enabled you to maintain friendships, or even create legitimate new ones. Make the case, in other words, for social networking's popularity to someone who is skeptical.

# If We Don't Regulate the Social Web, Someone Else Will
### Manish Mehta

**Let's Start Here•••▶** We live in an era when virtually everyone has an online presence of some sort. Even those of us who think we aren't an online presence might not be considering the fact that an eBay account, a PayPal account, or even an Amazon account amounts to an online profile. Users of these sites provide personal information, such as a billing address, financial information, and a location. More importantly, many people interact with these sites by rating items or sellers, and therefore they are making public their purchasing history, among other things. While most of us know that these companies protect our private financial information, we still must consider the implications of an online presence. Privacy, as a concept, is fluid, as Manish Mehta tells us in his essay. People who are Facebook users, even if they utilize privacy controls, can still be searched and found online. Even the most basic information (such as a school you're attending or the few friends Facebook publicizes) can tell far more about a person than he might realize. So it is only logical that since we live in the era of online profiles, accounts, and commerce, we should stop to consider the moral and ethical debate behind the idea of online privacy.

This is precisely what Mehta does in his piece. He ponders the implications of a world where people freely give information about themselves and still expect privacy. As you read the essay, observe how he makes the case for the importance of self-regulation, what the term means, and how it will impact our lives if it moves to the federal level.

Manish Mehta serves as Dell's Vice President of Social Media and Community, where he heads up strategy, social media and community, and search globally. Online operations have included all regional sites across the Asia-Pacific and Japan (APJ); Europe, the Middle East, and Africa (EMEA); and the Americas, including the United States, Latin America, and Canada. Mr. Mehta previously held various entrepreneurial roles at Dell. He was responsible for Dell's Global eBusiness and CRM strategy across all transactional and relationship businesses for Dell, reporting to Dell's Chief Marketing Officer. He served as an executive member of Dell Ventures, Dell's venture capital organization, where he held several board member and advisory board member positions with a number of private venture-backed startup companies. He regularly contributes to the *Huffington Post,* where this essay first appeared on June 22, 2010.

Excitement over the possibilities of the New can lead to exuberance, and exuberance—whether rational or irrational—can result in the kind of mistakes that stifle innovation. In social media, that moment has arrived. Our exuberance over the connections we can make with customers is prompting some companies to compromise their data security and privacy. The industry needs to take a step back now in order to ensure our ability to move forward later.

Consider the example of the nuclear power industry, where plant safety is analogous to social media's data privacy. Power plants were built to be safe, yet public concern mounted, boiling over when a major accident took place in 1979. The Nuclear Regulatory Commission stepped in and asked for major overhauls to power plant safety, making new plants prohibitively expensive. Not a single nuclear plant has been commissioned in the U.S. since.

> **analogous:**
> Able to be compared, or similar to something.

A leak or accident in the arena of privacy and data security in social media would cause, quite rightfully, a consumer outcry. If the companies didn't respond quickly and appropriately, regulators would need to get involved. The regulations could be more Draconian than customers were requesting. So for the sake of a short-term business gain on the part of a few players, the entire industry could be hobbled.

> **Draconian:**
> Cruel, unfair, or severe.

In her recent blogs and speeches, Danah Boyd, Social Media Researcher at Microsoft Research New England and a Fellow at Harvard University's Berkman Center for Internet and Society, makes the argument that privacy is not dead, even among kids. It's just different than we think. Privacy means user control. Users don't mind sharing their information with us—they're as interested in the exchange as we are. They just want to be the ones deciding which information they share.

As with any relationship, trust is key. And in this relationship, protecting customer information and preserving their choices about privacy is vital to maintaining that trust. The boundaries are evolving, and we don't know where they will eventually land, but we are all responsible for setting them together.

At first it sounds like an engineering question—privacy settings in software on web sites used by millions of people. But it's not an engineering question; it's a policy question. If companies set fair policies now, today, regulators won't have to impose restrictive policies later. Our vigilance will ensure that both companies and customers enjoy the freedoms of the social web for decades to come.

**vigilance:** Alertness or watchfulness.

---

**Let's Pause Here•••** ▶ Do you find it odd that Mehta compares the idea of regulating social media to the regulation of nuclear energy? How are the two related? Also, what is the warning he gives us about how outside regulators might negatively affect innovation? Clearly, Mehta is in favor of users working with companies to come to some sort of compromise, but what might that be?

---

**Let's Take It Further•••** ▼

1. In light of Mehta's article, where do you stand on the issue of privacy and regulation of privacy policies between users and companies? Is this a realistic goal? What, if anything, can users do to enter the dialogue between companies, and what information should they be able to share with one another?

2. Based on his language usage, as well as the examples he gives, to whom do you think Mehta is appealing by writing this article? How effective do you think his writing strategies are for convincing his audience of his point of view? How would it be different if he were addressing his essay to the industries he is discussing? What if he were addressing the government officials and agencies that have the power to regulate social media?

3. How much of your public profile(s) would you consider to be private information? Is there anything on your Facebook page, for example, that you wouldn't want your parents, potential employers, or even companies looking to do business with you to know about your personal life? If so, how do you currently keep these things private?

4. Do you agree with Mehta's assertion that outside regulation (for example, a set of federal laws) will end the innovation that is taking place within companies such as Twitter and Facebook? If so, how might these regulations stifle innovation? If not, how might innovators (think of app creators) skirt the regulations being imposed on them?

5. If you have an online profile, whether through Twitter, Facebook, or any other social networking site, take some time to classify the information you have placed online about yourself. Start with your interests, your "likes," and then move into groups of which you are a member, the apps you have installed, and the photographs and other forms of interaction (wall posts, comments) you regularly take part in. How much of your actual life is public? Have you noticed any trends in the groups, "likes," apps, and various other activities that you are engaging with regularly? What do these things say about you? What might a stranger be able to learn from your profile? Is there anything you wouldn't want a stranger to know? Compare your online representation of yourself to the "real you." How is it similar, and how is it different?

6. If you believe that companies and users might feasibly be able to work together to come to a set of privacy rules that meet everyone's liking, describe and explain the steps involved in such a transaction. What kind of information would you be willing to share with Facebook, and what private information would be okay for them to share with other companies? Understanding that many of these social websites provide a free service, and knowing that they must still be able to make money to provide the service, what would be fair ways for these companies to make money from their users without charging for a service?

7. Visit any of the major social websites and read their current privacy policy in full. Was there anything in the policy that surprised you or angered you? What do they reserve the right to know about you and share with other companies? What do they agree to keep private? Now that you've read the entire policy, do you agree with it? If not, what elements of the policy would you like to see changed, and why?

# mash**it**UP

Here is a series of essay and discussion topics that draw connections between multiple selections within the chapter. They also suggest outside texts to include in your essay or discussion. Feel free to bring in further outside texts, remembering the variety of texts (beyond articles) available to you.

1. Locate a celebrity Twitter feed or online profile of your choosing. Observe the ways in which this well-known person chooses to represent himself or herself online, given the information that most people know about this person because of his or her level of fame. What, if anything, is different about the person's online persona versus his or her real one? How might it be that the person is attempting to control people's perceptions of him or her by having an online persona?

2. So far, we have read articles that talk about the rise of social networking and the soon-to-be decline in "the social media era." Which of the following statements do you believe to be true: "The social media era will soon peak and be replaced by something else" ("The End of a Social Media Era?"), or "people, because of our narcissism, will continue to create online profiles of themselves in an effort to gain status" ("Virtual Friendship and the New Narcissism")? Argue your point of view based on the types of social media that exist and the ways in which they are constantly evolving.

3. Consider the cartoon "Social Media," and what it says about how people interact with one another both online and in real life. If social media threatens our physical interaction with tangible objects (i.e., e-readers as a threat to physical books), what might sites such as Facebook render obsolete in our personal interactions with people? What have they already rendered obsolete? Locate other political cartoons on social networking to see what contemporary artists criticize about social media.

4. Compare the "Virtual Friendship" essay's discussion on privacy to Mehta's essay about privacy concerns. Is there any similarity to the argument either author is making about our online personas and the danger of placing too much information about ourselves online? If the essays are making the same point, explain what that point is and how they go about making the same argument with differing techniques. If they present different opinions about privacy concerns, what are the concerns, and how do they make their point?

5. Find an outside source that has yet to be mentioned in this chapter that constitutes a virtual community or online social network. How is this service different than the ever-popular Facebook community? What purpose does it serve to its members that differs from either MySpace or Facebook? What site, if any, do you think has any chance at all of unseating Facebook from its current position of most-visited site in the world (over even Google, on occasion)?

6. Conduct a video interview or survey a group of people who use social media on a regular basis to determine the value of these technologies in their lives. How do the interviewees respond when asked about how their lives have changed since the advent of social media, and what role do these various media outlets play in their lives? Can any of them foresee a future where social media is less present than it is currently? Accompany your video with an essay that shows comparisons between the various answers you received in order to present a consistent opinion about the value of social media in modern-day life.

# Digital Communication                    Andy Singer

Andy Singer is a political cartoonist and the creator of the self-syndicated cartoon series titled *NO EXIT*, which he began in 1992. *NO EXIT* appears in dozens of newspapers, books, and magazines in the U.S. and abroad, including the *Funny Times*, the *Bay Monthly*, *Athens News*, *La Decroissance*, *Z Magazine*, *Random Lengths*, *Seven Days*, *Urban Velo*, and *Eugene Weekly*. He updates his *NO EXIT* site with 14 new cartoons every month at www.andysinger.com. This cartoon was originally published on February 16, 2010.

**NO EXIT**                    © **Andy Singer**

## DIGITAL COMMUNICATION

## Thinking About How We Communicate

Take a moment to look at the cartoon. Notice that it is titled "Digital Communication," which implies that the artist is making a statement about how we communicate with one another in a digital world full of blogs, Tweets, updates, and online commentary. Despite the fact that Andy Singer is referring to the process of communicating digitally, he chooses to reduce modern communication to four simple hand gestures—a peace sign, the middle finger, a thumbs-up, and a pointing finger. Each of these gestures can be read as a sign that carries meaning, as discussed in Chapter 1.

Now take into account the play on words that Singer is creating in the cartoon's title. At the root of the word "digital" is the word "digit," which also refers to digits on a hand (in other words, fingers). This wordplay shows that the artist is also discussing one of the most basic forms of communication: using fingers and hand gestures to stand in for more complex ideas. What might Singer be trying to convey by commenting on modern communication in these two different ways—as a primitive form of communication (with finger and hand gestures instead of language) and as a technological form of communication—both of which can be understood to fall under the definition of "digital"? Considering this fact, what meanings are attached to the gestures illustrated in the cartoon? Can you think of examples where each of these gestures is applied online in the form of words?

While it might offend some people even to see the middle finger displayed, there are surely equally flagrant displays of anger posted online with great regularity. The comment boards beneath virtually any online news story would be the easiest place to see this action on display. Where else might we use this gesture online, and in what context?

Now take a moment to consider the other ways in which we communicate online. Where are people being preachy or attempting to lay blame on an individual or group for a problem in our society (finger-pointing)? Where are we approving of things (thumbs-up) and where are people getting along and trying to build a community (the peace sign) rather than attacking one another (the middle finger)? Keep these thoughts in mind as you read the remaining selections in the chapter, and try to decide how accurate Singer is in his portrayal of modern communication. Have we really been reduced to little more than hand gestures when we live in a world of multimedia texts online that, at least in theory, allow us to communicate in more complex ways than ever before? If so, how? If not, how does Singer get it wrong?

# How Twitter Will Change the Way We Live

### Steven Johnson

**Let's Start Here•••▶** One common complaint of our modern, hyper connected world is that we are all disconnecting in real life. If you've ever heard or uttered that complaint, Johnson's essay that follows might come as a bit of a surprise. It is true that in a time when we communicate in fits and starts, small snippets of dialogue via text, comment, update, and Tweet, our means of communication are getting ever shorter and more compact. But is that a bad thing? Johnson argues the case that modern communication, specifically Twitter, is actually enabling a national dialogue that is both wide-reaching and intimate. How those two concepts can work together might seem baffling at first, but Johnson makes a point-by-point argument to defend his theory. Where it appears that conversation might be stifled by the limitations of the Twitter medium, it turns out the reality is that it is far more complex and engaging. As you read the article, focus on his examples of how Twitter is better in many ways as a source of information than Google. Also, observe the ways in which Johnson predicts, as his essay's title suggests, the way Twitter is changing how we communicate, and how it will change the way we interact with the Web itself.

Steven Johnson is the best-selling author of seven books on the intersection of science, technology, and personal experience. His writings have influenced everything from the way political campaigns use the Internet, to cutting-edge ideas in urban planning, to the battle against

21st-century terrorism. Steven was chosen by *Prospect* magazine as one of the "Top Ten Brains of the Digital Future." Johnson is a contributing editor to *Wired* magazine and was the 2009 Hearst New Media Professional-in-Residence at the Journalism School, Columbia University. He lectures widely on technological, scientific, and cultural issues. Johnson has also written for the *New York Times*, the *Wall Street Journal*, *The Nation*, and many other periodicals. This essay (which won the Newhouse School fourth annual Mirror Award) was the *Time* magazine cover article in June of 2009.

The one thing you can say for certain about Twitter is that it makes a terrible first impression. You hear about this new service that lets you send 140-character updates to your "followers," and you think, Why does the world need this, exactly? It's not as if we were all sitting around four years ago scratching our heads and saying, "If only there were a technology that would allow me to send a message to my 50 friends, alerting them in real time about my choice of breakfast cereal."

I, too, was skeptical at first. I had met Evan Williams, Twitter's co-creator, a couple of times in the dotcom '90s when he was launching Blogger.com. Back then, what people worried about was the threat that blogging posed to our attention span, with telegraphic, two-paragraph blog posts replacing long-format articles and books. With Twitter, Williams was launching a communications platform that limited you to a couple of sentences at most. What was next? Software that let you send a single punctuation mark to describe your mood?

And yet as millions of devotees have discovered, Twitter turns out to have unsuspected depth. In part this is because hearing about what your friends had for breakfast is actually more interesting than it sounds. The technology writer Clive Thompson calls this "ambient awareness": by following these quick, abbreviated status reports from members of your extended social network, you get a strangely satisfying glimpse of their daily routines. We don't think it at all moronic to start a phone call with a friend by asking how her day is going. Twitter gives you the same information without your even having to ask.

> **ambient:**
> Existing or present everywhere.

The social warmth of all those stray details shouldn't be taken lightly. But I think there is something even more profound in what has happened to Twitter over the past two years, something that says more about the culture that has embraced and expanded Twitter at such extraordinary speed. Yes, the breakfast-status updates turned out to be more interesting than we thought. But the key development with Twitter is how we've jury-rigged the system to do things that its creators never dreamed of.

In short, the most fascinating thing about Twitter is not what it's doing to us. It's what we're doing to it.

## The Open Conversation

Earlier this year I attended a daylong conference in Manhattan devoted to education reform. Called Hacking Education, it was a small, private affair: 40-odd educators, entrepreneurs, scholars, philanthropists and venture capitalists, all engaged in a sprawling six-hour conversation about the future of schools. Twenty years ago, the ideas exchanged in that conversation would have been confined to the minds of the participants. Ten years ago, a transcript might have been published weeks or months later on the Web. Five years ago, a handful of participants might have blogged about their experiences after the fact.

**philanthropists:** People who do charitable work to promote human welfare.

But this event was happening in 2009, so trailing behind the real-time, real-world conversation was an equally real-time conversation on Twitter. At the outset of the conference, our hosts announced that anyone who wanted to post live commentary about the event via Twitter should include the word #hackedu in his 140 characters. In the room, a large display screen showed a running feed of tweets. Then we all started talking, and as we did, a shadow conversation unfolded on the screen: summaries of someone's argument, the occasional joke, suggested links for further reading. At one point, a brief argument flared up between two participants in the room—a tense back-and-forth that transpired silently on the screen as the rest of us conversed in friendly tones.

At first, all these tweets came from inside the room and were created exclusively by conference participants tapping away on their laptops or BlackBerrys. But within half an hour or so, word began to seep out into the Twittersphere that an interesting conversation about the future of schools was happening at #hackedu. A few tweets appeared on the screen from strangers announcing that they were following the #hackedu thread. Then others joined the conversation, adding their observations or proposing topics for further exploration. A few experts grumbled publicly about how they hadn't been invited to the conference. Back in the room, we pulled interesting ideas and questions from the screen and integrated them into our face-to-face conversation.

When the conference wrapped up at the end of the day, there was a public record of hundreds of tweets documenting the conversation. And the conversation continued—if you search Twitter for #hackedu, you'll find dozens of new comments posted over the past few weeks, even though the conference happened in early March.

Injecting Twitter into that conversation fundamentally changed the rules of engagement. It added a second layer of discussion and brought a wider audience into what would have been a private exchange. And it gave the event an afterlife on the Web. Yes, it was built entirely out of 140-character messages, but the sum total of those tweets added up to something truly substantive, like a suspension bridge made of pebbles.

## The Super-Fresh Web

The basic mechanics of Twitter are remarkably simple. Users publish tweets—those 140-character messages—from a computer or mobile device. (The character limit allows tweets to be created and circulated via the SMS platform used by most mobile phones.) As a social network, Twitter revolves around the principle of followers. When you choose to follow another Twitter user, that user's tweets appear in reverse chronological order on your main Twitter page. If you follow 20 people, you'll see a mix of tweets scrolling down the page: breakfast-cereal updates, interesting new links, music recommendations, even musings on the future of education. Some celebrity Twitterers—most famously Ashton Kutcher—have crossed the million-follower mark, effectively giving them a broadcast-size audience. The average Twitter profile seems to be somewhere in the dozens: a collage of friends, colleagues and a handful of celebrities. The mix creates a media experience quite unlike anything that has come before it, strangely intimate and at the same time celebrity-obsessed. You glance at your Twitter feed over that first cup of coffee, and in a few seconds you find out that your nephew got into med school and Shaquille O'Neal just finished a cardio workout in Phoenix.

In the past month, Twitter has added a search box that gives you a real-time view onto the chatter of just about any topic imaginable. You can see conversations people are having about a presidential debate or the *American Idol* finale or Tiger Woods—or a conference in New York City on education reform. For as long as we've had the Internet in our homes, critics have bemoaned the demise of shared national experiences, like moon landings and "Who Shot J.R." cliff hangers—the folkloric American living room, all of us signing off in unison with Walter Cronkite, shattered into a million isolation booths. But watch a live mass-media event with Twitter open on your laptop and you'll see that the futurists had it wrong. We still have national events, but now when we have them, we're actually having a genuine, public conversation with a group that extends far beyond our nuclear family and our next-door neighbors. Some of that conversation is juvenile, of course, just as it was in our living room when we heckled Richard Nixon's Checkers speech. But some of it is moving, witty, observant, subversive.

**subversive:** Working behind the scenes to undermine or overthrow an idea, government, political ideology, or person.

Skeptics might wonder just how much subversion and wit is conveyable via 140-character updates. But in recent months Twitter users have begun to find a route around that limitation by employing Twitter as a pointing device instead of a communications channel: sharing links to longer articles, discussions, posts, videos—anything that lives behind a URL. Websites that once saw their traffic dominated by Google search queries are seeing a growing number of new visitors coming from "passed links" at social networks like Twitter and

Facebook. This is what the naysayers fail to understand: it's just as easy to use Twitter to spread the word about a brilliant 10,000-word *New Yorker* article as it is to spread the word about your Lucky Charms habit.

Put those three elements together—social networks, live searching and link-sharing—and you have a cocktail that poses what may amount to the most interesting alternative to Google's near monopoly in searching. At its heart, Google's system is built around the slow, anonymous accumulation of authority: pages rise to the top of Google's search results according to, in part, how many links point to them, which tends to favor older pages that have had time to build an audience. That's a fantastic solution for finding high-quality needles in the immense, spam-plagued haystack that is the contemporary Web. But it's not a particularly useful solution for finding out what people are saying *right now*, the in-the-moment conversation that industry pioneer John Battelle calls the "super fresh" Web. Even in its toddlerhood, Twitter is a more efficient supplier of the super-fresh Web than Google. If you're looking for interesting articles or sites devoted to Kobe Bryant, you search Google. If you're looking for interesting comments from your extended social network about the three-pointer Kobe just made 30 seconds ago, you go to Twitter.

## From Toasters to Microwaves

Because Twitter's co-founders—Evan Williams, Biz Stone and Jack Dorsey—are such a central-casting vision of start-up savvy (they're quotable and charming and have the extra glamour of using a loft in San Francisco's SoMa district as a headquarters instead of a bland office park in Silicon Valley) much of the media interest in Twitter has focused on the company. Will Ev and Biz sell to Google early or play long ball? (They have already turned down a reported $500 million from Facebook.) It's an interesting question but not exactly a new plotline. Focusing on it makes you lose sight of the much more significant point about the Twitter platform: the fact that many of its core features and applications have been developed by people who are not on the Twitter payroll.

This is not just a matter of people finding a new use for a tool designed to do something else. In Twitter's case, the users have been redesigning the tool itself. The convention of grouping a topic or event by the "hashtag"—#hackedu or #inauguration—was spontaneously invented by the Twitter user base (as was the convention of replying to another user with the @ symbol). The ability to search a live stream of tweets was developed by another start-up altogether, Summize, which Twitter purchased last year. Thanks to these innovations, following a live feed of tweets about an event—political debates or *Lost* episodes—has become a central part of the Twitter experience. But just 12 months ago, that mode of interaction would have been technically impossible using Twitter. It's like inventing a toaster oven and then looking around a year later and seeing that your customers have of their own accord figured out a way to turn it into a microwave.

One of the most telling facts about the Twitter platform is that the vast majority of its users interact with the service via software created by third parties. There are dozens of iPhone and BlackBerry applications—all created by enterprising amateur coders or small start-ups—that let you manage Twitter feeds. There are services that help you upload photos and link to them from your tweets, and programs that map other Twitizens who are near you geographically. Ironically, the tools you're offered if you visit Twitter.com have changed very little in the past two years. But there's an entire Home Depot of Twitter tools available everywhere else.

As the tools have multiplied, we're discovering extraordinary new things to do with them. Last month an anticommunist uprising in Moldova was organized via Twitter. Twitter has become so widely used among political activists in China that the government recently blocked access to it, in an attempt to censor discussion of the 20th anniversary of the Tiananmen Square massacre. A service called SickCity scans the Twitter feeds from multiple urban areas, tracking references to flu and fever. Celebrity Twitterers like Kutcher have directed their vast followings toward charitable causes (in Kutcher's case, the Malaria No More organization).

Social networks are notoriously vulnerable to the fickle tastes of teens and 20-somethings (remember Friendster?), so it's entirely possible that three or four years from now, we'll have moved on to some Twitter successor. But the key elements of the Twitter platform—the follower structure, link-sharing, real-time searching—will persevere regardless of Twitter's fortunes, just as Web conventions like links, posts and feeds have endured over the past decade. In fact, every major channel of information will be Twitterfied in one way or another in the coming years:

### News and Opinion

Increasingly, the stories that come across our radar—news about a plane crash, a feisty Op-Ed, a gossip item—will arrive via the passed links of the people we follow. Instead of being built by some kind of artificially intelligent software algorithm, a customized newspaper will be compiled from all the articles being read that morning by your social network. This will lead to more news diversity and polarization at the same time: your networked front page will be more eclectic than any traditional-newspaper front page, but political partisans looking to enhance their own private echo chamber will be able to tune out opposing viewpoints more easily.

### Searching

As the archive of links shared by Twitter users grows, the value of searching for information via your extended social network will start to rival Google's approach to the search. If you're looking for information on

Benjamin Franklin, an essay shared by one of your favorite historians might well be more valuable than the top result on Google; if you're looking for advice on sibling rivalry, an article recommended by a friend of a friend might well be the best place to start.

## Advertising

Today the language of advertising is dominated by the notion of impressions: how many times an advertiser can get its brand in front of a potential customer's eyeballs, whether on a billboard, a Web page or a NASCAR hood. But impressions are fleeting things, especially compared with the enduring relationships of followers. Successful businesses will have millions of Twitter followers (and will pay good money to attract them), and a whole new language of tweet-based customer interaction will evolve to keep those followers engaged: early access to new products or deals, live customer service, customer involvement in brainstorming for new products.

Not all these developments will be entirely positive. Most of us have learned firsthand how addictive the micro-events of our personal e-mail inbox can be. But with the ambient awareness of status updates from Twitter and Facebook, an entire new empire of distraction has opened up. It used to be that you compulsively checked your BlackBerry to see if anything new had happened in your personal life or career: e-mail from the boss, a reply from last night's date. Now you're compulsively checking your BlackBerry for news from other people's lives. And because, on Twitter at least, some of those people happen to be celebrities, the Twitter platform is likely to expand that strangely delusional relationship that we have to fame. When Oprah tweets a question about getting ticks off her dog, as she did recently, anyone can send an @ reply to her, and in that exchange, there is the semblance of a normal, everyday conversation between equals. But of course, Oprah has more than a million followers, and that isolated query probably elicited thousands of responses. Who knows what small fraction of her @ replies she has time to read? But from the fan's perspective, it feels refreshingly intimate: "As I was explaining to Oprah last night, when she asked about dog ticks . . . "

## End-User Innovation

The rapid-fire innovation we're seeing around Twitter is not new, of course. Facebook, whose audience is still several times as large as Twitter's, went from being a way to scope out the most attractive college freshmen to the Social Operating System of the Internet, supporting a vast ecosystem of new applications created by major media companies, individual hackers, game creators, political groups and charities. The Apple iPhone's long-term competitive advantage may well prove to be the more than 15,000 new applications that have been developed for the device, expanding its functionality in countless ingenious ways.

The history of the Web followed a similar pattern. A platform originally designed to help scholars share academic documents, it now lets you watch television shows, play poker with strangers around the world, publish your own newspaper, rediscover your high school girlfriend—and, yes, tell the world what you had for breakfast. Twitter serves as the best poster child for this new model of social creativity in part because these innovations have flowered at such breathtaking speed and in part because the platform is so simple. It's as if Twitter's creators dared us to do something interesting by giving us a platform with such draconian restrictions. And sure enough, we accepted the dare with relish. Just 140 characters? I wonder if I could use that to start a political uprising.

> **draconian:**
> Cruel, unfair, or severe.

The speed with which users have extended Twitter's platform points to a larger truth about modern innovation. When we talk about innovation and global competitiveness, we tend to fall back on the easy metric of patents and Ph.D.s. It turns out the U.S. share of both has been in steady decline since peaking in the early '70s. (In 1970, more than 50% of the world's graduate degrees in science and engineering were issued by U.S. universities.) Since the mid-'80s, a long progression of doomsayers have warned that our declining market share in the patents-and-Ph.D.s business augurs dark times for American innovation. The specific threats have changed. It was the Japanese who would destroy us in the '80s; now it's China and India.

> **augurs:**
> Foretells or predicts.

But what actually happened to American innovation during that period? We came up with America Online, Netscape, Amazon, Google, Blogger, Wikipedia, Craigslist, TiVo, Netflix, eBay, the iPod and iPhone, Xbox, Facebook and Twitter itself. Sure, we didn't build the Prius or the Wii, but if you measure global innovation in terms of actual lifestyle-changing hit products and not just grad students, the U.S. has been lapping the field for the past 20 years.

How could the forecasts have been so wrong? The answer is that we've been tracking only part of the innovation story. If I go to grad school and invent a better mousetrap, I've created value, which I can protect with a patent and capitalize on by selling my invention to consumers. But if someone else figures out a way to use my mousetrap to replace his much more expensive washing machine, he's created value as well. We tend to put the emphasis on the first kind of value creation because there are a small number of inventors who earn giant paydays from their mousetraps and thus become celebrities. But there are hundreds of millions of consumers and small businesses that find value in these innovations by figuring out new ways to put them to use.

There are several varieties of this kind of innovation, and they go by different technical names. MIT professor Eric von Hippel calls one "end-user innovation," in which consumers actively modify a product to adapt it to their needs. In its short life, Twitter has been a hothouse of end-user in-novation: the hashtag; searching; its 11,000 third-party applications; all those creative new uses of Twitter—some of them banal, some of them spam and some of them sublime. Think about the community invention of the @ reply. It took a service that was essentially a series of isolated micro-broadcasts, each individual tweet an island, and turned Twitter into a truly conversational medium. All of these adoptions create new kinds of value in the wider economy, and none of them actually originated at Twitter HQ. You don't need patents or Ph.D.s to build on this kind of platform.

This is what I ultimately find most inspiring about the Twitter phe-nomenon. We are living through the worst economic crisis in generations, with apocalyptic headlines threatening the end of capitalism as we know it, and yet in the middle of this chaos, the engineers at Twitter headquar-ters are scrambling to keep the servers up, application developers are releasing their latest builds, and ordinary users are figuring out all the ingenious ways to put these tools to use. There's a kind of resilience here that is worth savoring. The weather reports keep announcing that the sky is falling, but here we are—millions of us—sitting around trying to invent new ways to talk to one another.

**Let's Pause Here•••▶** Mr. Johnson makes an intriguing argument against the idea that Twitter, and online communication in general, is fracturing our society. Instead, he constructs an essay wherein he defines the aspects of Twitter that he feels are both exciting and innovative. As you think about the many points he makes in his essay, try to detail the ways in which the uses for Twitter that he observes and predicts are, in fact, changing the ways you communicate. What are the ways that users have innovated what seemed like a ridiculously compact system of com-munication? How have we managed to pack more into a brief message, rather than saying less and less (as the cartoon "Digital Communication" argues)? How do you interact with this me-dium? Whom do you follow? What conversations have you recently taken part in?

**Let's Take It Further•••▼**

1. Only two or three years ago, the idea of developing applications for someone else's products was almost non existent. Now, nearly every device and online service has tens of thousands (sometimes hundreds of thousands) of applications available, from an Oregon Trail app to a geneology app. Which sorts of apps do you use, and why? Can you think of any that have yet to be invented that would be of use to people?

2. Why does Johnson believe that our communications are actually getting more sophisticated and complex in nature, rather than what the "naysayers" predicted, which was a dumbing down of online conversations and dialogue? Do you believe that he is right or wrong?

3. Johnson strongly implies the possibility that Twitter might one day overtake the Internet gi-ant Google. In what ways would that be possible, based on the examples that he gives?

4. If the idea of a "super-fresh" Web is to be of any use, describe specific examples in which it would be far more helpful to have access to a conversation occurring now, versus the archival approach Google takes to cataloguing and searching the vast content of the Internet. Explain how the two processes (Twitter versus Google) vary and how one might be more useful than another, depending on the need of the user.

5. Research and describe other sorts of innovations that have occurred within the framework of Twitter since the article's publication. Explain how useful they have been, and to whom the innovation is most useful. Also, explain the process of how the innovations work.

6. Much has been made in the news of political protests being organized via Twitter. There have also been major news stories that broke on Twitter—with descriptions, photos, and real-time observations uploaded to the Web—that left news networks racing to get to a story they might not have even known was occurring. Find one such event and track the way the story broke, or how a particular event was organized. Then describe the type of information that was uploaded and how the event unfolded on Twitter. (Remember that all of these "conversations" are archived on Twitter and can often be found by using a hashtag, which is the # symbol.) You might also describe the media response to the event, once it came to their knowledge, as well as how mass media outlets have themselves incorporated Twitter's instantaneous nature into their own established formats.

7. Johnson describes a world where everyone will use Twitter to get news and updates on celebrities, as well as mundane events such as brief life updates from friends or relatives. Do you currently use Twitter for these purposes? If so, describe your daily interactions with Twitter and discuss a conversation you have taken part in recently that might never had occurred were it not for this medium of communication. Furthermore, explain and describe the way in which Twitter has improved an aspect of your life, if it has at all.

8. Construct a visual image or map of a Twitter conversation and explain the evolution of the conversation and its value. In other words, locate and define the manner in which the conversation began, how it grew and reached others, and what the end result was. For example, there is a project based out of New York City that provides pre paid cell phones to homeless people so they can document their daily lives. Using the cell phone, one homeless man created a Twitter account and subsequently located his daughter, whom he hadn't seen in years. Find a similar example of a conversation that had a clear beginning and a verifiable outcome.

# A Call to End Contraband Cell Phone Use
**Alexander Fox**

**Let's Start Here••• ▶** When most people discuss technology, it is with a sense of awe: at how rapidly it's changing, at the ways it has made life more convenient, even how electronics get smaller, faster, and better, while simultaneously getting cheaper. However, most of us rarely consider the ways technology can be used to cause harm or to break the law. For example, the benefits of cell phones and how they have enabled people to become more mobile, as well as more closely connected by virtue of carrying our phones with us, appear to far outweigh the negative consequences of having phones that can take photos, record video, text, connect to the Web, and even use hundreds of thousands of apps. The ways in which the technology of cell phones has changed our lives for the better make a discussion of the negative elements of cellular technology seem irrelevant, or perhaps even foolish.

However, Alexander Fox, a man who works in the corrections (prison) industry, sees cellular technology in a different light. In his article, he outlines the various ways cell phones are being criminally used, specifically in prisons, and the many potential negative outcomes. As you read his essay, determine whether you agree with the threats cell phones pose both in prison and to those outside of prison. Also, make note of the way Mr. Fox describes how prisoners interact socially and what kinds of social networks exist in the prison system.

---

Alexander Fox is the Director of Security Technologies for the Massachusetts Department of Correction and Chairman and Co-founder of the Northeast Technology and Product Assessment Committee (NTPAC). He occasionally contributes articles to the national magazine *Corrections Today*, which is where this essay first appeared in October of 2006.

As we continue to move forward into the new age of technology, a new dynamic in prison security and public safety has emerged. Drug trafficking, criminal organizations, money laundering, victim and witness intimidation, terrorism and facility escapes are just a few of the criminal activities that have long been conducted within the confines of correctional institutions. What has changed, however, is the method by which inmates are committing these crimes. For example, not too long ago, the use of cell phones was an unforeseen and unexpected element of these illicit activities. The implications for managing these critical situations are far reaching, potentially dangerous and would challenge any correctional administrator.

A unique characteristic of these present day crimes is that they are being facilitated by inmates using cell phones that are smuggled into correctional facilities. Although cell phones are generally considered contraband in prisons and strictly prohibited, they are finding their way into our correctional facilities at an alarming rate. To compound the concern is the fact that many of them are equipped with text messaging, GPS, cameras and Internet capabilities, which greatly increase the inmate's ability to orchestrate and carry out serious offenses in a much more sophisticated and dangerous manner. For example, in the past, a sex offender may have had the capability to write a threatening or offensive letter to his victim. Today, the use of a camera equipped cell phone would allow the offender to take offensive pictures and send them electronically to the victim, creating a much more traumatic and fearful situation for that person.

**contraband:** Prohibited or illegal goods or products.

Similarly, an inmate could now secretly plan and execute an escape with an accomplice by photographing escape routes and text messaging each other. In a worst case scenario, they could communicate in real time as to their whereabouts, potential detection issues and even give instructions that could have serious and potentially fatal consequences for individuals in the area. With the aid of this technology, the inmate's ability to succeed in the attempt is greatly increased.

The trend of contraband cell phones being introduced is not specific to just one state or region, it is a growing problem that faces the national community of corrections. The incidence of continued criminal activity via the use of cell phone technology by those we house within our prison systems is ever increasing. As correctional administrators we can probably all acknowledge at least one case of a cell phone being introduced into a facility within our own state. However, as they say, where there is one, usually there is more. Last year, in one state alone, there was a total of 135 cell phones confiscated. Although this number may or may not be an average representation across the board nationally, this problem is sure to escalate throughout the correctional community and adversely impact institutional security and public safety.

Given the sophisticated features of the technology, cell phones are becoming a hot commodity, some selling for as much as $1,000 to $2,000. Another reason cell phones are considered desirable is the fact that many states record inmate calls for security purposes. By bypassing institutional telephone monitoring systems, cell phones offer the inmate an alternative that allows them to conduct criminal activities without detection.

The problem is clear. The solution, however, is not so easy to attain. Many correctional experts are voicing concerns that agencies are not well prepared to deal with the problem, based on the limited available technology to detect and interfere with cell phones and cell phone usage within their facilities, as well as the current law prohibiting our ability to implement some solutions where they do exist. Presently, there are several technologies available that can interfere with the use of cell phones, thus preventing inmates from using them altogether. They include jamming, denial of service and passive interception. All of these, however, are prohibited by the Communications Act of 1934. The FCC is the regulatory agency for this law, but does not have the authority to grant waivers to law enforcement or correctional agencies, which would require congressional approval. This presents one of the most significant barriers to finding viable, sustainable solutions. The world has changed since 1934, but the law has not kept pace.

The good news is that although interference is prohibited, detection is not. There are several detection technologies that are currently in the prototype stage of development and are not yet widely available. Once they do become available, they may provide a valuable resource for corrections to combat this issue. Perhaps what is most promising is that the

National Institute of Justice has commissioned the Naval Surface Warfare Center to evaluate potential solutions and its report is currently pending.

The problem with cell phones in prisons is not going away. We can't afford to sit by idly while the problem escalates and wait for the consequences to catch someone's attention. As corrections professionals there are several things we can do to help improve the situation. We can work to find avenues to rally together to better articulate the gravity of the problem and the need to find solutions. We can try to change the current law, thus allowing us to implement existing solutions. We can also lobby for congressional support by way of securing grant funding to influence and stimulate the development and procurement of specific technologies that can be used under the current law.

Some states are already taking proactive measures to address the issue by establishing policies prohibiting the use of cell phones in institutions, introducing legislation that would criminalize the introduction of contraband cell phones, and enhancing searches of staff and visitors using magnetometers and pat searches. These commonsense approaches are ones we can all learn from and implement.

In addition to intervening in this situation, it is equally important that we recognize that cell phones are not likely to be the only technology that will present us with unique public safety challenges. We need to keep our eye on the ball and pointed toward the future by keeping up with the ever-changing technologies that will become available and potentially misused by the inmate population. By pursuing a broad range of strategies, we will be in a position to better manage technology-aided criminal activity in our institutions.

**Let's Pause Here•••▶**   What sort of reaction did you have to the potential negative situations described by Alexander Fox in his essay? Were there situations you had not imagined that he presented as possibilities? Why are illegal cell phones in prisons a threat to the public?

**Let's Take It Further•••▼**

1. Judging from Fox's list of potential crimes that might be committed, do you agree that cell phones should be outlawed in prisons? In what other ways might the presence of cell phones in prisons pose a threat?

2. Based on Fox's use of examples and word choices, who would you say his audience is? (Also note the place where the essay originally appeared.) How might his argument or his examples be different if he were trying to convince the general, voting public? What assumptions does he make about his audience that can be understood by his writing strategy?

3. Note that most of the scenarios Fox presents—victim harassment, planned escapes, orchestrating crimes to be committed on the "outside"—have always taken place as long as there have been prisons. Inmates can write letters, make phone calls, and in some states

even use email. How are cell phones a bigger threat than these other permitted methods of communication?

**4.** What other forms of technology might pose a threat if introduced within our prisons? What sorts of crimes might be committed using them?

**5.** Are there other forms of communication—based on Fox's argument—that should be banned in prisons? If so, what sort, and why?

**6.** Research the types of crimes most commonly committed by inmates in our penal system. Are the most common crimes the same as those seen as a major threat by Fox? If so, what are they? What is being done to combat the most common crimes committed in prisons?

**7.** Construct a scenario in which a prison inmate could commit a crime (using cell phones or another form of technology) that would affect someone who is not incarcerated. Detail and explain the process in which this could be achieved, as well as the means of preventing such a crime.

**8.** Watch a recent prison movie or TV show, such as *Stone, Oz,* or *Prison Break*, and observe the ways in which inmates interact with technology. Are the fears of anti technology advocates warranted, based on the depictions of prison life? What do these shows illustrate as the biggest technological threats in prisons, if any?

**9.** What rights, if any, do prisoners have to communicate with the outside world? If you believe the basic ability to communicate with family and loved ones exists, then what are some of the possible solutions to the root of Fox's argument, which is that inmate communication with the outside world poses a threat? Explain and describe alternatives, and also bring in outside sources to back up your opinion on the matter.

**10.** Research and describe other types of social networks that exist in American prisons. If the social media that we take for granted are not available to inmates in U.S. prisons, how do they network, and with whom? Do prison social networks mirror those on the outside in any way, or are they completely different? Compare the two—inmate and civilian—types of networks and explain how they are similar or different. Create a visual collage of images or video clips to illustrate the social networks within the prison system.

# Chatroulette Founder Andrey Ternovskiy Raises New Funding: "50,000 Naked Men"

**Austin Carr**

**Let's Start Here•••▶** In late 2009 and early 2010, a new form of social media blazed a quick path onto the world stage. This website, invented by a seventeen-year-old young man, took the world by storm. And then it seemed to disappear as quickly as it had surfaced. The name of the website was Chatroulette.

By taking an old idea (chat rooms) and combining it was a new twist (being randomly connected with strangers online), Andrey Ternovskiy stumbled on a brilliantly simplistic way to update the long-defunct method of online communication. What quickly followed were hundreds of high-profile news stories, celebrity sightings, public humiliations, faked suicides, and people shedding their clothes in large numbers. Oddly, though the Chatroulette experience was designed to be both random and instantaneous, an entirely new genre of YouTube video was born: the Chatroulette genre. In these videos, people recorded their Chatroulette experiences and posted them to YouTube. The impact and reach of this new service was surprisingly fast and long-reaching.

In the following essay, Austin Carr explores the rise and fall of the Chatroulette phenomenon. The essay also explores how the site's founder is evolving his business model to suit the needs of his fledgling business that experienced an overwhelming boom and bust in less time than it takes for most businesses to even get off the ground. As you read Carr's essay, note the methods he employs to define Chatroulette, as well as the ways he illustrates the service and its founder. Also, try to decipher whether or not Carr is pro- or anti-Chatroulette, or if he is objectively reporting on this company's successes and failures.

------

Austin Carr is an assistant editor for Fast Company, the Brooklyn-based online company (with a magazine of the same name) that features an editorial focus on innovation in technology, ethonomics (ethical economics), leadership, and design. This article first appeared on the Fastcompany. com website on January 12, 2011.

Following a week's worth of back and forth and blown off interviews, including one scheduled at 11 p.m. EST, Chatroulette founder Andrey Ternovskiy finally picks up his cell phone after several rings. It's early in Palo Alto, California, and Ternovskiy's voice is soft and raspy. He sounds like he's still half-dreaming.

Just a second—I can't talk very loudly because there are people sleeping in my room," he whispers in his Russian accent. "Alright, now I'm outside."

**evasive:**
The tendency to avoid contact with people.

The evasive, confined lifestyle isn't what you'd expect from Ternovskiy. Only months earlier, the 18-year-old had entertained drooling interest from the likes of Digital Sky Technologies and Fred Wilson, turning down million-dollar offers for his popular video-chatting service. The site was rocketing in popularity. Nearly every major media outlet wrote about Chatroulette. He met with the *New York Times*. *Good Morning America* explained his service to middle America. He got the feature treatment from *New York* magazine and *The New Yorker*, which gave him 4,500 words.

**fickle:**
Erratic or quick to change opinions.

But six months later, the fickle followers of Web fads have collectively hit the "next" button.

Since peaking in usership in the spring and early summer, Chatroulette has been hemorrhaging traffic, with visits plummeting close to 60% in the US, according to Quantcast. After a brief down period in late August, the site relaunched with improved safety features, and traffic appears to have bottomed out.

Ternovskiy now shares a one-bedroom apartment with two engineers that doubles as Chatroulette's headquarters. They all sleep and work there—that's why he's whispering and slipping outside to answer his phone.

The million-dollar offers have dried up, and critics have labeled the service a passing craze. Others have blamed the site's decline on its pornographic content—it's estimated one in every eight chats yielded R-rated material.

Ternovskiy still believes he can reclaim Chatroulette's prominence and VC interest. To do so, he's worked tirelessly to sanitize its image. "Since we've implemented the content-control system, the site has become cleaner, and more people are starting to use it," the founder tells *Fast Company*—traffic did begin to rise in October and November. "Now it's my job to shape the business into something more sustainable."

But Chatroulette can't fully wean itself off nudity yet. "You'll still see some naked men, about one every hour," Ternovskiy says. Of the roughly 500,000 visitors Chatroulette receives daily, about 10% are males itching to show their business. So Ternovskiy parlays that business into profit.

"Everyday, about 50,000 new men are trying to get naked," he says. "What we're doing is selling the naked men to a couple of websites—it's an investment for us."

When users flag someone enough times for indecent behavior (by clicking a button), the offender is automatically transferred to a partner site. Thanks to deals with adult dating services like FriendFinder.com, Chatroulette is earning cash hand over fist from the referral traffic.

"Basically, once we detect a person is naked, he'll be kicked from our service to another website," Ternovskiy says. "So, we're actually getting revenue from naked men right now."

These exhibitionists were a major headache for Ternovskiy before becoming a major source of income. Though helping to create buzz on the site initially (for better or worse), they were also a bandwidth drain, often nexting through as many as 800 users in just 15 minutes. According to Ternovskiy, Chatroulette is now earning $100,000 per month due to its refined business model and content-control system—all from "naked men." That's triple the site's monthly "mainstream" or "normal" revenue, as Ternovskiy refers to it.

It's also Ternovskiy's answer to whether he'd finally accepted outside investments. "50,000 naked men" has become "our investment," he says.

"I just didn't want to take investments—I feared that if I did the deals, my ideas would get pushed away. There are still offers, but they're valued proportionally less than offers back then, in terms of our traffic. So I think at this point, it's better for me to go on by myself."

Is he worried Chatroulette's novelty has worn off, leaving it to survive as an adult referral service? Does he regret not taking the offers he had on the table when they were significantly higher?

"It's really hard to say. I do believe the novelty has changed, even for me. It was like a movie: Everybody watched it, and then everybody else. Well, now that they've all watched it, they're less interested," Ternovskiy says. "After I declined the offers, I realized it was very difficult to execute something myself. I think I would accept the offers now, because I'm much more educated about it. But I'm not sure things would be better if I took the offers back then—I think traffic would've gone down anyway after the investment."

But the Moscow-born, high-school dropout isn't dwelling on the millions of dollars he might've lost. Living with his two coworkers in their one-bedroom, Ternovskiy is on a steady schedule: eat, sleep, and develop Chatroulette. ("Somebody needs to code, somebody needs to program, someone has to work," he says.) Last week, his team introduced a new feature called "skins," which provides alternating themes to the site's background. The blogosphere immediately lambasted the feature—as if the site needed more "skin," many joked—and criticized Ternovskiy for introducing such a basic upgrade.

> **lambasted:**
> Violently assaulted and mocked.

"It was just a minor change—it was five minutes of developer work," Ternovskiy retorts. "They made a joke of it—the idea was that Chatroulette sucks, you know, but I like it. I like the negative publicity because it gives me the freedom to work—I don't feel like I'm under a burden."

We hang up. Ternovskiy presumably settles in for a long day of coding with his roommates. Then an e-mail from him shows up shortly after our chat. He wants to make sure nothing he'd said would be misinterpreted.

"We are not desperate for investments," he wrote. "We are enjoying independence."

**Let's Pause Here•••▶** How familiar are you with the Chatroulette phenomenon? How did you first hear about it, if you were aware of its existence prior to reading Carr's essay? Whether or not you have used the service yourself, explain what the draw of such a social media service might be. What might account for the skyrocketing popularity of the site and its similarly swift decline?

**Let's Take It Further•••▼**

1. Based on Carr's descriptions of Chatroulette's founder, what sort of image is he trying to paint of the young man? How is Carr's representation of Ternovskiy consistent with the

popular culture image of entrepreneurial social media creators? Why do you think Carr provides the details that he does?

2. Based on the definitions, descriptions, and language used by Carr throughout his article, would you say he is supportive or critical of the Chatroulette site? Also, to whom might Carr be trying to appeal in terms of his audience? What descriptions, definitions, and examples does Carr give that prove the identity of his intended audience?

3. What reason might there be for "safety features" on a website like Chatroulette, based on Carr's definition of the site and the types of activities performed on it? Do you think it might have been the safety features or the "pornographic content" that contributed to the site's swift rise and equally speedy decline?

4. If you were in Ternovskiy's shoes, how would you feel about the site's breakneck ascent in popularity and its equally fast downturn? Would you have taken the earlier multi-million dollar offers made by companies interested in purchasing your website, or would you have passed the offers up, as the young founder did? How would you have responded when the offers suddenly dried up, and what would you do to rebuild your brand?

5. Is the image of the young, entrepreneurial social media founder that Carr paints consistent with the image that Ternovskiy tried to create of himself by turning down multi-million dollar offers? How might Ternovskiy have bought into the way social-media-creating icons are both portrayed and praised (or criticized) in popular culture? Did his actions help or hurt him, and how?

6. Is the current business model that Ternovskiy is attempting to integrate into his website—kicking naked people over to adult dating websites—a flawed model or a smart commercial move? Do you think that his making money off the remaining "50,000 naked men" on the website is a foolish one or one that will continue to generate income for Chatroulette? If so, explain and describe how he can grow this business model and adapt it as membership grows or shrinks. If not, propose and explain a better business model that will enable Chatroulette to become a more successful and profitable company.

7. Research and locate some of the early articles on Chatroulette that appeared in high-profile media outlets such as the *New York Times* and *The New Yorker*. What is the nature of the articles that emerged in the wake of Chatroulette's release, and how might the articles have helped or hurt the business that Ternovskiy was attempting to build? Describe whether the articles were critical or positive, and how the trajectory of the company's success and failure mirrored the way in which the media portrayed the social media in its infancy and as it grew in popularity.

8. Research and explore the various Chatroulette-related videos on YouTube and explain the trends that emerge among them. Based on what you observe, describe what might have contributed to the quick rise and/or decline of the website's popularity. What is the reputation of the social media service among the people who take part in it or comment on the YouTube videos?

9. The reputation of Chatroulette has shifted several times over the short lifespan of the website. Log on to Chatroulette and explain how the site currently operates. What sorts of safety features are there now? Describe how the website has been adapted to appeal to a different kind of audience than it initially appealed to (as described in Carr's essay). Observe and describe the types of people and experiences that can be viewed on the website currently, and then describe what trends, if any, emerge. Also, do you think this website will continue to become more popular, or has its relevancy passed? Back your opinion with outside sources as well as descriptions of your own video experiences.

# Facebook vs. FTC Round 2: Facebook Responds

Gregory Ferenstein

Those familiar with the history of Facebook—its inception in a Harvard dorm room, the many lawsuits leveled at its creator, and its current worldwide dominance as the social networking site of choice—will undoubtedly be aware of a long-standing argument between the service and its customers: the fight over privacy rights. In fact, more articles, essays, and news reports have been generated over Facebook and its privacy policies than any other Facebook-related issue.

While many Facebook users grumble each time some new update is made to the site that seems to further encroach on customer privacy, very few discontinue using the site. Privacy advocacy groups are formed within the site itself that quickly surge in number, then fizzle out after receiving few (or sometimes no) concessions from the company toward their demands. Because of this, in the steady push and pull between the ever-shifting Facebook privacy policy and users' ability to protect their personal information while still freely giving their most intimate life details, Facebook appears to have figured out a formula for setting the privacy bar precisely where the company wants it to be: push dramatically forward with some new change, then pull back slightly. This enables a steady forward motion for Facebook as it collects and classifies endless streams of information about its users.

Despite the fact that Facebook users have more or less given up on the fight about their rights to privacy, the Federal Trade Commission (FTC) has been attempting to rein in Facebook's ability to use, sell, and catalogue private user information for the company's financial benefit. It is a legal battle that has been going on for several years, and one with major financial ramifications for Facebook, Google, and other companies who collect, analyze, share, sell, or exploit their users' information and habits.

The following essay explores one of the latest progressions in the long battle between the FTC and Facebook over privacy issues. As you read Facebook's response to the FTC report (and the way the story is framed by Gregory Ferenstein), see whose opinion you agree with more—Facebook's or the FTC's.

---

Gregory Ferenstein is a writer and educator whose work focuses on technology, social media, and business. He has written for the *Christian Science Monitor*, CNN, the *Washington Post*, and Mashable.com, the online website devoted to social media. He is a contributing writer for *Fast Company*, where this essay originally appeared on February 23, 2011.

Facebook just released a 26-page retort to the Federal Trade Commission's preliminary report on privacy regulation—a report that social media firms see as an ominous approaching storm of chaotic bureaucracy. In summary, Facebook fears that government meddling could stifle both its ability to profit and smother the industry's progress on yet-unknown technological advancements.

**ominous:**
Foreboding or foreshadowing. A negative prediction.

**bureaucracy:**
A form of administration or oversight characterized by excessive rules, regulations, and red tape.

Facebook responded in mirror-image to the FTC; first, (respectively) reminding the FTC how much social media has done for the government itself, the advancement of democracy, and the growing cottage industry of social software:

## On Government

"In government, leaders use social media services to promote transparency, as evidenced by the nearly 140,000 followers of the White House Press Secretary's Twitter feed and the fact that more than 70 federal agencies have Facebook pages."

## On Democracy

"Advocates of democracy used Twitter to make their voices heard following the contested 2009 Iranian election, and Oscar Morales in Colombia famously employed Facebook to organize massive street demonstrations against the FARC terrorist group in 2008. Most recently, people in Tunisia and Egypt used social media to spread up-to-the-minute news, share videos of local events with the broader population, and mobilize online communities of thousands (and sometimes millions) behind a common cause."

## On Business

"Finally, the social web is a crucial engine for economic growth and job creation. Hundreds of thousands of application developers have built businesses on Facebook Platform. To take just one example, games developer Zynga, creator of the popular Farmville game, has more than 1,300 employees and has been valued at about $5.8 billion."

Second, it pleaded for the FTC to be optimistic about how ostensibly intrusive technologies end up benefiting the public:

**ostensibly:**
Outwardly appearing to be something it might not be.

## Caller ID

"Telephone companies originally collected and exchanged subscribers' telephone numbers solely for the purpose of completing telephone calls. But telephone companies later realized that they could use this information to display the calling party's telephone number and name to the call recipient, allowing the recipient to identify the caller in advance. Today, caller ID is an accepted and valued part of telephone communication, and few subscribers choose to block outgoing caller ID even though it is easy to do so."

## Facebook Newsfeed

"In 2006 Facebook launched a new feature called News Feed on every person's homepage. The product updated a personalized list of news stories throughout the day so users would know what their friends were posting. Before News Feed, people had to visit their friends' profiles to see what their friends were up to. Despite initial user skepticism when the product was first launched, News Feed is now—as any user would attest—an integral part of the Facebook experience."

## Google Flu Trends

"When the founders of Google began collaborating on a search engine research project in 1996, they probably did not envision that search queries about topics would one day become an early detection system for flu outbreaks. Today, Google Flu Trends can estimate flu activity one to two weeks more quickly than traditional surveillance systems involving virologic and clinical data, and may help public health officials and health professionals better respond to seasonal epidemics."

Finally, Facebook urged the FTC to be sensitive to the business implications of its decisions: "For Facebook—like most other online service providers—getting this balance right is a matter of survival," the report notes.

It continued, "Ultimately, the FTC's enforcement activities in the area of privacy must be guided by the realization that aggressive enforcement and imprecise standards can lead to more legalistic disclosures—and, as described above, chill economic growth—as companies seek to manage regulatory risk by over-disclosing, reserving broad rights, and under-innovating. To avoid these unintended consequences, the FTC should err on the side of clarifying its policies rather than taking aggressive enforcement action against practices that previously were not clearly prohibited."

**detriment:**
A source of damage or injury.

Both the FTC and Facebook have been light on data on experimental evidence—and both are obscuring a yet unrevealed future value (or detriment) associated with all of this sharing. Then again, forecasting problems into a very turbulent future is nearly impossible. Ultimately, both documents read like the fight will come down to a philosophical debate. And billions of dollars.

**Let's Pause Here•••▶** Prior to reading this essay, how familiar were you with the looming battle between the FTC and Internet companies who collect and utilize customers' private data? Do you see the potential courtroom battle as a positive or negative development, and why? Are there elements of Facebook's (or another social media site's) privacy policy with which you disagree or are uncomfortable agreeing to? What might those elements be, and what about the agreement between you and the social media site in question makes you feel uneasy?

1. Based on the tone and language used throughout his essay, as well as on how Ferenstein excerpts Facebook's response to the FTC report, who do you think the author sides with in the issue of privacy regulation? What specifically about the essay, including its construction and format, led you to understand which side Ferenstein is taking? What is the overall tone of the essay?

2. Based on the excerpts and presentation of Facebook's arguments by Mr. Ferenstein, do you find the overall argument that Facebook is using against the FTC to be effective? Which of the many Facebook examples that are excerpted in Ferenstein's essay do you find to be the most logical or effective, and why?

3. Explain how the "caller ID" comparison that Facebook makes in their response to the FTC is relevant to the overall argument of privacy. Do you agree with the comparison, or do you see the two issues as not compatible? Why or why not?

4. Do you agree with Facebook's assertion that "despite initial user skepticism" over the News Feed feature, it is now "an integral part of the Facebook experience" that users appreciate? How is the feature integral to the overall experience? How has it helped streamline the approach to using Facebook for users? How has it disrupted privacy? Do the positive elements of this feature outweigh the negatives? Why or why not?

5. Do you agree or disagree with Facebook's argument about the positive outcomes of "surveillance" of user information? Revisit the examples the company gives in the "Google Flu Trends" section of Ferenstein's essay, and decide whether the surveillance they are describing is good or bad for society.

6. Research and read the FTC preliminary results on Facebook and privacy (Google search: "Commercial Data Privacy and Innovation in the Internet Economy: A Dynamic Policy Framework. Docket No. 101214614-0614-01"), then research and read Facebook's response to the document (currently available at www.scribd.com/doc/47918734/Facebook-Comments-Commerce-Dept-Dynamic-Privacy-Framework). Which of the two sides do you agree with? Who do you think makes the better case for or against regulation of personal data? Cite examples from both documents to back your opinion, and explain who you think will win the legal battle, and why.

7. In its response to the FTC, Facebook makes its case by pointing out (among many other arguments) the ways that the government utilizes social media. Explain whether you believe this to be an effective argument on Facebook's part, and why. Research and illustrate the ways in which the government uses social media to reach out to citizens, and describe how government agencies have made an impact on U.S. citizens by engaging them using social media. Argue for or against Facebook's line of reasoning based on evidence of how the government does or does not use social media. Be sure to compare other government media (websites, e-mail, etc.) to governmental use of social media to illustrate which technique is most effective.

8. Locate and read the complete Facebook privacy policy or the policies of any other social media site or online service you regularly use in your daily life. Describe the nature of the privacy policy (e.g., is it designed to protect your privacy or to justify the company's use of your personal information?) and what, if anything, about the policy came as a surprise. How,

in other words, are users agreeing to allow companies to use their personal data? In light of the policy, would you reconsider using the social media site or online service whose policy you researched? If so, why? If not, list reasons and explain why you would be inclined to continue using a service because of (or despite) their privacy policy.

9. Facebook cites the people's uprisings in Iran and Colombia, which were organized via social networks such as Facebook and Twitter, as examples of the power of social media to influence and encourage democracy. What other major uprisings or democratic movements have occurred throughout the world thanks to Facebook, Twitter, or other social media outlets? Research, define, and describe one such movement whose success and origins were attributed to social media. Explain how social media was used, what the uprising was about, and whether the uprising was successful. Finally, explain whether social media continue to provide a platform or forum from which political movements can grow, and how they might continue to be used in this fashion.

10. Facebook repeatedly stresses the importance of its service for business growth, especially in terms of the business and production of Facebook apps. They cite only one example—app/games developer Zynga—as a multi billion dollar business that wouldn't exist without Facebook. Research other companies that created successful businesses thanks to Facebook and its Facebook Platform technology. Describe the service or product provided by the company, how many applications/games/services they have sold, and who the targeted consumers of the product are. Finally, explain whether the company could be as successful (or more successful) on any other platform or social media service.

# mash<sup>it</sup>UP

Here is a series of essay and discussion topics that draw connections between multiple selections within the chapter. They also suggest outside texts to include in your essay or discussion. Feel free to bring in further outside texts, remembering the variety of texts (beyond articles) available to you.

1. Several selections in this chapter seek to find deeper meaning in our relationships that we cultivate through computers (e.g., social networking). Describe the ways in which you think computers and social media might be making our lives better, or describe the ways in which they might be making our lives worse. Support your opinion with outside sources that provide evidence or documentation of positive or negative outcomes of social networking and social media.

2. Many detractors of social media (as mentioned in "How Twitter Will Change the Way We Live") fear the end of sophisticated communication, thanks to blogs, texts, and the hyper short information bursts of Twitter feeds. Despite this fear, several blogs and Twitter accounts have actually been turned into books themselves. Popular recent examples include the best-selling books *Sh\*t My Dad Says*, *Stuff White People Like*, and *I Hope They Serve Beer in Hell*. Locate and read any recent Twitter-to-book or blog-to-book best seller, then compare the printed version to the briefer online version. How did the core idea become expanded to encompass an entire book? How does this disprove (or prove) the fear that blogs and shorter media are ruining or improving book publishing?

3. The battle for the regulation of the Internet is currently in full swing. A portion of this has to do with "network neutrality" (i.e., preventing restrictions on content based on service provider or ability to pay), and some of it has to do with the issue of online privacy (Google, Facebook, Amazon, etc.). Choose which of these two issues is more important to you, research the current state of the legal battle, and discuss how you would like to see the issue resolved. Relate your preferred resolution to some manner in which you specifically use the Internet so that the legal issue you are discussing is relevant to your life.

4. Christine Rosen makes the case in her article, "Virtual Friendship and the New Narcissism," that people largely use social networking to build status and seek approval. If you disagree with her assessment of social networking, prove her wrong by describing how you interact with a social website, what it means to you, and how it affects your life in some constructive way. If you agree with Rosen's theory, describe your profile (or another specific person's public profile) to support her argument.

5. Using the Quantcast website (mentioned in the Chatroulette article by Austin Carr), track the current popular trends in Web browsing and see whether or not a recent major trend has emerged or shifted in the usage of the dominant sites mentioned in this chapter's selections. Describe which services are the most popular, define what those services are, and if a new service or social media platform has overtaken a formerly popular site, explain the reason for its rise.

6. Create a video or media collage that illustrates a "day in the life" of a person using social media. Conversely, you might film a "day in the life" of a person completely cut off from all forms of social media, as social media has been defined throughout this chapter. Whichever you choose, accompany your video with an essay that explains how woven into our everyday lives social media has become, as well as

whether you see this as inherently positive or negative, based on your observations over the course of creating your project.

**7.** View the film *The Social Network* and describe the way Mark Zuckerberg (the founder of Facebook) is portrayed in the film. Is he a hero or a villain? How have the filmmakers created a myth to accompany the rise of Facebook, and how accurate is the myth compared to reality? Research the story of Mark Zuckerberg, the early years of Facebook, the lawsuits, and the current status of the company, then compare these facts to the film's portrayal. In your opinion, does the film stay true to the Facebook story, or is it pro- or anti-Facebook propaganda designed to sway the audience's opinion one way or the other?

**Let's Connect •••▶** 🇫 "Like" our Facebook page for free, up-to-date, additional readings, discussions, and writing ideas on the topic of social media. Join other students and teachers across the country sharing in an online discussion of popular culture events. *American Mashup* is on Facebook at www.facebook.com/americanmashup.

# Mass Media

# Chapter 5

## Making the Cultural Connection

If there is anything we Americans love to criticize, it is our mass media. Because we live in a media-saturated culture, we are constantly in contact with one form of mass media or another. Many restaurants now have flat-screen TVs on their walls, as do coffee shops, libraries, bars, and even some public transportation systems. The mass media is so thoroughly engrained in our lives we sometimes interact with it and are unaware that we are doing so.

In terms of popular culture, there is probably nothing more powerful (in its ability to reach such large numbers of people and potentially influence them) than our mass media. The "mass media," as an entity, refers to our TV industry, our news industry, our music industry, our film industry, and other mass-media outlets such as magazines, famous blogs (TMZ or the *Huffington Post*, for example), radio stations, or news websites. Our media not only creates new trends, but also critiques them. The media is so important—and potentially so powerful—that even the White House has a press secretary who is basically a public relations guru for the office of the President of the United States. He is the middleman whose job is to represent the White House to the media.

Strangely enough, though most people understand that the vast majority of our media is in the business of entertaining, as a culture, we publicly decry them with great regularity when we feel as though they are not doing their job. One look at any popular news website's comments section will provide ample evidence of this trend. This begs the question, what is the mass media's job? What obligation do they have to their viewers, listeners, and consumers to accurately represent real life? What obligation do they have to be entirely objective in their presentation of news? This is the subject of wide debate, a subject that has generated hundreds of books, thousands of articles, and millions of blog posts in recent years alone.

Many Americans have a love–hate relationship with the mass media. We love it when they provide us with intriguing shows such as *Mad Men* or *Breaking Bad*, and we loathe them when we feel they exploit people or perpetuate stereotypes by producing shows such as *16 and Pregnant* or *Jersey Shore*. We love them when they report on stories with a political slant that matches our own political views, and we hate it when news reports seem to favor the other side. By now most everyone has heard someone say that we have nothing but liberal media, or, conversely, that all of our media is conservative or right wing. The reality is that the media plays all sides. If there is an audience for any popular viewpoint, there will be a media outlet to cater to that audience. Whatever the American people tune in to watch, whatever albums we buy or movies we attend, all of these things speak volumes about our culture. Quite simply, our media creates what we consume. What we are consuming from the media at any given time gives insight into the trends and concerns of popular culture as a whole.

For example, consider the genre of "reality television," which has reached an all-time peak in programming. There are shows in which real people compete against one another for fame and large sums of money. Some reality shows have become ingrained in our larger culture—as in the case of *Jon & Kate Plus 8*, in which we watched the triumphs and failures of a relationship as if it were our own. Morbidly obese people come on TV to suffer publicly at the hands of professional trainers in shows such as *The Biggest Loser*. Americans complain about the fact that it seems as though reality television has taken over the airwaves, but then we tune in to *The Apprentice, America's Got Talent, Worst Prom Ever*, and *Hoarders*. What does it tell us about our culture that we can't seem to get enough of other people's misery, or their unabashed quest for fame? Sure, people who watch *Survivor* might root for their favorite contestant, but the real entertainment is the backstabbing, the betrayals, and the hardships each person is subjected to throughout a season of the show.

Despite the common complaints about our mass media, it would seem that we *need* the mass media in our lives. We need our celebrity fix and our "true-life" stories. We need our political pundits screaming and crying about the end of the world. If we didn't need them, indeed, if we didn't want them, these shows and media personalities would not exist. And because of this, it can be argued that the mass media plays a very complicated role in our lives. Without it, we might not know as much about our larger popular culture as we do. The media is the filter through which we often view ourselves, and so the media is sometimes as important to us as looking into the mirror each morning before we leave the house.

What effect does this filter have on us? We see that there is no shortage of people who, like the person pictured here, are willing to humiliate themselves publicly for a few moments of fame. Why take such private matters and make them public? Perhaps it also shows us that we live in a

world in which the lines between media portrayals of "real life" and life itself are becoming blurred. Supermodel Naomi Campbell testifying before an international court during a war crimes trial? Comedian Stephen Colbert testifying before the United States Congress about immigration? Former Alaska governor Sarah Palin starring in a reality show on TLC about her life called *Sarah Palin's Alaska*? To some people, the very idea of these things crossing paths—an entertainer and the actual government— shows that we are getting to the point where the line between reality and staged productions is virtually nonexistent. This might not seem very important, but how are we ultimately going to determine what is real and what is not? When entertainers become politicians, and politicians become entertainers, how are we to determine what is an act and what is genuine?

This chapter raises these questions in many different ways. It discusses the moral obligations our media has toward us as a culture. We will consider the ethical responsibility of fictional TV shows to represent life accurately. We will try to determine whether TV (or other forms of mass media) actually has the power to change the way people think. After all, if there is no power in television or radio, if viewers and listeners are immune to the messages they are receiving, then why do politicians and major corporations spend tens of millions of dollars selling themselves to the American public? Finally, we will also consider how the media has affected what society views as normal and acceptable, as well as how the media chooses to represent our American culture on the whole.

The important thing to consider, however, is not only how the mass media affects us, but also how we interact with it in all of its various forms. It is no secret that we have the freedom of choice. We can turn off the television or the radio, and we can close a browser window or put down a magazine. So who is really to blame? Do we point a finger at the media that create our programs, films, articles, and blogs, or do we, as the consumers of mass media, have a larger role in the problem than we are willing to admit? This is the larger question to consider while reading the selections in this chapter.

# Simon Cowell                                    Taylor Jones

Taylor Jones is one of the world's most popular caricaturists. His work has appeared in magazines and newspapers all over the world. Originally posted to Politicalcartoons.com on January 20, 2008, this cartoon was published in response to the growing cultural backlash about Simon Cowell's perceived rudeness toward Americans who tried out for his hit show, *American Idol*.

# Thinking About Mass Media

Take a moment to look at the accompanying cartoon. Like most political cartoons, this drawing is attempting to make a statement about a topic that is popular in our culture. This cartoon's subject matter, which can be discerned at a glance, is mass media icon Simon Cowell, most famous for producing and hosting the wildly successful TV show, *American Idol*. Mr. Cowell, in many ways, is an apt representative of the media. He is more famous than many of the artists who are made stars overnight on his television shows (which include *The X Factor, Pop Idol, Britain's Got Talent, America's Got Talent*, and *American Idol*, among others). As is the case with most celebrities, Cowell is adored by some fans and loathed by others. Those who love him cite his ability for discovering talent and nurturing those artists in their careers. It is almost as if Cowell has a sixth sense when it comes to knowing what the public wants in a celebrity. But

"AMERICAN IDOL" JUDGE SIMON COWELL

those who hate him often say that he is too cruel in his public judgment of contestants, and that he brutally humiliates people who are only trying to achieve their dream of fame. Indeed, both sides have a valid argument.

But notice that the cartoon is more than just a picture of Simon Cowell and his famous sarcastic smirk. Hanging from his mouth is the body of a woman who holds a microphone. It's as though Mr. Cowell is munching on some surprised (shown by her body language) young woman who made the foolish mistake of getting too close to him. What then is the artist, Taylor Jones, attempting to say about Cowell? Is he judging or condemning Cowell? Or is he merely pointing out a fact: that Cowell chews up would-be stars without a second thought? Either way, what does it mean for our culture that this media icon is the face of modern reality television today? Why do people knowingly subject themselves to his criticisms? What are the risks of going on a show such as

*American Idol*, only to be harshly judged? Are the potential rewards worth the possibility of public humiliation?

Now, take a moment to consider our obsession with shows like *American Idol*. Perhaps you've heard the oft-quoted statistic that more people vote for *American Idol* contestants than in presidential elections. What does it say about our media- and fame-obsessed culture that tens of millions of people tune in to watch *American Idol* and to vote on their favorite contestants? What else should we be doing? Where else should our priorities lie?

# The Ethics of *Grey's Anatomy*    Mandy Redig

**Let's Start Here•••▶**  The issue of medical ethics is complicated, which is precisely why Mandy Redig explores the potential danger of a show such as *Grey's Anatomy* inaccurately depicting the realities of medicine. Rather than dissect *Grey's Anatomy*'s various (and mostly minor) medical inconsistencies (as many other writers have done), Redig focuses on larger ethical issues in her essay. She is also directly addressing the debate over the power of television to affect our perceptions of reality and the decisions that we make.

As you read the essay, observe the ways in which Redig validates her opinion and gives herself credibility. Also, make note of other ethical issues the show "gets wrong," if you are a fan of *Grey's Anatomy* or other medical dramas.

---

Mandy Redig is a medical student at Northwestern University working on her MD/PhD. She is a regular online blogger and occasionally blogs for the *Virginia Quarterly Review*, a national journal of literature and discussion that has been in circulation since 1925. The journal has a long history of publishing essays that discuss popular culture. This essay was published on May 27, 2009.

I know it's silly and not realistic and more than a little soap opera-ish, but I'll admit it: I'm kind of addicted to *Grey's Anatomy*.

The show started during my first year of medical school, and I could measure the progress of my medical education by how many flaws I could identify in each episode. For starters, no one looks that good in scrubs (turns out each actor has a custom-made pair); no one goes into the OR without wearing eye protection; and there's no such thing as a board-certified OB-GYN who also happens to do pediatric surgery. Not to mention what goes on in those call rooms. I've slept in them and trust me, sleep is the *only* thing that crosses anyone's mind in the middle of the night during a 36-hour call. But of course it's the escapism that makes the show worth watching—we like our glamorous physicians with their oh-so-not-real lives and loves. After all, if Meredith and Derek ever manage to work out their issues, will there even be a show?

**escapism:**
The habit of using entertainment or one's imagination to escape from reality or routines.

Doctors with perfect hair might make for great television, but when the setting is a hospital, even a fictional one, I think there are times when accuracy might count for more than entertainment. The medical subplots of even the most frivolous television shows revolve around issues that are very real for a great many people. Communication studies have shown that public attitudes about disease and decisions about screening tests like mammograms can be influenced by watching medical dramas. In the case of breast cancer awareness, this phenomenon of edutainment can work for the public good. When information about an issue of critical importance is not entirely accurate, problems arise.

I finally had the time to watch the *Grey's Anatomy* series finale online this weekend, and there's one bit I can't get out of my head. In the frantic moments at the end of the episode, one of the main characters goes into cardiac arrest following a risky neurosurgery for invasive cancer. Prior to the surgery and fully aware of her dismal prognosis, this character had signed a "do not resuscitate order," or DNR, the medicolegal document that makes known a patient's wish not to undergo resuscitation in the event of cardiopulmonary arrest. And yet in the drama of the moment, the chief of the hospital decides to overrule this patient's clearly stated wishes and instructs the medical

**prognosis:**
A medical prediction of a person's condition based on the professional opinion of a medical practitioner or doctor.

team to begin CPR. "Screw the DNR!" he proclaims, as the music crescendos and the final minutes of the episode slip away into a cliffhanger to be continued when the next season starts in the fall.

Signing a DNR order is a big deal. Many of the most difficult conversations in the wards of any hospital center around a patient's "code status." The decision to become DNR reflects a patient's wishes about death; there are few more personal and poignant decisions. As a member of the medical team, I also know that we spend a lot of time with patients and families talking about code status. When a DNR order is signed by a competent person, physicians absolutely do not have the right to revoke it.

Although most people have the impression from television and movies that a code almost always results in a good outcome, the reality is far different. Most people don't just wake up and become themselves again—there's unavoidable violence of cracking ribs and blood and tubes everywhere in that last-ditch effort to keep the heart pumping.

I realize that I am happily oblivious to the shortcuts portrayed in TV or films about any profession other than medicine, but I think the entertainment industry has an obligation to be accurate in matters of life and death.

Medicine happens to be what I know, and I know that real physicians don't "screw the DNR." Does that shortcut help make *Grey's Anatomy* a great TV drama? Definitely. But is it an accurate representation of an enormously complex ethical question? I don't think so.

**Let's Pause Here•••▶** How does Mandy Redig lend herself credibility as the author of this essay? Why does she believe that shows such as *Grey's Anatomy* owe it to their viewers to be more accurate about medical ethics? Are there other instances in television medical dramas where the show skirts an ethical issue?

**Let's Take It Further•••▼**

1. On the issue of the do not resuscitate order, are you in agreement with Redig on why it was so horrific that a character on *Grey's Anatomy* says, "Screw the DNR!"? Why is a DNR such an important document?

2. How important is it for shows like *Grey's Anatomy* to get it right when it comes to medical ethics? How much of it is the show's responsibility, especially if it is a fictional depiction of the world of medicine?

3. If communications studies show, as Redig states, that "public attitudes about diseases and decisions about screening tests like mammograms can be influenced by watching medical dramas," why might it be dangerous when medical dramas inaccurately depict a life-or-death medical situation?

4. Redig cites several examples of *Grey's Anatomy* being inaccurate in their depictions of medical situations. Can you locate and narrate how, in *Grey's* or similar shows, other instances of ethical dilemmas are "solved" in illegal or unethical ways (such as the impossibility of ignoring a DNR)? Construct an argument for how the ethical dilemma that is represented might be dangerous for the general public's perceptions of medicine. Explain how they could "get it right," while still allowing the show's plotlines to go undisrupted.

5. Redig argues that "the entertainment industry has an obligation to be accurate in matters of life and death." Do you agree with this statement? Argue for or against her opinion and locate an outside text or source that helps you support your claim.

6. Interview a medical professional or a professor who teaches in the medical field. Ask him or her how important it is that medical ethics are upheld and shown in a realistic manner on TV. Inform the person of the main idea behind Redig's essay, and see whether the person agrees or disagrees with her assessment of medical dramas and their moral obligations. Be sure to describe the experience of interviewing the person (including the questions you asked), as well as the responses that were given to your questions.

# The Gayest. Show. Ever.    Rob Sheffield

**Let's Start Here•••▶** These days, the idea of gay or lesbian characters on a television show may seem to be old hat. After the appearance of shows such as *The L Word*, *Queer as Folk*, *Will & Grace*, and *Queer Eye for the Straight Guy*, it would seem that hardly anyone would take notice of the "gayness" of a show. In fact, it is almost more strange *not* to see a gay or lesbian character on a sitcom or reality show than it is to see this demographic of America represented. Yet, despite all of this, Rob Sheffield declares *Glee* to be the "Gayest. Show. Ever." in the following *Rolling Stone* article.

As you read the article, try to determine whether Sheffield intends to mock the show or praise it. Look to his language and descriptions in order to decide what you believe his intentions to be.

---

Rob Sheffield is an author of two books and a music journalist who writes about music, television, film, and popular culture. Currently, he is a contributing editor at *Rolling Stone*, where he writes about popular culture. This article was first published in *Rolling Stone* on October 29, 2009.

Love it or hate it, you've got to give *Glee* credit: You have never seen this kind of show before. It's one thing for your *American Idols* and *So You Think You Can Dances* to bring professional showbiz camp to mainstream—sequined unitards, stripper heels, Siegfried and Roy production values. But it's another thing to dream up a Midwestern high school where these are the staples of everyday life. Everything about *Glee* is balls-to-the-wall camp: the ridiculous story lines, the bright pastels, the bitchy-pants dialogue. It sometimes makes me wonder if this is the gayest thing I've ever seen on TV—and I grew up watching *General Hospital*.

**camp:**
A style of creative expression often exaggerating sarcasm, absurdity, or something obviously artificial or out-of-date in order to be amusing.

The greatness of *Glee* is that it wastes no time trying to cater to any idea of how high schools actually are. *Bor-ing!* Instead, we get a big fat colorful fantasy of a school full of Ohio show-tune queens belting out their perky harmonies all over songs by Carrie Underwood, Journey and Kanye West, as well as old Broadway chestnuts from *Les Misérables*, *Cabaret* and *West Side Story*.

The best joke on *Glee* is the way it creates a gay teenage world in which no other world exists or is imaginable. It's not just the feel-good gay, it's punish-the-outside-world gay, openly hostile to the idea that some viewers out there might *not* be show-tune queens. If you have no idea who Kristin Chenoweth is, you can go watch something else, bitch.

Back in the 1980s, the flamboyant entertainer Peter Allen lamented, "Boy George makes Bette Midler and me look like this nice suburban couple." That's how *Project Runway* and *Gossip Girl* must feel about *Glee*.

In *Glee*'s alternate universe, the glee-club geeks actually win the respect of the jocks. In one episode, the football team wins a game because the gay placekicker drilled the team in the "Single Ladies" dance. After he nails the game-winning field goal, he comes out to his dad, telling him, "Being a part of the glee club and football has shown me I can be *anything!*"

Back in May, when *Glee* debuted after the *American Idol* finale, the cast's version of "Don't Stop Believin'" became a chart-topping hit. By now, every Thursday there's a new track from the *Glee* kids, whether it's their excellent version of Queen's "Somebody to Love" or their needles-in-the-eardrum rendition of Amy Winehouse's "Rehab." The cast has real musical-theater cred: Matthew Morrison, the teacher who gets the job of coaching the glee club, made his name on Broadway, and so did Lea Michele, the temperamental and thoroughly irritating Rachel.

The key is the way *Glee* takes the music so seriously, reveling in all the gory details of Top 40 excess. Every episode has at least two or three scenes of hyperchoreographed hysteria that are almost too tough to endure, especially when someone's singing. But I can't resist any TV this shameless, and the pain just makes it seem more hardcore and authentic to an actual high school glee club—kind of like the football violence in *Friday Night Lights*.

That's part of my fascination with *Glee*—it tests my pain threshold in a way I didn't think was possible for a network hit about a high school. Although the ads wishfully claim that this is some kind of guilty pleasure, it's really just the opposite—you have to have a cast-iron stomach to flog yourself through an entire hour of it.

For all the garishly lit sets, this is one bleak hour of TV. The story lines are relentlessly grim, as the kids deal with teen pregnancy and the teachers deal with failing marriages, money woes and alcoholism. None of the characters are all that likable or nice to each other. The dialogue aims for *Gossip Girl* levels of nasty artifice without ever really being all that funny.

**artifice:**
Fake or insincere behavior.

The most surprising part is that *Glee* goes out of its way to avoid being uplifting or conciliatory toward the casual viewer. There's no attempt to say, "Hey, America, give us a try and you might like us." The attitude is more like, "We are the monster you created, America, and now you shall taste our vengeance." For generations, high school students have mocked, scorned or (most likely) failed to notice the glee club. Now it's payback time. Every episode of *Glee* seethes with hostility under all the toe-tapping and finger-snapping: It's *Liza With a "Z"* meets *Carrie*.

**Let's Pause Here••• ▶** Sheffield asserts that *Glee* is unabashedly gay, on purpose. He even goes so far as to call it an "openly hostile" show that is "punish-the-outside-world" gay. What about his description of the show makes the show seem hostile? To whom is it hostile? And for what reason? Whether or not you see the show as hostile, how do you account for its wild success? What is *Glee*'s appeal?

**Let's Take It Further••• ▼**

1. Why is it so shocking that a show of this nature should be set in a Midwestern high school? Why does Sheffield think it's commonplace to see "sequined unitards, stripper heels, [and] Siegfried and Roy production values" on shows like *American Idol* and *Dancing with the Stars*, but to see it in an Ohio school comes as a shock?

2. Besides the fact that the show dares to have gay and lesbian high school students as its main characters, in what other ways does this show break the mold of standard television fare? Before this show, were there other shows with openly gay teenagers? If so, how were they represented differently than they are on *Glee*?

3. Consider the audience for whom Sheffield has written this essay (readers of *Rolling Stone* magazine). What word choices does Sheffield employ that prove he is aware of the demographic of *Rolling Stone* readers? What is the demographic that *Rolling Stone* caters to with their publication? How might have Sheffield shifted his tone, word choice, and observations about the show if this essay were originally published elsewhere (for example, in a national newspaper)?

4. Sheffield believes that the show is not asking to be liked. It is not apologizing for its existence. In fact, he even goes so far as to say that the show appears to scream, "We are the monster you created, America, and now you shall taste our vengeance." Do you agree that the show (based on its characters and story lines) does not try to play it safe when it comes to winning over fans? Is this show the natural by-product of our popular culture and our media obsessions? *Is* it a monster that we have created?

5. Find and interview a self-proclaimed "Gleek" (fan of *Glee*). During the course of the interview, inquire about the show's appeal. What is so entertaining about *Glee* to the person whom you are interviewing? Have the person explain whether *Glee* is merely entertainment, or if there is some other reason that the show has value to the viewer.

6. Construct a video collage or essay (using YouTube, a website, or a PowerPoint presentation) that proves or disproves Sheffield's point about the excessive nature (camp) of *Glee*. Using clips from the show itself, allow scenes from *Glee* to speak for themselves in supporting your point.

7. Locate and watch any of the other television shows that have gay or lesbian people as the show's main characters. Describe how *Glee* is different than the shows that came before it. Compare and contrast the way depictions of gay and lesbian characters differ between the two shows. Were the characters in the other show adults? Teenagers? In your opinion, would a show like *Glee* be able to exist without the shows that came before it? Why or why not?

**8.** Locate *Glee* fan videos/parodies online and give a detailed description of the types of video reactions to the show you encounter. What is the overall reaction to the show? Positive or negative? What reasons do online Gleeks give to explain their passion for the show? Do these videos help you to understand the draw of the show better or worse than Sheffield's article?

# "*CSI* Effect" Has Juries Wanting More Evidence
Richard Willing

**Let's Start Here••• ▶**  Forensic crime shows, such as *CSI*, have become a staple of American television. To many, this is a positive development, as it gives exposure to the complexities of a line of work that people used to ignore. Blood spatter expert? Before the days of *Dexter*, most people could not begin to explain such a field.

In the following essay, Richard Willing explores the impact that *CSI* and similar shows have had on our culture. He discusses the positive outcomes of these shows' popularity, as well as some of the dangers of public misconceptions of science. The one thing that becomes apparent is the power of television and the media to impact the minds of viewers, whether or not we realize it. To observe this process, read the following essay and see the real-life ways the show has impacted courtrooms across America. Note the demands juries now make in the courtroom when hearing cases. Also, take note of the manner in which prosecutors and defenders differ in their assessment of *CSI*'s impact on the legal system.

---

Richard Willing is a reporter for *USA Today* who writes about American culture and national news interest stories. This piece originally appeared on August 5, 2004, as a part of the *USA Today* "Nation" section.

Like viewers across the nation, folks in Galveston, Texas, watch a lot of TV shows about crime-scene investigators. Jury consultant Robert Hirschhorn couldn't be happier about that.

Hirschhorn was hired last year to help defense attorneys pick jurors for the trial of Robert Durst, a millionaire real estate heir who was accused of murdering and dismembering a neighbor, Morris Black. It was a case in which investigators never found Black's head. The defense claimed that wounds to the head might have supported Durst's story that he had killed Black in self-defense.

Hirschhorn wanted jurors who were familiar with shows such as *CSI: Crime Scene Investigation* to spot the importance of such a gap in the evidence.

That wasn't difficult: In a survey of the 500 people in the jury pool, the defense found that about 70% were viewers of CBS's *CSI* or similar shows such as Court TV's *Forensic Files* or NBC's *Law & Order*.

Durst was acquitted in November. To legal analysts, his case seemed an example of how shows such as *CSI* are affecting action in courthouses across the USA by, among other things, raising jurors' expectations of what prosecutors should produce at trial.

Prosecutors, defense lawyers and judges call it "the *CSI* effect," after the crime-scene shows that are among the hottest attractions on television. The shows—*CSI* and *CSI: Miami*, in particular—feature high-tech labs and glib and gorgeous techies. By shining a glamorous light on a gory profession, the programs also have helped to draw more students into forensic studies.

**glib:** Easygoing or informal acting.

But the programs also foster what analysts say is the mistaken notion that criminal science is fast and infallible and always gets its man. That's affecting the way lawyers prepare their cases, as well as the expectations that police and the public place on real crime labs. Real crime-scene investigators say that because of the programs, people often have unrealistic ideas of what criminal science can deliver.

**infallible:** Unable to make errors.

Like Hirschhorn, many lawyers, judges and legal consultants say they appreciate how *CSI*-type shows have increased interest in forensic evidence.

"Talking about science in the courtroom used to be like talking about geometry—a real jury turnoff," says Hirschhorn, of Lewisville, Texas. "Now that there's this almost obsession with the (TV) shows, you can talk to jurors about (scientific evidence) and just see from the looks on their faces that they find it fascinating."

But some defense lawyers say *CSI* and similar shows make jurors rely too heavily on scientific findings and unwilling to accept that those findings can be compromised by human or technical errors.

Prosecutors also have complaints: They say the shows can make it more difficult for them to win convictions in the large majority of cases in which scientific evidence is irrelevant or absent.

"The lesson that both sides can agree on is, what's on TV does seep into the minds of jurors," says Paul Walsh, chief prosecutor in New Bedford, Mass., and president of the National District Attorneys Association. "Jurors are going to have information, or what they think is information, in mind. That's the new state of affairs."

Lawyers and judges say the *CSI* effect has become a phenomenon in courthouses across the nation:

- In Phoenix last month, jurors in a murder trial noticed that a bloody coat introduced as evidence had not been tested for DNA. They alerted the judge. The tests hadn't been needed because the defendant had acknowledged being at the murder scene. The judge decided that TV had taught jurors about DNA tests, but not enough about when to use them.

- Three years ago in Richmond, Va., jurors in a murder trial asked the judge whether a cigarette butt found during the investigation could be tested for links to the defendant. Defense attorneys had ordered DNA tests but had not yet introduced them into evidence. The jury's hunch was correct—the tests exonerated the defendant, and the jury acquitted him.

- In Arizona, Illinois and California, prosecutors now use "negative evidence witnesses" to try to assure jurors that it is not unusual for real crime-scene investigators to fail to find DNA, fingerprints and other evidence at crime scenes.

- In Massachusetts, prosecutors have begun to ask judges for permission to question prospective jurors about their TV-watching habits. Several states already allow that.

- Last year in Wilmington, Del., federal researchers studying how juries evaluate scientific evidence staged dozens of simulated trials. At one point, a juror struggling with especially complicated DNA evidence lamented that such problems never come up "on *CSI*."

The *CSI* effect also is being felt beyond the courtroom.

At West Virginia University, forensic science is the most popular undergraduate major for the second year in a row, attracting 13% of incoming freshmen this fall. In June, supporters of an Ohio library drew an overflow crowd of 200-plus to a luncheon speech on DNA by titling it "CSI: Dayton."

The Los Angeles County Sheriff's Department crime lab has seen another version of the *CSI* effect. Four technicians have left the lab for lucrative jobs as technical advisers to crime-scene programs. "They found a way to make science pay," lab director Barry Fisher says.

## Shows' Popularity Soars

*CSI*, which begins its fifth season next month, was America's second-most-popular TV program during the season that began last fall, after the Tuesday edition of *American Idol*.

*CSI* and a spinoff, *CSI: Miami*, have drawn an average of more than 40 million viewers a week during the past TV season. *Law & Order*, whose plots sometimes focus on forensic evidence, has been the 13th-most-watched show during the 2003-04 season, averaging about 15 million viewers. On cable, the Discovery Channel, A&E and Court TV have programs that highlight DNA testing or the analysis of fingerprints, hair and blood-spatter patterns.

*CSI: NY*, set in New York City, is slated to premiere next month.

The *CSI* shows combine whiz-bang science with in-your-face interrogations to solve complex crimes. Some sample dialogue from actor David Caruso, the humorless monotone who plays investigator Horatio Caine on *CSI: Miami*: "He (the bad guy) doesn't know how evidence works, but you know what? He will."

The shows' popularity, TV historians say, is partly a result of their constant presence. Counting network and cable, at least one hour of crime-forensics programming airs in prime time six nights a week.

The stars of the shows often are the equipment—DNA sequencers, mass spectrometers, photometric fingerprint illuminators, scanning electron microscopes. But the technicians run a close second.

"It's 'geek chic,' the idea that kids who excel in science and math can grow up to be cool," says Robert Thompson, who teaches the history of TV programming at Syracuse University. "This is long overdue. . . . Cops and cowboys and doctors and lawyers have been done to death."

## Departing from Reality

Some of the science on *CSI* is state-of-the-art. Real lab technicians can, for example, lift DNA profiles from cigarette butts, candy wrappers and gobs of spit, just as their Hollywood counterparts do.

But some of what's on TV is far-fetched. Real technicians don't pour caulk into knife wounds to make a cast of the weapon. That wouldn't work in soft tissue. Machines that can identify cologne from scents on clothing are still in the experimental phase. A criminal charge based on "neuro-linguistic programming"—detecting lies by the way a person's eyes shift—likely would be dismissed by a judge.

But real scientists say *CSI*'s main fault is this: The science is always above reproach.

"You never see a case where the sample is degraded or the lab work is faulty or the test results don't solve the crime," says Dan Krane, president and DNA specialist at Forensic Bioinformatics in Fairborn, Ohio. "These things happen all the time in the real world."

Defense lawyers say the misconception that crime-scene evidence and testing are always accurate helps prosecutors. "Jurors expect the criminal justice system to work better than it does," says Betty Layne DesPortes, a criminal defense lawyer in Richmond, Va., who has a master's degree in forensic science.

She notes that during the past 15 years, human errors and corruption have skewed test results in crime labs in West Virginia, Pennsylvania, California, Texas and Washington state.

But prosecutors say the shows help defense lawyers. Jurors who are regular viewers, they say, expect testable evidence to be present at all crime scenes.

In fact, they say, evidence such as DNA and fingerprints — the staple of *CSI* plots — is available in only a small minority of cases and can yield inconclusive results.

"Defense attorneys will get up there and bang the rail and say 'Where were the DNA tests?' to take advantage of the idea that's in the juror's mind," says Joshua Marquis, a prosecutor in Astoria, Ore. "You've got to do a lot of jury preparation to defeat that."

Some prosecutors have gone to great lengths to lower jurors' expectations about such evidence.

In Belleville, Ill., last spring, prosecutor Gary Duncan called on seven nationally recognized experts to testify about scientific evidence against a man accused of raping and murdering a 10-year-old girl. The witnesses included specialists in human and animal DNA, shoe-print evidence, population statistics and human mitochondrial DNA, genetic material that is inherited only from one's mother and that seldom is used in criminal cases. Duncan won a conviction.

"I wanted to be certain the jury was clear on the evidence and its meaning," he says. "These days, juries demand that."

*CSI* producers acknowledge that they take some liberties with facts and the capabilities of science, but they say it's necessary to keep their story lines moving.

Elizabeth Devine, a former crime lab technician who writes and produces episodes of *CSI: Miami*, spoke at a training seminar for prosecutors last year in Columbia, S.C. She said that if the shows did not cut the time needed to perform DNA tests from weeks to minutes, a villain might not be caught before "episode five."

For all of *CSI*'s faults, some lab technicians say they have a soft spot for the TV version of their world. "It's great for getting people interested (in) careers" in forensic science, says Barbara Llewellyn, director of DNA analysis for the Illinois State Police.

Terry Melton, president of Mitotyping Technologies in State College, Pa., says the programs have made "jury duty something people now look forward to."

**cachet:**

Prestige or high-standing in people's opinion.

And Fisher says the shows have given "science types" like himself some unexpected cachet.

"When I tell someone what I do, I never have to explain it now," he says. "They know what a crime-scene (technician) does. At least, they think they do."

**Let's Pause Here•••▶** Perhaps you were well aware of crime shows and their popularity in our culture. As Willing says, crime shows run during prime time six nights a week, so these shows are hard to miss. If you are a fan of this genre of television, how has it affected your own expectations of law enforcement when it comes to solving crimes? How do you feel about the fact that a fictional show is having an impact in actual courtrooms across America? Should this be seen as a good or a bad development?

## Let's Take It Further••• ▼

1. Based on Willing's vocabulary and tone throughout his essay, would you say he believes these shows are doing more good or bad for our legal system? Does he favor one side over the other? If so, what in his writing leads you to believe Willing has a preference?

2. Willing implies that jurors' expectations might be putting a strain on our legal system, since the popularity of forensic crime shows has risen. What are some of the other "dangers" that an overly exposed (to crime TV) jury might pose to the legal system? For prosecutors? For defenders?

3. One of the most intriguing findings of Willing's essay is that TV has the power to change or influence the minds of its viewers. This is a topic that has been debated for years, with mixed results. Still, the evidence in the essay proves that—at least in terms of jurors and their exposure to crime TV—people's expectations and perceptions of the legal system have shifted because of shows such as *CSI*. If TV can indeed affect a person's expectations or worldview, how might this be a danger in light of other shows that are being aired? How might it be a positive development?

4. What was your reaction to the various courtroom examples given by Willing throughout his essay? Which of the examples do you see as a positive outcome of "the *CSI* effect"? Which of them do you see as negative outcomes of this phenomenon?

5. Watch an episode of *CSI* (or a similar crime show) and take notes on the process and methods used to establish the identity of the criminal. Using independent research, determine the "realism" of the show's scientific approach to forensic investigation and compare the show's science to the actual science. What did the show get "right"? What did they get "wrong"? How was the show's process different than the actual way forensics might have handled a similar case in real life?

6. Willing states that there has been a significant uptick in student interest in fields such as forensic studies. If your school has a forensic studies program, interview a forensic studies major to determine the reason behind his or her interest in the major. Determine whether the student is familiar with the crime show genre, as well as whether the decision to enter the program was the outcome or effect of viewing shows such as *CSI*. What are their expectations of the types of jobs they hope to get?

7. Research recent examples of how the "*CSI* effect" has positively affected the outcome of an actual court case. Describe the details of the case, as well as how it was affected specifically. How and why was this particular case attributed to *CSI*-influenced juries? Do you see this as a problematic or positive trend for future legal issues? Explain your opinion on the matter.

# Adult Situations

**Brett Fletcher Lauer**

**Let's Start Here•••▶** "Adult Situations" is a poem described by the author, Brett Fletcher Lauer, as "found text composed of movie descriptions from online TV guides." For anyone who has ever read the descriptions given by TV guides (whether online, in a newspaper, in the actual publication *TV Guide*, or on the TV Guide Channel), you will surely recognize the one-sentence format that Lauer utilizes in his poem.

By simply replicating word-for-word the sentences that appeared in the guides, Lauer allows the descriptions of the shows to speak for themselves. He also forces us to consider the meaning of these shows by purposely taking these one-line summaries out of context. We do not get the movie or sitcom title. We are not given the name of the channel on which the show airs. What is the result of this particular method that he employs in his poem? Does it make the shows seem better or worse than they most likely are?

---

Brett Fletcher Lauer is the Managing Director of the Poetry Society of America and a poetry editor at *A Public Space*. His poems have appeared in *Boston Review, Fence, Tin House*, and elsewhere. He lives in Brooklyn. This poem originally appeared in *Jubilat*, a literary journal. The poem is composed of lines extracted from descriptions of television shows in various TV guides.

A former soldier tries to rescue a kidnapped nuclear physicist from
    a terrorist who wants her to create warheads.
A corporate climber, whose boss and others use his apartment for
    hanky-panky, aids a young woman.
A litigious brother-in-law urges an injured TV cameraman
    to sue.

**litigious:**
A person who often engages in lawsuits.

A declared-dead man hides out with a widow after his
    wife and her lover botch his murder.
The Russian inventor of a new marine propeller falls in love with a
    woman in 1939 London.
The amateur sleuth has a killer, a gangster, and the police on his trail.
An assistant New York district attorney works and flirts with his
    adversary and her kooky artist client.
A checkout girl covering for a coworker faces danger from a drug
    dealer she double-crosses out of desperation.
Evil partners experiment on an infant and send his twin to a repu-
    table research nursery.
Four teenage outcasts use mental and physical powers to punish
    their high school tormentors.
An insurance salesman joins would-be heirs and the but-
    ler in a mansion with a millionaire's corpse.
Three inept private eyes try to catch a killer gorilla at a
    spooky mansion.

**inept:**
Incompetent or unfit.

A law-enforcement officer from Earth seeks vengeance for his
   brother's mysterious death on Mars.

A dishonest lawyer must prove he is not a killer.

Genetically engineered piranha head for a beach resort.

A man takes singing lessons from drag-queen neighbor.

People hide in a house from carnivorous walking corpses revived
   by radiation fallout.

An innocent couple face life in prison after false accusations of child
   molestation.

Explosives ace helps woman get revenge in Miami.

A giant mutated lizard wreaks havoc in New York.

An undercover policeman tries to thwart an old friend, now a Los
   Angeles gang leader.

David and Kathy spend half of their third date lying and the other
   half confessing.

A mystery writer and her friends are stalked by a faceless throat-
   ripper in a haunted house.

Rival reporters mix romance with work as they hunt an apartment-
   house killer.

A doctor injects himself with ape fluid and turns hairy; he needs
   human fluid to turn back.

While blackmailing a corrupt police officer, a man becomes involved with two women.

No-frills policewoman is ordered to protect a pampered actress who
   has witnessed a murder.

From a sanitarium morgue slab, a corpse tells how she died
   and who was involved in her death.

> **sanitarium:**
> A rest or rehab-
> ilitation facility.

Sent to a Wyoming summer camp, troublemaking surfer twins
   are mistaken for forest-ranger recruits.

A fourteen-year-old orphan becomes an NBA basketball player after
   he finds a pair of magic sneakers.

An all-powerful New York gossip columnist gives a press agent
   some dirty work.

A woman gives etiquette lessons to her reluctant granddaughter
   who is heir apparent to a throne.

A conspirator turns an arrogant ruler into a llama.

---

**Let's Pause Here••• ▶** What do you think Lauer's purpose is in composing this poem?
How is it different from other poems you have encountered? Why do you think the author chooses
to call his poem "Adult Situations"? What about the various show descriptions is "adult"? How do
you think Lauer intends the word "adult" to be understood?

## Let's Take It Further••• ▼

1. Did you recognize any of the plotlines from films and/or TV shows you have seen? If so, is it strange to see them summarized in one sentence? What is the effect of seeing a 30-minute sitcom or a 2-hour film reduced to one sentence?

2. What do the language and length of these descriptions say about the expectations of *TV Guide*'s audience? How is *TV Guide* appealing to their readers' emotions with language? How might Lauer be playing with this concept by selecting the lines that he has, especially in the context of the TV rating phrase "adult situations"?

3. Which of the descriptions seem like something you would want to watch? Which of them seem too absurd even to bother watching? Were you surprised at some of the descriptions? Were any of them so far-fetched that it would be hard even to imagine such a show? If so, why?

4. What do you think Lauer is saying about our mass media by taking their own words and publishing them out of context? What does it say about TV viewers, since we undoubtedly watch the very shows being described, even if we don't recognize them in this context?

5. Choose any of the lines in the poem and try to construct a plausible plot to accompany it. On which channel might such a show appear? What might the purpose of such a show be? Who might be the ideal audience for the show? How would you classify the show among the other genres of TV shows (reality, game, drama, etc.)?

6. Watch any show or film on television. When you finish, attempt to summarize the plot of what you just watched in one sentence. Explain what difficulties you face in what might first seem to be an easy task. Next, go to the cable TV guide (or any other online TV guide) and see how they summarized the movie or show. How similar was your description to the one given by the TV guide? How was your interpretation of the show/movie different from the one given by the show itself?

7. Search YouTube for video reviews of books and shows, and use a similar reviewing format to construct a video review and description of a television show. Explain whether you recommend the show and what it is that makes the show worthy of recommending.

8. Construct a visual collage (video, PowerPoint, or website) that uses news headlines and descriptions from print and online news sources in the same manner employed by Lauer in his poem. As Lauer did with "Adult Situations," explain where these sentences came from, and then include in the essay what you are trying to comment on about the nature of news and mass media.

# mash**UP** essay

The following essay is this chapter's Mashup selection. Keeping in mind our definition of a Mashup essay in Chapter 2 (an essay that includes multimedia texts, as well as multiple writing strategies), observe the way the author, James Parker, utilizes multimedia texts. For example, he refers to multiple television reality shows, many of which have been around for several years, as well as the spin-offs of reality shows (for example, how *Flavor of Love* contestant "New York" eventually landed her own show, called *I Love New York*). There are also several references to famous popular culture events (the Rodney King beating) and bygone celebrities (Tila Tequila, the MySpace queen). But Parker takes it one step further by bringing in the once-famous radio show, *Loveline*, which has been on the air nearly 30 years and even had a brief, 4-year television run on MTV. For reasons that will become apparent, Parker focuses on reality television because of the nature of his essay. But he also seeks out—and includes in his essay—books written on the subject of reality television, as well as books and articles written by Dr. Drew Pinsky, who is the primary focus of Parker's essay. The vast variety of television and radio shows, as well as texts about reality TV and its contestants, serve an important purpose in Parker's essay: they show that Parker is quite familiar with the genre of reality television and also familiar with scholarship that takes reality television and its participants as the subject of its research. The result is that Parker's credibility is strong, and we feel as though we are in good hands as we read his essay.

Parker also employs many writing strategies to help him make a more sophisticated argument for the value of Dr. Drew's latest show, *Celebrity Rehab*. For example, Parker uses a definition–illustration approach to writing in order to describe what *Celebrity Rehab* is, as well as

**Mashup Essay Flowchart**

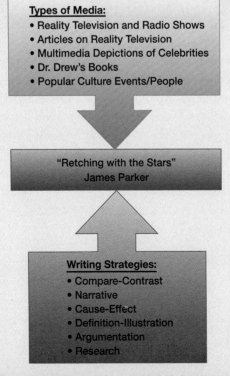

what events transpire on the show. He also regularly brings in other reality television and radio shows to compare to the format, content, and value of *Celebrity Rehab*, which is where he utilizes the comparison-contrast writing strategy. This allows him to justify his opinion that *Celebrity Rehab* is not only a show worth watching, but also a reality show that might even have more value than a run-of-the-mill reality show (the argumentation strategy). Part of the power of Parker's essay is the way he uses the "if–then" technique to show the outcome of fame on celebrities that have long since passed out of the public eye (the cause-effect strategy). Finally, you should also note how Parker includes extensive outside sources (the research writing strategy) to bring scholarship into his discussion of both celebrities and reality television. Parker weaves all of these writing strategies together seamlessly, and the result is an intriguing and thought-provoking assessment of a show that might otherwise not seem to be all that important.

When you begin writing a Mashup essay of your own in response to the selections in this chapter, revisit Parker's essay to generate ideas for multimedia texts and multiple writing strategies. Use the flowchart to see the ways in which Parker employs the various writing strategies and multimedia texts he utilizes in his writing.

## Retching with the Stars                    James Parker

### Let's Start Here••• ▶

It appears as though reality television is here to stay. At least that's what anyone who watches the TV Guide Channel for more than five minutes might say, judging by the glut of reality shows. From would-be celebrities who appear on shows for a chance to break into Hollywood, to "real-life" people opening up their lives for television cameras, there is now a reality show for just about every topic one can imagine. Swapping spouses, pregnant teenagers, drunks getting arrested, outlandish "Sweet 16" parties, neighbors pitching in to rebuild someone's fire-damaged home, all of these (and much more) are a button-push away from being paraded across the screen.

But there is one show that stands out among the rest—one show that, according to James Parker, is the reality show we should *all* be watching, if for no other reason than it shows the downside of celebrity. It shows the wreckage of fame in an unrelenting manner. That show is *Celebrity Rehab*.

According to Parker, *Celebrity Rehab* is a long-overdue attack on reality TV itself. He believes that if our fame-obsessed media and culture were only to watch the various former celebrities who appear on the show, addictions in tow, then maybe—just maybe—we might reconsider the value of celebrity, fame, and media portrayals of celebrity life as nothing but glitz, glamour, and adoring fans.

As you read the essay, observe the ways in which Parker describes the show's participants, and even the show's host, Dr. Drew. Does he feel sorry for them, or are they a source of amusement? Does he see this show as entertainment, or as a cultural critique that is leveled at our media and ourselves?

---

James Parker is a contributing editor for *The Atlantic Monthly*, where this essay first appeared in November 2009.

At the monument to the Last Postmodern Philosopher, who was assumed into heaven after watching Season One of *Laguna Beach*, the celebrities are gathering to pay tribute: lumbering Donald Trump, with his volume always set wrong; tiny-footed Tila Tequila. There's Paris Hilton, sleek as a seal; and a cartwheeling Flavor Flav! Applause greets them all, and shouted questions, the usual brouhaha. With the arrival of one man, however, a fresh note is heard from the crowd—a note of supplication. Hands are out-thrust, seeking the curative touch. Here, the people seem to feel, is someone with answers, someone with *powers*. Who is he, this smiling thaumaturge? We must investigate. For despite his mildness and evident sanity, and his perpetual bedside manner, reality TV has in its long roster of loonies produced no more exotic figure than Dr. Drew Pinsky.

> Parker uses these bygone celebrities as a text to prove how quickly people can rise and fall in the realm of fame and celebrity.

> **supplication:**
> A humble act of worship.

> **thaumaturge:**
> A person who can perform miracles.

Dr. Drew is the service director of the Chemical Dependency/Residential Treatment Center at Las Encinas Hospital in Pasadena, California. He is a board-certified internist and addictionologist, 51 years old, tall, neutrally handsome, and fit as a fiddle. His voice is even, his face without pores, and when he tilts his head his semi-frameless glasses catch the light like faraway windshields. He favors khaki slacks, light-mauve or powder-blue shirts, and nice ties. For 25 years he has hosted the nationally syndicated radio show *Loveline*—toneless voices of teens, some of whom can barely phrase their distress, calling in with misunderstood gayness or drug queries or parent problems or never-ending boners, each issue calmly and compassionately addressed in the Pinsky baritone.

> Parker uses description as a writing strategy to vividly illustrate the various defining characteristics of Dr. Drew that he finds relevant to his essay.

This is the youth of the nation, and Dr. Drew is listening. In his 2003 book, *Cracked: Life on the Edge in a Rehab Clinic*, he decried the "orgiastic mythos of sex, mayhem and cool

> By researching and providing a little background about the show *Loveline*, Parker is able to show how Dr. Drew has evolved as a public figure over the past 25 years.

clothes" whipped up by "the most successful creative figures in our culture, from the producers of reality TV to the editors of *Maxim*," and outlined his basic message to today's kids:

> Life isn't all about fun and sex . . . Slow down. Listen to your inner voice when it comes to right and wrong. Think for yourself. Be more human.

Mental health, he wrote in *Cracked*, "is about accepting reality on reality's terms."

All of which, one might think, would tend to make his next move—a VH1 reality show called *Celebrity Rehab With Dr. Drew*—something of a surprise. But no: just part of the program. Appalled by *The Osbournes* and *The Anna Nicole Show*, wherein (as he wrote in this year's *The Mirror Effect: How Celebrity Narcissism Is Seducing America*) the loopiness of the subjects was paraded "without acknowledging all the circumstances underlying their dysfunction," Dr. Drew decided upon a cultural intervention: a show in which addicted celebrities would weep, puke, "act out," shudder sweatily through days of withdrawal, and then, in harrowed sobriety, face the music. As he is fond of saying: "There's no free lunch with Mother Nature!"

Twenty-one days of treatment at the Pasadena Recovery Center, under Dr. Drew's supervision, with a camera crew present: that's the formula. And as far as ratings go, it seems to be working: a third season is in production, to be aired in early 2010. The lineup changes, of course. If the cast of Season One—a porn star, an Ultimate Fighter, a Baldwin brother, Brigitte Nielsen—resembled a colonization pod en route to the surface of a freshly invaded planet, Season Two's addicts were more disarming. We met gentle Rodney King, infamously beaten by the LAPD in 1991 and still prone to demolishing himself with intoxicants; Steven Adler, leakily lovable, ejected from the Guns N' Roses drum stool and having sad dreams that someone was kicking his dog; and Sean Stewart, troubled son of Rod.

The rehab vibe, however, the smell of generalized debility, is a constant. Peering from beneath hoods, wearing sweatpants, clutching blankets, huddling sideways in their chairs as if centrifugally dislodged from their own lives, the celebs tell their stories at group sessions. The stories, of abuse and neglect, are very sad: sometimes Dr. Drew is literally panting with empathy. Then after each session, in the facility's little Californian back

---

Parker uses Drew's own book to show how Drew views the world of celebrity and its effects on young people and celebrities alike.

It is this show that Parker will spend the vast majority of his essay describing and explaining for his readers, using the definition-illustration writing strategy.

Parker uses Drew's latest book to explain how it mirrors the message of Drew's new *Celebrity Rehab* show.

**narcissism:**
Love of one's own body or looks; self-love or adoration.

Parker researches the various stories attached to each celebrity's achievement of fame so that their failures displayed on Drew's show can be contrasted with earlier moments of greatness.

**empathy:**
Understanding or sensitivity.

garden, they sit amid lush, dark leaves and smoke like chimneys, if such furrowed, ritualistic intensity can be attributed to chimneys. And they fall to pieces, punctually. Amber Smith, a stately beauty from Season Two, seemed more or less unafflicted until we saw her going through detox—jackknifed over the trash can and probing her epiglottis with a long finger. Season Three will feature Heidi Fleiss, Dennis Rodman, and the ex-bassist from Alice in Chains.

My favorite addict so far? Gary Busey, by a mile. "The Businator," as his fellow patients called him—or, when he'd pissed them off, "Dr. Abusey." With bull-at-the-gate physical presence, a born-again ex-cokehead blowing hoarse gusts of religion ("I speak from a spiritual land that I live in!"), Busey on *Celebrity Rehab* seemed to rise in slashes of charcoal and orange crayon from the pages of Flannery O'Connor, twice as potent as the characters he played in *Point Break* and *The Firm*. He spoke in parables and the personalized acronyms he calls "Busey-isms"—SOBER, for example, breaks down Busey-style as "Son Of a Bitch, Everything's Real!" (Sean Stewart inquired at one point if there was a Busey-ism for *colonoscopy*. "Not yet," replied Busey, "but I got one for *poop*.") He got into an awful fight with Jeff Conaway (Kenickie in *Grease*; painkillers), after which he promised, before the group, to pray for him. "Oh, shove it up your ass!" said Conaway. "Everybody knows you're crazy." Later, in the garden, the two old troupers had a rapprochement. "I know you love me," grumbled Conaway. "One hundred and fifty percent," breathed Busey. "My love for you lives 5,000 miles past heaven." Conaway looked at him: "If it just stopped at heaven," he said, "that's enough for me." The Businator's mental "filter" was damaged in a motorcycle accident he suffered in 1988—or so suggested Dr. Charles Sophy, a colleague of Dr. Drew's who appeared in Season Two wearing no socks. (I found this remarkable in a medical man: between trouser hem and refulgent loafer, a gleam of bronzed ankle.)

As a healer, Dr. Drew is fascinating. On the surface his approach is scientific and slightly Dawkins-oid: in *Cracked* he briskly locates the source of addiction in "a tiny region of the brain called the nucleus accumbens," and suggests that the emotional dissociation of the trauma victim is "an evolutionary remnant of the risky strategy of feigning death."

But go below, and you'll feel the cunning of the rural exorcist. Drugs are presences ("I like them," says a patient. "They like you," Dr. Drew tartly reminds him), and addiction is a demon. That's your disease talking, he tells patients;

> Notice how as Parker's essay goes on, he still uses descriptive writing to explain what each celebrity is most famous for and what their addiction is.

> **rapprochement:**
> Establishing cordial or friendly relations with a person.

> Many of these moments are featured throughout Parker's essay, where he employs the narrative writing strategy to show how celebrities on the show interact and how the show progresses in each episode.

that's your addiction talking. Your disease is waiting for you to slip up. If I could script one scene for *Celebrity Rehab*, it would feature a scarecrow-haired addict falling to her knees in the white hallway of the Pasadena Recovery Center and crying out— raspingly, chthonically, her voice not her own—*Let us alone; what have we to do with thee, thou Dr. Drew? Art thou come to destroy us?*

**chthonically:**
Hellishly or demonically.

The black magic of reality TV, however, may be beyond the control of even so mighty a medicine man as Dr. Drew. Yes, he has plumbed the pathologies of the culture: in *The Mirror Effect*, he reports that he and his co-author, Dr. Mark S. Young, administered a test called the Narcissistic Personality Inventory (NPI) to 200 celebrities, and were grimly vindicated by the results ("reality TV personalities are more narcissistic than any other group, with a very high average score of 19.45"). And yes, he bemoans the passing of "the old phenomenon of public shame." But can he be sure that his televised merry-go-round of vomiting celebs will have the proper effect? Might not the deeper message of the show, the one that hits the viewer right in her "mesolimbic reward center," be: *Get high, young person; get fucked up; and then, when you can't do that anymore, commend your spirit into the hands of Dr. Drew?*

**vindicated:**
Justified or proven to be correct.

This is a central argument of Parker's piece. He uses the argumentation writing strategy to illustrate the value of Drew's show to both the celebrities featured on it and its viewers.

Nor is his ministry foolproof. After *Celebrity Rehab* Season Two came *Sober House*, another nine-parter, aired earlier this year, that pursued several of the Pasadena alumni into a "sober living" facility. This was a horrible show: removed somewhat from the structuring therapeutic gaze of Dr. Drew, untethered from the PRC's tight routine, the addicts succumbed bitchily to the dark side of the reality-TV dynamic. They also succumbed, or resuccumbed, to their addictions. Amber Smith got drunk again. Poor Steven Adler, nodding out on heroin but still standing, knees half-bent and arms akimbo, appeared momentarily to be practicing some kind of narcotic tai chi. Is it possible that being on television was not good for these people?

Here Parker employs the compare–contrast writing strategy to show how Dr. Drew's show and its spinoff (which doesn't feature Dr. Drew) are dramatically different from each other.

But Dr. Drew is no doubt right about everything. That the culture is clinically narcissistic, wallowing before the idol Ego, who would deny? Sanity, let there be sanity. Let moderation prevail.

On the other hand, my nucleus accumbens is twitching: I want that third season. I can't wait to see Heidi Fleiss throw up into a plastic bin.

## Let's Pause Here••• ▶

After reading this essay, do you agree with James Parker's viewpoint that *Celebrity Rehab* is a show that was inevitable because of our cultural and mass media obsession with fame? What value might there be in a show that displays broken people—specifically celebrities—wrestling with their addictions? Does it seem to you that Parker is deriving pleasure from the experience of watching *Celebrity Rehab* even while he is discussing the show's importance? Why do you think he titles his article "Retching with the Stars"?

## Let's Take It Further••• ▼

1. Are you familiar with any of the celebrities mentioned in Parker's essay as *Celebrity Rehab* participants? If so, how do you feel about the state that they are in currently? Would you watch the show to see these people? If so, why? If not, why not?

2. What might have led these celebrities down their paths of addiction, and what does it say about their addiction to fame that they would come onto a rehab show and display their most vulnerable side for the world to publicly watch? Which of their addictions is greater, the substance to which they are addicted or the pull of fame? Why?

3. What is your reaction to Dr. Drew, who, in several books he has written, has attacked our celebrity-obsessed media as well as other potentially damaging addictions? Do you feel that he is genuinely trying to do good, or do you believe he is exploiting the show's participants for some other reason? Regardless of which side you take, back up your opinion with selections from Parker's essay.

4. Parker makes a point of describing Dr. Drew as "an exotic figure" among the "long roster of loonies" that have been produced by reality television. What does he mean by this statement? What is so exotic about Dr. Drew, compared to the other people Parker describes in the opening of his essay? Why does Parker use the word choices that he does to describe the various failed celebrities, as well as Dr. Drew? How do Parker's descriptions have an effect on the reader?

5. Parker states that, in his opinion, *Celebrity Rehab* is something of a "cultural intervention." What do you believe he means by this, based on your understanding of the word *intervention*? What is our society addicted to that would warrant an intervention (recall Dr. Drew's findings that reality television personalities are "more narcissistic than any other group" of people)? How might we go about "breaking ourselves" of our addiction? Why does it even matter?

6. Discuss the evolution of reality television over the years. Pick a now-defunct reality show that was at one time popular and compare it to a wildly popular reality show currently on the air. How are the two shows different? How do the subjects of each, the participants, the locations, and even the purposes of the two shows differ? Do you see reality television evolving in a positive or negative way? Why? Judging from the trajectory of the two shows (whether they are getting more "brutal" or more "meaningful"), where do you see reality television in five years? What might the shows be about in the future?

7. Using as much detail as possible, describe the appearance of a "celebrity" as you envision one such person in your head. List and explain what you see as the traits of a celebrity. Next, watch an episode of *Celebrity Rehab* (on Hulu or YouTube) and describe the state of the participants in as much detail as possible (revisit Parker's essay to see an example of this). How are these two images—the real versus the imagined—at odds with one another? What was your reaction to the differences between the "broken" celebrities on the show and the ideal image of a celebrity that you carry in your mind?

8. Parker quotes Dr. Drew as lamenting the fact that the "old phenomenon of public shame" no longer exists in our culture. Given the rise of would-be celebrities on YouTube, many of whom post sometimes humiliating videos of themselves in an effort to get famous, can you cite specific instances of people chasing fame that prove they no longer care about public humiliation? Is there a now-famous person that you can describe who became famous because of their shameless self-promotion on YouTube? Or, if you disagree with Dr. Drew's complaint, can you find evidence (also on YouTube) to argue against his belief that we no longer have public shame?

9. Choose a celebrity who has succumbed to the underside of fame (addiction, etc.) and do research online to find images of them during the height of their fame. Locate other images as the celebrity slowly fell victim to whatever was the cause of their downfall and then create a photo collage (either print or video by using YouTube, PowerPoint, or a website) that shows the celebrity's progression from fame to failure. Write an essay that both describes and explains the various points in the celebrity's life that you have chosen to include in the photo collage. Be sure to compare and contrast the differences in the current and former versions of the celebrity's life.

# mash**it** UP

Here is a series of essay and discussion topics that draw connections between multiple selections within the chapter. They also suggest outside texts to include in your essay or discussion. Feel free to bring in further outside texts, remembering the variety of texts (beyond articles) available to you.

1. There are many mass media icons besides Simon Cowell (the subject of the cartoon at the beginning of this chapter). Identify another media icon and explain the role he or she plays in our culture by answering the following questions: Who is the person you have chosen as a media icon? What is it that this person is known for in the media? Does he or she have a "following" of viewers, supporters, or admirers? What is the role this person plays in our popular culture?

2. Both "*CSI* Effect" and "The Ethics of *Grey's Anatomy*" are working on the assumption that television affects viewers' perceptions of reality.

Locate another cultural phenomenon (in any mass media outlet) that has reached the popularity of these two shows and discuss the ways in which the show might be a benefit or a danger to society. Make your case by providing evidence from the show, as the authors of both articles did.

3. Research and locate real-life (i.e., nonfiction) medical studies that have been shown to greatly influence popular opinion as well as people's medical decisions in the same way that several authors in this chapter claim mass media can affect its consumers' decisions. Explain the difference between how people react to a movie or television show versus how they react to a real medical study. Which do you believe to be more dangerous or more of a threat out of the two influential sources, and why?

4. The general premise of "Retching with the Stars" is that we watch the aftermath of fame as celebrity participants come onto the show to air their demons. Once a person is in the public eye and is famous, the addiction to fame might be more powerful than any actual drug itself. Working with Parker's premise, locate a once famous person who has fallen from his or her pinnacle of fame and unraveled before the public eye (e.g., through drug addiction, run-ins with the law, or dismal relationships, to name a few). How has the person changed? What is he or she doing in terms of a profession? What is known about the person? Is he or she suffering from addictions, a criminal past, or any other downfall similar to the participants of *Celebrity Rehab*? Is the person merely living a "normal" noncelebrity life? Based on your discoveries, explain how the knowledge you've gained about this person affected you. Were you disappointed? Happy? Why did this person matter to you in the first place, and how has that changed with your research?

5. We have discussed the ways in which TV affects people's lives and their decisions, but television is only one aspect of the media. Can you locate other forms of media that have the power to affect their audiences? Explain the type of media you have chosen and prove the ways in which this particular form of media has influenced its audience. Did it affect its audience in a positive or a negative fashion?

6. How has television changed public opinion about issues such as homosexuality? Revisit Sheffield's essay about *Glee* and observe the ways in which he argues his case for it being a groundbreaking show. What other television shows are on the air that have changed public perceptions about once taboo topics?

7. Compare the YouTube video "10 Celebrities Caught on Tape with Drugs" in the "Heroes and Celebrities" chapter to the representation of famous people with addictions in an episode of *Celebrity Rehab*.

Also contrast the way celebrities are presented in the two sources. Explain how both illustrate the potentially "dark" side of fame and which you believe to be more successful at portraying this dark side.

## Award Worship
Brian Fairrington

Brian Fairrington is a political cartoonist for the *Arizona Republic* a newspaper based out of Phoenix, Arizona. He is nationally syndicated by Cagle Cartoons, Inc. This cartoon first appeared on December 25, 2009.

## Thinking About Mass Media Values

Take a moment to look at the accompanying cartoon. Notice that it is titled "Award Worship," which implies that the media sometimes places a higher value on our celebrities than more important things in life (such as a cure for cancer). It is apparent that the artist, Brian Fairrington, is critiquing the media. What do you think his criticism of the media is? What in the cartoon leads you to believe this? How do you know that it's the media he's critiquing?

As a society, we like to hold our media to a high standard, expecting them to produce "newsworthy" stories so that we keep in touch with what is going on in the world around us. We express disdain when a story about Lindsay Lohan getting busted for drugs—yet again—runs on the news headlines for days, and yet some devastating natural disaster or our ongoing wars in the Middle East barely warrant a mention. However, it is no secret that news outlets, and media outlets in general (our film, music, magazine, radio, and television industries), tailor their programming to get the highest ratings. If this is true, what does it say about us, as a culture, that a news story like the one shown here would be interrupted for a much less important story about an awards ceremony?

Many people plan theme parties that are centered around awards ceremonies such as the Oscars, Tonys, Emmys, or MTV Awards. Perhaps you've even held or attended a similar theme party. Why is it that we are far more likely to have an Oscar party than a NASA shuttle launch party? How is one more interesting than the other?

If there is the desire on our part for our media to be moral and to weed out the unimportant stories for us, then whom might the blame fall on when our mass media outlets continue to add celebrity news to the "regular" news? How guilty are the rest of us if the stories we follow and share with one another online are stories that really don't matter in the grand scheme of life? If there is an oil spill in the Gulf of Mexico, shouldn't that outweigh Tiger Woods's extramarital affairs?

Take another look at the cartoon. Is Fairrington only critiquing the mass media, or is he also critiquing American society? If so, what is his critique of us, and how is he doing it in such a limited space? Finally, if it came down to watching either the Oscars or an interview with a scientist who helped find a cure for cancer, which of the two shows would you watch? Why? What does either selection say about you as a consumer of culture, as well as your own role in the media and what it produces?

# Biebered! How "Team Edward," "Team Jacob," & Justin Bieber Killed the American Man
Shana Ting Lipton

**Let's Start Here•••▶** It is nearly impossible to go through an entire day without coming across an image in a grocery store, on a billboard, on television, or even on a news website, of one of the many young celebrities who is considered a hot commodity by our media. Powerhouse media outlets such as Disney churn out child stars with great regularity. We have our Britneys and our Justins, our Mileys and our Zacs. Disney alone creates more child stars than just about any other mass media outlet that exists. They hold a near-monopoly on all things related to childhood.

Shana Ting Lipton has an axe to grind with Disney and our media-laden culture in general. In her essay, Lipton defines for us what she sees as a "youth obsessed" culture. The sexualizing of youth, as she sees it, poses a great danger for our society because it upends the "normal" cycle of life, which is to say that everybody ages and we should not deny that fact. Observe her critique of the media, as well as our own role in the youth-as-sex-objects craze that she argues has reached a fever pitch. As you read Lipton's essay, see if you can identify underage boys and girls who are the objects of desire in our media, and try to determine whether there is an actual threat if Lipton is correct in her assessment of our media and our culture.

---

Shana Ting Lipton is an editor, feature writer, content producer, and cultural strategist who grew up in Los Angeles. Her L.A. and L.A.-related articles have been published in regional, national, and international publications for over a decade. This essay originally appeared in the *Huffington Post* on July 6, 2010.

Wine glass in-hand, at a cocktail party held by my architect friends, I systematically build my case like a lawyer. A handful of us graduate-level educated folks are engaged in a heated debate. We hit a stalemate as emotions run high. "Team Edward!" I chant for the last time. "Team Jacob!" yells a pregnant 30-something woman who works at a museum.

The *Twilight* movies—not politics, culture or science—dominate our social interactions.

It's not until hours later, in the clear and sober light of day, that it fully dawns on me. Like so many others in LA—frankly, in this country—I have been sucked into touting the brand of Lolita-banging pubescent porn spoon-fed to me by the studios, the publicists, Hollywood; in short, the youth-obsessed American media.

In the realm of movie stars, someone grown-up and classically masculine like George Clooney or Daniel Craig should make my knees weak. Instead, I've been Biebered, and Eclipsed—somehow swindled with kid gloves into seeing the fresh-faced and zit-challenged as romantic ideals and larger-than-life sex symbols.

I'm clearly not alone, if the "soccer mom" demographic of *Twilight* movie fans is any indicator. And this, incidentally, goes way beyond the "cougar" designation championed by Demi Moore and Ashton Kutcher. Justin Bieber and the other boyish heartthrobs make the *Punk'd* star look like Sean Connery.

This trend is of course non-gender-biased as teeny-bopper tarts like Miley Cyrus are also part of it. However, the zeitgeist's female counterpart has forever been in existence in the U.S. (and to a large degree in "little girl lovin" France and Japan).

**zeitgeist:** The cultural, intellectual, and moral climate that defines a particular period of time (e.g., 1980s).

Young girls like a pre-teen Brooke Shields, the *Poison Ivy* era Drew Barrymore, the Olsen twins, and most radically JonBenet Ramsey, have always been part of the accepted (but disturbing) media landscape. Wasn't it Marilyn Monroe's "baby talk" that made her rise above some of the other equally gorgeous actresses of her day?

It's not shocking that this long-time adoration for youth has extended into the male realm. One might argue that it already did eons ago with the Greek's pedaphillic social mores. It's just that now—the playing field having been leveled—no one can cry sexism.

**pedaphillic:** Defined by a sexual attraction of adults to children.

We can see this for what it is: an unhealthy (in my opinion), unabashed across-the-board Youth Mania. When *SNL* invites teens Bieber and Taylor Lautner to host, and NPR runs a "Team Edward or Team Jacob?" piece you know it's hit the tipping point into total societal dysfunction.:

> **unabashed:** Shameless or unembarrassed.

Here in LA, it has reached epidemic proportions. The Land of the Lost Boys, this town is rife with 50-year-old skaters or surfers sporting baggies and backwards baseball caps—hoping to "live up to" the youthful ideal.

Whether they're middle-aged entertainment lawyers, ad agency directors or tech company founders, they look like aging members of a boy band. And though it's great that they want to retain an energized and youthful spirit, there is something undeniably sad and stunted about this media-fueled but self-accepted regression.

I'm not suggesting that we all—men and women—go back to the uptight grown-up days of *Mad Men*. With so many health-conscious, fit people in our midst (who don't look their age—some without plastic surgery and Botox), I just wonder why we—Hollywood and the media nation—are stuck in such a shallow and inappropriate groove.

At the end of the day, I guess I'm just a little afraid of the lack of age-appropriate boundaries. I'm scared for the teens—who, with hormones coursing through their bodies, will always lean towards sexual teasing and enticement. I'm afraid for the adults on the receiving end, who seem to have a form of age dysmorphia which could not only land them in jail, but block their personal growth and progress.

Most of all, I'm afraid for myself. If I don't remove those root beer goggles with which the media has provided me, the next guy I end up rubbernecking could be the son of the man I'm meant to end up with.

**Let's Pause Here••• ▶** Lipton makes an intriguing argument about our media obsession with celebrity youth as overly sexualized. Do you agree with her assessment? Can you think of any other examples of underage celebrities whose photo shoots, album covers, movie posters, costumes, lyrics, or other aspects of their entertainment careers make them seem to be objects of desire? What's the difference between a young person in the media—a person who is young and just happens to be famous—and a young person who is purposely portrayed as a sex object? Can you find an example of both?

**Let's Take It Further••• ▼**

1. Lipton says that we are being "spoon-fed" the idea that young people should be objects of desire, specifically by the American media. Can you find any examples in recent times that support her critique? What, specifically, about your example proves her to be correct? In other words, how are these young people being presented to us as "larger-than-life sex symbols"?

**2.** Based on Lipton's word choice and language, whom do you believe her audience to be? How might she address a different audience of young adults or men, for example, if she wanted to make the same point to them?

**3.** Lipton cites her fears of adult men and women who, when obsessed with younger people, might "block their personal growth and progress." What do you think she means with this statement? How might being obsessed with, intrigued by, or even attracted to someone much younger block an adult's personal growth or progress?

**4.** In describing the effects of this trend on the men and women around her, Lipton states that there is "something undeniably sad and stunted" about a man in his fifties, for example, who would try to mimic the styles and fashions of a much younger person. What is sad about people not acting their own age? Is it really that big of a threat to our identities as adult men and women that our media is obsessed with youth, or is Lipton blowing it out of proportion?

**5.** Choose any current celebrity youth (male or female) and locate images, articles, Twitter feeds, news stories, or even clips from their shows or videos. Describe the ways in which the young person is being portrayed (either by the media or himself or herself). Is he or she wearing inappropriate clothing or in suggestive poses (and how would you define inappropriate or suggestive)? How is the celebrity you've chosen depicted differently (or similarly) in the media than his or her adult counterparts? Decide whether you agree with Lipton's assessment, and use the outside texts that you've located to prove or disprove her theory.

**6.** According to Lipton, one of the most offensive elements of this recent trend is that it has become so normal to be youth-obsessed that even women have begun to see young men as sex objects. She claims objectifying someone (or seeing him or her as only a sex object) is now a non-gender-biased activity. In other words, where people used to complain about men chasing after much younger women, now women are guilty of the same. If that is true, what accounts for the media's treatment of "real-life" women—such as the infamous teacher, Mary Kay Letourneau, who ended up sleeping with a much younger student and then ultimately marrying him—versus men who do the same? Locate the *60 Minutes* interview with Ms. Letourneau and watch the way Barbara Walters interviews her. Then, try to imagine the same sort of interview occurring if a man were being interviewed about the same crime. How would the treatment be different? Is, as Lipton says, the idea of sexualizing young people as non-gender-biased as she suggests?

**7.** Because of the "cougar" phenomenon, would you argue that relationships with vast age differences have become normal to the extent that they are no longer that big of a deal? Has society shifted its opinions on this issue, or is the media just making it seem normal? Choose any of the more famous celebrity relationships in which one person is at least a generation apart from the other (e.g., Demi Moore and Ashton Kutcher, Michael Douglass and Catherine Zeta-Jones, Ellen DeGeneres and Portia de Rossi, Harrison Ford and Calista Flockhart) and research what the media reaction was in the beginning of the relationship. Then, compare it to a more recent relationship of the same sort and make the argument for whether there has been any change in how the media portrays these relationships.

# The *Notting Hill* Effect: How Romantic Comedies Can Harm Your Love Life

**David Derbyshire**

**Let's Start Here••• ▶** Whether or not you are a fan of romantic comedies, most likely you have seen one. In fact, they are often viewed as the perfect date-night activity, and it isn't at all abnormal for girls' night get-togethers to include a romantic comedy for entertainment. But there is a danger to watching these films, according to Derbyshire's article. Movies such as *Pretty Woman* and *The Proposal* give their viewers a skewed outlook on what real relationships are like. Most of us probably do not give a second thought to the movies we watch, but David Derbyshire feels that we should.

In his essay, Derbyshire cites the research of Scottish scholars and warns us of the potential negative outcomes of something as innocent as viewing a movie. As you read the essay, try to determine what your own expectations of relationships are, and from where these expectations originated.

---

David Derbyshire has worked for the *Daily Mail* (a popular British newspaper) as Environment Editor since June 2007. He has worked on UK national newspapers since 1996—first as the *Daily Mail's* Science Correspondent, then as the *Daily Telegraph's* Science and Medical Correspondent, and more recently as the *Daily Telegraph's* Consumer Affairs Editor. This essay first appeared in the *Daily Mail* on January 26, 2009.

They have long been regarded as the perfect movie for a first date.

But according to a study, romantic comedies such as *Bridget Jones's Diary* and *Notting Hill* could be bad for your love life.

Rather than being harmless entertainment, "rom-coms" give people unrealistic—and potentially unhealthy—expectations about real-life relationships, scientists say.

Researchers found that those who watched romantic comedies were more likely to believe in predestined love than those who preferred other genres of movie.

They were also more likely to believe that perfect relationships happen instantly, and were less likely to believe that couples need to work at relationships.

Watching just one romantic comedy is enough to sway people's attitudes to romantic love, they found.

Dr. Bjarne Holmes, who led the research, said: "We are not being killjoys—we are not saying that people shouldn't watch these movies. But we are saying that it would be helpful if people were more aware and more critical of the messages in these films.

"The problem is that while most of us know that the idea of a perfect relationship is unrealistic, some of us are still more influenced by media portrayals than we realize."

For the first part of the study, Dr. Holmes and colleagues at the Family and Personal Relationships Laboratory at Heriot Watt University, Edinburgh, studied 40 box office hits from 1995 to 2005 including *You've Got Mail, The Wedding Planner, Maid in Manhattan* and *While You Were Sleeping.*

Most mainstream comedies depicted couples falling instantly in love and promoted the idea of fate—the notion that there is just one perfect mate out there, they found.

And people were far more forgiving of cheating than they are in real life, they found.

"There's a notion of destiny and couples in romantic comedies immediately understand each other," said Dr. Holmes. "If you think that's how things are, you are setting yourself up to be disappointed."

In a second study, Dr. Holmes asked around 100 student volunteers to watch *Serendipity*—the 2001 romantic comedy starring Kate Beckinsale and John Cusack, while 100 watched a David Lynch drama.

In a questionnaire after the film ended, students watching the rom-com were far more likely to believe in fate and destiny than those who had watched the "straight" film.

A third study found that fans of romantic comedies had far stronger beliefs in predestined love.

**Let's Pause Here••• ▶** Is Derbyshire correct in his criticism of romantic comedies? Why might it be necessary for us to be more critical of the messages in the movies we watch, particularly romantic comedies? Are we really so open to the power of the media that it can change the way we see something as important and valuable as a relationship? Can you think of any examples to prove this one way or the other?

**Let's Take It Further••• ▼**

1. Who do you believe Derbyshire envisions as his audience, based on the way he addresses the reader? What specific language or passages lead you to understand the type of person to whom Derbyshire speaks within his essay? If this was published in a men's magazine such as *GQ*, how might his language and word choices differ from the current version of his essay?

2. Derbyshire quotes the head researcher, Dr. Holmes, as saying that people who base their expectations of love on these movies are "setting [themselves] up to be disappointed." How might a person be disappointed by a romantic comedy if she or he buys into the ways relationships are portrayed in these types of films?

3. Dr. Holmes is also quoted as saying that most of us understand that "the idea of a perfect relationship is unrealistic." Do you agree with that statement? Do you believe there is no "perfect mate" out there? Do you agree with the concept of love at first sight? In what ways do you think real-life relationships differ from those depicted in romantic comedies? Even if you realize movie relationships are "unrealistic," do you still wish you had one as perfect and romantic as those in movies?

4. If you have ever been on a first date and gone to a romantic comedy, did you have higher expectations of the relationship on which you were embarking because of the film? Did you cringe when you realized you could never live up to the attributes of either the male or female character? How did it affect the date, if at all?

5. Watch a recent (within the last two years) romantic comedy of your choosing. What is the message that the movie gives its viewers about love? Is it realistic, in your opinion? Why or why not? Be sure to describe the basic plotline—how the couple meets, how they get together, and what the outcome of their relationship is—and then discuss the manner in which the movie portrays relationships in general. What sorts of elements of the relationship do not strike you as accurate or realistic about real-life relationships? How does a "good" relationship start in the film? How is a "good" relationship defined? What effect does it have on your expectations of relationships?

6. Locate the original research study done by Dr. Holmes and his colleagues. After researching the study, decide whether you agree with his findings, and explain why. Then, conduct a similar study on your own, asking questions of people who do and do not watch romantic comedies. How are your results the same or different from Dr. Holmes's findings? After conducting research, has your opinion of the "danger" of these rom-coms changed? If so, how did that happen, and if not, why not? Be sure to describe the type of research you did and the methods you used.

7. Compare an older (ten years or more) romantic comedy with a more recent one (within the last two years). Has the message of this genre of film changed at all over the years? How are the movies similar or different in the ways in which they depict relationships, as well as the outcomes of the relationships?

8. Compare and contrast the ways in which relationships and the concept of love are represented in "dude" films, such as *Super Bad* or any of *The Hangover* movies, with the ways they are represented in the romantic comedies such as those featured in Derbyshire's essay. How does each genre represent relationships to their audience? What messages do they give in terms of the concept of "love at first sight" or even the idea of monogamy? Which gives a more realistic version of love and relationships, and how does it accomplish this?

# Guitar Hero: More Than a Video Game

**Christopher Palmeri**

**Let's Start Here•••** ▶ By this point, Guitar Hero and similar play-along music games have firmly established themselves as a media form in their own right, alongside other types of video games, which have begun to mimic other enduring forms of mass media in many ways (particularly by inundating the consumer with advertisements). Many people would never have guessed that music games would become a source of revenue for the music industry in a similar way in which sporting games have created licensing income for sports bodies such as the NFL, the NBA, or even NCAA sports teams.

Christopher Palmeri, in the following informative essay, describes the rise of Guitar Hero and its significance in our culture—not only as a cultural phenomenon, but also as a new media outlet. As you read the essay, see how many of his predictions have come true, and consider the popularity of games such as Guitar Hero. What makes these sorts of games so appealing? How might they change both the gaming and the music industry landscape?

---

Christopher Palmeri is a reporter for Bloomberg News based out of Los Angeles, and a Senior Correspondent to *Business Week* who has written for the magazine since 2000. Before that he worked for *Forbes* magazine for 13 years, the last 6 as Houston Bureau Chief. He writes about toys, energy, housing, casinos, fashion, finance, art, and anything else he thinks will make a good story. The following story first appeared in *Business Week* on October 29, 2007.

Metallica fought digital downloads fiercely. But the heavy metal act was a lot more accommodating when the people behind Guitar Hero came calling. The game allows you to play along to popular music, and its publishers wanted Metallica to make its songs available. A gusher of longing fan e-mails helped tip the balance. So did the fact that two of drummer Lars Ulrich's sons are Guitar Hero addicts. When the game's latest edition, Guitar Hero III, appears in stores on Oct. 27, players will be able to channel their inner rock god with Metallica's hit "One."

The music industry is like a mosh-pit casualty, battered on one side by song-swiping file sharers and on the other by competing entertainment options, including, yes, gaming. Record companies looking for new ways to sell and promote their music can't have helped noticing that Guitar Hero was the most popular game in the U.S. for the first eight months of this year, according to NPD Group. In November a Viacom-owned rival called Rock Band will join Guitar Hero. This holiday season the two games are expected to sell a combined 3.5 million copies (at $100 and up). And everyone from the Sex Pistols to former Guns N' Roses axman Slash wants in.

Gaming won't save the music industry. But the major labels see it as another way to introduce people to artists, new and old, and build anticipation for tours, where increasingly they will find their revenue. There even has been discussion of including a "buy button" in the games for impulse purchases. "This is our core demographic, the people who play video games 30 hours a week," says George White, Warner Music Group's head of digital sales. "It's very important for us to maintain their share of mind."

Guitar Hero was a surprise hit when it appeared in late 2005. The game won a following among people who can't play a lick of guitar but have always wanted to, as well as fans of music-related TV shows such as *American Idol* and *Hannah Montana*. As avatars perform onscreen, players join in on a guitar featuring five buttons that are punched in time to cues from the game. You win points by hitting the right buttons. For the game's architects, the best news was that Guitar Hero's appeal transcended hard-core, shoot-'em-up geeks: Parents bought the game for their kids and ended up playing, too. (You know who you are.)

**transcended:** Rose above.

Game companies and Big Media took notice. In May, 2006, game giant Activision bought Guitar Hero publisher RedOctane for $100 million. Four months later, Viacom paid $175 million for Harmonix Music Systems, which developed Guitar Hero but didn't own it. For Viacom, Harmonix created Rock Band, which also features a microphone, bass, and drums.

The first iteration of Guitar Hero featured re-recorded songs because it was cheaper than licensing the real thing. "We weren't sure it would make much of a difference," says Harmonix CEO Alex Rigopolus. Players demanded the real recordings. In May Guitar Hero II began selling downloads at $6 per package of three songs. Both Guitar Hero III and Rock Band will include original and re-recorded tracks in their games and will release downloads after that.

**iteration:** Version, occurrence, or incarnation.

It's doubtful that the record companies will make a lot of money selling downloads through the games. But the promotional bang could be significant—even for acts that broke up three decades ago. This summer, the Sex Pistols re-recorded a version of *Anarchy in the U.K.* for Guitar Hero III. The game's release will coincide with a short Sex Pistols tour and a 30th anniversary edition of the Pistols' album *Never Mind the Bollocks*, released by Virgin Records.

## "You Can Do All Sorts of Stuff"

The great thing about games is that you can dress up promotions as rewards for playing skill. Players who reach a certain level on Guitar Hero III will unlock video interviews with their favorite guitarists, including Tom Morello of Rage Against the Machine and Bret Michaels, whose band Poison will perform a rooftop concert above a Best Buy in Los Angeles on the night of Guitar Hero III's release.

For its part, Viacom can use shows on its MTV, Nickelodeon, and Country Music Television networks to build excitement around Rock Band—and vice versa. Promos for the recent MTV Video Music Awards featured backstage clips of bands playing the game, including the Gym

Class Heroes, who almost missed receiving their award because they were too distracted. "Our heritage is music," says Van Toffler, who runs Viacom's music-related cable networks. "We'll do a whole bunch of games around music and dancing and seamlessly integrate them on air."

That's just the beginning of the promotional opportunities, some say. "Why not have Coca-Cola sponsor a free download?" asks Michael Pachter, a video game industry analyst at Wedbush Morgan Securities. "You can do all sorts of stuff you can't do with traditional video games."

How do musicians feel about being part of a game? Slash says he was "giddy with excitement" when he heard Activision wanted to feature him as a character in Guitar Hero III. Slash donned a motion-capture suit and recorded some original licks for the game. Reached on tour with his band, Velvet Revolver, Slash said: "I'm on a bus in New Mexico. I've got nothing to do but play video games."

**Let's Pause Here••• ▶** Do you find it odd that an *actual* guitar hero, Slash, of the band Velvet Revolver (and formerly of the rock and roll power band Guns N' Roses), is a fan of a game whose sole purpose is to make regular people feel as though they are rock gods? Other famous musicians have also professed their love for these games. Why is this a strange occurrence?

**Let's Take It Further••• ▼**

1. How do you feel about games becoming sources of revenue not only for the music industry, but also for "sponsors" such as Coca-Cola, as Palmeri suggests? Do you find it offensive that gamers are being subjected to advertisements on a game for which they have paid $100 or more? Why or why not? Either way, how should this particular form of media differ from, or become the same as, other forms of mass media in regard to advertising?

2. In the essay, George White (Warner Music Group's head of digital sales) is quoted as saying, "It is very important for us to maintain [gamers'] share of mind." What does White's statement "share of mind" mean? Do you see anything disturbing about his statement? If so, why?

3. Palmeri points out his belief that Guitar Hero and similar games "won't save the music industry." Do you agree with that statement? What other means might there be for the music industry to be "saved"?

4. If you have played or are an avid fan of Guitar Hero, describe its appeal. What do you think has made the game such a huge success? How is it different from playing a real guitar, and what might the appeal be when your only fans are virtual people cheering on the screen? What might account for the game's appeal even among "non-gamers" (e.g., women, parents, or even actual rock stars)?

5. Locate another video game of your choice and observe and describe the ways in which this particular form of media has begun to evolve in such a way that it now mirrors many other

forms of mass media. Conversely, if you believe that this form of media is different from other forms of mass media, use your observations to justify that opinion. Then explain whether you find this similarity/difference to mass media to be a positive or negative development, and why you hold the opinion that you do.

6. One element of Palmeri's essay deals with the video game aspect of Guitar Hero, while another deals with the issue of how people in American culture acquire music. With the record industry constantly lamenting plummeting sales, and with recent occurrences of bands such as Cake topping the Billboard sales charts with a mere 40,000 albums sold, it is obvious that American society has shifted to other formats of music. Briefly discuss the manner in which you acquire music, and if you prefer this method of music consumption over the traditional CD/vinyl formats. What is the dominant format for listening to music currently? What are the benefits of that format over the other formats (vinyl, CD, MP3, streaming, etc.)?

7. Always on the lookout for new ways to tempt potential customers into purchasing music, the recording industry and other entrepreneurial companies have begun to formulate brilliant ways of introducing people to new music—the job radio stations used to largely do for them. Music streaming websites, such as Last FM, allow virtually anyone to set up a streaming radio station and DJ her own playlists. iTunes created a "Genius" feature that gives suggestions for new bands based on your listening habits. Pitchfork media started a blog (and an annual music festival in Chicago) devoted to unearthing indie bands and introducing them to a wider audience. MySpace, once the sparkly playground of pre-teens and spammers, is now mostly bands and musical artists hawking their wares to a larger audience. Select any of these services, preferably one you have not used before, and spend a week with it in your free time. Were any of the services helpful in introducing you to new music? If so, how did they succeed? How accurate were Last FM DJs or the iTunes "Genius" service at making suggestions you actually liked, based on your current musical tastes? Would you recommend any of these services to other music lovers? Describe the process of using the service for a week, as well as how the service you chose actually works, and mention any surprises or annoyances you encountered along the way.

# The Video-Game Programmer Saving Our 21st-Century Souls    Jason Fagone

**Let's Start Here •••▶**    When most of us think of video games, certain images might enter our minds. For example, when we think of the game Guitar Hero, we can visualize a person playing a plastic guitar as though he is in an actual band. Or, when we think of a person who spends several hours a day playing games such as World of Warcraft or Halo, we might wonder what would compel someone to give so much of her time to a game. One answer is that we play games for entertainment—to escape from our everyday lives, as Jason Fagone states in his essay. The gaming industry is a multibillion dollar mass media enterprise that makes its money off our desire to be entertained and to escape, like so many other forms of media. In addition, it has become a given that the more realistic a game is, the more successful it will be.

However, there is a game programmer who is upending the basic concept of games-as-entertainment, games-as-mass-media, and even realism in games. He wants us to feel complex human emotions. This is probably a foreign idea to most people—that a game can make us *feel* something other than possibly an adrenaline rush. Fagone outlines how such a thing is possible, and how it might already be happening now. Consider, as you read his essay, whether Fagone's assessment of the man who wants to change video games as we know them is correct and what that might mean for us and how we interact with games or even machines.

---

Jason Fagone is a journalist and author of two books who lives in Philadelphia, Pennsylvania. He writes about science, sports, and culture. His work has appeared in *GQ, Wired, Esquire, Philadelphia, The Atlantic Monthly, Slate, Kill Screen,* the *New York Times, Play* magazine, *The Penn Stater, Wharton Magazine, Etiqueta Negra,* and *Deadspin.* This essay originally appeared in *Esquire's* November 2008 "Best and Brightest" issue.

What if, back in the day before TVs were in every waiting room and bedroom and bar, before the perpetual buzz of blue background noise changed the way we think and speak, before the easy escapism of *M\*A\*S\*H* and Wolf Blitzer and *Ice Road Truckers,* before our leaders began to speak to us like third-rate voice-over actors—what if some influential genius had recognized the threat and stood up and yelled *Stop*?

The next dominant communications medium in America is undeniably even more potent than TV. It presents our brains with beguiling tasks. It commandeers our circuitry. And we can actually issue commands back.

That's the promise and the terror of this new form. We can interact with its entertainments. We can summon new layers of noise and color. The American video game is enabling us to live out deeper escapist fantasies than TV ever has. Right now we're mainly using this new medium to imagine that we are space aliens and NFL quarterbacks and mercenaries with hearts of steel. But it doesn't have to be this way.

A naked kid and a freakishly tall man walk in a meadow. The meadow is their front yard. It pokes up from among the sheared lawns of upstate New York's Route 11B like a Mohawk, purposeful and defiant. The kid's hair is long and blond and, on first glance, feminine. He wears orange rain boots, his uncircumcised penis free in the breeze. The tall man wears military-style cargo pants and a red T-shirt that says MONTREAL INTERNATIONAL GAME SUMMIT. He's barefoot. His dirty-blond hair is spiky from not showering. A cop pulls into his driveway. The man chats with the cop. The cop says he just got a call about a "tall guy and a naked girl down by the gas station" and dropped by to investigate.

The tall man is amused.

The cop—burly, bearded, the sitcom essence of small-town cop—doesn't need to ask the tall man what he does for a living. He already knows. Everyone in this town knows. The tall man is famous here in Potsdam, New York, an aging hamlet near the Canadian border, because of his meadow. The meadow inspired a court case and made the front pages of the local newspapers. The tall man fought a village ordinance that required him to cut his meadow to a height of ten inches. He represented himself in court, and it came out after the trial that this man earned a living by making video games. Which didn't make much sense to the town's inhabitants, like this cop here, who's got to be having a hard time reconciling the tall man's career in computers with the apparently Luddite lifestyle on display: the meadow, the tiny ranch home it obscures, the naked hippie kid, the wife standing on the porch with the red hair and freckles and fiery green eyes, and the baby in a cloth sling. Later today, the tall man will hold the baby off the front porch, above the cedar bushes, and whisper "*Pssssss, pssssss*" in his ear, and the baby will pee into the bush, on command, just like that. Pavlovian.

> **reconciling:**
> Getting two incongruous or incompatible ideas to agree with each other.

> **Luddite:**
> One who is against technological change or advances.

> **Pavlovian:**
> A reaction that is conditioned or programmed into a person.

The cop seems to be buying what the tall man is saying. He gets back in his squad car, pulls back onto 11B, and drives away, satisfied that the tall man is weird, yes, but harmless.

In 2007, the tall man, whose name is Jason Rohrer, uploaded a free game to his Website. It used a mere two megabytes of disk space and a thin horizontal stripe of color on the screen. So simple. In Passage, you're this little pixelated guy. You live in the stripe of color. The stripe is twelve pixels tall. It's green. All else is blackness. Your job is to move up and down and left and right through the stripe—the "forest"—in search of treasure chests, sort of like in the Legend of Zelda.

As you walk, the stripe shimmers and flickers, the fuzzy pixels in front of you scroll into sharpness, and the pixels you've already traveled blur in your wake. The stripe is your whole world. But soon you have to make a choice: share the world or keep it to yourself. You meet a girl. Your fat-pixeled soul mate. Link up with her and a heart explodes. You're in love. Now she sticks to you as you move through the forest, less easily than before. It's a trade-off: You can get more treasure by staying single, but bond with your "wife" and you earn double the points for every step you take.

If you're like most people, you'll choose the comforts of companionship. Only, as you trudge across the stripe, something happens. Your pixels begin to fade, gray out. Your hair recedes by degrees. Your wife slurs into a matronly shape. It hits you: This is going to happen to me. Age, decrepitude, ugliness.

Also: At least I won't be alone. Somebody loves me. Ha-ha-ha.

Then—*thwack*—she dies.

Jesus. Weren't expecting that. There's a tombstone with a little cross. Then—*thwack*—you die, too.

The first person to cry playing Passage was Rohrer himself, as he was programming it. All that summer, he watched one of his neighbors die of cancer. She was a nice old woman with a beautiful garden. "Her whole life, she had said if she ever got cancer, she wouldn't want to go through chemotherapy," Rohrer says. "But once it happened to her, she changed her mind. . . . We watched her go through chemotherapy, and she essentially just rotted away. And she died in six months anyway." It wasn't only sad. It was irrational. So Rohrer, a few months shy of his thirtieth birthday, made a game about the inevitability of death. "Yes, you could spend your five minutes trying to accumulate as many points as possible," he wrote in a twelve-hundred-word creator's statement, "but in the end, death is still coming for you."

Some players didn't know what to make of Passage. The video-game blog Kotaku wrote, "It's a weird little game, but sweet, and worth spending a couple of minutes with. But weird." For others, though, it was a revelation. Games don't have to be bloated and huge and violent. They can be small and quiet and deep. Writers struggled for metaphors; to the tech blog Boing Boing, Passage was "a pregnant, forlorn sentence" of a game, while a reviewer from *Wired* opted for "a superb and tightly crafted sonnet," gushing, "More than any game I've ever played, it illustrates how a game can be a fantastically expressive, artistic vehicle for exploring the human condition."

**existential:**
Relating to the idea of being concerned with existence or the state of existing.

Passage was sad, it was sincere, it was personal, it was mysterious, it was existential, and for all these reasons, it was new. The big boys of gaming, a universe away from Potsdam, e-mailed it to one another. Clint Hocking, a designer at Ubisoft best known for Tom Clancy's Splinter Cell, was so blown away by Passage that he made it a focus of his Game Developers Conference talk earlier this year. In front of an audience full of the industry's most influential game designers, Hocking growled, "Why can't we make a game that fucking *means something*? A game that *matters*? You know? We wonder all the time if games are art, if computers can make you cry, and all that. Stop wondering. The answer is yes to both. Here's a game that made me cry. It did. It really did."

He put up a slide of Passage.

Then he put up a slide of another small indie game, the Marriage, coded by Rohrer's friend Rod Humble. The Marriage uses brightly-colored circles and squares to model . . . a marriage. Humble claims to have made it after going through "a really heavy Kandinsky period."

"I think it sucks ass that two guys tinkering away in their spare time have done as much or more to advance the industry this year than the other hundred thousand of us working fifty-hour weeks," said Hocking.

Here was a cute video game that made jaded men weep by commanding a sophisticated and rare power that lay—where? Where in those two megabytes, those twelve pixels?

"I am prepared to believe that video games can be elegant, subtle, sophisticated, challenging, and visually wonderful," Roger Ebert, the world's most famous film critic, wrote in 2005. "But I believe the nature of the medium prevents it from moving beyond craftsmanship to the stature of art. To my knowledge, no one in or out of the field has ever been able to cite a game worthy of comparison with the great dramatists, poets, filmmakers, novelists, and composers...video games represent a loss of those precious hours we have available to make ourselves more cultured, civilized, and empathetic."

> **empathetic:**
> Characterized by the ability to relate to or sympathize with another person or his circumstances.

This is what the video-game industry lacks. Not money; it rakes in $40 billion globally per year, even more than Hollywood. Not influence; it's got a lock on the hearts and minds of America's eighteen- to thirty-four-year-old males. What it lacks is legitimacy. The video game in 2008 is a ghettoized creative form, more ghettoized even than comic books; at least comics have their hipster auteurs, their graphic novelists, their Chris Wares and Daniel Clowses and Brian K. Vaughans. But there are no video-game auteurs whose names ring out in the wider culture.

> **ghettoized:**
> Isolated or considered lowbrow.

According to Jason Rohrer, the reason for this is simple: "Ebert's right." Games suck. Game companies have spent so many years trying to make skulls explode complexly and water ripple prettily that they haven't invested any time in learning how to make games that are as emotionally dense as the best novels and films. Most games are a waste of time. Soulless. Empty. Rohrer is far from the only game-maker who believes this. In fact, a growing number of game-makers in positions of power at large companies—Electronic Arts, Ubisoft, etc.—aren't interested in continuing to defend the industry against its critics. Because, one, it's hard to see how the critics are wrong, hard to see how Halo 3 and Grand Theft Auto IV aren't what they seem to be. Murder simulators. *Really fun* murder simulators. And, two, if you're a middle-aged game-maker and you're going to see *Children of Men* on the weekend with your wife and kids and getting your mind blown, you hit a point where you *want* to do something better, more important, than making blood flow realistically.

In truth, ambitious game-makers want it to be true that games are polluting the minds of our youth, because that means games really are touching our brains in sophisticated ways, and therefore games have room to grow. Like Passage, they can be art.

And if this new breed of emotional game can also rake in the cash, well, all the better. Under way right now is a high-stakes race to create the

*Citizen Kane* of video games: an "AAA" title (the industry's equivalent of a big-budget summer movie) that also pushes the needle forward artistically. The best current contender is a project code-named LMNO, part of Stephen Spielberg's development deal with Electronic Arts, which has been described as *North by Northwest* meets *E.T.* Your character in the game will be a spy who encounters a mysterious, sexy woman. How much help she offers will be dependent upon how well you cultivate her as your partner and guide. Essentially, LMNO aims to be the first major video game whose action will not pivot on jumping puzzles or twitch-reflex fusillades but on a nuanced relationship.

As it turns out, the expert that Spielberg's partners hired to serve as an "idea guy"—a guy who "sort of instinctively thinks this way," according to the project's creative director at Electronic Arts, Doug Church—is Jason Rohrer.

And Rohrer's happy to do it, of course. To consult for EA and Spielberg. Who wouldn't be? But while he thinks the game is "very, very cool," ultimately it's just a gig. Because it's not Rohrer's goal to make big games. Because making a big-budget emotional game now is a lot like trying to run before you can walk. Premature. Because the video-game industry lacks something even more crucial than respect: a basic grammar of emotion. Film has it, novels have it, songs have it: heroes to idolize and imitate, codified bodies of knowledge you can soak up over a lifetime or try to have dumped into you at an M.F.A. program or film school. But a game-maker is in a different position altogether. Nowhere to look. No place to start. "We just have no idea," says Chris Hecker, who spent the last five years working alongside gaming god Will Wright on the hugely ambitious, sprawling Spore. "The question I have is, Are games in fifty years going to be recognizable? Is there a game we'll look back at in fifty years and say, yeah, that was the model?"

**codified:**
Systematized or classified.

**audacious:**
Daring or bold.

Here is Jason Rohrer's audacious bet: no. The models don't exist. So he's setting out to build them.

"I don't know if you can smell me yet, but by the end of the day, you will probably be able to."

Rohrer doesn't use deodorant. He washes his hair only twice a month. He doesn't put on a new pair of clothes in the morning, because he gave most of his clothes away years ago. He owns four pairs of boxer shorts. If he owned any more, he or his wife would have to spend more time washing them, which would make them both more reliant on electricity to run the washer. He keeps his fridge unplugged for the same reason. No fridge, no meat; no meat, no spoilage in an electrical storm. Open the fridge and all you see are vegan grains. "There, that's quinoa. You had quinoa before? It's really good." He bakes a loaf of bread every other morning and feeds it to his family at lunch, along with lentil soup. Every day, same lunch. For weeks at a time. The alternative is to starve. Despite his consulting fee from EA, the family budget is $14,500 a year, the income pieced together from PayPal donations from his Website, freelance writing consulting, occasional speaking fees, and monthly checks from his "patron," a wealthy software-industry figure who has taken a liking to his games.

To some extent, Rohrer fits the profile of a game-maker: a computer dork who is more seduced by comic books and movies than by dreams of becoming a legendary hacker or a dot-com millionaire. And Rohrer, who studied artificial intelligence at Cornell, is a dork through and through. But even within the small yet growing dork **vanguard** of indie game-makers—a vanguard that includes Rohrer and Rod Humble and a guy called "Cactus" and Ian Bogost, an associate professor of digital media at Georgia Tech, and Jonathan Blow, who pumped $180,000 of his life savings into Braid, a game about the nature of time and existence and quantum mechanics—Rohrer is "pretty fringe," according to Bogost. The other indie guys don't live in meadows.

> **vanguard:** Leaders or people on the frontlines of a movement.

But there's a deep logic to the way he lives. If he didn't live this way, he couldn't make the games he makes. By carefully constructing an alternate reality, bit by bit, Rohrer has been able to make the same creative leap that many artists have made in the past. His games start with an emotion, an observation about the poignancy of a certain set of trade-offs inherent to being alive; Rohrer then figures out how to abstract and encode these trade-offs using math and images. This is why Rohrer's games, while sharing a common aesthetic—often pixelated, retro cute, allusive to video-game hits of the past—feel so different from one another.

At dinner one night, he asks his wife if she thinks it would be fun to be immortal—she says she thinks it would get boring—so he makes a game, Immortality, in which you're this little stick figure who has to build a tower to the heavens; the game grants you the powers of immortality, then makes you yearn to have those powers taken away. He's surfing online and comes across that YouTube video of the "Don't tase me, bro" guy, and he's so freaked out by the tyranny of the police that he cries, and when he's done crying, he codes a game called Police Brutality that puts you in the room with the "Don't tase me" dude and challenges you to organize an unarmed insurrection. He makes a Super Mario Brothers–type game called Gravitation about his relationship with the kid in the meadow, his five-year-old son, Mez.

And it's hard to see the art in these games unless you play them and struggle with them and try to figure out what the games mean. It doesn't help to watch over his shoulder as he codes a game on his beat-down Dell laptop, in his humid home office with the peeling linoleum floor and the

**arcadian:**
A pleasing or enjoyable scene in nature.

window overlooking the arcadian wilderness of his back-yard meadow. Watch him code his latest sketch, a game about regret, and what do you see?

Tuesday, there's an idea on a scrap of paper: "Mistakes you make, early on, haunt you through some game me-chanic later." Thursday, there's a map of a maze. Later that day, the maze is populated with bunnies and squirrels; in the game, you have to feed the animals from a pouch full of different foods, and if you feed them the wrong food, they die, and you "regret it." Rohrer adds some additional texture; the dead animals come back as "ghosts," and you can either feed them or avoid them. If you feed them, they just come back later. Lesson: Regret is pointless. Move on. Friday, there's a nearly completed video game. It doesn't give an inch. It doesn't tell you how to play it, how to get a high score, how to win. You have to figure that out for yourself. The game, in its own small way, is trying to reverse decades of infantilism in video games and culture, in which you get coins for doing stupid shit. It's not going to coddle: *awesome job!*

And when you do figure it out, it's a tiny epiphany, and maybe you understand something about regret that you didn't understand before. You're seeing its inner workings laid out before you, yet you still can't figure out *how he's doing it*. Ian Bogost calls this "procedural rhetoric": It's the art ghost in the machine. Asking where it comes from is like asking Hemingway, *Papa, why'd you put the comma there and not there?* Papa would turn around and punch you in the nose. The game is art not because it's beautiful like a poem, but because it's as difficult to explain as a poem—some ungraspable mélange of pixels, sounds, characters, and your own brain's response.

**mélange:**
Assortment.

And if you don't get it? Well, you're lost. So maybe you log on to Kotaku or IndieGames.com and chide Rohrer for "this little slice of emo pie." Or maybe you really unload: "Jason Rohrer is a pretentious jerk. Now, to be an indie art-film maker, you have to be pretty preten-tious. To be an indie art-game maker is another thing entirely. You have to have your head shoved so far up your own ass that you can eat your heart. Wow Jason Rohr. I hate you."

**ascetic:**
A spiritual practice wherein a person denies himself material objects and activities deemed unnecessary.

Rohrer is trying to make art in a medium that most peo-ple *don't even think is capable of art*. He can create this space of pure freedom, as artists have done in the past—isolation, in-trospection, ascetic poverty. But ultimately he has to send these works out into the world, and people have to respond to them. And right now the audience doesn't know what to do with them.

This is why video games need a figure like Rohrer so badly: an au-teur. A person of great energy, courage, ego, and, yeah, pretentiousness—pretentiousness with a purpose—to just show up every day and sit in his broken office chair, the one held together with the rubber band and the clothespin, and read the nasty comments about him online, and laugh so hard that he almost scissors his chair into plastic confetti, and then open the coding window on his shitty laptop and conjure that image of a disapproving, cranky cultural critic, "cracking the whip in the back of my mind," before launching into work on his next game, a game that's itching for a fight—difficult, heady, a game inspired by the philosopher W. V. Quine—a game about "consciousness and isolation and some other things I can point at desperately but cannot quite name."

**Let's Pause Here•••▶**  What is your initial response to Fagone's article? Does the possibility of games becoming a meaningful form of media intrigue or even excite you? Do you feel that there's a possibility that one day we will interact with our machines in meaningful ways, as Fagone suggests, or will it always just be a machine taking our input and giving us feedback? If games were to become meaningful, would you play them?

**Let's Take It Further•••▼**

1. If you were the author of this essay, what would you have asked Jason Rohrer about his life, his philosophy, or any other question related to this article's topic?

2. Several people in the essay—including the Ubisoft designer, Clint Hocking, and even Fagone himself—claim that Passage made them cry. Why is it so strange to think of this emotion being associated with video games? How are video games different from other media and art forms (movies, music, paintings, or theater, to name a few) that regularly make people emotional? What would a game have to do to engage a person on such a deeply emotional level?

3. Visit Jason Rohrer's website (http://hcsoftware.sourceforge.net/jason-rohrer) and read more about his philosophies on games, life, and the lifestyle he has chosen for himself and his family. Do you agree or disagree with his worldview and values? Do you like that he wants to make games legitimate and meaningful (and the reasons he gives for this desire), or do you see it as pointless?

4. Why do you think that it might be important if machines (and more specifically video games) could make us feel? If Rohrer and the others like him who are described in this article succeed at making games "matter," as well as making our interactions with machines more "meaningful," how might this be a positive or a negative development? Be sure to consider the fact that other forms of mass media already have the ability to evoke intense emotional responses from their consumers.

5. Download and play the game described at the beginning of the essay, Passage (simply Google "Passage Game"). What was the experience of playing this game like for you? How was it different from or similar to the way Fagone and others described it? Was it an emotional experience, or not?

**6.** Download any of Jason Rohrer's games from his website (they are all free, but you can choose to donate). Play the game a few times, read his "creator's statement," and write a review of the game, keeping in mind that you should describe the game, how it's played, and what—if any—emotional reaction you had to it.

# mash**it**UP

Here is a series of essay and discussion topics that draw connections between multiple selections within the chapter. They also suggest outside texts to include in your essay or discussion. Feel free to bring in further outside texts, remembering the variety of texts (beyond articles) available to you.

**1.** Revisit the cartoon "Award Worship" and watch an awards ceremony. Then compare the manner in which an awards ceremony is produced (paying special attention to the "red carpet" portion of the show) to the manner in which a news broadcast is produced. Which is the bigger event, and why do you think that is? Are awards results featured on "regular" news shows (i.e., not purely entertainment news)? Create a video or print collage that compares the difference in each type of show's footage that you locate.

**2.** If the "Team Edward/Team Jacob" debate, and the *Twilight* phenomenon in general, is any indication of our cultural obsessions (as Lipton argues it is), in what ways are these obsessions sexual in nature? What other major popular culture phenomena mirror the inappropriate objectification of young people to society as a whole (rather than, say, marketing teens to teens)?

**3.** Many times when a form of media actually gets its audience to shift its opinions on a subject (such as relationships, or the capabilities of the law or medicine), a name is given to it, such as "the *CSI* Effect" or "The *Notting Hill* Effect." Locate another form of mass media and discuss the ways in which you have noticed it changing the minds of its audience (its viewers, listeners, or subscribers). What would you name the "effect" that it has on its audience?

**4.** Revisit the essay, "The *Notting Hill* Effect" and compare the author's description of romantic comedies to the genre of romantic movies that attempts to upend the common notion of "love at first sight," such as *Juno* or *500 Days of Summer*. In what ways to these films go against the ideas of rom-coms, as outlined by Derbyshire in his essay? How do they succeed in illustrating more realistic romantic relationships? Which of the two types of romantic movies are better entertainment, and why?

5. Research on IMDB.com the "17 Best Romantic Comedies" as chosen by the website's viewers and film critics. Read the summaries of each and see how many of the most recent films are "unrealistic" about love (as Derbyshire asserts) and how many are more cynical or "realistic" in their representation of love and relationships. Is there a notable trend in these films toward one view over another? If so, which direction do these films appear to be heading? Do you see this as a positive or negative development, and why?

6. The issue of media ethics was raised several times throughout this chapter. The debate, as it turns out, assumes that our media has the power to influence our thoughts and opinions. If that is the case, then what is the media's obligation to "get it right," and how (if at all) should they be held accountable? How much of the debate should be turned back on the audience itself? Do we have a responsibility, as consumers of media, to identify and remember what is fiction and what is reality, or does the responsibility lie solely with the media?

7. Compare the concept at work in the cartoon "Digital Communication" (located in the Social Media chapter) to the Jason Fagone essay "The Video-Game Programmer Saving Our 21st-Century Souls." How are the two central ideas of each piece saying the same thing? And how are they different? Can both ideas be correct, or is one more accurate, in your opinion?

8. Search some of the other "indie" video game programmers mentioned in the Fagone article and play one of their games. How was the experience different from playing a Rohrer game? In what ways was it similar? Who do you think is the better programmer, and why?

9. Search YouTube for the "Don't tase me, bro" video mentioned in the Fagone article. What was your emotional response to the video as you viewed it? Next, visit Jason Rohrer's page and download his response, "Police Brutality." How is Rohrer responding to the video (by using video games as a mass media tool), and what does his game ask players to do in response to the police brutality depicted in the YouTube video? What do you feel his opinion is on the video, based on his game? Are you in agreement, or do you disagree? Did your opinion change after playing his game?

**Let's Connect •••▶** 📘 "Like" our Facebook page for free, up-to-date, additional readings, discussions, and writing ideas on the topic of the mass media. Join other students and teachers across the country sharing in an online discussion of popular culture events. *American Mashup* is on Facebook at www.facebook.com/americanmashup.

# Chapter 6

# Sexuality and Relationships

## Making the Cultural Connection

In America, we have a strange relationship with sex. Our cultural perceptions of sex and sexuality are simultaneously puritanical and freewheeling. On the one hand, our culture is hypersexual. Everywhere we turn, we are met with sexualized images of men and women selling us products, showing us how to look beautiful, reminding us of this most basic aspect of our nature. Our malls have Victoria's Secret. Our buses have ads for shows such as *Desperate Housewives*, where the female stars stare at passersby with sultry looks on their faces. The dashing men of AMC's hit show *Mad Men* have little more than sex and advertisement on the brain, and women swoon over their characters. Television shows abound that feature sex as their primary subject matter—*Big Love*, *The L Word*, and *Real Sex*, to name just a few. Late night commercials remind us that we're single and should be looking for a romantic fling. Website ads point us to places to meet "willing" men and women.

On the other hand, ours is a culture that also likes to pretend as though sex is not constantly on our minds. We rarely speak of sex publicly, and when we do it's considered scandalous or in bad taste. Preachers and community leaders warn of the pitfalls of sex, of the monumental devastation sex can cause in someone's life. When public figures—whether celebrities or politicians—stray from their marriages or have affairs, we are quick to tear them down and strip them of their power. We do this because they remind us of the reality of our existence in America. In a highly sexualized culture, it would stand to reason that people will succumb to the many temptations constantly presented to them.

As if the shows, the movies, the television ads for alcohol, and the Internet pornography weren't enough, we have other cultural events, such as Halloween or Spring Break, that have become little more than veiled excuses to allow people to dress and act in ways they normally wouldn't in "real life." When it comes to Halloween, for example, everything, particularly in the realm of female costumes, is "sexy." There are sexy cops and sexy witches, sexy fairies and sexy athletes, sexy sailors and sexy animals. Everywhere we look, it's sex, sex, sex. We have public school teachers sleeping with their students, *Girls Gone Wild*, *To Catch a Predator*, lurid public affairs, football stars and congressmen texting nude pictures of

themselves, and senators who troll for affairs on Craigslist. We have websites like "Hot or Not?" and Facebook and smartphone apps designed solely for flirtation.

The conundrum of living in the United States and navigating our culture's dual infatuation and repulsion toward sex is trying to figure out the real role that sex plays in our lives. If we cannot speak of it publicly (other than to denounce someone's sexual activities for being different than our own), then where and when can we? That is the purpose of this chapter: to afford you the opportunity to reflect on sex, sexuality, and their meaning in our lives. We will discuss the nature of sex in America today, including the current sexual trends among teens and our latest public objects of desire. We will talk about the positive aspects of sex, as well as the potential dangers of some recent trends.

However, this chapter is more than simply about sex. It will also highlight the dilemma of sex versus love in our modern world, as well as relationships and their roles in our lives. It includes selections that speak to the issue of having a crush on someone that goes unnoticed, or romantic advice to help the lonely, single person find a mate. You might notice a trend in some of the selections that is probably not surprising: many of them allude to the troublesome state of marriage in our country, which currently has the highest divorce rate in the world (hovering around 50%). Instead of merely pointing out this well-known fact, the selections in the relationship portion of the chapter will focus on *why* the American institution of marriage is so threatened from within. Several of the essays will attempt to provide alternatives to traditional marriage or ways to tweak the existing structure so that couples might stay together longer. Some selections question the validity of monogamy, others explain the virtues of abstinence, and still others discuss the growing popular trend among young people of avoiding marriage altogether.

Because of our country's complex relationship with both sex and relationships, with sexual identity and the trends among our youth, this chapter will necessarily leave many subjects out. There are simply too many varieties of relationships and sexual lifestyles and practices to mention here, but these essays and multimedia texts are a starting point, a springboard from which the dialogue on sex, sexuality, and relationships can be discussed in open and meaningful ways. We will question what sex means to us as individuals and as a larger culture. We will ponder the validity of traditional relationships and look at their modern alternatives in an effort to define and discuss the nature of relationships and the many ways in which love and lust intertwine.

The important thing to keep in mind, however, isn't just that sex and sexuality are ever-present in our society, but also why. Why is it that we Americans like to think about sex, to watch sex, even to have sex, but then we bristle at the mention of sex education or young people experimenting with one another? What does it say about our society that we don't like to speak publicly about sex, but then we express outrage when the teen pregnancy rate suddenly spikes or we hear of yet another adult exploiting her power to take advantage of children? Who is really to blame? Do we indict our schools and our television stations? Should we regress to more "pure" times when both men and women dressed more conservatively and television shows offered us safe yet bland programming? Do we throw our hands up at the state of marriage today, or do we try to consider realistic ways to update and modernize marriage to better match our country's current culture? Is there wisdom in waiting to marry? Can young people have meaningful relationships? These, among others, are the topics we will explore in this chapter.

# And the Love?

**Angel Boligan**

Angel Boligan is a political cartoonist and conceptual artist. He is the daily editorial cartoonist for the *El Universal* newspaper in Mexico City and is one of Mexico's top, award-winning cartoonists. His work is internationally syndicated by Cagle Cartoons. This cartoon was first published in *El Universal* on October 19, 2010.

www.boligan.com

## Thinking About Sexuality

Take a moment to look at the cartoon. Like most political cartoons, this drawing is attempting to make a statement about a topic that is popular in our culture. This cartoon's subject matter, which can be discerned at a glance, is the concept of love versus lust, or even noncommittal sex versus sex in the context of a relationship. This is a topic that has been debated over the years, but seems to be more and more relevant as our culture becomes ever more sexualized by exposure to sex on television, in film, and, of course, on the Internet.

Sex—the act of two people being physically intimate with each other—is of course a topic of great interest to all humans, but in our culture it appears to some as though the divide between sex and love grows greater with each passing day. People say they want love—that they are looking for Mr. or Mrs. Right—but the images we are shown most frequently are sexualized images (scantily clad women and hulking, semi-nude men) of people who are held up as the model men and women we should aspire to be.

While sex is most certainly a part of the human condition in that it is something nearly all humans will experience in one form or another, it becomes much more complicated when love is introduced into the equation. For some people, sex is easier if love is out of the equation. And yet, when this occurs, others who are romantics see the sexual activity as crude. Some people cannot fathom having sex outside the context of a meaningful and committed relationship. These are the two poles, the opposite extremes in point of view when it comes to sex and relationships.

Take a closer look at the cartoon. Notice some of the finer details. Cupid is standing behind the couple, obviously downtrodden, as evidenced by his posture. That image, as well as the blinking hotel sign, proves that the sexual encounter that is about to take place will contain very little, if any, actual "love." Also, notice the outfits that both people are wearing. What does it further say about the encounter that the woman is dressed the way she is? What does it say about the encounter that the man is dressed the way he is, and that he's gesturing for Cupid—a universal character associated with love—to get lost? Based on the cartoon's title, as well as the action being depicted in the cartoon, what do you think Angel Boligan is trying to say about the state of modern love in our culture? What leads you to believe that this is his point? Does Boligan's opinion become clearer in the actions of the man or the woman? Either way, what does it mean for modern love, and even for our culture's public opinion of sex, that Boligan has drawn up this cartoon to comment on the state of love versus lust in our culture? What solution, if any, do you believe Boligan might be offering up? Or do you believe it is more of a simple comment on our highly sexualized culture?

Now, take a moment to consider your opinion on the issue of love versus lust in both popular culture and in college culture. What does it say about our culture that college and sex seem to be synonymous with one another? What about the theory that many people look to find their life partners while attending college? Which of the two does college culture, and even American popular culture, seem to favor over the other?

# Is Sex Interesting?
Wallace Shawn

**Let's Start Here•••▶** While it may come as a surprise that there are people who make a living writing specifically about sex, there is, in reality, a vast market that caters to people and their sexual interests that goes beyond lingerie stores, adult bookshops, and Internet pornography sites. In fact, there is an entire genre of literature that seeks to understand, on a scholarly and meaningful level, the role that sex plays in our lives and culture beyond the mere biological purpose for the act of intercourse.

Despite this fact, there is still such a taboo in our culture against speaking publicly about sex that the author of the following essay feels it necessary—even after more than 40 years of seriously writing about sex—to justify his line of work to his readers. Still, the essay is more than just one writer justifying his preferred writing subject. It is also a candid discussion of the reasons why sex is still considered a taboo topic in a country where sex and sexuality are obviously of great interest to our culture.

As you read the essay, observe the ways in which Wallace Shawn discusses why it's even necessary to write about sex. See if you can determine what he believes to be the cause of the cultural taboo on sex in public dialogue. Also, take note of the way in which Mr. Shawn manages to break down sex as an important and necessary part of nature, regardless of one's personal beliefs toward sex and its appropriateness in various venues.

---

Wallace Shawn is an American actor, writer, author, voice artist, and stand-up comedian. His best-known film roles include Vizzini in *The Princess Bride* (1987) and debate teacher Mr. Hall in *Clueless* (1995). Shawn has pursued a parallel career as a playwright whose work is often dark, politically charged, and controversial. The following essay first appeared in *Harper's* magazine in the August 2009 issue.

For whatever reason, and I don't remember how it happened, I am now what people call "sixty-four years old," and I have to admit that I started writing about sex almost as soon as I realized that it was possible to do so—say, at the age of fourteen—and I still do it, even though I was in a way the wrong age then, and in a different way I guess I'm the wrong age now. Various people who have liked me or cared about me—people who have believed in my promise as a writer—have hinted to me at different times in my life that an excessive preoccupation with the subject of sex has harmed or even ruined my writing. They've implied that it was sad, almost pitiful, that an adolescent obsession should have been allowed to **marginalize** what they optimistically had hoped might have been a serious body of work.

> **marginalize:** Make unimportant or trivial.

Meanwhile, people I don't know very well have tended over all those decades to break into a very particular smile, one I recognize now, when they learn that I've written something that deals with sex—a winking smile that suggests a trivial, silly, but rather amusing topic has been mentioned. I suppose it goes without saying that James Joyce, D. H. Lawrence, and others were expanding the scope of literature and redrawing humanity's picture of itself when they approached this subject at the start of the twentieth century. But by the time I came along, many of my friends were embarrassed on my behalf precisely because the topic I was writing about seemed so closely associated with an earlier era.

Why is sex interesting to write about? To some, that might seem like a rather dumb question. Obviously, when someone interested in geology is alone in a room, he or she tends to think a lot about rocks. And I imagine that when many geologists were children, they put pictures having to do with rocks on their bedroom walls. And I would have to guess that geologists find it fun to sit at a desk and write about rocks. So, yes, I find it enjoyable. But apart from that, I still find myself wondering, "Why is it interesting to write about sex?"

**bourgeois:**

Middle-class people defined by materialistic pursuits and a concern for being respected.

One reason is that sex is shocking. Yes, it's still shocking, after all these years. At least, it's shocking to me. Even after all these years, most bourgeois people, including me, still walk around with an image of themselves in their heads that doesn't include—well—that. I'm vaguely aware that while going about my daily round of behavior I'm making use of various mammalian processes, such as breathing, digesting, and getting from place to place by hobbling about on those odd legs we have. But the fact is that when I form a picture of myself, I see myself doing the sorts of things that humans do and only humans do—things like hailing a taxi, going to a restaurant, voting for a candidate in an election, or placing receipts in various piles and adding them up. But if I'm unexpectedly reminded that my soul and body are capable of being swept up in an activity that pigs, flies, wolves, lions, and tigers also engage in, my normal picture of myself is violently disrupted. In other words, consciously, I'm aware that I'm a product of evolution and I'm part of nature. But my unconscious mind is still partially wandering in the early nineteenth century and doesn't know these things yet. Writing about sex is really a variant of what Wordsworth did; that is, it's a variant of writing about nature or, as we call it now, "the environment." Sex is "the environment" coming inside, coming into our homes and taking root inside our own minds. It comes out of the mud where the earliest creatures swam; it comes up and appears in our brains in the form of feelings and thoughts. It sometimes appears with such great force that it sweeps other feelings and other thoughts completely out of the way. And on a daily basis it quietly and patiently approaches the self and winds itself around it and through it until no part of the self is unconnected to it.

Sex is of course an extraordinary meeting place of reality and dream, and it's also—what is not perhaps exactly the same thing—an extraordinary meeting place of the meaningful and the meaningless. The big toe, for example, is one part of the human body, human flesh shaped and constructed in a particular way. The penis is another part of the body, located not too far away from the big toe and built out of fundamentally the same materials. The act of sex, the particular shapes of the penis and the vagina, are the way they are because natural selection has made them that way. There may be an adaptive value to each particular choice that evolution made, but from our point of view as human beings living our lives, the various details present themselves to us as arbitrary. It can only be seen as funny that men buy magazines containing pictures of breasts but not magazines with pictures of knees or forearms. It can only be seen as funny that demagogues give speeches denouncing men who insert their penises into other men's anuses—and then go home to insert their own penises into their wives' vaginas! (One might have thought it obvious that either both of these acts are completely outrageous or neither of them is.) And yet the interplay and

**arbitrary:**

Existing by chance, or random.

**demagogues:**

People in positions of power who exploit popular prejudices and false claims.

permutations of the apparently meaningless, the desire to penetrate anus or vagina, the glimpse of the naked breast, the hope of sexual intercourse or the failure of it, lead to joy, grief, happiness, or desperation for the human creature.

> **permutations:**
> Major or important changes by rearranging existing elements.

Perhaps it is the power of sex that has taught us to love the meaningless and thereby turn it into the meaningful. Amazingly, the love of what is arbitrary (which one could alternatively describe as the love of reality) is something we human beings are capable of feeling, and perhaps even what we call the love of the beautiful is simply a particular way of exercising this remarkable ability. So it might not be absurd to say that if you love the body of another person, if you love another person, if you love a meadow, if you love a horse, if you love a painting or a piece of music or the sky at night, then the power of sex is flowing through you.

Yes, some people go through life astounded every day by the beauty of forests and animals; some are astounded more frequently by the beauty of art; and others by the beauty of other human beings. But science could one day discover that the ability to be astounded by the beauty of other human beings came first, and to me it seems implausible to imagine that these different types of astonishment or appreciation are psychologically unrelated.

Sex has always been known to be such a powerful force that fragile humanity can't help but be terribly nervous in front of it, so powerful barriers have been devised to control it—taboos of all varieties, first of all, and then all the emotions subsumed under the concepts of jealousy and possessiveness, possessiveness being a sort of anticipatory form of jealousy. (A recent survey of married people in the United States found that when asked the question "What is very important for a successful marriage?" the quality mentioned most frequently—by 93 percent—was "faithfulness," while "happy sexual relationship" came in with only 70 percent. In other words, to 23 percent of the respondents, it seemed more important that they and their partner should not have sex with others than that they themselves should enjoy sex.) Sex seems capable of creating anarchy, and those who are committed to predictability and order find themselves inevitably either standing in opposition to it or trying to pretend that it doesn't even exist.

> **subsumed:**
> Placed within something larger or more comprehensive.

My local newspaper, the *New York Times*, for example, does not include images of naked people. Many of its readers might enjoy it much more if it did, but those same readers still might not buy it if such images were in it, because it could no longer present the portrait of a normal, stable, adequate world—a world not ideal but still good enough—which it is the function of the *Times* to present every day. Nudity somehow implies that anything could happen, but the *Times* is committed to telling its readers that many things will not happen, because the world is under control, benevolent people are looking out for us, the situation is not as bad as we tend to think, and although problems do exist, they

> **benevolent:**
> Defined by doing good things.

can be solved by wise rulers. The contemplation of nudity or sex could tend to bring up the alarming idea that at any moment human passions might rise up and topple the world we know.

But perhaps it would be a good thing if people saw themselves as a part of nature, connected to the environment in which they live. Sex can be a humbling, equalizing force. It's often been noted that naked people do not wear medals, and weapons are forbidden inside the pleasure garden. When the sexuality of the terrifying people we call "our leaders" is for some reason revealed, they lose some of their power—sometimes all of it— because we're reminded (and, strangely, we need reminding) that they are merely creatures like the ordinary worm or beetle that creeps along at the edge of the pond. Sex really is a nation of its own. Those whose allegiance is given to sex at a certain moment withdraw their loyalty temporarily from other powers. It's a symbol of the possibility that we might all defect for one reason or another from the obedient columns in which we march.

**Let's Pause Here•••▶** What are your initial reactions to the basic premise of Shawn's essay—that sex is a logical and even necessary topic of public discussion? Do you feel he does a good job of proving the legitimacy of writing about sex as a topic to be taken seriously? Do you agree with the idea that sex and sexuality should be seen as less taboo by our society? Why or why not?

**Let's Take It Further•••▼**

1. Shawn begins his essay by stating that most people—even his friends—view writing about sex as "trivial" and "silly." What might be trivial or silly about it? And, if you see it as trivial or silly, what do you feel is the appropriate venue to seriously discuss sex and its relevance in our lives?

2. Shawn also makes the statement that "sex is shocking." If that's true, what is so shocking about sex? Or is it just shocking when people speak on the subject publicly, as Shawn has done throughout his entire writing career? Why, after more than 40 years of writing on the subject, is it still necessary for Shawn to prove his writing is "legitimate"?

3. Based on his tone, as well as how he constructs his argument, can you determine who Mr. Shawn intends to reach as his audience? Is he trying to engage people who are for or against a public discussion of sex? Do his vocabulary, examples, or lines of logic reveal the age group he intends to engage? How might the conversation be different if it were originally published elsewhere?

4. Do you agree with the idea that sex is simply a part of nature, as this essay argues? Why do you agree or disagree with this statement? If it *is* a part of nature, like the other natural activities Shawn outlines, then what is it about discussing sex that makes it such a shocking or titillating part of nature? Can you locate examples in popular culture of how people are publicly shocked (or pretend to be) when discussing human sexuality?

5. Shawn likens the parts of the anatomy associated with sex (human genitalia) to the rest of our bodies, saying that *all* parts of our body are fundamentally made of the same materials. And so, the forearm is virtually the same as a breast. The big toe is basically the same as the penis. If that is true, then what is it about our "private" parts that makes them so

mentally stimulating? Is it the fact that they are kept private? What makes some body parts more intriguing than others?

6. The author of this essay also alludes to societal taboos (or "powerful barriers" against certain practices) concerning sex and sexuality. People feel these activities are to be kept secret, despite the fact that large swaths of the population engage in them. What are some of our current sexual taboos in American culture? What makes them taboo? Research and describe sexual practices/beliefs that were at one time considered taboo that are now quite normal (or, conversely, practices that were once normal that are now considered taboo). Explain what you think accounts for these shifts in the perceived normalcy or strangeness of these practices.

7. Locate the sexual survey put out by the Kinsey Institute (one of the leading institutes of sexual study in the United States) in 2010, as well as its accompanying report. (This information can be found at kinseyinstitute.org.) Note the ways society has shifted from earlier surveys, which can also be found at the website. Discuss the findings of the most recent survey and how well you believe it reflects the reality of sex in America among younger people, based on your own research (i.e., a similar survey of students at your college).

8. One of the most intriguing points about sex and its power in our culture that Shawn makes is in his observation that "when the sexuality of the terrifying people we call 'our leaders' is for some reason revealed, they lose some of their power—or sometimes all of it—because we're reminded...that they are merely creatures like the ordinary worm or beetle." There is no shortage of examples of people in positions of power who lose their stature because their sexual affairs come to light. Locate one such leader and describe the position he or she once held, what particular element of his or her sexuality was discovered, and how it affected his or her career. Also, explain why you think this particular person's personal life led to his or her downfall (in other words, how it was at odds with the person's public persona).

9. Create a video or image collage of popular culture reactions in the mass media to a public figure who broke a societal taboo regarding sex. In an accompanying essay, describe the situation, as well as why there was such a public outcry. What was the outcome of the event? Do you feel that the public figure in question deserved to be publicly decried, or should the person have been treated in a kinder manner, and why? Find an example of the media treating another public sex scandal differently and explain what you see as the reason for a different treatment.

# Sex at Dawn: Why Monogamy Goes Against Our Nature    Thomas Rogers

**Let's Start Here•••** ▶ In a culture as obsessed with sex and sexuality as our seems to be, where sexual images permeate virtually every aspect of our daily lives, there appears to be a new sexual revolution, of sorts, occurring beneath our noses. The fact that a highly sexualized (or at least sexually charged) culture places such a high cultural value on monogamy might baffle some people. And yet it is one of the most strongly held points of view when it comes to relationships—that we and our partners are to remain monogamous.

In the following essay, which is one part book review, one part interview, Thomas Rogers explains the theory behind a recently released book that attempts to get to the root of the cultural currency that we lend monogamy, as well as where this concept stemmed from in our past. He also sits down with one of the book's two authors and asks pointed questions in an effort to force the author to back many of the claims made in the book. The outcome is a candid—albeit possibly disturbing or disappointing—discussion of the role and purpose of monogamy in American culture. As you read his essay, note the way Rogers illustrates the book's main points, as well as the types of questions he asks of Christopher Ryan, one of *Sex at Dawn*'s two authors.

---

Thomas Rogers is a regular contributor to *Salon*, where he writes on topics that include sexuality, popular culture, politics, and celebrities. The following interview and book review were first published at Salon.com on June 27, 2010.

According to Christopher Ryan and Cacilda Jethà, the authors of the new book *Sex at Dawn: The Prehistoric Origins of Modern Sexuality*, the state of the American marriage is awfully grim. We have a stratospheric divorce rate and a surge of single parents. Couples who stay together are often trapped in sexless, passionless unions. An entire industry—from couples therapy to sex supplements—has emerged to help people "rekindle the spark" without straying from the confines of monogamy.

But Ryan and Jethà also have a theory for what's causing this misery: From a biological perspective, men and women simply aren't meant to be in lifelong monogamous unions. In *Sex at Dawn*, which uses evidence gathered from human physiology, archaeology, primate biology and anthropological studies of pre-agricultural tribes from around the world, they argue that monogamy and the nuclear family are more recent inventions than most of us would expect—and far less natural than we've come to believe.

Before the advent of agriculture, they argue, prehistoric humans lived in a much less sexually possessive culture, without the kind of lifelong coupling that currently exists in most countries. They also point to the bonobos, our closest relatives, who live in egalitarian and

**egalitarian:**
The belief in equality for all humans.

peaceful groups and have astronomical rates of sexual interaction, as evidence of our natural inclinations. While Ryan and Jethà's book (Ryan is a psychologist, and Jethà a practicing psychiatrist, in Spain) is often a bit scattered and hard to follow, its provocative argument is also impossible to dismiss.

Salon spoke to Ryan over the phone from Barcelona about the problem with American marriages, why gay men understand relationships better than straight men, and the hidden meaning of human testicle size.

*You paint a bleak picture of the state of marriage in the West, particularly in the United States. What makes it so bad?*

Marriage in the West isn't doing very well because it's in direct confrontation with the evolved reality of our species. What we argue in the book is that the best way to increase marital stability, which in the modern world is an important part of social stability, is to develop a more tolerant and realistic understanding of human sexuality and how human sexuality is being distorted by our modern conception of marriage. Certainly growing up in the '70s and '80s there were very few kids I knew whose parents weren't divorced at least once. The economic, emotional, psychological cost of fractured relationships is a major problem in American society—with single mothers and single-parent families.

*You argue that much of this misery stems from changes that occurred when humans developed agriculture, around 8000 B.C. What happened?*

The advent of agriculture changed everything about human society, from sexuality to politics to economics to health to diet to exercise patterns to work-versus-rest patterns. It introduced the notion of property into sexuality. Property wasn't a very important consideration when people were living in small, foraging groups where most things were shared, including food, childcare, shelter and defense. It makes perfect sense that sexuality would also be shared—why wouldn't it be when paternity wasn't an issue?

When you have agriculture, men started to worry about whether or not certain children were theirs biologically, because they wanted to leave their accumulated property to their own child. At that point, people also made a very clear connection between sexual behavior and birth. Lots of people didn't have a very clear understanding of the cause and effect of sex and birth, but when you have domesticated animals living side by side with people, they start to notice that the characteristics of a certain male that has mated with a certain female show up in the offspring.

*One of the central ideas of much biological and genetic theory is that animals will expend more energy protecting those they're genetically related to—siblings, parents, offspring—as opposed to those they're not related to. Why wouldn't that apply to humans?*

There are many, many exceptions to that rule in nature. One of the exceptions we talk about in the book are the vampire bats that share blood with each other. They go out and they suck the blood at night and then they come back to the cave and the bats that didn't get any blood will receive blood from other bats. They share, and that has nothing to do with genetic connection. And in terms of animals that are much more closely related to humans, when you look at bonobos and their promiscuous interaction, it's virtually impossible for a male to know which of his offspring are related to him biologically. So to say that there's this inherent concern with paternity within our species, I just don't see evidence for that.

*Does this mean that humans didn't form couples before the advent of agriculture?*

Because human groups at the time knew each other so well and spent their lives together and were all interrelated and depended upon each other for everything, they really knew each other much better than most of us know our sexual partners today. We don't argue that people didn't form very special relationships—you can see this even in chimps and bonobos and other primates, but that bond doesn't necessarily extend to sexual exclusivity. People have said that we're arguing against love—but we're just saying that this insistence that love and sex always go together is erroneous.

**exclusivity:**
Being exclusive, or devoted to one thing.

**erroneous:**
Containing errors.

*Given that these people have been dead for thousands of years, and we don't have a fossil record of sexual activity, isn't this hard to prove?*

The evidence comes from several different areas. We look at preagricultural people who have been studied today and horticultural people who have been studied by anthropologists. There's a fair amount of information about the sexuality of people who haven't been deeply exposed to Western influence. There are accounts from travelers and colonialists, first-contact accounts from historical records, that we rely on. But you can also extract a great deal of information from the human body itself—from the design of the penis to the volume of the testicles to the sperm-producing potential of the testicular tissue and the way we have sex.

*What does our testicle size tell us about the way we have sex?*

Our testicles aren't as big as those of chimps and bonobos, but our ejaculation is about four times as big in terms of volume. The theory is that when males compete on the level of the sperm cell, they develop much larger testicles, because in promiscuous animals, the sperm of the different males is competing with the sperm of other males to get to be the first to the egg. And the fact that our testicles are not as small relative to our body as the monogamous gibbon or gorillas reinforces the idea that we have been non-monogamous for a long time.

Plus the design of our penis strongly suggests that it evolved to create a vacuum in the female reproductive system, thereby pulling out the semen of anyone who was there previously. There are all kinds of indications of sperm competition in the human male. And one of the things that we suggest in the book that no one else has suggested is that because the testicles are genetically the part of the body that adapts fastest to environmental pressure, it's quite possible that our testicles are much smaller than they were as recently as fifteen or twenty thousand years ago, to reflect the historical cultural imposition of monogamy. And of course we all know that sperm count is dropping precipitously even as we speak.

> **precipitously:**
> A steep descent.

*But that drop in sperm count has been reported over the last few decades, and I don't think American culture has becoming less sexualized since the 1950s—I think the opposite is true.*

Well, it's hard to say because it's only been measured for about the last 100 years. So it's very difficult to know what was happening before that. But yeah, it does seem to be plummeting faster and faster, and there are indications that it has a lot to do with industrial contaminants in the environment, and antibiotics and growth hormones in the food supply and so on.

But I think there's this bifurcation of American culture where you've got the liberalization on one side with states passing gay marriage, but then you have other states veering off in the other direction. I think the Bill Clinton and Lewinsky situation could

> **bifurcation:**
> Division into two parts or branches.

have been such a great opportunity for the culture to grow up instead of wasting so much time and money and political capital in this investigation of a victimless crime. If the Clintons had gone on their *60 Minutes* interview and just said, "You know what, our sex life is nobody's business but ours," I think the country would have been so much better off.

*I think from a cultural standpoint the idea of strict monogamy has far less currency within the gay male world than it does within the straight world. I'm a gay man, and I think probably about half the gay male couples I know are in open relationships. Why do you think that is?*

First of all, they're both men, so they both know what it's like to be a man. They both know from experience that love and sex are two very different things, and it seems that for women the experience of sexuality is much more embedded in narrative, in emotion, in emotional intimacy. But also it's really hard to judge what women would be like if they hadn't been persecuted for the last five or six thousand or ten thousand years for any hint of infidelity.

Gay men in the United States have also by definition gone through a process of self-examination. The whole process of coming out is a process of integrating sexuality into your life in a way that takes courage, and it's not something that happens naturally. I think gay people have an advantage because they've already gone through a process of saying: "Look, my sexuality is what it is. I'm not ashamed of it. I'm going to live openly and in accord with it." That puts them on a different level than most heterosexual people who are able to pass along and pretend that they fit into the normal parameters.

*It seems like many Americans, in particular, have a very strong notion that a marriage must remain monogamous at all costs—and that any infidelity is grounds for divorce. In other countries, like France, for example, that doesn't seem to be the case.*

I've been living off and on for almost 20 years here in Barcelona, and from outside, the United States looks very adolescent, in a positive and negative sense. There's its adolescent energy—its idealism—but there's also an immaturity and intolerance toward the ambiguity of life and the complexity of relationships. The American sense of relationships and sexuality tends to be very informed by Hollywood: It's all about the love story. But the love story ends at the wedding and doesn't go into the 40 years that comes after that.

**ambiguity:**
Uncertainty.

*So if monogamous marriage isn't the right arrangement for us, what is?*

We're not really arguing for any particular arrangement. We don't even really know what to do with this information ourselves. What we're trying to do in the book is give people a more accurate sense of where we came from, why we are the way we are, and why certain aspects of life feel like a bad fit. I think a lot of people make a commitment when they're in love, which is a sort of a delusional state that lasts a couple of years at most. I think it was Goethe who said that love is an unreal thing, and marriage is a real thing, and any confusion of the real with the unreal always leads to disaster.

All we're really hoping for is to encourage more tolerance and more open discussion between men and women about sexuality and about marriage, and to come to see that marriage isn't about sex. It's about things that are much deeper and more lasting than sex, especially if you have children. And the American insistence on mixing love and sex and expecting passion to last forever is leading to great suffering that we think is tragic and unnecessary.

**Let's Pause Here•••▶** Based on his questions, do you feel that Rogers agrees or disagrees with the theories put forth by the book *Sex at Dawn* and its authors? Which question or questions lead you to believe that he is siding with them or challenging their views? How do you feel about the book, based on the reading that Rogers gives of it in the book review portion of the essay? Is it something that you would be interested in reading? Why or why not?

**Let's Take It Further•••▼**

1. Thomas Rogers begins his review by pointing out the "awfully grim" state of marriage in America today. What does Rogers mean by this statement? Why is this a sentiment that occurs so often in the media, as well as in several essays in this chapter? Do you agree that the state of marriage is grim? If so, why? If not, why not?

2. Based on the examples he gives and the language he uses in his responses, to whom is Christopher Ryan trying to appeal with his argument? To whom is Rogers, the interviewer and reviewer of Ryan's book, trying to appeal with his presentation of the book? Are they in agreement or do they hold different viewpoints on the topic of monogamy? Use examples from the selection to back your point.

3. Christopher Ryan, when asked about the origins of monogamy, points out that the practice likely first arose from humans becoming an agricultural society. At this point in our history, Ryan argues, "men started to worry about whether or not children were theirs biologically, because they wanted to leave their accumulated property to their own child." Does this explanation make sense to you as a turning point in human history? Why or why not? How would it have made sense in earlier hunter-gatherer periods of history to be concerned (or not to be concerned) with the paternity of one's offspring?

4. What is your opinion of the various biological and evolutionary examples given by Ryan throughout the interview? Which of them made sense, and which of them went against logic? Did the interview change your opinion on the issue of monogamy, or does your opinion remain the same? Why or why not?

5. Ryan also states that before the advent of agriculture, human groups spent so much time together that they actually "knew each other much better than most of us know our sexual

partners today." Do you find any truth in that statement? How can Ryan make that statement, and can you prove or disprove it with any modern-day examples?

6. Why do you think that the Clintons did not publicly declare the words that Ryan suggested they should have ("Our sex life is nobody's business but ours")? Why would such an action have been fruitless or impossible? Or, might it have had the effect that Ryan claims it would?

7. Thomas Rogers, in his introduction and review of the new book, mentions the thriving sex and relationship industry that is designed to help monogamous couples put the spark back into their relationship. Research some of these companies and see how they profess to "rekindle the spark" in a monogamous relationship. Choose one or two that you think might actually be useful (remembering that the industry is made up of movies, books, therapists, "marital aids,"—in other words, toys—as well as TV shows, advice columns, and much more), and explain the ways you think these products might actually help and how they might accomplish that goal. Or, choose one or two of these services that you think would be useless in repairing an ailing marriage or committed relationship, and explain and describe the shortcomings of the service(s) or product(s) and why they would fail.

8. Based on Rogers's interpretation of *Sex at Dawn* and your own reading (which will require you to locate all or at least significant portions of the text), what questions would you ask the authors of this book that Rogers neglected to ask? List at least five questions, along with the explanation behind why you would ask each question. Also, for each question, discuss what you hope the answers to your questions might reveal, either in terms of flaws in the book's logic or ways the authors could better prove their points about monogamy.

9. In response to the interview's first question, Ryan tells Rogers, "the economic, emotional, and psychological cost of fractured relationships is a major problem in American society." It goes without saying (and can easily be proven) that the divorce rate in our country continues to climb. In fact, it would be a very rare occurrence for someone in modern America not to have been directly affected by divorce, either through her parents or the parents of someone who she is close to being divorced. If you have direct experience with divorce, explain and outline (giving specific examples) the various ways in which the divorce has heavy economic, emotional, and psychological costs, as Ryan asserts in his answer. You might even compare the outcomes of a divorce to the family dynamic of a nuclear family that is still together.

10. Christopher Ryan refers to America as a somewhat "adolescent" culture. In the negative sense, he believes that our culture dangerously ties love and sex together, and that we get these notions from Hollywood. His theory is that Hollywood romance films show impossibly romantic relationships and give people unrealistic ideals for love, relationships, and their partners, as evidenced by the fact that most romantic movies end at the wedding and show little to none of the actual marriage. If the marriage is the hard part, the part where relationships fracture, then it would make sense that Hollywood depicts this aspect of relationships as well. However, according to Ryan, they don't. Prove or disprove his theory by locating Hollywood films that depict not only the romantic years or months (or even days) leading up to a wedding, but also the years following. (See also "The *Notting Hill* Effect" in the "Mass Media" chapter.) How are marriages themselves (not weddings) depicted in films? Do they prove or disprove Ryan's statements about our adolescent outlook on relationships?

11. Conduct a multimedia interview (video/sound/images) that asks the respondents to explain the value of monogamy. Once you have interviewed enough people that an obvious trend (or trends) emerges, explain whether the trend and reasoning behind people's beliefs and values in monogamy match the explanations given by Ryan in his interview responses. How is he correct in his assertions of why we value monogamy? How, if at all, is he incorrect?

# Alarming Sex Trends Among Teens Today
### Shannon Lane

**Let's Start Here•••** ▶ Young people who are going through or have recently been through puberty are overwhelmed by hormonal changes in the body. This is not news. However, what *might be* news to some people is that every generation of young people to come of age in the United States—indeed, in the entire world—has its own trends in fashion, music, and, yes, even sex.

Of course, this is not surprising to the people who grew up when these trends were the norm, but for their parents (who surely had sexual trends of their own in their youth), the idea that their young adult children might be curious and experimenting can be terrifying. This is simply one of the great fears of parenthood: that a child might be engaging in sexual activity that is different from trends in the parents' own time. For some parents, the very idea that a child might be engaging in sexual activity of *any* kind is enough to pass shudders through their bodies.

Shannon Lane, the author of the following essay, is one such parent. In her essay, "Alarming Sex Trends Among Teens Today," she points out a couple of recent trends that took her by surprise. As you read the article, try to determine the authenticity of her claims. Are the trends she is highlighting trends of which you were aware? Regardless of whether you have heard of these trends (or others), see if you can understand and empathize with the points she is trying to make to parents who worry about their children being sexually active.

---

Shannon Lane is a regular contributor to *Helium*, a website devoted to citizen journalism, where she has published more than 150 articles on writing, publishing, parenting, sexuality, and gender identity. A self-proclaimed "Southern woman" who is proud of her North Carolina upbringing and traditional values, Lane has been designated a *Helium* "Marketplace Premier Writer." The following essay was first published to the *Helium* website on January 17, 2010.

I want to educate other parents of teens out there about two of the most disturbing sexual trends being promoted and practiced today. You can read Dr. Phil's transcripts about the many shows on the this subject. Other children have told me about these things as well. The children view these games as fun and innocent forms of interacting with their friends and peers. The Internet and cell phones are used at an alarming rate to sexually communicate pornographic materials. The children are not having physical intercourse through these channels and that is the main argument among their age group today. Pictures are not hurting anyone and no one is getting pregnant or passing around sexually transmitted diseases. Another very accepted form of physical contact is oral sex. This is very popular and encouraged among our teenage community. They will debate with adults on this issue that it is not much different than kissing someone on the mouth with their tongue and no one is getting pregnant.

Most disturbing is the ease of Internet. Adolescent pornography has exploded among young children who photograph themselves in what they truly believe is the privacy of their own home. By posting these images online they have a very false sense of security. With these actions they are gaining not only popularity among their peers but they have also found out that they can make money from them . . . Big Money. The new pimp of the today is the sixteen-year-old boys or girls that can acquire pornographic images and sell them out on the extremely open market. In their young minds, these are nothing more than harmless images. They do not completely understand the possible repercussions from such behavior. Young girls by the thousands and thousands have knowingly and willingly sold pornographic materials of themselves and others. These things are done directly under their parents' noses. With the deep knowledge and understanding of computer technologies these teens can drive the Internet like a bright red sports car. Passwords, secret e-mails, access from multiple computers. They know how to hide what they are doing. The small little cell phone in their pocket could be holding hundreds of images and never to be found without the proper password.

Another eye-opening conversation with a teen had me at a complete loss for words. This was when I learned about the very popular "Rainbow Party." A rainbow party is held and all participants are willing and aware that they will be engaging in an open forum of oral sex and random intercourse. The young ladies have a code of color now among them and it is widely understood. The color of a girl's lipstick is indicative of her willingness and ability to perform oral sex. The young men at the rainbow party will afterwards have the evidential marks of lipstick from the party activities. It is a competition among each gender as to how many different shades they can give and receive. A huge amount of pornographic pictures are circulating the Internet that captured these acts. The frightening part again is that these photos are not only a way to gain popularity from peers, but to benefit from the money that is being thrown around on the Internet. The new place to hide money is the ever-popular PayPal, very easy to set up and manage through different e-mail accounts. I just re-

**indicative:**
Serves to indicate.

ceived my debit card from PayPal, so now there is no need for anyone to leave a paper trail of financial exchanges. These children are starting these behaviors at unthinkable young ages. Do not think that for one minute it cannot happen to your child. It can happen to anyone's child. Their young impressionable minds are made for the ultimate adventures. They are so full of the unknown. Talk to them, be open to listening and not just hearing. Tell them about some of the fears you have for them. Let them know you care about their behavior and why. And most importantly that you understand the pressures they are under in their stage of life. They are normal, curious, and confused.

**Let's Pause Here•••▶**    Do you think that Lane's essay warrants the alarm that her tone (word usage) might suggest? Whether or not you were aware of current or recent teen sex trends, do you see them as a threat or a normal teen experience in sexual experimentation? Why or why not? Do you feel that Lane's generalizations (and occasional lack of evidence) give her piece credibility, or do they lessen her warning to parents? What sort of evidence would you like to see her present?

**Let's Take It Further•••▼**

1. Who do you think the intended audience of Lane's piece is supposed to be? How can you determine who her audience is? What do you think the purpose of her essay is for her audience? Is her tone merely informative, or is there more here than a simple informational piece? What is the overall message behind Lane's short essay?

2. Lane makes the assertion that young people who take part in exchanging pornographic photos and videos via cell phones and Internet connections argue that since they are "not having physical intercourse" through virtual channels, there is nothing dangerous about these activities. Do you agree with Lane's point about how young people justify this trend? What *is* the justification or logic that young people gave her, based on her essay? If you know of a different "popular" argument, what is it?

3. In another major point in her essay, Lane argues that young people compare oral sex to "not much different than kissing someone on the mouth with their tongue." Have you heard a similar argument to this as well? Or do sexually active young people consider oral sex to be an act of actual sex? Whether or not it is different, where do these definitions of sex come from?

4. According to Lane, young people not only share nude pictures and videos of themselves, but they do it in order to gain "popularity among their peers." If this is true, how would sharing nude pictures of oneself gain one popularity? In your own school experience (or those of young people whom you know), were people who took part in this activity deemed popular or shunned? Why?

5. Lane alludes to Dr. Phil's television show, which has featured many teen sex trends in recent years. Research Dr. Phil's transcript (printed accounts of each show's dialogue)

archives, as suggested by Lane, to see the many teen sex trends he has featured on his show. Define and describe a few of these sex trends that are featured on *Dr. Phil*. Which of the trends are worthy of parental alarm, and why? Which of these trends do not warrant parental alarm, and why? Support your opinion with outside sources.

**6.** Throughout her essay, Lane warns parents that their children do not understand the repercussions of, for instance, disseminating nude photographs and videos of themselves online. What are some of the potential repercussions of taking part in this activity? Among peers? Among relatives or loved ones? On potential relationships? How about possible repercussions on the person's adult future? Find and cite examples of the damage that has resulted in a similar case.

**7.** Research the current sex trends among teens and discuss any more recent trends that have not been on the radar, so to speak, of cultural figures such as Dr. Phil, who is the go-to source for many parents when it comes to these sorts of topics. What are these trends? Define and describe them. Who takes part in them? What do they hope to accomplish? What are the positive and negative effects or outcomes?

**8.** Are there methods about which Shannon Lane is not aware that young people use to bypass the security precautions their parents might take to protect them from the sorts of activities outlined in her essay? For example, Lane speaks of young people actually selling pictures of themselves using PayPal or of having multiple email accounts, passwords, and so on. What methods has she overlooked? Describe how young people today manage to thwart their parents' protective measures. Conversely, you might describe better methods for parents to thwart their children's schemes.

# Three Sex Crime Arrests Among Stickam.com Users So Far This Year

Brad Stone

**Let's Start Here•••▶** While there are certainly many sexual trends among young people today, one of the more commonly known recent trends is the use of Stickam to broadcast live video feeds of pornographic imagery. Several years ago, when Stickam was a budding company, the author of the following essay, Brad Stone, pointed out the fact that the company, which makes its services available to users aged 14 and up, was owned by a well-known Internet pornography conglomeration of companies based out of Japan. Stone thought it suspicious that this service was linked to questionable companies, and he raised his doubts in an earlier column.

Fast forward a couple years, and sure enough, what Stone was afraid might happen had come true. This is what the following article addresses: the negative outcomes of a service such as Stickam, which lends itself easily to one of the trends mentioned in one of this chapter's earlier essays.

The cases mentioned in Stone's essay are among the first publicly known cases stemming from this particular website, but more are certainly to follow. As you read the essay, see if you can determine why it is that this particular service is being targeted, versus other live-feed resources available through most instant messaging services, email services, and even cell phone services. What about Stickam lends itself to abuse more than the other video-conferencing or online cam feed websites or services? Is there cause for alarm?

---

Brad Stone is an American journalist and writer. Before moving to Bloomberg in late 2010, he was a longtime technology correspondent for the *New York Times.* He also worked at *Newsweek.* In 2003, he published his first book, *Gearheads,* about the combat robot culture. On August 5, 2007, Stone published a story in the *New York Times* exposing *Forbes* editor Daniel Lyons as "Fake Steve Jobs," the author of *The Secret Diary of Steve Jobs.* The following essay, published in the *New York Times* as a follow-up to an article on the same subject two years earlier, first appeared on October 15, 2009.

Two years ago, I wrote about Stickam.com, a live video start-up that former employees and public documents said was owned by a Japanese pornography operator.

The article asked if a company with that unusual pedigree could keep a live-video site free from smut and keep its large community of teenage users safe from all the potential abuses.

This year, three arrests have underscored why that question needs to be asked.

Earlier this week, Dan Goodin of *The Register* wrote about Lawrence Joseph Silipigni Jr., who was recently indicted on nine felony counts on charges of using Stickam to trick underage girls into removing their clothes and performing sexual acts live on the Web.

Mr. Silipigni video-recorded at least one such session and later posted the video to the Web. Two other teenage Stickam users subsequently came forward to say Mr. Silipigni tricked them as well, according to court documents. Mr. Silipigni told the F.B.I. he collected more than 100 webcam videos of girls he met on Stickam by posing as a teenage boy. In Stickam's defense, Kate Sowell, from the agency Lewis PR, said it was Stickam itself that reported the incident to authorities.

But this was not the first time sex crimes involving minors had been committed live on Stickam.

In February, a popular Stickam user named Jonathan Hock, age 20, was said to have sexually assaulted his unconscious girlfriend while broadcasting it live on his Stickam feed. Mr. Hock ended the broadcast himself, according to Christopher Stone, who runs the gossip site StickyDrama and recorded video of the event, because he said he recognized a crime was being committed. Stickam terminated Mr. Hock's account when it later learned of the incident. Mr. Hock has been held without bond in Arizona since his arrest and is awaiting trial.

Finally, in June, a multiagency sexual crimes task force arrested Richard Allen Chaney, 23, from Costa Mesa, Calif., for persuading a 14-year-old girl to engage in live-video sex acts on Stickam. Mr. Chaney is also accused of arranging an in-person meeting with this minor on Stickam and having sex with her.

To be sure, monitoring the activities of 30,000 online members at the same time is daunting (although other live-video sites like Justin.TV don't seem to have this kind of problem). But Stickam has never addressed its connections to pornography, nor is it transparent about the critical issue of its monitoring procedures.

Over the summer, I e-mailed a few questions about Stickam's safety practices to Steven Fruchter, its chief executive. (Mr. Fruchter was formerly director of information security at Hypermedia Systems, another in the same family of firms owned by the Japanese pornography company). I asked Mr. Fruchter via e-mail what the standard was for monitoring live feeds on Stickam, what actions the company takes to prevent crimes or stop them once they are in progress and how many staff members they have devoted to policing content.

After a back-and-forth exchange with Lewis PR, representatives of Stickam reported that Mr. Fruchter did not want to answer those questions.

**Let's Pause Here••• ▶** Perhaps you've heard of the social media service Stickam (or others that are similar), and how it differs from sites such as YouTube or camera messaging services. Whether or not you have, how do you feel about the cases mentioned in Stone's essay? Were you aware of the potential dangers of Stickam's service? Do you feel that the evidence Stone gives to support his opinion is sufficient to make his case?

**Let's Take It Further••• ▼**

1. Since the mass popularity of the Internet first rose in the mid- to late-Nineties, there have always been instances of predators lurking for young, unsuspecting boys and girls to manipulate by posing as young men and women themselves. How are the Stickam crimes different than previous crimes committed using services such as MySpace or even the chat rooms of the past? What makes this more dangerous? Or is Stickam merely the latest Internet phenomenon to be exploited by predators?

2. What is the purpose of Stone's essay, and how does he go about proving his point? What is it that he wants from his readers? How does the manner in which he defines Stickam and explains its dangers help you understand his target audience? If he were trying to warn a separate audience (say, potential future Stickam users), how might have his language and writing strategy have been different?

3. The idea that young people are falling prey to predators goes directly against what Lane's earlier essay states are purposeful acts on the part of the teens who transmit their images

intentionally. If it is a trend to do this, at what point does it become exploitation or a crime on the part of the viewer? At what point is it a crime on the part of the person transmitting the images (assuming they are knowingly and purposely doing so, as suggested by the scholarship on this particular trend)?

4. Stone makes a point of saying that a similar service, Justin.TV, does not have the same policing issues that Stickam seems to have. What might the reason for this be? Explain and describe—by comparing and contrasting—how the two services are different. Why can one be more easily exploited than the other, both by the person broadcasting and the people viewing?

5. Research the outcomes of the three cases mentioned in Stone's article. Describe the punishments (or lack thereof), and give your opinion about whether you feel they were appropriate to the crimes. Be sure to cite other similar situations in popular culture to help you back your opinion. What should the punishments have been, if you think they should have been more severe, and why?

6. Use research to locate other specific instances of social media abuse and exploitation that have arisen since the three cases addressed in Stone's essay. What were the outcomes of those cases? Compare and contrast how they were different or similar to the ones he mentions. Is there a trend emerging in the types of crimes being prosecuted since those mentioned by Stone? If so, what is that trend? What might it mean in terms of potential danger for teens in the future?

7. In his essay, Stone mentions that he emailed a Stickam representative about the methods they use for monitoring live feeds. Though his emails went unanswered, Mr. Stone implies that Stickam should be held liable for what their users do on their service. Do you believe that sites like Stickam have the legal responsibility to monitor their users' activities? If so, explain the process of how might they go about doing this and what their actions should be when they find violations. What might a violation be? Should consenting adults be allowed to use the service in a sexual manner? If you believe that Stickam should not be held liable for its users' actions, then who should be? And how might the service's users be held accountable?

8. Google the title of this essay (which originally appeared on the *New York Times* blog in October of 2009) and scroll down to the comments portion of the blog post. There you will find that varying opinions are listed on the topic, as is often the case with blog posts on such a sensitive subject. Find one or two comments that stand out to you as particularly logical or, conversely, outrageous, and engage the comment by proving or disproving the poster's opinion using outside sources. Or, if there were any that stood out to you as surprising because they raise a point of view you might never have considered, explain why that particular post was a surprise and how it helped to shed a different light on the subject.

9. Put Stone's theory of danger to the test by logging on to Stickam and viewing a large sampling of live video feeds, enough to support or refute his claims that the site is a danger to teens. In an essay, define and describe potential security flaws of the site, as well as the types of behaviors of users on the website. Was it as dangerous a site as Stone claims it to be? If so, explain how. If not, refute Stone's claims by citing evidence from your video research.

# mash**it**UP

Here is a series of essay and discussion topics that draw connections between multiple selections within the chapter. They also suggest outside texts to include in your essay or discussion. Feel free to bring in further outside texts, remembering the variety of texts (beyond articles) available to you.

1. Compare the essay on teen sex trends by Lane to Stone's essay on Stickam. Where do you stand on the issue of sex trends? In general, should parents be alarmed? If so, what trend or trends should parents be alarmed by, and how might they keep their teens from taking part in them? If you think that parents have no cause for alarm, explain the types of trends that exist and why they are not alarming. Be sure to locate outside sources that enable you to make your claim about trends and their existence, rather than merely relying on hearsay or opinion.

2. Locate and read the text *Sex at Dawn* and discuss whether you agree with the book's main points on monogamy and its role in human relationships. If you agree, choose three or four main points and discuss how they prove the relative newness of monogamy as a facet of human long-term relationships. If you disagree, find three or four main points to refute the authors' claims about the "unnatural" qualities of monogamy.

3. Locate and read Dawn Eden's book, *The Thrill of the Chaste*, and compare her angle in promoting chastity to that of another pro-chastity celebrity or organization. Who is more successful at getting across an effective message? What, specifically, about their methods makes one superior to the other? What suggestions would you give either one to make their message more effective to their target audiences?

4. Compare the book *Sex at Dawn* to the book *The Thrill of the Chaste*. Which of the two books makes a better case for their cause, based on the evidence each provides? How might one book learn from the other's argumentation writing strategies? Which specific examples (or evidence) given were superior, and what specifically was superior about them? How well did each author represent his or her own work in his or her respective interviews featured in this chapter?

5. Locate other works by Wallace Shawn (author of the essay "Is Sex Interesting?") and read about some of the other specific sexual topics he raises in his writing. Then, locate another instance of sex writing (from a columnist, blog, essay, or other media) and compare the tone and content of the two writers. Which writer takes the subject matter more seriously? What are the types of topics each writer discusses? Is

either writer "silly or trivial," as Shawn says people often think of sex writing? Why or why not?

6. Stickam is the focus of Brad Stone's article on sex crimes that have taken place recently over the Internet. There are, of course, far more venues where teens and others take part in sex trends that sometimes end in criminal charges for either participants or viewers, and sometimes both. Locate another online venue that allows a popular sex trend to take place that has come under the scrutiny of the law or the public. Describe how the service or website works, as well as how users are exploiting it to take part in whatever sex trend you are identifying. Find a case that has resulted in criminal charges and/or prison time, and explain the nature of the case. Finally, advocate for or against the site or service being shut down or regulated, based on the methods of exploitation and the criminal cases that have developed from the service.

# "If We're Going to Be Friends with Benefits..."
### William Haefeli

William Haefeli is a native of Philadelphia, Pennsylvania, who has been a cartoonist for *The New Yorker* since his first drawing was accepted in 1998. His work has appeared in several collections of modern cartoonists, including *The Mammoth Book of the Funniest Cartoons of All Time* (2006). The following cartoon was first published in *The New Yorker* on December 8, 2008.

*"If we're going to be friends with benefits, I want health and dental."*

# Thinking About Relationships

Take a moment to look at the accompanying cartoon. It is apparent that the artist, William Haefeli, is referring to a relationship practice of people being "friends with benefits," which is widely known to mean a sexual relationship without an "actual" relationship attached to it. The phrase "friends with benefits" implies that there are negative aspects of relationships that both parties want to avoid. What might those aspects of a relationship be, and why would people want to avoid them? How is Haefeli referring to this practice, as well as its results, in this cartoon? What is the inherent joke of the cartoon, which can be discerned by what the woman is saying to the man?

As a society, we romanticize relationships of all sorts. When we are young, we seek to have relationships where labels such as "boyfriend" and "girlfriend" are attached to them. We want exclusive relationships so that we can feel as though we belong to someone and that they belong to us in some fashion. As we mature, stereotypes emerge (often depicted in Hollywood movies and in popular songs) that, for instance, women long for steady, committed relationships, and men are terrified of committing to one person, or "settling down." Like the sex industry, so too is there a multi-billion dollar industry devoted to helping people define relationships, find suitable partners, begin relationships, maintain relationships, and deal with fractured and even terminated relationships.

And yet, despite the fact that the reality of relationships and the Hollywood versions of them tend to be at odds, we still seek them out. Those who do not seem concerned about relationships raise the eyebrows of their friends and family, who wonder what might be "wrong" with the person who isn't consumed with the desire to have a boyfriend or girlfriend, or even to be married and have children. For many, part of the college experience is doing just that: seeking a lifelong partner from the vast number of similarly aged people, so that a relationship can be kindled and maintained—in all hopefulness—for the rest of one's life.

But there is another aspect in popular culture, particularly youth culture, that Haefeli's cartoon is engaging: the notion that there are several different "levels" and complications when it comes to relationships. People identify relationships on one end of the scale as "just talking," "hanging out," and "hooking up," whereas on the other end of the scale there is "dating," "seeing," and being "committed to" someone. This phenomenon has even been given value by Facebook and other social networking sites that feature a wide variety of "relationship status" features.

Look to Haefeli's cartoon again to see how he is bringing the different shades of relationships into the discussion. Obviously, from the postures of the characters, they have recently completed (or are about to begin) a sexual act, and the woman is using this particular moment to put forth her terms of the relationship. Why would she request "health and dental" benefits? In some ways, the phrase is obviously a pun on the "benefits" one gets when employed with a good company. But is there more to it? How is Haefeli, for example, critiquing the various roles the two people in a "friends with benefits" relationship play? Does the relationship take on the tone of a business transaction, as though a person were negotiating benefits for a job, and if so, how might that show what Haefeli is trying to say about the nature of this sort of relationship arrangement?

Is Haefeli only critiquing people, like the man in the cartoon, who are unwilling to commit, or is he also critiquing relationships and sexual culture in American society? How might it be hypocritical that the one "benefit" of friendship would be sex? If two people were to engage in such a relationship, what would be the benefits beyond sexual encounters, if there are any?

# Nice Guys Finish Last                        Ask Chauntel

**Let's Start Here•••** ▶  Relationship advice has been around in one form or another as long as people have been in relationships. What used to be talk among friends, asking for help pertaining to things that are going wrong with one's relationship has now become a multi media affair. There are radio DJs, such as Delilah, whose callers frequently air their relationship grievances while seeking her opinion. There are newspaper and magazine columnists who receive letters and emails and answer them accordingly. There are television shows, websites, blogs, and even apps, all designed to give people a place to turn for advice.

And, of course, there is also YouTube, the home of thousands of would-be relationship advisors who seek to improve the love lives of their viewers. A quick search for "relationship advice" on YouTube results in over 45,000 hits, but a more thorough search for specific types of relationship issues will result in hundreds more. Why the need for relationship advice? Because for those to whom relationships are important, a third-party perspective on something as emotional as a relationship might very well be the difference between the end of a relationship or it being "saved" from falling apart.

One of the more popular relationship advisors on YouTube is Chauntel, who takes viewer questions and responds to them via video posts. The one featured here is a rather common question, one that Chauntel even admits to hearing all the time. Despite its commonness, the question persists, and Chauntel's take on the question is both entertaining and thought-provoking. As you watch the video, jot down (in two columns) the parts of her answer that you agree with, as well as the parts of her answer you disagree with. See which answers make sense and which do not.

"Ask Chauntel" is the name of Chauntel's YouTube relationship advice channel, which was founded in September 2008. Since forming the channel, Chauntel has posted over 70 advice videos that range in subject from dating tips to teenage pregnancy. The format of her channel is to answer user-submitted relationship questions. She also founded and maintains the relationship-advice-themed website askchauntel.com. The following video was first published to YouTube on January 17, 2009.

**Search on YouTube: "Relationship Advice: Nice Guys Finish Last. Ask Chauntel!"**

http://www.youtube.com/watch?v=kliCdij205c

**Let's Pause Here•••** ▶ Have you ever heard the question that is posed to Chauntel by the viewer? If so, what do you think about the way in which Chauntel systematically breaks down her answer to give a multi faceted response to the question asked? Were you satisfied with her overall answer? If you were the one who had asked the question, would you have been satisfied then?

**Let's Take It Further•••** ▼

1. Do you agree with Chauntel's assertions that "nice guys" seem not to possess the qualities sought after in a man? If so, why is it that nice guys don't display the qualities women seek? And, if not, how is it that nice guys do display the qualities she says women seek?

2. What is your impression of the "tips" that Chauntel provides? Do they seem helpful and realistic? Are they detailed enough? Why or why not?

3. Based on the nature of Chauntel's responses, who do you believe her audience to be? What about her language, video formatting, and the general discussion that she leads shows the

age group she is trying to reach? How about in terms of gender? To whom would Chauntel be of most use?

4. Does it strike you as contradictory that Chauntel would say that women want men who "aren't controlling," but that they still want to be "controlled"? How can sense be made of these two opposing statements, or does she undermine her credibility by (apparently) canceling out her advice with the two statements?

5. Make a list (regardless of whether you are a man or a woman) of the traits that you believe a woman looks for in a man. Explain the traits and why each is important, and then compare your list to the five qualities/traits that Chauntel lists in her video. How are yours similar? How are they different? What, ultimately, is the difference between what you see as important or desirable in a man and what Chauntel does? Is there a common ground?

6. Survey a mixed-gender group of students to see what they look for in partner for a relationship. How do men and women differ in what they desire in a person? How are they similar? Do any of the traits they look for strike you as unrealistic? What do men primarily seem concerned with in their potential partners? What do women seem primarily concerned with in theirs?

7. View the many comments beneath Chauntel's YouTube video to see how people have responded to her advice. Do men tend to agree with her assessment of the whole "nice guy" versus "bad boy" issue? If so, why? If not, why not? Also, do women seem to agree with her responses, or are they in disagreement with her? Why or why not? Ultimately, where do you stand on the issue? Does Chauntel get it right, or not?

8. Solicit relationship questions from your schoolmates or peers and create a video response to two or more of the questions you feel most qualified to answer. Create the video as a solo or group collaboration project. Accompany it with an essay that describes the process of making the video, how you decided which questions you were most qualified or experienced to answer, and what you hope the outcome of the project might be. Post the video to YouTube and incorporate any comments you receive into your discussion of the entire experience.

# mash**UP** essay

The following essay is this chapter's Mashup selection. Keeping in mind our definition of a Mashup essay in Chapter 2 (an essay that includes multimedia texts, as well as multiple writing strategies), observe the way the author, Libby Copeland, utilizes multimedia texts. For example, the central text to which her essay refers is a college newspaper article written by Matt Brochu for the University of Massachusetts's newspaper, the *Massachusetts Daily Collegian*. Copeland also visits the online version of the article where she culls information for her essay from the comments section beneath Brochu's article—a resource of over five hundred individual posts from readers. Besides extracting a narrative—or story line—and common themes from the comments themselves, Copeland takes her research a step further by contacting a number of the posters themselves and interviewing them for her essay. The result is that Copeland unearths the before-and-after stories that stemmed from Brochu's original article, as well as people's responses to it. Finally, Copeland interviews the author of the original article, asking follow-up questions to his article and the massive number of responses it received in a few short months.

The strength in Copeland's essay is her willingness to seek out not only the original article, the online version, and the responses to it, but also the sources of so many of the online comments. Rather than simply speculate on the outcome of the comments and the people who posted them, she went an extra step to contact the posters to see what their particular stories were and what the results turned out to be. This makes for a more credible and engaging paper, a more complete and far-reaching essay, because the people involved in this hopelessly romantic affair get to tell their stories and outcomes.

One of the most enjoyable elements of the essay is that, unlike many newspaper essayists ("Boy Friend..." originally appeared in the *Washington Post*), Copeland employs more than just a straightforward definition-informative approach. She does, indeed, utilize this particular writing strategy by informing the reader of the content of Brochu's original article and the story behind it. She also explains the way a comment section below an online article works to help the reader visualize and understand this element of her essay, in the event that we haven't seen a comments section online. Finally, she also explains what a "friend crush" is, for those who've never heard the term or experienced such a thing themselves.

But, in addition to the definition-informative writing strategy, Copeland uses several others, which she seamlessly weaves into her larger narrative of Matt Brochu and his popular newspaper column that seemed to strike a nerve with readers worldwide. One such strategy she employs is the narrative writing method, which allows Copeland to literally tell the stories of Matt Brochu and the four other young people she features in her essay. This allows us to see some of the real people behind the event, rather than just writing about this article out of context. Copeland also uses the descriptive writing strategy to paint a vivid picture of the emotions felt by several of the respondents who posted beneath Brochu's article. By using this technique she is able to appeal to her readers on a more emotional and personal level, because she even draws from her own experience to illustrate the effects of this sort of unrequited crush on a person who is oblivious.

In terms of using research in her writing (the research writing strategy), Copeland not only researches the article and goes online to read and catalogue the responses to Brochu's article, she also manages to track down several of the respondents and interview them. The best bit of research that she does, however, is to locate Matt Brochu himself and get him to tell her readers (and, indirectly, his readers as well) the outcome of the affair that he wrote about in the first place. In doing her research, Copeland also employs the compare-contrast writing strategy as she takes the time to divide the responses into those of men and women, the cynics and the romantics, even the people who agree and disagree with Brochu's proposed method of making the object of one's crush aware of one's infatuation.

Ultimately, the essay as a whole is a cause-effect essay that repeatedly shows us examples of various causes and their effects. For example, there's Brochu's crush, and the effect of him writing an article. There's the article being posted online and shared, and the subsequent outcome of over five hundred comments. There are the people who read the comments

**Mashup Essay Flowchart**

<u>Types of Media:</u>

- U of Massachusetts Newspaper Column
- Online Version of Same Brochu Essay
- Personal Interview w/ Matt Brochu
- Online Comment Forum
- Reference to Greek Mythology (Tantalus)
- Follow-Up Interviews with Several Commenters

"Boy Friend: Between Those Two Words a Guy Can Get Crushed"
Libby Copeland

<u>Writing Strategies:</u>

- Definition-Informative
- Descriptive
- Narrative
- Cause-Effect
- Compare-Contrast
- Research

and decided to take action in their own personal situations, and on, and on. The result is a complex, engaging, and sophisticated essay about an emotionally difficult topic.

When you begin writing a Mashup essay of your own in response to the selections in this chapter, revisit Copeland's essay to generate ideas for multimedia texts and multiple writing strategies. Use the accompanying flowchart to see the ways in which Copeland employs the various writing strategies and multimedia texts she utilizes in her writing.

## Boy Friend: Between Those Two Words a Guy Can Get Crushed

**Libby Copeland**

**Let's Start Here•••** ▶ Anyone who has reached adulthood has most likely experienced the sort of relationship that is outlined in the following essay. We have all had our secret crushes, our infatuations, our strange attractions to people who may or may not be good for us. And, for those of us who have had a crush on a friend, the simultaneous awkwardness and torture are nearly unbearable. The good news—if there can be good news in such a situation—is that you are not alone.

In fact, this emotional turmoil is suffered by people all over the world, as proven by the following essay. Libby Copeland, writer for the *Washington Post*, stumbled upon an article by a college student named Matt Brochu that, as it turned out, had been forwarded to and resonated with people all over the world. So taken was Copeland with the story-behind-the-story, and the outpouring of responses to Brochu's own article, that she decided to write a story of her own.

What follows, then, is an essay in which Copeland narrates a tragic tale of one person's hopeless romance and the international acclaim his story gained. While you read the article, see how much of the Brochu story you can relate to, regardless of whether you've been the person with the crush or the one who (oblivious or not) refused to let it go anywhere.

---

Libby Copeland is a staff writer for the *Washington Post*. She started her career with the *Post* in 1998 as an intern in the Style department, and now covers Washington politics. In 2005, she was awarded—by the American Association of Sunday and Feature Editors—the Feature Specialty Reporting award for large circulation papers. She has appeared on MSNBC, CNN, and NPR. The following essay was originally published in the *Washington Post* on April 19, 2004.

| | |
|---|---|
| Copeland situates the main idea of the entire essay by alluding to the Greek mythological character Tantalus. | The worst kind of temptation, as Tantalus found out, is the sort that's closest, the fruit that's barely out of reach. This holds true for infatuation, which is why the cruelest crush is one between friends. |

We call this the friend-crush, and it happens when one member of a platonic relationship secretly harbors a desire for something more. The friend-crush survives through crying jags and significant others and drunken walks home. And when it ends, it often goes out with a humiliating fizzle, accompanied by something like, "I can't date you, Jason/Bobby/Steven/Mike. I value our friendship too much."

Apparently, no one talks about the friend-crush, about the fact that it's quite common, that it usually seems to be the guy doing the crushing, and that it is endemic to high schools and college campuses. Last autumn a college kid named Matt Brochu wrote about it in his school newspaper, and it was as if he'd just translated the Rosetta Stone of adolescent longing.

When Brochu's column ran in the University of Massachusetts paper in November, a cry of recognition arose from the young people of this nation. At last, someone had given voice to their silent suffering. Through instant messaging, the column spread from Amherst, Mass., to Boston to Austin to Muncie to Berkeley. It spread to England and Belgium and to a Navy enlistee in the middle of the Pacific Ocean and to a woman in eastern Canada who "almost cried" when she read it.

The Web site for the *Massachusetts Daily Collegian*, where Brochu's column was posted, was flooded. A typical column gets at most 1,000 readers in one month. Brochu's got 570,000 hits from November to March.

The column was an anatomy of Brochu's real-life crush, embellished by past experiences and by a sprinkling of imagination. Brochu, now a 21-year-old senior, fell into infatuation last summer, after he became friends with a girl from his home town of East Longmeadow, Mass. She was three years younger, an incoming freshman at UMass and—the way Brochu tells it—burdened by a boyfriend who wasn't good enough for her. (They never are.) She was flirtatious and beautiful and had an air of innocence. She and Matt wound up in psychology class together, where they chatted through each seminar and Brochu's roommate took notes for both of them. Then she broke up with her boyfriend.

Brochu started writing. When he finished, the column was effusive and tragic the way love paeans usually are. It was called "What she doesn't know will kill you," and it was written in the second person and filled with references specific to

---

**endemic:**
Belonging to a particular group of people.

Copeland first cites what will be the primary research source for the entire essay: Brochu's original article.

This paragraph sets up a writing strategy that Copeland repeatedly employs throughout the entirety of her essay—the cause-effect strategy—by showing how people were affected by Brochu's original piece.

Copeland also repeatedly uses the website version of the article (and the comments/reactions from readers) as an additional primary text in her essay.

**embellished:**
Decorated or elaborated upon to make more attractive.

**effusive:**
Expressing excessive emotion, or very emotional.

**paeans:**
Songs that praise or glorify.

his slice of generation. *You met her a few months ago, and somehow she managed to seep into your subconscious like that "Suga how you get so fly" song. . . . She's gorgeous, but gorgeous is an understatement. More like you're startled every time you see her because you notice something new in a "Where's Waldo" sort of way.*

It described how a crush works on memory, causing the desirer to remember everything ever told to him by the object of his desire. It talked about the guy's everyday indecisions, such as what to get the girl for her birthday and whether to instant-message her at any given moment. It talked of "that cute little scar on her shoulder," and her love for calzones, and her utter obliviousness to his ardor. It talked of her boyfriend, the "tool," who didn't appreciate her.

Again, Copeland explores the cause (Brochu's article) and its effect (large reader response from around the world).

Collegian Web site readers are allowed to write responses to articles. Most columns get three or four. Brochu's column got over 500, nearly all in gratitude and praise. Eventually, the exhausted editor running the feedback section told readers they couldn't write in any more. But the old messages are still up there, steeped in the drama of young love.

"Thank you for showing me that I'm not alone on this in this crazy world," wrote someone under the name "Hobbes."

Copeland also uses the online responses to Brochu's article as texts themselves.

"By the time I finished it, I was speechless and light-headed from the truthfulness of it all," wrote "Abel."

"i laughed when i saw resemblances of myself, yet inside i was really crying," wrote "Krunk."

Readers were inspired by the end of Brochu's column, a romantic call to arms that included a blank space where each reader could write the name of his beloved. The last lines are these: *Now cut this out, fill in her name, and give it to her, coward. Just let me know how it works out.*

"Damn, I wish I could be so eloquent," wrote "P. Che." "Maybe it really is worth a shot no?"

Brochu thought so. He'd made up his mind to tell the girl.

**Talmudic:**

Deeply philosophical interpretation (usually in a religious sense).

Unlike the infatuation from afar, the friend-crush is especially powerful because the romance seems so almost possible. By its very nature, the friend-crush encourages Talmudic dissections of the beloved's psyche, hashing and rehashing of missed opportunities, optimistic interpretations of neutral behavior.

There's Brad Clark, 17, of Glen Burnie, who years ago became friends with a girl he had a crush on and tried to ask her out via a passed note. She wrote back, "I think you're really cool so we can be friends but I have a boyfriend."

For a week, Clark listened to moody Dashboard Confessional songs and analyzed the note over and over. He considered the phrase, *But I have a boyfriend.*

"*Have.* That's not a very strong word there," he thought.

There's Carl M. Schwarzenbach, a 17-year-old high school junior in Southwick, Mass., who had a crush on a certain girl since the first moment he saw her, 2 1/2 years ago, on the first day of school. It was the beginning of fifth period, choir class, at 12:03 p.m., as he recalls. He was a freshman. She was a senior. She was blond and beautiful and wearing a black tank top and jeans. They became close. Schwarzenbach says they kissed a few times, but they stayed just friends.

"She always had this mind-set that she was afraid of commitment and she didn't want to commit to anything 'cause she was afraid she would hurt me," Schwarzenbach says.

When Brochu's column came out, Schwarzenbach e-mailed it to the girl, with her name filled out in the blank. She's in college now, and they haven't seen each other much. She e-mailed him back, in pink, as always.

"She just said, uh, that it was really, really sweet and it made her smile," Schwarzenbach says. "I think it might have brought us a little closer."

The friend-crush is largely a phenomenon of adolescence, when hope is more persuasive then experience. Though it happens in high school, it blossoms in college, when a new culture shakes everything up. College is when you consider important questions like: Is there such a thing as a platonic back rub? Is there such a thing as a long-distance boyfriend?

It might have to do with the coed dorm setting, where near-strangers are thrust into an intimacy previously reserved for family. (Suitemates pass by in towels.) It might be the fluidity of college dating, in which nothing is defined, and in any case, no one knows what the definitions mean. Are you friends? Are you taking it slow? One person's "seeing each other" is another person's "dating each other," which is another person's "hanging out," which is another person's "friends with benefits."

Consider the experience that countless college guys have had. At a party, a certain girl—one you thought was taken—seems to be flirting with you. She takes your arm when you walk her home. The next day, when you

---

*By applying research to her writing and locating the people who posted responses to Brochu's article, Copeland enhances her essay in the telling of various responders' personal stories.*

*Each of these responders' stories retold by Copeland is an example of using the narrative writing strategy.*

*These two paragraphs use the definition-informative writing strategy to define and explain the concept of a "friend crush" and to explain the differing definitions people apply to several levels of "relationship."*

instant-message her with the vaguely suggestive "I had a nice time last night," she says, "Me, too," and then mentions her boyfriend. What could it possibly mean?

Brian Murphy, a freshman at Robert Morris University in Pittsburgh, met a girl from his dorm on move-in day, and they became best friends. They walked to class together, ate lunch and dinner together, went to parties together. After parties, they had a ritual where they would go back to her room and cuddle. Murphy fell for her, hard. He says it was the kind of situation where—forced to choose between going out with guy friends and staying in with her to watch a chick flick—he'd watch the chick flick.

But she had a boyfriend of three years.

Murphy and the girl shared one guilty kiss, then they went home for Christmas break. During the break, Murphy read Brochu's column, and inspired by it, resolved to tell the girl how he felt. He made a scrapbook filled with pictures of the two of them. When they came back to school, he gave her the scrapbook and confessed his feelings.

"Get over me," she said. She said she had realized how much she loved her boyfriend.

Murphy was crushed.

"It's definitely the first time that I ever fell in love," he says.

Love is like wealth, or the world food supply. Some people hog it; others get nothing at all. To scroll down the feedback column below Matt Brochu's article is to realize how much love goes unrevealed, unrecognized and unrequited. If only there were some mechanism for spreading love around, everybody could get enough.

Instead, the postings sit static in cyberspace, declarations of love to people who may never read them.

"I've seen the sun rise over the mountains of Vermont and seen it set over the Caribbean. I've swam with tropical fish and seen the view from the top of Katahdan. But none of that even begins to compare to how beautiful she is."

"Katie Norris—if you ever read this, you know how I felt about you during that first month when I was in Mexico . . . look me up sometime. . . . I'd still like to try again."

"Shandie although i only just met you it seems like u are the one . . . dang girl ur perfect"

Some female readers, impressed by Brochu's way with words, try to woo the author himself.

"As a woman that constantly prays for a man with those sensitive values and beautiful words, you definitely took the right approach with this lucky lady. And as a little side note . . .

Copeland employs the compare-contrast writing strategy to illustrate the different reactions readers had to the text and subsequent comments.

if she didn't think she was as lucky as everyone thought she was; I would love to hear back from you."

A reader incensed by the number of girls praising Brochu writes:

"Girls, stop saying you hope to find someone like the guy who wrote this . . . you already have but you call them your best friend and what you don't know is that they are In Love with you."

The feedback column is a strange sort of conversation, taking place among 500 strangers over the course of months. Readers post responses that reference other posts and debate the efficacy of Brochu's just-tell-her approach. All the theories on love present themselves. There are the cynics. They write that if romance hasn't happened yet, it isn't meant to. They suggest that women want jerks more than "nice guys," and they question whether it's even possible to move from friendship to love. They offer cautionary tales.

> Copeland sees this "conversation" as a text that can be read, which she frequently references in her essay.

"I guess all good stories aren't supposed to have a happy ending and all heroes are not supposed to win," writes a fellow named "Ryan," who posts a harrowing account of running two miles in the rain to a woman's house to declare his love. The woman listened, then told him they were better off as friends. "It was a long walk home that day, the rain. . . . laughing at me in a steady and harsh flow."

But there are more romantics than cynics. A girl writes in to reconsider the "dateability" of guys who are "right under my nose." Another writes in to say she knows a guy has a crush on her and she thinks she feels the same way, but she needs to take it slow. Some confess their love to the people they like, and contacted later, two guys say it actually worked out.

> Copeland also uses the compare-contrast writing strategy (as well as the classification strategy) to show the differences between responses from "romantic" people and "cynical" people.

Someone named "Kate" writes: "As heard one thousand times before . . . amazing article. But, answer us all one question, because we're all dying to know . . . did you get the girl?!"

The answer is: After the story ran, Brochu sent the link over instant messaging to his crush. She wrote back, asking who the column was about. He sent her a cautious, rambling set-up, which he saved, along with her responses, so that he could analyze them later. His set-up started like this:

> "First off, I'm not really obsessed with this girl, I'm just interested, and I have been since the day I met her, and she doesn't have to worry about letting me down easy, b/c I'm not the type of person to let

things get awkward and let it ruin the friendship we already have, b/c she's gotta realize. . . ."

It went on like this for a while. Then: "So yeah, it's you, sorry I had to make things all weird."

She called it the "sweetest thing" she'd ever read and the "nicest thing" that had ever happened to her, and they agreed to sleep on it and talk the next day.

She called him.

"You never know whether to believe it or not, whether she was letting me down nicely," Brochu says. She talked about her long relationship with her ex-boyfriend, and how she didn't want to get into something serious, and how she felt she'd get too serious with Brochu.

"She said that she could only hang out with people in that way that she couldn't see herself getting to like," Brochu says.

It hurt, but the strange thing is, it hurt only for two days and then Brochu was over it. He says it was as if a light switch inside of him was turned off. He wonders now how much of the crush was just him enjoying the chase, the thrill of the unattainable.

"I think it goes to show that my crush was just building upon itself from me not knowing," he says. "It was completely constructed."

They're still friends, and Brochu says he's totally over her.

Anyway, he's dating someone now. Or, seeing someone. He doesn't quite know what to call it. At the very least, they're hanging out.

> The final usage of the cause-effect strategy answers the often-posed question (by online responders and Copeland alike), so what was the outcome of Brochu's article on his crush?

**Let's Pause Here•••▶**     What was your overall impression of Copeland's essay? Were you able to relate to it in an emotional way? If so, what emotions did you feel as you read it? Why do you think Brochu's original article spread all over the world? What about its appeal was so strong that it was able to reach into the hearts of people who encountered it and cause them to respond to it and share it with friends?

**Let's Take It Further•••▼**

1. Why do you think that Libby Copeland begins her article by making the comparison to the Greek mythological character of Tantalus (whose story is that he was punished by the gods and doomed to forever be tortured with food and water just out of his reach)? How does it

compare to the other statement that Copeland makes ("the cruelest crush is the one between friends")? What does she mean by this statement?

2. Based on the format and logic of this essay, as well as the writing strategies and texts used by Copeland throughout, who does it appear Copeland seeks to address with her writing? What specific comments or questions does she write that help you understand to whom she is speaking? How is her audience different from Brochu's intended audience? Or are they trying to reach the same people?

3. Have you ever found yourself in a situation similar to Brad Clark, as described by Copeland, where he mulled over every word of a rejection letter trying to give it new meaning? What is so tragic about the fact that he lingers on every word so much that they seem to shift in meaning? How is his reading of the note accurate or inaccurate?

4. Copeland characterizes the vast majority of the respondents to Brochu's essay as either "cynics" or "romantics." Which of the two would you consider yourself, and why? How likely is it, in your opinion, that one of these "friend crushes" can ever end well? Why do you believe that?

5. Copeland makes the case for college as the time where people consider questions such as the following: "Is there such a thing as a platonic back rub? It there such a thing as a long-distance boyfriend?" Are there other similar questions about relationships and sexuality that are common to the college experience? What are they and what is their purpose?

6. One of the more intriguing lines in Copeland's essay is when she says, "Love is like wealth, or the world food supply. Some people hog it; others get nothing at all." How does this quote relate to the essay's main topic, and what do you think she means when she uses this analogy? Can you think of real-life examples that prove her analogy to be true?

7. Locate the original article by Matt Brochu at the *Massachusetts Daily Collegian* and respond to it. How do you feel Brochu gets it right when it comes to his illustration of this "friend crush" phenomenon? If you disagree with his assessment, how might he have better portrayed it? Also, read the various comments and choose five to ten that most agree with your perspective on the issue. Use them to back your opinion by incorporating their quotes into your own argument about friend crushes and how to solve (or avoid) them.

8. Circulate the Brochu article among a small group of friends and ask them to respond to it in writing or in person (via video or audio). Explain the types of reactions that people had to it, and classify them into groups according to their responses. How did the men respond? How about the women? Who, if anyone, was angered by the article, and why? Who, if anyone, was emotionally moved? How were the responses similar, and how were they different? Finally, discuss the impact of Brochu's article overall and explain why you think it resonates so deeply through the various types of people you interviewed.

9. Create a "friend crush" Facebook group or blog that links to (or references) Brochu's online version of the article and start a discussion to generate comments to his article (be sure to invite friends to participate). What kinds of responses did you receive, and how many people took part in the conversation? Was there a general consensus in the nature of the responses the group members contributed? Describe the types of interactions between group members in your essay, and include screen captures of the responses that stood out from the rest of the members or represented the opinions of many.

# The Rise of the Financial Divorce   Yaran Noti

**Let's Start Here•••▶** As has become apparent in recent years, the institution of marriage is in the midst of troubling times in America. On the most basic level, this can be observed through the stellar rise in divorce rates over the past 30 years. A person would be hard-pressed to go through her list of friends and not encounter several people who are the children of a divorced couple, and maybe she has been through a divorce herself.

In light of the recent rise in divorce rates in our country, people have begun to seek alternatives to marriage, such as having children out of wedlock, living together without marrying, or even forgoing marriage and childbirth altogether. Within the realm of marriage, many couples are trying a variety of creative techniques to address what they see as the most problematic areas of marriage, or the areas that cause the most rifts, emotional distress, and eventual dissolution of marriages.

In the following essay, Yaran Noti documents the rise of one such trend, which he terms the "financial divorce." Noti explains how some couples have discovered that the core of their marital woes can be traced to money, and he explains the steps they are taking to alleviate this problem from their marriage. Noti points out some of the many ways that people who agree to a "financial divorce" go about separating their incomes and monetary obligations in order to maintain some semblance of freedom in the face of economic stress in a marriage.

As you read the essay, observe the manner in which Noti illustrates the various approaches men and women take to reducing financial stress in their marriages, as well as the way he makes comparisons to couples who choose to share the financial burdens of marriage. Also, pay attention to the way Noti compares and contrasts the pros and cons of this sort of marital arrangement.

---

Yaran Noti is a contributor to *Details* magazine, where he writes about popular culture trends, sexuality, relationships, family, and fashion. He is also the assistant editor of MyFDB.com (My Fashion Database). The following essay first appeared in *Details* magazine's March 2009 issue.

Kevin, 39, a vice president at a Chicago Internet company, likes to spend money. During the six years he's been married, he's surprised his wife, Dawn, 37, by coming home with purchases—power tools, shoes, and even a Nissan Pathfinder—that he neglected to mention to her beforehand. "She was out of town and I just bought the new car and picked her up at the train station in it," he says.

Not telling your spouse that you've dropped tens of thousands of dollars on an SUV would be a source of terminal conflict in most marriages, but Kevin and Dawn have a secret that keeps his spending (and her thriftiness) from getting in the way of their marital bliss—they keep completely separate finances.

Kevin, who makes considerably more than Dawn, splits their $2,800 monthly mortgage payment evenly with his wife. They keep their own checking accounts, have their own credit cards, and save separately for the future. "She wasn't too thrilled about the car," Kevin says, "but I paid for it, so she didn't have too big of a problem."

Purchasing decisions—involving everything from toilet paper to a vacation home—are common flash points for spouses, and as the economy falters, discussions about them only become more fraught. "The No. 1 thing couples divorce over is money," says Leah Hanson, director of the Har*money* program, a Boston counseling service that teaches couples how to communicate about finances. "Recessions and rising prices result in divorce." To guard against that eventuality, many couples are becoming kitchen-table accountants who go fifty-fifty on every major bill and keep what's left for their own purposes.

Christian Farrell, a 33-year-old associate planning director at an advertising company, alternates weekly grocery duty with his wife, Rebecca, 32. They each write a check for half the rent on their Hoboken, New Jersey, apartment, and they keep track of the utility payments they make and settle up at the end of the month. Since they make similar money and have separate credit cards, the personal spending habits of one elicit little more than a shrug from the other.

"My wife likes spending on vacations and trips more than I do," Christian says. "But we don't fight about money, because most of the stuff we buy we individually control."

Kevin's experience has been similar. "With separate finances, not every little thing is scrutinized. There's less to argue about."

For some financially unyoked couples, dividing responsibilities is more complicated than making a fifty-fifty split. Marc Bliss, 40, a research-deployment manager for IBM in Knoxville, Tennessee, makes significantly less than his wife, Jerilyn, 40, a vice president of communications for a cable-television company. She brings in around 65 percent of the total household income, and so she pays 65 percent of the expenses.

"It doesn't make sense for us to split things evenly. We've used a percentage system for our entire six-year marriage, and we never really argue about money," Marc says.

Having financial independence doesn't mean just being free to splurge or filling notebooks with calculations to maintain economic equity. For Chad Randle—a 37-year-old restaurateur in Maryland with two children—the joy of separate finances comes from being able to simply buy the small stuff rather than let his wife play domestic tastemaker.

"I'm not going to drink cheap beer," Randle says. "I'm going to drink Guinness. It's not like I have 10 cases of Guinness in the garage, but even if I did, to hell with her."

For guys like Randle—who keeps his own savings account and who pays the mortgage while his wife, Christine, 38, ponies up for utilities and child care to even things out—the thought of freedom from having to re-port back about, account for, and defend their expenditures is what leads them to separate financially from their wives.

"I have a couple of guy friends who are the big breadwinners in their families but their wives put them on allowances," Marc Bliss says. "If they knew, they would envy me, because I spend my money any way I want."

But according to Lisa Peterson, president of Lantern Financial, LLC, roommate-style monetary arrangements can cause trouble down the road. With the financial pie split in half, couples who dream of a vitamin-commercial-quality retirement may not realize that while one spouse is saving to have enough cash to retire to the French Riviera, the other is snapping up a new iPhone every time there's an upgrade.

Eve Kaplan of Kaplan Financial Advisors in Berkeley Heights, New Jersey, has seen the separate-finances approach go awry. "I met a wife who was talking about having another child, and her husband was talk-ing all about himself—now and in retirement," Kaplan says. "If one per-son has enough money to last them to 95 and the other is going to run out at age 70, what happens then?"

In the meantime, as the economy continues to flatline, guys like 44-year-old John Hall—a fitness professional in Chicago who pays the mortgage and utilities while his wife takes care of her own incidentals and credit cards—are taking a hard-nosed approach to short-term financial woes.

"My wife works at a mortgage brokerage, so she's been financially strapped," he says. "But I'm like, 'Hey, that's on you. Those are your bills. Don't bitch to me about your bills.'"

**Let's Pause Here••• ▶** What is your reaction to the tone that several of the men exhibit when explaining the reason for their financial divorce, versus the tone of the women in the same situ-ation? Do they vary in their reasoning or perspective of this arrangement, or are their views the same? Do you think Noti, based on his depiction of this particular marital arrangement, is a supporter of financial divorce, or is he against it?

**Let's Take It Further••• ▼**

1. According to Noti, for many of these people featured in the essay, "the thought of freedom from having to report back [to one's spouse] about . . . expenditures is what leads them to

separate financially." Do you think this is a legitimate reason to financially divorce? Why or why not?

2. There are several variants on the idea of "financial divorce" in Noti's article. How do you feel about the 50/50 split approach compared to the percentage approach? If you had to choose a financial divorce, which of these would be the preferred arrangement, and why?

3. Are there other reasonable solutions to the issue of finances in marriage (and the problems that stem from this) that you can come up with in response to the problem? What sorts of ideas do you have? How might a couple implement them?

4. How do the language and examples Noti uses help you determine the angle he takes in his essay? Does he appear to be for or against arrangements such as the "financial divorce" as solutions to modern marital issues? How do you think the essay's original place of publication affected the writing strategies Noti employs throughout his article? How might it have been different if he were informing a more general audience? What if it were originally published in a women's magazine?

5. What are some of the potential pitfalls and benefits of having a financial divorce in a marriage? Describe and compare some of the pros to the cons and make the case for which arrangement is better—financial divorce or "traditional" financial responsibility. Which would you use in your own marriage, and why? If you are unmarried, you may want to speak to a married couple about the types of financial responsibilities a couple faces when they are married to generate possible ideas.

6. In his article, Noti quotes Eve Kaplan of Kaplan Financial Advisors, who posits a scenario where one spouse has been frugal and saved enough for a lengthy retirement, while the other has saved much less. She says: "If one person has enough money to last them to 95 and the other is going to run out at age 70, what happens then?" Speculate on Kaplan's question and explain how you would respond to such a situation. Describe how would you respond if you were the one who had saved less. How would you respond if you were the one who'd saved more? What possible solutions to this problem are there? Outline a potential process and explain how it might be a viable solution.

7. What other sorts of marriage arrangements are couples trying in order to make their marriages last? Research the various arrangements and choose one that strikes you as realistic. Describe the marital dilemma that the arrangement is trying to address, and explain how the arrangement is supposed to work. Then, explain whether you believe this arrangement might be a successful remedy to the problem it is attempting to address.

8. Interview two or more married couples and ask them what types of alternative approaches to standard marital issues they use (if you use video or audio for your interview, include them with your essay). Compare the different approaches to one another and describe each. Then, choose which method you feel has the best chance of being the most successful as an approach to working out marriage issues.

# *August Farewell:*
# *The Last Sixteen Days of a*
# *Thirty-Three-Year Romance*

David G. Hallman

**Let's Start Here •••▶** So far this chapter has dealt with different types of relationships in various stages of development. However, one unfortunate truth about relationships is that they inevitably end. Sometimes relationships end when two people break up or separate, and sometimes they end when one person dies. Naturally, the end of any relationship—whether a gay or straight relationship, a dating relationship or a marriage—is a difficult event to cope with for the people involved. But a relationship that ends because of something as definitive and final as death is perhaps the most devastating ending of them all. After all, regardless of the nature of a relationship, when two people split up who are both still alive, they can still hold out hope that the relationship might be repaired or redeemed. Not so with a death.

In the following essay (excerpted from Hallman's 2011 memoir by the same title), David G. Hallman narrates the experience of standing by hopelessly while his partner of 33 years dies from pancreatic cancer. As difficult as this experience undoubtedly was, Hallman still manages to find redemptive moments within the final days of his partner's life. While you read the essay, observe the manner in which Hallman depicts the events of his partner's final days, as well as how Hallman intersperses memories of better times within the experience of his partner's life ending.

---

David G. Hallman lives in Toronto and has worked for more than 30 years on the national staff of The United Church of Canada, carrying a wide range of social justice responsibilities. In addition to his work in Canada, he also served from 1988 to 2006 as the Coordinator of the World Council of Churches Climate Change Programme based in Geneva, which involved him in UN global negotiations on climate change. Hallman is the author and editor of many articles and books on ecological themes, including *A Place in Creation: Ecological Models in Science, Religion and Economics* (1992), *Ecotheology: Voices from South and North* (1994), *Spiritual Values for Earth Community* (2000) and a major study paper on *Climate Change and Poverty: Science, Theology, and Ethics* (2005) for the National Religious Partnership on the Environment. Hallman's partner of 33 years, William Conklin, died in August 2009, two weeks after being diagnosed with pancreatic cancer. The following is an excerpt from Hallman's memoir, *August Farewell: The Last Sixteen Days of a Thirty-Three-Year Romance,* in which he chronicles the final days of his partner's life interspersed with vignettes from their life together. His first novel, *Searching for Gilead,* was published in the fall of 2011.

## Friday, August 7

After the x-ray is finished and the technician thanks Bill for the new joke, she pages an orderly to deliver us to the next testing site. Bill's bed is wheeled to a distant wing in the hospital and we are placed in the corridor queue for a CAT scan. There are several patients ahead of us but the line moves pretty expeditiously and within fifteen minutes or so a technician comes into the hall and asks Bill if he is William Conklin. This time I am not allowed to go into the room with him but am directed to a nearby waiting room.

**queue:** A waiting line of people.

**expeditiously:** Promptly and efficiently.

I wonder if he is telling her the dead duck joke.

For the first time today, Bill and I are separated. I have nothing to do but sit and wait. And think.

I replay the day's activities in my mind. It has been frenetic since Bill's early morning wake-up call. Because of the pace, I have not digested the implications of the activities. We are here at the hospital because Bill's doctor was concerned about the most recent test's results. We are now in the medical imaging department because the emergency room doctor was concerned about what we told her about Bill's recent history and about what she saw when she examined him.

**frenetic:** Frenzied or frantic.

Maybe we are finally going to get some solid answers as to what is going on with Bill.

But now as I sit here wondering what the CAT scan may show, I find myself having qualms about whether I really want to know after all.

**qualms:** Feelings of uneasiness.

One way or another, we marked the major transitions in our lives. The happier ones, we invariably celebrated with parties. Over the years, Bill and I did a lot of entertaining. We enjoyed hosting people in our home. Call it the Adelle-Lillian gene. We both could recall many grand soirées organised by our mothers.

In December 2000, we gathered friends and family for a three-fold celebration: the inauguration of a new millennium, the year of my fiftieth birthday and the cusp of the year of our twenty-fifth anniversary. We began the planning early and soon realised that the scope of our ambitions would strain the physical capacity of our Stratford house as well as the energies that we could bring to the food preparation. We already had a trip to Paris scheduled for late November and didn't fancy coming home from a week of Louvre-D'Orsay-Pompidou-Garnier-Bastille and having to throw ourselves into canapé recipes.

The solution—outsource the work to a hotel. A block from our Stratford house stood the venerable Queen's Inn. The edifice may have seen better days but the dining room had a

**edifice:** Building structure.

**cantilevered:**
Supported by a large piece of wood or metal that sticks out from a structure, such as a balcony.

**fastidiousness:**
Neatness and orderliness.

**minutiae:**
Smallest or most minor details.

cozy atmosphere with large cantilevered windows draped in red velvet, enough tables to seat one hundred plus, a parquet section of the floor large enough for the dancing styles of a range of ages and the kitchen could assemble a grand buffet that was equal parts tasty and tasteful. The multiple groups of friends that we were inviting from Toronto could stay overnight right there at the hotel relieving us of any obligation to convert our house into a one-night bed and breakfast. With characteristic queenly fastidiousness, we worked out the minutiae of details with the hotel's catering manager and then left for Paris.

Stratford was blanketed with a fresh snowfall on the party night, not so much to cause problems for the out-of-towners making the drive but sufficient to project a charming seasonal ambiance with all the Christmas lights strung along the main street. An hour or so before the party began, Bill and I walked the block from our house carrying our tuxedo suit bags and checked into the room that we had reserved for ourselves. Of course, we needed a room of our own to allow for the changes of clothes from formal dinner wear to after-dinner-let-loose-and-party wear. As the hosts, we had to set a high standard.

It was a wonderful party. Everyone thought so. Late in the evening, Bill and I circulated around the room with a tray teeming with simple and elegant Christmas decorations that we had bought in Paris to give our guests as a memento of the evening. I treasure a photograph from the party of my parents dancing arm in arm, Mom with the Christmas corsage on her wrist that we had bought for both our mothers. It was the last dancing occasion before Mom's deteriorating mobility put an end to that post-retirement form of exercise.

The one sour note (literally) of the evening was the DJ that we had hired supposedly on good recommendation. I thought his selection of dinner and dancing music was okay. My partner didn't. At times, Bill was almost apoplectic. But sufficient wine and the effusiveness of our guests who were clearly enjoying themselves mitigated his distress, for the most part at least. When I or any friend referred to that party in subsequent years, Bill would say, "remember that bloody DJ?"

**apoplectic:**
Furious.

**effusiveness:**
Expressing excessive emotion.

## Monday, August 17

I'm sitting beside the bed trying to swab Bill's lips without disturbing him. His eyelids flicker. He is awake. "Hello my darling. You seem to have had a relatively tranquil day today. I think that you've been asleep most of it." I'm not expecting any response. Conversation is pretty much a thing of the past.

He surprises me with a few soft sounds that are other than his usual breathing noises. He looks directly at me, his eyes not fully open but with his pupils focused and clear and plaintive. I'm not sure that I can trust my judgment. Is he trying to communicate or am I just projecting my emotional state onto him? He moves his fingers and tightens slightly his grip on my hand. It is not my imagination.

> **plaintive:**
> Expressing sorrow, sadness, or suffering.

"I know dear. You want to go. And you're ready to go. And you're at peace about going."

Almost but not quite inaudibly he says, "yeah."

I take a deep breath and hold his gaze. "I want you to go because I know we both believe that it will be to a better place than the pain-filled place where you are now."

"You're right", he says slightly more distinctly.

"I'll be a major mess for a long time but I'm strong and we've got lots of friends who will help me. I'll eventually be all right. I want you to know that. You can go without worrying about me."

"Okay" he murmurs and closes his eyes.

"Happy anniversary my darling. I love you so much," I whisper, tears streaming down my face.

## Wednesday, August 19

Bill loved learning languages. Partly, it was the musician in him, the beauty of hearing the word spoken or sung.

Spanish had a big place in his heart. He spoke Spanish to any Hispanic he met on the street. He jabbered away to a Mexican friend in Stratford. He had long gossipy conversations with the housekeeper at the guest house in Puerto Vallarta where we spent every February. He enjoyed conversations with the Spanish-speaking staff at Verve, the new condominium building we moved into in October 2008.

About ten years ago after regaling his mother with endless stories of how much at home he felt when we were travelling in Mexico and how easily the language seemed to come to him, she looked him in the eye and said, "I guess it is about time I told you something."

"What?"

She hesitated. "You're grandfather is not who you think you grandfather is."

"What!"

"Hardly anyone in the family knows about this. I've never told you or anyone else about this except your dad of course. Frankly, I've always been pretty embarrassed about it." Long pause. "You know that my mother, your grandmother, was not all that keen on family life." Bill had heard lots of stories over the years about the two marriages, about how she would dump off her kids at relative's homes when she tired of them,

**vaudeville:**

Turn of the 19th/20th-century variety shows.

a little bit about her life in vaudeville. "Well, she had an affair and bore two children out of wedlock. I was one of
them."

"Oh my God. Are you serious?"

"This is not something I would joke about," she said
sternly.

"Sorry. Sure. Please go on."

"My father, your grandfather, your real grandfather, was Mexican."
Bill sat dumbstruck. After a moment, she asked, "Are you upset?" He just
stared at her incredulous. Bill at a loss for words. Imagine. Adelle ven-
tured on, "I guess my mother met him through the show business. He
was a trick rider with a travelling Mexican rodeo. Apparently, his stage
name was Mexican Joe."

Bill exploded in laughter, jumped up and kissed his mother and
started dancing around the room. "This is fantastic. Absolutely incredible. I'm part Mexican. That explains so much. Do you know anything
more about him?"

"Only his name and what I've told you."

"I'm thrilled Mom."

"And I'm relieved I guess. Now we don't have to talk about it
anymore."

Bill's most recent project was to teach himself Italian. He loved
travelling in Italy, he loved the operas of Verdi and Puccini, he loved
the films of Fellini and Visconti, he loved Italian design. He decided
that he just had to speak and understand the language fluently. He took
night school courses and had workbooks from which he taught himself

**culmination:**

The final or end result of something.

the grammar and vocabulary. For Bill, the culmination of
learning Italian was going to be to be able to read Dante's
*The Divine Comedy* in the original. He wanted to go to Italy
soon and spend a year studying Italian and art. He didn't
make it.

## Sunday, August 23

I meet Mario in the hall outside our door. I need to prepare him. He and
Bill have been good friends jabbering away in Italian as Bill spent the past
few years in his new linguistic endeavor. But I hadn't been able to get
through to Mario to tell him about Bill's diagnosis. He had been away
from home. Yesterday, he picked up my messages and called me back.
Now he is here to visit. And to say goodbye. I tell him that I believe Bill is
very near death. Mario is in shock. I take him into the apartment. It is a
very difficult visit. He holds Bill's hand and sobs. Bill's right eye is open.
I detect tears rolling down his cheek.

**Let's Pause Here•••▶** What was your overall reaction to the tone of Hallman's memoir excerpt? How do you feel about the way that Hallman manages to be both sad and accepting about the death of his partner? What, in particular, stood out about the way that Hallman managed to narrate such a difficult experience? What types of emotions do Hallman's writing style and subject matter evoke in you as a reader? Was there anything surprising or shocking about the essay? Was there anything that you didn't expect to encounter in the essay?

**Let's Take It Further•••▼**

1. Based on the subject matter and the events that Hallman narrates (as well as his language and writing style choices), whom do you think he envisions as his primary audience? People who are losing a relationship to death? People who are losing a relationship in general? Do you think that his audience is meant to be readers of a particular sexual orientation, or is this meant to address the universal experiences a person would have when watching a partner die?

2. Which events do you think Hallman describes better, the sad times or the happy times? Which does he describe more often? Why do you think he takes this particular approach to writing about this event?

3. Why do you think Hallman doesn't specifically mention the fact that he was in a homosexual relationship with Mr. Conklin? Did you notice that it was a homosexual relationship being described? Why does it not matter for this essay whether Hallman raises the issue of homosexuality?

4. How does it make you feel that Mr. Conklin is making jokes despite the fact that he is facing death? Why do you think he does this? What does it say about him as a person that he uses humor to cope with something as terrible as dying? How is his outlook different from Hallman's?

5. If you've ever experienced a meaningful relationship ending, narrate your experience in a style that is similar to Hallman's (i.e., journal format). Be sure to describe both the positive and negative events, rather than only focusing on the negative. What, if anything, did you learn from the experience? How did it help you with future relationships, if it did at all?

6. Whether or not you have ever experienced the end of a relationship, explain the process one might go through in order to cope with the loss and to move on eventually. Be sure to give specific steps and advice, and give thorough descriptions of each step and each piece of advice.

7. Compare two relationships that you've been in to one another. What were the positive elements of both? What were the negative elements? Overall, which of the two was a better experience and why? What relationship advice might you be able to offer your reader based on your experiences in the two relationships that you are describing?

8. Describe and narrate a major transition or event in your life that wasn't necessarily a relationship ending. What, if anything, did you learn from the experience? How has your life changed—for better or for worse—since the event you are describing? How might you do things differently were you to find yourself in a similar situation in the future?

# Young Adults Delaying Marriage for Long-Term Relationships

Leah Finnegan

**Let's Start Here•••▶** The following essay discusses the rising modern trend among young people of avoiding or delaying marriage. As it turns out, the reasons younger people are avoiding marriage are fewer than their older counterparts (who have also begun to put off marriage or avoid it altogether), but they are every bit as important to the trend. Rather than focusing on the negative reasons for the decline in marriage rates among young people (as is common among writers who discuss this issue), this essay points out how experts are *optimistic* about the trend of declining marriage rates and older marrying ages.

In this brief essay, Leah Finnegan compares the generational differences on this issue, as well as showing two opposing views on the idea of delayed marriage. As you read the essay, observe its tone, style, and intended audience.

---

Leah Finnegan is a native of Chicago, Illinois, and is the editor of *HuffPost College*, a division of the *Huffington Post*. She also writes for the *Morning News*, an online magazine published daily since 1999. The following essay was first published to the *Huffington Post* website on June 23, 2010.

Young adults are waiting longer than ever to tie the knot, leaving many experts optimistic about the future of marriage.

Whereas Baby Boomers married in their early 20s, today the average age for making it official is 26 for women and 28 for men. Significant reasons for holding off the institution include later financial independence, increased instance of sex before marriage and an uptick in unmarried cohabitation.

*USA Today* talked with a host of marriage experts, many of whom saw the light of this trend:

"There's a certain wisdom in lengthy courtships," says Gary Hoppenstand, professor of American Studies at Michigan State University. "If it lasts three, four, five, six or seven years, they feel like there's something there to support a marriage that will last."

Michael Johnson, emeritus professor of sociology at Pennsylvania State University, says the combination of a certain maturity level and the ability to work out problems before committing may help young people avoid the marital mistakes of the Baby Boomer generation.

But others questioned if waiting too long could be a waste of time. As Johns Hopkins University sociologist Andrew Cherlin said, "It's good to get to know your partner before marrying, but one wonders how long you need."

**Let's Pause Here••• ▶**    Were you surprised by the idea that there are experts who would be optimistic about young people avoiding or delaying marriage? Why or why not? Why is it that people tend to focus on the negative reasons behind the growing trend of avoiding marriage? Which is the better viewpoint to have, and why?

**Let's Take It Further••• ▼**

1. Who is the intended audience for Finnegan's short essay, based on its original publication and the language used throughout? What specific techniques does this essay employ that makes its audience apparent? How were you able to determine Finnegan's intentions?

2. Why might the idea of young adults waiting longer to get married make experts feel "optimistic about the future of marriage"? How does the next generation of married couples play a role in marriage's future?

3. Finnegan cites three main reasons as the cause for younger people holding off on the ceremony: "later financial independence, increased instance of sex before marriage and an uptick in unmarried cohabitation." Which of these three, in your opinion, seems most likely to be the greatest cause for the decline in marriage among younger people? Why do you believe this to be so?

4. One expert, Gary Hoppenstand, states that "there's a certain wisdom in lengthy courtships." How does this statement and his subsequent statement help support the idea of a person who intends to get married eventually but wants to test out the couple's compatibility first? What is to be gained in a courtship of many years? What, if anything, might be lost?

5. On the opposing side, another expert in the article puts it this way: "it's good to know your partner before marrying, but one wonders how long you need." While his statement could be read in a variety of ways, take the question at face value. Map out a timeline with benchmarks for how long a person might actually need to live with someone in order to get to know a partner before committing to marriage (if he or she intends to commit at all). Explain the timeline and its benefits.

6. Interview a member of the "Baby Boomer" generation (defined roughly as someone born between 1946 and 1964) and ask him or her to define what some of the "mistakes" of his or her generation were in relation to marriage (as suggested by Finnegan's essay). Allow the person to read Finnegan's essay and respond to the general theory that younger generations are responding to what they see as the mistakes of previous generations. Whether the person agrees or disagrees with this notion, ask him or her how his or her generation has positively or negatively affected the current trends in marriage, if at all. In your essay, compare the interviewee's response to the main idea of Finnegan's essay. Also, list, define, and describe the "mistakes" given by the interviewee in his or her responses. Next, interview a person from a younger generation (anyone born after 1965) and take the same approach to his or her interview. What is your final assessment of Finnegan's theory? *Has* the Baby Boomer generation made an impact on the marital and relationship decisions of subsequent generations?

# mash<sup>it</sup>UP

Here is a series of essay and discussion topics that draw connections between multiple selections within the chapter. They also suggest outside texts to include in your essay or discussion. Feel free to bring in further outside texts, remembering the variety of texts (beyond articles) available to you.

1. Compare the relationship advice in the Ask Chauntel YouTube video to the advice in the Matt Brochu piece featured in Libby Copeland's article. How are the two different at giving advice? Who do you feel does a better job, and why? Also, view the comments to Brochu's article and compare the comments to Chauntel's video. Which of them seems to be better at reaching their target audience, and how do they manage to do this?

2. A common theme that emerged in two separate selections in this chapter (Thomas Rogers's essay and David G. Hallman's essay) was that heterosexual couples might do well to look to the manner in which homosexual couples maintain their relationships. In his interview of *Sex at Dawn* author Christopher Ryan, Rogers asks several questions that allow Mr. Ryan to make the case for how homosexual relationships (specifically those that do not place a heavy emphasis on monogamy) prove his theory to be true by the very nature of their success. So too, in his memoir does Hallman speak to the benefits of brutal honesty in a relationship, explain why this approach to a relationship might be a more successful approach. Conversely, if you disagree with the potential solutions this offers, research sources to back your opinion. Locate outside sources (articles, blog posts, or conduct personal interviews) to see how people feel about this open approach once its pros and cons are explained in your paper.

3. One trend among young people when it comes to their relationships (briefly alluded to in several of the essays in this chapter) is the idea of labeling relationships in their different phases. For example, when young people begin to first have an interest in one another—and sometimes even after there has been one or more sexual encounters—this phase is often referred to as "talking." As the relationship evolves, it moves from "talking" to "hanging out" to "dating," and so on. Outline the various phases or stages in a relationship from its beginning to its end in currently used terms, explaining each term and what it means, as well as giving an example for each along the way. There are many texts to which you can turn for further examples and

definitions—from UrbanDictionary to YouTube—and a variety of online and print sources. You may also consider interviewing friends and peers to come to a consensus on the true meaning of the relationship terms you intend to include in your article.

4. Interview a member of a generation prior to yours about the views the person has concerning unmarried people cohabitating. Does the person approve or disapprove? Does the person see any logic in it? What does the person see as potential positives and negatives, other than any possible moral issues? Then, interview a person from your generation and see what his or her views are on the issue. Explain how the two differ and how they are similar. How does it appear that society has changed over the years in its acceptance of these sorts of activities?

5. In the spirit of Brad Stone's "*Sex at Dawn*: Why Monogamy Goes Against Our Nature" book review/interview, find a recent book (within the last two years) on any subject having to do with sex or relationships. Once you have completed the book, give it a review that includes the following: the basic premise or main idea of the book, the topic's application to our culture and lives, the argument that the author is making for or against any particular kind of action or new discovery in that field, and whether you find the book to be helpful or potentially helpful and to whom. Incorporate into your review questions you would like to ask the writer if you were ever to meet him in person.

6. Locate other political cartoons that address current cultural issues dealing with sexuality and/or relationships and "read" the cartoon to explain the artist's intentions and message. Be sure to give some background on the issue itself in order to help your reader understand the cartoon's relevance. What, specifically, in the cartoon makes it apparent what the subject or topic is? What images show his or her opinion? What about text, if there is any? What does it enable the artist to say about the topic he or she is addressing?

7. Copeland's essay speaks to the issue of dating, in general. Find other texts (multimedia or otherwise) that address the issue of dating (rather than sex or relationships). Compare these other texts to Copeland's selection in this chapter and explain which is more honest and more useful for someone who hopes to understand the experience of dating.

**Let's Connect····** ▶  "Like" our Facebook page for free, up-to-date, additional readings, discussions, and writing ideas on the topics of sexuality and relationships. Join other students and teachers across the country sharing in an online discussion of popular culture events. *American Mashup* is on Facebook at www.facebook.com/americanmashup.

# Violence

# Chapter 7

## Making the Cultural Connection

Everybody loves a good fight. We, as Americans, have birthed many violent institutions (such as the WWE, UFC, WBO, and NFL, to name a few of the most popular sporting bodies) that appeal to the voyeuristic inclination in so many of us to watch someone take a beating, just so long as we aren't the ones on the receiving end of a fist, or a foot, or a hard tackle. One need only observe the rapid rise of Ultimate Fighting Championships to see the popularity of violent sports. Certainly, this love of violence—or, more accurately, obsession with violence—is not only the property of America. But it's not too far of a stretch to see how we've taken older sports such as the gladiator contests of ancient Rome, or the jousting tournaments of Medieval Europe, and one-upped them.

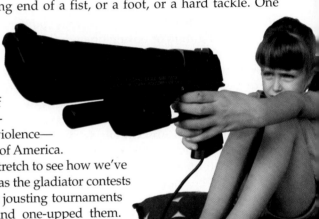

America, a country founded on and bound up in violence, glorifies it and engages in it in our own peculiar way.

And we like to do things big here. Whether we are building the world's tallest skyscrapers or the biggest cars and trucks, everything has to be massive. Otherwise it just wouldn't be American. We like our oversized meal portions, our all-you-can-eat buffets, our sprawling houses, and our IMAX movies. We even like our celebrities to be larger than life. It goes without saying, then, that we would apply this same concept to our sports.

Consider the idea of the Old West. We often look back on those years in our history as a time of unrelenting violence, and we praise the heroes who stepped in and "tamed the Wild West." We like seeing justice, and we like seeing the good guy win, but we really want to see a good fight along the way. Some of us even secretly root for the bad guy.

Maybe fighting or boxing or any of the other "contact" sports, as the most brutal of them are called, are not your thing. Consider this, then: How many times have you driven by an accident and slowed down to see the damage? How many times have you seen a fight break out at school—whether between women or men—and walked away with absolutely no interest? Were you the least bit interested to see the photos of prisoner abuse leaked from Abu Ghraib, such as the one shown here? In fact, the *Saw* movies, which are an amazingly lucrative slasher franchise, dwell on the very nature of violence. They get to the core of how violent humans can possibly be, mostly by placing characters in a "me or him" situation where somebody has to die a horrific death. Even the Saw videogame plays to this notion of violence and disfigurement. Why else have a dismembered leg on the game's cover? These types of images are disturbing, but something deep within us makes it seem as though we are hardwired to at least take a look, even if the thought of violence repulses us.

Here's a common refrain most people have heard: "America is going down the tubes." Or, replace the word "America" with any other location,

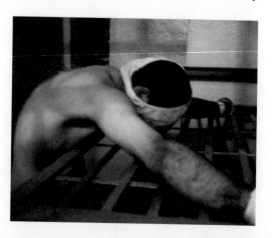

such as Chicago, Atlanta, or the suburbs of any major city. The idea is that our world and our own country have never been more violent than they are now. People like to think that years ago we were all laid back, peaceable creatures and that each generation is becoming more reckless and brutal. Most every generation thinks that those who come after them are more violent or morally shady than previous generations. Perhaps you've heard your grandparents, or someone from an older generation say, "Back in my day a fight was just a fight. We didn't stab or shoot anyone. There was honor," or some variation of that complaint. The general idea of that statement is that the world is so heartless and cruel, and humans are so dishonorable and capable of hurting one another, it will surely all come crashing down around us at any given moment. This notion is not at all new.

In reality, America—and the rest of the world—has always been a violent place. Our history is violent. The way we became America is steeped in violence. The way we remain America will inevitably require future violence. We are no different than any other country in that respect. We have had to defend ourselves against threats. We have even had to defend against threats from within. Truthfully, we wouldn't be the country we are today without this history. In terms of military might, we are still the most powerful nation in the world. We have a lot of weapons, and we aren't afraid to use them. This fact has been proven time and time again.

America, as much as we profess to abhor violence, continues to engage in violence on a mind-boggling number of levels. We have powerful gangs. We have a powerful military. Our riot police and S.W.A.T. teams are among the most feared, and most capable, on the planet. Ours is a land rife with school shootings and domestic abuse. Sanctioned violent sports and underground illegal sports abound within our borders. National news regularly reports police brutality, riots, gang rapes, and employees who shoot up the businesses where they work. We have schoolyard brawls and we have drug-related violence. It never seems to end, and we just can't seem to look away. And yet, strangely, many of us are complacent in the face of violence.

Surely there is a reason? Surely we're not the most violent country on the planet? Some would say that we are, without a doubt. Others would say, turn on the news and you'll see social unrest all over the world, so what can be done about it? They would say murders and rapes, police brutality, riots and robberies, all happen everywhere. In a sense, both sides of the argument are correct. But neither side could deny that here, in America, we have our own particular brand of violence. It's almost as if we need it, as if it is some sort of drug we find ourselves craving. Need a little proof? Watch any 30-minute news broadcast on a television station of your choice. See what the lead story is. Chances are it involves somebody getting harmed in some way. Why? Because television producers know that we need our fix, and they're more than willing to give it to us.

This chapter will explore America's long-standing relationship with violence. We will try to discover what it means to us. We will try to understand the ways in which it infiltrates our culture and then consider what this means in terms of our national and personal identities. Some selections will try to get to the root cause of our violent tendencies, while others will attempt to find the sources of violence in order to begin the process of alleviating them. Some selections will implicate us as passive bystanders to various types of violence, while others will illustrate how we *do* act, though we could do more. There are essays that will actually make the case for why we aren't violent enough, and there are texts that make it seem as though it is a miracle if a person can make it through the day without encountering, or falling victim to, an act of violence.

## School Zone

**Jim Day**

Jim Day was an artist at the *Las Vegas Review-Journal* for 30 years. He was the newspaper's graphics editor before becoming a full-time political cartoonist. Before moving to Las Vegas, he worked as a newsroom illustrator for the (Norfolk) *Virginian-Pilot* and was also the editorial cartoonist for the *St. Joseph* (Mo.) *News-Press*. He is internationally syndicated with Cagle Cartoons. "School Zone" originally appeared in the *Las Vegas Review-Journal* in 2008.

# Thinking About Violence

Take a moment to look at the accompanying cartoon. Like most political cartoons, this drawing is attempting to make a statement about a topic that is in the news. The topic, which can be discerned quickly, is about school shootings. We know this because we can see one of the familiar "school zone" signs that line a road leading to a school, as well as a gun in the middle, where there would normally be figures of students walking to school. Of course, the purpose of the school zone sign—the way it is intended to be read—is as a warning to drivers to be on the lookout for children walking to school, since children tend to be easily distracted and not necessarily on the lookout for drivers.

Considering that these signs are supposed to serve as a warning to motorists, what might Jim Day be saying about schools? Whom is he warning, and what is he warning his audience about? How does he go about placing this message within the single frame of a still drawing? What do you think the artist's opinion on the subject of school shootings might be? How were you able to "read" this from a drawing with only two words? Note that the cartoon was first published in 2008. How many school shootings have occurred since 2008? Who were the shooters, and what were their motives?

Now, take a moment to consider other types of warning signs one might put up around schools to make a political statement, in light of any recent news related to schools in America. What other topics might need to be addressed about our schools and the idea of violence? If you were to be given an assignment where your instructor gave you this exact same cartoon, but with a blank sign, what might you draw in the photo to illustrate a political statement that you'd want to make about our schools?

# *Bowling for Columbine*    Michael Moore

**Let's Start Here•••▶**   Most people have heard of the famous Hollywood documentary filmmaker, Michael Moore, and many of us have seen one or more of his controversial documentaries. Love him or hate him, Mr. Moore gets people talking. And that's a good thing.

Consider the following YouTube video clip, which is excerpted from Moore's 2002 movie, *Bowling for Columbine*. The film is Moore's lengthy and complicated explanation of what may have caused the now-infamous Columbine school massacre on April 20, 1999. In this clip, Moore puts forth his version of why America is more violent than other cultures. Keep in mind that he is performing satire, which means he is purposely exaggerating to make his point. If that's the case—that he is partially joking and partially serious—how does it help him make his point? Or does it hurt his message? Which parts of the clip are jokes, and which parts are serious? Finally, as you watch this short segment, see if you can determine what Moore believes to be at the root of our nation's violent tendencies.

---

Michael Moore is an American filmmaker, author, and liberal political commentator. He is the director and producer of *Bowling for Columbine, Fahrenheit 9/11, Sicko,* and *Capitalism: A Love Story,* four of the top nine highest-grossing documentaries of all time. In September 2008, he released his first free movie on the Internet, *Slacker Uprising,* documenting his personal crusade to encourage more Americans to vote in presidential elections. He has also written and starred in the TV shows *TV Nation* and *The Awful Truth. Bowling for Columbine* brought Moore international attention as a rising filmmaker and won numerous awards, including the Academy Award for Best Documentary Feature, the Independent Spirit Award for Best Documentary Feature, a special 55th Anniversary Prize at the 2002 Cannes Film Festival, and the César Award for Best Foreign Film. The film was first released in 2002.

Search on YouTube: *"Bowling for Columbine*—The History of the United States of America"
http://www.youtube.com/watch?v=Zqh6Ap9ldTs

**Let's Pause Here•••▶** First of all, do you agree or disagree with Michael Moore's theory of why Americans are so violent? Which parts of his "history" do you find offensive, unbelievable, or perhaps even humorous? Do you feel there were parts of his telling that struck you as accurate or inaccurate? Was the cartoon too short, too long, or just about right? How might the cartoon's narrator influence the audience, and what might it say about whom Moore is trying to mock or illustrate in a negative light?

## Let's Take It Further••• ▼

1. What problems arise from Michael Moore's boiling down of United States' history to a three-minute cartoon? What significant portions of our history did he leave out, and why?

2. Why do you think Moore chose to make the cartoon's mascot a bullet? What do you think of the mascot's accent? How is the accent supposed to represent Americans in general, or a more specific group of Americans? Based on the choice of the narrator—both as a bullet and also its accent—who does Moore consider his audience to be? What words, phrases, or even historical events that Moore chooses reveal his point of view on the subject of violence and American history?

3. Do you believe the connections Moore makes between fear, and violence as a reaction to fear, are accurate? In other words, is America a nation of people who are paranoid about one another, or is he purposely exaggerating? Do you see any merit to his argument about who and what the general population of America fears? If so, which elements of his argument seem legitimate, and which elements are exaggerated purposely? Why would he exaggerate elements of American history?

4. How do you feel about Moore's depiction of white people as terrified and all other ethnic groups as subdued, nonviolent characters? Does this generalization of white Americans help or harm Moore's overall message? What about the fact that Moore himself is white? Does that change your perception of his depiction of white people? How might it be different if he weren't white?

5. The final image of everyone in the "All-American" family holding a gun—including the baby—is a fairly blunt image. What is your reaction to the way Moore depicts modern Americans as gun-toting paranoid citizens? Is there any truth to this? If so, can you think of any recent examples?

6. Conduct research on any of the time periods Moore depicts in his brief cartoon. Bring in historical sources to fill in the gaps he left out. Use this information to prove/disprove Moore's depiction of any particular era in American history (e.g., the Civil Rights movement of the 1960s) by comparing and contrasting Moore's version of events to the actual events themselves.

7. Map the timeline of the cartoon. In three minutes Moore covers more than 230 years of American conflicts and history. Follow the timeline and compare it to the timeline of American history, pointing out why you believe he stopped to illustrate and discuss certain events and ignored others. (One helpful illustrated timeline of American history can be found here: www.animatedatlas.com/timeline.html) Which significant historical events in our history does he skip? Why do you think he skips the events that he does? What is the result of Moore choosing the eras in American history that he does?

8. If you agree with Moore's theory of fear, and violence as a response to fear, argue alongside him while adding examples from current mass media news stories (or other texts) that prove his point. If you disagree with his theory of fear, locate mass media and multimedia texts that prove Americans do not live in perpetual fear, or that we do not resort to violence as a first reaction.

9. If you disagree with Moore's theory of why we are violent and all carry guns, construct an argument against him by giving examples of guns providing necessary protection, or even

how guns have been used simply as methods of deterring crime in recent years. Avoid a discussion of gun control laws, instead focusing on actual events in recent news that prove the value of guns in terms of allowing a person to defend himself against a crime.

10. Create your own "History of America" video or image collage, focusing on a specific time period in American history that directly relates to causes of fear and/or violence in modern America. Accompany your collage with an essay that explains why you picked the historical period that you did, as well as what you are attempting to say about violence in America today.

# Teen Fight Clubs Worry Police

**WLUK Fox 11 News**

**Let's Start Here•••▶** When is fighting okay, and when is it morally incorrect? When is it legal, and when is it illegal? The following news broadcast attempts to answer these questions by showing a growing trend in their Green Bay, Wisconsin, community: teen fight clubs. In response to the mixed martial arts craze sweeping the nation, which shows no sign of slowing, teenaged men are organizing underground fight clubs. Observe the ways in which the newscasters choose to inform their audience of the trend by paying attention to the interview clips they use.

Fox 11 WLUK is a television station based out of Green Bay, Wisconsin. The following video originally aired on June 25, 2009.

**Search on YouTube: "Teen Fight Clubs Worry Police"**

http://www.youtube.com/watch?v=Bx3ZYme7R10

**Let's Pause Here•••▶** Where do you stand on the issue of fighting? Is it ever warranted? Should it be avoided no matter what? If so, why? What might these clubs offer to the young men who take part in them? In other words, according to the young man's explanation for the purpose of the fight club, what are these clubs doing for these young men? Is the sort of circumstance explained by the young man in the interview one that would be an instance of justified fighting? Why or why not?

**Let's Take It Further•••▼**

1. Are there flaws in either side's argument in this news clip? If so, which side is flawed, and what are the flaws? Which side do you agree with more?

2. Despite the fact that the news clip was made for a general viewing audience, are there elements of the broadcast that show the audience to whom they are most trying to appeal? Are they trying to warn young men against fight clubs, or warn parents? Are they merely attempting to inform their audience of the existence of fight clubs, or are they actually trying to choose one side over the other?

3. Consider Captain Jeff Sanborn's statement: "Can two adults, with consent, go in and start fighting? Yes, they probably could." Knowing that it wouldn't necessarily be illegal for two adults to consent to fighting, does it change your opinion about whether fighting is always bad? Does it change your stance on the fight clubs the story is featuring?

4. Consider the way Declan O'Connell begins his justification of organizing fight clubs with the following statement: "I don't drink at all. I refuse to. And I don't do drugs at all." Why would he preface his pro–fight club stance with this assertion? What does this do for his credibility and opinion?

5. Which side do you find yourself agreeing with by the end of this brief broadcast, if you agree with one over the other? Give specific examples from the clip that convinced you. If you could ask either side a follow-up question, what would you want to ask?

6. What is the difference, morally, ethically, or legally, between "sanctioned" fight clubs (e.g., Ultimate Fighting Championships) and a fight between two consenting adults in the privacy of their own home? Is one more justified or "acceptable" than the other? If so, why? Make the case by providing examples to support your point of view.

7. Consider Mr. O'Connell's statement about how he gets a "rush" out of fighting. It appears as though this is how he gets his "high," which is the reason most people use drugs and alcohol. Research and describe the physical process of how a person gets high, then compare it to the manner in which O'Connell describes his reasons for seeking the adrenaline rush in his statement. Can a rush of adrenaline be used to get high? If so, might O'Connell be addicted to adrenaline? Does this make him an "addict" in any way? Can people become addicted to something like violence?

8. Is the issue being confronted in this news story the legality of fight clubs, or do you believe they are arguing that a teenager organizing them is what is so tragic, offensive, or unbelievable? How might the news clip have been different if the fight club organizers were adult males, or even females for that matter? How might the officer's opinion have differed, if at

all? (See also "Alarming Sex Trends Among Teens Today" in the "Sexuality and Relationships" chapter, to observe how teens cause alarm for other adults.) What other ways are teen trends depicted in the media that make the trend seem detrimental to teens throughout the country?

9. Conduct research to see whether you can locate a real fight club in or nearby your community. In what ways is it different from or similar to the club described in this newscast? What reasons does the club give for its existence? What does it offer the people who become members? Do you agree or disagree with the reasons given for the club's existence?

10. If you were going to organize an underground fight club, how would you go about doing it? Illustrate the process of putting the group together, where you would meet, how it would function, and so on. Describe who you would invite and why. How would you justify its existence? Explain what you would like the club to offer to its members and what you hope it would accomplish, beyond simply providing a venue for people to fight one another.

11. If you were going to produce this news feature and wanted to get people to disagree with teen fight clubs, how might you have done it differently? If you wanted people to think that fight clubs aren't so horrible, how would you have produced the news clip then? Revisit the news clip and dissect the ways in which it is for or against the fight club in question. Explain how you could add or remove content to convince the viewer of one side's argument over the other.

# Fight Club
### Chuck Palahniuk

**Let's Start Here•••▶** The novel *Fight Club* (1996) became a cult classic after it was turned into a film in 1999. Since then, a number of real fight clubs have appeared, such as those mentioned in the previous news story, many of which have been attributed to people copying the book. Despite Chuck Palahniuk consistently stating that he was not advocating violence, the clubs continue to appear to this day.

This chapter, excerpted from Palahniuk's novel, explores the purpose of the novel's fight club, specifically giving reasons for its creation and how it helps the members to improve their lives. Observe the solutions the text offers up, and see if you find any valid reason behind the club's existence and its stated purpose.

---

Chuck Palahniuk is a freelance journalist and author of 12 books of fiction, nonfiction, and short stories. Two of his novels—*Fight Club* and *Choke*—were adapted into major motion pictures. He began his career as a journalist in 1986, quitting in 1988, then doing volunteer work in the Portland, Oregon, area. The following excerpt is Chapter 6 from the 1996 novel *Fight Club* (Owl Books).

Two screens into my demo to Microsoft, I taste blood and have to start swallowing. My boss doesn't know the material, but he won't let me run the demo with a black eye and half my face swollen from the stitches inside my cheek. The stitches have come loose, and I can feel them with my tongue against the inside of my cheek. Picture snarled fishing line on the beach. I can picture them as the black stitches on a dog after it's been fixed, and I keep swallowing blood. My boss is making the presentation from my script, and I'm running the laptop projector so I'm off to one side of the room, in the dark.

More of my lips are sticky with blood as I try to lick the blood off, and when the lights come up, I will turn to consultants Ellen and Walter and Norbert and Linda from Microsoft and say, thank you for coming, my mouth shining with blood and blood climbing the cracks between my teeth.

You can swallow about a pint of blood before you're sick.

Fight club is tomorrow, and I'm not going to miss fight club.

Before the presentation, Walter from Microsoft smiles his steam shovel jaw like a marketing tool tanned the color of a barbecued potato chip. Walter with his signet ring shakes my hand, wrapped in his smooth soft hand and says, "I'd hate to see what happened to the other guy."

The first rule about fight club is you don't talk about fight club.

I tell Walter I fell.

I did this to myself.

Before the presentation, when I sat across from my boss, telling him where in the script each slide cues and when I wanted to run the video segment, my boss says, "What do you get yourself into every weekend?"

I just don't want to die without a few scars, I say. It's nothing anymore to have a beautiful stock body. You see those cars that are completely stock cherry, right out of a dealer's showroom in 1955, I always think, what a waste.

The second rule about fight club is you don't talk about fight club.

Maybe at lunch, the waiter comes to your table and the waiter has the two black eyes of a giant panda from fight club last weekend when you saw him get his head pinched between the concrete floor and the knee of a two-hundred-pound stock boy who kept slamming a fist into the bridge of the waiter's nose again and again in flat hard packing sounds you could hear over all the yelling until the waiter caught enough breath and sprayed blood to say, stop.

You don't say anything because fight club exists only in the hours between when fight club starts and when fight club ends.

You saw the kid who works in the copy center, a month ago you saw this kid who can't remember to three-hole-punch an order or put colored slip sheets between the copy packets, but this kid was a god for ten minutes when you saw him kick the air out of an account representative twice his size then land on the man and pound him limp until the kid had to stop. That's the third rule in fight club, when someone says stop, or goes limp, even if he's just faking it, the fight is over. Every time you see this kid, you can't tell him what a great fight he had.

Only two guys to a fight. One fight at a time. They fight without shirts or shoes. The fights go on as long as they have to. Those are the other rules of fight club.

Who guys are in fight club is not who they are in the real world. Even if you told the kid in the copy center that he had a good fight, you wouldn't be talking to the same man.

Who I am in fight club is not someone my boss knows.

After a night in fight club, everything in the real world gets the volume turned down. Nothing can piss you off. Your word is law, and if other people break that law or question you, even that doesn't piss you off.

In the real world, I'm a recall campaign coordinator in a shirt and tie, sitting in the dark with a mouthful of blood and changing the overheads and slides as my boss tells Microsoft how he chose a particular shade of pale cornflower blue for an icon.

The first fight club was just Tyler and I pounding on each other.

It used to be enough that when I came home angry and knowing that my life wasn't toeing my five-year plan, I could clean my condominium or detail my car. Someday I'd be dead without a scar and there would be a really nice condo and car. Really, really nice, until the dust settled or the next owner. Nothing is static. Even the *Mona Lisa* is falling apart. Since fight club, I can wiggle half the teeth in my jaw.

Maybe self-improvement isn't the answer.

Tyler never knew his father.

Maybe self-destruction is the answer.

Tyler and I still go to fight club, together. Fight club is in the basement of a bar, now, after the bar closes on Saturday night, and every week you go and there's more guys there.

Tyler gets under the one light in the middle of the black concrete basement and he can see that light flickering back out of the dark in a hundred pairs of eyes. First thing Tyler yells is, "The first rule about fight club is you don't talk about fight club.

"The second rule about fight club," Tyler yells, "is you don't talk about fight club."

Me, I knew my dad for about six years, but I don't remember anything. My dad, he starts a new family in a new town about every six years. This isn't so much like a family as it's like he sets up a franchise.

What you see at fight club is a generation of men raised by women.

Tyler standing under the one light in the after-midnight blackness of a basement full of men, Tyler runs through the other rules: two men per fight, one fight at a time, no shoes no shirts, fights go on as long as they have to.

"And the seventh rule," Tyler yells, "is if this is your first night at fight club, you have to fight."

Fight club is not football on television. You aren't watching a bunch of men you don't know halfway around the world beating on each other live by satellite with a two-minute delay, commercials pitching beer every ten minutes, and a pause now for station identification. After you've been to fight club, watching football on television is watching pornography when you could be having great sex.

Fight club gets to be your reason for going to the gym and keeping your hair cut short and cutting your nails. The gyms you go to are crowded with guys trying to look like men, as if being a man means looking the way a sculptor or an art director says.

Like Tyler says, even a soufflé looks pumped.

My father never went to college so it was really important I go to college. After college, I called him long distance and said, now what?

My dad didn't know.

When I got a job and turned twenty-five, long distance, I said, now what? My dad didn't know, so he said, get married.

I'm a thirty-year-old boy, and I'm wondering if another woman is really the answer I need.

What happens at fight club doesn't happen in words. Some guys need a fight every week. This week, Tyler says it's the first fifty guys through the door and that's it. No more.

Last week, I tapped a guy and he and I got on the list for a fight. This guy must've had a bad week, got both my arms behind my head in a full nelson and rammed my face into the concrete floor until my teeth bit open the inside of my cheek and my eye was swollen shut and was bleeding, and after I said, stop, I could look down and there was a print of half my face in blood on the floor.

Tyler stood next to me, both of us looking down at the big O of my mouth with blood all around it and the little slit of my eye staring up at us from the floor, and Tyler says, "Cool."

I shake the guy's hand and say, good fight.

This guy, he says, "How about next week?"

I try to smile against all the swelling, and I say, look at me. How about next month?

You aren't alive anywhere like you're alive at fight club. When it's you and one other guy under that one light in the middle of all those watching. Fight club isn't about winning or losing fights. Fight club isn't about words. You see a guy come to fight club for the first time, and his ass is a loaf of white bread. You see this same guy is here six months later, and he looks carved out of wood. This guy trusts himself to handle anything. There's grunting and noise at fight club like at the gym, but fight club isn't about looking good. There's hysterical shouting in tongues like at church, and when you wake up Sunday afternoon you feel saved.

After my last fight, the guy who fought me mopped the floor while I called my insurance to pre-approve a visit to the emergency room. At the hospital, Tyler tells them I fell down.

Sometimes, Tyler speaks for me.

I did this to myself.

Outside, the sun was coming up.

You don't talk about fight club because except for five hours from two until seven on Sunday morning, fight club doesn't exist.

When we invented fight club, Tyler and I, neither of us had ever been in a fight before. If you've never been in a fight, you wonder. About getting hurt, about what you're capable of doing against another man. I was the first guy Tyler ever felt safe enough to ask, and we were both drunk in a bar where no one would care so Tyler said, "I want you to do me a favor. I want you to hit me as hard as you can."

I didn't want to, but Tyler explained it all, about not wanting to die without any scars, about being tired of watching only professionals fight, and wanting to know more about himself.

About self-destruction.

At the time, my life just seemed too complete, and maybe we have to break everything to make something better out of ourselves.

I look around and said, okay. Okay, I say, but outside in the parking lot.

So we went outside, and I asked if Tyler wanted it in the face or in the stomach.

Tyler said, "Surprise me."

I said I had never hit anybody.

Tyler said, "So go crazy, man."

I said, close your eyes.

Tyler said, "No."

Like every guy on his first night in fight club, I breathed in and swung my fist in a roundhouse at Tyler's jaw like in every cowboy movie we'd ever seen, and me, my fist connected with the side of Tyler's neck.

Shit, I said, that didn't count. I want to try it again.

Tyler said, "Yeah it counted," and hit me, straight on, *pow*, just like a cartoon boxing glove on a spring on Saturday morning cartoons, right in the middle of my chest and I fell back against a car. We both stood there, Tyler rubbing the side of his neck and me holding a hand on my chest, both of us knowing we'd gotten somewhere we'd never been and like the cat and mouse in cartoons, we were still alive and wanted to see how far we could take this thing and still be alive.

Tyler said, "Cool."

I said, hit me again.

Tyler said, "No, you hit me."

So I hit him, a girl's wide roundhouse to right under his ear, and Tyler shoved me back and stomped the heel of his shoe in my stomach. What happened next and after that didn't happen in words, but the bar closed and people came out and shouted around us in the parking lot.

Instead of Tyler, I felt finally I could get my hands on everything in the world that didn't work, my cleaning that came back with the collar buttons broken, the bank that says I'm hundreds of dollars overdrawn. My job where my boss got on my computer and fiddled with my DOS execute commands. And Marla Singer, who stole the support groups from me.

Nothing was solved when the fight was over, but nothing mattered.

The first night we fought was a Sunday night, and Tyler hadn't shaved all weekend so my knuckles burned raw from his weekend beard. Lying on our backs in the parking lot, staring up at the one star that came through the streetlights, I asked Tyler what he'd been fighting.

Tyler said, his father.

Maybe we didn't need a father to complete ourselves. There's nothing personal about who you fight in fight club. You fight to fight. You're not supposed to talk about fight club, but we talked and for the next couple of weeks, guys met in that parking lot after the bar had closed, and by the time it got cold, another bar offered the basement where we meet now.

When fight club meets, Tyler gives the rules he and I decided. "Most of you," Tyler yells in the cone of light in the center of the basement full of men, "you're here because someone broke the rules. Somebody told you about fight club."

Tyler says, "Well, you better stop talking or you'd better start another fight club because next week you put your name on a list when you get here, and only the first fifty names on the list get in. If you get in, you set up your fight right away if you want a fight. If you don't want a fight, there are guys who do, so maybe you should just stay home.

"If this is your first night at fight club," Tyler yells, "you have to fight."

Most guys are at fight club because of something they're too scared to fight. After a few fights, you're afraid a lot less.

A lot of best friends meet for the first time at fight club. Now I go to meetings or conferences and see faces at conference tables, accountants and junior executives or attorneys with broken noses spreading out like an eggplant under the edges of bandages or they have a couple stitches under an eye or a jaw wired shut. These are the quiet young men who listen until it's time to decide.

We nod to each other.

Later, my boss will ask me how I know so many of these guys.

According to my boss, there are fewer and fewer gentlemen in business and more thugs.

The demo goes on.

Walter from Microsoft catches my eye. Here's a young guy with perfect teeth and clear skin and the kind of job you bother to write the alumni magazine about getting. You know he was too young to fight in any wars, and if his parents weren't divorced, his father was never home, and here he's looking at me with half my face clean shaved and half a leering bruise hidden in the dark. Blood shining on my lips. And maybe Walter's thinking about a meatless, pain-free potluck he went to last weekend or the ozone or the Earth's desperate need to stop cruel product testing on animals, but probably he's not.

**Let's Pause Here•••▶** What sort of reaction did you have to the depictions of violence within the text? Was it more or less emotional than witnessing violence on TV, film, or even in real life? Why do you suppose the men want the club kept a secret? What might keeping it a secret accomplish?

**Let's Take It Further•••▼**

1. What purpose, according to the text, does the actual club itself serve for the men who attend? What do they gain physically, spiritually, and emotionally?

2. Whom do you think the author, Chuck Palahniuk, sees as his audience? Is he only trying to appeal to men through his descriptions of violence and fighting, or is there a message that women can also take away from the novel? Why do you think the novel itself is classified on Amazon as a "Men's Adventure" book?

3. What is the purpose behind the rules of fight club? How do they function to protect not only the club, but also its members? Are there rules that do not make sense, or do they all seem to serve the same purpose of protecting the group and its members? If you had to add or remove any of the rules, what would they be, and why?

4. Do you agree with the ideas expressed in this chapter to justify fight club and its existence? Why or why not? How is the club justified, and what might it do to better explain the benefits it provides its members?

5. What do you think about the fact that the men all feel as though they're symbolically fighting someone or something? Why would they do this, and what purpose might it serve? How do you feel about the things they specifically mention that they are fighting against? Do the people and things that the men list make sense as things to fight against? Why or why not?

6. Explore the idea of these men becoming "gods" for the few moments when they are fighting. How does this help them struggle with the idea of being completely anonymous in real

life? What is the benefit of being "god-like," and how does violence offer them this brief moment of greatness?

7. Research and locate interviews with the author, Chuck Palahniuk, that specifically deal with the public reaction to his first novel, *Fight Club*. How does Palahniuk feel about the fact that real men started real fight clubs in response to his novel? Does he agree or disagree with this outcome? Do you agree or disagree with Palahniuk's answers in his interviews? How much are artists responsible for how people respond to their work, if at all?

8. *Fight Club* asserts throughout its pages, in a roundabout way, that the club seeks to empower men. How, exactly, might modern American men be feeling powerless? Find passages mentioned in the chapter that address the woes of modern American men, and then use real-world examples from popular culture multimedia sources to prove or disprove your viewpoint about how men are perceived and represented in popular culture. Are the reasons Palahniuk gives for men's dissatisfaction legitimate? How does he get it right or wrong?

9. *Fight Club* also points out, in this chapter and the book as a whole, the absence of fathers in many of today's modern families. Even President Obama (a by-product of a fatherless family himself) has noted this in several of his speeches, and he has repeatedly encouraged men to be more actively involved in the lives of their children, regardless of their relationship status with the mother of their children. Locate statistics and articles, as well as popular culture references (such as films and music), that discuss this issue of fathers absent from their children's lives. What impact does it have on the children? How accurate are the assertions being made by the novel about the impact of absent fathers?

10. This chapter also discusses the concept of beauty, or how men and women look to the media to determine what makes us beautiful or aesthetically pleasing in terms of our culture's opinions, hence the desire for these men to buck that trend and fight because it is "nothing anymore to have a beautiful stock body." Much has been written on the idea of the media affecting a person's self-image and definitions of beauty (see also "I Won. I'm Sorry." in the "Identity Construction" chapter of this textbook). Locate some of these popular culture sources and describe the process of how one defines one's image based on media impressions. Do you agree that our popular culture plays a significant role in how both men and women define what beauty is? How does our mass media show young men and women what is "beautiful" and desirable? Is the media to blame for people's negative impressions of themselves, or is the media being targeted unfairly? Why or why not?

11. Watch the film adaptation of *Fight Club* and compare the solutions to modern male woes being offered up in the film versus those offered up in the novel excerpt here. Which do you feel is more realistic as a set of solutions? Which do you feel more accurately portrays the types of issues that American men face when it comes to identity? How does violence in either (or both) provide a solution?

# Common Sense Makes a Comeback in Classrooms

*USA Today*

**Let's Start Here•••▶** For most modern-day students, the phrase "zero tolerance" has become a regular part of attending school. These rules, and sometimes laws, were initially generated as a reaction to what was seen as an escalating problem of school violence nationwide. Zero-tolerance policies reached a fever pitch after the 1999 Columbine massacre, as more and more schools tried to come up with ways to keep similar horrific events from occurring in their buildings. The positive side of this—for school administrators—was that they were able to enact sweeping rules that allowed them to remove students who were perceived as a threat.

Perhaps there were many Columbine-like incidents that were averted because of these policies. However, most people—and certainly news organizations—began to notice that students were being expelled, suspended, and even arrested for infractions as minor as bringing a set of nail clippers to school, or drawing a picture of a gun. The following article discusses the impact of zero-tolerance rules in the classroom. As you read it, try to determine the sorts of infractions you believe should fall under the definition of zero tolerance and which actions should be punishable in lesser ways than blanket expulsions and arrests.

---

The following essay was written by the editorial staff of *USA Today*, America's first national newspaper (founded in 1982). This editorial essay first appeared in print on November 11, 2009.

For 15 years, "zero tolerance" policies have been the norm in the nation's public schools. The policies took off with a 1994 federal law that called for a one-year expulsion for any student who brings a firearm to school. After the 1999 Columbine massacre, states tightened their rules further. Zero-tolerance policies expanded beyond weapons to include drugs, alcohol, and sexual harassment. By one credible estimate, 80% of schools now have them in one form or another.

Though well-intentioned, too often zero tolerance treats minor offenses and major abuses in the same thoughtless way. Across the nation, kids are regularly suspended, expelled or sent to alternative education for such things as bringing over-the-counter pills to school for menstrual cramps, pinching a friend's bottom, or taking an empty shell casing to show-and-tell.

The policies are inflexible instruments that assume school officials have no brains and students have no rights. They teach children that rigid adherence to the rulebook is more important than wisdom or judgment.

**transgressions:**
Violations of a law or rule.

Now, at long last, there are encouraging signs that a backlash is building against overreacting to minor transgressions with outsize punishments:

- This fall, when Delaware first-grader Zachary Christie, 6, proudly brought his Cub Scout camping utensil—a combined knife, fork and spoon—to school, he was suspended and ordered to an alternative school for 45 days. A sadly typical case, but this one had a happier ending than most: After news reports, and protests from parents and classmates, it turned out that authorities' hands weren't tied so tightly after all. Zachary's suspension was reduced to five days.

- In June, the U.S. Supreme Court confirmed what should have been obvious all along—that a middle school had no right to strip search a 13-year-old girl who was suspected of possessing prescription-strength ibuprofen tablets in violation of anti-drug rules. The court's 8-1 ruling provided legal ammunition for schools to turn away from zero-tolerance policies.

- Some states are revisiting their zero-tolerance policies, and activists are lobbying for change. Consider the evolution of Fred Hink, who heads a group called Texas Zero Tolerance. When a Korean girl was suspended from his local school for having a Korean pencil sharpener that resembled a box cutter, Hink's initial reaction was to write a letter to the *Houston Chronicle* saying she got what she deserved. But after meeting the girl's mother and a neighbor whose daughter was also suspended for a minor transgression, Hink changed his mind.

Texas Zero Tolerance helped push through a law requiring schools in the state to consider intent, self-defense, past disciplinary history and whether the child has special needs before acting. Florida has also relaxed zero-tolerance laws.

To be sure, there are times when severe punishments are appropriate, as when students smuggle guns or deal illegal drugs. But zero tolerance makes it all too tempting for schools to view all kids as problems—not developing human beings who can make mistakes. Far better to gear punishments to fit the crime than to cast common sense out the window.

**Let's Pause Here•••▷** Judging from events that have occurred since the enactment of zero-tolerance policies, would you say these rules and laws have done more harm or good? What accounts for more shootings at schools such as Virginia Tech, Northern Illinois University, or the University of Alabama? Notice that this article doesn't mention anything about the "major" infractions that were punished by these laws. What is your opinion of the fact that the editors mostly point out abuses of the zero-tolerance laws, but make little mention of instances where zero-tolerance policies prevented a disaster? Does this article strike you as being for or against zero-tolerance laws?

## Let's Take It Further•••▼

1. What are your thoughts about the fact that the article makes no mention of the reason school shootings and violence occur in the first place? Do you feel it is addressing the appropriate issues for the causes of school violence? If not, what should the editorial be addressing?

2. Judging by the examples given and the language used throughout the editorial essay, who is the essay's target audience? Parents? Teachers? Students? Lawmakers? How might the language and examples given differ for each type of audience?

3. How do you feel about Mr. Hink's reversal in opinion of a little girl who he thought "got what she deserved" when she was suspended? How does he justify his opinion reversal? Do you think it has been fully justified, or does he owe a better or more complete explanation? Why or why not?

4. *USA Today* states that zero-tolerance policies are "inflexible instruments that assume school officials have no brains and students have no rights." How do these laws imply school officials "have no brains"? How do they imply that students "have no rights"?

5. Were you, or someone you know, subjected to any of your school's zero-tolerance rules? If so, describe the events that took place, as well as the punishment and the parents' or community's reaction. Was the reaction of the school fair or was it overkill, as in the examples given by the *USA Today* editorial staff? Explain and describe the approach taken by the school as well as the approach they should have taken.

6. Locate the zero-tolerance policies in your hometown school district. What rules do they have in place? Do you feel they are fair rules that take students' rights into account? If not, can you generate and describe a scenario where these rules could potentially abuse students' rights? How should the rules be adjusted to account for potential real-life situations?

7. Choose from one of the examples of student zero-tolerance infractions mentioned in the article. What might have been a more fair process for handling the infraction rather than the punishment given to each student? Describe the process and the outcome for what you see as a more logical or fair solution.

8. If you believe that zero-tolerance rules are a good tool for stopping school violence, locate one or more instances where these rules actually helped to avoid a potential occurrence of school violence. Describe the scenario that took place, as well as how the zero-tolerance rule stopped a potentially violent situation from occurring. Does this particular event justify the existence of zero-tolerance laws? Why or why not?

9. Conduct an audio or video interview of high school or college students regarding zero-tolerance laws. What are the students' opinions of zero-tolerance laws or rules in schools? Are they seen as a positive or a negative reality, and what would they do to improve the rules themselves, if anything? Are more students for or against these rules? Why or why not? What do they see as the benefits? What do they see as the potential negative elements of these rules?

# In Defense of the Fistfight          Chris Jones

**Let's Start Here•••▶**          In this era of lawsuits and zero-tolerance policies, most people do anything they can to avoid a fight, even if defending oneself is entirely warranted. But many of us have secretly wished, at some point or another, that there would be no repercussions if we lashed out against someone who offended us, harmed us, or even threatened someone we love. Defending oneself is a natural reaction to a confrontation, but many people avoid it despite this fact.

Enter Chris Jones, who, in the following article, has decided enough is enough. He believes that our tendency toward peacefulness actually empowers people who would otherwise be less confrontational. And, quite simply, he has decided that fighting might be a good thing after all. As you read his essay, decide how you feel about the clever approach Jones takes to advocating violence. See if his experience and his argument resonate with you.

---

Chris Jones is an author of two books of nonfiction and a journalist who began his career as a sportswriter for the *National Post*, where he won an award as Canada's outstanding young journalist. He joined *Esquire* as a contributing editor and sports columnist, and became a writer-at-large when he won the 2005 National Magazine Award for Feature Writing for the story that became the basis for his book *Too Far from Home: A Story of Life and Death in Space*. His work has also appeared in *The Best American Magazine Writing* and *The Best American Sports Writing* anthologies. He lives in Ontario, Canada. The following piece originally appeared in *Esquire* magazine in December 2007.

This whole thing started—or maybe it ended—with these guys engaging in some ritualistic, Hare Krishna clapping shit. They were sitting at a table across the bar from my buddy Phil and me. We were trying to enjoy a quiet pint in our quiet local on a quiet evening, but these hippies wouldn't quit with their clapping. Swear to God, they might as well have been crashing cymbals in my ears.

I asked them politely to stop. "Make us," they said, and then they clapped louder, smiling their dirty-toothed smiles at us, twisting our nipples. One of them was named Jericho, I picked up. He was a skinny bearded guy who looked as though he'd wear Guatemalan mittens in winter. "Jerry," I said when they finally took a break, "come on over here, have a chat." He did, and shortly thereafter, he loosed a throat pony into my face. It was Jerry's bad luck that I had resolved to start punching people again.

It wasn't a snap decision. I'd reached the end of the road after what seemed like a perpetual assault from life's Jerichos—the sorts of assholes who not only act like assholes but celebrate their assholedom: the grease spot who gave me the forearm shiver in our recreational soccer league and said, "It's a man's game, bitch"; the walnut-headed midlife crisis in his convertible who cut me off and then gave me the finger. It felt like they had me surrounded, clapping in concentric circles. I mean, Jesus, a skinny bearded hippie named after a biblical city had just spit in my face.

How'd we get here? Blogs are part of it, along with the incessant frothing of TV pundits and reality-show contestants, especially that lippy midget from *The Amazing Race*: Everybody thinks they're above being edited. And the saddest part is, the Jerichos are right to feel bulletproof.

**hokum:**
Pretentious and unrealistic nonsense.

Somewhere along the way, we've evolved into a culture without consequence, taught so much hokum about the bigger man walking away. Yet to appease us, we've also been told that what goes around comes around. What kind of contradictory horseshit is that—that one day, accounts will be settled, but by the universe? I like karma as much as the next guy, but lately, watching my city behave more and more like an Internet comments thread in the midst of a flame war, I've grown tired of waiting for the planets to balance the ledger. It's like we've started playing hockey without the enforcers, and all the scrubs are tripping up the skaters with impunity. You know why Wayne Gretzky could be Wayne Gretzky? Because everybody knew that Dave "Cementhead" Semenko would fill you in if you fucked with his friend.

Too bad life changes when we take off our skates—constrained by fear of cops, by fear of lawyers, by fear of the wife, all of our judges. Not anymore.

**asinine:**
Extremely foolish, or resembling a jackass.

I would submit, Your Honor, that if someone is doing something demonstrably asinine, and I ask them to stop it, please, and they say, "Make us," they've entered a binding oral contract whereby I am permitted, even obligated, to try to make them.

And so, before I wiped his spit off my face, I grabbed Jericho by his beard and dragged him outside. By the time I had him squared up, I saw all that I needed to see to know that I'd found a new habit: the regret on his once-smiling face. I was surprised by how good it felt, and I stopped for a second, frozen under the streetlights, satisfied that Jericho was about to make like the walls of that bitch city, and that I was about to settle my own accounts.

**Let's Pause Here•••▶** How well do you think Chris Jones makes his case for advocating fistfights? Did you find yourself nodding in agreement, or were you horrified by the notion he puts forward? What is your impression of the way he characterizes the men who were antagonizing him? How did you feel about the way he characterizes himself and his friend? What is your opinion of Jericho by the end of the article? What is your opinion of Chris Jones? How much of what he says about the state of the world (people feeling "bulletproof") do you believe to be true?

## Let's Take It Further••• ▼

1. What might the ramifications of Mr. Jones's proposal be if everyone took him up on it? Would there be more fighting, or less? Would it solve the dilemma that he describes throughout his essay? If so, how? If not, why not?

2. How might Jones have written this piece differently if he were speaking to a more general audience? Based on where the piece was originally published, as well as his word choices and descriptions that he employs throughout, whom would you say is his intended audience?

3. What do you think about the "causes" of people treating each disrespectfully with no fear of any sort of retaliation, as Jones describes them? Do you agree with what the causes are for people mistreating one another or being rude with no fear of retaliation? Do you think there are additional causes that Jones fails to mention? What, if anything, did he leave out of his argument?

4. Did you identify more with Jericho or with Jones and his friend? In other words, whose side do you understand better? How, for example, might Jericho have differently described the same situation? Who is more in the right if Jones described it exactly as the situation occurred?

5. Is there an unspoken code that people usually adhere to in order to avoid fights? If so, what is it? For example, why might people choose to avoid a fight in a public setting, such as in a bar or at a school? What is the purpose of this code? How does it allow America to function as a nonviolent society, if it has any bearing on our society at all?

6. Is there anything else Jones might have done other than dragging the guy outside and fighting him? If so, what were Jones's other options (especially considering his point about people "asking for it")? What would you have done if you found yourself in a similar situation?

7. If you have ever found yourself in a situation similar to the one Jones writes about, describe the scene and how you reacted to antagonism. Also discuss, in detail, what you might have done differently, in light of Jones's article and his argument. In other words, what process would you (or do you) use to avoid confrontation, and why? Would you consider resorting to violence based on Jones's explanation of why it is becoming necessary? Explain how and why you would agree with Jones if you find yourself in a similar situation in the future.

8. Whether or not you agree with Jones's proposition, state your viewpoint on the issue of fighting and then support it by giving examples of what you see as necessary or unnecessary violence. Also compare and contrast the positive and negative consequences to fighting, as depicted in popular culture media outlets. Defend whichever of the two you think makes more sense, and explain why by using multimedia sources.

9. The era of litigation—or frivolous lawsuits—we currently live in has caused businesses and people to walk on eggshells, always on guard against exposing themselves to a potential suit. Locate information about the now-famous "McDonald's Coffee" lawsuit, which many identify as the turning point in modern legal confrontations. Then, locate and describe some of the other famous "frivolous lawsuits" and discuss why you think they might not have been warranted. Finally, define how—if at all—these sorts of lawsuits might factor into the argument Jones makes in his essay.

10. Choose one of the "causes" Jones lists for how Jericho became the confrontational and disrespectful man illustrated in the essay. Watch some of the shows (or types of shows) that Jones lists, read the blogs, or listen to the talk-show hosts and take notes on the content and tone of the information being presented. Explain whether you agree with Jones's assertion that these forms of media are making people feel justified in being disrespectful to one another, with no fear of repercussions. How does Jones's argument echo the sentiment of mass media outlets after the Tucson shooting of Congresswoman Giffords and others in January of 2011? What is a potential solution for these causes?

11. Show Jones's essay to someone you know. See what his or her reactions are as the person reads it. Then, interview the person and ask his or her opinion on the argument Jones makes. Feel free to use the discussion topics above to generate questions for your interview. Report your findings, including describing the person's reaction to the article.

Here is a series of essay and discussion topics that draw connections between multiple selections within the chapter. They also suggest outside texts to include in your essay or discussion. Feel free to bring in further outside texts, remembering the variety of texts (beyond articles) available to you.

1. Locate the lyrics to Eminem's song "The Way I Am." See how many of the previous selections' themes and messages he addresses directly. What does he say about the power of entertainment to evoke violence and the burden of responsibility? Why does he think it's strange that people noticed Columbine but didn't pay nearly as much attention to all the school shootings that occurred prior to that one particular shooting? What is it about the Columbine massacre that was so different from other school shootings? Do you ultimately agree or disagree with Eminem's point about the Columbine shooting and its aftermath?

2. Is there a difference in how men and women engage in violence? Search YouTube for fights between men and fights between women. Compare and contrast the two, and explain the differences, if any exist. Also, compare news stories of violence by women (such as the school shooting in Alabama by a female professor) to the depictions of violence by Pompa in his poem "The Body as Weapon, as Inspiration," which appears later in this chapter. How are the two similar or different? Are women as equally violent as men? Why or why not?

3. We have read essays that say we are too violent, and we have read selections arguing that we are not violent enough. So, which is it? Are we not violent enough? Have we all become weaklings too terrified to defend ourselves for fear of injury or lawsuits? Or are we more violent than ever before, just as older generations have been saying about each subsequent generation? Which of the previous selections makes a better case on this issue? Regardless of where you stand on the issue, locate outside texts to support your viewpoint.

4. Using research techniques, find a news story or TV broadcast about an instance of notable violence and try to determine the alleged criminal's motivations behind his or her act of violence. This will be easier if you locate a criminal who later got caught and gave an explanation, such as in a television or newspaper interview, or if you locate a case that is about to end or has recently ended. Do any of the explanations that you encounter agree with or justify the opinions given in any of the previous selections? If so, how does the case mirror any of the selections in this chapter so far?

5. Compare Moore's theory of the causes of violence in "A Brief History of the United States" to Jones's theory in his essay "In Defense of the Fistfight." Why are they so different? Who do you feel makes his case better? Which of them offers up a better solution?

6. Compare the "Teen Fight Club" newscast to the excerpt from the novel *Fight Club*. Is there any similarity to the purpose of the two fight clubs, as outlined in the interview of the fight club organizer and the narrator's own words in the novel excerpt? How are the two fight clubs similar in terms of what they provide their members? How are they different? Do you think the teen fight club may have been influenced by the movie, or by something else?

7. Find an outside source that you believe contributes to violence in our society. The only stipulation is that the media source must be mainstream enough to be readily available to the general public (i.e., mass media outlets as defined in the "Mass Media" chapter). Make the case for how the mass media source (music lyrics, games, TV shows, etc.) might incite people to violence, whether or not it is a subtle or blatant invitation to action. Discuss how you see it as subtle or blatant, and the ways in which the source "incites" or "encourages" violence.

8. Create a video or image collage that illustrates elements of mass media that encourage or advocate violence as a solution to commonplace problems and explain the ways in which these texts might cause someone to consider violence. How do you suggest that viewers of these multimedia texts engage with them without becoming violent? What other texts can you suggest that show the negative outcomes of violence?

# Jaywalker

TAB (Thomas Boldt)

Thomas Boldt (TAB) was born in Southern Prussia to a family of shepherds. Having survived the Industrial Revolution, he came to Canada only to find the market for shepherds on the verge of collapse. TAB was a cartoonist for *The Calgary Sun* until 2008, where the following cartoon originally appeared on February 6, 2008. He is internationally syndicated by Cagle Cartoons.

## Thinking About Abuses of Power

When we think of violence, we usually conjure up images of people harming one another in situations that might potentially be easily avoided (such as those mentioned in the first half of this chapter). While there is certainly no shortage of that sort of violence in our society, we hear more and more of people who are in positions of power abusing that power, which is the focus of this chapter's second half. Like the cartoon pictured here, which features a policeman "tasing" an elderly woman, there are stories regularly featured in the news that tell of people harming helpless or defenseless people by abusing the power afforded to them by their position—whether they are police personnel, soldiers, lawyers, teachers, coaches, or priests, to name a few examples.

This cartoon addresses the issue of police brutality without using the phrase at all. Instead, the artist asks us to read the image itself to see that he is illustrating this all-too-common occurrence. To be sure, TAB is not saying that all police officers are violent or abusive, but when it comes to people in positions of power abusing the helpless or defenseless, this sort of violence takes on a more sinister and troubling meaning to us. Why is abuse or violence in this sort of situation more problematic than everyday instances of violence? What is it about someone abusing his power that makes the violence even worse than it would have been anyway?

Note that the cartoon is titled "Jaywalker," which is a person who walks outside of a crosswalk or ignores the "don't walk" signal that most crosswalks feature. Why do you think TAB, the cartoonist, decided to call the drawing "Jaywalker" rather than something else? What imagery does he use to make a point about the "crime" being committed here? What is the *true* crime: the jaywalking, the tasing, or the people in the background commenting on the event? For example, why do you think the jaywalker is an elderly woman, rather than a teen in baggy clothes? Also, why is the couple's dialogue disturbing, if you see it that way? How does TAB make his point without being preachy?

One element of the couple's discussion that might give a viewer pause is that they are discussing who is at fault in this scenario. They basically approve of the policeman's treatment of the woman by judging her actions rather than his. At the heart of the cartoon is also the issue of complacency, which is the act of doing little or nothing when we witness something disturbing, illegal, or immoral. How is this couple being complacent? Do you agree or disagree with their statements, and why? What should they be saying or doing in place of what they are saying?

Now, take a moment to consider some other elements of TAB's drawing. For instance, what punishment, if any, should be given to the woman for breaking the law? Are there circumstances under which this sort of action on the policeman's part is warranted? If so, what might those situations be? What is the effect of drawing an old woman walking a poodle, rather than another type of citizen? How is TAB trying to affect our understanding of police brutality by incorporating the mildly absurd image of the old woman and her dog both being electrocuted by the officer? If you were asked to draw a cartoon depicting police brutality, what would you draw, and what would your point be about this particular act of violence? Consider the messages embedded in this drawing as you read the remaining selections in this chapter.

# mash**UP** essay

The essay that follows is this chapter's Mashup selection. Keeping in mind our definition of a Mashup essay in Chapter 2 (an essay that includes multimedia texts, as well as multiple writing strategies), observe the way the author, Jed Perl, utilizes multimedia texts. For example, he refers to the Abu Ghraib torture photographs that can easily be found online, and he reads these photographs as texts. He also refers to books written on the subject of art, and the mass media responses (in print, online, and on TV) to the Abu Ghraib photo leak. What other sorts of outside, multimedia texts does Perl use to make his argument?

In addition to the types of texts that Perl uses, observe the manner in which he constructs his argument in favor of censoring war photography (the argumentative essay strategy). You should also note the way Perl employs description to create vivid images of the Abu Ghraib photos (the descriptive essay strategy), as well as the manner in which he compares war photography to art (the compare-contrast writing strategy). Finally, you should also note how Perl includes extensive outside sources (the research writing strategy), as well as showing the potential outcome of further publication of war photographs (the cause-effect writing strategy), to aid in his classification (the classification writing strategy) of the Abu Ghraib photographs as a different kind of photography than the high art they have been compared to on occasion since their release.

**Mashup Essay Flowchart**

**Types of Media:**
- Court Documents and Proceedings
- Abu Ghraib Photos
- Editorials on Abu Ghraib Photos
- Articles Discussing "Trophy" Phenomenon
- Blogs
- Book: *The Abu Ghraib Effect*

⬇

**"Picture Imperfect"**
Jed Perl

⬆

**Writing Strategies:**
- Argumentative
- Compare-Contrast
- Cause-Effect
- Classification
- Descriptive
- Research

By employing multiple writing strategies and incorporating a wide variety of multimedia texts, Perl manages to construct a thoughtful, sophisticated, and engaging case in favor of the Bush and Obama administrations' decision to censor these photographs. Not only does he incorporate his own expert opinion (Perl is an expert in the art field who has published several books on the subject), he systematically uses other texts to back his stance. In an effort to weaken the opposing arguments in favor of releasing all the Abu Ghraib photos, Perl also deconstructs the positions of the people who have made the case that these photos are necessary to see, as well as the positions of those who have made comparisons between these photographs and the violent works of some of art's greatest masters.

When you begin writing a Mashup essay of your own in response to the selections in this chapter, revisit Perl's essay to generate ideas for multimedia texts and multiple writing strategies. Use the accompanying flowchart to see the ways in which Perl employs the various writing strategies and multimedia texts he utilizes in his writing.

# Picture Imperfect     Jed Perl

**Let's Start Here••• ▶**    The infamous leaked Abu Ghraib photographs (one pictured here), which are the subject of the following essay, shocked and enraged the world when they first emerged in 2004. They embarrassed the United States, which had already been humbled by the lack of a quick and resounding success in the two wars we continue to wage in Afghanistan and Iraq. More importantly, what the photos showed was the ugly side of war that most people know exists but turn away from because of the discomfort caused by having a public discussion of torture.

So the international conversation on torture and prisoner abuse began. A debate has since ensued over the ethics and morals of war, the responsibility of soldiers, the responsibility of military leadership, and even the very definition of torture. The following essay gets to the root of the photographs' importance in this discussion, as well as why it is important that they be made public, or, conversely, kept secret. Keep in mind as  you read Perl's essay that he approaches the subject as an art expert as well as an engaged citizen. If you feel so inclined, and if you have never seen the photographs in question, take a moment to Google "Abu Ghraib photos" and familiarize yourself with them. Also, as you read the essay, observe the way Perl describes these photos and reads them as texts in order to counter the viewpoints of those who believe we would benefit from releasing them all to the general public.

Jed Perl was a contributing editor to *Vogue* in the 1980s and has been the art critic for *The New Republic* since 1994. He has also authored and coauthored numerous books on art criticism and artistic movements. This essay first appeared in *The New Republic* on June 17, 2009.

These are the primary "texts" that Perl will use throughout the entire essay, which he will read by utilizing his skills as a professional art critic and historian.

What is there to say about photographs we have not seen? There is a good deal to say, when those photographs document the abuse of prisoners in Iraq and Afghanistan. The U.S. government has in its possession as many as 2,000 images that have not been made public, a cache that will add to, but probably not significantly alter, the story we know from the photographs and videos first seen five years ago, taken as U.S. military personnel brutalized prisoners at Abu Ghraib. The lawsuits

These lawsuits are other texts that will be used occasionally by Perl to argue his opinion on the matter of whether to publicize the photos.

demanding the release of these photographs under the Freedom of Information Act date back to the middle years of the Bush administration, and now, the Obama administration, after initially agreeing to a court-ordered release, has reversed course, citing the security of our troops and the danger of giving further material for propaganda to terrorists in the Arab world. The arguments of the American Civil Liberties Union and other organizations that support release cannot be taken lightly. The courts have already concluded, in a number of decisions, that even the possibility that these photographs might endanger American troops does not justify their being withheld. Some have said Obama realizes that the release of the photographs will occur sooner rather

Perl sets up his overall argument for the rest of the essay, which he continues in the opening lines of the next paragraph.

than later and has been mostly trying to avoid their being published on the eve of his trip to Egypt. So is the Obama administration standing in the way of the truth? If we do not see these photographs, are we being denied some information that we need to have now? I am not convinced.

Photographic truth is a particular kind of truth, and that is the case even when the photograph has not been doctored or edited. In going back to the courts to urge that these pictures not be released, the Obama administration is acknowledging this very fact. The argument against releasing them is not that they are not truthful, but, rather, that they represent an aspect of the truth about U.S. behavior in Iraq that Islamic militants will be able to use to cre-

Perl also uses the repetition and reproduction of these images online and in the news as texts.

ate lies about the United States. The repetition of images on television and the Internet—and this is as much the case with our 24/7 news cycle as with the propaganda campaigns of Islamic militants—is a form of editorializing that, by its very nature, reshapes the photographic image, which in the first place represents a singular act of brutalization or the results of a particular sequence of acts.

The argument has been made that the wide distribution of torture photographs helps to concentrate the public's imagination, rendering ideas of brutality and suffering concrete. This is surely true, but it is also true that the public can become inured to even the most violent pictures, can claim image overload, can simply turn away. Photographic images should never become a substitute for the development of the moral imagination, for the ability to comprehend horrors we have not ourselves experienced or for which there is little or no documentation. Sometimes we need to believe things we cannot see, not as a matter of religious faith but of moral conviction.

> **inured:**
> Accustomed to pain or discomfort.

Everybody can call to mind some of the photographs from Abu Ghraib. There is the shot of Lynndie England, the boyish military prison guard, holding a leash at the other end of which is a naked prisoner flat on the floor, pulled half out of his cell. And there is another photograph of a prisoner, his head covered by a conical hood, his outstretched arms attached to wires, standing on a box. These pictures derive from a three-month period, October to December 2003, that has been the subject of a number of military trials and convictions. That these pictures were taken by the perpetrators, as trophies of a kind, has been, for some viewers, nearly as unsettling as the abuse itself. Here is a glimpse of a mentality that Americans did not want to see, certainly not in their countrymen. From a legal point of view, the self-satisfied looks on the faces of the torturers as they pose for the camera certainly reveals a good deal about their mental state. But the ugliness of the self-documentation—the guys-and-gals-having-a-wild-time-together side of the photographic record—can also confuse the issue. The stupidity of the photographs should not be allowed to detract from their monstrousness, which is exactly what Rush Limbaugh and callers on his show were trying to do when they argued that this was just frathouse stuff, people letting off steam, horsing around.

> Perl uses the descriptive writing strategy to paint a vivid picture of the photographs themselves.

> Perl uses Rush Limbaugh's radio talk show and his listeners' responses as texts.

Photographs, in and of themselves, do not necessarily tell us very much. A certain kind of photographic literalism has made it easier for some to argue that these were isolated acts. All there is, so this argument goes, is in the photograph. What you see is what you get. But the grotesque particularity of certain shots can be said, if not to exactly distort the truth, then certainly to skew the truth. There are several close-up photographs of a male prisoner's nipple with a smiley face inscribed

> Perl uses the compare-contrast writing strategy to show the difference between photographs and the reality they are depicting.

in what looks like magic marker. The pop culture sadism is sick-making, no question about it, but if you linger too long here you are succumbing to a diversion. The picture cannot tell us who encouraged or ignored such behavior, or who was responsible for creating an atmosphere in which such things took place. While much of what we know about the lawless conduct of some American soldiers in Iraq comes from these photographs, more probably derives from non-photographic sources: from military documents, congressional testimony, evidence of many kinds. Certainly, the photographs should not be considered without captions. To study them without being aware of the circumstances under which they were produced is to accept them as autonomous images with their own integrity, and that is obscene.

In the five years since these pictures were first seen on "60 Minutes," there have been a number of efforts to decode them, and some of the interpretation strikes me as not so much mistaken as beside the point. It is easy to see that TV news, which is always looking for the next flashpoint, can collapse a complex story into an image that, however horrific, is only one piece of evidence in a story that is even more terrible, if understood in its entirety. But there is also a danger in lingering for too long over the individual photographs, in submitting them to psychological or sociological or art-historical analysis. Soon after the first pictures from Abu Ghraib were released, they were compared to online S&M pornography, and the suggestion was made that soldiers who had not seen Internet porn would have never thought of the leashes, the stress positions, the mortifying nudity, the simulated sex. I worry that this recourse to theories about the psychology of the perpetrators, this effort to give their pathological behavior a sociological setting, can blunt the plain horror of what was done, can make it all seem somehow interesting, the material for a novel or a movie. There have also been comparisons made between the Abu Ghraib photographs and Robert Mapplethorpe's photographs of consensual S&M sex, and this is another line of thinking I find inherently troubling, a form of aggrandizement. The very mention of Mapplethorpe's name adds interest, even cachet to these abhorrent acts. Why dress up the ugly truth? My feeling is that violent power relationships are inherently appealing to certain individuals, and that there could have been military police on duty at Abu Ghraib who felt the urge to act as they did even without a little nudge from Internet porn.

---

*This is an example of Perl's usage of the cause-effect writing strategy.*

*Another use of multimedia texts by Perl to justify and strengthen his argument.*

*This entire paragraph uses the classification strategy. Perl classifies various types of art, artistic periods, and well-known masters. He uses these classifications to show how the Abu Ghraib photos don't fit these classifications.*

**recourse:**
Turning to for help or aid.

**aggrandizement:**
Making greater or more powerful.

**cachet:**
An official seal of approval or quality.

I also resist the connections that have been made between photographs from Abu Ghraib and various works of art, whether Goya's *Disasters of War* or Picasso's *Guernica*. The impulse to see connections between the art of the past and photographic images taken without any conscious thought of creating art can be very strong, especially among those who are familiar with the art in the museums. Sometimes the associations are almost impossible to avoid. Who can forget the news photograph taken at Kent State in 1970, with a young woman kneeling over the body of a student who has just been shot to death, her arms outstretched and mouth open in horror, in a pose that might have come straight out of the iconography of ecstasy and grief in Hellenistic art? But what precisely does this comparison tell us except that the artists of the past were acute observers of human behavior? A recent book by the art historian Stephen F. Eisenman, *The Abu Ghraib Effect*, traces certain gestures and situations that we encounter in the Abu Ghraib images all the way back to the Greeks, and, although Eisenman is very judicious about the connections that he makes, I cannot help wishing that he would have left the pictures from Abu Ghraib as what they are, namely evidence of particular, terrible things done by particular men and women at a particular moment. When heinous acts are associated with artistic acts, there is a danger of amelioration, or, at least, the appearance of amelioration.

Whatever the courts decide, however, we would do well to remember that we can expect too much from photography, that we need to respect the limits of photographic truth. Living in a society that is as widely and vibrantly uncensored as ours, we have an obligation to consider the value of self-censorship, of a reticence or discretion that can shape the onslaught of information. While we cannot achieve knowledge without information—this is a fundamental fact in any democratic society—information does not always advance knowledge, and photographic information in its raw form can mean many different things. We did not need the Abu Ghraib photographs to tell us that men and women do terrible things. The significance of these pictures is particular, specific. And their specificity should be approached with a certain reticence. We must not aggrandize the torturer's photographic acts of self-aggrandizement. And then there is the matter of the privacy of the victims, some of whom may well recognize themselves in these photographs and, I would presume, would not want such images disseminated

**Sidebar notes:**

Famous war-related paintings that Perl uses as texts to contrast the Abu Ghraib photos.

Perl returns to the descriptive writing strategy to again illustrate the contents of a photograph.

**iconography:** The study of religious or sacred images (specifically in relation to art).

Perl researches a fellow art historian's text in order to argue against how it lends credibility to the Abu Ghraib photos.

**judicious:** Shows sound judgment or wisdom.

**amelioration:** Approving them or making them better than they are.

**reticence:** Silence or lack of speaking out.

**aggrandize:** Lend or give power to.

**self-aggrandizement:** Self-empowerment.

around the world. No wonder some of the photographs have been published with the faces or genitals blurred, a distortion of photographic truth that brings home to us in the most immediate way the reality of these awful images.

Photographs turn current events into historical events. Precisely because photographers operate in the moment, their work has the effect of emphasizing the speed with which the present becomes the past. If this is a paradox, it is one that everybody embraces when they rush to see the photographs of the vacation or the party—to see what they've just experienced reframed as a story. It is surely true that, in order for the full historical record of American terror and abuse in Iraq and Afghanistan to finally be revealed, all the photographs in the possession of the U.S. government will need to be seen. But, even if some of the photographs show us significantly different aspects of what went on, it is unlikely that our understanding will be significantly altered, and, in any event, the fragmentary reports of what these photographs contain do not suggest that major revelations are in store. What we have already seen in the photographs from Abu Ghraib will not be better understood by seeing more photographs, that is for sure. Photography can provide evidence. But people have to make the judgments.

**paradox:**
An idea that contradicts itself and therefore cannot be true.

**Let's Pause Here•••▶** Perl makes an interesting and passionate argument about why these photographs are important to the larger discussion of American soldiers torturing and also human nature. Do you feel he is correct in assigning so much meaning and importance to the photographs? Or do you think he is making a big deal out of something we would rather just put behind us? What do you think other people in the world think about our soldiers not only abusing prisoners, but also documenting it in a trophy-like manner, as Perl suggests? How do you feel about this event? What do you think the soldiers were hoping to accomplish both by the torture and the documenting of it in photographs? Do you agree with Perl's assertion that the 2,000 photographs the government has in its possession should be kept classified?

**Let's Take It Further•••▼**

1. What was your reaction when you read about or saw the Abu Ghraib photographs? Describe how they made you feel, and explain the reason why.

2. Why does Perl so dislike the comparison that has been made between these photographs and art? Is it merely because of his art background, or is there another reason he is so adamantly against comparisons being drawn between the torture photos and the works of great painters? Do you agree or disagree with Perl's stance on the issue of art comparisons to the photos?

3. How do you feel knowing there are more than 2,000 additional photographs documenting torture of prisoners? What could be the justification for so many photographs being taken?

4. Who is Perl's audience, based on the argument that he presents as well as his language and writing strategies? How can you tell whether he is speaking to the general public, the Obama administration, soldiers, civilians, or people from other countries? How might have his writing strategies and texts used throughout his essay differed for each of these audiences?

5. Do you agree with the author's assertion that the Obama administration should not release the more than 2,000 photos of prisoner abuse by American soldiers and hired personnel? If so, why? If not, why not? Locate other texts addressing this topic and incorporate them into your essay to back your own opinion on the matter.

6. What do you believe the pictures say about the people who took them? Locate texts written by either psychologists or social behaviorists who have discussed the "trophy" phenomenon described in this article. How are these soldiers displaying traits of the trophy phenomenon, or are they attempting to make some other form of statement?

7. Research the outcome of the Abu Ghraib torture trials. How appropriate do you feel the punishments were for these actions? Too harsh? Too lenient? What reason or justification did the various soldiers who stood trial for these photographs give for taking the pictures? Explain their rationale, and discuss whether you agree with their reasoning. Were there people who took the fall for their fellow soldiers or people higher up the chain of command, or did everyone involved get punished? Do you feel there are others who should be brought before the courts in relation to the photographs? Be sure to include descriptions of the photographs to make them present in the essay you are writing.

8. Is there ever a time when torture is justified? If so, explain and describe a scenario that you believe justifies torturing people. What type of torture is justifiable in this circumstance? What other options might be used first? What procedures do you think should be followed and exhausted before resorting to torture? Define and describe which techniques are justifiable and which are unacceptable under any circumstances. Then explain why.

9. Analyze one or more of the Abu Ghraib photographs. Try to make sense of what is being portrayed. What is the photograph "saying"? In other words, by observing the position of the people in the photo—both the soldiers and the prisoners—see if you can figure out what the meaning is behind the particular photo. What do you think the soldiers are saying to the viewers (even if they intended to be the photo's only viewers)? What message might they be trying to portray to the enemy (either those in the photos or those who might see them in the future)? You may even use a book on body language to help decipher what is being said.

10. How was the media and public reaction to the Abu Ghraib photographs different from the reaction to the photographs of the U.S. Army "Kill Team" photographs leaked in early 2011? Locate articles on the Web related to both photograph leaks and compare and contrast the outcomes of both. Which event caused a larger national (and even international) furor? Why was one seen as worse than the other? Which event do you think was more horrific, and why?

11. Create a video or image collage consisting of the Abu Ghraib (and possibly other) torture photographs. Then, construct a series of interview questions for your peers or schoolmates about violence and torture in order to determine whether they agree or disagree with torture or violence overall. Use the same series of questions before and after they view the photo collage and see if their opinions change. Be sure to document and describe what their responses are to the photographs as well. Describe the experience in your final essay and illustrate what, if anything, you took away from the entire process.

# Texas Manhandle

**Let's Start Here•••▶** The selections in the chapter thus far have dealt with the abuse of power by law enforcement and military personnel toward prisoners. However, a far more common form of power abuse that we are exposed to in popular culture is police brutality toward regular citizens who may or may not have broken the law. There are, of course, several famous cases of police brutality. The Rodney King case, spanning 1991–1993, is one of the most notorious, but there have been several instances of police brutality video recorded in the years following that event.

Though the selection that follows is about police brutality, it was not recorded and therefore did not receive as much public or media attention. This essay is an affidavit from a lawsuit filed on behalf of 12-year-old Dymond Milburn, which alleges police brutality toward her on the day described. Pay close attention to the manner in which the alleged victim and alleged perpetrators of brutality are depicted within this document. Reserve your judgment of who is in the wrong until the end, if you can.

———————————————

Dymond Milburn, at the time of this lawsuit, was a 12-year-old African American girl accused of "resisting arrest," who was beaten by four police officers from the Galveston, Texas, police department. The following court document is from a lawsuit filed in December 2007 in Galveston, Texas, against Sergeant Gilbert Gomez and officers Justin Popovich, Sean Stewart, and David Roark, on behalf of plaintiffs Emily Milburn and her daughter, Dymond. On September 15, 2006, police arrived at Dymond's middle school and arrested her for assaulting a public servant, a charge that stems from Dymond's struggling during the incident described below.

On the night of August 22, a blue van drove up while Dymond Milburn, an African American, was in the front yard of her home. At the time, Dymond was twelve years old and an honor student taking advanced classes at her middle school. She was five feet six inches tall and weighed 120 pounds and was wearing a T-shirt and red athletic shorts.

Four officers exited the van. They were not in uniform and did not identify themselves as police. One officer grabbed Dymond and said, "You're a prostitute. You're coming with us." An officer later said he suspected she was a prostitute because of the "tight shorts" she was wearing. Dymond's shorts were not tight.

Dymond grabbed a tree and started yelling, "Daddy, daddy." One officer covered her mouth while the others tried to handcuff her. Dymond's mother and father heard her cries and rushed outside, where they found their daughter holding onto the tree with one arm while two officers struck the back of her head with a flashlight, hit her neck and throat, slapped her across the face, and told her to get off the tree.

"That's our daughter. She's twelve!" Dymond's father said.

"I don't care if she's twenty-two, thirty-two, or forty-six," said an officer. "Tell her to calm down."

Dymond's parents asked the officers if they could comfort their daughter but were told no.

The family's five-month-old puppy bit one officer's leg. He threatened to shoot it if they did not grab it.

Dymond's parents took her to the emergency room for treatment. A physician found that she suffered injuries from multiple blows to the head, face, neck, lower back, left shoulder, and left hip area. She suffered a contusion to the back of the head (where she was struck with a flashlight). There were abrasions on her arm and wrist. Her throat was swollen; she experienced nausea, vomiting, difficulty swallowing, and hoarseness of voice due to her being struck in the throat. She had black eyes, scalp lacerations, and tenderness of the vertebrae. She experienced double vision and hearing loss. Dymond also had blood in her ear, a bruised nasal septum, and a nosebleed.

Since the incident, Dymond has had regular nightmares in which police officers are raping her, beating her, and cutting off her fingers. Dymond sought psychological treatment and was diagnosed with posttraumatic stress disorder. Her fear has prevented her from participating in normal activities such as going outside to play, which she no longer considers safe.

The Milburns eventually learned that the dispatch call the officers were responding to reported three white female prostitutes soliciting men half a block from the family's home.

**Let's Pause Here•••▶**     Observe the way the various "actors" in the above affidavit are depicted. Why do you suppose Dymond is not only described as "African American," but also as an "honors student taking advanced classes"? What does this do for you as a reader, if anything? Do you consider what is being described above as police brutality? If so, why? If not, why not?

**Let's Take It Further•••▼**

1. Why do you suppose the lawsuit points out that the officers in question were not in uniform and did not identify themselves as police? How, if at all, does it change your perspective of what happened?

2. What is the effect of the language used in this affidavit when it describes the alleged actions of that day? Is there a bias toward one side over the other? If so, who is this biased against? How does this relate to the fact that it was filed on behalf of the plaintiff, Dymond Milburn?

3. How did the event being described make you feel as you read it? Point out specific "scenes" being described to which you had an emotional response and explain what that emotional response was and why.

4.  Why would the lawsuit bother to describe how Dymond was dressed? How is it relevant to the case? Is it relevant to the case how the arresting officers were dressed? Why or why not?

5.  Look for other language in the article that is an attempt to appeal to a reader's emotions. Which descriptions, if any, do you feel are purposely placed into the story to sway your opinion one way or another? Did any of these particular descriptions of the people in the lawsuit manage to shed light on the situation? If so, what were they?

6.  Scour the article for language designed to appeal to a reader's emotions and explain how the language accomplishes this. Specifically point out examples of emotional language and descriptions and explain how they evoke a response in you as a reader. Who is the audience the document is designed to appeal to? Which places, if any, did you feel an emotional response (anger, disgust, annoyance, etc.)? Which of these responses do you think are intentionally sought by the author of this document, and which of these are responses to the situation itself?

7.  Dymond's lawyer claims she was diagnosed with PTSD. Locate the definition of PTSD and how it is caused, and explain what the term means. Then explain how Dymond's experience and the aftermath, based on the descriptions given in the affidavit, conform or do not conform to the definition of PTSD. How does the diagnosis of PTSD alter the circumstances of the case, if at all?

8.  Research the Dymond Milburn case and describe its outcome. Do you feel that justice was served? Why or why not? What specifically happened in the trial (and verdict) that you agree or disagree with? Describe the reaction of the community based on texts available to you. How does this case compare to similar verdicts in police brutality trials?

9.  How would you define police brutality? Locate any of the many well-known instances of police brutality and read the stories about them. Choose one in particular and compare-contrast the case to Dymond's. How are those situations similar to Dymond's? How are they different? What, do you suppose, might be a reason for the incidents in question to have been viewed by the police officers as justified? What trends emerge among the cases you located, if any?

# No Jail Time for Cop Who Pummeled Bartender

**Matt Walberg**

**Let's Start Here•••▶**   Of the many police brutality cases that have come to the public's attention in the last few decades, most of them have been focused within a handful of large police departments in major U.S. cities (the most notorious include Los Angeles, New York City, New Orleans, and Chicago). Among these most troubled departments in the country—in terms of frequency of allegations raised against the department—the Chicago Police Department has had some of the highest-profile cases in recent years.

The following article, written by Matt Walberg, is the outcome of a lengthy trial of alleged police brutality in Chicago, Illinois, against a woman named Karolina Obrycka. Mr. Walberg, who covered the trial from the beginning to its end for the *Chicago Tribune*, recounts the major events of the trial as well as the story's history. As you read the article, observe the descriptions he gives of the officer and the plaintiff in the case, Karolina Obrycka.

---

Matt Walberg is a reporter and writer for the *Chicago Tribune*. He covers criminal courts in the city of Chicago. The following article first appeared in the *Chicago Tribune* on June 23, 2009.

A Chicago police officer avoided jail time today for pummeling a woman who was tending bar, even though prosecutors produced a previously unseen video showing him beating someone else at the bar hours earlier.

Anthony Abbate was sentenced to two years probation for beating Karolina Obrycka in February of 2007. He could have gotten up to five years for the attack, which was captured by the bar's security camera and shown around the world.

Judge John Fleming said he decided against jail because he did not believe the crime was serious enough and throwing Abbate behind bars would not be a deterrent to others.

"If I believed that sending Anthony Abbate to prison would stop people from getting drunk and hitting other people, I'd sentence him to the maximum," the judge said. "But I don't believe that is the case."

Fleming also imposed a curfew of 8 p.m. to 6 a.m. for Abbate, who declined to say anything to the judge before he was sentenced. The cop must also attend anger management classes, undergo alcohol evaluation, and perform 130 hours of community service.

Fleming said he would like Abbate to perform the service in a homeless shelter.

In arguing for prison time, prosecutors produced a previously unseen video from the bar hours before Obrycka was attacked showing Abbate beating someone else.

In the video, a man in the bar can be seen speaking with Abbate for a few seconds, after which Abbate grabs the man, slams him against a wall and then throws him across the room. The man crashes to the floor and into the bar stools, and Abbate stands over him as the man tries to shimmy away on his back.

Assistant State's Attorney LuAnn Snow said the attack was one of three unprovoked assaults in the span of 6 hours, a violent window into "a day in the life of Anthony Abbate." Authorities did not charge Abbate with the other two alleged attacks.

Snow said it was "by the grace of God" that Obrycka wasn't more severely injured.

In a brief statement to the court, Obrycka said the attack has left her fearful, has affected her marriage and left her unable to trust others.

"It was terrifying to be attacked by such a big man," Obrycka told Fleming. "I tried to protect myself, but I was helpless."

As time passed, "I thought about the beating a lot," she said. "I had nightmares about it, I try to avoid thinking about the beating, but I was helpless again . . . I pulled away from people close to me. I was irritable and angry, [and] I was fearful of other people. If someone walked behind me, I would jump, and unexpected noises made me jump, too.

"The world didn't feel like a safe place anymore," Obrycka said. "I also started to have anxiety attacks which I never had before. When something would remind me of the beating, I would start to feel nauseated, then vomit. My head hurt, my hands became numb and then I would start to sweat and shake."

"My world still feels changed because of this beating," she continued. "I have a hard time trusting people, including my husband. Our marriage is very difficult. I'm still irritable and suspicious . . . I'm working very hard to recover from this beating, but it is harder than I could ever imagine."

Before handing down his sentence, Fleming said "any adult in the world" would know better than to act as Abbate did, but said he did not believe that a term of imprisonment was appropriate.

He noted that Abbate had no prior criminal history, and his crime did not involve a handful of other factors that under the law would justify a sentence greater than probation.

**delineated:**
Outlined.

"He didn't cause serious harm—the doctor said it was bumps and bruises," Fleming said as he delineated the reasons why probation was the correct sentence.

He said the widespread media attention was immaterial in reaching his decision.

"The fact that this 30-second video has probably been seen by more people than any other crime in the world does not make it a greater crime," Fleming said.

Fleming asked Abbate if he wanted to say anything but Abbate declined. The officer left the courthouse with his father and his fiancé, refusing to comment to reporters.

Obrycka said outside the courtroom that she wished Abbate had said he was sorry.

"I'm very disappointed that he didn't apologize for what he did," she said, adding that she was also disappointed in the sentence he received.

Abbate had faced several charges, including intimidation, conspiracy and communicating with a witness, and official misconduct. But prosecutors dismissed most of them before the trial began.

Fleming dismissed the two counts of official misconduct and found Abbate guilty of aggravated battery.

The police department is seeking to have Abbate fired, and the Independent Police Review Authority has recommended that he be dismissed, according to Superintendant Jody Weis. The case is up before the Police Board on July 7.

"I don't think anyone who behaves like that should be a police officer," Weis said after the sentencing.

But Weis said he was not going to recommend the officer's case to federal authorities because he was off-duty at the time. "I would be shocked if the Department of Justice pursued [the case]" he said.

Mark P. Donahue, head of the Fraternal Order of Police, had little comment about the sentence except to say, "He had his day in court, and like it or not, the results are what they are."

**Let's Pause Here•••▶** How did you react as you read the accusations against the police officer, Anthony Abbate? What was your reaction to the reasons given by the judge for sentencing Abbate to probation? Do you think that his sentence was fair? What is your reaction to the verdict in this particular case (in terms of the various charges that Abbate faced and the one count for which he was found guilty)? Is it appropriate, outrageous, or not at all surprising? How was this story different from other news reports of alleged police brutality?

**Let's Take It Further•••▼**

1. Mark P. Donahue, head of the Chicago Chapter of the Fraternal Order of Police, responded to the sentencing by stating, "[Abbate] had his day in court, and like it or not, the results are what they are." What does he mean by this statement and how does it relate to the Obrycka case? Is his statement appropriate to this situation? Why or why not?

2. Based on Walberg's language and descriptions throughout the entire article—both of the officer and Karolina Obrycka—were you able to detect a preference for an outcome on his part? How does he attempt to appeal to his readers using descriptions and various writing strategies? Is he successful? Why or why not?

3. What does it tell you about her expectations of the trial's outcome that Obrycka describes her life since the beating in the manner that she does? In other words, how has the beating affected Mrs. Obrycka, and how might her life continue to be affected because of the case's outcome? Should any of her statements have factored into the judge's decision for sentencing Officer Abbate? Why or why not?

4. Is there any merit to the judge's reasoning for giving Abbate probation rather than the five-year maximum sentence? How would you respond to his statement that follows if you had the opportunity to address the judge: "If I believed that sending Anthony Abbate to prison would stop people from getting drunk and hitting other people, I'd sentence him to the maximum. But I don't believe that is the case."

5. Explain how the article paints Obrycka and Officer Abbate as "texts" that can be read. Compare the different descriptions of both people in the article, and explain how the texts of these people may or may not have had an outcome on the sentencing. Revisit earlier articles on this case—by Matt Walberg as well as other reporters—to see the various ways Obrycka and Abate were portrayed throughout the trial.

6. Compare Karolina Obrycka as a text in this article to Dymond Milburn as a text in the "Texas Manhandle" selection. How are both plaintiffs being represented as texts in a similar way,

and how are they being represented differently? What is the outcome of this technique for the plaintiffs? Does it help or hurt them, ultimately? Do you feel both cases exploit the idea of people as texts? Does the media play a role in this as well, or are the interpretations of these two plaintiffs as texts only done within the context of the court system?

**7.** Locate Walberg's article on the *Chicago Tribune* website and view both videos mentioned in the article (the Obrycka beating and the additional beating hours earlier). How does the prosecutor's statement, "[the videos are] a day in the life of Anthony Abbate," get illustrated by both videos? What do the videos say about Officer Abbate as a text, and how might it explain what "a day in [Abbate's] life" might mean?

**8.** Locate both videos online, as well as the original Walberg article featured here, and read the commentary beneath each video and the article. What are the overall trends that emerge in the public's response to the crimes featured in the video? How do they react to the knowledge that Officer Abbate was not charged with the previous two assaults the same evening as the Obrycka beating? Illustrate the types of recommendations people have for appropriate forms of punishment, as well as the rationale for those who feel Officer Abbate received an appropriate sentence.

**9.** Locate a case of police brutality where an officer or officers were found guilty and compare it to another case where the officer or officers were acquitted. How were the trials handled differently in both cases? What was similar and different in terms of the alleged crimes? Which turned out to be the worse of the two? Why did one trial end in acquittal and one end in a guilty verdict? Describe and explain the situation surrounding each, as well as the type of evidence offered in each case. What was the public reaction to both verdicts and how were the reactions similar or different?

# "The Body as Weapon, as Inspiration," "The Performer," and "Police Dog"
### Paul Martínez Pompa

**Let's Start Here•••▶**    When most people think of poetry, we tend to think of it as a form of writing that is romantic both in subject matter and in language. While there is a great deal of poetry that deals with love and romance, there is also poetry that occasionally goes to darker places. The following three poems, which are excerpted from a collection of poetry titled *My Kill Adore Him*, deal with three different forms of violence: police brutality, street toughness, and even acts of terrorism.

As you read the poems, observe the way the poems are narrated, paying close attention to the manner in which Paul Martínez Pompa describes the events he is depicting in each. Be aware of the point of view used (in other words, who is telling the story) and the language used to describe the various people featured in the poems.

Paul Martínez Pompa is the author of *My Kill Adore Him* (University of Notre Dame Press, 2009), which was selected by Martín Espada for the 2008 Andrés Montoya Poetry Prize. His chapbook, *Pepper Spray*, was published by Momotombo Press in 2006. Martínez Pompa's poetry and prose have been anthologized in *Telling Tongues* and *The Wind Shifts: New Latino Poetry*. He earned degrees from the University of Chicago and Indiana University, where he served as a poetry editor for *Indiana Review*. The following poems are excerpted from his book, *My Kill Adore Him*.

## THE BODY AS WEAPON, AS INSPIRATION

The body as weapon, as inspiration
when she walks into a Jerusalem market
and explodes herself. Not so much
the explosive force, but the shrapnel

a year ago that tore through her
mother's chest and maimed her
brother's legs. Her father was spared
unnecessary pain—instantly dead under

the collapse of ceiling joists & plywood.
Somehow she survived. Now only a scar
on her forehead and an unofficial apology
from the State. Soon men will fall

to the ground with ringing in their ears.
There will be tiny fragments of glass
& bone caught in the skin of the undead.
There will be retaliation strikes,

missile bombardments, another round
of bulldozers. And there will be a poet
thousands of miles away, excited
by the burden of writing this thing.

## THE PERFORMER

I play it chingon in full length
mirrors. Mad doggin' my reflection—
some kind of *don't fuck with me*
skin language. Rollin hard on
suburban boulevards. Scare

the white off kids, teachers shake
their heads. Almost beggin' for a beat
down. Toy gun real enough
to fear. Step to the mirror, pull out my
*what-chu gonna donow?*

Pray he backs down, punks out.
Everyone watching, the gun
trembles in the mirror. Pistol whip.

He goes down. All the kids cheer
my head thick with e—g—o.

## POLICE DOG

it's all just
play to wrap

your mouth
around a man's

wrist barely
break skin

to growl tug
hold on till

the officers
arrive only then

do things
get serious

**Let's Pause Here•••▶**    What is your initial reaction to these poems, based on your expectations of poetry? How do these poems differ from other poems you have encountered in the past? What is the purpose behind the various points of view Pompa uses in his three poems? Does it make them more emotional, or is the subject matter of the three pieces emotional enough without the added layer of a person's perspective being shown? What do you think Pompa is trying to say about these different forms of violence—terrorism, police brutality, and the idea of street toughness?

**Let's Take It Further•••▼**

1.  In "Police Dog," why do you think that Pompa states "it's all just play" when describing the violence the police dog inflicts on the person, only to state later that when the police officers arrive, "only then do things get serious"? What do these two statements imply?

2.  In "The Performer," what is being "performed," and by whom? For whom is he performing? What does the performer hope to accomplish? What does the last line of the poem, "My head thick with e—g—o," imply about both the performer and the purpose of his performance?

3.  In "The Body as Weapon, as Inspiration," what is Pompa describing? How does he explain what might make someone want to commit an act of terrorism? Do you agree with his theory, or do you think there is never a reason to justify such an act? How is the body being used as a "weapon"? How is it an "inspiration"?

4.  Research the idea of how police dogs are to be used, not only for locating drugs or bodies, but also how they are supposed to intimidate alleged criminals with their ferocity. Next, discuss the way Pompa illustrates police dogs being used in his poem. How are the two similar, and how are they different? What is the purpose of how Pompa depicts them in this poem?

5.  Locate a story of a woman who has committed a terrorist act in recent years, specifically a suicide bombing. See if you can find the background story on the person and compare it to

the background story Pompa illustrates in his poem. Are the stories similar or different? How might you account for the motivation to commit such an act, based on the explanations given in both the poem and any news story you were able to locate?

6. If you have ever experienced any act of violence at the hands of someone else (or witnessed an act of violence), describe the situation as you remember it. Are there any similarities to the poems above? If so, what are they? If it was completely different, attempt to reconstruct the situation and explain how and what you learned.

# Losing Is for Losers Michael Kinahan

**Let's Start Here•••▶**  There are many ways that a person in a position of power can abuse their position. While someone who is a coach might not be seen as being in a position of power by an outsider, anyone who has ever been coached in a sport realizes that person does indeed hold a great deal of power over players. In recent years there have been stories of coaches who have abused their players, with varying outcomes. Sometimes a coach is fired, and sometimes the community rallies around the person to defend him or her.

The following brief text is an email from a soccer coach to the families of his team of seven-year-old girls. He was later forced to resign, but claimed that the email was a satire. Remember that satirical writing makes a serious point by disguising it within the context of a joke or some other far-fetched idea. If, indeed, Mr. Kinahan is engaging in satire, what do you think he is trying to say about those who are either rabid about sports or who think violence and sports are inextricably linked? If you do not see his email as a satirical comment on the nature of sports (and its inherent violence), then attempt to make the case for how this represents an abuse of power as you read the following email.

---

Michael Kinahan was a coach of a soccer team for girls aged seven and under in Scituate, Massachusetts. The following is excerpted from a March 2009 email to the children's parents. After parents complained to league officials, Kinahan resigned, saying in his resignation letter that the email was meant to be "a satire of those who take youth sports too seriously for the wrong reasons." The email was obtained by the (Quincy, Massachusetts) *Patriot Ledger*. It was reprinted in *Harper's* magazine in September 2009.

Congratulations on being selected for Team 7 (forest-green shirts) of the Scituate Soccer Club! My name is Michael, and I have been fortunate enough to be selected to coach what I know will be a wonderful group of young ladies.

Okay, here's the real deal: Team 7 will be called Green Death. We will only acknowledge "Team 7" for scheduling and disciplinary purposes. Green Death is not a team but a family (some say cult) that you belong to forever. We play fair at all times, but we play tough and physical soccer. We have some returning players who know the deal; for the others, I only expect 110 percent at every game and practice. We do not cater to superstars but prefer the gritty determination of journeymen who bring their lunch pail to work every week, chase every ball, and dig in corners like a Michael Vick pit bull.

Some say soccer at this age is about fun, and I completely agree. I believe, however, that winning is fun and losing is for losers. Ergo, we will strive for the W in each game. Although we may not win every game (excuse me, I just got a little nauseous), I expect us to fight for every loose ball and play every shift as if it were the finals of the World Cup. As I spent a good Saturday morning listening to the legal-liability BS, which included a thirty-minute dissertation on how we need to baby the kids and especially the refs, I was disgusted. The kids will run, they will fall, get bumps and bruises, even bleed a little. Big deal; it's good for them (but I do hope the other team is the one bleeding). If the refs can't handle a little criticism, then they should turn in their whistles. My heckling of the refs actually helps them develop as people. The political-correctness police are not welcome on my sidelines. America's youth are becoming fat, lazy, and noncompetitive because competition is viewed as "bad." I argue that competition is crucial to the evolution of our species and our survival in what has become an increasingly competitive global economy and dangerous world. Second-place trophies are nothing to be proud of. They serve only as a reminder that you missed your goal; their only purpose is as an inspiration to do that next set of reps. Don't animals eat what they kill? (And yes, someone actually kills the meat we eat—it isn't grown in plastic wrap.) And speaking of meat, I expect that the ladies be put on a diet of fish, undercooked red meat, and lots of veggies. No junk food. Protein shakes are encouraged, and while blood doping and HGH use is frowned upon, there is no testing policy. And at the risk of stating the obvious, blue slushies are for winners.

These are my views and not necessarily the views of the league (but they should be). I recognize that my school of thought may be an ideological shift from conventional norms. But it is imperative that we all fight the good fight, get involved now, and resist the urge to become sweatxedo-wearing yuppies who sit on the sidelines in L.L. Bean chairs sipping mocha-latte-half-caf-accinos while discussing reality TV and home decorating with other feeble-minded folks. I want to hear cheering, I want to hear encouragement, I want to get the team pumped up and know they are playing for something.

**cognizant:**
Aware.

We are all cognizant of the soft bigotry that expects women, and especially little girls, to be dainty and submissive; I wholeheartedly reject such drivel. My overarching goal is to develop ladies who are confident and fearless, who will stand up for their beliefs and challenge the status quo. Girls who will kick ass and take names on the field, off the field, and throughout their lives. I want these girls to be winners in the game of life. Who's with me?

Go Green Death!

**Let's Pause Here••• ▶**     Did you find yourself horrified or amused by the email? If so, why? What did you think of the tone of the piece? Did it strike you as serious and offensive, or obviously playful and joking? Note the way he tries to rile up the girls and even compares how he envisions them acting as similar to "a Michael Vick pit bull." What do you suppose is his purpose in addressing the team in such a manner? Was this, or was it not, an abuse of power?

**Let's Take It Further••• ▼**

1. Do you believe it was fair for the coach to be asked to resign, based on the content of this email? If you believe it was the right thing to do, explain why he should have resigned. If you believe he should have been able to keep his job coaching this girls' team, explain why.

2. Who do you think the true audience of this email was meant to be, based on the language and examples used by Coach Kinahan? Was it the girls? Their parents? "Rabid" fans of sports? All of the above?

3. If you agree that the piece is satire, as the coach claims it was, what is he satirizing? Cite specific lines that show his opinion on matters such as violence in sports.

4. How would you have reacted if the same email was sent to your daughter? Would you have been offended or amused? Why? If you had to explain to a child what the coach meant with his email, how would you do that?

5. Are we not allowed to have a sense of humor when dealing with children, or is that considered taboo? If so, why? What, in particular, about the coach's obvious humor was in bad taste? What was acceptable humor, and why?

6. Observe and underline all the violent imagery in the text of the email. Then, locate other sports articles, reporting, or even on-air commentary, and compare it to the language of the email. How is it the same and how does it differ? If the audience were different, would the email have been less offensive? How is the coach working within the language and parameters of "sports talk" in the construction of this email?

7. Should children be protected from competitiveness, or does the coach's point about lack of competition resulting in "fat, lazy" kids ring true? If so, why? Locate sources that discuss this topic to back your opinion, and describe the issue of modern coaching techniques for children (see also "In Defense of the Fistfight" earlier in the chapter). What other claims from the coach can you back or refute using additional sources?

8. How do you feel about the coach's comments regarding the parents of children who play sports? Do such parents adhere to his descriptions, or do they differ? In what ways are they the same or different? Use personal examples and descriptions as well as stories in the news and mass media to back your claims.

9. Kinahan is also directly referencing parents who get so caught up in the sport that they commit acts of violence. Locate a recent example of an outbreak of violence at a children's sporting event and see how the person committing the act justifies it to the authorities or media. Do you agree with his or her position? Is violence in the presence of children ever justified? How does Coach Kinahan's email address this topic of overzealous parents?

**10.** Construct a satirical "rally" or "pep talk" video, in the spirit of Kinahan's email, that mimics the serious versions of the same. What elements of sports and its competitiveness and potential violence are you addressing, and how does your video accomplish this? If there are "right" reasons to take sports seriously (as implied by Kinahan's justification of his email by saying he was satirizing those who take sports seriously for the "wrong reasons"), what are those, and how does your video critique the "wrong" reasons as well? What do you hope people take away from your video?

# Offensive Play
**Malcolm Gladwell**

**Let's Start Here•••▶** While direct violence toward a person is certainly one form of abuse, so too can it be abuse to do nothing in the face of harm to those whose lives are supposed to be protected. This is one of the implied accusations within the following essay that simultaneously discusses the aggressive nature of football and compares it to the violence of dogfighting.

In the following selection, excerpted from a larger article by the same title, Malcolm Gladwell asks uncomfortable questions about our national passion for violent sports. Exploring the national outrage that resulted from the 2007 arrest of football quarterback Michael Vick for dogfighting, Gladwell draws a comparison between the way dogs are treated in dogfighting and the way NFL players are treated within their own sport. The comparisons are eerily similar. Strangely, most of the general public sees dogfighting as a moral outrage, and yet we do little or nothing in the face of the devastating injuries suffered by humans in the sport of football. Gladwell sees this as an act of complacency (and hence abuse) on the part of fans and those in the highest managerial positions in the NFL and makes the case for how we should reconsider this sport in a new light.

So we end this chapter with a moral question: What makes one of these forms of violence worse than the other? For that matter, what makes any form of violence worse than another? As you read this final selection, consider this question in light of the dogfighting versus football issue, and also in terms of all the forms of violence addressed within this chapter.

---

Malcolm Gladwell is a writer for *The New Yorker* and a best-selling author based in New York City. He has been a staff writer for *The New Yorker* since 1996. He is best known for his books *The Tipping Point* (2000), *Blink* (2005), *Outliers* (2008), and *What the Dog Saw: And Other Adventures* (2009). Gladwell's books and articles often deal with the unexpected implications of research in the social sciences and make frequent and extended use of academic work, particularly in the areas of psychology and social psychology. The following essay first appeared in *The New Yorker*'s October 19, 2009, issue.

One evening in August, Kyle Turley was at a bar in Nashville with his wife and some friends. It was one of the countless little places in the city that play live music. He'd ordered a beer, but was just sipping it, because he was driving home. He had eaten an hour and a half earlier. Suddenly, he felt a sensation of heat. He was light-headed, and began to sweat. He had been having episodes like that with increasing frequency during the past year—headaches, nausea. One month, he had vertigo every day, bouts in which he felt as if he were stuck to a wall. But this was worse. He asked his wife if he could sit on her stool for a moment. The warmup band was still playing, and he remembers saying, "I'm just going to take a nap right here until the next band comes on." Then he was lying on the floor, and someone was standing over him. "The guy was freaking out," Turley recalled. "He was saying, 'Damn, man, I couldn't find a pulse,' and my wife said, 'No, no. You were breathing.' I'm, like, 'What? What?'"

> **vertigo:**
> A confused or dizzy sensation of the mind.

They picked him up. "We went out in the parking lot, and I just lost it," Turley went on. "I started puking everywhere. I couldn't stop. I got in the car, still puking. My wife, she was really scared, because I had never passed out like that before, and I started becoming really paranoid. I went into a panic. We get to the emergency room. I started to lose control. My limbs were shaking, and I couldn't speak. I was conscious, but I couldn't speak the words I wanted to say."

Turley is six feet five. He is thirty-four years old, with a square jaw and blue eyes. For nine years, before he retired, in 2007, he was an offensive lineman in the National Football League. He knew all the stories about former football players. Mike Webster, the longtime Pittsburgh Steeler and one of the greatest players in N.F.L. history, ended his life a recluse, sleeping on the floor of the Pittsburgh Amtrak station. Another former Pittsburgh Steeler, Terry Long, drifted into chaos and killed himself four years ago by drinking antifreeze. Andre Waters, a former defensive back for the Philadelphia Eagles, sank into depression and pleaded with his girlfriend—"I need help, somebody help me"—before shooting himself in the head. There were men with aching knees and backs and hands, from all those years of playing football. But their real problem was with their heads, the one part of their body that got hit over and over again.

"Lately, I've tried to break it down," Turley said. "I remember, every season, multiple occasions where I'd hit someone so hard that my eyes went cross-eyed, and they wouldn't come uncrossed for a full series of plays. You are just out there, trying to hit the guy in the middle, because there are three of them. You don't remember much. There are the cases where you hit a guy and you'd get into a collision where everything goes *off*. You're dazed. And there are the others where you are involved in a big, long drive. You start on your own five-yard line, and drive all the way down the field—fifteen, eighteen plays in a row sometimes. Every play: collision, collision, collision. By the time you get to the other end of the field, you're seeing spots. You feel like you are going to black out. Literally, these white explosions—*boom, boom, boom*—lights getting dimmer and brighter, dimmer and brighter.

"Then, there was the time when I got knocked unconscious. That was in St. Louis, in 2003. My wife said that I was out a minute or two on the field. But I was *gone* for about four hours after that. It was the last play of the third quarter. We were playing the Packers. I got hit in the back of the head. I saw it on film a little while afterward. I was running downfield, made a block on a guy. We fell to the ground. A guy was chasing the play, a little guy, a defensive back, and he jumped over me as I was coming up, and he kneed me right in the back of the head. *Boom!*

"They sat me down on the bench. I remember Marshall Faulk coming up and joking with me, because he knew that I was messed up. That's what happens in the N.F.L: 'Oooh. You got effed up. Oooh.' The trainer came up to me and said, 'Kyle, let's take you to the locker room.' I remember looking up at a clock, and there was only a minute and a half left in the game—and I had no idea that much time had elapsed. I showered and took all my gear off. I was sitting at my locker. I don't remember anything. When I came back, after being hospitalized, the guys were joking with me because Georgia Frontiere"—then the team's owner—"came in the locker room, and they said I was butt-ass naked and I gave her a big hug. They were dying laughing, and I was, like, 'Are you serious? I did that?'

"They cleared me for practice that Thursday. I probably shouldn't have. I don't know what damage I did from that, because my head was really hurting. But when you're coming off an injury you're frustrated. I wanted to play the next game. I was just so mad that this happened to me that I'm overdoing it. I was just going after guys in practice. I was really trying to use my head more, because I was so frustrated, and the coaches on the sidelines are, like, 'Yeah. We're going to win this game. He's going to lead the team.' That's football. You're told either that you're hurt or that you're injured. There is no middle ground. If you are hurt, you can play. If you are injured, you can't, and the line is whether you can walk and if you can put on a helmet and pads."

Turley said that he loved playing football so much that he would do it all again. Then he began talking about what he had gone through in the past year. The thing that scared him most about that night at the bar was that it felt exactly like the time he was knocked unconscious. "It was identical," he said. "It was my worst episode ever."

In August of 2007, one of the highest-paid players in professional football, the quarterback Michael Vick, pleaded guilty to involvement in a dog-fighting ring. The police raided one of his properties, a farm outside Richmond, Virginia, and found the bodies of dead dogs buried on the premises, along with evidence that some of the animals there had been tortured and electrocuted. Vick was suspended from football. He was sentenced to twenty-three months in prison. The dogs on his farm were seized by the court, and the most damaged were sent to an animal sanctuary in Utah for rehabilitation. When Vick applied for reinstatement to the National Football League, this summer, he was asked to undergo psychiatric testing. He then met with the commissioner of the league, Roger Goodell, for four and a half hours, so that Goodell could be sure that he was genuinely remorseful.

"I probably considered every alternative that I could think of," Goodell told reporters, when he finally allowed Vick back into the league. "I reached out to an awful lot of people to get their views—not only on what was right for the young man but also what was right for our society and the N.F.L."

Goodell's job entails dealing with players who have used drugs, driven drunk and killed people, fired handguns in night clubs, and consorted with thugs and accused murderers. But he clearly felt what many Americans felt as well—that dogfighting was a moral offense of a different order.

Here is a description of a dogfight given by the sociologists Rhonda Evans and Craig Forsyth in "The Social Milieu of Dogmen and Dogfights," an article they published some years ago in the journal *Deviant Behavior*. The fight took place in Louisiana between a local dog, Black, owned by a man named L.G., and Snow, whose owner, Rick, had come from Arizona:

> The handlers release their dogs and Snow and Black lunge at one another. Snow rears up and overpowers Black, but Black manages to come back with a quick locking of the jaws on Snow's neck. The crowd is cheering wildly and yelling out bets. Once a dog gets a lock on the other, they will hold on with all their might. The dogs flail back and forth and all the while Black maintains her hold.

In a dogfight, whenever one of the dogs "turns"—makes a submissive gesture with its head—the two animals are separated and taken back to their corners. Each dog, in alternation, then "scratches"—is released to charge at its opponent. After that first break, it is Snow's turn to scratch. She races toward Black:

> Snow goes straight for the throat and grabs hold with her razor-sharp teeth. Almost immediately, blood flows from Black's throat. Despite a serious injury to the throat, Black manages to continue fighting back. They are relentless, each battling the other and neither willing to accept defeat. This fighting continues for an hour. [Finally, the referee] gives the third and final pit call. It is Black's turn to scratch and she is severely wounded. Black manages to crawl across the pit to meet her opponent. Snow attacks Black and she is too weak to fight back. L.G. realizes that this is it for Black and calls the fight. Snow is declared the winner.

Afterward, Snow's owner collects his winnings; L.G. carries Black from the ring. "Her back legs are broken and blood is gushing from her throat," Evans and Forsyth write. "A shot rings out barely heard over the noise in the barn. Black's body is wrapped up and carried by her owner to his vehicle."

It's the shot ringing out that seals the case against dogfighting. L.G. willingly submitted his dog to a contest that culminated in her suffering and destruction. And why? For the entertainment of an audience and the chance of a payday. In the nineteenth century, dogfighting was widely accepted by the American public. But we no longer find that kind of transaction morally acceptable in a sport. "I was not aware of dogfighting and the terrible things that happen around dogfighting," Goodell said, explaining why he responded so sternly in the Vick case. One wonders whether, had he spent as much time talking to Kyle Turley as he did to Michael Vick, he'd start to have similar doubts about his own sport.

In 2003, a seventy-two-year-old patient at the Veterans Hospital in Bedford, Massachusetts, died, fifteen years after receiving a diagnosis of dementia. Patients in the hospital's dementia ward are routinely autopsied, as part of the V.A.'s research efforts, so the man's brain was removed and "fixed" in a formaldehyde solution. A laboratory technician placed a large slab of the man's cerebral tissue on a microtome—essentially, a sophisticated meat slicer—and, working along the coronal plane, cut off dozens of fifty-micron shavings, less than a hairbreadth thick. The shavings were then immunostained—bathed in a special reagent that would mark the presence of abnormal proteins with a bright, telltale red or brown stain on the surface of the tissue. Afterward, each slice was smoothed out and placed on a slide.

The stained tissue of Alzheimer's patients typically shows the two trademarks of the disease—distinctive patterns of the proteins beta-amyloid and tau. Beta-amyloid is thought to lay the groundwork for dementia. Tau marks the critical second stage of the disease: it's the protein that steadily builds up in brain cells, shutting them down and ultimately killing them. An immunostain of an Alzheimer's patient looks, under the microscope, as if the tissue had been hit with a shotgun blast: the red and brown marks, corresponding to amyloid and tau, dot the entire surface. But this patient's brain was different. There was damage only to specific surface regions of his brain, and the stains for amyloid came back negative. "This was all tau," Ann McKee, who runs the hospital's neuropathology laboratory, said. "There was not even a whiff of amyloid. And it was the most extraordinary damage. It was one of those cases that really took you aback." The patient may have been in an Alzheimer's facility, and may have looked and acted as if he had Alzheimer's. But McKee realized that he had a different condition, called chronic traumatic encephalopathy (C.T.E.), which is a progressive neurological disorder found in people who have suffered some kind of brain trauma. C.T.E. has many of the same manifestations as Alzheimer's: it begins with behavioral and personality changes, followed by disinhibition and irritability, before moving on to dementia. And C.T.E. appears later in life as well, because it takes a long time for the initial trauma to give rise to nerve-cell breakdown and death. But C.T.E. isn't the result of an endogenous disease. It's the result of injury. The patient, it turned out, had been a boxer in his youth. He had suffered from dementia for fifteen years because, decades earlier, he'd been hit too many times in the head.

> **disinhibition:** The loss of being able to stop oneself from doing something seen as prohibited or in bad taste.

McKee's laboratory does the neuropathology work for both the giant Framingham heart study, which has been running since 1948, and Boston University's New England Centenarian Study, which analyzes the brains of people who are unusually long-lived. "I'm looking at brains constantly," McKee said. "Then I ran across another one. I saw it and said, 'Wow, it looks just like the last case.' This time, there was no known history of boxing. But then I called the family, and heard that the guy had been a boxer in his twenties." You can't see tau except in an autopsy, and you can't see it in an autopsy unless you do a very particular kind of screen. So now that McKee had seen two cases, in short order, she began to wonder: how many people who we assume have Alzheimer's—a condition of mysterious origin—are actually victims of preventable brain trauma?

McKee linked up with an activist named Chris Nowinski, a former college football player and professional wrestler who runs a group called the Sports Legacy Institute, in Boston. In his football and wrestling careers, Nowinski suffered six concussions (that he can remember), the last of which had such severe side effects that he has become a full-time crusader against brain injuries in sports. Nowinski told McKee that he would help her track down more brains of ex-athletes. Whenever he read an obituary of someone who had played in a contact sport, he'd call up the family and try to persuade them to send the player's brain to Bedford. Usually, they said no. Sometimes they said yes. The first brain McKee received was from a man in his mid-forties who had played as a linebacker in the N.F.L. for ten years. He accidentally shot himself while cleaning a gun. He had at least three concussions in college, and eight in the pros. In the years before his death, he'd had memory lapses, and had become more volatile. McKee immunostained samples of his brain tissue, and saw big splotches of tau all over the frontal and temporal lobes. If he hadn't had the accident, he would almost certainly have ended up in a dementia ward.

Nowinski found her another ex-football player. McKee saw the same thing. She has now examined the brains of sixteen ex-athletes, most of them ex-football players. Some had long careers and some played only in college. Some died of dementia. Some died of unrelated causes. Some were old. Some were young. Most were linemen or linebackers, although there was one wide receiver. In one case, a man who had been a linebacker for sixteen years, you could see, without the aid of magnification, that there was trouble: there was a shiny tan layer of scar tissue, right on the surface of the frontal lobe, where the brain had repeatedly slammed into the skull. It was the kind of scar you'd get only if you used your head as a battering ram. You could also see that some of the openings in the brain were larger than you'd expect, as if the surrounding tissue had died and shrunk away. In other cases, everything seemed entirely normal until you looked under the microscope and saw the brown ribbons of tau. But all sixteen of the ex-athlete brains that McKee had examined—those of the two boxers, plus the ones that Nowinski had found for her—had something in common: every one had abnormal tau.

The other major researcher looking at athletes and C.T.E. is the neuropathologist Bennet Omalu. He diagnosed the first known case of C.T.E. in an ex-N.F.L. player back in September of 2002, when he autopsied the former Pittsburgh Steelers center Mike Webster. He also found C.T.E. in the former Philadelphia Eagles defensive back Andre Waters, and in the former Steelers linemen Terry Long and Justin Strzelczyk, the latter of whom was killed when he drove the wrong way down a freeway and crashed his car, at ninety miles per hour, into a tank truck. Omalu has only once failed to find C.T.E. in a professional football player, and that was a twenty-four-year-old running back who had played in the N.F.L. for only two years.

"There is something wrong with this group as a cohort," Omalu says. "They forget things. They have slurred speech. I have had an N.F.L. player come up to me at a funeral and tell me he can't find his way home. I have wives who call me and say, 'My husband was a very good man. Now he drinks all the time. I don't know why his behavior changed.' I have wives call me and say, 'My husband was a nice guy. Now he's getting abusive.' I had someone call me and say, 'My husband went back to law school after football and became a lawyer. Now he can't do his job. People are suing him.'"

> **cohort:**
> A group of people with a shared trait or identifier.

McKee and Omalu are trying to make sense of the cases they've seen so far. At least some of the players are thought to have used steroids, which has led to the suggestion that brain injury might in some way be enhanced by drug use. Many of the players also share a genetic risk factor for neurodegenerative diseases, so perhaps deposits of tau are the result of brain trauma coupled with the weakened ability of the brain to repair itself. McKee says that she will need to see at least fifty cases before she can draw any firm conclusions. In the meantime, late last month the University of Michigan's Institute for Social Research released the findings of an N.F.L.-funded phone survey of just over a thousand randomly selected retired N.F.L. players—all of whom had played in the league for at least three seasons. Self-reported studies are notoriously unreliable instruments, but, even so, the results were alarming. Of those players who were older than fifty, 6.1 per cent reported that they had received a diagnosis of "dementia, Alzheimer's disease, or other memory-related disease." That's five times higher than the national average for that age group. For players between the ages of thirty and forty-nine, the reported rate was nineteen times the national average. (The N.F.L. has distributed five million dollars to former players with dementia.)

"A long time ago, someone suggested that the [C.T.E. rate] in boxers was twenty per cent," McKee told me. "I think it's probably higher than that among boxers, and I also suspect that it's going to end up being higher than that among football players as well. Why? Because every brain I've seen has this. To get this number in a sample this small is really unusual, and the findings are so far out of the norm. I only can say that because I have looked at thousands of brains for a long time. This isn't something that you just see. I did the same exact thing for all the individuals from the Framingham heart study. We study them until they die. I run these exact same proteins, make these same slides—and we never see this."

McKee's laboratory occupies a warren of rooms, in what looks like an old officers' quarters on the V.A. campus. In one of the rooms, there is an enormous refrigerator, filled with brains packed away in hundreds of plastic containers. Nearby is a tray with small piles of brain slices. They look just like the ginger shavings that come with an order of sushi. Now McKee went to the room next to her office, sat down behind a microscope, and inserted one of the immunostained slides under the lens.

"This is Tom McHale," she said. "He started out playing for Cornell. Then he went to Tampa Bay. He was the man who died of substance abuse at the age of forty-five. I only got fragments of the brain. But it's just showing huge accumulations of tau for a forty-five-year-old—ridiculously abnormal."

She placed another slide under the microscope. "This individual was forty-nine years old. A football player. Cognitively intact. He never had any rage behavior. He had the distinctive abnormalities. Look at the hypothalamus." It was dark with tau. She put another slide in. "This guy was in his mid-sixties," she said. "He died of an unrelated medical condition. His name is Walter Hilgenberg. Look at the hippocampus. It's wall-to-wall tangles. Even in a bad case of Alzheimer's, you don't see that." The brown pigment of the tau stain ran around the edge of the tissue sample in a thick, dark band. "It's like a big river."

McKee got up and walked across the corridor, back to her office. "There's one last thing," she said. She pulled out a large photographic blowup of a brain-tissue sample. "This is a kid. I'm not allowed to talk about how he died. He was a good student. This is his brain. He's eighteen years old. He played football. He'd been playing football for a couple of years." She pointed to a series of dark spots on the image, where the stain had marked the presence of something abnormal. "He's got all this tau. This is frontal and this is insular. Very close to insular. Those same vulnerable regions." This was a teen-ager, and already his brain showed the kind of decay that is usually associated with old age. "This is completely inappropriate," she said. "You don't see tau like this in an eighteen-year-old. You don't see tau like this in a *fifty*-year-old."

McKee is a longtime football fan. She is from Wisconsin. She had two statuettes of Brett Favre, the former Green Bay Packers quarterback, on her bookshelf. On the wall was a picture of a robust young man. It was McKee's son—nineteen years old, six feet three. If he had a chance to join the N.F.L., I asked her, what would she advise him? "I'd say, 'Don't. Not if you want to have a life after football.'"

At the core of the C.T.E. research is a critical question: is the kind of injury being uncovered by McKee and Omalu incidental to the game of football or inherent in it? Part of what makes dogfighting so repulsive is the understanding that violence and injury cannot be removed from the sport. It's a feature of the sport that dogs almost always get hurt. Something like stock-car racing, by contrast, is dangerous, but not unavoidably so.

In 2000 and 2001, four drivers in Nascar's élite Sprint Cup Series were killed in crashes, including the legendary Dale Earnhardt. In response, Nascar mandated stronger seats, better seat belts and harnesses, and ignition kill switches, and completed the installation of expensive new barriers on the walls of its racetracks, which can absorb the force of a crash much better than concrete. The result is that, in the past eight years, no one has died in Nascar's three national racing series. Stock-car fans are sometimes caricatured as bloodthirsty, eagerly awaiting the next spectacular crash. But there is little blood these days in Nascar crashes. Last year, at Texas Motor Speedway, Michael McDowell hit an oil slick, slammed head first into the wall at a hundred and eighty miles per hour, flipped over and over, leaving much of his car in pieces on the track, and, when the vehicle finally came to a stop, crawled out of the wreckage and walked away. He raced again the next day. So what is football? Is it dogfighting or is it stock-car racing?

Football faced a version of this question a hundred years ago, after a series of ugly incidents. In 1905, President Theodore Roosevelt called an emergency summit at the White House, alarmed, as the historian John Sayle Watterson writes, "that the brutality of the prize ring had invaded college football and might end up destroying it." Columbia University dropped the sport entirely. A professor at the University of Chicago called it a "boy-killing, man-mutilating, money-making, education-prostituting, gladiatorial sport." In December of 1905, the presidents of twelve prominent colleges met in New York and came within one vote of abolishing the game. But the main objection at the time was to a style of play—densely and dangerously packed offensive strategies—that, it turns out, could be largely corrected with rule changes, like the legalization of the forward pass and the doubling of the first-down distance from five yards to ten. Today, when we consider subtler and more insidious forms of injury, it's far from clear whether the problem is the style of play or the play itself.

The most damaged, scarred, and belligerent of Michael Vick's dogs—the hardest cases—were sent to the Best Friends Animal Sanctuary, on a thirty-seven-hundred-acre spread in the canyons of southern Utah. They were housed in a specially modified octagon, a one-story, climate-controlled cottage, ringed by individual dog runs. The dogs were given a final walk at 11 P.M. and woken up at 7 A.M., to introduce them to a routine. They were hand-fed. In the early months, the staff took turns sleeping in the octagon—sometimes in the middle, sometimes in a cot in one of the runs—so that someone would be with the dogs twenty-four hours a day. Twenty-two of Vick's pit bulls came to Best Friends in January of 2008, and all but five of them are still there.

What happens at Best Friends represents, by any measure, an extravagant gesture. These are dogs that will never live a normal life. But the kind of crime embodied by dogfighting is so morally repellent that it demands an extravagant gesture in response. In a fighting dog, the quality that is prized above all others is the willingness to persevere, even in the face of injury and pain. A dog that will not do that is labelled a "cur," and abandoned. A dog that keeps charging at its opponent is said to possess "gameness," and game dogs are revered.

In one way or another, plenty of organizations select for gameness. The Marine Corps does so, and so does medicine, when it puts young doctors through the exhausting rigors of residency. But those who select for gameness have a responsibility not to abuse that trust: if you have men in your charge who would jump off a cliff for you, you cannot march them to the edge of the cliff—and dogfighting fails this test. Gameness, Carl Semencic argues, in "The World of Fighting Dogs" (1984), is no more than a dog's "desire to please an owner at any expense to itself." The owners, Semencic goes on,

> understand this desire to please on the part of the dog and capitalize on it. At any organized pit fight in which two dogs are really going at each other wholeheartedly, one can observe the owner of each dog changing his position at pit-side in order to be in sight of his dog at all times. The owner knows that seeing his master rooting him on will make a dog work all the harder to please its master.

This is why Michael Vick's dogs weren't euthanized. The betrayal of loyalty requires an act of social reparation.

Professional football players, too, are selected for gameness. When Kyle Turley was knocked unconscious, in that game against the Packers, he returned to practice four days later because, he said, "I didn't want to miss a game." Once, in the years when he was still playing, he woke up and fell into a wall as he got out of bed. "I start puking all over," he recalled. "So I said to my wife, 'Take me to practice.' I didn't want to miss practice." The same season that he was knocked unconscious, he began to have pain in his hips. He received three cortisone shots, and kept playing. At the end of the season, he discovered that he had a herniated disk. He underwent surgery, and four months later was back at training camp. "They put me in full-contact practice from day one," he said. "After the first day, I knew I wasn't right. They told me, 'You've had the surgery. You're fine. You should just fight through it.' It's like you're programmed. You've got to go without question—*I'm a warrior. I can block that out of my mind.* I go out, two days later. Full contact. Two-a-days. My back locks up again. I had re-herniated the same disk that got operated on four months ago, and bulged the disk above it." As one of Turley's old coaches once said, "He plays the game as it should be played, all out," which is to say that he put the game above his own well-being.

Turley says he was once in the training room after a game with a young linebacker who had suffered a vicious hit on a kickoff return. "We were in the cold tub, which is, like, forty-five degrees, and he starts passing out. In the cold tub. I don't know anyone who has ever passed out in the cold tub. That's supposed to wake you up. And I'm, like, slapping his face. 'Richie! Wake up!' He said, 'What, what? I'm cool.' I said, 'You've got a concussion. You have to go to the hospital.' He said, 'You know, man, I'm fine.'" He wasn't fine, though. That moment in the cold tub represented a betrayal of trust. He had taken the hit on behalf of his team. He was then left to pass out in the cold tub, and to deal—ten and twenty years down the road—with the consequences. No amount of money or assurances about risk freely assumed can change the fact that, in this moment, an essential bond had been broken. What football must confront, in the end, is not just the problem of injuries or scientific findings. It is the fact that there is something profoundly awry in the relationship between the players and the game.

"Let's assume that [the leading C.T.E. researchers] are right," Ira Casson, who co-chairs an N.F.L. committee on brain injury, said. "What should we be doing differently? We asked Dr. McKee this when she came down. And she was honest, and said, 'I don't know how to answer that.' No one has any suggestions—assuming that you aren't saying no more football, because, let's be honest, that's not going to happen." Casson began to talk about the research on the connection between C.T.E. and boxing. It had been known for eighty years. Boxers ran a twenty-per-cent risk of dementia. Yet boxers continue to box. Why? Because people still go to boxing matches.

"We certainly know from boxers that the incidence of C.T.E. is related to the length of your career," he went on. "So if you want to apply that to football—and I'm not saying it does apply—then you'd have to let people play six years and then stop. If it comes to that, maybe we'll have to think about that. On the other hand, nobody's willing to do this in boxing. Why would a boxer at the height of his career, six or seven years in, stop fighting, just when he's making million-dollar paydays?" He shrugged. "It's a violent game. I suppose if you want to you could play touch football or flag football. For me, as a Jewish kid from Long Island, I'd be just as happy if we did that. But I don't know if the fans would be happy with that. So what else do you do?"

Casson is right. There is nothing else to be done, not so long as fans stand and cheer. We are in love with football players, with their courage and grit, and nothing else—neither considerations of science nor those of morality—can compete with the destructive power of that love.

**Let's Pause Here••• ▶**  Gladwell's depictions of Turley and his symptoms are disturbing, to say the least. What does it do for our impression of "untouchable" or "indestructible" NFL stars to get such honesty from both Turley and Gladwell? How does it affect you as a reader that Gladwell lets Turley speak for himself and narrate his own experiences? How did the ending of the article—implicating rabid fandom as one of the reasons the problem of serious football injuries won't go away—help to cement Gladwell's point or disrupt it? In the end, which do you see as more morally reprehensible: the damage inflicted on dogs that dogfight, or the damage inflicted on athletes who compete in contact sports?

**Let's Take It Further••• ▼**

1. What is our moral obligation, as fans of violent or dangerous sports, to protect the players from damage? What is our obligation to them in their later years, long after they've left the game, if any? How about those in positions of power, such as NFL commissioner Roger Goodell? What does he owe to players as the head of the NFL?

2. Is there any solution to the conundrum presented in this story: football will never stop being violent because people will always want to see it and the violence that occurs? How can the sport remain interesting and engaging without permanently injuring those who play it?

3. Is Gladwell's target audience simply rabid fans of football and violent sports, or is he trying to reach a more general audience? How does his inclusion of the dogfighting issue allow him to bring in an audience that wouldn't necessarily be interested in the issue of football otherwise? What is the effect on readers of viewing these two sports side by side? Do you feel his writing strategy has helped or hurt his cause?

4.  Of the many gruesome descriptions in the story, did you find yourself more bothered by the depictions of dogfights or the injuries (especially long-term injuries) sustained by humans in football? If so, why? Another way to view the issue is to question why animal rights activists are not always as active or vocal about human rights. Why might that be? What logic do animal rights activists give about how it sometimes *appears* as though they might value animal life over human life?

5.  Note the hesitation on the part of scientists to explicitly state that C.T.E. in aging football players is the direct result of playing football. Why the hesitation, in your opinion? Why do you think that these scientists will not directly blame the heavy hits and the many repetitive lesser hits for the brain damage done to football players? What would happen if they made this direct claim?

6.  Do you feel Gladwell is morally opposed to one sport more so than the other, or is he equally against both? How does his bias for one over the other (if it indeed exists) come through in his discussion of the two sports?

7.  Locate some of the articles pertaining to the Michael Vick arrest. What was the public's attitude toward him and his crimes? Locate responses to the Gladwell article online. Have there been similar public outcries over the injuries sustained by football players? What accounts for the differences in tone and reaction to the two sports? Which do you feel is more important, and why? Locate this entire essay online (at *The New Yorker*'s website) and read the parts that have been omitted from this version of the essay. Using Gladwell's research as a foundation, expand on it to make his case stronger or to refute his main point.

8.  If you believe it to be true, make the case for why dogfighting is more unethical than contact sports, or vice versa. There are plenty of sources that make the case for both sides, in light of Vick's arrest, so locate some to back your opinion. Be sure to use multimedia texts, as well as the online discussions of the issue, to back your opinion.

9.  Why do you think people so enjoy watching violent sports? If you enjoy them yourself, try to articulate to the best of your ability how and why you enjoy the game(s). Be sure to describe and explain your favorite violent sport, if you are a fan of more than one. Then, locate case studies that show how and why we are drawn to violence and the "safety" of violent sports. Also, justify the damage to the athletes and players of violent sports. Why should the public not be more concerned for them than we are? Or, conversely, why should we be more concerned, if that's what you believe?

10. What do you think the NFL should do in light of this article? List a specific process or series of actions you believe will accurately, adequately, and fairly address the risk of injury inherent to NFL players and their sport. Before addressing this issue, be sure to locate Gladwell's entire article (on *The New Yorker*'s website) to see the further research he includes in his longer essay. You might also interview athletes to see what their opinion on the matter is as well.

11. Compare another violent sport involving animals to any other human contact sport, addressing the injuries, known long-term effects, and moral issues in the manner that Gladwell does in the above article. Try to persuade your reader to see one as worse than the other. Be sure to locate research on the effects of both sports on human athletes and animals, and define the sports and describe them for your reader.

12. Put Gladwell's theory to the test by viewing football (or any other contact sport) "hits" or tackles on YouTube and compile them into a video collage. How do viewers of the sport

respond to these hits online, and do their responses shed light on our desire to see athletes inflict pain on one another? If further safety measures are enacted, how might it negatively affect the fan base's interest in the sport? What, if anything, do you see as the solution?

# mash**it**UP

Here is a series of essay and discussion topics that draw connections between multiple selections within the chapter. They also suggest outside texts to include in your essay or discussion. Feel free to bring in further outside texts, remembering the variety of texts (beyond articles) available to you.

1. Compare the concept of revenge in "The Body as Weapon, as Inspiration" to the Abu Ghraib article, "Picture Imperfect," and the photos Perl's article discusses. Are the photos portraying a manifestation of revenge? If so, what is it revenge for? If not, what is the purpose of the photos? How is revenge, as a concept, working in the Pompa poem? Is there truth behind the Obama administration's (as well as the previous Bush administration's) assertion that more released photos will spur future violence? If so, use "The Body as Weapon, as Inspiration" to illustrate the connection between what might "inspire" someone to acts of terror.

2. Discuss the concept of intimidation in "No Jail Time for Cop Who Pummeled Bartender" and "A Call to End Contraband Cell Phone Use" (which is located in the "Social Media" chapter of the textbook). How are people in both selections seeking to intimidate others? How are they different in their methods, outcomes, and reasoning? Is one form of intimidation worse than the other, and, if so, why?

3. Compare the poem "Police Dog" to the lawsuit "Texas Manhandle." In what way are these two texts documenting the same phenomenon? How do they differ in approach, and language, if they do? What sorts of solutions, if any, are there to the issue of police brutality?

4. Discuss the concept of bullying in "No Jail Time for Cop Who Pummeled Bartender" and revisit the It Gets Better Project website (see the Identity Construction chapter). How is the concept of bullying central to the reactions of people to the outcome of the Obrycka case, as well as the purpose for the "It Gets Better" website and book?

5. Compare the reaction to "Losing Is for Losers" with "Offensive Play." Which of the two generated a bigger reaction (from yourself or your classmates)? Which one sparked a bigger outcry in the media or the community featured in the selections? What might this say about Gladwell's assertion that we seem to not care about our NFL players

as much as animals? Why would a satirical email about children cause parents to demand the coach's resignation, but the scientific evidence suggesting a connection between football and severe brain disease or injury be treated as not nearly as important?

6. One line in "Losing Is for Losers" states that "America's youth are becoming fat, lazy, and noncompetitive because competition is viewed as 'bad.'" Compare that to the earlier essay by Chris Jones, "In Defense of the Fistfight," and Jones's explanation for why we are all weak and cocky. Are Jones and Kinahan making the same point (in other words, agreeing with one another), or are they making different points? How are their points similar or different? Do you agree with their points, or can you locate another cause unrelated to what either writer identifies as the culprit?

7. Discuss the issue of judging pictures without knowing the accompanying story (as raised in "Picture Imperfect"). How do the pictures throughout this chapter (and the textbook as a whole) influence your reaction to the articles they accompany? Do they make you more averse to the selection or more intrigued to read it? Apply that same process to pictures in other forms of media (magazines, newspapers, blogs, and even newscasts). What work are the photographs doing for the stories they accompany? How accurately are they portraying the story of the photo itself?

8. One of America's most high-profile police departments currently under the national media microscope is the New Orleans Police Department, which, ever since Hurricane Katrina hit, has been plagued with accusations of police brutality that even include the murder of unarmed citizens. Locate articles about the current cases against members of the New Orleans Police Department and compare them to the cases featured in this chapter. How are the cases similar, and how are they different? Are the officers in these cases being treated any differently than officers in other high-profile cases around the country? If so, how? If not, how are these cases being handled differently?

9. Locate and watch the "Don't Tase Me, Bro" video on YouTube and then read the essay "The Video-Game Programmer Saving Our 21st-Century Souls" (in the "Mass Media" chapter) to see how Fagone describes the game programmer's response to that particular event in American history. How does Jason Rohrer's reaction to violence strike you? Play (and record yourself playing, to use for illustration purposes) the game that Rohrer created in response to the event and explain how it affected you, as well as what you see as Rohrer's goal in creating the game. (Rohrer's game, called "Police Brutality," is available for free online through his website: http://hcsoftware.sourceforge.net/jason-rohrer.)

What does he hope to accomplish with his game, and do you think it is working? Why or why not?

10. Locate and create a collage of YouTube videos related to the Iraq and Afghanistan wars that depict acts that you think are questionable or morally wrong. Incorporate the comments on these videos as a way of proving your point one way or the other about the power of videos and images to incite people to violence (as argued, in part, in Perl's essay "Picture Imperfect"). Describe the reactions of people to the videos online and whether you see them as problematic or justified. Be sure to explain why.

**Let's Connect •••▶** 	 "Like" our Facebook page for free, up-to-date, additional readings, discussions, and writing ideas on the topic of violence. Join other students and teachers across the country sharing in an online discussion of popular culture events. *American Mashup* is on Facebook at www.facebook.com/americanmashup.

# Chapter 8

# Alcohol and Drugs

## Making the Cultural Connection

Americans are not alone in our predisposition to drugs and alcohol. Addictions abound in every corner of the world. But what sets us apart from so many other countries is how tightly drugs and alcohol are woven into the fabric of our national identity. You need not look far for proof. Simply turn on a Top 40 radio station and listen to the lyrics of every third or fourth song. There's a good chance that many of them will feature drugs, alcohol, or partying in some fashion. In fact, *Billboard*'s top ten hits for the week of February 5, 2011, featured eight songs that directly reference drinking, smoking, doing drugs, and

### SELECTIONS IN THIS CHAPTER

partying in general ("Black and Yellow," "What's My Name?," "Hold It Against Me," "Tonight (I'm Lovin' You)," "We R Who We R," "Raise Your Glass," "The Time (Dirty Bit)," "Hey Baby (Drop It to the Floor)").

It is widely known that law enforcement agencies step up their patrols on virtually every national holiday because when we have a holiday, there is sure to be someone consuming too many drugs or too much alcohol, or both. Why? Because a party means getting messed up. Time off from work, a break in classes, or a day on which the entire nation observes a federal holiday—all of these mean one thing: time to party.

We have even had several presidents who struggled with addictions to drugs and alcohol in their prepresidential years. President Clinton famously claimed that when he smoked weed in the Sixties he "didn't inhale," while President Obama, during his election campaign, said, "When I was a kid I inhaled frequently. That was the point." Even President George W. Bush had his own struggles with alcohol and cocaine addiction, which came back to haunt him briefly during his first election campaign. That's how "American" it is to seek a high or a reprieve from the stressors of everyday life.

Most people are drawn to the "badness" of alcohol and drugs because we are told from our earliest years that drinking and drugs are bad. Then, we spend the rest of our childhood and adolescent years being bombarded with images of how "good" or "fun" or "cool" it is to be drunk or high. It's no matter then that there's so much confusion over these mixed messages. It almost begs for young people to try these things out, if only to see what the big deal is.

Among Americans, drugs and alcohol are sometimes front-and-center because we have been raised in a culture in which alcohol advertising trumps all other forms of advertising during sporting events, major and minor. So we drink while we tailgate outside of a game, and we drink while we watch games on television. Drinking and sports fandom appear to go hand-in-hand. Beyond sporting events, alcohol advertisements are all around us. They are on billboards, in magazines, on TV, on the Web, on radio stations, on racecars and boxing rings. Simply put, we are constantly reminded that alcohol exists, and we are encouraged to consume it.

Because of our country's long history with drugs and alcohol, it should come as no surprise that we rank our colleges according to "party school" status. We grow up watching college movies in which fraternities, sororities, drinking, drugs, and sex seem as though they are the sole purpose for going off to school. There are startlingly few films about college life that do not reference drinking or drugs in some fashion. It is in itself a genre of filmmaking, and we expect, as viewers of these films, to be shown people puking, passing out, making fools of themselves, and making decisions they regret. And now, we even post the "real-life" versions of these events on YouTube and our Facebook profiles for the whole world to see. And so,

the story being told in this picture is an all-too-familiar one.

We, as Americans, have even mastered the art of the drinking game, which is to say that one of the great American pastimes is to invent ways to drink more by playing games that force us to drink as punishment. Yes, we do love our alcohol.

Think for a moment of the thousands of terms and phrases there are for being under the influence of alcohol. People get wasted, plowed, tanked, sloshed, annihilated, soused, steamed, plastered, faded, twisted, and also drunk. This is just the tip of the terminology iceberg. Drunk terms are as colorful and varied as the people who use them. It's safe to say our language has more synonyms for drunkenness and being high than any other concepts.

We are also a country inundated with drug epidemics of one sort or another. We have had meth epidemics, crack epidemics, heroin epidemics, and cocaine epidemics. And still we soldier on. We have dozens of cultural icons who have succumbed to their drug addictions—musicians, writers, actors, politicians—but rather than being held up as an example of the negative consequences of drug use, they are somehow twisted into figures of greatness who simply passed before their time.

There is another side to this particular part of our popular culture. For all of the ways we praise, glorify, and wonder at drug and alcohol consumption, there are those of us who see it as our mission to eradicate these bad habits from our culture. We have a drug war that has been raging for over a hundred years. Our prisons are full of men and women who have fallen on the wrong side of the drug war. We have outlawed alcohol, and then reneged on the law. We have spawned organizations such as Mothers Against Drunk Driving (M.A.D.D.) and Students Against Drunk Driving (S.A.D.D.), and have had antidrinking and antidrug campaigns such as the "Just Say No" and D.A.R.E. initiatives. And yet the wars continue to this day.

What does it say about our society that we have engrained alcohol and drugs so deeply into our social fabric? How is it that a would-be lawyer who regularly consumed large quantities of alcohol and took advantage of women could become a cultural icon, the way Tucker Max has become? How does he have two best-selling books, one of which has been made into a movie, if we don't have some sort of national fascination with alcohol and the ridiculous actions it causes us to perform? Why do college students line their dorm room walls with posters of Bob Marley smoking a huge joint and long-dead musicians who fell to their various addictions?

This chapter raises these questions in many different ways. It discusses the nature of alcohol in our culture, and, more specifically, among college students. It addresses both sides of the decades-old drinking age debate, and dispenses advice for those who will drink no matter what, regardless of whether it's legal. You will be asked to consider the trend of posting public humiliation online, and trends in drinking games, and what they mean to us. We will try to determine whether drugs should be legal, and whether "enhancing" ourselves with drugs is a good or a bad thing. After all, we have plenty of legal drugs—alcohol, tobacco, and caffeine, to name a few. Who gets to determine which ones should be legal and why? Finally, you will also be asked to consider how drugs and alcohol have infiltrated our American culture on the whole, and why we cannot seem to stop drinking, smoking, shooting up, popping, chewing, and huffing—even when it's made illegal and potentially comes with punishments such as hefty prison sentences.

The important thing to consider, however, isn't just what role drugs and alcohol play in our society, but also why. Why is it that we are all well aware of the dangers of these substances, and yet we continue to use them as though we are indestructible? What does it say about our society that just south of our border thousands of people are being killed every year as drug cartels jockey for the best positions and entryways to deliver their products to our waiting American mouths, arms, noses, and stomachs? These are the larger questions to consider as you read the selections in this chapter.

# College Drinking
Mike Keefe

Mike Keefe's work has ranged from auto assembly line work, the U.S. Marines, and graduate school in mathematics. Keefe has been the editorial cartoonist for *The Denver Post* since 1975. Throughout the Nineties he was a weekly contributor to *USA Today* and a regular on America Online. His nationally syndicated cartoons have appeared in Europe, Asia, and in most major U.S. news magazines and hundreds of newspapers across the country. He has won top honors in the Fischetti, National Headliners Club, Society of Professional Journalists, and Best of the West contests. He was a John S. Knight Fellow at Stanford University and is a past president of the Association of American Editorial Cartoonists. He was a juror for the 1997 and 1998 Pulitzer Prizes in Journalism. Keefe is the author of the books *Running Awry, Keefe-Kebab,* and *The Ten-Speed Commandments.* He was co-creator (with *Pittsburgh Post-Gazette* cartoonist Tim Menees) of the nationally syndicated comic strips, *Cooper* and *Iota.* The following cartoon originally appeared in *The Denver Post* on September 28, 2004.

## Thinking About Alcohol

Take a moment to look at the accompanying cartoon. Like most political cartoons, this drawing is attempting to make a statement about a topic that is popular in our culture. This cartoon's subject matter, which can be discerned at a glance, is the issue of excessive (or binge) drinking on American college campuses. As most college students likely know, drinking is such a part of college culture that students often talk about little else in terms of weekend plans. Students drink to excess at parties, in dorm rooms, in the parking lots of college sporting events, and, of course, in bars.

Drinking is so synonymous with college that many people see it as a part of the entire college experience. There are classes to attend, fraternities and sororities to join, sports teams to root for, and drinking that must be done. In fact, drinking is such a part of college culture that students pride themselves on their national rankings—not in academics or even in sports, but in where they are ranked in terms of "party schools."

Lately, there has even been a new push nationwide to lower the drinking age. The reason is that drinking among college students is such a pressing issue that some schools are uncertain how to combat the problem. Lowering the drinking age is seen as one potential solution.

But notice that the cartoon is more than just a drawing of college students partying. The newspaper headline is directly addressing the issue of alcohol-related deaths on American college campuses. The man and woman enjoying an outdoor meal in a café are discussing the dilemma of college drinking and deaths the same way people discuss any other news story. Based on the couple's conversation, what do you believe the artist, Mike Keefe, is attempting to say about the issue of college binge drinking (and the subsequent alcohol-related deaths) in American culture? Does Keefe's opinion come out in the words of the man or the woman? Either way, what does it mean that the café employees are dragging a man out of the restaurant by his feet, apparently for smoking a cigarette? How are the two issues (college drinking and public smoking) being compared? Is the issue of college drinking unfixable, as the man says? Or is it merely a matter of our popular culture shifting its opinion on the issue of college (and underage) drinking? What solution do you believe Keefe might be offering up?

Now take a moment to consider your opinion on the issue of underage drinking and alcohol's role in college culture. What does it say about our culture that college and drinking seem to go hand-in-hand? What other alternatives are there? Is this an issue that will ever be resolved to everyone's satisfaction? How might the banning of smoking in public buildings by many states be related to the issue of both underage drinking and college binge drinking?

# The Ultimate Drunk People Compilation Video Ever
### jackginger06

**Let's Start Here•••▶** There is something about human nature that draws us to a tragic event. We slow down to look at car accidents, stop to watch a fight, point and laugh at the person too inebriated at a party to walk. Because of this part of our nature, there are hundreds of thousands of videos on YouTube of people in various states of embarrassment and pain. So it stands to reason that one of the most popular videos on YouTube, with well over 40 million views, is the awkwardly titled "The Ultimate Drunk People Compilation Ever," which is a collage of publicly drunk people doing severely drunken things.

Of course, drinking plays a large role in American culture. We are inundated with ads for alcohol in magazines, on billboards, and during commercial breaks. And in these ads—whether pictures or video—we see beautiful people drinking responsibly. Then there is the down side to drinking: the embarrassing stumble, the drunken fights and ramblings, the passing out, the regretful decision, the DUI, the untimely death. It is only natural that our inclination for observing tragic or uncomfortable events would lead people to watch YouTube for an endless supply of public humiliation that drunk people provide.

Watch the video "The Ultimate Drunk People Compilation Ever" and see whether it causes you to cringe, to laugh, or to think twice about drinking too much in public.

---

Little is known about YouTube user jackginger06. The following video is the only one he has ever uploaded. To date, the video has accrued more than 40 million views. The video was originally uploaded to YouTube on October 24, 2007.

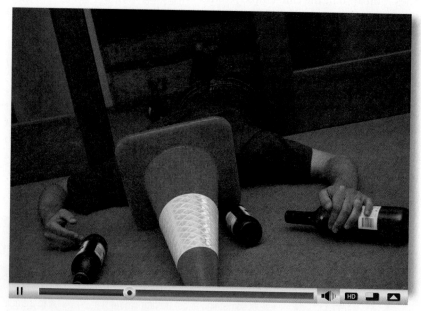

**Search on YouTube: "Ultimate Drunk People Compilation Video Ever"**

http://www.youtube.com/watch?v=tZmDWItBziM

**Let's Pause Here•••▶** Do you think this video is funny or disturbing? What do you think jackginger06 intended by posting this video? Is it merely to serve as entertainment, or is there something more that can be taken away from watching this video?

**Let's Take It Further•••▼**

1. What do you think might be the cause of this video's popularity? Why are we drawn to watching these events over and over again? What (if anything) do you feel for the various people featured in the video?

2. Based on the depictions of drunkenness, as well as the sound track to the short video, what message do you think jackginger06 is attempting to send to his audience? Is he merely

providing entertainment, or is there a message about drinking and public drunkenness embedded in the video that goes beyond the humor of this embarrassing behavior? Who do you think his audience might be? Potential drinkers? Young people? Alcoholics? What about his video allows you to read the intentions of YouTube user jackginger06?

3. In an era in which it appears that people are constantly being filmed (by both public and private cameras), how might this video serve as a warning to would-be public drinkers?

4. This video is a representation of the potentially negative side of drinking. It features people harming themselves, getting arrested, even acting as though they've completely lost their minds. Why might people be drawn to drinking even when there is the potential to be so publicly humiliated?

5. Google the term "drunk people" and search some of the sites that appear. Choose one or two of the websites that appear and describe the content of each site. What does the purpose of these sites appear to be? How do people react to the site (for example, the comments beneath each picture or video)? How did you "read" the website to determine its purpose? Again, is it merely meant for entertainment? Or is there a message that can be read from the site's presentation? Who built the site, and does this reveal anything about the site's intentions?

6. Find a video on YouTube that shows other instances of embarrassment or public humiliation. Do you believe the video is merely poking fun at someone's embarrassing moment, or that it could be used to serve as a warning or possibly even an educational tool to help people avoid the same types of behaviors? Describe why you believe this. Feel free to use the comments at the bottom of the video to help prove your opinion. Be sure to discuss and describe the site's elements (music, graphics, etc.) to help make your case.

7. If you were to make a video showing similar clips of people humiliating themselves under the influence of drugs or alcohol, how might you portray these images in order to show the viewers the downsides of this sort of behavior? Or, conversely, how might you use the footage to show the positive side of drinking? What steps would you take (including the sound track, for example) to get your message across with your video? Accompany your video with an essay explaining your intentions and detailing the site's various elements and how they help you achieve your goal.

# Lessons for a Young Drinker    Tom Chiarella

**Let's Start Here•••▶** Young people drink. Not all of them, of course, but many do. The dangers of drinking are regularly documented and featured in news stories, by groups such as Mothers Against Drunk Driving, and even by campus safety groups at American colleges and universities. Most people are quite used to hearing stories of DUI accidents, fights, arrests, and many other negative activities associated with drinking. But if it were *all* bad—if drinking only led to trouble—then people would not do it. So there must be something positive about it. And, for all of the negativity, there are plenty of people who drink and do not get into trouble of any sort.

Tom Chiarella, the author of the following article, realizes that young people drink, whether or not people try to stop them. He realizes, of course, that there are negative consequences. But he also understands that there are positive elements to drinking. In "Lessons for a Young Drinker," Chiarella is honest about the fact that many young people drink. Instead of trying to dissuade young people from drinking, he takes a different approach: he offers advice to would-be drinkers. He discusses the pros and cons of alcohol, as well as the entertainment and potential danger it can provide.

As you read the article, note how his tone is different than the tone of most other informational commercials, essays, articles, or conversations you have encountered that warn about drinking. Regardless of whether you drink alcohol, see if anything in the following article strikes you as good advice or bad advice.

---

Tom Chiarella is a fiction writer, sports writer, essayist, writer-at-large for *Esquire*, and visiting professor at DePauw University in Greencastle, Indiana. Besides hundreds of articles in *Esquire* since 1996, his magazine work has appeared in *The New Yorker, Golf Digest,* Forbes.com, *Links, O: The Oprah Magazine, Washington Golf Monthly, Indianapolis Monthly, The London Observer* and *Men's Style* (Australia), and has been syndicated internationally in 19 different countries. He is the recipient of a National Magazine Award. Chiarella has also twice appeared in the *Best American Magazine Writing* anthologies (2004 and 2009). This essay first appeared in *Esquire* magazine in the May 2009 issue.

Look, drinking is pretty damned fun. This must be said. Yes. Women look better. The ocean looks bluer. We know. And your jokes? Way better, right? Man, laughs are just way better. I mean, right? You just start to like where you are, no matter where that is. It can make you good with the world. And this really can be a good thing. Seriously.

When you start, drinking is all about expansion, escape, getting out. The act feels transgressive, edgy, puissant. You stand on the fringe of some piece of adolescent geography—a parking lot, a quarry, the roof of a rattletrap garage—and furtively take a pull of brandy; you hit the leftover champagne glasses at a cousin's wedding, creep to the attic with filched bourbon or a backpack loaded with beers long forgotten on the top shelf of some garage refrigerator. This, in turn, forces you into some iconic poses—leaning against the hood of a car, hitting on a 40, throwing back a shot like you were born doing it, levering a beer bottle with two fingers.

When you look back on your world with some booze in you—at your family, at your home, at your troubles—you'll find yourself a little unhinged from expectation, from fear. This is undeniably heady. For a while, for a long while maybe, you surprise yourself. You're braver. Sharper. You

**transgressive:**
In violation of a law or boundary.

**puissant:**
Empowering.

**furtively:**
Stealthily or sneakily.

say some shit you shouldn't. You say some things that must be said. You sing better. You tell more truths. Things seem to get done when you drink. You feel located in the moment and the moment is all that matters. It feels good out there, beyond the rules, beyond the hand-me-down lessons of school and work, and yes, you'll take another pull.

Understand, from the get-go, these are fun illusions.

The young drinker is usually not self-aware. Observe yourself and take notes. That's a key to drinking: don't stop looking. When you are less drunk than everyone else, look around. When you are more drunk than anyone else, look at your own dumb ass in the mirror. To persist, you must make a style out of it. Don't slouch. Don't slosh. Make rules: I don't drink beer from boots. Don't chug. Don't shotgun. Don't hoot. Like that. Walk into a bar as if you've been there before. When entering a crowded joint, know your poison. Order simply and clearly. If the bar is uncrowded, if the bartender is smart and attentive, ask for recommendations. Draft your own lessons. Learn from your mistakes. Quickly. You get a couple when you start. After that it's on you.

Lose the urgency, too. Drinking should not be the event in itself.

There is no lesson plan, but you have to learn. No authoritative how-to. That's your job. Everyone in a bar is a kind of how-to. How to handle it, how to share it, and how to let it go. Drinking must be mastered, or it will master you.

Every once in a while, you'll turn around and you'll encounter that guy, any one of many guys, really—the shouter, the stumbler, the puncher, the teary guy, the sleepy drunk, the ass-grabber, the chest-poker, the jab-bermouth, the spitter, the wobbly fool. One version or another, he's always there. Really look then. Understand that that guy doesn't know what he is, doesn't know what he looks like, what people say about him. Fair warning: You'll probably be every one of those guys eventually. Figure out that you don't have to be.

Quit. For some period of time, anyway. A week. A month. Three years. Whatever it takes. Just walk away. Study the absence. Feel it. In some ways, you'll find you're right back on the outside. Know what it means to not drink, too.

Start again if you want. Be better at it this time.

Eventually you'll have your patterns of control and eccentricity. Some of this is luck, some of it persistence.

At some point, you'll drink only gin in the summer, whiskey all winter. Or you'll make batches of cocktails for friends. You'll buy rounds, for the women at the jukebox, for the whole goddamned place. You'll stock your own bar and reconsider olives, cocktail onions, and the importance of limes. You'll have a good bottle of whiskey in your desk drawer at work so long that you'll forget it's there. And some bartender, somewhere, will work your drink the minute you tug your way in. You'll make one brief, well-considered toast a year, though people will ask for more. You'll have your own philosophy about the relative harmlessness of mixing liquors, about why you order a beer behind your shot, about drinking at the beach.

When asked, you'll offer this stuff up. Young drinkers need to know. And the music in the bar will rise, inflating the circus tent of the evening once more. Then your round arrives. That menagerie of clinking highballs. Nice. Maybe then you'll look over the shoulders of the young drinkers, at the women, or at the ocean. That's when you'll say, because of it all and despite it all: Drinking is pretty damn good.

**Let's Pause Here•••▶**  What did you think of the tone that Chiarella uses in addressing the "young drinker"? Was it surprising to you that he begins his essay by stating that "drinking is pretty damned fun"? What do you think of his honesty when addressing the topic of young drinkers? Is it an effective way to get potential young drinkers to take him seriously, or does it seem like he is pandering (or trying too hard)? How was the essay different from media depictions of drinking that are normally directed at young people?

**Let's Take It Further•••▼**

1. Chiarella states that when young people first start drinking, it is "all about expansion, escape, getting out." What do you think he means by this statement? Can you think of examples of people drinking for any of these reasons? What might they be expanding on, escaping from, or getting out of by drinking?

2. Though Chiarella states in the essay's title that his audience is "young drinkers," in what way does he consistently address or engage this audience by his choice of words, examples given, and his general approach to the subject? Is he only addressing young drinkers, or does he appeal to other audiences at the same time? If so, who might those audiences be, and how are you able to identify who they are, based on his writing strategies?

3. Why do you think that Chiarella gives a list of the benefits of drinking, only to turn around and call them "fun illusions"? Is he saying that drinking is bad, like most other adults say to young men and women, or does he mean something else by that statement?

4. Do you believe that Tom Chiarella is actually advocating drinking among young people, or is he merely offering advice for those who will drink regardless of warnings and laws? Is his approach realistic or dangerous? Why do you believe it to be one or the other?

5. Chiarella suggests that young drinkers make rules, and then he gives some examples. What do you think the purpose is behind the rules that he suggests? How might these change the actions of a young drinker, for better or for worse? Can you generate more potential rules to add to the list that he gives in his essay? How would your rules help a young drinker to not make foolish mistakes?

6. Chiarella also talks about how every drinker will inevitably encounter "that guy," and then he goes on to list the types of drinkers who are "that guy" (or "that girl," as the case may be). If

you've ever encountered (or worse, been) "that guy," describe which type of person you encountered and give specific details about how he or she acted. What was the outcome of the encounter? And how might you "figure out that you don't have to be" any of the negative drinkers he suggests exist?

7. Chiarella also suggests that all young drinkers quit for a period of time. Based on his explanation of why, what do you think is the purpose of his suggestion? If you are a drinker, or if you know one, quit for a period of time or encourage the drinking person who you know to quit for a period of time (and document how long that period of time is), and then document how your (or the other person's) perception of drinking changes. Make the observations that Chiarella suggests you make, and discuss what, if anything, changed about your view of alcohol. Be sure to include descriptions of the before and after scenarios of drinking and your relationship with alcohol before, during, and after the experiment. Did anything change in your perception of alcohol or drinking? If so, what did you notice?

8. Create (and post on YouTube) a video of advice for drinkers (whether they are old or young). Feel free to scour YouTube for video clips that you can sample and include in your own video, or film drinking situations (parties, bars, etc.) that you are attempting to illustrate. Be sure to accompany your video with an essay that details the process and what you are attempting to accomplish with the video. Is it supposed to warn against negative behaviors, or is it pointing out ways to be responsible and have fun? What is the overall lesson to be learned from your video?

# Quicker Liquor: Should We Lower the Drinking Age?
**Darshak Sanghavi**

**Let's Start Here••• ▶**  There are two sides to every debate, and certainly the "drinking age" debate is no exception. Powerful cultural figures (such as politicians, community leaders, and university administrators) have chimed in on the national debate, especially in recent years as binge-drinking and alcohol-related deaths and crimes have begun to rise more rapidly. Many of these crimes and fatalities occur on the campuses of American colleges, which has led to a heightening of the debate by college administrations. In light of a recent initiative proposed by presidents of some of our country's leading universities, Darshak Sanghavi wrote this essay to argue against lowering the drinking age.

As you read his essay, note the way in which his approach to the drinking age argument differs from the popular arguments for lowering the drinking age. Also, observe the way he raises the opposing side's argument and discredits it with research, which is a sophisticated debating skill. By the end of his article, see whether you agree or disagree with his point of view on the argument.

---

Educated at Harvard College and Johns Hopkins Medical School, Darshak Sanghavi completed his clinical fellowship at Harvard Medical School and Children's Hospital Boston after working for several years as a pediatrician for the U.S. Indian Health Service in Navajo country. Currently, he is the chief of pediatric cardiology at UMass Medical School. He has published many scientific papers on topics ranging from the molecular biology of cell death to tuberculosis transmission patterns in Peruvian slums, and speaks widely on medical issues. A frequent writer, television, and radio guest featured on many respected national venues, Sanghavi also serves on the advisory board of *Parents* magazine, is a member of the Lluminari expert network, is *Slate's* health care columnist, and was a visiting media fellow of the Kaiser Family Foundation. His recent book, *A Map of the Child: A Pediatrician's Tour of the Body* (Henry Holt), was an acclaimed bestseller that tells the stories of children's developing bodies. The following essay first appeared in *Slate* on August 26, 2008.

Last week, a coalition of presidents from more than 100 colleges and universities called on authorities to consider lowering the legal drinking age. The so-called Amethyst Initiative, founded by a fed-up former president of Middlebury College, asserts that "twenty-one is not working" because the current drinking age has led to a "culture of dangerous, clandestine binge-drinking" on college campuses. "How many times," they rhetorically ask, "must we relearn the lessons of prohibition?"

**rhetorically:**
Asking for effect, with no answer wanted or expected.

These academic heavyweights—who include the presidents of institutions like Duke, Spelman, Tufts, and Johns Hopkins—believe that lowering the legal drinking age can promote more responsible alcohol use. The familiar argument is that singling out alcohol to make it off-limits is odd, since 18-year-olds may legally join the military, vote, buy cigarettes, and watch porn. Meanwhile over the past decades, binge-drinking has soared among young people. The 1984 federal law that helps determine the legal drinking age is up for renewal next year, and the college presidents believe this law "stifles meaningful debate" and discourages "new ideas" to stop binge-drinking, like allowing kids over 18 to buy alcohol after a course on its "history, culture, law, chemistry, biology, neuroscience as well as exposure to accident victims and individuals in recovery."

It's a nice to think that simply lowering the drinking age would make college students behave better (as well as cheer loudly). But the Amethyst Initiative—named for the gemstone believed by ancient Greeks to stave off drunkenness—has naively exaggerated the benefits of a lower legal drinking age. They ignore some of the implications of their recommendations, fail to acknowledge their own complicity in the campus drinking problem, and ultimately gloss over better solutions to bingeing. Kind of like addicts might.

**complicity:**
Association with an unlawful act by virtue of not addressing or ending the problem.

In truth, the higher drinking age saves lives and has little relation to college bingeing. Some history: After her daughter was killed by an intoxicated driver, Candy Lightner founded Mothers Against Drunk

Driving and successfully lobbied for the 1984 National Minimum Drinking Age Act (the law that's up for reauthorization in 2009), which gave full federal highway funds only to states that set the minimum age to purchase or consume alcohol at 21 years. Most states immediately complied, setting the stage for a national experiment.

According to the federal study Monitoring the Future, underage drinking dropped instantly. From 1977 to 2007, the percentage of 12th graders drinking at least monthly fell from 70 percent to 45 percent—almost immediately after the law was enacted, and lastingly. Fatal car crashes involving drunk young adults dipped 32 percent, resulting in 1,000 fewer lives lost per year. Impressively, this decrease occurred despite minimal efforts at enforcement; the mere presence of the law was protective. The relationship is likely causal. In 1999, by comparison, New Zealand lowered the drinking age from 20 to 18, and while alcohol-related crashes involving 15- to 19-year-olds subsequently fell, they declined far less than in the overall population. Today, all major public health authorities, including the American Medical Association, Centers for Disease Control, National Highway Traffic Safety Board, and surgeon general, support the higher drinking age.

> **causal:**
> One event caused by the other.

We also know that kids in more permissive parts of the world don't drink more responsibly. A magisterial 760-page review from the Institute of Medicine in 2004 noted dryly, "As the committee demonstrates in this report, countries with lower drinking ages are not better off than the United States in terms of the harmful consequences of youths' drinking." Those romantic visions of Irish lasses demurely drinking a glass of ale or sophisticated French teens sipping wine just don't reflect reality.

> **magisterial:**
> Authoritative.

Still, the college presidents signing the Amethyst statement aren't hallucinating about the American version of the problem: There are more binge drinkers on campuses today. Among college students, the percentage of "frequent-heavy" drinkers remained stable from 1977-89, at about 30 percent. However, bingeing began increasing steadily throughout the late 1990s, long after the legal age was increased.

So if we can't blame the drinking age, what's going on? It's key to understand that there are huge disparities in bingeing, depending on where you live and go to school. State bingeing rates vary three- to four-fold, with middle-American states like Michigan, Illinois, and Minnesota far outpacing coastal areas like Washington state, North Carolina, New York, and New Jersey. David Rosenbloom, a professor of public health at Boston University who studies alcohol use, told me bingeing rates at colleges even in the same city can differ dramatically.

> **disparities:**
> Fundamentally at odds with each other or unmatched.

The reasons aren't very complicated: The strongest determinants of college bingeing are weak state and campus alcohol control policies (the regulatory environment) and the presence of lots of bingeing older adults (a locale's overall drinking culture). Impressively, states that severely restrict the promotion of alcohol and its purchase in large quantities—for example, by requiring registration of keg sales, restricting happy hours and beer-pitcher sales, and regulating advertising like billboards—have half the college bingeing rate of states that don't.

In addition to lobbying for these kinds of local laws, college presidents could also promote alcohol education (obviously) and racial and ethnic on-campus diversity (less obviously). As one might expect, alcohol education does help; for example, a brief educational program at the University of Washington reduced long-term binge-drinking in high-risk students. Additionally, young whites drink far more than young African-Americans and Latinos, men drink more than women, and younger students drink more than older students. When mixed, all the groups moderate their alcohol consumption; thus, colleges with greater student diversity have less bingeing across the board.

There's a faster and more effective way to reduce underage drinking—and bingeing—as well: Forget the drinking age debate and sharply increase excise taxes on beer, the preferred choice of underage drinkers. (In real dollars, taxes on liquor, and especially beer, have dropped substantially over the past 30 years.) Just as higher cigarette taxes trump all other methods of curbing smoking among young people, higher alcohol taxes stop kids from drinking too much.

David Rosenbloom notes that the five states with the highest beer taxes have half the binge drinking of other states. In 2004, the Institute of Medicine concluded, with characteristic understatement, that the "overall weight of the evidence" that higher taxes reduce alcohol abuse and related harm to young adults is "substantial." Just as gasoline taxes today don't fully reflect the societal costs of carbon emissions, alcohol taxes are too low, argue economists P.J. Cook and M.J. Moore, since they cover less than half of alcohol's external costs, including damage done by drunk young drivers.

Of course, in the end a lot of teens will binge-drink, no matter what the law says. But that's not an argument against making the legal age 21 years old to buy and consume it. (After all, a third of high-schoolers have smoked marijuana, and few people want to legalize it for them.) Rather, the current law is best viewed as a palliative medical treatment for an incurable condition. Chemotherapy can't cure terminal cancer, but it can make patients hurt a little less and perhaps survive a little longer. Similarly, the current drinking age undeniably reduces teen binge-drinking and death a little bit, without any bad side-effects. When there's no complete cure, though, desperate people are vulnerable to the dubious marketing hype of snake-oil peddlers—which is all the Amethyst Initiative is offering up now.

**palliative:**
Masks problem by treating symptoms.

**dubious:**
Questionable.

**Let's Pause Here••• ▶** How do you feel about the tone Sanghavi uses in his essay (for example, calling the opposing side "naïve" and calling college students "kids")? Does it affect your reading of the essay? What do you think of Sanghavi's argument for maintaining the current drinking age and the way in which he supports it? In what ways is it different than the standard "pro" age-lowering arguments, especially in terms of the "evidence" both sides use to back their respective stances on the issue? Regardless of whether you approve or disapprove of drinking (or underage drinking), what points does Sanghavi make that you agree with? Which ones do you disagree with?

**Let's Take It Further••• ▼**

1. Sanghavi argues that college presidents are ignoring the actual cause of binge drinking and turning a blind eye to the real problems on their respective campuses by pressing for the acceptance of the Amethyst Initiative. Do you agree that it is the job of colleges to regulate the drinking of their students? If so, why? If not, whose job is it to address the issue of underage drinking and binge-drinking? How would they go about doing this?

2. What is the effect of Sanghavi using (and refuting) some of the common arguments used by people who advocate lowering the drinking age? How does this illustrate who he is intending to reach with his argument? Is his audience university administrators? Students? Parents? How do Sanghavi's writing strategies, examples, and language reveal who he is trying to reach with his argument?

3. What sorts of "dangerous, clandestine binge-drinking" occurs on your campus, if any? Do you agree with the premise of the Amethyst Initiative (and Sanghavi), which assumes this is a campus-wide dilemma facing all of our nation's schools, or do you think (based on your own college experience) that it is being blown out of proportion?

4. How do you feel about the various statistical examples given by Sanghavi throughout his essay? Which of them surprised you or went against your expectations? Why or how did it go against the statistical outcome you expected? Did it change your opinion on the issue of the drinking age, or did your opinion remain the same?

5. Note the way in which Sanghavi raises the other side's arguments and refutes their claims. How does this approach to debating strengthen or weaken his argument?

6. Sanghavi cites the Amethyst Initiative's statement that students over 18 should be allowed to buy and consume alcohol after taking a course on its "history, culture, law, chemistry, biology, neuroscience as well as exposure to accident victims and individuals in recovery." If such a course were required alongside a law that lowered the drinking age to 18, how might it actually encourage responsible behavior? What, specifically, is listed in this quote that you feel would be an effective educational tool? How might such a course be taught, and what would the sources be to provide the information listed in the quote above?

7. The Amethyst Initiative has, at its core, a lengthy document that outlines the problems associated with both underage drinking and binge-drinking on college campuses. Though it is a long document that supports the initiative's stance, it is systematically broken into much smaller sections that address the problems and their potential solutions. Locate the document online and choose one of the solutions offered up by the initiative. How realistic is this particular solution to the problem? Discuss in detail the ways that the solution might succeed and/or fail if it is adopted by college campuses.

8. Interview students on your campus to see what solutions they offer up as ways of solving the problem of underage drinking. If their answer is to lower the drinking age, ask them if they have any other solutions. The benefit to this approach is that it would be interesting to see what other ideas students might have (other than the commonplace suggestion of lowering the drinking age) that could potentially help curb either underage drinking or alcohol-related crimes.

9. Through your campus police, community websites, and activist organizations, research the elements that Sanghavi lists in his essay that contribute to the "drinking culture" of a particular school in order to determine your school's identifying characteristics. For example, Sanghavi lists advertising, local drinking culture, drink specials, law enforcement, geography, and many other factors that directly affect a school's culture of alcohol consumption. Also, locate the drinking statistics and alcohol-related illnesses and crimes, as well as interviewing classmates, to get a better picture of your campus's relationship with drinking. How would you define your school? Provide details that explain and illustrate the drinking environment on your campus, the level of social acceptability, the presence of alcohol at school functions, and so forth. Finally, explain how these traits of your particular school prove or disprove Sanghavi's argument about campus binge-drinking, and discuss which of the factors could be eliminated or altered to improve the school's drinking environment. Is Sanghavi correct in his assessment of the situation? Can administrators or local officials change any of the factors that contribute to your school's drinking culture? If so, how? If not, why not?

# proper credentials are needed to join
### Charles Bukowski

**Let's Start Here•••▶**  Charles Bukowski, a nationally renowned writer of over 60 books of poetry, fiction, and essays, was famous for his hard-drinking lifestyle. His poems regularly featured alcohol as their subject matter, in addition to regular appearances of drugs, prostitutes, and his interaction with society's "low-life" members. If there is anyone who is an "authority" on drinking, it would be Charles Bukowski.

In the following poem, Bukowski rants about alcohol, drinkers—specifically young drinkers—and the idea of "real" drinkers versus "fakes." As you read the poem, see if you can determine which of these two groups Bukowski identifies with and what he is saying about the opposite side. Also, see if you can determine how he feels about drinking and alcohol in general.

---

Henry Charles Bukowski was a German-American poet, novelist, and short story writer. His writing was influenced by the social, cultural, and economic ambience of his home city of Los Angeles. It is marked by an emphasis on the ordinary lives of poor Americans, the act of writing, alcohol, relationships with women, and the drudgery of work. Bukowski wrote thousands of poems, hundreds of short stories, and six novels, eventually having over 60 books in print. In 1986, *Time* called Bukowski a "laureate of American lowlife." The following poem is from his 2005 collection of poetry titled *The Flash of Lightning Behind the Mountain* (Ecco).

## proper credentials are needed to join

I keep meeting people, I am introduced to
them at various gatherings
and
either sooner or later
I am told smugly that
this lady or
this gentleman
(all of them young and fresh of face,
essentially untouched by life)
has given up drinking;
that
they all have
had a very difficult time
of late
but
NOW
(and the NOW
is what irritates me)
all of them are pleased and proud
to have finally
overcome all that alcoholic nonsense.

I could puke on their feeble
victory. I started drinking at the age of
eleven
after I discovered a wine cellar
in the basement of a boyhood
friend
and
since then
I have done jail time on 15 or
20 occasions,
had 4 D.U.I.'s
have lost 20 or 30 terrible
jobs,
have been battered and left for
dead in several skid row
alleys, have been twice

hospitalized and
have experienced numberless wild and
suicidal
adventures.

I have been drinking, with
gusto, for 54 years and intend to
continue to
do so.

and now I am introduced
to these young,
blithe, slender, unscathed,
delicate creatures
who

**vanquished:**

Defeated or overcome.

claim to have vanquished the
dreaded evil of
drink!

what is true, of course, is
that they have never really experienced
anything—they have just
dabbled and they have just
dipped in a toe, they have only pretended to really drink.
with them, it's like saying that
they have escaped hell-fire by blowing out
a candle.

it takes real effort
and many years to get damn good
at anything
even being a drunk,
and once more
I've never met one of these reformed young drunks
yet
who was any better for being
sober.

**Let's Pause Here•••▶** How does this poem differ from other poems that you've read, either for classes or for leisure reading? Why do you think Mr. Bukowski titles the poem "proper credentials are needed to join"? What does he mean by "credentials," and what group do these credentials allow a person to join? What do you think Bukowski's view of alcohol is? Does he seem proud or ashamed of his more than 50 years of drinking? What kind of tone does he take toward less experienced drinkers?

## Let's Take It Further•••▼

1. Did you find the poem to be amusing or offensive? What about the poem was amusing, and what about the poem was offensive? Was it offensive because of his professed professionalism? Did it offend you as a drinker or a nondrinker?

2. Based on his language and discussion of drinking, who do you think Bukowski is addressing in his poem? How are you able to determine his audience, and what is he trying to tell them?

3. Do you feel that Bukowski was advocating drinking, or was he trying to raise another point? What might he have been saying about alcohol in general? Is he glorifying it, or does this poem serve another purpose?

4. Note Bukowski's list of "accomplishments" in relation to drinking. What is the effect of seeing this list? Do you find yourself admiring him or pitying him? Why? How do other people you know boast about their drinking "accomplishments" in a similar or different fashion than Bukowski?

5. Though he was a very prolific writer, Charles Bukowski's hard living took a toll on him in many different ways, not the least of which was his physical appearance. Locate pictures of Mr. Bukowski online at various stages in his life, and see whether his appearance might serve as a warning. Compare the young Bukowski to the old Bukowski and describe the differences using specific details from the pictures. How do you feel the statements he makes in this poem are related to the way he changed over the years? How does it affect your opinion of the "coolness" of drinking and/or drug use, if at all?

6. Do you agree or disagree with Bukowski's assessment of young versus old drinkers? How does it affect your opinion on the matter that he was 65 at the time this poem was written and had been drinking for 54 years, if it does at all? Explain the difference between young and old drinkers, both in terms of types and quantities of alcohol consumed, as well as the behaviors of older versus younger drinkers. Also, discuss his definitions of "professional" versus "amateur" drinkers and how he is correct or incorrect in his explanation of the differences between the two.

7. Show this poem to a friend or acquaintance who drinks. How did the person respond to the poem? Was he or she offended or amused by Bukowski's obvious disdain toward young (or fake) drinkers? Does the person have "adventures" that compare to Bukowski's on any scale? Or does he or she admit that he or she will never reach the level of Bukowski's commitment to be "damn good" at being a drunk? How does the person define a "real" versus a "fake" drinker?

8. Locate another Bukowski poem on drinking and compare it to the poem in our chapter. What is his opinion on alcohol based on both poems? What role does it play in his poetry? Do bad things always happen when he drinks, or is he an advocate of drinking because it makes his life good? Use lines from both poems to prove your point.

9. Write a poem about your experience (or lack of experience) with alcohol consumption, as well as what your opinions are on the issue of "professional" versus "amateur" drinking, and "responsible" versus "irresponsible" drinking. Accompany your poem with an essay that explains your intentions and the message about drinking that you are attempting to achieve with your poem.

# How intelligent & cool I think I am based on the number of drinks I've had.

**Darling Stewie**

**Let's Start Here••• ▶** Anyone who has ever been around drinkers has most likely heard statements such as "she's an angry drunk" or "he's a sleepy drunk." There are many theories and scientific studies that attempt to shed light on people's behaviors when under the influence of alcohol, with widely varying results. But it is widely known that the more people drink, the less "cool" and "intelligent" they can become.

In the following chart, Web and graphic designer Darling Stewie creates her own take on the levels-of-drunkenness issue by critiquing the way her intelligence and coherence devolves with each drink she consumes. It is, naturally, supposed to be a joke, but see if there is any truth to the idea of how people's judgment and intelligence shift as they consume more alcohol. Also note the various types of popular culture references that she makes, as well as how the references go from "intellectual" to borderline nonsensical.

---

Darling Stewie is a Web and graphic designer, a writer, and a self-professed "tattooed princess nerd" who lives and works in Northeastern Pennsylvania. This chart was created by Darling Stewie and originally posted to her website, www.darlingstewie.com, on May 30, 2011.

**Let's Pause Here••• ▶** As we have discussed multiple times in this chapter, college and drinking are often viewed as being part and parcel of one another. So, too, do college-aged students become more politically active (or aware), as well as more exposed to cultural figures who they might have never encountered otherwise. Taking that into account, how is Darling Stewie's drunk chart addressing both the activity of drinking alcohol and the idea of intellectual conversation? Is this meant only to be a joke, or is there an element of the chart that sheds light on the true nature of how alcohol affects a drinker's intelligence?

**Let's Take It Further••• ▼**

1. Based on the venue where this chart was first published, as well as the language and imagery used throughout the graphic, who do you think is the intended audience of the cartoon? What message, if any, do you think the author is trying to get across to her site's visitors? Is she merely trying to be humorous, or are there other motives at work here? Might there be something serious that a viewer can take away from the drawing? If so, what might that be?

2. In what ways do you believe the chart is serious about the different "types" of personalities that emerge when a person is drunk? In what ways is Darling Stewie merely joking? Based

# How intelligent & cool I think I am based on the number of drinks I've had.

"I'd definitley vote libertarian but I just feel too strongly about social issues to vote for Ron Paul. Animal rights & environmental responsiblitiy are so crucial to the future of society. Oh yes I do have a blog & a tumblr."

"Yeah 'cuz I think if women want to have an abortion it's like totally cool. Come on like some dude in a suit is gonna tell me what I can do with my body? No way that's not cool. I'm the mom I like get what's up."

"I read a Howard Zinn book! Also & you know who is cool? Harry Potter. That kid was like ZOOM on a broom. I wanna to Hogwarts like soooo bad. I would steal all thur horcruxes. It's funny that it says Whore in the name of a Horcrux too HAHAHAHAHHAH OH MAN!!!"

"Robots go booooooooop. Boop Zoop boop. Like how R2D2 got second place. Zooooooop. Za Za Zoop. But da guyz on dere say no luts just BLOW UP ALDERON LET'S JUST BLOW DID UP. THAT IS OPPRESSION MAN. OPRESHHH..UN....."

<3 darlingstewie.com

on your experience (if you have had any) with a drunk person, how is the chart accurate? How is it inaccurate?

3. The chart uses language that references popular culture figures and events. How is the author of this chart showing the way her intelligence devolves as the number of drinks grows? In other words, how are the references early on in the drawing different from those that come later?

4. Research scholarly sources that seriously address the same issue that this chart addresses using humor—the different personalities and behaviors that emerge when a person drinks. According to the research, what is the cause behind heightened personality traits that

emerge when a person is under the influence of alcohol? How does alcohol physically affect a person's cognitive abilities? Compare how accurate the chart is, based on academic research. Also, compare and contrast how the academic findings are different from or similar to the chart.

5. Browse the Darling Stewie website and choose one video, picture, or other medium that can be read both as a humorous and a serious message about some aspect of our popular culture. Describe the selection and the ways it portrays both ideas. How does Darling Stewie achieve this with the selection you've chosen? What is she joking about, and what is serious about the selection you've chosen to discuss?

6. Research one of the popular culture references mentioned early in the chart and one mentioned later in the chart. Compare and contrast the two popular culture references, making sure to describe who or what each popular culture reference is. How is one a more "intellectual" reference than the other, and why?

7. Create a chart of your own and accompany it with a video or pictures to illustrate the various levels of drunkenness and experiences that accompany them. Be sure to identify the types of personalities drunk people display according to your own observations, and illustrate the way they become more or less "intelligent" as the consume more alcohol.

# mash**UP** essay

The following essay is this chapter's Mashup selection. Keeping in mind our definition of a Mashup essay in Chapter 2 (an essay that includes multimedia texts, as well as multiple writing strategies), observe the way the author, Mina Kimes, utilizes multimedia texts. For example, she refers to multiple well-known advertising campaigns and the marketing firms behind them (such as the KFC "Doubledown" campaign). Kimes also makes several references to websites that are pushing a new trend in drinking games (brosicingbros.com, which is no longer available) and even their spinoffs (iceashton.com). But Kimes takes it a step further by going to the sources of these Internet trends themselves. She interviews the creator of brosicingbros.com, as well as marketing spokespeople for Smirnoff's parent company, Diageo. Not only does the author explain the phenomenon of "icing," she also researches the outcome, digging up videos and photos of "icings" that have been posted to the Internet and describing them for her readership. Finally, Kimes turns to a variety of blogs (Goldman Sachs employee blogs, as well as pop culture blogs that follow and comment on Internet trends) to illustrate the evolution of this particular trend that has recently emerged. The vast variety of online sources Kimes utilizes, as well as the way in which she contacts all parties involved in (or affected by) this trend, serve an important purpose in her essay: they show that Kimes is a thorough reporter of this new phenomenon. The result is that Kimes's credibility is strong, and we feel as though we are in knowledgeable and capable hands as we read her essay.

Kimes also employs many writing strategies to help her make a more sophisticated assessment of this latest craze in drinking games, "icing." For example, she uses a definition-informative approach to writing in order to describe what "icing" is, as well as how it came to be in the first place. She then follows the evolution of the trend, from its beginnings to its mutations, tracking with great detail the way in which the game starts at colleges in the South and spreads throughout the country. To do this, she utilizes the cause-effect writing strategy, which enables her to show the drinking game's course from its start to its state at the time the essay was published. Kimes also used the techniques of descriptive essay writing to paint a clear picture of some of the "icing" scenarios and game strategies that have appeared online. One way in which she proves her understanding of the "icing" trend is that she also describes, step-by-step, the way the game is played, its various rules, and what its outcomes are (the process-analysis writing strategy). But most of the essay's strength lies in the fact that Kimes does not settle for her own interpretation of this new phenomenon that began on college campuses and has worked its way into our nation's most

**Mashup Essay Flowchart**

**Types of Media:**
- Smirnoff Marketing/Smirnoff Liquors
- Various Blogs
- Personal Interviews with Meme Creator and Diageo
- Websites
- Advertising Campaigns
- Research into Marketing Agencies

"'Don't Ice Me, Bro!' When Memes Hit the Marketplace"
Mina Kimes

**Writing Strategies:**
- Process-Analysis
- Descriptive
- Definition-Informative
- Cause-Effect
- Illustration
- Research

prestigious banks and even celebrity lifestyle. Instead, she does extensive research (the research writing strategy) to determine the trend's origins, as well as the creator's intent. She even goes so far as to interview representatives of Smirnoff and other marketing firms to see what they think of the recent drinking fad. In the end, Kimes weaves all of these writing strategies together seamlessly, and the result is an intriguing and thought-provoking assessment of a trend that might appear to be meaningless, but which speaks volumes about our culture of alcohol, our fondness of drinking games, and even the power of ideas or trends to take hold and spread.

When you begin writing a Mashup essay of your own in response to the selections in this chapter, revisit Kimes's essay to generate ideas for multimedia texts and multiple writing strategies. Use the flowchart to see the ways in which Kimes employs the various writing strategies and multimedia texts she utilizes in her writing.

# "Don't Ice Me, Bro!" When Memes Hit the Marketplace

Mina Kimes

**Let's Start Here•••▶** If drinking is a deeply rooted part of not only college culture but also the larger popular culture of America, then drinking games, in all their variations, are an intrinsic part of the drinking experience for young drinkers. The games shift and change according to a person's age and region of the country, but some of the more popular drinking games in recent years would include cornhole, beer pong, quarters, flippy cup, and Edward 40hands. Of course, one popular variation on the idea of a drinking game is to incorporate drinking as a form of "punishment" into already long-established games such as poker. Others play variations in which they watch a program, such as an episode of *The Daily Show*, and then drink each time a certain word or phrase appears.

But a recent drinking phenomenon has taken hold and spread using a fairly unconventional means: the Internet. Where once these sorts of drinking activities were spread by word of mouth and passed from one group of people to another, now an online trend has emerged that has the game of "icing" taking the country by storm.

In the following article, Kimes is interested not only in tracking the evolution of this recent meme, but also in attempting to understand what this recent trend (and trends to come) might mean for liquor companies, for drinkers, and for the future of advertising itself. (Incidentally, a "meme," in the context of this article, is a trend that usually is created and evolves exclusively on the Internet, mostly with the rapid spread and manipulation by people who encounter it.)

According to Kimes, the implications of a meme such as "icing" go far beyond a new drinking game. She believes that alcohol marketers and other people interested in reaching the college demographic are keeping a close eye on this particular trend to see how it might change the marketing landscape as we know it.

As you read the essay, observe the ways in which Kimes describes the game's creators, its rules and evolution, and even how widely it has spread in such a short period of time. Also, try to determine whether Kimes advocates the drinking game itself or if there is another purpose to her essay.

---

Mina Kimes has been writing since high school and blogged throughout her college days at Yale University. Ms. Kimes has been a freelance journalist for *Fortune* magazine since 2009. This article first appeared in *Fortune* on May 26, 2010.

---

John Ryan didn't see it coming. The Scottsdale, Ariz.based software engineer, 27, had just returned to his office from lunch. Seconds later, his project manager crept up to his desk, holding a ticking time bomb: A 24 oz. bottle of Smirnoff Ice. "You've been iced," he said.

> Kimes begins her essay with the narrative writing technique, as she tells a small anecdote about the experience of being "iced."

As his boss delightedly snapped pictures with his cellphone, Ryan popped the cap, got on one knee, and chugged it. "It was rough," he says.

"Icing"—or "getting iced"—is a drinking game that's rapidly gaining popularity amongst office workers, tech and media types, and college students. The rules are simple: If a person sees a Smirnoff Ice, he or she must get down on one knee and chug it, unless they happen to be carrying their own Smirnoff, in which case they can "ice block," or refract the punishment back onto the attacker. In order to dupe people into stumbling across the beverage, participants have devised creative ways of presenting them with Ices, like strapping the bottles to the backs of dogs or burying them in vats of protein powder.

> Kimes employs the definition-informative approach to explain what "icing" is and how the game works.

The trend first took hold on college campuses in the South, but it's trickled up both coasts, where icings have been spotted at the offices of companies like Yelp! and IAC's College Humor. Bankers, too, have embraced the fratty fad: An ice attack was recently reported at Goldman Sachs, and *Fortune* has learned of icings at Florida-based investment bank Raymond James and New York City hedge fund D.E. Shaw.

> Kimes uses the idea of memes, or Internet trends, as a text.

As homemade videos and snapshots of people imbibing Smirnoff Ice appeared on the Internet last week, bloggers speculated that the meme was the work of Smirnoff, which is owned by British alcohol giant Diageo. But representatives for both Diageo and its advertising firm, JWT, say they aren't involved. "The icing phenomenon is consumer generated,"

> The responses—videos and pictures—are texts as well.
>
> **imbibing:** Drinking.

Kimes uses research to allow Smirnoff's parent company, Diageo, to respond to the meme.

says Zsoka McDonald, a Diageo spokeswoman. She adds: "Some people think it's fun. Diageo never wants underage icing."

Again, Kimes employs research to interview the creator of the brosicingbros.com website.

The creator of brosicingbros.com, the foremost authority on icing, says, "I've heard absolutely nothing from them." The brains behind the site, "Joe," is a 22 year-old recent college graduate who lives near Columbia, S.C. (he requested anonymity because he's looking for a job—Internet marketing firms, take note).

### The Bro-Eds Behind It

This is one of many instances where Kimes utilizes the cause-effect writing strategy to show the way the meme of "icing" spread.

Joe says he first heard about icing from fraternity members at the nearby College of Charleston, and decided to import it to his own school about six weeks ago. With the help of his frat brothers, the business major spread the word around campus and created brosicingbros.com to host pictures. "A bro is a college-age person," he says. "They like to hang out. A lot of them drink beer and wear backwards baseball caps. A lot of them drive SUVs and listen to Dave Matthews Band."

Here, in the course of the interview, "Joe" uses the definition-informative strategy to define and describe a "bro."

Bros are also "alpha consumers," at least on campus, which may be why the trend spread so quickly. "There are certain individuals that define social structures and drive the decisions other consumers make," says Dr. Heather Honea, a marketing professor at San Diego State University. "Infiltrating the fraternity or sorority market could be ideal."

Within weeks, Joe says, "BrosIcingBros" became a hit, so much so that his classmates were carrying protective Smirnoff Ices in their backpacks to ward off attacks. The game spread to other college campuses in the South. Joe—who pays for the site with Google Ads—says he gets as many as 100 submissions a day now. With the help of two friends, he sifts through e-mails for pictures of creative icings.

More recently, he says, he's received submissions from people in New York City, where interest amongst advertising and media types has hit a fever pitch. There are already spin-off memes: iceashton.com entreats visitors to ice Ashton Kutcher, the king of Twitter (Coolio, the rapper, has already been iced).

Another example of the meme responses as texts.

Colin Nagy, the creator of iceashton.com and a partner at Manhattan social media marketing agency Attention, says memes like his could prolong the trend. "It's like introducing more oxygen into a fire," he says. So far, Kutcher remains elusive.

## Smirnoff: Bro Is Me?

In some ways, the meme seems like a gift to Smirnoff: Free publicity powered by a marketing gimmick that's generated solely by consumers. Such authenticity is rare, advertising gurus say, but also risky. After all, "icing" is predicated on a negative message about the drink. Bros (allegedly) dislike Smirnoff Ice, which is why they derive pleasure from forcing it on each other.

> **predicated:**
> Founded or based.

Surprisingly, this could actually be good for the brand, so long as the game places more emphasis on its femininity than its alleged bad taste. "It's being positioned as a girlie product," says Honea. "If that's the association [Smirnoff] wants, then it's a positive thing for the brand."

The game could also create a new association for the product—humor. Consumers sometimes support products and ideas ironically, propelling fads like "Rickrolling," which introduced a younger generation to 80's singer Rick Astley. KFC's DoubleDown sandwich, better known for its absurdity than its flavor, has been a hit for KFC, which recently extended its tenure through the summer.

> More examples of memes as texts.

Such love affairs are typically short-lived, but can generate longer-term interest in a brand. Bros might find that they actually enjoy the beverage. "I have been iced with the mango flavor of Smirnoff Ice, and I have to say it's not that bad," says Joe.

So far, the trend has yet to visibly impact sales of Smirnoff Ice. Workers at grocery stores in South Carolina and New York said they hadn't seen much of an effect. "[Smirnoff Ice] is doing okay, not too much," said an employee at Yesol Market, a bodega located in New York's financier-heavy Murray Hill neighborhood. According to researchers IRI, sales of Smirnoff Flavored Malt Beverages, which includes the Ice drinks, are up 1.6% over the last month, while other flavored malt beverages are up 12%. Last year, volumes of Smirnoff Ice sold in the U.K. were down 20%.

> Kimes explores the meme's effect on Smirnoff sales by using the cause-effect strategy.

Diageo's McDonald says the company has been spending more time marketing its new Smirnoff Mixed drinks, which came out in the spring and have done well. "The real growth we're seeing in the segment is through new products," she says.

## Bro with the Flow

So far, Smirnoff has steered clear of the game—a smart move, advertising experts say, since it could ruin its authenticity. But as the trend grows, it runs the risk of breeding ill will towards the brand, or, worse, associating it with binge or underage drinking. Alcohol companies have come under scrutiny recently from groups like the World Health Organization for marketing booze through social media.

"The challenge with consumer-generated messaging is that you lose control," Honea says. For example, in 2006 Chevrolet invited users to create their own commercials for the Chevy Tahoe; consumers responded by devising messages that critiqued the SUV as hurting the environment.

Smirnoff must walk a delicate line in addressing the meme, says Honea. "You have to figure out a way to be a partner as opposed to an adversary," she says.

**adversary:**
Opponent or enemy.

The typical lifecycle of an Internet meme is short—as brief as a couple of weeks, according to Sandy Smallens, EVP of Oddcast, a New York-based social marketing agency that has developed Internet campaigns for brands like eTrade and McDonald's. But Smallens think memes like BrosIcingBros can last longer because they create a feedback loop between Internet usage and real world experience. He expects corporations to try and follow suit.

Kimes does market research by interviewing an upper-level employee of a major marketing firm to discuss memes and their impact on marketing products.

"We're gonna see more of this," says Smallens. "Now that everything can be delivered through digital media, what's the last authentic thing? Spontaneous experience." These bros, he says, are at the vanguard of the next phase in social media: real life.

**vanguard:**
Front line.

---

**Let's Pause Here•••▶** Notice the constant play on the word "bro" throughout the article. What do you think is Kimes's intention in creating puns of well-known phrases, such as "woe is me," by inserting the word "bro" into them? Do you believe that Kimes is advocating this particular drinking game, or drinking games in general, or is there another purpose to this essay? What does she accomplish, in terms of discussing this particular meme, by writing this essay? Why do you believe that she ends the article saying that the "vanguard of the next phase of social media [is] real life," and what does that statement mean? How does all of this relate to the marketing potential of memes?

---

**Let's Take It Further•••▼**

1. Kimes argues that some memes evolve and last for a while, while others go "extinct" within a matter of weeks. Have you heard of "icing," or has this particular meme gone extinct? What other memes do you know of that have gone extinct? What does it say that the website mentioned in this very essay (brosicingbros.com) has already been shuttered?

2. The article asserts that "bros" on college campuses are seen as "alpha consumers," and Kimes quotes a marketing professor who states that "infiltrating the fraternity or sorority market could be ideal." What does the statement "alpha consumer" mean, and why might marketing companies (particularly of alcohol) see fraternities and sororities as an "ideal" market? What are the roles of fraternities and sororities on campus? How effective are they at setting trends?

3. Who is the audience to whom Kimes is appealing in her essay? Is this information intended for use only by drinkers, businessmen, or even potential marketers? What is the effect of the examples she gives and the language (including the aforementioned puns) she uses on her overall message about drinking games and memes?

4. Notice that Kimes tells marketing firms to "take note" of "Joe," the brains behind the website brosicingbros.com. Why do you think she makes this statement? What is it about "Joe" that might be valuable to marketing firms?

5. How do you feel about Smirnoff's parent company, Diageo, stating that "Diageo never wants underage icing" when asked about their involvement in the meme? Why do you think they made the "underage" distinction, and yet didn't shy away from the idea of drinking games, which promote excessive drinking by virtue of their very existence? Do you feel they are happy with this recent trend? Do you think their statement is sincere?

6. Kimes mentions a few recent (at the time of the essay's publication) online memes in addition to "icing," such as the absurd online popularity of the KFC Doubledown and the YouTube practice of "Rickrolling" that swept the Web by storm. There have been many other memes since these, such as the Tiger Woods "Cigar Guy," the Antione Dodson "Bed Intruder Song," and the Charlie Sheen "Tiger Blood" crazes. What other sorts of memes have occurred since these? How did they start, and how did they evolve? What exactly is their purpose, and how are you able to discern this? Describe the process of how they began, how they mutated and changed, and where they ended up. Be sure to describe what the meme is, in the same manner Kimes uses in her article.

7. The role of humor in the marketing of alcohol is briefly mentioned by Kimes in her essay. What role do you feel humor plays in selling alcohol? In what ways do alcohol companies employ humor in their various advertising campaigns to make their products seem both attractive enough to drink and "cool" enough to make jokes about? Locate an alcohol marketing advertisement (online, TV, radio, magazine, billboard, or any other medium) that uses humor to sell its product. Describe the product and the way they use humor to sell it, as well as who you believe their market to be. What sort of humor do they use to sell the product?

8. Kimes quotes Honea (the marketing professor) as saying that the game of "icing" positions Smirnoff Ice as "a girlie product." This is why it is a form of punishment for "bros" to "ice" each other. The implication is that they are not supposed to like "girlie" drinks. In the realm of alcohol advertisement, how does a company position their product as more appealing to one gender over another? How does each gender learn what the "manly" and the "girlie" drinks are? If you believe it is through marketing, locate an advertisement that clearly targets women or men and explain how the ad accomplishes this. "Read" the ad to explain the ways the ad makes a particular alcoholic product appealing to women or men. If you believe there are other ways men and women determine (or learn) the drinks that are appropriate for each gender, explain how and from where this is learned.

9. According to Kimes, alcohol companies do not want to be associated with "binge or underage drinking." She adds that groups like the World Health Organization have begun criticizing these companies for "marketing booze through social media." Explain why a company that makes and markets alcohol would not want to be seen as promoting excessive drinking. How would it be different than any other company promoting its product? If the whole point of advertising is to promote a product so people will buy it (and presumably lots of it) and consume it, why do alcohol companies have to walk such a thin line? Also, why would an alcohol company be criticized for marketing through social media? How is this any different from marketing on TV, on billboards, in magazines, and online in general?

10. In the same fashion that Kimes dissects the "icing" trend, identify and describe a drinking game that is particular to your own campus or community. How does it work? What is its purpose? What are its rules? Where did it begin, and how did it grow in popularity? Who are the types of people who use the game? Ultimately, decide whether the game will have lasting effects on your school or community (either positive or negative), and discuss the future of the game as you see it.

# mash**it**UP

Here is a series of essay and discussion topics that draw connections between multiple selections within the chapter. They also suggest outside texts to include in your essay or discussion. Feel free to bring in further outside texts, remembering the variety of texts (beyond articles) available to you.

1. In his essay, "Lessons for a Young Drinker," Chiarella tells his audience that "drinking must be mastered, or it will master you." Compare that sentiment, as well as his overall message for young drinkers, to the point of Bukowski's poem "proper credentials are needed to join." How are the two selections similar, and in what ways are they at odds with one another? How is the advice of Chiarella's piece working alongside the message in Bukowski's poem?

2. Compare the essay on drinking age ("Quicker Liquor: Should We Lower the Drinking Age?") to an essay that advocates lowering the drinking age and determine which one makes the better case. Find outside sources that help to support your viewpoint. How might the YouTube videos of drunk people help to make Darshak Sanghavi's point for him? How do mass media depictions of underage drinking (or drinking in general) play a role in this debate?

3. Compare Bukowski's poem "proper credentials are needed to join" and some of his other drinking poems to the work of writer Tucker Max,

who many critics have dubbed a "Bukowski ripoff." Max, who is the author of the book-turned-movie *I Hope They Serve Beer in Hell*, is wildly popular among the younger drinking set (and equally loathed by campus activist groups). How do the two men write about alcohol? What is the purpose of alcohol for each of them, and what kinds of events occur when they are drunk? Describe which of the two is "better" or "worse," and in what way.

4. Research depictions of drinking in college movies by watching any college movie from the last five years. Do these films promote drinking? If so, how? Why, in your personal experience, do people associate drinking and college? Is it just because of our popular culture, or is there something else at work here? Are movies to be blamed as part of the problem, or are they merely mirroring the reality of the college experience?

5. If the premise of the cartoon "College Drinking" is intended as a sign of what's to come (i.e., society will come to see drinking the way some now see smoking), how might this take place? Research outside sources to see how campuses and communities are trying to stifle binge drinking. Do you think it is possible that one day campuses will ban drinking the same way many establishments have banned smoking? Will our society ever look on drinking with the same disdain that we now have for the once-popular smoking? Why or why not?

6. Examine depictions of drinking in popular culture (music, TV, film, advertisements, social media, clothing, etc.) and discuss the way messages on drinking are given to the general public. How are messages on drinking (whether positive or negative) spread to different age groups, ethnicities, or even social classes? How does the message shift from one group to another in order to get the maximum impact out of advertising or illustrating the pros and cons of drinking to each audience?

7. Compare Sanghavi's discussion of the complacency of college presidents on the issue of underage drinking to the argument Gladwell makes in his essay "Offensive Play" (see the "Violence" chapter). How are the two both abuses of power, and what roles should each set of leaders play in the situations being illustrated? Who is failing a bigger population or abusing their power more, and why?

8. Visit drinking game websites, or locate drinking game videos or apps, and use these to support or refute Sanghavi's arguments about drinking age, responsibility, and mature drinking. Do the sites reinforce or counter Sanghavi's points? How could Sanghavi change his argument to better reflect the reality of drinking, specifically in relation to college culture and alcohol consumption?

# Phelps Olympic Sponsors

**Randy Bish**

Randy Bish is an American editorial cartoonist working for the *Pittsburgh Tribune-Review*. He is the recipient of a Golden Quill Award and was a 2002 winner in the Iranian International Cartoon Contest. Bish began working for the *Pittsburgh Tribune-Review* in 1985, where he draws seven weekly cartoons. In addition, his editorial cartoons have appeared in the *Orlando Sentinel*, the *21st Century Business Herald* in China, and *Reakja* in Poland. News programs, including *Good Morning America*, Fox News, C-Span, and *CNN Headline News*, have used his editorial cartoons. His cartoons are syndicated by the Pennsylvania Newspaper Association and have been syndicated by United Media. Bish's cartoons have been published in *Attack of the Political Cartoonists* and *The Best Political Cartoons of the Year 2005*. His artwork was used for the cover of *Best Editorial Cartoons of the Year* in 1998. The following cartoon was originally published in the *Pittsburgh Tribune-Review* on February 4, 2009.

# Thinking About Drugs

Take a moment to look at the accompanying cartoon. The title of the cartoon is "Phelps Olympic Sponsors," which is a reference to Olympic gold medalist Michael Phelps. It is apparent that the artist, Randy Bish, is referring to the scandal that Phelps became embroiled in when pictures of the world-famous swimmer surfaced on the Internet that showed him taking bong hits at a party. The ensuing drama led to many of Phelps's corporate sponsors dropping him, despite his record-breaking eight gold medals won at the 2008 Beijing Olympics. How is Bish referring to the scandal, as well as its results, in this cartoon? How do the pop culture figures of Cheech and Chong allow us to understand what the cartoonist is trying to say about Phelps as well as the outcome of his weed-smoking scandal?

As a society, we try to hold our athletes to high standards, and we regularly subject them to drug screens (particularly for "performance enhancing" drugs like anabolic steroids). This is due in part to feeling that athletes should be "worthy" of their high salaries by abstaining from drugs. We also feel that enhancing one's performance is cheating, since many athletes train long, grueling hours for even the slightest competitive edge that steroids could provide with minimal effort. In other words, it is considered to be unsportsmanlike. But it is also because these public figures are viewed as role models for younger aspiring athletes, and we do not want our athletes to set a bad example by using drugs.

However, despite the anger toward Phelps and other famous athletes caught "doping" or doing "recreational" drugs, the use of steroids, marijuana, and countless other drugs pervades not only our popular culture, but also our college campuses nationwide. Students pop pills to make it through the crunch of final exams. They smoke pot in their dorm rooms and experiment with other drugs, all as yet another part of the "college experience."

On the whole, drugs play every bit as large of a role in our society as alcohol does. Countless famous actors, musicians, writers, athletes, and politicians have died untimely deaths by succumbing to drug addictions. Despite the fact that the war on drugs has been being waged in our country for nearly a hundred years, the popularity of drugs in all aspects of our popular culture doesn't seem to be diminishing whatsoever—though specific epidemics (cocaine, crack, meth) seem to come and go.

Look to Bish's cartoon again for proof of this fact. Did you know, when you first viewed this cartoon, who the characters Cheech and Chong are? Do you know what they are famous for? How might they hypothetically be "sponsors" for someone like Phelps, and what explanation can be given for their fame?

Is Bish only critiquing athletes like Phelps, or is he also critiquing American society? How might it be hypocritical of our society that we demonize someone like Phelps and yet we give the characters "Cheech and Chong" a long, healthy career in movies, glorifying the very activity that Phelps's sponsors use as the excuse to drop him from their payrolls? What does our persistent drug use say about us as a culture, despite the nearly 100 year war against drugs?

# Is It Fair to Be Angry at Lindsay Lohan?

**Mary Elizabeth Williams**

**Let's Start Here•••▶** It is nearly impossible to go through an entire day without coming across a story on a news website, on TV, or being shared on Facebook that features yet another of our many celebrities who are in trouble with the law for drugs or alcohol, or both. They are in rehab one day and out the next. They are photographed being arrested for driving drunk. Their mug shots are plastered all over the Web. But still they persist. And occasionally we stop and wonder, what's wrong with these people? If they have so much going for them—money, fame, lucrative careers in sports, movies, or some other form of entertainment—why do they constantly risk losing it all by using drugs and alcohol?

Some of us feel sorry for our troubled celebrities, while others choose to more or less boycott them. But either way, it is tragic to see so much talent and good fortune wasted. And it is also offensive to many that celebrities are blatantly given lighter punishments for breaking the law than "normal" people would be given.

These are the dilemmas of drug use in our culture that Mary Elizabeth Williams addresses in her article, "Is It Fair to Be Angry at Lindsay Lohan?" As you read the essay, observe the tone and language Williams uses throughout her discussion to determine what her answer is to the question posed in the title of her essay.

---

Mary Elizabeth Williams is a writer, consultant, and radio commentator. The publications she writes for with regularity include Salon.com, the *New York Times*, the *New York Observer, TV Guide, Smith*, and *Yoga Journal*. She is a popular culture critic for PRI's morning show *The Takeaway* and is a regular pop culture commentator for the CBC. She is the author of the book, *Gimme Shelter: My Three Years Searching for the American Dream*. The following essay first appeared in *Salon* on September 27, 2010.

An addict can be the biggest jerk in the world. An alcoholic can rip out your heart and steal your wallet. If you want to know what it means to be frustrated, disgusted, and straight up perplexed, invest a little of your time and energy in an active substance abuser. And if said possessor of a wagon he or she just can't stay on has been granted every opportunity to go straight—counseling, support, stints at the best rehabs—and can't manage something as simple as not getting falling-down messed up, well, that person has got to be a world-class ungrateful piece of crap. Yeah, we're talking about you, Lindsay.

Seemingly minutes after serving two weeks in jail for a probation violation stemming from her 2007 DUI, the most famously troubled actress/

self-tanning entrepreneur was back in rehab for the umpteenth time. And right on cue upon her release, she flunked her latest drug test earlier this month and wound up back in handcuffs.

Last week, as she prepared to head back on her apparent hamster wheel of jail, rehab and subsequent partying, she stated via Twitter, "I am so thankful for the support of my fans, loved ones and immediate family, who understand that I am trying hard, but also that I am a work in progress, just as anyone else. I am keeping my faith, and I am hopeful. . . . Thank you all!!!"

Yet with every reliably timed relapse, her claims of "trying really hard" ring increasingly false. There's Lindsay, the desperate-to-improve-her-public-image starlet volunteering at a Los Angeles outreach center—and tweeting conspicuously about her good works. There's Lindsay, the woman with every envy-inspiring advantage in the world, gazing gorgeously from the cover of the current Vanity Fair and moaning that she is "literally falling apart." And there's the hollow-eyed young woman with an uncanny resemblance to the actress crouching in a corner and clutching a syringe. She sure doesn't look like a woman trying hard. She looks like a woman who has selfishly wasted a hundred more opportunities to pull it together than most substance abusers ever get in a lifetime, one who, were she not beautiful and wealthy, would be selling her food stamps for cough syrup. You can see why she pisses people off, why so many people think that pretty face looks like it could use a book or two thrown at it.

That's the way it works with addiction. And depression. And lots of other conditions that aren't friendly and noble and can contaminate everybody in the sufferer's circle. The compulsions to do exactly the most self-destructive thing in the world don't just make the addict despise him- or herself; they do a bang-up job shutting everybody else out as well. You can watch, helplessly, wondering how someone could not want wellness enough, could not love you enough, could choose a bottle or a powder over career or family or everything good so close within reach.

A friend recently had her heart broken by a great man, a talented man with a kid and loving parents, who decided that after a long time of being clean that he preferred the company of heroin. What kind of a loser throws all that away? If you're fortunate enough to not be wired that way, it's damn near unfathomable to accept that it's because something powerful inside that person wants him or her dead.

But self-destruction is a two-way relationship between a person and his or her own demons, and plenty of people somehow do manage to get the upper hand. Whether it's through rehab or 12-step programs or therapy or sheer force of will, the world is full of men and women who work very, very hard every day at being functional and succeed. So it's easy to point and say, Christ, Lindsay, if Eminem and Russell Brand can do this, what's your holdup?

Unfortunately sobriety is not transferable. And the fact that Lohan is still very much a protected figure with easy access to all the temptations available to a Hollywood beauty can only add obstacles to her path. It's not easy to be the diabetic at the candy factory. Maybe she needs somebody to let her wake up in her own urine a few times, to not post her bail, and not let her be on the cover of magazines looking more like the Princess of Monaco than a serial rehab truant. Then again, maybe none of that would make a lick of difference. Because for all Lohan's privilege, addiction is an equal opportunity condition. It doesn't care how much money or fame or sex appeal a person has; it just wants everything she's got. And as grim as it is to look at someone in a tailspin and see so much that's ugly and selfish, it's harder still to see so much that is talented or funny or just plain good, locked inside a human being drowning in a sea of poison.

**Let's Pause Here•••▶** Williams asks the question "Is it fair to be angry with Lindsay Lohan?" within the title of the essay itself. What is her answer to that question, according to this essay? Do you agree with her answer or disagree with it? Why? Is her tone one of pity for celebrities with addictions, or is it a tone of anger? What words or phrases in particular does Williams use in her essay that prove she feels pity or anger?

**Let's Take It Further•••▼**

1. If we are to hold our celebrities to some sort of moral standard, what should that standard be? Should we be allowed to judge them or be angry with them when they get in trouble with the law, specifically over drug or alcohol problems? If so, why?

2. Though it is obvious that in some ways Williams is voicing her frustrations to Lindsay Lohan herself, who else is she trying to engage with her discussion of whether it is fair to judge Lohan—or other addicts for that matter? Based on Williams's writing strategies and appeals to logic, how might she be trying to influence her audience? In other words, what does she hope to achieve in terms of her audience's opinion on the matter of addiction?

3. One of Williams's main points is that she feels celebrities are treated as though they're above the law because of their status as celebrities. Do you agree with this point? If so, why do celebrities "get off easy," while everyday people get in far more trouble for the same crimes and infractions? Should this be allowed? If you disagree, why should celebrities be allowed more chances than "normal" citizens, and when is enough enough? To what types of privileges should they be entitled?

4. Williams complains that the treatment of Lindsay Lohan by popular magazines and Hollywood in general (glamorous photo shoots, continued roles in films) might be the cause of her constant relapses into addiction. She argues that if Lohan were to "wake up in her own urine a few times, not [have someone to] post her bail, and not [be allowed] on the cover of magazines," perhaps Lohan would have a wake-up call. Do you agree with her proposal? How might allowing Lohan to realize the state of her addiction help her to overcome her drug and alcohol demons?

5. Williams cites Ms. Lohan's regular Tweets about her struggle with drugs and her community service activities. Because this information is public and archived on Twitter, locate Lindsay Lohan's Twitter feed and observe the unfolding of events (arrests, rehabs, relapse, charity activities, and everyday activities) from Ms. Lohan's perspective. Describe how her view of things differs from the public record regarding any (or all) of her arrests, stints in rehab, and legal woes. How do her Tweets reflect the perspective of the public or the media? How aware does Lohan seem to be of the criticisms being leveled toward her? Do her Tweets support Williams's overall argument about addiction, or do the Tweets undercut Williams's overall point?

6. There has been no shortage of celebrities who have publicly been through the dark side of addiction and appeared back on top. Williams cites the cases of Russell Brand and Eminem as celebrities who have overcome their addictions. Locate another celebrity who has publicly wrestled with addiction and all of its trappings (including arrest, rehab, and even public humiliation) and describe his or her battle with addiction, the costs of his or her addiction, how the celebrity managed to fight it, and how he or she is back on top of his or her career.

7. Research the legal ramifications for a "normal" person involved in alcohol- or drug-related infractions. Describe the process that a normal person is entitled to, as well as the potential punishment that occurs for these crimes. Then compare them to any well-known celebrity case in which the celebrity was treated differently. Describe and explain the differences in treatment between the two, and explain the reason why you believe one is treated more harshly than the other.

8. Locate interviews with other well-known celebrities who have conquered addictions (see also "Celebrity Rehab" in the "Heroes and Celebrities" chapter) and describe the ways that they define and narrate their own processes of overcoming addictions. How does Williams's argument agree with or go against the celebrity's own sense of what an addict is, as well as what loved ones and friends should do to either influence, support, or intervene in a person's addiction?

# The Parable of Prohibition    Johann Hari

**Let's Start Here•••▶** Most people are familiar with the period in U.S. history known as Prohibition. In the early 20th century, the 18th Amendment to the Constitution briefly outlawed the consumption and sale of alcohol. In the years following, organized crime took hold in the U.S. as bootleggers and gangsters sold alcohol to a public who, quite frankly, wanted to drink. The effects of Prohibition were severe and long-lasting, and eventually the 18th Amendment was repealed because the government realized the futility in outlawing alcohol in a country where so many people wanted to drink.

In the following essay, Johann Hari gives a brief history of the era of Prohibition and shows how and why it was a short-lived moment in our history. Hari also draws a comparison between the prohibition of alcohol and the current prohibition of illegal narcotics, in an effort to explain how there are lessons learned from prohibition that might apply to illegal narcotics. Convinced of the connection between the two "prohibitions," Hari points out the many ways the prohibition of drugs has led to (and continues to lead to) a rise in organized crime, drug wars, and skyrocketing incarceration of average citizens. Hari sees this as a story that is being retold before our eyes, but the only "character" who has changed is drugs standing in for alcohol.

As you read the essay, observe the many ways Hari draws comparisons between the era of Prohibition and our current drug prohibition. Also, pay attention to the way he uses actual events and outcomes in our nation's history to draw a parallel between the two wars on drugs and on alcohol.

---

Johann Hari is an award-winning journalist who writes twice-weekly for *The Independent*, one of Britain's leading newspapers, and the *Huffington Post*. He is a contributing writer for *Slate*, and regularly appears on the BBC's *Newsnight Review*. His work has also appeared in the *New York Times*, the *Los Angeles Times*, *Le Monde*, *Le Monde Diplomatique*, *The New Republic*, *El Mundo*, *The Guardian*, *The Melbourne Age*, the *Sydney Morning Herald*, South Africa's *Star*, *The Irish Times*, and a wide range of other international newspapers and magazines. He has reported from Iraq, the Gaza Strip, the Congo, Bangladesh, India, Venezuela, Rwanda, Peru, Ethiopia, Mexico, the Central African Republic, Syria, and the United States. The following essay originally appeared in *Slate* on June 3, 2010.

**ineradicable:**
Impossible to get rid of or remove.

Since we first prowled the savannahs of Africa, human beings have displayed a few overpowering and ineradicable impulses—for food, for sex, and for drugs. Every human society has hunted for its short cuts to an altered state: The hunger for a chemical high, low, or pleasingly new shuffle sideways is universal. Peer back through history, and it's everywhere. Ovid said drug-induced ecstasy was a divine gift. The Chinese were brewing alcohol in prehistory and cultivating opium by 700 A.D. Cocaine was found in clay-pipe fragments from William Shakespeare's house. George Washington insisted American soldiers be given whiskey every day as part of their rations. Human history is filled with chemicals, comedowns, and hangovers.

And in every generation, there are moralists who try to douse this natural impulse in moral condemnation and burn it away. They believe that humans, stripped of their intoxicants, will become more rational or ethical or good. They point to the addicts and the overdoses and believe they reveal the true face—and the logical endpoint—of your order at the bar or your roll-up. And they believe we can be saved from ourselves, if only we choose to do it. Their vision holds an intoxicating promise of its own.

Their most famous achievement—the criminalization of alcohol in the United States between 1921 and 1933—is one of the great parables of modern history. Daniel Okrent's superb new history, *Last Call: The Rise and Fall of Prohibition*, shows how a coalition of mostly well-meaning, big-hearted people came together and changed the Constitution to ban booze. On the day it began, one of the movement's leaders, the former baseball hero turned evangelical preacher Billy Sunday, told his ecstatic congregation what the Dry New World would look like: "The reign of tears is over. The slums will soon be only a memory. We will turn our prisons into factories and our jails into storehouses. Men will walk upright now, women will smile, and the children will laugh. Hell will be forever rent."

The story of the War on Alcohol has never needed to be told more urgently—because its grandchild, the War on Drugs, shares the same DNA. Okrent alludes to the parallel only briefly, on his final page, but it hangs over the book like old booze-fumes—and proves yet again Mark Twain's **dictum**: "History doesn't repeat itself, but it does rhyme."

> **dictum:**
> Observation or saying.

There was never an America without chemical highs. The Native Americans used hallucinogens routinely, and the ship that brought John Winthrop and the first Puritans to the continent carried three times more beer than water, along with 10,000 gallons of wine. It was immediately a society so soaked in alcohol that it makes your liver ache to read the raw statistics: By 1830, the average citizen drank seven gallons of pure alcohol a year. America was so hungry for highs that when there was a backlash against all this boozing, the **temperance** movement's initial proposal was that people should water down their alcohol with opium.

> **temperance:**
> In favor of moderation or altogether abstaining from alcohol consumption.

It's not hard to see how this **fug** of liquor caused problems, as well as pleasure—and the backlash was launched by a furious housewife from a small town in Ohio. One Sunday in 1874, Eliza Thompson—a mother to eight children, who had never spoken out on any public issue before—stood before the crowds at her church and announced that America would never be free or godly until the last whiskey bottle was emptied onto the dry earth. A huge crowd of women cheered: They believed their husbands were squandering their wages at the saloon. They marched as one to the nearest bar, where they all sank to their knees and prayed for the soul of its owner. They refused to leave until he repented. They worked in six-hour prayer shifts on the streets until the saloonkeeper finally appeared, head bowed, and agreed to shut it down. This prayer-athon then moved around to every alcohol-seller in the town. Within 10 days, only four of the original 13 remained, and the rebellion was spreading across the country.

> **fug:**
> Stuffy atmosphere.

It was women who led the first cry for Temperance, and it was women who made Prohibition happen. A woman called Carry Nation became a symbol of the movement when she traveled from bar to bar with an oversize hatchet and smashed them to pieces. Indeed, Prohibition was one of the first and most direct effects of the movement to expand the vote. This is one of the first strange flecks of gray in this story. The proponents of Prohibition were primarily progressives—and some of the most admirable people in American history, from Susan B. Anthony to Frederick Douglass to Eugene V. Debs. The pioneers of American feminism believed alcohol was at the root of men's brutality toward women. The anti-slavery movement saw alcohol addiction as a new form of slavery, replacing leg irons with whiskey bottles. You can see the same left-wing prohibitionism today, when people like Al Sharpton say drugs must be criminalized because addiction does real harm in ghettos.

Of course, there were more obviously sinister proponents of Prohibition too, pressing progressives into weird alliances. The Ku Klux Klan said that "nigger gin" was the main reason that oppressed black people were prone to rebellion, and if you banned alcohol, they would become quiescent. An echo of this persists in America's current strain of prohibition. Powder cocaine and crack cocaine are equally harmful, but crack—which is disproportionately used by black people—carries much heavier jail sentences than powder cocaine, which is disproportionately used by white people.

**quiescent:**
Submissive or obedient.

**disproportionately:**
Out of proportion with another group.

It was in this context that the Anti-Saloon League rose to become the most powerful pressure group in American history and the only one to ever change the Constitution through peaceful political campaigning. It was begun by a little man called Wayne Wheeler, who was as dry as the Sahara and twice as overheated—and a political genius, maneuvering politicians of all parties into backing a ban. He threatened them by weaving together a coalition of evangelicals, feminists, racists, and lefties—the equivalent of herding Sarah Palin, the National Association of Women, David Duke, and Keith Olbermann into one unstoppable political force.

With the implementation of the 18th Amendment in 1920, the dysfunctions of Prohibition began. When you ban a popular drug that millions of people want, it doesn't disappear. Instead, it is transferred from the legal economy into the hands of armed criminal gangs. Across America, gangsters rejoiced that they had just been handed one of the biggest markets in the country, and unleashed an armada of freighters, steamers, and even submarines to bring booze back. Nobody who wanted a drink went without. As the journalist Malcolm Bingay wrote, "It was absolutely impossible to get a drink, unless you walked at least ten feet and told the busy bartender in a voice loud enough for him to hear you above the uproar."

So if it didn't stop alcoholism, what did it achieve? The same as prohibition does today—a massive unleashing of criminality and violence.

Gang wars broke out, with the members torturing and murdering one another first to gain control of and then to retain their patches. Thousands of ordinary citizens were caught in the crossfire. The icon of the new criminal class was Al Capone, a figure so fixed in our minds as the scar-faced King of Charismatic Crime, pursued by the rugged federal agent Eliot Ness, that Okrent's biographical details seem oddly puncturing. Capone was only 25 when he tortured his way to running Chicago's underworld. He was gone from the city by the age of 30 and a syphilitic corpse by 40. But he was an eloquent exponent of his own case, saying simply, "I give to the public what the public wants. I never had to send out high pressure salesmen. Why, I could never meet the demand."

By 1926, he and his fellow gangsters were making $3.6 billion a year—in 1926 money! To give some perspective, that was more than the entire expenditure of the U.S. government. The criminals could outbid and out-gun the state. So they crippled the institutions of a democratic state and ruled, just as drug gangs do today in Mexico, Afghanistan, and ghettos from South Central Los Angeles to the banlieues of Paris. They have been handed a market so massive that they can tool up to intimidate everyone in their area, bribe many police and judges into submission, and achieve such a vast size, the honest police couldn't even begin to get them all. The late Nobel Prize winning economist Milton Friedman said, "Al Capone epitomizes our earlier attempts at Prohibition; the Crips and Bloods epitomize this one."

> **banlieues:**
> Outskirts.
>
> **epitomizes:**
> Becomes a definitive symbol or representation of something else.

One insight, more than any other, ripples down from Okrent's history to our own bout of prohibition. Armed criminal gangs don't fear prohibition: They love it. He has uncovered fascinating evidence that the criminal gangs sometimes financially supported dry politicians, precisely to keep it in place. They knew if it ended, most of organized crime in America would be bankrupted. So it's a nasty irony that prohibitionists try to present legalizers—then and now—as "the bootlegger's friend" or "the drug-dealer's ally." Precisely the opposite is the truth. Legalizers are the only people who can bankrupt and destroy the drug gangs, just as they destroyed Capone. Only the prohibitionists can keep them alive.

Once a product is controlled only by criminals, all safety controls vanish and the drug becomes far more deadly. After 1921, it became common to dilute and re-label poisonous industrial alcohol, which could still legally be bought, and sell it by the pint glass. This "rotgut" caused epidemics of paralysis and poisoning. For example, one single batch of bad booze permanently crippled 500 people in Wichita, Kan., in early 1927—a usual event. That year, 760 people were poisoned to death by bad booze in New York City alone. Wayne Wheeler persuaded the government not to remove fatal toxins from industrial alcohol, saying it was good to keep this "disincentive" in place.

> **disincentive:**
> Something that keeps a person from doing something unwanted or undesirable.

Prohibition's flaws were so obvious that the politicians in charge privately admitted the law was self-defeating. Warren Harding brought $1,800 of booze with him to the White House, while Andrew Mellon—in charge of enforcing the law—called it "unworkable." Similarly, the last three presidents of the United States were recreational drug users in their youth. Once he ceased to be president, Bill Clinton called for the decriminalization of cannabis, and Obama probably will too. Yet in office, they continue to mouth prohibitionist platitudes about "eradicating drugs." They insist the rest of the world's leaders resist the calls for greater liberalization from their populations and instead "crack down" on the drug gangs—no matter how much violence it unleashes. Indeed, Obama recently praised Calderon for his "crackdown" on drugs by—with no apparent irony—calling him "Mexico's Eliot Ness." Obama should know that Ness came to regard his War on Alcohol as a disastrous failure, and he died a drunk himself—but drug prohibition addles politicians' brains.

**platitudes:**
Overused, meaningless, or stale remarks.

By 1928, the failure of Prohibition was plain, yet its opponents were demoralized and despairing. It looked like an immovable part of the American political landscape, since it would require big majorities in every state to amend the Constitution again. Clarence Darrow wrote that "thirteen dry states with a population of less than New York State alone can prevent repeal until Haley's Comet returns," so "one might as well talk about taking a summer vacation of Mars."

**demoralized:**
Morale was destroyed.

Yet it happened. It happened suddenly and completely. Why? The answer is found in your wallet, with the hard cash. After the Great Crash, the government's revenues from income taxes collapsed by 60 percent in just three years, while the need for spending to stimulate the economy was skyrocketing. The U.S. government needed a new source of income, fast. The giant untaxed, unchecked alcohol industry suddenly looked like a giant pot of cash at the end of the prohibitionist rainbow. Could the same thing happen today, after our own Great Crash? The bankrupt state of California is about to hold a referendum to legalize and tax cannabis, and Gov. Arnold Schwarzenegger has pointed out that it could raise massive sums. Yes, history does rhyme.

Many people understandably worry that legalization would cause a huge rise in drug use, but the facts suggest this isn't the case. Portugal decriminalized the personal possession of all drugs in 2001, and—as a study by Glenn Greenwald for the Cato Institute found—it had almost no effect at all. Indeed, drug use fell a little among the young. Similarly, Okrent says the end of alcohol prohibition "made it harder, not easier, to get a drink. . . . Now there were closing hours and age limits, as well as a collection of geographic proscriptions that kept bars or package stores distant from schools, churches

**proscriptions:**
Imposed rules or restrictions.

and hospitals." People didn't drink much more. The only change was that they didn't have to turn to armed criminal gangs for it, and they didn't end up swigging poison.

Who now defends alcohol prohibition? Is there a single person left? This echoing silence should suggest something to us. Ending drug prohibition seems like a huge heave, just as ending alcohol prohibition did. But when it is gone, when the drug gangs are a bankrupted memory, when drug addicts are treated not as immoral criminals but as ill people needing health care, who will grieve? American history is pocked by utopian movements that prefer glib wishful thinking over a hard scrutiny of reality, but they inevitably crest and crash in the end. Okrent's dazzling history leaves us with one whiskey-sharp insight above all others: The War on Alcohol and the War on Drugs failed because they were, beneath all the blather, a war on human nature.

**utopian:**
Defined by a belief in perfect, most likely impossible, societies.

**glib:**
Lacking substance.

**blather:**
Foolish talking.

---

**Let's Pause Here••• ▶**  Do you think that the comparison Johann Hari makes between the prohibition of alcohol and the war on drugs is an appropriate comparison? In what ways are the two wars similar, based on the information given in Hari's essay? In what ways are they different? Do you believe that the outcome of the war on drugs will be the same as the outcome of the 18th Amendment, or are there factors that make this particular "war" different? Are there lessons that we can take away from the prohibition of alcohol that might be helpful in our current war against drugs? If so, what are they?

---

**Let's Take It Further••• ▼**

1. In the beginning of his essay, Hari makes the claim that "human history is filled with chemicals, come-downs, and hangovers." If we take him at his word (and believe the brief examples he gives), how might this help us put into perspective the current role of drugs in our popular culture today? Are things getting better, worse, or do they seem the same as the examples Hari gives us? Explain your answer and why you believe things are the same or different than at earlier moments in history.

2. Given the way most people (and even many history texts) perceive the Puritans, why is it surprising to learn that they brought with them, on their first trip across the Atlantic, "three times more beer than water, along with 10,000 gallons of wine"? How does it change your perspective of the Puritans and the way in which they were viewed as "moralists" of their time?

3. Is the primary audience that Hari seeks to engage those who are for or against the legalization of drugs? How can you discern who he intends to sway one way or the other, based on his writing strategies, his examples given, and the general way he aligns the two types of prohibition?

4. Hari describes how slavery abolitionists saw alcohol as "a new form of slavery, replacing leg irons with whiskey bottles." How might alcohol be a form of slavery? How can the two be compared, and should they be? What is the power (or the point) in comparing slavery to alcoholism?

5. Like the results of Prohibition, so too—claims Hari—has the war on drugs created a "massive unleashing of criminality and violence." Find recent examples in the news of the criminality and violence that have been unleashed due to the illegality of drugs. Describe the type of violence and explain how it is drug related. How might legalizing drugs put a stop to the events you are describing?

6. Every generation, according to Hari, has its own "moralists" who seek to fight what she calls our "natural impulse" to use both drugs and alcohol. Who are our moralists today that are leading the fight against drugs? What logic are they using to fight it, and how does it compare to the examples of the Prohibition-era moralists that Hari describes early in his essay?

7. Research the history of the "war on drugs" and explain its origins. Who coined the phrase, and what was the logic behind the national push for outlawing narcotics? Every war has its successes and failures, so give specific examples of how the war on drugs has been a success and how it has failed. Make the case for why you believe the war is ultimately a failure or if it is a success. Should we keep fighting it? Why or why not?

8. According to Hari, the state of California has been experiencing such budgetary woes that the state decided to put forth a public referendum in the 2010 election (Prop. 19) to legalize and regulate drugs to earn money on the taxation of drugs—much like they do with alcohol and tobacco. Research the public referendum and the stance Governor Schwarzenegger took on the issue, as well as the outcome of the election on this particular issue and why it succeeded or failed. Then make the case for why you believe it was a good or a bad idea and how it might be implemented in other states or the country as a whole.

# Private Dwyer's Last Breath
**Roxanne Patel Shepelavy**

**Let's Start Here•••▶** There are numerous well-known substances that people are commonly addicted to in our culture. It is quite common to hear the terms "crack-head," "meth-head," "pot-head," and even "pill-head." But beneath the surface of our popular culture, many less-common drug addictions seem to fly beneath the radar. "Huffing," or the practice of inhaling toxic fumes from paint, glue, gasoline, and other chemical compounds, is one such below-the-radar addiction. Disturbingly, Roxanne Patel Shepelavy unearths a story that is tragically commonplace but not well known: the use of inhalants (specifically Dust-Off) by veterans of the Iraq and Afghanistan wars.

In her essay, Shepelavy traces the life of one such veteran, Private First Class Joseph Dwyer—who was once an icon of the heroism and righteousness of the Iraq War—and his downward spiral into madness and addiction. She follows Dwyer's rise to heroism, his humility, his abandonment, and the way he succumbed to his demons. What follows is a modern-day tragedy of the unseen damage a war has on its soldiers, and a discussion of our responsibility to these people. As you read the essay, observe the tone that Shepelavy takes on the subject. Is she being judgmental? If so, whom is she judging, and why? Who is to blame for our veterans' widespread addiction to Dust-Off, alcohol, and other narcotics?

---

Roxanne Patel Shepelavy is an award-winning freelance magazine writer whose work has appeared in *Details, Self, Glamour,* and *Philadelphia* magazines. She specializes in narrative investigative pieces about health, medical ethics, crime, and social issues. This selection originally appeared in *Details* in July 2009.

It was only a moment in what would become the long war. The invasion of Iraq was barely a week old, and Private First Class Joseph Dwyer's squadron had beaten back a 24-hour barrage of attacks from Saddam's army. The fighting had just ended on March 25, 2003, when a hysterical cry filled the relative quiet. An Iraqi man ran toward the Americans carrying a half-naked boy bleeding from an ugly gash in his leg. Dwyer, a 26-year-old medic on his first tour of his first war, saw the terror on the kid's face. He knew there could be Iraqi soldiers ready to open fire. Still, he dashed out to meet the man, cradled the boy to his barrel chest, and gently carried him to safety.

**exuding:**
Oozing.

A moment like so many others. But an *Army Times* photographer captured this one: Dwyer rushing back, exuding concern and purpose and, yes, heroism. Some 12 hours later, the picture was on *Nightline*, on the front pages of newspapers around the country, everywhere from Dwyer's hometown on New York's Long Island to the base where he trained in El Paso, Texas, to Robbins, North Carolina, where his new wife awaited his return. It became the first iconic image of the conflict. Behold the U.S. soldier carrying an injured boy. Dwyer became a symbol of the noble, necessary war waged by "liberators." The next day, when he learned of his fame, in the field once again, he laughed at the absurdity. "I was just one of a group of guys," he told the *Military Times*. "I wasn't standing out more than anyone else."

**iconic:**
Symbolic.

Private Dwyer never intended to be a front-page story when he enlisted, a few days after September 11, 2001. He was just another patriotic American. He'd almost lost a brother in the attacks on the Towers. And he'd vowed to his family that "nothing like this is ever going to happen to my country again." In Iraq, Dwyer did more than his part. When the U.S. invasion started, he was attached to the Third Squadron of the Seventh Cavalry, at the "tip of the tip of the spear" crossing into Iraq. The Cav was deep in the shit most every day. As the 500-vehicle convoy made its way from Kuwait to Baghdad, Dwyer and his fellow soldiers left a trail of Iraqi corpses along the dusty road. Ninety-two days after arriving in country, he started for home. He didn't feel like a hero. He felt like a murderer, alone and afraid, left to cope in the only way he could, with the aid of this war's drug of choice. Again he would become a reluctant symbol.

A hot day, bright and dusty, with the echo of bombs in the distance and the enemy everywhere but nowhere to be seen. Dwyer drove down a nearly empty street. A cardboard box caught his eye. He'd seen this before, an innocuous-seeming carton that turned out to be a bomb. He swerved into a nearby road sign, then caught his breath and looked around. There was no bomb, no Iraqi insurgents, no one aiming a machine gun at him. He wasn't in Baghdad. He was back in El Paso, a desert town with a military base, where he was again stationed.

**innocuous:**
Harmless.

In January 2004, six months after leaving Iraq behind, Dwyer started having flashbacks. They woke him from sleep in a cold sweat. Even in the light of day his mind returned to the battlefields—the smoky stench of spent ammo, the rattle of the radio, the sight of bloated bodies. For a while he was nothing more than an unfortunate statistic, one of the thousands of Iraq-war veterans diagnosed with post-traumatic stress disorder.

According to a 2008 RAND Corporation study, 18.5 percent of Iraq and Afghanistan veterans suffer from PTSD or major depression and

19.5 percent report a "probable traumatic brain injury," which can lead to other mental-health issues. That amounts to more than 300,000 vets already—before the surge returns from Iraq. And a great many of those soldiers have gotten inadequate treatment or no treatment at all. "We were trained in how to deal with a sucking chest wound," says Adam Beard, a former cavalry captain. "But we weren't trained for how to spot a mental-health problem. We didn't really talk about it."

A year after his return, Dwyer thought he'd found some peace. Never particularly religious, he happened on a prayer breakfast at the base and was struck by a Bible passage, 2 Corinthians 5:17: "If anyone belongs to Christ, there is a new creation. The old things have gone; everything is made new." Raised Roman Catholic, Dwyer started attending a Southern Baptist church with his wife, Matina, taking the verse's message to heart. He was ready to be saved. On a Sunday morning in December 2004, he followed his pastor into a shallow wading pool, where the pastor dipped him backward until the water ran over Dwyer's head. He cried, praying for the promised cleansing of his soul.

He was granted no such miracle. The flashbacks turned darker and came more frequently, and with them the doubts. *Not even God can save me.* Dwyer stopped going to church and was consumed by thoughts of his certain damnation. Nothing made the anguish go away—not time, or the therapist he saw every six weeks, or the antidepressants he'd started taking. So he got something that did. One afternoon, when Matina was at work, he reached for a can of Dust-Off.

He put the nozzle to his mouth. He pushed the trigger and inhaled deeply. As he unleashed a chilly stream of vapor, a pressurized pffffffffft, the compressed air—used to clean computer keyboards—filled his lungs, limiting the oxygen to his brain. And suddenly Dwyer wasn't at war anymore. He felt giddy and light-headed . . . at peace. He knew huffing was dangerous: Within seconds of even the first hit, Dust-Off can cause cardiac arrest. Which is why, at first, the soldier kept his habit to a minimum. One can lasted days, letting him sleep and function normally. Soon, though, he needed 10 cans a day, chasing the 20-minute high with hit after hit, often late into the night.

Matina came home after work one afternoon to find a strange hissing sound coming from the computer room. When she went to check it out, Dwyer greeted her with wild eyes. When she returned a short while later, he had a can of Dust-Off hidden behind his back. Matina was baffled. She'd occasionally seen Dwyer drunk, but she couldn't believe he'd try something as depraved as huffing. "What would possess you to even think about doing that?" she asked.

"Nothing else works," he said. "This makes the flashbacks stop. I need it."

Huffing, it turns out, is this war's easy escape. On most bases in Iraq, it's nearly impossible to find booze or drugs. But there's an endless supply of Dust-Off in the desert, where the godforsaken sand is everywhere. It gets into rifles and computer keyboards and GPS devices the way a war gets into a G.I.'s head, triggering malfunctions. Dust-Off expunges the grit.

"It's a thing that people do when they're bored," says one Iraq vet, who recalls his buddies buying Dust-Off from the base supply store in shifts so they wouldn't draw attention to themselves. At night in the barracks, they gleefully traded hits off the canisters, giggling, while the rumbles of the war faded into the distance.

For troubled soldiers, Dust-Off can be a quick solace, getting them "out of Iraq for two minutes," as one officer told *Stars and Stripes* in 2007, when he banned the substance from barracks after a huffing soldier went into convulsions. "These guys are using anything that will help them avoid dealing with the traumatic events they experienced," says Keith Armstrong, a therapist at the San Francisco Department of VA Medical Center. "It's not really surprising that they're huffing."

Chief medical examiner Craig Mallak of the Armed Forces Medical Examiners System says 39 active-duty soldiers and marines have died from inhalant abuse since the war started, including a depressive 22-year-old officer who was found in his trailer with a half-empty can of Dust-Off under him. But it's hard to gauge the full sweep of the problem. "Since most people huff alone, we don't know how many soldiers are doing it," Mallak says. "We only see them when they die." A year ago, Mallak persuaded the Army and the Air Force to purchase only Dust-Off canisters laced with horrid-tasting bitterants. Posters and TV spots now warn soldiers about huffing's perils. As of early June, just one active-duty soldier had died from the practice this year, compared with seven in all of 2008.

**bitterants:**
Chemical additive which results in foul taste or smell.

Whatever highs Dust-Off delivered to Dwyer, they were short-lived. Despite Matina's pleas, he insisted on buying a handgun to add to the loaded pistol and two rifles he kept in their small apartment. He never said exactly what he feared, just that the war had somehow followed him home. "I have to protect myself," he told Matina. "I did things to save myself over there. Now they're coming to get me."

On the evening of October 6, 2005, Dwyer was home alone in the El Paso apartment, cleaning his 9mm. He had been sitting with Matina and a fellow soldier earlier, but both felt compelled to leave because of his continual huffing. The soldier was so troubled by what he saw that he phoned the base for help. Two first sergeants drove to the apartment, and Dwyer greeted them at the door. When one tried to enter, Dwyer got spooked. He locked the dead bolt and fired a few warning shots through the door, then aimed at the ceiling, where he heard insurgents clamoring on the roof. He called Matina on her cell phone. "I'm sorry I have to do this to you," he said. Then he fired his gun again.

"Joseph! Joseph!" Matina screamed, convinced her husband had killed himself.

A few minutes later, he came back on the line. "They're here!" he shouted. "They're surrounding me! They're on the roof!"

By the time the El Paso police arrived, Dwyer was hunkered down, holding a mirror out the window to track the insurgents. On the phone with the swat team, he tried to order an air strike while firing up to 300 rounds inside his living room. After three hours, the police finally talked him out of the apartment. Embarrassed, Dwyer acknowledged what was glaringly obvious: He was sick. He spent 45 days in the psychiatric ward at the Fort Bliss medical center. Afterward, he was honorably discharged from the Army, at the rank of specialist, and in March 2006 he moved with Matina to Pinehurst, North Carolina.

After his standoff with the police, Dwyer promised Matina he was done with huffing. He was ready to get help. He had a good reason: In May, his daughter, Meagan, was born. But after several months of therapy at the VA clinic in North Carolina, the new father was no better. In fact, he'd gotten worse—a development he blamed, in part, on being assigned a new therapist every couple of months. When he closed his eyes, he witnessed unspeakable things happening to Meagan in Iraq, horrors he refused to share with Matina.

At his wife's insistence, he had left his guns in Texas. But soon after Meagan's first birthday, Dwyer purchased a semi-automatic rifle. He also picked up a can of Dust-Off; soon he was snorting cocaine as well. When Matina realized he'd relapsed, she took Meagan, and the gun, and left for her parents' house. A few days later, Dwyer called her, out of his head. "I'm coming up there to get my gun," he told her. "And one of us is going to die." Once he'd regained his faculties, he had no recollection of the phone call. "It almost killed him," Matina recalls. In tears, he apologized and promised again to get help.

But the VA medical center in Durham was full, and the Army couldn't help because he'd been discharged. Even before the war, the VA's health system—the biggest in the country—had been overwhelmed. With staggering numbers of new veterans since 2003, it was now under constant siege. To meet the demand, President Obama plans to increase funding by $25 billion over the next five years, opening the door to some 500,000 more vets. But five years is a long time to wait for change—especially when this war's soldiers have been coming home for six.

Dwyer finally found what he needed at a VA-run substance-abuse program on Long Island, where he spent eight months with soldiers like him. He devoted hours every day to therapy, willingly confronting, for the first time, what he'd seen and done in Iraq. On the phone with Matina, he finally confessed to the thing he could not get past, the one moment of the war that forever changed him. Not the heroic moment. Something else. Near the end of his tour, his unit was assigned to search for Saddam and his criminal cohorts. On a dark night during a raid, Dwyer burst into a house, kicked open a door, and saw someone rush toward him. He fired his gun. Then he looked to see who he'd killed: an unarmed woman. In front of her young child. "I killed a lady, a mother," he told Matina. "I don't understand how I could become someone who would do that, just . . . kill . . . like an animal. How can God forgive that? How?"

He returned home on March 1, 2008. Six days later, Matina found him in the computer room, huffing. She turned around, picked up Meagan, and walked out. Alone, Dwyer spiraled. He had bored a hole through a closet wall to make a bunker, and he took to hiding in it with a gun when he felt threatened. Every morning, he called a taxi to drive him to a computer store, where he bought a supply of Dust-Off. On the night of June 28, he called a taxi to take him to the hospital. When the driver arrived at his house, Dwyer shouted that he couldn't get up. The police arrived a few minutes later and broke down the door. They found him on the floor, lying in his own feces, surrounded by empty cans of Dust-Off. "Help me, please," Dwyer groaned. "I'm dying. . . . I can't breathe." As the paramedics rolled him to the ambulance, he took his last breath. Five years after surviving war, Dwyer had huffed himself to death.

The famous soldier from those first heroic days of the war was suddenly news again. On the website legacy.com, hundreds of strangers wrote tributes to him, some with prayers—pleas—for his death to resonate, to keep others from suffering as he did. Mt. Sinai, Dwyer's Long Island hometown, named a street after him; a family friend formed a nonprofit in his name to raise money for disabled vets. Dwyer was no longer just one American soldier suffering from PTSD; he was, again, a symbol— but this time, a symbol of how we treat our heroes. "There should have been more help here for Joseph," Matina says. "He was all alone and felt like nothing could help him, like nothing had worked. He never really came home at all."

**Let's Pause Here•••▶** Undoubtedly, Shepelavy's essay is a tragedy. In fact, it is many simultaneous tragedies occurring in one person's life. In your opinion, what is the story's biggest tragedy? Why do you believe it to be so? It is most certainly an informative essay about the dangers of "huffing," but what other dangers is the author pointing out in addition to this one?

**Let's Take It Further•••▼**

1. Do you feel that Shepelavy's descriptions of war, the events that haunt the soldiers, and the process (and purpose) of huffing Dust-Off do a successful job of portraying the experiences

of people like Private Dwyer? What about her descriptions allows readers to begin to understand the horrors of Dwyer's life? Were you emotionally moved by any of her descriptions? If so, which one(s)?

2. Based on the tone of the story, as well as the sometimes uncomfortable descriptions of drug use and its effects, who would you say that Shepelavy is attempting to appeal to in this essay? The general public? Soldiers? Military leadership? Politicians? What is the overall goal of her essay? Which writing strategies (and texts) does Shepelavy specifically employ in order to accomplish her goal? How effective are the strategies that Shepelavy uses?

3. Think of the numbers cited in this essay. If there are more than 300,000 veterans returning from the two wars discussed in this article, how might their addiction to substances become a public crisis? How might it be alleviated?

4. Adam Beard, a former cavalry captain, is quoted in the essay as saying, "We didn't really talk about mental-health problems." Why do you think mental health isn't a subject of wide or open discussion in the military? How might that change in the future, or can it?

5. Throughout the essay Shepelavy describes how Private Dwyer tried several options to cope with the horrors of war, including religion, therapy, alcohol, and Dust-Off. Obviously, none of these options was successful. In light of that, and the recent national discussion of veterans of the two wars in the Middle East, what do we owe our returning soldiers for their service, and how can we help them reintegrate into society when returning from combat? What sorts of programs are being suggested and what is the likelihood of their success based on the research and reactions to the proposed services for veterans? What sorts of programs would you propose as potential solutions, and how might they be implemented?

6. Locate an Iraq or Afghanistan war veteran on your campus and interview him or her. Ask him or her about the prevalence of Dust-Off huffing and see if the veteran is aware of its widespread use among soldiers and veterans. Ask the person what the reason for its popularity might be, and compare his or her response to the explanations given by the men and women quoted in Shepelavy's article. How accurate is her essay in its depictions of the epidemic of huffing? How does she get it right or wrong, according to the person you interviewed? What solution might there be?

7. Shepelavy illustrates for the reader how Private Dwyer, early in his deployment, became an icon of the Iraqi conflict, as well as "a symbol of the noble, necessary war." How does the photo that she describes (located at the beginning of Shepelavy's essay) turn Private Dwyer into this symbol? What about the photo might resonate with its viewers? "Read" the photograph to look for messages that can be found within the photo and to determine what "story" the photograph tells about Dwyer, the war, and our nation's stated rationale for being in Iraq.

8. Create a multimedia text that explores a drug trend that is negatively impacting a specific segment of the American population and illustrate how the drug works, who is using it, the effect it is having, and any possible solutions. Feel free to incorporate video or audio interviews, pictures, statistics, and any other texts that help to illustrate the trend and its impact on the community that you are featuring in your essay.

# Lessons from the Celebrity Doping Scandal

Daniel Engber

**Let's Start Here•••▶** In recent years the drug war has taken an interesting twist: Congress has held many hearings on the issue of professional athletes "doping" to enhance their athletic performance in their sport. While some have argued that this isn't even an issue that should be addressed by the U.S. Congress, others, like the author of the following essay, feel that another problem is being caused by the publicity behind the doping trials: the media is equating HGH and anabolic steroids. To Daniel Engber, this is a crime in itself because it helps feed what he sees as a national misconception about the major differences between the two drugs.

To set the record straight, Engber uses the recent celebrity doping scandal (in which several high-profile celebrities were found to be using HGH) to illustrate the dramatic differences between the two drugs—in terms of their use, their benefits, and their side effects. Engber also argues that the "doping" epidemic is neither as prevalent nor as dangerous as the media has made it out to be, precisely because of the differences between the two drugs. Observe the ways in which he outlines the differences, and see if you agree with his assessment of our current doping "epidemic."

---

Daniel Engber writes and edits science coverage for *Slate* magazine. He has also written for *Discover, SEED, Popular Science*, and the *Washington Post*, among other publications. His proposal for a scientific approach to professional basketball was featured in the *New York Times Magazine*'s "Year in Ideas." This essay originally appeared in *Slate* on January 15, 2008.

Congress heard testimony today on the rampant use of performance-enhancing drugs in Major League Baseball, but the biggest steroid news of the week comes from the entertainment world. According to a report published Sunday in the Albany Times-Union, an ongoing drug investigation in New York and Florida has turned up the names of five prominent entertainers—Mary J. Blige, 50 Cent, Timbaland, Wyclef Jean, and Tyler Perry. According to the newspaper, anonymous sources reveal that "Blige and other stars were shipped prescribed human growth hormone or steroids," and four of the five received shipments of both drugs.

You may not be shocked to learn that celebrities take illegal drugs or artificially enhance their looks. But this dog-bites-man story supports the notion that we're in the midst of a national doping epidemic—born in the locker room and spreading through health clubs, concert venues, and even suburban schoolyards. (At a 2005 congressional hearing on steroid use in football, Rep. Tom Davis, R-Va., claimed that one in 14 *middle-school girls* have tried anabolic steroids.) In particular, it reinforces a central myth of the war on doping: that all performance-enhancing drugs are the same, and it's just as bad to take human growth hormone as it is to shoot up with Deca-Durabolin.

As I've pointed out before, HGH and anabolic steroids are as different as marijuana and black-tar heroin. Growth hormone helps you lose fat and put on lean body tissue—it's great for bare-chested stage acts—but it doesn't improve athletic performance. (In fact, let's stop calling it a "performance-enhancing" drug, once and for all.) Anabolic steroids, on the other hand, have been shown to increase strength and cardiovascular fitness: They give athletes a real edge in competition.

HGH also has very mild side effects, compared with steroids. Taking growth-hormone injections may cause reversible joint pain, carpal tunnel, and proto-diabetes. Press accounts often cite claims from anti-HGH crusaders like Thomas Perls that it causes cancer and other grave health problems—but these have been more clearly associated with acromegaly patients (who naturally overproduce HGH) than patients on controlled dosages. Meanwhile, anabolic steroids have been shown to cause testicular shrinkage, increased risk of stroke and cardiovascular disease, and other maladies. Steroids might also cause aggressive, dangerous behavior, as suggested by the murder-suicide of Chris Benoit.

> **acromegaly:**
> Visit http://en.wikipedia.org/wiki/Acromegaly for a full definition of this disease.

> **maladies:**
> Ailments, diseases, or sicknesses.

(Even baseball's Mitchell report—the *hadith* of the doping jihad—admits that human growth hormone isn't as bad as steroids. The introduction concedes that HGH doesn't really enhance performance, and its listed side effects don't sound as awful as the ones for steroids.)

> **hadith:**
> Authoritative document declaring war.

Federal law (for once) appropriately reflects the relative risks associated with these drugs. Anabolic steroids are Schedule III controlled substances, which means it can be a crime even to possess them. But you won't get in trouble in the United States for having a few vials of human growth hormone: The feds can only go after the dealers (under the Food, Drug, and Cosmetic Act) for selling meds without a proper prescription.

But those who prosecute the war on doping tend to ignore these differences. When you lump together HGH and anabolic steroids, the problem seems much bigger and more immediate. According to the *Times-Union*, the celebrity dopers exposed on Sunday were among "tens of thousands of people who may have used or received prescribed shipments of steroids and injectable human growth hormone in recent years." The newspaper blithely assumes that anyone who's using HGH is also using anabolic steroids, though it's not at all clear which of these masses were using which drugs. The article goes on to make the nonsensical claim

> **blithely:**
> Casually or without appropriate thought.

that "the use of steroids and human growth hormone . . . illustrates how pervasive steroids use in the United States has become."

News reports on doping confuse the two drugs with alarming regularity. An earlier *Times-Union* story about the same investigation in New York and Florida described the seizure of "mail-order steroids" at the home of former pitcher Jason Grimsley. But a search warrant affidavit posted on the Smoking Gun shows that federal agents seized two kits of human growth hormone, not anabolic steroids.

Coverage of the celebrity doping scandal in other newspapers treats HGH and steroids as if they were interchangeable. The *New York Times* describes how "the drugs" have some legitimate uses, but "misuse of the drugs can be harmful." The Associated Press declared without qualification that "athletes use steroids and human growth hormone to get bigger, faster and stronger," and that "the drugs lure other people with their supposed anti-aging qualities."

**conflated:**
Confused or inappropriately fused two conflicting ideas.

*Slate* is just as guilty. We conflated the two medications in a feature called "The Steroids Social Network," which listed the baseball players and trainers named by confessed drug dealer Kirk Radomski in the Mitchell report. In fact, more than one-third of the 53 players were accused of taking HGH only and have never been linked to steroids.

How did this confusion become so widespread? First, both drugs are being dispensed by the same crooked doctors and pharmacies. (And, in many cases, doctors do prescribe both drugs to the same patient.) When federal agents raid an "anti-aging" clinic in Florida, they aren't so concerned with the specific meds that went to each user; they're gathering evidence for a broader case against the dealers. Embedded reporters watch the feds seize thousands of pounds of documents from file cabinets and dumpsters, and then file ambiguous copy about the sales of performance-enhancing drugs, "including steroids and human growth hormone."

**ambiguous:**
Uncertain or doubtful.

**rhetoric:**
Language.

Second, the rhetoric of a war on drugs makes it impossible for a league commissioner or politician to draw any real distinctions between doping agents. Neither Bud Selig nor the lawmakers who questioned him today can risk appearing soft on performance enhancers, even when it comes to a soft drug like HGH. Now Sen. Chuck Schumer, D-N.Y., and Rep. Stephen Lynch, D-Mass., are trying to codify this dunderheaded posturing: Each has introduced a bill to amend the Controlled Substances Act so that human growth hormone would be equivalent to anabolic steroids under federal law.

**codify:**
Classify.

**dunderheaded:**
Ill-conceived or idiotic.

That would be a disturbing development. At this point, the federal drug laws are the only rational voice left in the doping debate.

**Let's Pause Here•••** ▶  Now that you have finished the essay, why do you believe Engber is so determined to set the record straight about the differences between HGH and anabolic steroids? Do you feel as though you truly understand the differences between the two? Did you understand the difference between the two drugs prior to reading this article, or did you (like the many media outlets he cites) believe the drugs were the same? Would you say that Engber is pro-HGH, based on his treatment of the drug, or is he merely anti-anabolic steroids? What is it about his approach to the essay that leads you to believe he is pro-HGH or only anti-anabolic steroids?

**Let's Take It Further•••** ▼

1. How do you feel about the fact that Congress has taken on the issue of doping among athletes? Do you feel that they are the appropriate body to address this issue? If so, why should our federal government use its time to concern itself with athletes who use drugs to cheat? If not, who should address the issue?

2. Judging from Engber's passionate discussion of the difference between HGH and anabolic steroids, who do you think he is trying to convince of the difference? The general public? Politicians? Other journalists? What specific language and writing strategies does he utilize to make his case, not only for the difference between the two drugs, but also for the importance of understanding how both work? In other words, what are the "lessons [to be] learned from the celebrity doping scandal"?

3. Engber goes to great lengths to explain how HGH isn't as "bad" as anabolic steroids, saying that HGH "helps you lose fat and put on lean body tissue," rather than enhancing athletic performance. In light of that description, do you think HGH should be acceptable (even legal) for celebrities who rely on their bodies for their careers (for example, musicians who perform in little or form-fitting clothing and who are expected to be attractive)?

4. If HGH is a weight-loss aid and anabolic steroids enhance performance, why shouldn't they both be considered "cheating"? Why is one worse than the other? Or should they both be considered similar drugs?

5. Why is the following statement, quoted in Engber's essay, considered to be a "nonsensical claim"? "The use of steroids and human growth hormone . . . illustrates how pervasive steroids use in the United States has become." What about the quote makes no sense? How does it illustrate the very point that Engber has been making throughout his essay?

6. Research and describe in detail the application, the physical benefits, and the side effects of HGH and anabolic steroids. Then compare your findings to the manner in which Engber describes the drugs. Is his depiction of HGH and anabolic steroids accurate? If so, how does he get it right? If not, how does he wrongly describe the drugs? How is each drug used, and is one application more acceptable than the other? Why or why not?

7. In his essay, Engber labels Thomas Perls as an "anti-HGH crusader," for his criticism of the drug. Locate any of Perls's work on the subject and describe the ways he is or is not against HGH. Is Engber correct in his assessment of Perls as an "anti-HGH crusader," or has he

misinterpreted Perls's intentions in his research? How is he correct or incorrect about Perls's intentions?

**8.** Engber claims that "news reports on doping confuse the two drugs with alarming regularity." Locate news reports about the subject of steroids and doping, and see if they do, in fact, regularly confuse the two drugs. If they do, why might it be problematic and possibly even dangerous if our media continues to confuse the two drugs? What might it mean for everyday citizens? Could it result in jail time? Lack of access to HGH? And how might it affect people who medically require either drug to treat a disease or illness?

**9.** Should athletes be allowed to take HGH, based on Engber's argument about its difference from anabolic steroids, or should they not be allowed to take either drug? If so, what is the reason you believe athletes should be allowed to take HGH? If not, why do you believe HGH should be banned? Why should or shouldn't athletes be held to a different standard than other entertainers?

# More Students Turning to "Smart" Drugs
**Michelle Trudeau**

**Let's Start Here•••▶** Like alcohol, drugs have long been a part of college culture. Drugs such as marijuana, ecstasy, cocaine, and acid have risen and fallen in popularity over the years, with marijuana winning out as the most common drug of choice on college campuses nationwide. However, in recent years, the trendiest campus drug is Adderall (and similar ADHD prescription drugs), which is being bought and sold with alarming regularity, regardless of the level of prestige a school has or the background of the students who attend.

Michelle Trudeau, in a recent NPR report, briefly discusses the rise in the popularity of "smart drugs," as many call them. She maps out the ways that students use the drugs, and why they are popular. She also illustrates that this drug culture is unlike many other drug cultures, in that the users take these drugs to do *better* at school, rather than to take time off or escape from school (as is the case with most other drugs). Observe the way Trudeau, in her informative essay, explains the draw of these drugs for students, as well as how she attempts to dissuade students from using "smart drugs."

---

Michelle Trudeau is a contributing correspondent for National Public Radio (NPR) who began her radio career in 1981 filing stories for NPR from Beijing and Shanghai, China. She began working as a science reporter and producer for NPR's *Science Desk* in 1982. Trudeau's news reports and feature stories, which cover the areas of human behavior, child development, the brain sciences, and mental health, air on NPR's *Morning Edition* and *All Things Considered*. Trudeau has been the recipient of more than 20 media broadcasting awards for her radio reporting from such professional organizations as the American Association for the Advancement of Science, the Casey Journalism Center, the American Psychiatric Association, World Hunger, the Los Angeles Press Club, the American Psychological Association, and the National Mental Health Association. The following selection was a featured story on NPR on February 5, 2009.

They're commonly called "smart drugs" or "study drugs." Scientists call them "cognitive enhancers." Drugs like Adderall and Ritalin, generally prescribed for attention-deficit disorder, are increasingly being used by college students to help them study despite serious side effects, researchers say.

Adderall, nicknamed "Addy" by students, is the most popular study drug on college campuses around the country, according to scientists. Students say the drug boosts cognitive function and enables them to study for hours with full concentration without getting fatigued.

## Illegal and Popular

One student says she took her first Adderall during her freshman year when she was cramming for tests. She and other students asked that their names not be used because using or selling these drugs without a prescription is a felony.

"I would take it, and in about a half an hour, all of a sudden, looking at my journal which had all my assignments, I'd look at it and say, cool, OK," she says. "And I'd start to get more excited about work."

Popping an "Addy" made her feel motivated, eager to hit the books. "When I was sitting down to study, I wouldn't be restless. I wouldn't be thinking about the TV or listening to music. I would just be completely channeled into what I was doing," she says. "I was very focused."

And Adderall didn't make her feel jittery or anxious, like when she drank strong coffee. "I functioned very, very well under it. Anything I did was productive. It was a perfect kind of transition into a study mentality, and I could keep that up for hours," she says.

## Buying and Selling

Students say Adderall and its cousin Ritalin are easy to get—bought and sold in the library, the cafeteria, the dorm, pretty much anywhere on campus. The going rate, they say, is typically $5 a pill. Unless it's exam week. Then, supply and demand kicks in and the price can shoot up to $25 a pill.

They say the main source for the drugs are students who have prescriptions to treat their attention-deficit disorder. One such student says he has been on Adderall for his ADD since high school. Now a college senior, he's still getting his prescription for 60 pills a month. He's supposed to take two pills a day but says he doesn't like taking the medicine unless he has to pull an all-nighter. So he has more pills than he needs.

"I usually just give it to my friends," he says. "I don't really want to charge them for something that I'm not even taking. It's just like extras."

He explains that he doesn't like taking his Adderall because of the side effects he experiences, such as insomnia and loss of appetite.

## The Down Side

Although Adderall and Ritalin might sound like wonder drugs that can help students study for hours, the drugs are amphetamine-based. That means they can be habit-forming, according to Martha J. Farah, director at the Center for Cognitive Neuroscience at the University of Pennsylvania.

Farah has studied the use of Adderall and Ritalin on college campuses and collaborated on writing a recent commentary in the journal *Nature*. In the article, Farah describes a college survey in which as many as 25 percent of students on some college campuses have used these study drugs in the past year. She says she understands the drugs' appeal because they do measurably increase concentration and motivation. This is what makes studying for hours on end, or any kind of intellectual work, more engrossing and more rewarding.

But she cautions: "It's also a little worrisome, because basically that extra motivation that you feel when you're using these drugs is the result of the drugs' effects on the brain's reward system."

Scientists have found the drugs increase the brain chemical dopamine. And as they target the brain's reward center, Farah says, there can be trouble. "These are serious drugs with serious side effects," such as severe sleep deprivation and rare heart problems, she says. But most importantly, she says, the drugs can be addictive.

## A Student Cautions Others

One college senior recalls using Adderall frequently during her freshman and sophomore years.

"I started to notice my own addictive behaviors," she says, adding that she began using the drug more and more. "The more you use it, the more you want to use more of it."

She knew she was becoming addicted and that she wouldn't be able to afford her habit. So she decided to stop using Adderall. "It takes away your own coping skills and your own ability to evolve your own study skills and work ethic. So it's kind of an easy way out." And she says it made her feel "like a lesser person," relying on the drug to do well. During her last two years of college, she says, she's stayed away from Adderall—and gotten good grades.

**Let's Pause Here•••▶** Do you feel Trudeau makes a better case in this essay for using "smart drugs," or does the essay succeed at warning students of the pitfalls of taking drugs such as Adderall and Ritalin? In other words, after reading this essay, do the drugs' pros outweigh their cons? Why or why not?

## Let's Take It Further••• ▼

1. Trudeau explains that Adderall and other ADHD drugs are widely used on college campuses to improve studying. In your experience at college, is this statement accurate? If so, how is the statement correct? If not, how is your experience (or campus) different?

2. Does it seem that this piece of reporting is directed more toward parents, students, school officials, or some other group of people? Which details and writing strategies reveal the primary audience of the piece, as intended by Trudeau?

3. Students, according to Trudeau, claim that Adderall and Ritalin are easily obtained on college campuses. Have you found this to be true? Has anyone on your campus ever offered you the drugs? If you wanted to purchase them, where would you go to get them?

4. Strangely, the description of the benefits of Adderall and Ritalin seems very similar to the benefits of caffeine, which is a legal drug. The "difference" between the two, according to Martha J. Farah, who is quoted in the essay, is that ADHD drugs can be habit forming. Is caffeine addictive? If so, then is there any difference between the two drugs? What are the negative side effects of caffeine, for example?

5. Do you believe that Adderall and Ritalin should be legal or illegal, based on the descriptions of the drugs and the side effects listed in this essay? Do further research into both the benefits and the side effects of these types of drugs and use it to support your stance. Why might the drug be bad or good for college students?

6. Interview someone who takes ADHD drugs illegally (meaning the person hasn't had the drug prescribed to him or her), and ask the person some of the previous discussion questions. Have the person describe the difference between his or her academic performance when taking the drug versus his or her performance when not taking the drug. How does the person obtain it? Has the person noticed a dependency on the drug? Are there negative consequences or side effects that the person can describe? Does he or she believe the drug should be legal? Why or why not? How is the person's story different from the subjects interviewed by Trudeau, or is his or her story the same?

7. Survey a large sample of students at your college about drug use to determine if ADHD drugs are as widespread on college campuses as Trudeau's report implies. Construct an anonymous survey and describe the questions you included in it. What percentage of students surveyed admitted to drug use? What types of drugs did they use? Why did they use them? What are the most common drugs used on your campus? What do your findings say about your campus, and how is drug use on your campus similar to or different from the national trend described in Trudeau's essay?

# mash<sup>it</sup>UP

Here is a series of essay and discussion topics that draw connections between multiple selections within the chapter. They also suggest outside texts to include in your essay or discussion. Feel free to bring in further outside texts, remembering the variety of texts (beyond articles) available to you.

1. Note that in his essay "Lessons from the Celebrity Doping Scandal," Engber calls our federal drug laws a "rational voice," while Hari, in her essay "The Parable of Prohibition," says our current federal drug laws are as dangerous as prohibition laws that led to crime and violence in the early 20th century. Which of these two perspectives of the federal drug laws is more accurate, in your opinion? What evidence can you locate to support your claim?

2. Compare the tragic story of Private Dwyer in the essay by Shepelavy to other public cases of recent war veterans who have returned home and succumbed to addiction, depression, and mental anguish. There have been many widely documented cases featured in popular magazines, on websites, in TV news magazines, and in other media outlets. Locate another instance of a troubled Iraq or Afghanistan war veteran and compare his or her story to Dwyer's. How are they similar? What differs in the circumstances of their life stories? Does a pattern begin to emerge in our war vets who return home that you feel should be addressed? If so, what is it, and how should it be addressed?

3. How has the mass media represented our culture of drug use in movies, songs, and literature in recent years? Is drug use glorified by the media (as they are often accused of glorifying alcohol consumption), or are we warned against the potential downsides of drugs? Give examples of mass media representations of drugs that support your claim.

4. What other drug epidemics is our country facing—either throughout our entire culture or some smaller element of our culture, such as college campuses—that were not mentioned in this chapter? Research the epidemic and explain its causes, its locations, and how it is affecting whatever group of people is abusing it.

5. In the sprit of Tom Chiarella's "Lessons for a Young Drinker," compose an essay that dispenses advice about some sort of drug or alcohol experience to warn against the potential pitfalls. Try to address why people are drawn to it in a realistic sense, so the reader will not see it as a sermon as much as realistic advice. Feel free to include multimedia texts, such as YouTube videos or celebrity Tweets, that document the pros and cons of your topic.

6. Find a political cartoon that addresses any current political issue that relates to drugs or alcohol and "read" the cartoon to explain the artist's intentions and message. Be sure to give some background on the issue itself in order to help your reader understand the cartoon's relevance.

7. In a rare instance of merging both the "jock" and "stoner" images, Michael Phelps is a hero to both athletes and pot smokers alike. Research the story of Phelps's rise to fame and his subsequent drama involving the "bong hit" photos that surfaced on the Internet. How has the situation been resolved? Is he still seen as a hero to athletes? To

stoners? How has he managed to reconcile the two images? In other words, what TV appearances and other pop culture events has Phelps attended, and what does that say about how he wants to be read as a text? Has he reconciled the two seemingly opposite worlds of athletics and drug use? Or has he become an icon of one more so than the other?

8. Are there college drug trends that exist on today's college campuses that have not been described or addressed in this chapter? If so, identify and define a recent drug trend and explain the drug, how it works, and who takes it. Also, explain its purpose and usage among college students. Is it the result of a larger national trend, or is it specific to your particular campus or region? Reference Trudeau's piece for ways to construct your discussion.

**Let's Connect•••▶** ⓕ "Like" our Facebook page for free, up-to-date, additional readings, discussions, and writing ideas on the topics of alcohol and drugs. Join other students and teachers across the country sharing in an online discussion of popular culture events. *American Mashup* is on Facebook at www.facebook.com/americanmashup.

# Chapter 9

# Advertising and Shopping

## Making the Cultural Connection

There is nothing more American than the overwhelming urge to shop. We shop to pass the time, to update our wardrobes, to make ourselves feel better, and simply to buy more stuff. We are, in short, a consumer culture. Some people argue that we are the most consumptive culture in the world. So it would stand to reason that we also have one of the world's most lucrative and sophisticated advertising markets. However, despite the fact that we claim to despise companies pitching us their products, advertising has become something of a cultural art form anyway. We have television shows about marketers (*Mad Men*) and people who are put to the ultimate marketing tests in order to secure a job with real estate mogul Donald Trump (*The Apprentice*). But we also

### SELECTIONS IN THIS CHAPTER

have advertising institutions that have become national points of pride. Each year's Super Bowl ads, for example, have become a cultural event themselves. We look forward to them, we rank them, and we discuss our favorites the next day at school or at work. Perhaps we have even learned to enjoy advertising in some ways.

But there is more to advertising than simply entertainment. After all, American companies don't waste hundreds of millions of dollars a year to merely entertain us. They want our money, and they know how to get it. On the surface, when we think of advertisements, we often think of commercials on TV, Web banners, and print ads in magazines and newspapers. However, the more we stop and pay attention, the more we realize that advertisements are everywhere. Movies have products placed in them, video games feature brand-name products within the games themselves, even our clothing is advertising for the brands that we wear. We are all, in a sense, walking ads in one way or another. And we are awash in advertising from the moment we rise in the morning until we go to sleep at night. In fact, many of us are so used to being overwhelmed by advertising that we hardly notice there is rarely a moment in any given day where something isn't prompting us to purchase a product or where we aren't reminded of a particular brand's existence. Even our popular songs regularly feature name-brand alcohol, clothing, restaurants, cars, and hotel chains.

Most of us rarely stop to consider the power of ads and what it says about us that we are so easily swayed by them. We rarely consider the reality that we are tempted with advertising from birth until death. The image of children glued to a television screen, soaking up commercial after commercial—like the one included here—is so commonplace that people often jokingly refer to television sets as "babysitters."

But there is power behind advertising—it is not as innocent as the picture might make it appear—and there is a palpable attempt on the part of marketers to get consumers to identify with (and stay loyal to) products and brands on a personal level so that we continue to return to them again and again. They want to hook us young and keep us for life.

On the other hand, some might argue, how difficult of a job do advertisers really have when we Americans love to shop and buy things? It goes without saying that many Americans assume they are going to buy a new car as soon as their current car loan is paid off. It goes without saying that schoolchildren expect to have a new wardrobe each year when school begins. It goes without saying that we will spend thousands of dollars over the holidays to show our loved ones how much we care for them. We will buy our love interests gifts on Valentine's Day, on anniversaries, on birthdays, and, well, just because, because buying things for someone means you love that person. Much of this is the result of a lifetime of programming. It is the result of the advertising culture in which we live, a practice that we're more than happy to oblige because we love to shop.

Just how important is shopping in our culture? Think of the many phrases applied to shopping. Women sometimes joke that they need to go to the mall for some "retail therapy," which implies that the very act of shopping can relax a person. People encourage one another to "shop 'til you drop," which shows that we can conceive of shopping as an all-day activity, albeit one that brings a welcome exhaustion. The famous phrase "Black Friday," which refers to the biggest shopping day of the year (the day after Thanksgiving), used to refer to the idea that companies would go out of the red (a deficit) and into the black (a profit). But today, it's

widely perceived as a negative term for the year's most brutal shopping event. We see stampedes and fights, people lining up for hours to save a few dollars, and mothers beating one another in the aisles of a toy store for the year's "must have" toy.

Such is the price and the honor of living in the United States and navigating our culture's love affair with product consumption. We must consume, but then we inevitably consume too much. We claim to despise advertising, but we empower it by sometimes viewing it as entertainment, and also by purchasing the products that we are being tempted with.

It is this national dilemma that this chapter will seek to address. You will be given the opportunity to observe the role that advertising plays both in our larger popular culture and in your personal tastes and purchasing habits. We will see that there is more to the science of advertising than simply pushing a product or service. And we will even observe how the phenomenon of advertising plays out in the political sphere. There will be moments of clarity as you discover that your seemingly personal preference for something might very well be the by-product of exposure to advertisements in your younger years. You will also be given many opportunities to dissect advertisements themselves to search for the deeper message being conveyed in them.

However, this chapter covers more than simply advertising and its role in our lives. It will also highlight our national habit—some might even say obsession—with shopping. You will be shown that there is far more to the act of shopping, more meaning and manipulation, than you previously assumed. Perhaps you'll learn something about yourself along the way. For example, as you read "The Science of Shopping," you will inevitably begin to become more aware of the shopping experience itself, and the theater that it entails.

The important thing to keep in mind, however, isn't just that we are a nation of consumers who succumb to the trickery of advertising, but also why. Why is it that we Americans like to consume and collect and purchase things that we don't need? What does it say about our society that we have television channels devoted to shopping, such as QVC, which highlight our national obsession with buying and having things, even if they might serve no meaningful purpose in our lives? Who is really to blame? Is it the advertisers, or is it the government that implores us to shop? Is it the credit card companies or our parents who dropped us off at the mall on weekends? And how does all of this relate to an economy whose success is judged by how much money we are spending on things we don't necessarily need? Is there a way for America to exist without a consumer-based economy? Should advertisers be regulated or held accountable for their role in all of this? These, among other questions, are the topics we will explore in this chapter as we attempt to gain insight into our relationship with both advertising and shopping.

# Consumer Product Head

Andy Singer

Andy Singer is a political cartoonist and the creator of the self-syndicated cartoon series titled *NO EXIT*, which he began in 1992. *NO EXIT* appears in dozens of newspapers, books, and magazines in the United States and abroad, including: *The Funny Times, The Bay Monthly, Athens News, La Decroissance, Z Magazine, Random Lengths, Seven Days, Urban Velo,* and *Eugene Weekly.* He updates his *NO EXIT* site with 14 new cartoons every month at www.andysinger.com. This cartoon was originally published on October 28, 2010.

# Thinking About Advertising

Take a moment to look at the accompanying cartoon. Like most political cartoons, this drawing is attempting to make a statement about a topic that is popular in our culture. This cartoon's subject matter, which can be discerned at a glance, is the concept of product identity, or, more specifically, the way in which we consumers identify with various products and how they, in turn, play a role in how we identify ourselves. While this might seem to be a confusing statement at first, most American consumers are inherently aware of the various facets of the previous statement, even if we haven't ever specifically articulated it.

Advertising—the act of marketing to a specific consumer group by a company who is selling a product—is, of course, something that so thoroughly infiltrates our daily existence that we hardly even notice the countless media and methods we are subjected to on a daily basis. We have banner ads on websites; text ads beside our private emails; spam advertising in our email inboxes; junk mail in our physical mailboxes; billboards, radio, and TV commercials; and even ads that we inadvertently pay to watch in one form or another (such as at the beginning of a movie or ads placed within video games). While our popular culture seems to understand—and perhaps even embrace—that we will constantly and forever be bombarded with ads, many of us rarely take the time to consider what the ads are trying to do beyond selling us a product.

Most companies, whether they are selling high-end goods (such as luxury cars and clothing) or low-end goods (such as cereal or cheap toys), are actually trying to gain lifetime customers. If they can get you to do what Andy Singer is pointing out in the above cartoon—that is, to identify yourself with their product—then they can count on your loyalty for as long as their product is relevant to your life. Think about the loyalties you have now. You have a preference in phone carriers, clothing brands, food, and probably even cars. If you were to take a thorough accounting of the brands with which you most identify yourself, and the various aspects of your life that they address, you might be very surprised to find how meaningful and important some brands and products are to your identity.

Now, take a closer look at Singer's cartoon. Notice some of the finer details. The "head" in the cartoon is obviously a composite of a variety of products. How many of them do you recognize? How many of the objects that comprise the "head" are items or services that you could not live without? What does it say about our society that goods and services are so important to us that we identify with them on a personal level? What do you think Singer is saying about our very American obsession with owning things? For example, how many of the objects pictured are things that are necessary for living a fruitful and meaningful life? How many are simply "perks" or add-ons that really play no significant or meaningful role in our existence? Now, to really see the power of advertising, note that the products shown above have no particular brand associated with them. Did you, in your viewing of the cartoon's details, find yourself associating specific brands with singular objects? Why do you think you did this? How does it show the power of advertising?

Finally, and perhaps most importantly, consider the words written at the top of the cartoon: "The products I buy help define me." In what way do you feel that your identity is formed by things you buy? How does one brand speak differently about you over another one? In other words, are there brands you wouldn't be caught dead wearing because they go against your own self-image? If so, how and why? You'll likely be surprised to find that no matter how important or unimportant the things you own are to you, you still most likely identify some part of your personality with the things you own, and vice versa. And this is precisely what advertising is about—making the things you own tell a story about you. Companies want their products to become a part of the "text" that you are presenting to others. If they can get your loyalty, if they can get you to identify with their products, then they have most likely gained a customer for life. This is what makes the countless billions of dollars spent on advertising worth it to the advertisers in the long run. It is a small cost to pay for the lifetime of spending they hope to gain from you.

Now, take a moment to consider your opinion on the issue of advertising and identity in popular culture. What does it say about our culture that we willingly buy into the identity a brand puts forth about itself? How about those people who purposely seek to avoid aligning themselves with a particular brand? What sorts of brands could they buy that would go against the push by companies to gain lifelong customers? Are there any brands that do not advertise, and, in doing so, seem to go against the popular culture addiction to brands and their identities? If so, how would a consumer find out about their existence?

## "I'm a Mac. I'm a PC."  Apple Inc.

**Let's Start Here•••▶** The first chapter of this textbook spent a brief amount of time discussing the wildly popular "I'm a Mac. I'm a PC." ad campaign by Apple in the mid-2000s. Now we will take the time to pick apart 15 of the Apple ads that are collected on YouTube in one location. There are, of course, many more of these ads, but this is a good sampling.

Keeping in mind our discussion of advertisements as texts that are purposely trying to persuade their viewers, observe the various ways Apple does this in the following ads. It is no accident, as mentioned previously, that Apple used a middle-aged man dressed in ill-fitting clothes to represent the outdated and uncool world of PCs that run Microsoft products. But the following ads go further in their critique of Apple's largest competitor. The ever-present element in all the "I'm a Mac" ads is that Macs are cool and PCs are, at best, inconvenient and associated with boring work. However, each ad addresses a particular flaw in both PCs and Microsoft products, while simultaneously praising Apple's superiority.

The campaign was such a huge success that it even spawned a whole genre of ad parodies online, thousands of which are posted on YouTube. Some critique Apple's pretentiousness, while others defend what they see as the superiority of PC and Windows-based computing. Nearly every ad parody uses satirical means either to poke back at Mac or to reinforce many of the messages Apple had already put forth in their own ads. Other ads use the same approach—the compare-contrast method utilized in every "I'm a Mac" ad—to critique other companies, politicians, and corporate entities and even to prove which comic book "universe" was superior to the other (as in DC Comics versus Marvel).

As you view the following 15 ads, note the main message in each 30-second TV spot, as well as the roundabout way in which Apple critiques its competitors without blatantly stating that their product is better.

Apple Inc. is an American multinational corporation that designs and markets consumer electronics, computer software, and personal computers. The company's best-known hardware products include the Macintosh line of computers, the iPod, the iPhone, and the iPad. As of May 2010, Apple is one of the largest companies in the world and the most valuable technology company in the world, having surpassed Microsoft. Established on April 1, 1976, in Cupertino, California, and incorporated January 3, 1977, the company was previously named Apple Computer, Inc., for its first 30 years, but removed the word "Computer" on January 9, 2007, to reflect the company's ongoing expansion into the consumer electronics market. For reasons as various as its philosophy of comprehensive aesthetic design to its distinctive advertising campaigns, Apple has established a unique reputation in the consumer electronics industry. This includes a customer base that is devoted to the company and its brand, particularly in the United States. *Fortune* magazine named Apple the most admired company in the United States in 2008, and in the world in 2008, 2009, and 2010. The company has also received widespread criticism for its contractors' labor, environmental, and business practices.

Search on YouTube: "Buy a Mac (15 Ads in 1 Pack) HQ"

http://www.youtube.com/watch?v=C5zOla5jDt4

**Let's Pause Here•••▶** Who do you think the intended audience of the Mac ads is supposed to be? How can you determine who their audience is? Are they trying to convince people who are undecided about the superiority of one brand over another, or are they trying to convert Windows PC users into Apple product users instead? Is the tone of the ads merely informative, or are there other underlying messages at work?

**Let's Take It Further•••▼**

1. Do you find yourself entertained or offended by the tone of the ads? What is the reason for your opinion? Is it the ads themselves or your own personal preference of computer platform, operating system, or brand?

2. Other than the differences in age and appearance between the two actors in these ads, what other subtle messages does Apple use to show PC as being outdated? How do they accomplish this?

3. Which of the 15 Apple ads do you feel gets its message across most effectively, and how? In your own personal experience, which of the computing issues that Apple raises in their ads do you feel is the most relevant to your own computing experiences?

4. Locate and choose a Microsoft ad on YouTube that attempts to address the effectiveness of the "I'm a Mac" ads by painting a more positive picture of their products and services. Explain which of the ads you think is better, Microsoft's or Apple's. Describe which elements of the advertisement you feel make a better case for their product and explain the effectiveness of the ad that you feel is superior and why.

5. Throughout the various Apple ads, Apple warns of the deficiencies in its competitor's products. How do the ads use humor to get their message across, rather than merely pointing out their competitor's flaws? Choose two or more of the Apple ads and explain the particular facet of their competitor that they are critiquing, as well as how they make the point without directly slandering the brand and product they are competing against. Be sure to read into the various elements of the ads that get their point across through both blatant and subtle messages.

6. Browse through some of the "I'm a Mac" parody videos and choose two or three of your favorites. What elements of the "I'm a Mac" commercial format do the parodies mirror? What are they critiquing? Are these as effective, more effective, or less effective than the original ads that they are parodying?

7. Design your own "I'm a Mac" parody video ad and explain the two items that you will be comparing. How are they similar and how are they different? Which of the two items is superior and why? How will you critique the "lesser" item without directly attacking it in order to follow the same format that Apple applies to their commercials? Which do you hope to convince your audience to choose in watching the video?

# Super Bowl XLV Commercials   NFL FanHouse

**Let's Start Here•••▶**   One of the greatest institutions in American popular culture is Super Bowl advertisements. There are several reasons that this has grown into a cultural phenomenon, but the biggest reason is that for several decades the NFL Super Bowl has regularly been one of the most watched televised events annually. In fact, in 2011, the Super Bowl reached its highest rating ever, with an estimated 111 million viewers worldwide. With audiences of this size, it's no wonder that networks carrying the biggest sporting event in the world can fetch rates over $2.5 million for a mere 30 seconds of advertising. Because of these sky-high prices, it stands to reason that companies would want the most bang for their buck, and so the norm has become that those companies willing to spring for these 30 second spots would put their best and brightest advertising minds to work on what will undoubtedly be one of the most watched commercials of the year.

Perhaps you've heard people mention how they enjoy the ads more than the game itself. This is a common enough occurrence, most likely because the ads are sometimes works of art and small films in themselves. In the hours following the Super Bowl, people begin ranking what they considered to be the best ads of the game. Television shows the next morning do the same, and people at work and at school compare notes on their favorites.

The following videos compose one such list. Users of the NFL-sanctioned website NFL FanHouse (www.nflfanhouse.com) ranked the top ten ads of the 2011 Super Bowl in descending order, and the list has been viewed and commented on by hundreds of thousands of users. As you watch this top ten list, see if a particular theme emerges in the ads. For instance, are most of the ads using humor to sell their product, or some other method of emotional appeal? Which types of products are represented in the range of advertisements featured in the video?

---

The following ten TV advertisements originally aired during Super Bowl XLV (45) in early 2011.

**The advertisements are located here:**

http://superbowlads.fanhouse.com/2011/

**Let's Pause Here•••▶**     If you watched the 2011 Super Bowl, do you agree with NFL FanHouse's list of top ten videos? Which did they leave out of the lineup that you thought deserved to be there? Which of them should have been removed from the list? Whether or not you watched the event, what about these videos is so entertaining that people would willingly subject themselves to advertisements? How, for example, do companies who advertise during this event counter our natural impulses as consumers of television to turn away from advertisements?

## Let's Take It Further•••▼

1. Of the videos featured in the top ten list, which was your favorite, and why?

2. Why do you believe that viewers of the Super Bowl are so enamored with the advertisements that occur during the breaks in the game? What is it about these particular ads that is so different from ads that run during regular television programming?

3. Though each ad is pushing a different product or service, all aired during the same televised event. This would imply that each of these companies is trying to reach the same audience. Based on the subject matter, the language and imagery used, and the tone of each ad, who do you think the primary target audience is for all of these companies? What, specifically, is the common theme or strategy that reveals the target audience? Who is the most successful at reaching this particular audience?

4. If you were to make a top ten list of Super Bowl ads (or ads from any major televised event, such as the Olympics or the FIFA World Cup), what criteria would you use? What types of ads would you include, and what types of ads would you exclude from your list?

5. Make an argument to justify the expense of $2.5 million for 30 seconds of television advertising during the Super Bowl. What benefits, other than the more than 100 million live viewers, do these ads have, especially in the YouTube era, where ads might take on a life of their own? How might this justify what amounts to $83,333.33 per second of advertising, not to mention the cost of production on the advertisement itself?

6. Choose your two favorite ads of the top ten list and explain why they were the best ads. What, specifically, about these ads appealed to you? Explain how the two ads stood out from the rest, as well as the way in which they positioned their products within the context of the commercial. How do these ads make their products appealing? What, if anything, about the ads might make someone disinterested in their products?

7. In what ways do Super Bowl television ads vary from other forms of advertisement? Choose any other media in which companies advertise to show comparisons and find differences between the two methods of advertising. How does the media that is not television vie for a viewer's attention? Which is more effective as a method of advertising, and why?

8. Choose any of the companies whose products are being advertised in the top ten list and seek out more recent or earlier ads (preferably ones created for the Super Bowl). In what way has the message about their product stayed the same over the last few years? In what way has the product's message shifted? Are there elements of the advertisements that show how popular culture and societal norms have shifted over the years? If so, how were you able to determine this, and how do the advertisements reflect a shift in our popular culture?

# Ethnic Marketing: McDonald's Is Lovin' It

**Burt Helm**

**Let's Start Here•••▶** One of the most iconic American companies—McDonald's—has always held a respectable lead over its other fast-food competitors because of the masterful advertising that they have developed for decades now. The Golden Arches are featured prominently at sporting events, on billboards, and on TV, and they spring into the air of nearly every single town in America. According to the McDonald's website, the corporation has over 32,000 stores globally and opens a new franchise roughly every four hours. So it is no wonder that those in advertising business look to this corporate behemoth's every move in order to mimic their models of advertising.

Most of us have grown up with McDonald's in some fashion. Perhaps the Happy Meal was a staple of your childhood diet. Or maybe you can remember some of their more catchy jingles or advertising campaigns. Either way, if you go online and watch old McDonald's commercials from the Eighties and Nineties, you'll see a significant difference between the ads of those decades and ads from the last ten years. The biggest difference: the ads tend to be much more "diverse" and "urban."

The following essay, by Burt Helm, explains how and why McDonald's decided to diversify not only their advertising but also their customer base. The rationale, and the resulting advertisements, product developments, and outcomes might surprise you. As you read the essay, observe the manner in which Helm explores the ways that McDonald's purposely borrows from minority cultures because they see minorities as "trend setters" in the United States. Keep in mind the current McDonald's advertising campaigns, as well as campaigns from your childhood and through the years.

---

Burt Helm is the marketing department editor for *BusinessWeek*. Prior to this position, he was a staff writer for *BusinessWeek Online*, a position he assumed in September 2004. Previously, Helm held positions at *Inc.* and *Maxim*. The following essay appeared in *BusinessWeek*'s July 8, 2010, issue.

The music industry has long sold black culture to white Americans. Now McDonald's is doing much the same. It's taking cues from African Americans, Hispanics, and Asians to develop menus and advertising in the hopes of encouraging middle-class Caucasians to buy smoothies and snack wraps as avidly as they consume hip-hop and rock 'n' roll.

"The ethnic consumer tends to set trends," says Neil Golden, McDonald's U.S. chief marketing officer. "So they help set the tone for how we enter the marketplace." Golden says preferences gleaned from minority consumers shape McDonald's menu and ad choices, which are then marketed to all customers.

The fast-food giant's strategy is a departure from the way companies typically market to American households. Usually, a company works with an agency to develop advertising aimed at the general market, then turns to boutique multicultural agencies to create versions tailored to blacks, Hispanics, or Asians. McDonald's still creates ads specially tailored to minority groups, as it has for over 30 years, but minorities exert an increasingly influential role in its mainstream advertising as well. The company thinks they provide early exposure to new trends.

"Most companies think they can box in Latinos, box in African-Americans, and then run the general market ad," says Steve Stoute, chief executive of Translation, which advises brands, including McDonald's, on how to reach young adults. "McDonald's will take an ad that could be primarily geared toward African-Americans and put a general market advertising dollar behind it."

The move reflects a demographic shift under way in the U.S. as a whole. As whites head toward minority status by mid-century, according to Census Bureau projections, Hispanics, Asians, and black populations are growing faster. California and Texas, the two largest states, are already "majority minority," meaning white non-Hispanics make up less than 50 percent of the population.

Its low prices have helped fuel McDonald's recent strong performance, even as the rest of the restaurant industry struggles to recover from the recession. But Golden says his minority-shapes-majority marketing strategy is paying off, too. U.S. sales rose 1.5 percent in the first three months of the year, thanks to the success of new menu items and, he says, an improved perception of the brand among all ethnic groups.

Golden says he first discovered how dramatically minority tastes can influence mainstream preferences when he oversaw McDonald's marketing in the U.S. West in the 1990s. His team had developed products aimed at Hispanics called the "Fiesta Menu," which included guacamole and spicy beef tortas. After the launch, the items sold well enough in Hispanic neighborhoods—but sales rose more than expected in Orange County and specifically Laguna Beach, an area that was more than 90 percent white. "The intended consumer said, 'We sure appreciate what you're trying to do, nice try.'" Golden recalls. "But [the Fiesta menu] overperformed in the general market."

Golden went on to create a strategy for the U.S. business that he calls "Leading with Ethnic Insights." Working with Jonah Kaufman, a McDonald's franchisee who has 13 restaurants on Long Island, N.Y., Golden doubled the spots designated for minority franchisees on the national advertising committee, which advises on and approves ads. McDonald's also uses a disproportionate number of blacks, Hispanics, and Asians in focus groups. Later, marketers are asked to imagine how they would sell a product if the U.S. population were only African American, Hispanic, or Asian. They look for differences to McDonald's general market plan.

**disproportionate:** A number that doesn't mirror the proportion of these groups to the whole of larger culture.

That sensitivity has already influenced new products. The fruit combinations in McDonald's latest smoothies, for instance, reflect taste preferences in minority communities. And when the company started heavily advertising coffee drinks last year, the ads emphasized the indulgent aspects of sweeter drinks like mochas, a message that resonated with blacks, says Golden.

In fact, many of McDonald's ads now feature only African Americans. Of the 10 most-aired TV ads from the past 12 months, compiled by ad tracker Nielsen IAG, five had all-black casts. While the ads usually push specific products or deals, many use situations aimed directly at ethnic consumers. In a recent commercial called "Big Day," a young boy at a wedding looks bored while watching the bride and groom kiss and jump over a broom—an African American matrimonial tradition. His eyes light up, however, when he gets to his seat and finds a Happy Meal.

> **matrimonial:** Relating to a marriage.

**Let's Pause Here•••▶** Prior to reading this essay, how aware were you of the recent practice of McDonald's "borrowing" trends from minority cultures and incorporating them into their advertising? Were you surprised, humored, or offended to learn of this practice? Do you think this is an ethical thing to do? Why or why not? Overall, how do you feel about the fact that—despite the ethics of "borrowing" from minority cultures—this tactic has paid off handsomely for the company (and other companies that mirror this approach to advertising)?

**Let's Take It Further•••▼**

1. Why do you think it is that "the ethnic consumer tends to set trends," as McDonald's chief U.S. marketing officer states in Helm's piece? Do you think this is a truthful statement? If so, how? If not, what's to account for the wild success of this approach to advertising?

2. Despite the fact that "ethnic consumers" are who McDonald's borrows from, the company still airs the same advertisements all over the country, even places where the minority group in question is extremely small in number. Judging from the explanations given by McDonald's executives for these sorts of advertisements and their successes, who do you think they are attempting to target as their market? What messages do McDonald's ads send about their products, and how do they appeal to different audiences?

3. Do you find it strange, humorous, or even offensive that "boutique multicultural agencies" exist whose job it is to target specific ethnic markets? Regardless of your reaction to this knowledge, explain why you think such places might exist and the reason companies might utilize their services.

4. What do you think accounts for the fact that McDonald's introduces products and menus designed to appeal to one ethnic group (for example, the "Fiesta Menu"), only to find that it becomes wildly popular with a completely different ethnic group? What might account for this phenomenon?

5. Helms begins his essay with the following general statement: "The music industry has long sold black culture to white Americans." Research this statement and find sources (for example, the book of essays titled *Everything but the Burden* by Greg Tate) that either support or refute this statement. Whether the statement is proven true or false by your research, explain where you stand on the issue of the appropriateness of such a practice. In other words, do you think it is ethically or morally correct or incorrect to borrow from other cultures, especially if the purpose is to sell the ideas to a different culture? What might be unethical about such a practice?

6. Locate McDonald's commercials on YouTube and see how they borrow from other cultures. Describe the specific elements of other cultures (such as cultural traditions or even actors of varying ethnicities) that appear in the commercials and the effect that this might have on viewers. Does it make their ads seem genuinely inclusive of many different types of people, or does it seem like they are trying too hard? Explain your impression by pointing out specific details (music, actors, language, clothing, etc.) that allow you to read the advertisements' intentions.

7. Visit a McDonald's in your community and take a look at their menu choices. Which of the menu choices, language, and even pictures seem to support this statement by Helm: "Preferences gleaned from minority consumers shape McDonald's menu and ad choices." Describe the menu's (and the store's) presentation, as well as the options it offers, and explain which elements might have been borrowed from another culture and why. Is it obvious that the borrowing has occurred? Or has the company managed to seamlessly integrate these details with the rest of the restaurant's image?

8. Research a "boutique multicultural [advertising] agency" and explain how these companies market themselves to other companies. How, for example, do they explain which ethnic group (or other niche, for that matter) they specialize in marketing toward? What services do they offer other companies? How do they give themselves credibility? After answering these questions, give your opinion on whether or not you see these marketing firms as a positive or negative development in our culture, and why.

9. What other companies employ "ethnic marketing" strategies to increase their sales not only to minority groups, but to majority groups by "borrowing" trends? Choose one company and—using the same writing strategies that Helm employs throughout his essay—explain the manner in which the company you have selected incorporates minority cultures and trends into their advertisements. Be sure to include visual examples of how the company does this (either print or video ads).

# Best Viral Ad Campaigns for 2010

Time.com

**Let's Start Here•••▶** Up to this point, the chapter has primarily focused on advertisements for products and services, since these are the most commonplace ads that we come across in our daily lives. However, as most people are well aware, when election season comes around there is a whole genre of advertising that deals solely with politics. Still, despite the fact that these ads are designed to present politicians and their platforms to the general public, they often bear a surprising amount of similarity to conventional advertising. As the most successful television commercials attempt to engage their audience on an emotional level, so too do political ads. Many of them can even be read, quite easily, as texts that represent the issues of their time.

The following political ads were selected by Time.com as the top viral political campaign videos during the 2010 midterm elections. Though the purpose of the list's creation was primarily to entertain Time.com readers, it still provides an intriguing look into the many ways advertising culture and popular culture have affected the world of political advertisement.

As you watch the sampling of 29 political ads featured in this list, observe the ways in which these ads are similar to traditional television advertising. Also, see if you can determine the issues that were in the forefront of the political spectrum during the 2010 election campaign as trends emerge among the various advertisements.

---

*TIME* magazine, on their website, Time.com, regularly features "Best of" lists that categorize everything from advertising to fashion to politics. These "Best of" lists are intended to be brief glimpses into popular culture trends in America. This particular list comprises primarily political campaigns for the 2010 midterm elections. The captions that accompany each video on the Time.com website were written by *TIME* magazine bloggers Feifei Sun, Katy Steinmetz, and Christina Crapanzano.

Search on Time.com: "Best Viral Ad Campaigns for 2010"

http://www.time.com/time/specials/packages/completelist/0,29569,2012290,00.html

**Let's Pause Here•••▶** Though the winners of this particular election have long been decided, which of these ads do you feel are strong enough to sway voters? Which, if any, of these candidates would you have voted for, based on their messages? Overall, did the ads strike you as serious or funny? Were they entertaining in any way, and if so, how? What do you suppose might be the reason that these ads all went viral, despite the fact that several of the candidates ended up losing in the election?

1. What do you feel the purpose is for the blurbs written by the *TIME* bloggers that accompany each of the political ads? How does the tone of the writing show the author's intention behind critiquing the advertisements? Are they fair representations of the ads, or are they misrepresenting them in some way?

2. What are the most common themes and issues that emerged in these ads? How do they reflect the political landscape of the time? What issues were at the forefront of the political landscape during the 2010 midterm election, judging by the content of these political advertisements?

3. How relevant are the topics of these political advertisements now? Are any of these issues still in the forefront of our national political dialogue?

4. Based on the language and tone of the caption that accompanies each video, who would you say is the target audience of the *TIME* bloggers? Are they more pro-Republican or pro-Democrat? Or, do they not seem to lean one direction more so than the other? How can you tell to whom these bloggers intend to appeal, based on the videos they selected and commented on?

5. In what way do these political hopefuls give their credentials that make them viable and "vote worthy" candidates in the eyes of the public? Why do you suppose they use the credentials that they do (beyond their political work experience) in terms of trying to get voters to trust them? Which ones matter to you and which of them seem irrelevant?

6. Though many of the ads in this list are purposely making attempts at humor or camp (which is to say that they are knowingly attempting to create absurd and sometimes meaningless ads for the sake of catching the viewer's attention and drawing it to the candidate), many of the commercials follow the formulas for success that traditional television advertising employs. Choose a few ads that you feel are trying to mirror the approach taken by conventional commercials made by companies advertising their products or services, and discuss the ways the political advertisements you've chosen mirror conventional advertising. How do they attempt to engage and manipulate the viewer's opinions and emotions in a similar manner in which companies advertise their products and services?

7. According to the accompanying text of these political ads, many of the commercials in this list are paying homage to other well-known viral videos from YouTube. Locate one of the videos in the list that gives a nod to another famous viral video and then watch the video that it is mimicking. What elements of the original video is the political ad copying? How are the two videos similar, and how are they different? Which video is more effective overall, and why? Why use these techniques at all in a political advertisement?

8. Many of the political ads in this list quite purposefully use symbolic imagery to get a subtler message across. For example, an ad that used a bald eagle might be attempting to appeal to a person's sense of patriotic pride. Choose three commercials from the Time.com list and discuss the symbolic imagery being used to get messages across. What specific images are being used, and how are they being presented to the viewer? What are the implications of the images? Are they positive or negative? Finally, how are the images working with the overall political stance that the candidate is taking? Do they mirror or support the person's stance, or is it a different or opposing message?

9. The Time.com list features a wide spectrum of political ads, representing politicians from different parties who are running for a variety of offices. Despite your own political leanings, which of the ads most resonated with you, and why? In other words, which of the messages do you agree with, and which of the candidates do you feel make the strongest case for why they should be elected? Which of them, if any, do you believe were hurt by their own advertising?

10. Within this list of 29 viral ads are several subgenres of political advertising. Some are the classic "attack" ads, others are parodies of well-known videos or methods of advertisement, while others still are video résumés for the candidate. Revisit the list of political ads and categorize them into the various forms of advertising under which they fall. Describe each category and briefly explain why each video belongs in each category. Then, point out any trends you notice that emerge from within the various ads you've categorized, and explain why you feel these trends are significant.

11. Create your own political advertisement, based on an issue that is relevant to our time. The ad can be funny or serious, or it can parody one of the viral ads here (or another recent viral video). Accompany your advertisement with an essay that explains the issue you are attempting to discuss, as well as what elements of the advertisement are meant to be symbolic representations of political issues or ideas. How does it compare to the other videos in this list, and what effect do you hope the advertisement will have on the viewer?

# A Mashup Portfolio of Advertisements
**Various Companies**

**Let's Start Here•••▶** Though most of the advertisements featured in this chapter so far have been video advertisements, since these are becoming the most common form we encounter with great regularity (online, on film, and on TV), the format of print advertising is alive and well. In light of this, we will observe some of the most innovative and provocative ads from recent years.

What follows in this small sampling of print ads for a variety of different companies and organizations is a series of five print advertisements that first appeared in magazines and billboards across the country. You will most likely note that some of these ads are for companies, while others were created by (and for) nonprofit organizations with particular agendas. Nevertheless, what all of these ads have in common is the fact that they carry messages that are both immediate and obvious, while also subtle and clever when viewed more than once or at great length.

As you view (and read) each of the following ads, locate the name of the company or organization that paid for the advertisement. Next, identify the message behind each ad. In other words, what is the company or organization trying to get across to its audience? Finally, observe the subtler details that were not immediately apparent at first glance, and note how it changes the message of the advertisement.

*All Hot Wheels® images and art are owned by Mattel, Inc. © 2011 Mattel, Inc. All Rights Reserved.*

**Let's Pause Here•••▶** What was your first reaction as you viewed each of these advertisements? Did any of them shock you or entertain you? If so, how? Which of the advertisements do you think did the best job of getting its message across, and why? Which of the ads accomplished the most creative and innovative use of space and best took advantage of the limitations of a static, print ad?

## Let's Take It Further••• ▼

1. In what ways do all of these print ads use the visual aspect of being a two-dimensional print to draw your eye in one particular direction? What, for example, was the first thing you noticed about each?

2. Based on each message's sponsor, as well as the types of images depicted in these advertisements, who do you think the audience for each ad is meant to be? What, specifically, about each ad proves who the ad is trying to address or engage?

3. How do these advertisements use humor to appeal to viewers? Are the attempts at humor successful, or do they hurt their overall message in any way?

4. Which—if any—of the advertisements use shocking or disturbing images to get your attention? Is this an effective technique? If so, how does it help the ad's intentions? If not, how does the use of a "shock factor" keep the ad from achieving its goal?

5. Explain the ways in which one or more of these advertisements make references to popular culture events to add meaning (or an additional story line).

6. Choose one of the ads in this portfolio and dissect it for meaning, intention, and message. How, for example, is the eye drawn into the advertisement by placement of objects within the frame? How are words being used (if they are present), and in what ways is a message or messages being given to the viewer that shows the intention of the company or organization? What outside or popular culture references are being made within the advertisement itself? How does this outside reference add to or detract from the power of the advertisement to reach its audience? What is the ad's overall effect on the viewer, and do you think it is a successful advertisement, or is it failing to get across a clear message? How, if at all, would you have changed the advertisement to make it more "catchy" or effective?

7. Google any of the following phrases to find aggregator sites that feature "best of" lists of print ads (end each phrase with the year of interest to you): "most innovative print ads," "most daring print ads," "funniest print ads," "most evocative print ads," "sexiest print ads," or "most offensive print ads." Choose a list and from that list choose your favorite two or three ads of the list. Discuss who made the ads, what the ads are trying to accomplish, and why you believe each ad you chose is the most "successful" of the group. Also, "read" the advertisement and describe how it gets its message across by explaining the visual methods employed in each.

8. Choose your favorite and least favorite ads of those featured here and explain why they stood out as the best and worst ads. Compare and contrast the advertisements with one another to illustrate what, specifically, appealed to you or turned you away from their message. Explain how the two ads stood out from the rest (in both positive and negative ways), as well as the way in which they positioned their messages within the context of a one-frame, nonmoving print ad. How do these ads make (or fail to make) their messages stand out? What, if anything, about the ads might make someone disinterested in their organization or product? What was each ad's biggest strength and weakness?

9. In what ways do these print ads vary from other genres of advertisement? Choose any other media in which companies advertise to show comparisons and find differences between the two methods of advertising. How do the print media grab and hold their viewers' attention? Which is more effective as a method of advertising, and why? What are the strengths and weaknesses of each form of advertisement?

10. Compose a print ad of your own for a nonprofit organization that gets the overall purpose of the organization across in one frame (as these ads do). Be sure to use imagery that grabs the viewer's attention and use minimal wording. Accompany your print ad with an essay that explains how you constructed the advertisement, how you intend your advertisement to be read, and who you hope to engage as an audience. Discuss the various elements of your advertisement that might not have been noticed at first glance, and explain how you hope your viewer will react or what you hope the outcome of the advertisement to be.

# mash**UP** essay

The following essay is this chapter's Mashup selection. Keeping in mind our definition of a Mashup essay in Chapter 2 (an essay that includes multimedia texts, as well as multiple writing strategies), observe the way the author, Eric Schlosser, utilizes multimedia texts. For example, the central concept to which his essay refers is advertising (primarily on television) directed toward young, easily influenced children. Schlosser also utilizes the very same tools that marketers do as they learn to master their trade: marketing journals and magazines, as well as well-regarded books on the specific subject of marketing to children. But Schlosser, rather than simply critiquing children's marketing from the sidelines, allows various advertisements and marketing sleight-of-hand techniques that are directed at children to speak for themselves. He also utilizes two major national surveys that were conducted on children to study the effects of marketing, as well as interviewing corporate executives from the very businesses that seek to attract children (for example, an executive from Burger King). Schlosser even discusses a failed federal law that child advocates attempted to get passed in the late Seventies, in order to show the power of those who lobbied for companies that market to children and the stations who profit from selling them advertising time. The result is a well-rounded article that allows the people most guilty of manipulating children with marketing to damn themselves by virtue of blatantly publishing articles and books that discuss the mechanisms for exploiting youngsters.

The strength in Schlosser's essay is his willingness to seek out a wide variety of sources to back his opinion that marketing to children is both unethical and dangerous. Rather than simply bashing these companies who market to children in an attempt to gain lifelong customers, Schlosser patiently weaves together his argument for how and why this is a questionable practice, using many sources that prove his points and lend his opinion credibility. This makes for a more engaging and thought-provoking argument, a more sophisticated and important essay, because it is hard to argue with the facts he gives us that illustrate how marketing to children is a major business with serious and long-lasting results.

One of the most intriguing elements of the essay is that Schlosser employs more than just a straightforward argumentative approach in his writing. The major thrust of the essay is, indeed, that Schlosser wants to persuade his readers to see how marketing to children is unethical, but this is cushioned in the midst of several other writing strategies that he employs. In addition to the argumentation writing strategy, Schlosser uses several others, which he simultaneously utilizes in order to show the wide-reaching scope and importance of this article in the lives of anyone who has ever watched children's television or has children who are subjected to manipulative marketing techniques. One such strategy Schlosser employs is the definition-informative writing method, which allows him to explain a variety of marketing techniques, marketing strategies, and even the terminology employed when referring, for example, to the various stages of "nagging" that children use to coerce their parents into purchasing something for them. This allows us to see some of the reality behind the scenes in the world of marketing, as well as to help us understand how serious and lucrative the business world deems marketing geared toward children to be. Schlosser also uses the descriptive writing strategy to illustrate the many different techniques that marketing researchers use in order to extract information from children about their preferences and tastes. By using this technique he is able to allow his readers to see the extent to which marketers are willing to go in order to decode the minds of children so they can figure out the best product pitch to use on them.

In terms of using research in his writing (the research writing strategy), Schlosser not only researches the marketing practices used on children, he also goes a step further and chooses to include books, articles, interviews, surveys, expert opinions, and even the movement in the late Seventies to write legislation that would regulate marketing to children. In doing his research, Schlosser also employs the classification writing strategy as he discusses the different types of advertising directed at children and how it fits into the larger scheme of television advertising in general. He also employs the cause-effect writing strategy by showing the outcomes of children's advertising on children themselves, which proves that children can indeed be manipulated into forging brand identities at a young age and remain loyal to those brands for the rest of their adult lives.

Ultimately, the essay as a whole is an argumentation essay that reiterates the author's main point in a variety of intriguing and effective ways. For example, we are shown in the two surveys of children that these ads do affect them, and we are shown how marketers intend for children to harass their parents into purchasing items for them. Schlosser further cements his argument by ending his essay with the statistics that show why television advertising is such a powerful force: because children spend more time watching television than doing anything else, other than sleeping. But, the most successful aspect of his essay is that he avoids being preachy and instead lets the surveys, the articles, the quotes, the figures, and the words of advertisers make the case against themselves.

When you begin writing a Mashup essay of your own in response to the selections in this chapter, revisit Schlosser's essay to generate ideas for multimedia texts and multiple writing strategies. Use the flowchart to see the ways in which Schlosser employs the various writing strategies and multimedia texts he utilizes in his writing.

## Mashup Essay Flowchart

**Types of Media:**
- Marketing Experts
- Marketing Journals and Magazines
- Marketing Books
- Marketing Firms
- A Proposed Federal Law
- Children's Television Networks
- Corporate Executive Interviews
- Marketing Surveys

"Kid Kustomers"
Eric Schlosser

**Writing Strategies:**
- Classification
- Descriptive
- Definition-Informative
- Cause-Effect
- Argumentation
- Research

# Kid Kustomers

**Eric Schlosser**

**Let's Start Here•••▶** Anyone who grew up watching television—which is, of course, a staple of childhood in American popular culture—is familiar with children's television advertising. Of course, as children, we do not give any thought to advertisements designed to catch our attention. We either notice the ads or we don't. We are either intrigued by the cereal, the toys, the movies, and the clothing being advertised, or we turn the channel when the commercials come on. Still, despite the fact that children do not think about the advertisements geared toward them, it turns out that a great deal of thought goes into children's advertising on the part of the advertisers themselves.

In fact, it is the thought process behind children's advertising, as well as the science behind capturing customers at the youngest age possible, that is the subject of the following essay. Eric Schlosser, author of the wildly successful book *Fast Food Nation* (from which the following essay is excerpted), dissects the science of marketing to children and all of its purposeful trickery. Though his book focuses on the business of fast food, this particular selection shows how fast food companies (as well as other businesses) have built their empires on the impressionable young minds of child television viewers.

We are shown that all things related to children and seeing them as customers are not as innocent as they might first appear. Instead, Schlosser paints a disturbing picture of the nature of doing business with children as your prime customers. While you read the article, see how many of the various methods of advertising you were exposed to as a child, and consider the impact these ads had on you then, as well as the brands you are most loyal to now.

---

Eric Schlosser is an investigative journalist and author of several nonfiction books of investigative journalism, most notably *Fast Food Nation* (2001), which was made into a film in 2006, *Reefer Madness* (2003), and *Chew On This* (2007), which is a young adult book adapted from *Fast Food Nation*. The following essay first appeared in Schlosser's book *Fast Food Nation*.

| | |
|---|---|
| Schlosser begins his essay by using the definition-informative writing approach to explain the field of children's marketing. | Twenty-five years ago, only a handful of American companies directed their marketing at children—Disney, McDonald's, candy makers, toy makers, manufacturers of breakfast cereal. Today children are being targeted by phone companies, oil companies, and automobile companies as well as clothing stores and restaurant chains. The explosion in children's advertising occurred during the 1980s. Many working parents, feeling guilty about spending less time with their kids, started spending more money on them. One marketing expert |

has called the 1980s "the decade of the child consumer." After largely ignoring children for years, Madison Avenue began to scrutinize and pursue them. Major ad agencies now have children's divisions, and a variety of marketing firms focus solely on kids. These groups tend to have sweet-sounding names: Small Talk, Kid Connection, Kid2Kid, the Gepetto Group, Just Kids, Inc. At least three industry publications— *Youth Market Alert*, *Selling to Kids*, and *Marketing to Kids Report*—cover the latest ad campaigns and market research. The growth in children's advertising has been driven by efforts to increase not just current, but also future, consumption. Hoping that nostalgic childhood memories of a brand will lead to a lifetime of purchases, companies now plan "cradle-to-grave" advertising strategies. They have come to believe what Ray Kroc and Walt Disney realized long ago— a person's "brand loyalty" may begin as early as the age of two. Indeed, market research has found that children often recognize a brand logo before they can recognize their own name.

> Schlosser uses these companies (and similar publications) as research sources. To him, their names are also texts that explain their marketing approach to children.

> The idea that marketers purposely market to children to gain lifetime customers is central to the essay's main argument.

The discontinued Joe Camel ad campaign, which used a hip cartoon character to sell cigarettes, showed how easily children can be influenced by the right corporate mascot. A 1991 study published in the *Journal of the American Medical Association* found that nearly all of America's six-year-olds could identify Joe Camel, who was just as familiar to them as Mickey Mouse. Another study found that one-third of the cigarettes illegally sold to minors were Camels. More recently, a marketing firm conducted a survey in shopping malls across the country, asking children to describe their favorite TV ads. According to the CME KidCom Ad Traction Study II, released at the 1999 Kids' Marketing Conference in San Antonio, Texas, the Taco Bell commercials featuring a talking chihuahua were the most popular fast food ads. The kids in the survey also like Pepsi and Nike commercials, but their favorite television ad was for Budweiser.

> Schlosser reads this entire ad campaign (and Joe Camel) as a text.

> This source is vital because of the many lawsuits and several pieces of legislation that resulted from it.

> Schlosser uses this and several other marketing texts to support his argument.

The bulk of the advertising directed at children today has an immediate goal. "It's not just getting kids to whine," one marketer explained in *Selling to Kids*, "it's giving them a specific reason to ask for the product." Years ago sociologist Vance Packard described children as "surrogate salesmen" who had to persuade other people, usually their parents, to buy what they wanted. Marketers now use different terms to explain the intended response to their ads—such as "leverage," "the nudge factor," "pester power." The aim of

> To Schlosser, Packard's groundbreaking research illuminates the science of marketing toward children.

most children's advertising is straightforward: Get kids to nag their parents and nag them well.

James U. McNeal, a professor of marketing at Texas A&M University, is considered America's leading authority on marketing to children. In his book *Kids As Customers* (1992), McNeal provides marketers with a thorough analysis of "children's requesting styles and appeals." He classifies juvenile nagging tactics into seven major categories. A *pleading* nag is one accompanied by repetitions of words like "please" or "mom, mom, mom." A *persistent* nag involves constant requests for the coveted product and may include the phrase "I'm gonna ask just one more time." *Forceful* nags are extremely pushy and may include subtle threats, like "Well, then, I'll go and ask Dad." *Demonstrative* nags are the most high-risk, often characterized by full-blown tantrums in public places, breath-holding, tears, a refusal to leave the store. *Sugar-coated* nags promise affection in return for a purchase and may rely on seemingly heartfelt declarations like "You're the best dad in the world." *Threatening* nags are youthful forms of blackmail, vows of eternal hatred and of running away if something isn't bought. Pity nags claim the child will be heartbroken, teased, or socially stunted if the parent refuses to buy a certain item. "All of these appeals and styles may be used in combination," McNeal's research has discovered, "but kids tend to stick to one or two of each that proved most effective . . . for their own parents."

McNeal never advocates turning children into screaming, breath-holding monsters. He has been studying "Kid Kustomers" for more than thirty years and believes in a more traditional marketing approach. "The key is getting children to see a firm . . . in much the same way as [they see] mom or dad, grandma or grandpa," McNeal argues. "Likewise, if a company can ally itself with universal values such as patriotism, national defense, and good health, it is likely to nurture belief in it among children."

Before trying to affect children's behavior, advertisers have to learn about their tastes. Today's market researchers not only conduct surveys of children in shopping malls, they also organize focus groups for kids as young as two or three. They analyze children's artwork, hire children to run focus groups, stage slumber parties and then question children into the night. They send cultural anthropologists into homes, stores, fast food restaurants, and other places where kids like to gather, quietly and surreptitiously observing the behavior of prospective customers. They study the

The classification writing strategy breaks down the seven common types of children's nagging.

academic literature on child development, seeking insights from the work of theorists such as Erik Erikson and Jean Piaget. They study the fantasy lives of young children, they apply the findings in advertisements and product designs.

Dan S. Acuff—the president of Youth Market System Consulting and the author of *What Kids Buy and Why* (1997)—stresses the importance of dream research. Studies suggest that until the age of six, roughly 80 percent of children's dreams are about animals. Rounded, soft creatures like Barney, Disney's animated characters, and the Teletubbies therefore have an obvious appeal to young children. The Character Lab, a division of Youth Market System Consulting, uses a proprietary technique called Character Appeal Quadrant analysis to help companies develop new mascots. The technique purports to create imaginary characters who perfectly fit the targeted age group's level of cognitive and neurological development.

Children's clubs have for years been considered an effective means of targeting ads and collecting demographic information; the clubs appeal to a child's fundamental need for status and belonging. Disney's Mickey Mouse Club, formed in 1930, was one of the trailblazers. During the 1980s and 1990s, children's clubs proliferated, as corporations used them to solicit the names, addresses, zip codes, and personal comments of young customers. "Marketing messages sent through a club not only can be personalized," James McNeal advises, "they can be tailored for a certain age or geographical group." A well-designed and well-run children's club can be extremely good for business. According to one Burger King executive, the creation of a Burger King Kids Club in 1991 increased the sales of children's meals as much as 300 percent.

> **proliferated:** Increased rapidly in number.

> This is a valuable research source because of the importance of kids' clubs to many fast-food chains' business models. The Burger King executive's words prove the power of these advertising and data collection methods.

The Internet has become another powerful tool for assembling data about children. In 1998 a federal investigation of Web sites aimed at children found that 89 percent requested personal information from kids; only 1 percent required that children obtain parental approval before supplying the information. A character on the McDonald's Web site told children that Ronald McDonald was "the ultimate authority in everything." The site encouraged kids to send Ronald an e-mail revealing their favorite menu item at McDonald's, their favorite book, their favorite sports team—and their name. Fast food Web sites no longer ask children to provide personal information without first gaining parental approval; to do so is now a

> Schlosser reads the McDonald's website as a text, particularly in how it encourages children to interact with it.

This is an example of Schlosser employing the cause-effect writing strategy to show the outcome of the public's disapproval of data mining from children.

violation of federal law, thanks to the Children's Online Privacy Protection Act, which took effect in April of 2000.

Despite the growing importance of the Internet, television remains the primary medium for children's advertising. The effects of these TV ads have long been a subject of controversy. In 1978, the Federal Trade Commission (FTC) tried to ban all television ads directed at children seven years old or younger. Many studies had found that young children often could not tell the difference between television programming and television advertising. They also could not comprehend the real purpose of commercials and trusted that advertising claims were true. Michael Pertschuk, the head of the FTC, argued that children need to be shielded from advertising that preys upon their immaturity. "They cannot protect themselves," he said, "against adults who exploit their present-mindedness."

The FTC's proposed ban was supported by the American Academy of Pediatrics, the National Congress of Parents and Teachers, the Consumers Union, and the Child Welfare League, among others. But it was attacked by the National Association of Broadcasters, the Toy Manufacturers of America, and the Association of National Advertisers. The industry groups lobbied Congress to prevent any restrictions on children's ads and sued in federal court to block Pertschuk from participating in future FTC meetings on the subject. In April of 1981, three months after the inauguration of President Ronald Reagan, an FTC staff report argued that a ban on ads aimed at children would be impractical, effectively killing the proposal. "We are delighted by the FTC's reasonable recommendation," said the head of the National Association of Broadcasters.

The following paragraph shows the descriptive writing and definition-informative writing strategies. Schlosser describes the large role television (and its advertising) plays in children's lives and informs his reader of statistics about children's television consumption.

The Saturday-morning children's ads that caused angry debates twenty years ago now seem almost quaint. Far from being banned, TV advertising aimed at kids is now broadcast twenty-four hours a day, closed-captioned and in stereo. Nickelodeon, the Disney Channel, the Cartoon Network, and the other children's cable networks are now responsible for about 80 percent of all television viewing by kids. None of these networks existed before 1979. The typical American child now spends about twenty-one hours a week watching television—roughly one and a half months of TV every year. That does not include the time children spend in front of a screen watching videos, playing video games, or using the computer. Outside of school, the typical American child spends more time watching television than doing any other activity except sleeping. During the course of a year, he or she watches more than thirty thousand TV commercials. Even the nation's youngest children are watching a great deal of television. About one-quarter of American children between the ages of two and five have a TV in their room.

**Let's Pause Here•••** ▷ What was your overall impression of Schlosser's essay? Were you surprised by the amount of thought and work that goes into marketing products and services to children, or did you suspect that it was this way before you read this essay? Why do you think Schlosser feels it is important to let adults know the realities of marketing to children? Does it change your opinion of these companies in any way? If so, how did the essay change your opinion of companies that market to children? If not, how did the essay fail to result in a change of opinion on your part?

**Let's Take It Further•••** ▽

1. Schlosser makes the point early in his essay that children really first became a significant buying force in the Eighties when their parents felt guilty for not spending enough time with them and subsequently began to spend more money on them to make up for it. Based on your experience, would you agree or disagree with that assessment of modern parenting? Is it still true today that parents spend money on their children to make up for lost time? Or is there some other reason spending might have spiked in the Eighties?

2. Though Schlosser's essay is both informative and also arguing about the unethical marketing toward children, he uses various writing strategies and examples that suggest his audience is more than simply parents. Based on his language, examples, and other writing strategies, who else might Schlosser be targeting with his essay besides parents? Which elements of his essay lead you to believe who his audience might be?

3. Working with the concept that Schlosser discusses, which is that advertisers purposely want "cradle to grave" advertising to hook consumers young and keep them for life, what ads do you most remember from your childhood television-viewing experience? How many of these ads resulted in you "nagging" your parents to buy their advertised product for you? Which of these products or companies do you still do business with today, and why?

4. Schlosser cites a now-famous study showing that children recognized Camel's mascot, Joe Camel, as easily as they recognized Mickey Mouse. He then goes on to say that of all the cigarettes sold illegally to minors, one-third of these were Camel brand cigarettes. Do you feel that this figure proves or disproves the power of advertising to children? How could the Joe Camel character have influenced minors to smoke?

5. According to children's marketers, businesses seek to turn youngsters into "surrogate salesmen" who coerce their parents into purchasing products. Do you find this practice to be brilliant or cruel on the behalf of marketers? Why? Were you a surrogate salesman

for a company when you were a child? If so, for whom, and how did you accomplish this? In other words, which sort of "nagging" technique did you employ?

6. Schlosser states that the companies who used to market to children were those with products that they specifically wanted children to buy. He goes on to say that now, in the modern era of children's marketing, young people are being targeted by companies that have products that don't necessarily matter to children. Yet they still advertise to them. Watch children's television programming and make note of the ads that are from companies (such as those Schlosser discusses early in his essay) whose products are not related to childhood interests. Describe the company and their advertisement, as well as how they are marketing their product or service for children in hope of hooking "cradle to grave" customers. How do these ads differ from the more traditional companies that would logically market to children? Are they effective in achieving their goals?

7. Since Schlosser's book was first published, large strides have been made in marketing as a whole. The science has improved as people give personal information more willingly on social networking sites, as well as shopping websites. Research a children's marketing firm, or read recent findings In children's marketing journals to determine how marketing toward children has changed in the years since *Fast Food Nation* was first published. Explain how marketing has changed and whether you think it has gotten more manipulative or less manipulative than the techniques discussed in "Kid Kustomers." What new angles have been discovered and exploited? Explain how the philosophy of marketing to children has changed, if it has at all.

8. Survey a child or small group of children to see which brands they are loyal to already. Try to determine how they were first introduced to the company in question, and explain why they feel loyalty (or preference) to one brand over another. Explain the process you went through to glean information from the child or children that you interviewed. Finally, play several ads for them (some from children's television and some from adult television) and see which ads they better respond to and why. Ask them to explain the appeal of one product over another. How do your findings differ from Schlosser's, or how do they reinforce the argument he puts forth in his essay?

9. The Character Lab—a company that helps corporations create imaginary characters for children—is but one in a large constellation of children's marketing firms. Locate another such firm whose sole focus is children and marketing, and explain what the company's particular specialty is and what process they use to market to children. For example, the Character Lab uses "proprietary" techniques, such as the "Character Appeal Quadrant" mentioned by Schlosser, to fit characters to specific age groups. What does the marketing firm you have researched specialize in? Describe how they set themselves apart from other children's marketing firms. Do you believe the methods they use will be effective in manipulating children? Why or why not?

10. Schlosser explains that children's clubs are especially effective at capturing the attention of kids and coercing them into giving up personal information about themselves. He uses the example of the Disney Mickey Mouse Club and the Burger King Kids Club, then explains how these clubs have provided valuable benefits to the companies that created them. What is a modern-day equivalent of these clubs? Locate one such club and

explain how it operates, what the supposed benefits are for the kids who join, and what products they are pushing. Explain the mechanisms of the club and how they extract information from children, as well as how they entice children to buy their product or service. Finally, explain whether you believe this particular club's practices to be ethical, and why.

11. Construct an advertisement (either video or print images) designed to appeal to children specifically. Besides utilizing the explanations and techniques explained throughout Schlosser's essay, research sources (such as the publications mentioned in this essay) that deal with children's marketing. Explain the product or service you are marketing, as well as how you are employing methods explained in Schlosser's essay and the other sources you located. What do you hope the outcome to be, and how are you trying to achieve it?

# mash it UP

Here is a series of essay and discussion topics that draw connections between multiple selections within the chapter. They also suggest outside texts to include in your essay or discussion. Feel free to bring in further outside texts, remembering the variety of texts (beyond articles) available to you.

1. Locate ad parodies, or "spoofs" (either in print or video), of other famous advertisements and compare the parodies to the original advertisements. You can locate print ad parodies by Googling the phrases "print ad parodies" or "print ad spoofs." Which elements of the original ad are the parodies copying? Are they making fun of the original advertisement itself, or merely mirroring a technique employed in the original ad? Which is more successful at achieving its goal?

2. Locate consumer-generated advertisements online (such as ads produced for the Doritos Super Bowl "make your own ad" contest) and compare them to professional ads for the same companies. In what significant ways are the amateur ads different than professional ones? What similar themes emerge within the ads you've located? How do the ads appeal to viewers' emotions in a similar way to the company's professional ads (for example, humor, sex, or shock value)? Which elements of marketing that are used in professional television ads do the consumer-generated ads mimic?

3. Revisit the *Bowling for Columbine* YouTube selection in the "Violence" chapter and compare it to the political ads in the "Best Viral Ad Campaigns for 2010" selection featured in this chapter. How are some of the political videos exploiting or playing to the very thing that Moore is describing in the clip featured in the "Violence" chapter? Which of

the two sources is more accurate in its assessment of Americans and what we fear? Which one are you able to take more seriously, and which one seems to "get it wrong" when playing to our national fears?

4. Locate and read Schlosser's popular book *Fast Food Nation* and discuss the way children's marketing plays a role in the current fast-food empires of our country's most successful restaurants. Then, explain your preference for fast food and whether you have held this preference from childhood. Which of these restaurants' advertising most intrigued you as a child, and how?

5. Watch an adult television station for an hour and make note of the advertising, including the companies advertising, the products and services offered, as well as the types of ads that are shown. Then, watch a children's television station for an hour and do the same for the commercials featured on that channel. Finally, compare the types of companies advertising, as well as the ways in which the advertising for adults was similar or different from that for kids.

6. Compare the viral political ads in the Time.com list to campaign ads from other elections (either those since 2010 or those prior to 2010), which can be easily located on YouTube. Explain how the ads are similar and how they differ, in terms of political content (or message), imagery, tone, and even genre.

7. Create your own print or video ad for a product or political campaign, using the techniques illustrated by the many advertisements in the first half of this chapter. Accompany your advertisement with an essay that explains what you hope to accomplish with your advertisement, and who your audience is that you are attempting to reach. Describe the process of creating the ad, as well as the message you are trying to get across to your viewer.

# Shared Sacrifice

R. J. Matson

R. J. Matson is the editorial cartoonist at the *St. Louis Post-Dispatch*, *The New York Observer*, and *Roll Call*. His cartoons and illustrations have appeared in many other publications, including *The New Yorker*, *The Nation*, *MAD Magazine*, *City Limits*, *The Daily News*, *The Washington Post*, *Washington City Paper*, *Capital Style*, and *Rolling Stone*. He received a B.A. from Columbia University in 1985 and won a national Scholastic Press Association Award for cartoons he contributed to the *Columbia Daily Spectator*. He moved to Washington, D.C., in 1985 to work as a reporter for *States News Service*. In 1986 he became the staff illustrator at *Roll Call* and the editorial cartoonist at the *Montgomery County Sentinel*. He was the art director of *The Washington*

*Monthly* from 1986 to 1988. R.J. returned to New York City when he became the editorial cartoonist at the *New York Observer* in 1989. He was recently the Secretary of the National Cartoonists Society, the Chairman of the New York Metro Chapter of the NCS, and a member of the Board of Advisors of the Museum of Comic and Cartoon Art in Manhattan. The following cartoon first appeared in the *St. Louis Post-Dispatch* on December 21, 2006.

## Thinking About Shopping

Take a moment to look at the accompanying cartoon. It is apparent that the artist, R.J. Matson, is giving a nod to two different popular culture icons: Santa Claus and Uncle Sam. Most people recognize Uncle Sam as a sort of informal mascot for the United States. And, for those who have seen the famous "I Want You" poster entreating citizens to join the military, it is understood that this action is only alluded to when the government, represented by Uncle Sam, is ordering us to do something as a country in order to support our way of life. Of course, it goes without saying that Santa Claus represents the holiday season at the end of each year, with a particularly strong tie to Christmas. So, if these two icons are being simultaneously used, what do you think Matson is attempting to say about the role of shopping in American popular culture? How is Matson using the power of Uncle Sam, and how is he using the power of Santa? What is the inherent message of the cartoon, which can be discerned by the words above and below Uncle Sam/Santa?

As a society, we have thoroughly given ourselves over to the notion of shopping and the power it holds in our lives. We understand that we, as Americans, identify ourselves by the activity of shopping. We have nicknames such as "Black Friday" for national sales events. We understand that every Christmas there will be shortages of whatever toy is popular at the moment, and that it is quite likely that a fight will break out, maybe even a devastating injury will occur—and yet we will not be swayed from shopping because it is what we do. We shop to relieve stress, to prepare ourselves for the upcoming school year, and even to show our affection for someone. We are trained from a very young age that shopping is a magical and nearly religious experience, which can be seen in the eyes of youngsters taken on their earliest shopping experience. They reach for shiny objects on bottom shelves (placed there just for them). They beg their parents, pleading and whining and screaming, for objects they want but do not need. And so the cycle goes.

Still, despite the fact that the act of shopping is so thoroughly entrenched in our national identity, these words in the above cartoon were *actually* uttered by President George W. Bush on December 12, 2006, when he told Americans that the solution to the looming recession was to "go shopping more." Considering that we love to shop in the first place, why might our government ask us to shop *more*? What kind of country do we live in that, in order for its economy to thrive, it relies heavily upon its citizens spending vast sums of money on things they might not even need or want?

There is another aspect in our popular culture, particularly in our popular political culture, that Matson's cartoon is engaging: the notion of a nation pulling together in "shared sacrifice," as the cartoon is titled. How might this idea of "shared sacrifice," a term frequently employed during times of national hardship, be related to the idea of a nation of shoppers being asked to keep shopping? Where does the term "sacrifice" play into this commandment? Does each citizen actually owe it to one another to shop for our nation's larger well-being? If so, how and why?

Now, revisit the cartoon for a moment to see how Matson blends the images of Uncle Sam and Santa. Why do you believe that Matson has chosen to include the Santa imagery? Why wasn't it enough to just simply have Uncle Sam order Americans to shop and leave it at that? Could it be that Santa is associated with the heaviest shopping season of the year? If so, in what ways is Santa (and the year-end holiday season) associated with the joys, obligations, and possibly even financial hardships of shopping in excess for others? How does this change the message of the cartoon? How would it have been different if Matson had only used the iconic imagery of either Santa or Uncle Sam, but not both? What is the effect of using the two together?

Finally, it is worth noting that most Americans probably do not need to be reminded that we like to shop. Still, it is interesting to see how Matson toys with the idea of government edicts (or commandments) while still playing up the joy of gift purchasing and gift giving. If you were to create a cartoon about shopping and its role in our daily lives, what might you include in your drawing? Why do you think it is so important to us, and how could you go about illustrating its importance?

# The Science of Shopping    Malcolm Gladwell

**Let's Start Here•••▶** Shopping is one of the great American pastimes. In fact, malls—the mecca of shopping in our culture—themselves play a significant role in most Americans' lives from an early age. Most of us were exposed from a very young age to the bright lights, the sales, and the sheer amount of products being sold all in one spot. A particular teenage rite of passage (not too unlike getting a driver's license at 16) is the ritual of going to the mall every weekend to hang out. The purpose isn't necessarily to shop, as much as it is to spend time with friends, catch up on gossip, flirt, and maybe buy a snack. Still, all those years of exposure add up, and so the mall and the shopping experience become a part of our identity.

One thing most of us likely didn't pay attention to during those teen years of hanging out at the mall was the placement of objects in store windows. Maybe you noticed a sale sign, or a mannequin. Perhaps you even went into a store and tried on clothes. But what you probably didn't notice was how objects and products were arranged in the store itself. If you didn't notice, it's because you weren't supposed to notice.

After reading Malcolm Gladwell's essay, you probably will notice from now on.

As it turns out, researchers study the habits of shoppers, the "dance" of shopping (which is the way in which customers physically interact with the store and its products), and even the speeds at which we walk. These and other specific shopping habits are analyzed and explained by Gladwell in the following essay. You might be surprised at some of the techniques employed, and the lengths that companies will go to in order to learn their customers' habits and to coerce them into spending more time in their stores and, hopefully, buying more products during each visit.

While you read the essay, make note of the practices Gladwell illustrates that come as a surprise to you. Also, see whether you can determine if Gladwell is merely informing his audience about the science behind our shopping experiences, or if he is suggesting that anything unethical is occurring in the practice of this secretive "science."

---

Malcolm Gladwell is a writer for *The New Yorker* and a best-selling author based in New York City. He has been a staff writer for *The New Yorker* since 1996. He is best known for his books *The Tipping Point* (2000), *Blink* (2005), *Outliers* (2008), and *What the Dog Saw: And Other Adventures* (2009). Gladwell's books and articles often deal with the unexpected implications of research in the social sciences and make frequent and extended use of academic work, particularly in the areas of psychology and social psychology. The following essay first appeared in *The New Yorker's* November 4, 1996, issue.

# 1.

Human beings walk the way they drive, which is to say that Americans tend to keep to the right when they stroll down shopping-mall concourses or city sidewalks. This is why in a well-designed airport travelers drifting toward their gate will always find the fast-food restaurants on their left and the gift shops on their right: people will readily cross a lane of pedestrian traffic to satisfy their hunger but rarely to make an impulse buy of a T-shirt or a magazine. This is also why Paco Underhill tells his retail clients to make sure that their window displays are canted, preferably to both sides but especially to the left, so that a potential shopper approaching the store on the inside of the sidewalk—the shopper, that is, with the least impeded view of the store window—can see the display from at least twenty-five feet away.

**canted:**
Tilted or set at an angle.

Of course, a lot depends on how fast the potential shopper is walking. Paco, in his previous life, as an urban geographer in Manhattan, spent a great deal of time thinking about walking speeds as he listened in on the great debates of the nineteen-seventies over whether the traffic lights in midtown should be timed to facilitate the movement of cars or to facilitate the movement of pedestrians and so break up the big platoons that move down Manhattan sidewalks. He knows that the faster you walk the more your peripheral vision narrows, so you become unable to pick up visual cues as quickly as someone who is just ambling along. He knows, too, that people who walk fast take a surprising amount of time to slow down— just as it takes a good stretch of road to change gears with a stick-shift automobile. On the basis of his research, Paco estimates the human down-shift period to be anywhere from twelve to twenty-five feet, so if you own a store, he says, you never want to be next door to a bank: potential shoppers speed up when they walk past a bank (since there's nothing to look at), and by the time they slow down they've walked right past your business. The downshift factor also means that when potential shoppers enter a store it's going to take them from five to fifteen paces to adjust to the light and refocus and gear down from walking speed to shopping speed— particularly if they've just had to navigate a treacherous parking lot or hurry to make the light at Fifty-seventh and Fifth. Paco calls that area inside the door the Decompression Zone, and something he tells clients over and over again is never, ever put anything of value in that zone—not shopping baskets or tie racks or big promotional displays—because no one is going to see it. Paco believes that, as a rule of thumb, customer interaction with any product or promotional display in the Decompression Zone will increase at least thirty percent once it's moved to the back edge of the zone, and even more if it's placed to the right, because another of the fundamental rules of how human beings shop is that upon entering a store—whether it's Nordstrom or Kmart, Tiffany or the Gap— the shopper invariably and reflexively turns to the right. Paco believes in the existence of the Invariant Right because he has actually verified it. He has put cameras in stores trained directly on the doorway, and if you go to his office, just above Union Square, where videocassettes and boxes of Super-eight film from all his work over the years are stacked in plastic Tupperware containers practically up to the ceiling, he can show you reel upon reel of grainy entryway video—customers striding in the door, downshifting, refocusing, and then, again and again, making that little half turn.

> invariant: Unchanging or consistent.

Paco Underhill is a tall man in his mid-forties, partly bald, with a neatly trimmed beard and an engaging, almost goofy manner. He wears baggy khakis and shirts open at the collar, and generally looks like the academic he might have been if he hadn't been captivated, twenty years ago, by the ideas of the urban anthropologist William Whyte. It was Whyte who pioneered the use of time-lapse photography as a tool of urban planning, putting cameras in parks and the plazas in front of office buildings in midtown Manhattan, in order to determine what distinguished a public space that worked from one that didn't. As a Columbia undergraduate, in 1974, Paco heard a lecture on Whyte's work and, he recalls, left the room "walking on air." He immediately read everything Whyte had written. He emptied his bank account to buy cameras and film and make his own home movie, about a pedestrian mall in Poughkeepsie. He took his "little exercise" to Whyte's advocacy group, the Project for Public Spaces, and was offered a job. Soon, however, it dawned on Paco that Whyte's ideas could be taken a step further—that the same techniques he used to establish why a plaza worked or didn't work could also be used to determine why a store worked or didn't work. Thus was born the field of retail anthropology, and, not long afterward, Paco founded Envirosell, which in just over fifteen years has counseled some of the most familiar names in American retailing, from Levi Strauss to Kinney, Starbucks, McDonald's, Blockbuster, Apple Computer, A.T. & T., and a number of upscale retailers that Paco would rather not name. When Paco gets an assignment, he and his staff set up a series of video cameras throughout the test store and then back the cameras up with Envirosell staffers—trackers, as they're known— armed with clipboards. Where the cameras go and how many trackers Paco deploys depends on exactly what the store wants to know about its shoppers. Typically, though, he might use six cameras and two or three trackers, and let the study run for two or three days, so that at the end he would have pages and pages of carefully annotated tracking sheets and anywhere from a hundred to five hundred hours of film. These days, given the expansion of his business, he might tape fifteen thousand hours in a year, and, given that he has been in operation since the late seventies, he now has well over a hundred thousand hours of tape in his library. Even in the best of times, this would be a valuable archive. But today, with the retail business in crisis, it is a gold mine. The time per visit that the average American spends in a shopping mall was sixty-six minutes last year—down from seventy-two minutes in 1992—and is the lowest number ever recorded. The amount of selling space per American shopper is now more than double what it was in the mid-seventies, meaning that profit margins have never been narrower, and the costs of starting a retail business—and of failing—have never been higher. In the past few years, countless dazzling new retailing temples have been built along Fifth and Madison Avenues—Barneys, Calvin Klein, Armani, Valentino, Banana Republic, Prada, Chanel, Nike Town, and on and on—but it is an explosion of growth based on no more than a hunch, a hopeful multimillion-dollar gamble that the way to break through is to provide the shopper with spectacle and more spectacle. "The arrogance is gone," Millard Drexler, the president and CEO of the Gap, told me. "Arrogance makes failure. Once you think you know the answer, it's almost always over." In such a competitive environment, retailers don't just want to know how shoppers behave in their stores. They have to know. And who better to ask than Paco Underhill, who in the past decade and a half has analyzed tens of thousands of hours of shopping videotape and, as a result, probably knows more about the strange habits and quirks of the species Emptor americanus than anyone else alive?

## 2.

Paco is considered the originator, for example, of what is known in the trade as the butt-brush theory—or, as Paco calls it, more delicately, le facteur bousculade—which holds that the likelihood of a woman's being converted from a browser to a buyer is inversely proportional to the likelihood of her being brushed on her behind while she's examining merchandise. Touch—or brush or bump or jostle—a woman on the behind when she has stopped to look at an item, and she will bolt. Actually, calling this a theory is something of a misnomer, because Paco doesn't offer any explanation for why women react that way, aside from venturing that they are "more sensitive back there." It's really an observation, based on repeated and close analysis of his videotape library, that Paco has transformed into a retailing commandment: a women's product that requires extensive examination should never be placed in a narrow aisle.

Paco approaches the problem of the Invariant Right the same way. Some retail thinkers see this as a subject crying out for interpretation and speculation. The design guru Joseph Weishar, for example, argues, in his magisterial "Design for Effective Selling Space," that the Invariant Right is a function of the fact that we "absorb and digest information in the left part of the brain" and "assimilate and logically use this information in the right half," the result being that we scan the store from left to right and then fix on an object to the right "essentially at a 45 degree angle from the point that we enter." When I asked Paco about this interpretation, he shrugged, and said he thought the reason was simply that most people are right-handed. Uncovering the fundamentals of "why" is clearly not a pursuit that engages him much. He is not a theoretician but an empiricist, and for him the important thing is that in amassing his huge library of in-store time-lapse photography he has gained enough hard evidence to know how often and under what circumstances the Invariant Right is expressed and how to take advantage of it.

> **assimilate:**
> To take in and comprehend.

> **theoretician:**
> A person who theorizes or constructs theories.

> **empiricist:**
> A person who relies on observations or experiences.

What Paco likes are facts. They come tumbling out when he talks, and, because he speaks with a slight hesitation—lingering over the first syllable in, for example, "re-tail" or "design"—he draws you in, and you find yourself truly hanging on his words. "We have reached a historic point in American history," he told me in our very first conversation. "Men, for the first time, have begun to buy their own underwear." He then paused to let the comment sink in, so that I could absorb its implications, before he elaborated: "Which means that we have to totally rethink the way we sell that product." In the parlance of Hollywood scriptwriters, the best endings must be surprising and yet inevitable; and the best of Paco's pronouncements take the same shape. It would never have occurred to me to wonder about the increasingly critical role played by touching—or, as Paco calls it, petting—clothes in the course of making the decision to buy them. But then I went to the Gap and to Banana Republic and saw people touching and fondling and, one after another, buying shirts and sweaters laid out on big wooden tables, and what Paco told me—which was no doubt based on what he had seen on his videotapes—made perfect sense: that the reason the Gap and Banana Republic have tables is not merely that sweaters and shirts look better there, or that tables fit into the warm and relaxing residential feeling that the Gap and Banana Republic are trying to create in their stores, but that tables invite—indeed, symbolize—touching. "Where do we eat?" Paco asks. "We eat, we pick up food, on tables."

> **implications:**
> Significance or deeper meaning.

Paco produces for his clients a series of carefully detailed studies, totaling forty to a hundred and fifty pages, filled with product-by-product breakdowns and bright-colored charts and graphs. In one recent case, he was asked by a major clothing retailer to analyze the first of a new chain of stores that the firm planned to open. One of the things the client wanted to know was how successful the store was in drawing people into its depths, since the chances that shoppers will buy something are directly related to how long they spend shopping, and how long they spend shopping is directly related to how deep they get pulled into the store. For this reason, a supermarket will often put dairy products on one side, meat at the back, and fresh produce on the other side, so that the typical shopper can't just do a drive-by but has to make an entire circuit of the store, and be tempted by everything the supermarket has to offer. In the case of the new clothing store, Paco found that ninety-one percent of all shoppers penetrated as deep as what he called Zone 4, meaning more than three-quarters of the way in, well past the accessories and shirt racks and belts in the front, and little short of the far wall, with the changing rooms and the pants stacked on shelves. Paco regarded this as an extraordinary figure, particularly for a long, narrow store like this one, where it is not unusual for the rate of penetration past, say, Zone 3 to be under fifty percent. But that didn't mean the store was perfect—far from it. For Paco, all kinds of questions remained.

Purchasers, for example, spent an average of eleven minutes and twenty-seven seconds in the store, nonpurchasers two minutes and thirty-six seconds. It wasn't that the nonpurchasers just cruised in and out: in those two minutes and thirty-six seconds, they went deep into the store and examined an average of 3.42 items. So why didn't they buy? What, exactly, happened to cause some browsers to buy and other browsers to walk out the door?

Then, there was the issue of the number of products examined. The purchasers were looking at an average of 4.81 items but buying only 1.33 items. Paco found this statistic deeply disturbing. As the retail market grows more cutthroat, store owners have come to realize that it's all but impossible to increase the number of customers coming in, and have concentrated instead on getting the customers they do have to buy more. Paco thinks that if you can sell someone a pair of pants you must also be able to sell that person a belt, or a pair of socks, or a pair of underpants, or even do what the Gap does so well: sell a person a complete outfit. To Paco, the figure 1.33 suggested that the store was doing something very wrong, and one day when I visited him in his office he sat me down in front of one of his many VCRs to see how he looked for the 1.33 culprit.

It should be said that sitting next to Paco is a rather strange experience. "My mother says that I'm the best-paid spy in America," he told me. He laughed, but he wasn't entirely joking. As a child, Paco had a nearly debilitating stammer, and, he says, "since I was never that comfortable talking I always relied on my eyes to understand things."

**debilitating:** Impairing a person's ability to function normally.

That much is obvious from the first moment you meet him: Paco is one of those people who look right at you, soaking up every nuance and detail. It isn't a hostile gaze, because Paco isn't hostile at all. He has a big smile, and he'll call you "chief" and use your first name a lot and generally act as if he knew you well. But that's the awkward thing: he has looked at you so closely that you're sure he does know you well, and you, meanwhile, hardly know him at all. This kind of asymmetry is even more pronounced when you watch his shopping videos with him, because every movement or gesture means something to Paco—he has spent his adult life deconstructing the shopping experience—but nothing to the outsider, or, at least, not at first. Paco had to keep stopping the video to get me to see things through his eyes before I began to understand. In one sequence, for example, a camera mounted high on the wall outside the changing rooms documented a man and a woman shopping for a pair of pants for what appeared to be their daughter, a girl in her mid-teens. The tapes are soundless, but the basic steps of the shopping dance are so familiar to Paco that, once I'd grasped the general idea, he was able to provide a running commentary on what was being said and thought. There is the girl emerging from the changing room wearing her first pair. There she is glancing at her reflection in the mirror, then turning to see herself from the back. There is the mother looking on. There is the father—or, as fathers are known in the trade, the "wallet carrier"—stepping forward and pulling up the jeans. There's the girl trying on another pair. There's the primp again. The twirl. The mother. The wallet carrier. And then again, with another pair. The full sequence lasted twenty minutes, and at the end came the take-home lesson, for which Paco called in one of his colleagues, Tom Moseman, who had supervised the project. "This is a very critical moment," Tom, a young, intense man wearing little round glasses, said, and he pulled up a chair next to mine. "She's saying, 'I don't know whether I should wear a belt.' Now here's the salesclerk. The girl says to him, 'I need a belt,' and he says, 'Take mine.' Now there he is taking her back to the full-length mirror." A moment later, the girl returns, clearly happy with the purchase. She wants the jeans. The wallet carrier turns to her, and then gestures to the salesclerk. The wallet carrier is telling his daughter to give back the belt. The girl gives back the belt. Tom stops the tape. He's leaning forward now, a finger jabbing at the screen. Beside me, Paco is shaking his head. I don't get it—at least, not at first—and so Tom replays that last segment. The wallet carrier tells the girl to give back the belt. She gives back the belt. And then, finally, it dawns on me why this store has an average purchase number of only 1.33. "Don't you see?" Tom said. "She wanted the belt. A great opportunity to make an add-on sale . . . lost!"

**nuance:**
Subtle distinctions and variations of something.

**asymmetry:**
Not balanced or evenly proportioned.

**deconstructing:**
Dissecting or picking apart to examine.

**3.**

Should we be afraid of Paco Underhill? One of the fundamental anxieties of the American consumer, after all, has always been that beneath the pleasure and the frivolity of the shopping experience runs an undercurrent of manipulation, and that anxiety has rarely seemed more justified than today. The practice of prying into the minds and habits of American consumers is now a multibillion-dollar business. Every time a product is pulled across a supermarket checkout scanner, information is recorded, assembled, and sold to a market-research firm for analysis. There are companies that put tiny cameras inside frozen-food cases in supermarket aisles; market-research firms that feed census data and behavioral statistics into algorithms and come out with complicated maps of the American consumer; anthropologists who sift through the garbage of carefully targeted households to analyze their true consumption patterns; and endless rounds of highly organized focus groups and questionnaire takers and phone surveyors. That some people are now tracking our every shopping move with video cameras seems in many respects the last straw: Paco's movies are, after all, creepy. They look like the surveillance videos taken during convenience store holdups—hazy and soundless and slightly warped by the angle of the lens. When you watch them, you find yourself waiting for something bad to happen, for someone to shoplift or pull a gun on a cashier.

The more time you spend with Paco's videos, though, the less scary they seem. After an hour or so, it's no longer clear whether simply by watching people shop—and analyzing their every move—you can learn how to control them. The shopper that emerges from the videos is not **pliable** or **manipulable**. The screen shows people filtering in and out of stores, petting and moving on, abandoning their merchandise because checkout lines are too long, or leaving a store empty-handed because they couldn't fit their stroller into the aisle between two shirt racks. Paco's shoppers are **fickle** and headstrong, and are quite unwilling to buy anything unless conditions are perfect—unless the belt is presented at exactly the right moment. His theories of the butt-brush and petting and the Decompression Zone and the Invariant Right seek not to make shoppers conform to the desires of sellers but to make sellers conform to the desires of shoppers. What Paco is teaching his clients is a kind of slavish devotion to the shopper's every whim. He is teaching them humility. Paco has worked with supermarket chains, and when you first see one of his videos of grocery aisles it looks as if he really had—at least in this instance—got one up on the shopper. The clip he showed me was of a father shopping with a small child, and it was an example of what is known in the trade as "advocacy," which basically means what happens when your

**pliable:**
Easily swayed or convinced.

**manipulable:**
Able to be manipulated.

**fickle:**
Erratic or frequently changing opinions.

four-year-old goes over and grabs a bag of cookies that the store has conveniently put on the bottom shelf, and demands that it be purchased. In the clip, the father takes what the child offers him. "Generally, dads are not as good as moms at saying no," Paco said as we watched the little boy approach his dad. "Men tend to be more impulse-driven than women in grocery stores. We know that they tend to shop less often with a list. We know that they tend to shop much less frequently with coupons, and we know, simply by watching them shop, that they can be marching down the aisle and something will catch their eye and they will stop and buy." This kind of weakness on the part of fathers might seem to give the supermarket an advantage in the cookie-selling wars, particularly since more and more men go grocery shopping with their children. But then Paco let drop a hint about a study he'd just done in which he discovered, to his and everyone else's amazement, that shoppers had already figured this out, that they were already one step ahead—that families were avoiding the cookie aisle. This may seem like a small point. But it begins to explain why, even though retailers seem to know more than ever about how shoppers behave, even though their efforts at intelligence-gathering have rarely seemed more intrusive and more formidable, the retail business remains in crisis. The reason is that shoppers are a moving target. They are becoming more and more complicated, and retailers need to know more and more about them simply to keep pace.

> **formidable:** Causing fear, paranoia, or a sense of dread.

**4.**

This doesn't mean that marketers and retailers have stopped trying to figure out what goes on in the minds of shoppers. One of the hottest areas in market research, for example, is something called typing, which is a sophisticated attempt to predict the kinds of products that people will buy or the kind of promotional pitch they will be susceptible to on the basis of where they live or how they score on short standardized questionnaires. One market-research firm in Virginia, Claritas, has divided the entire country, neighborhood by neighborhood, into sixty-two different categories—Pools & Patios, Shotguns & Pickups, Bohemia Mix, and so on—using census data and results from behavioral surveys. On the basis of my address in Greenwich Village, Claritas classifies me as Urban Gold Coast, which means that I like Kellogg's Special K, spend more than two hundred and fifty dollars on sports coats, watch "Seinfeld," and buy metal polish. Such typing systems—and there are a number of them—can be scarily accurate. I actually do buy Kellogg's Special K, have spent more than two hundred and fifty dollars on a sports coat, and watch "Seinfeld." (I don't buy metal polish.) In fact, when I was typed by a company called Total Research, in Princeton, the results were so dead-on that I got the same kind of creepy feeling that I got when I first watched Paco's videos.

**innocuous:**
Harmless or
inoffensive.

On the basis of a seemingly innocuous multiple-choice test, I was scored as an eighty-nine-per-cent Intellect and a seven-per-cent Relief Seeker (which I thought was impressive until John Morton, who developed the system, told me that virtually everyone who reads *The New Yorker* is an Intellect). When I asked Morton to guess, on the basis of my score, what kind of razor I used, he riffed, brilliantly, and without a moment's hesitation. "If you used an electric razor, it would be a Braun," he began. "But, if not, you're probably shaving with Gillette, if only because there really isn't an Intellect safety-razor positioning out there. Schick and Bic are simply not logical choices for you, although I'm thinking, You're fairly young, and you've got that Relief Seeker side. It's possible you would use Bic because you don't like that all-American, overly confident masculine statement of Gillette. It's a very, very conventional positioning that Gillette uses. But then they've got the technological angle with the Gillette Sensor. . . . I'm thinking Gillette. It's Gillette."

**predilections:**
An established
or consistent
preference for
something.

He was right. I shave with Gillette—though I didn't even know that I do. I had to go home and check. But information about my own predilections may be of limited usefulness in predicting how I shop. In the past few years, market researchers have paid growing attention to the role in the shopping experience of a type of consumer known as a Market Maven. "This is a person you would go to for advice on a car or a new fashion," said Linda Price, a marketing professor at the University of South Florida, who first came up with the Market Maven concept, in the late eighties. "This is a person who has information on a lot of different products or prices or places to shop. This is a person who likes to initiate discussions with consumers and respond to requests. Market Mavens like to be helpers in the marketplace. They take you shopping. They go shopping for you, and it turns out they are a lot more prevalent than you would expect." Mavens watch more television than almost anyone else does, and they read more magazines and open their junk mail and look closely at advertisements and have an awful lot of influence on everyone else. According to Price, sixty percent of Americans claim to know a Maven.

The key question, then, is not what I think but what my Mavens think. The challenge for retailers and marketers, in turn, is not so much to figure out and influence my preferences as to figure out and influence the preferences of my Mavens, and that is a much harder task. "What's really interesting is that the distribution of Mavens doesn't vary by ethnic category, by income, or by professional status," Price said. "A working woman is just as likely to be a Market Maven as a nonworking woman. You might say that Mavens are likely to be older, unemployed people, but that's wrong, too. There is simply not a clear demographic guide to how to find these people." More important, Mavens are better consumers than most of the rest of us. In another of the typing systems, developed by the California-based SRI International, Mavens are considered to be a subcategory of the consumer type known as Fulfilled, and Fulfilleds, one SRI official told me, are "the consumers from Hell—they are very feature oriented." He explained, "They are not pushed by promotions. You can reach them, but it's an intellectual argument." As the complexity of the marketplace grows, in other words, we have responded by appointing the most skeptical and the most savvy in our midst to mediate between us and sellers. The harder stores and manufacturers work to sharpen and refine their marketing strategies, and the harder they try to read the minds of shoppers, the more we hide behind Mavens.

**5.**

Imagine that you want to open a clothing store, men's and women's, in the upper-middle range—say, khakis at fifty dollars, dress shirts at forty dollars, sports coats and women's suits at two hundred dollars and up. The work of Paco Underhill would suggest that in order to succeed you need to pay complete and concentrated attention to the whims of your customers. What does that mean, in practical terms? Well, let's start with what's called the shopping gender gap. In the retail-store study that Paco showed me, for example, male buyers stayed an average of nine minutes and thirty-nine seconds in the store and female buyers stayed twelve minutes and fifty-seven seconds. This is not atypical. Women always shop longer than men, which is one of the major reasons that in the standard regional mall women account for seventy percent of the dollar value of all purchases. "Women have more patience than men," Paco says. "Men are more distractible. Their tolerance level for confusion or time spent in a store is much shorter than women's." If you wanted, then, you could build a store designed for men, to try to raise that thirty-percent sales figure to forty or forty-five percent. You could make the look more masculine—more metal, darker woods. You could turn up the music. You could simplify the store, put less product on the floor. "I'd go narrow and deep," says James Adams, the design director for NBBJ Retail Concepts, a division of one of the country's largest retail-design firms. "You wouldn't have fifty different cuts of pants. You'd have your four basics with lots of color. You know the Garanimals they used to do to help kids pick out clothes, where you match the giraffe top with the giraffe bottom? I'm sure every guy is like 'I wish I could get those, too.' You'd want to stick with the basics. Making sure most of the color story goes together. That is a big deal with guys, because they are always screwing the colors up."

When I asked Carrie Gennuso, the Gap's regional vice-president for New York, what she would do in an all-male store, she laughed and said, "I might do fewer displays and more signage. Big signs. Men! Smalls! Here!" As a rule, though, you wouldn't want to cater to male customers at the expense of female ones. It's no accident that many clothing stores have a single look in both men's and women's sections, and that the quintessential nineties look—light woods, white walls—is more feminine than masculine. Women are still the shoppers in America, and the real money is to be made by making retailing styles more female-friendly, not less.

To appeal to men, then, retailers do subtler things. At the Banana Republic store on Fifth Avenue in midtown, the men's socks are displayed near the shoes and between men's pants and the cash register (or cash/wrap, as it is known in the trade), so that the man can grab them easily as he rushes to pay. Women's accessories are by the fitting rooms, because women are much more likely to try on pants first, and then choose an item like a belt or a bag. At the men's shirt table, the display shirts have matching ties on them-the tie table is next to it-in a grownup version of the Garanimals system. But Banana Republic would never match scarves with women's blouses or jackets. "You don't have to be that direct with women," Jeanne Jackson, the president of Banana Republic, told me. "In fact, the Banana woman is proud of her sense of style. She puts her own looks together." Jackson said she liked the Fifth Avenue store because it's on two floors, so she can separate men's and women's sections and give men what she calls "clarity of offer," which is the peace of mind that they won't inadvertently end up in, say, women's undergarments. In a one-floor store, most retailers would rather put the menswear up front and the women's wear at the back (that is, if they weren't going to split the sexes left and right), because women don't get spooked navigating through apparel of the opposite sex, whereas men most assuredly do. (Of course, in a store like the Gap at Thirty-ninth and Fifth, where, Carrie Gennuso says, "I don't know if I've ever seen a man," the issue is moot. There, it's safe to put the women's wear out front.)

The next thing retailers want to do is to encourage the shopper to walk deep into the store. The trick there is to put "destination items"—basics, staples, things that people know you have and buy a lot of—at the rear of the store. Gap stores, invariably, will have denim, which is a classic destination item for them, on the back wall. Many clothing stores also situate the cash/wrap and the fitting rooms in the rear of the store, to compel shoppers to walk back into Zone 3 or 4. In the store's prime real estate—which, given Paco's theory of the Decompression Zone and the Invariant Right, is to the right of the front entrance and five to fifteen paces in—you always put your hottest and newest merchandise, because that's where the maximum number of people will see it. Right now, in virtually every Gap in the country, the front of the store is devoted to the Gap fall look—casual combinations in black and gray, plaid shirts and jackets, sweaters, black wool and brushed-twill pants. At the Gap at Fifth Avenue and Seventeenth Street, for example, there is a fall ensemble of plaid jacket, plaid shirt, and black pants in the first prime spot, followed, three paces later, by an ensemble of gray sweater, plaid shirt, T-shirt, and black pants, followed, three paces after that, by an ensemble of plaid jacket, gray sweater, white T-shirt, and black pants. In all, three variations on the same theme, each placed so that the eye bounces naturally from the first to the second to the third, and then, inexorably, to a table deep inside Zone 1 where merchandise is arrayed and folded for petting. Every week or ten days, the combinations will change, the "look" highlighted at the front will be different, and the entryway will be transformed.

Through all of this, the store environment—the lighting, the colors, the fixtures—and the clothes have to work together. The point is not so much beauty as coherence. The clothes have to match the environment. "In the nineteen-seventies, you didn't have to have a complete wardrobe all the time," Gabriella Forte, the president and chief operating officer of Calvin Klein, says. "I think now the store has to have a complete point of view. It has to have all the options offered, so people have choices. It's the famous one-stop shopping. People want to come in, be serviced, and go out. They want to understand the clear statement the designer is making."

> **coherence:** Logical and visually appealing sense of order.

All this imagemaking seeks to put the shopping experience in a different context, to give it a story line. "I wish that the customers who come to my stores feel the same comfort they would entering a friend's house—that is to say, that they feel at ease, without the impression of having to deal with the 'sanctum sanctorum' of a designer," Giorgio Armani told me. Armani has a house. Donna Karan has a kitchen and a womb. Ralph Lauren has a men's club. Calvin Klein has an art gallery. These are all very different points of view. What they have in common is that they have nothing to do with the actual act of shopping. (No one buys anything at a friend's house or a men's club.) Presumably, by engaging in this kind of misdirection designers aim to put us at ease, to create a kind of oasis. But perhaps they change the subject because they must, because they cannot offer an ultimate account of the shopping experience itself. After all, what do we really know, in the end, about why people buy? We know about the Invariant Right and the Decompression Zone. We know to put destination items at the back and fashion at the front, to treat male shoppers like small children, to respect the female derrière, and to put the socks between the cash/wrap and the men's pants. But this is grammar; it's not prose. It is enough. But it is not much.

**Let's Pause Here•••▶** What was your overall impression of Gladwell's essay? Were you surprised to learn the amount of time, money, and brainpower that goes into the shopping experience? Were you aware of this science prior to reading Gladwell's explanation of it? How many of the shopping habits that he describes do you take part in as a consumer?

**Let's Take It Further•••▼**

1. Gladwell makes a point of explaining that Paco Underhill—the leading force in retail advertising at the time this essay was published—observes shoppers and collects data, but that he isn't interested in constructing theories to explain shoppers' actions. But Gladwell is interested in the possible theories rather than simply recording the data. In light of Gladwell's preference, consider the phenomenon of the "Invariant Right." Do you have any explanations or theories that might make sense of this habit in shoppers? What might account for our tendency to enter a building and turn (or look) right?

2. Based on the writing strategies and examples that Gladwell employs throughout his essay, who do you think his target audience is? Shoppers or retailers? Advertisers or Mavens? How does he appeal to one of these groups more than another? What is the dominant message of the overall essay?

3. How do you feel about Paco Underhill's observation that women will stop shopping immediately when brushed from behind—what he calls the "butt-brush theory"—while looking at items in a store? What might explain this phenomenon?

4. Gladwell goes to great lengths to explain the appeal of merchandise tables in stores. At the time that he published this essay, the Gap and Banana Republic were among a small group of retailers that used this particular consumer-friendly approach to shopping. Which other popular retail chains use this method now? Why do you think it has caught on? Do you agree with the explanation given by Gladwell about the appeal of tables, or is there some other appeal that he fails to mention?

5. Do any of the retail terms for customers mentioned in this essay strike you as strange or offensive? For example, how do you feel about the fact that fathers are called "wallet carriers" by people in the retail trade?

6. Do you agree with Gladwell's point about shoppers inherently understanding the "undercurrent of manipulation" in the shopping experience? If you are aware of the purposeful manipulation, how have you noticed it during your own shopping experiences? What do you do to push back, or to not fall victim to the manipulation of retailers?

7. Go to a mall and observe the habits of shoppers in a similar fashion employed by Paco Underhill. Which of his observations did you witness? What additional observations did you make about shoppers that weren't mentioned in Gladwell's essay? What might the habits that you observed tell you if you were in the retail industry and attempting to better understand your customers?

8. If you are in agreement with Calvin Klein's Madison Avenue store architect, John Pawson, when he states, "People who enter [the store] are given a sense of release," and that

"they are in a calm space," then explain the way in which the act of shopping is a relief from the worries of life. How, for example, does the experience of walking into a store to potentially spend money allow you to feel better about your life, your job, or anything else that might be causing you stress? Give specific descriptions of the process of shopping—from the moment you make the decision to go shopping until the moment you return home with your purchases—that illustrate the calming effects of shopping.

9. Locate a "retail anthropology" book or journal and see what new trends have been observed in shoppers since the publication of this essay. How have shoppers adapted to the way retailers attempt to manipulate them with their store geography? What new techniques are retailers employing to keep customers in their stores longer and purchase more products? Finally, go visit a retail space and explain how they are (or are not) implementing the latest retail anthropology findings. Are the methods being employed actually effective? Why or why not?

10. Explain the work that Paco Underhill is doing these days. How does he continue to change the geography of retail? Describe specific ways in which he explains how to incorporate his findings into a business strategy. Are there other notable people who have risen in the field of retail science since this essay's publication? How have marketing programs (and college courses offered) changed to address Underhill's scientific findings in this budding field of study?

11. Gladwell describes a savvy shopper as a "Market Maven," which is someone who is not easily manipulated, who keeps track of prices, who knows which products are superior in quality, and so on. If you know a Market Maven (or if you are one yourself), explain the ways in which he gathers information on products, services, shopping trends, and even retailers. Why do you respect this person's opinion when he gives suggestions about where to shop, what prices are fair to pay, and any other shopping advice he might give you? How does the Maven's advice differ from "regular" shoppers you know?

12. How has the act of shopping (as well as the existence of "Market Mavens") changed in light of online retail sales, rating systems, and communities of shoppers? In other words, how might a rating and review system, such as those featured on Amazon and similar sites, change the ways in which Mavens can use their expertise to influence other people's shopping habits? Locate Mavens on Amazon (who the site calls its "Top Reviewers") and view some of the many thousands (as is usually the case) of their ratings and reviews. How good is their advice? How thorough are their reviews? How have other shoppers responded favorably (or unfavorably) to the advice and suggestions of the Mavens? How might future marketing and advertising people account for the Mavens' power in the era of online shopping and advice?

13. Write a review (or create a video review) of a product or service available online and discuss the positives and negatives of the item you are reviewing. Be sure to view other online reviews or ratings and follow a similar format. Accompany your review with an essay that explains how you are attempting to praise the product or service, as well as how you are attempting to illustrate any flaws or shortcomings that a business would be unlikely to disclose themselves.

# Should We Admire Wal-Mart? Some say it's evil. Others insist it's a model of all that's right with America. Who are we to believe?

Jerry Useem

**Let's Start Here•••▶** One important element of the shopping experience—and a key to marketing and advertisement's core reasons for existence—is the choices we consumers make about where we shop and what we buy. For some consumers, the decision to shop at a store is just as important as what they are going to the store to buy. Those who prefer organic foods are more likely (and often more willing) to pay higher prices and shop at stores that specifically cater to them. Those who are looking for the lowest possible price (without as much concern with, say, quality or business ethics) will likely be less concerned with a store's reputation and more interested in simply who carries the cheapest goods.

For people who are politically motivated enough to consider the ethics of a particular business (for example, Starbucks and their commitment to fair trade), the way a business conducts itself, pays its employees, and works with local communities is every bit as important (if not more so) than the best value for each dollar spent.

At the heart of the debate on business ethics, one company has consistently been both praised and denounced as it continues its stellar rise to worldwide dominance. That company is Wal-Mart, an international corporate giant with humble beginnings in Bentonville, Arkansas. As the discount chain has grown in number and market power (it currently has more than 8,900 stores in 55 countries), the amount of praise and criticism toward the company has grown to match its wildly successful business model.

In the following essay, Jerry Useem (an editor-at-large for *Fortune* magazine), dissects the Wal-Mart phenomenon in an attempt to get to the bottom of the question, "is Wal-Mart bad or good?" What follows is an essay that shows both sides of the debate. It explores the business practices that many people believe to be killing off the "mom and pop" businesses in the communities where Wal-Mart opens stores, and it examines the business practices that have allowed the company to thrive—even in cultures (such as China) that have been historically anticapitalist. As you read the essay, put aside your current beliefs about the company and see which side has a more logical- and ethical-sounding argument by the time you reach the end of Useem's essay.

---

Jerry Useem is the senior editor-at-large for *Fortune* magazine and writes about finance, business, business ethics, general management, and corporate enterprise. His articles have focused on subjects including crisis leadership, the history of the CEO, why companies fail, New York

Yankees manager Joe Iorre, and such Fortune 500 standards as General Electric, Wal-Mart stores, and Boeing. Useem was previously a senior writer at *Inc.* magazine and a casewriter and researcher at Harvard Business School. His writing has also appeared in such publications as the *Boston Globe, Wired, The American Prospect,* and *Business 2.0,* while his commentaries have been heard on National Public Radio. Useem is also a coauthor of the best-selling *Upward Bound: Nine Original Accounts of How Business Leaders Reached Their Summits.* This piece originally appeared in *Fortune* magazine for the week of March 8, 2004.

There is an evil company in Arkansas, some say. It's a discount store—a very, very big discount store—and it will do just about anything to get bigger. You've seen the headlines. Illegal immigrants mopping its floors. Workers locked inside overnight. A big gender discrimination suit. Wages low enough to make other companies' workers go on strike. And we know what it does to weaker suppliers and competitors. Crushing the dream of the independent proprietor—an ideal as American as Thomas Jefferson—it is the enemy of all that's good and right in our nation.

> **proprietor:** Business owner.

There is another big discount store in Arkansas, yet this one couldn't be more different from the first. Founded by a folksy entrepreneur whose notions of thrift, industry, and the square deal were pure Ben Franklin, this company is not a tyrant but a servant. Passing along the gains of its brilliant distribution system to consumers, its farsighted managers have done nothing less than democratize the American dream. Its low prices are spurring productivity and helping win the fight against inflation. It is America's most admired company.

Weirdest part is, both these companies are named Wal-Mart Stores Inc.

The more America talks about Wal-Mart, it seems, the more polarized its image grows. Its executives are credited with the most expansive of visions and the meanest of intentions; its CEO is presumed to be in league with Lex Luthor and St. Francis of Assisi. It's confusing. Which should we believe in: good Wal-Mart or evil Wal-Mart?

> **polarized:** Broken into two opposing parts.

Some of the allegations—and Wal-Mart was sued more than 6,000 times in 2002—certainly seem damning. Yet there's an important piece of context: Wal-Mart employs 1.4 million people. That's three times as many as the nation's next biggest employer and 56 times as many as the average FORTUNE 500 company. Meaning that all things being equal, a bad event is 5,500% more likely to happen at Wal-Mart than at Borders.

One consistent refrain is that Wal-Mart squeezes its suppliers to death—and you don't have to do much digging to find horror stories. But while Wal-Mart's reputation for penny-pinching is well deserved, so is its reputation for straightforwardness—none of the slotting fees, rebates, or other game playing that many merchants engage in. Nor has it ever been accused of throwing around its buying power improperly, as Toys "R" Us (and, long ago, A&P) was for demanding that its suppliers not sell to rivals.

Another rap on Wal-Mart—that it stomps competitors to dust through sheer brute force—seems undeniable: Studies have indicated a decline in the life expectancy of local businesses after Wal-Mart moves in. But this morality play is missing some key characters—namely, you and me. The scene where we drop into Wal-Mart to pick up a case of Coke, for instance, has been conveniently cut. No small omission, since the main reason we can't shop at Ed's Variety Store anymore is that we stopped shopping at Ed's Variety Store.

Evil Wal-Mart's original sin, then, was to open stores that sold things for less. This was a powerful idea but hardly a new one. The basic discipline of discounting had been around for at least a century—honed by department stores in the 1870s, by the Sears and Montgomery Ward catalogs in the 1890s, and then by chain stores like Woolworth and A&P. Though founder Sam Walton added a twist—a small town, he realized, could support a big store—he didn't invent the rules of discounting. He just followed them better than anyone else.

**consultancy:** An agency that provides consultations and advice to companies.

Not surprisingly, that's how the people running Good Wal-Mart see their story. They cast their jobs in almost missionary terms—"to lower the world's cost of living"—and in this, they have succeeded spectacularly. One consultancy estimates that Wal-Mart saves consumers $20 billion a year. Its constant push for low prices, meanwhile, puts the heat on suppliers and competitors to offer better deals.

That's a good thing, right? If a company achieves its lower prices by finding better and smarter ways of doing things, then yes, everybody wins. But if it cuts costs by cutting pay and benefits—or by sending production to China—then not everybody wins. And here's where the story of Good Wal-Mart starts to falter. Just as its Everyday Low Prices benefit shoppers who've never come near a Wal-Mart, there are mounting signs that its Everyday Low Pay (Wal-Mart's full-time hourly employees average $9.76 an hour) is hurting some workers who have never worked there. For example, unionized supermarkets in California—faced with studies showing a 13% to 16% drop in grocery prices after Wal-Mart enters a market—have been trying to slash labor costs to compete, triggering a protracted strike. The $15 billion in goods that Wal-Mart and its suppliers imported from China in 2003, meanwhile, accounted for nearly 11% of the U.S. total—contributing, some economists argue, to further erosion of U.S. wages.

Where you stand on Wal-Mart, then, seems to depend on where you sit. If you're a consumer, Wal-Mart is good for you. If you're a wage earner, there's a good chance it's bad. If you're a Wal-Mart shareholder, you want the company to grow. If you're a citizen, you probably don't want it growing in your backyard. So, which one are you?

And that's the point: Chances are, you're more than one. And you may think each role is important. Yet America has elevated one above the rest.

The consumer—as an entity with distinct rights and wishes—didn't exist before the first mass retailers called it into being. Even then it met with resistance. Early in the last century, a mayoral candidate in Warsaw, Iowa, proposed to fire city employees caught shopping from a catalog; in the 1930s, 27 states imposed special taxes on chain stores. But as organized labor began its slow decline, a new type of political activity—consumer activism—came to the fore. Other countries passed laws that protected workers and the small businesses that employed many of them. But in America, antitrust laws were designed to protect consumers.

> **fealty:**
> To be intensely faithful.

Wal-Mart swore fealty to the consumer and rode its coattails straight to the top. Now we have more than just a big retailer on our hands, though. We have a servant-king—one powerful enough to place everyone else in servitude to the consumer too. Gazing up at this new order, we wonder if our original choices made so much sense after all.

> **servitude:**
> Enslaved by someone or used by someone without any freedom on the used person's part.

This growing unease with the cost of "low cost" is the No. 1 threat facing Wal-Mart. And the company has begun to get it. "Shoppers could start feeling guilty about shopping with us," says spokeswoman Mona Williams. "Communities could make it harder to build our stores." Hence a flurry of corrective actions. Wal-Mart's new television spots advertise happy employees instead of low prices. It has ramped up its PR and lobbying efforts. And its leaders have begun to take external criticism more seriously. As Robert Slater quotes CEO Lee Scott in Slater's recent book, *The Wal-Mart Decade*, "Instead of throwing [a critical] article in the trash and saying it's inaccurate, we now say, 'Is it possible that this is true?'"

How far Wal-Mart's self-examination will go remains to be seen. A corporation can't be expected to stop growing, as many critics would like. But it can be expected to live up to its own rhetoric. Consider Ford Motor Co. Founder Henry Ford had a mix of motives when, in 1914, he announced the $5 day—a stunning increase over the prevailing wage. But among them was his recognition that the promise of a car for Everyman would ring hollow if his own workers couldn't afford one. Now Wal-Mart has been brought face to face with its own contradiction: Its promises of the good life threaten to ring increasingly hollow if it doesn't pay its workers enough to have that good life.

It's important that this debate continue. But in holding the mirror up to Wal-Mart, we would do well to turn it back on ourselves. Sam Walton created Wal-Mart. But we created it, too.

**Let's Pause Here•••▶** What is your initial reaction to Jerry Useem's essay on Wal-Mart? Did it in any way change your opinion or understanding of the company that you held prior to reading the essay? If so, how did your opinion of the company shift over the course of the essay? Do you think more or less of the company now? How familiar were you with the many woes that Wal-Mart has faced over the years in terms of bad publicity and lawsuits against the corporation? Do you think Wal-Mart is being treated fairly or unfairly by the media?

**Let's Take It Further•••▼**

1. Do you think that Jerry Useem maintains an objective—or nonjudgmental—attitude toward Wal-Mart in his essay? Does his treatment of the company seem fair, or does he seem to choose one side of the debate over the other? What about the manner in which he divides his time between the pros and cons of Wal-Mart proves his objectiveness, or, conversely, his judgment of the corporation?

2. Judging by the language Useem uses, as well as the manner in which he addresses the reader, who do you think Useem is attempting to bring into a more fair debate about Wal-Mart and its business practices? What does it mean that the essay was originally published in *Fortune* magazine? Does it change the way Useem has to address the issue of business ethics in his essay? How might it have been different if this were originally published in a different publication, such as a nationwide newspaper or TV news channel?

3. Why do you think Useem makes the following statement: "The scene where we drop into Wal-Mart to pick up a case of Coke, for instance, has been conveniently cut"? What does it mean for us as readers, and as American consumers? How does this idea, plus the last lines of Useem's essay ("Sam Walton created Wal-Mart. But we created it, too."), implicate us as playing a role in the Wal-Mart phenomenon?

4. What sorts of conversations have you overheard (or engaged in yourself) about the topic of Wal-Mart and its effect on communities both small and large? How do you feel about the company on the whole? For example, do lower prices trump everything else? Or would you be willing to pay higher prices if the company were to better pay its employees and suppliers?

5. According to Useem, "Wal-Mart's new television spots advertise happy employees instead of low prices." What do you think is the reason that the company has shifted its advertising of low prices into showing happy employees? What does that particular advertising strategy do for the store chain, especially in terms of the debate being discussed by Useem throughout his essay?

6. If Wal-Mart is indeed guilty of unethical business practices, how does that affect your impression of the store and whether you should shop there? Does it matter at all whether the places you shop are treating their employees well? How do a business's practices play into your decision about whether to shop there?

7. Research the types of lawsuits or public condemnation that have been leveled at Wal-Mart and discuss the outcome of one particular lawsuit or issue. How does the case prove that Wal-Mart's business practices are or are not ethical? How do the lawsuit's allegations and outcomes affect your opinion of the company for better or worse?

**8.** According to Mona Williams of Wal-Mart, one major concern the corporate giant faces is that "shoppers could start feeling guilty about shopping with us . . . [and] communities could make it harder to build our stores." Research the treatment of Wal-Mart by a major city where the discount chain was attempting to open stores (for example, Chicago, L.A., New York City, and Boston have all had very public battles with Wal-Mart). What arguments did the city have against Wal-Mart opening within their city limits? Do you agree or disagree with the arguments the city put forth? What was the outcome of the public disagreement? In other words, which one got their way, Wal-Mart or the city?

**9.** Research (by interviewing people in your community and finding local data from your Chamber of Commerce, for example) the effect Wal-Mart has had on your community or one nearby to prove or disprove the accusation that Wal-Mart squeezes out local competition when it enters the market. How many businesses existed prior to Wal-Mart entering the community, and how many of them shut their doors? How much did the average income in your community rise or fall after Wal-Mart's arrival? Finally, based on your findings, explain whether you believe Wal-Mart to be bad for or good for a community. Will (or should) this knowledge have any impact on your impression of the store and whether you will shop there? Why or why not?

**10.** Interview Wal-Mart employees and/or customers to determine their positions on the company and its business ethics. Do people who work for the company enjoy working there? Are there particular things they would like Wal-Mart to do in the community or for its employees? How do customers feel about the company, and how aware (if at all) are they of the various accusations made toward Wal-Mart about its business practices? How does this information help to shape your opinion of the company, if at all?

**11.** Visit the website www.walmartwatch.org to see some of the accusations being made currently toward Wal-Mart. Research one of the particular accusations and see how the company is addressing it, either in court or on its own website. Compare walmartwatch.org's representation of the company to the way the company represents itself online and in advertisements. Who makes a more convincing case? Describe the particular issue you research about Wal-Mart, and explain the story behind it and how it has progressed over time, if it has progressed at all.

# mash**it** UP

Here is a series of essay and discussion topics that draw connections between multiple selections within the chapter. They also suggest outside texts to include in your essay or discussion. Feel free to bring in further outside texts, remembering the variety of texts (beyond articles) available to you.

**1.** In his essay "The Science of Shopping," Malcolm Gladwell describes a particular kind of consumer that he defines as a "Market Maven."

In his best-selling book, *The Tipping Point*, which focuses on trends and the people who create them, Gladwell further explores the categories of people who have power when it comes to the purchasing decisions that others make. Read the first few chapters of the book, where he explains the various types of people who influence trends (among them the Maven), and apply these categories of people to the process of shopping specifically, explaining what their roles would be in shaping a shopping trend or fad.

2. "Kid Kustomers" focuses on advertising specifically geared toward children, while "The Science of Shopping" focuses on the ways retailers market to adults. Combine these two ideas and visit a children's store to see how retail anthropology is applied to the arena of children's retail stores. What are the similarities and differences between children's and adults' retail stores, and what do you think accounts for them?

3. As we saw in the essay "Ethnic Marketing: McDonald's Is Lovin' It," McDonald's leads the field of advertising in the manner in which they incorporate trends from minority groups into their advertising campaigns. Research other forms of "niche" marketing (or marketing to a smaller group of people who are defined by some trait that separates them from American culture at large) and see the ways in which marketers cater to whichever niche group you have decided to discuss. Are the methods used offensive or flattering? How effective is niche marketing on the groups that are being targeted?

4. Of all the comic strips that have been published over the years, none deals more directly with our culture of shopping and advertising than the nationally syndicated comic strip *Cathy*, which recently concluded after 34 years in print. Locate some of the comic strips that deal with Cathy's shopping addictions, her vulnerability to advertising, and the complicated feelings of guilt and relief that she felt whenever she shopped. Explain the role of shopping in her life and how it mirrors the role of shopping in our popular culture.

5. Locate other political cartoons that address current cultural issues dealing with consumerism and "read" the cartoon to explain the artist's intentions and message. Be sure to give some background on the issue itself in order to help your reader understand the cartoon's relevance. What, specifically, in the cartoon makes it apparent what the subject or topic is? What images show his or her opinion? What about the text, if there is any? What does it enable the artist to say about the topic he or she is addressing?

6. Compose a video or image collage made up of advertisements that together deliver specific messages to the viewer. For example, many scholars regularly attack advertising and the media in general as

giving people unattainable standards of beauty by regularly featuring models whose beauty might be impossible to achieve without surgery or even starving oneself. You should be sure to find a variety of ads for several different companies and products. Break down the particular trend or theme that emerges and explain what message is being portrayed to the viewer. Also, discuss whether you see the trend or message as positive or negative, and why.

7. Draw your own cartoon that addresses our cultural obsession with shopping and/or our love of advertising. Then explain how your cartoon illustrates consumer culture or advertising culture and its current place in our larger popular culture. What, specifically, in your cartoon makes it apparent what the subject or topic is? What images show your opinion? What about text you chose to include, if there is any? What do you hope the viewer will take away from your cartoon?

**Let's Connect •••▶** "Like" our Facebook page for free, up-to-date, additional readings, discussions, and writing ideas on the topics of shopping and advertising. Join other students and teachers across the country sharing in an online discussion of popular culture events. *American Mashup* is on Facebook at www.facebook.com/americanmashup.

# Chapter 10

# Heroes and Celebrities

## Making the Cultural Connection

Of the many popular culture elements with which most people are familiar, few are as widely observed and discussed in day-to-day life as the role of celebrities in American society. Entire industries have risen up around celebrities—from gossip magazines to paparazzi-style websites. Fans of any particular celebrity can obsessively follow the person's Tweets, scour the Internet for pictures or information, and even emulate the

## SELECTIONS IN THIS CHAPTER

way the celebrity dresses or acts, all with minimal work. So, too, do some heroes become celebrities in our culture. In fact, the ideas of heroes and celebrities are often so closely intertwined that at times it is difficult to make a distinction between the two. At the heart of this chapter is a search for where these two concepts intersect.

Consider, for example, the subject of this chapter's essay on the Navy SEALs who killed America's most-wanted criminal—Osama bin Laden. To many, these men are heroes who finally completed the nearly ten-year manhunt for the 9/11 mastermind. And yet, because of the nature of their work, which requires anonymity for safety reasons, few people know who these actual men are that comprise Navy SEAL Team 6. Nevertheless, these men are widely regarded as heroes, and they have been elevated to the status of international celebrities, despite there being no actual men to shower with praise. They are celebrities as an idea, rather than specific men with identities that can be made public. It is without question that their actions were heroic, but we will never know who these men actually are. Which begs the question, are these anonymous men celebrities if they cannot come forward to receive the accolades that our culture and media so wish we could give them? Are they more than heroes?

This chapter also seeks to address the differences between how our culture praises both heroes and celebrities. For example, what sorts of actions warrant the term "heroism"? How does a person or group of people become a celebrity for their heroic acts, and how—if at all—does a celebrity become a hero? Is one more meaningful than the other? Is one entitled to more praise? If you stop to consider that some people might consider heroes more worthy of praise than celebrities because their actions are, by definition, more important to people, because they actually make a difference in people's lives, then perhaps it becomes apparent that heroes play a more important role in our culture than celebrities. And yet, often heroes fall out of the public eye much more quickly than celebrities. This chapter will also address the notion of the "unsung hero," or a person who does heroic and noble things without being noticed or praised. This, to many, is the ultimate act of heroism—to do good work for the sake of doing good work, rather than praise. We are impressed that people do noble deeds with no need for adoration or recognition. This chapter also asks you to question what makes a person a hero. Saving lives? Aiding those in need? Lifting people out of unfortunate circumstances? It will also allow you to consider the definitions of heroes and heroism, as well as how we define the concept of fame and celebrity.

Though most of us understand the inherent value in heroism and wouldn't necessarily balk at being labeled a celebrity hero, we understand that there is a fundamental difference between a celebrity and a hero. For some, the idea of praising heroes seems much more legitimate than praising celebrities. After all, if we merely praise someone because she entertains us and because she is famous, it might seem to many as if this is a hollow or meaningless form of praise.

When it comes to celebrities and fame, many of us, for example, entertain the idea of being famous and becoming a celebrity. This is a common enough fantasy for most Americans. But the important thing to consider is what it actually means to *be* a celebrity. The concepts of celebrity and fame are not as simple as they might appear on the surface. After all, a person can become famous in many ways. The trick is to *remain* famous, or—better yet—to remain relevant. When most of us think of celebrities, we envision the glamorous men and women of Hollywood who entertain us with their acting, or the musicians whose work moves us emotionally. These are the celebrities with sticking power, the ones who generate movies and TV shows and albums that constantly keep them in the celebrity discussion, on the swiftly moving radar of popular culture. Sometimes when we think of celebrities we think of famous politicians, or even athletes. But there are many fleeting celebrities who are often only known for a brief while—though for that small amount of time they are widely known. Remember the White House "party crashers," the "Octomom" (pictured here), or the "Balloon Boy"? All of these people were major national stories and instant celebrities who slipped out of the public eye just as quickly as they entered—virtually overnight.

Our popular culture has a strange relationship with celebrities. If there were ever a perfect example of a love-hate relationship, the way we treat our celebrities would be it. On the one hand, we celebrate the rise of

a celebrity whenever he or she does something that warrants fame—a brilliant role in a movie, or a song that we cannot get out of our heads, for example. On the other hand, when a celebrity slips up and publicly breaks the law or otherwise humiliates himself in the all-encompassing way that some celebrities are prone to doing, we judge him harshly and quickly. It would seem that our culture feels that fame is something to be earned and constantly deserved. One public gaffe, one moral misstep, and we rush to pull our celebrities down from their pedestals and back into the mire of everyday existence alongside us.

So what explains these awkward and sensitive parameters of fame? How is it that we can worship a celebrity one moment and then reduce her to obscurity over the smallest mistake? And how is it that some celebrities are allowed to make colossal slip-ups and retain their fame, while others are pushed aside for minor infractions? Why do we sometimes praise a celebrity who fails and then attempts a comeback, while for others we do everything in our power to resist accepting a celebrity who has fallen out of favor for one reason or another? Who makes the judgment call, and why do we even bother holding them to a standard different than those to which we hold ourselves? These are some of the questions this chapter will seek to address as we pick apart the meaning of the word celebrity and the reasons that celebrities are important to our lives.

Besides celebrities and fame, we will discuss the importance of heroes to our culture and how they too sometimes become celebrities in their own right. We will dissect the roles that heroes play in our culture, and

how the iconic images such as the 9/11 flag raising pictured here become permanently etched into the collective memory of American popular culture the same way in which this famous Iwo Jima flag raising photograph has remained a long-lasting image of heroism for seven decades.

When memorable events such as these occur, we document heroism in an effort to later decipher what these events mean to our larger culture. For example, did these men raising flags in both instances understand the symbolism behind their actions? And how does the unity and bravery of these men come together around the flag, our nation's symbol? Is it the destruction around them that makes these images more meaningful, more heroic? In what way do these images and the stories that go with them compare and contrast with one another? How do we agree as a culture on the ways in which we most want to remember events such as these and attach something positive to an overwhelmingly negative event? These are the elements of heroism and celebrity that we will explore throughout the entirety of this chapter.

There is, of course, a large difference between heroes and celebrities, which this chapter will also address. We will discuss how celebrities are created and the ways in which we praise and critique them. We will discuss the meaning of heroism and how we give credibility to their actions by celebrating their acts of kindness, bravery, and selflessness. We will discuss how heroes sometimes become celebrities, and even the ways in which we create mythologies to attach to our national heroes.

Of course, the question is, at the end of the day, why do either heroes or celebrities matter? Why do we need people greater than ourselves to praise, whether or not the praise is deserved? How important are these larger-than-life people to our popular culture as a whole, and what role do they play in Americans' opinions of our country and ourselves? If someone's heroic actions go unnoticed, are they any less heroic or more heroic than a well-known act of heroism? If a celebrity commits an act of heroism (such as Sean Penn famously taking a motorboat to New Orleans in the aftermath of Hurricane Katrina to rescue stranded citizens), is it in any way cheapened by the fame that they have already achieved? Is it any less heroic? Is it more heroic? Ultimately, we will discover that it is a very American characteristic to want to praise individuals for their accomplishments. But we also have the tendency to occasionally celebrate the fall of a celebrity just as strongly as we might desire to applaud a hero. A famous person whom we adore one day might be loathed and cast aside the next. A person who does a good deed might become a media darling. We need our celebrities and our heroes.

The most important thing to keep in mind as you proceed through this chapter is that even though we might occasionally be hard on our celebrities, we seem to have some unexplained fascination with beautiful, successful people who are living a life most of us will never lead. In fact, in the essay titled "Superhero Worship," we will discover that the need to worship something or someone more glamorous than ourselves—even if it is a fictional character—is just as much a part of our American identity as hamburgers and French fries, as baseball and apple pie. Perhaps this is why we need our heroes as well—so that we can praise someone legitimately. We need someone or something to worship, to remind us that America is a land of celebrities and heroes. Perhaps we will not come up with any definitive answers to these questions, but we will at least begin to understand how these two elements of popular culture intermingle with one another, and maybe we will be more forgiving toward our celebrities and each other for our faults. And maybe we will find heroes all around us.

## Ground Hero

J. D. Crowe

J. D. Crowe, who has been a political cartoonist for over 29 years, is the author of, most recently, a book spanning four years of his work, titled *Smell the Love.* He lives in Fairhope, Alabama, where he is a cartoonist for the *Mobile* (Alabama) *Press-Register.* Mr. Crowe's cartoons have appeared in the *New York Times, The Washington Post,* and on CNN and CBS Sports. Mr. Crowe also contributes to the *Los Angeles Times, Sacramento Bee, Fort Worth Star-Telegram, Nonprofit Times, Counseling Today,* and *San Diego Magazine.* Online, his work can be viewed on Cagle's Professional Cartoonists Index (www.cagle.com). His cartoons are nationally syndicated with Artizans. This cartoon first appeared in the *Mobile Press-Register* on May 5, 2011.

GROUND HERO

# Thinking About Heroes and Heroism

Take a moment to look at the accompanying cartoon. Like most political cartoons, this drawing is attempting to make a statement about a topic that is popular in our culture. This cartoon's subject matter, which can be discerned at a glance, is the concept of heroism. The artist takes 9/11—and all the meaning attached to that particular event in American history—as his subject matter to show two different types of heroes. Of course, the events of 9/11, beyond being horrific and unimaginable, were also a major turning point in our nation's sense of identity. Americans united together in response to the event, and we widely praised those who came to the aid of the World Trade Center and Pentagon victims, as well as demanded action against our attackers. We needed heroism on that day and the days following, and there has been no shortage of men and women who rushed in to fill the void. From that particular event, many heroes have emerged.

It is worth noting that another outcome of 9/11 was the emergence of a different kind of hero. Police officers and firefighters became the symbol of the ultimate American hero for risking their lives to come to the aid of 9/11 victims. NYPD and FDNY became synonymous with bravery, self-sacrifice, and heroism. Police officers and firefighters have long been held high in the estimation of popular culture for their daily sacrifices made protecting their fellow citizens. But this event was different. More shocking. More immense. So the response to the acts of heroism displayed on 9/11 were equally immense. There were parades and memorial ceremonies. There were interviews and TV specials. Full-page spreads in newspapers and magazine covers all over the world. America embraced its new heroes, and many of them became celebrities in their own right.

Of course, this cartoon is addressing 9/11 heroes by depicting a firefighter shaking hands with another hero now associated with 9/11: a member of the Navy SEAL team that executed a late-night raid that resulted in Osama bin Laden's death. Why do you think the artist chose to bring these two types of heroes together in the same frame? What effect does this have on you as you view the drawing? Consider, for example, the manner in which Crowe depicts both men in the drawing. How does he praise heroism without going overboard or being melodramatic? How does he manage to depict solemnity and dignity in the form of a cartoon?

Now, take a closer look at Crowe's drawing. Notice some of the finer details. Why do you suppose he chose to name the cartoon "Ground Hero"? In what way is he playing with the notion of "Ground Zero," that now-famous phrase that describes the site where the Twin Towers fell? Is there a reason he chooses to blur the cartoon rather than have a sharp image of both figures? What is the effect of this particular choice on you as a viewer? Why do you suppose he has the two men shaking hands? What does this gesture imply about the seriousness of Crowe's subject? How would you choose to depict heroism in a drawing if you were asked to do so? Can you think of figures in American culture that are equally as heroic as those pictured in Miller's drawing? How, for example, would you begin to determine who is heroic and worthy of being praised for her heroism? As you continue reading the chapter, keep these questions in mind, particularly those that address how we define heroes and what acts are considered heroic.

# SEALs Who Killed Bin Laden Remain Secret Heroes in Hometown    William Selway

**Let's Start Here••• ▶** As we discussed in the chapter's introduction, the events of 9/11 have had a massive impact on American culture and identity for reasons that are both obvious and mysterious. For one, many people were shocked by the realization that America could be vulnerable to such an attack. After all, we are and remain one of the world's most militarily powerful countries. So how is it that we can have been taken by surprise?

Add to these thoughts the fact that one man, Osama bin Laden, publicly took credit for the 9/11 attacks, and it becomes clear how he became both a symbol for the 9/11 attacks, as well as the number one target for retaliation. Not only did bin Laden take credit, he also gloated by regularly releasing videos decrying the power and ethics of the United States. He released videos from hiding, taunting the United States and inflaming the shocked and horrified citizens of America who demanded that he be brought to justice.

In early May of 2011, justice was finally served. A team of elite soldiers—Navy SEALs—stormed the compound where bin Laden was hiding and eventually killed the world-famous terrorist and founder of al-Qaeda. What followed was an international celebration for what amounted to a nearly ten-year manhunt. The Navy SEAL team was praised for their bravery and success in most corners of the world. And yet, by virtue of their elite status, none of the SEALs came forward. But they were praised and deemed heroes despite this fact.

The following essay, by William Selway, describes the nature of fame and heroism in regard to these men whose identities will forever remain unknown. As you read the essay, observe the manner in which Selway describes the people whom he interviews, as well as the way in which these people speak about the anonymous heroes. Try to determine whether it is correct that these men remain anonymous, as well as whether praising them might be doing the opposite of what is intended by potentially placing these men in danger. Also, consider the idea of how the mythology behind unknown heroes grows larger than the stories of known heroes, due to the nature of the actual people being unknown.

---

William Selway is a Bloomberg News reporter who is responsible for coverage of municipal finance and state and local government in California. Selway, a University of Arizona graduate, has been with Bloomberg News in San Francisco since 2000, where he covered technology in the wake of the Internet bubble's collapse, the recall of Governor Gray Davis, and the fight over gay marriage, among other stories. His stories have won awards from groups including the Investigative Reporters and Editors, the New York Press Club, and the Society of American Business Editors and Writers. Before joining Bloomberg, he worked at *Dow Jones*, the *Bond Buyer* and *AFX News*. The following article first appeared for Bloomberg News on May 3, 2011.

As jets screamed over Naval Air Station Oceana behind his used-car lot in Virginia Beach, Richard DeBerry Jr. said he knows a member of Navy SEAL Team Six, the elite, secretive unit that killed Osama bin Laden.

That friendship still won't get him any details of the nighttime raid on the Pakistan compound of the terrorist who eluded capture for a decade.

"We're not even going to try to pick his brain about it—he's not going to say a thing," DeBerry, 33, said in an office lined with baseball caps from Navy servicemen who bought cars. "You get drunk with them and they won't tell you a thing about what happened on their missions. They don't even tell their wives."

The SEAL team emerged as local heroes, if discreet ones, in Tidewater, Virginia, where a complex of military bases sprawls from the shipyards in Norfolk to the Dam Neck compound where part of the unit is based.

**reconnaissance:**
Surveying enemy territory to gain information about the enemy and its forces.

The SEALs trace their roots to World War II, when they surveyed beaches and cleared obstacles for Allied amphibious landings. Today, SEALs—the name stands for Sea, Air and Land—perform commando assaults, unconventional warfare, reconnaissance and intelligence-gathering.

## Professionalism in Uniform

Such special operations forces have played a key role since the beginning of the conflict against al-Qaeda in Afghanistan in 2001, when they worked with the Northern Alliance against the Taliban.

"You've got a process of evolution since Vietnam that has not only created a more professional military but a far more professional group of intelligence operatives and special forces," said Anthony Cordesman, a national-security analyst with the Center for Strategic and International Studies in Washington.

The SEAL strike team flew May 1 in helicopters to bin Laden's Abbottabad compound under the cover of darkness, and during a 40-minute raid worked its way through the structure, confronting and killing him on a top floor, according to White House counterterrorism adviser John Brennan and other administration, defense, and intelligence officials. President Barack Obama and national security officials listened to an audio feed and heard the code words that let them know bin Laden was dead.

## SEALs and Delta

In Virginia Beach, the base of bin Laden's killers in a heavily guarded compound isn't marked by name. Its Army counterpart is Delta Force, headquartered at Fort Bragg, North Carolina. The teams are part of the Joint Special Operations Command, which also oversees the Army's 160th Special Operations Aviation Regiment with helicopters to get the commandos to work and the 75th Ranger Regiment with infantry shock troops to back up the commandos with more firepower.

Around Virginia Beach, a city of about 433,000 dominated by strip malls and suburban sprawl around the military bases, there were no signs of public tribute to the SEALs who killed America's most-wanted man.

Service members were loath to discuss it. One told a reporter that the mention of a bar as a gathering spot for SEALs might get it blacklisted by the military, lest it tip off enemies wishing to retaliate.

Around the town dominated by military, their families, and businesses that cater to them, residents said in interviews that their joy at the death of bin Laden was tinged with anxiety as troops are still waging two wars launched in the wake of the attacks on Sept. 11, 2001.

## Joy and Melancholy

Standing on the lawn outside her mobile home, Marilyn Hargiss, 60, recounted her mixed emotions at the news of the terrorist's death. She said her son-in-law is overseas with the Navy, which has kept him from his three daughters and year-and-a-half-old son for more than three months.

"I'm proud of our military," she said. "They wouldn't let up and they kept looking until they found him."

Diamond Desmond, 33, served eight years in the Navy—"the best of the armed services in my opinion"—leaving in 2007 after eight years. She said that while serving on a carrier she helped ferry troops to Iraq and saw the devastation firsthand during 18 months when she was posted to the Navy's medical center in Bethesda, Maryland.

Desmond, while working at a lingerie store near the Oceana base, said another terrorist would likely take bin Laden's place, and that his death provides slim solace to those who lost loved ones in war.

## Continuing Fire

"I'm excited that they caught him," she said. "There's still going to be a long list. It's going to be never-ending. Someone's going to step up."

DeBerry, the car dealer, said he has more than half a dozen relatives and friends in uniform.

"It's an uncomfortable feeling," he said. "What's going to happen next?"

"We don't feel this is the end," he said. "Not at all, the fire's just getting started now."

Hargiss said her pleasure at bin Laden's demise was tempered by the continuing struggle.

"Once the dust settles and we get past all the celebrating, they'll start wondering, what now? What's next?" she said. "I'd like to bring those kids home."

**Let's Pause Here•••▶** What was your overall impression of the essay? Do you think the manner in which Selway constructs his essay does justice to the men he is attempting to praise? Or do you believe that all the attention might have the opposite effect? Whether or not you agree with their actions—which have been debated at great length since the killing of bin Laden—do you think they should be praised and rewarded in some fashion? Should there be a national recognition, or do you think that the praise these men received in the media following the killing was sufficient?

**Let's Take It Further•••▼**

1. How is it that the mythology of these men has grown or shifted in the time since the killing of bin Laden? In what ways has the story grown larger and more heroic, or has it grown less heroic and faded from memory? What do you think might account for the shift in story?

2. Whom do you believe to be Selway's intended audience in his essay? Is he attempting to address the general public or members of the military? Based on his writing strategies, how are you able to determine Selway's intended primary readership?

3. What is your reaction to the mixed emotional responses by the military people featured in Selway's article? Why do you believe they are more reserved in their celebration? How valid are their expressed concerns over the fallout from the killing of bin Laden?

4. Does heroism need to be acknowledged to be legitimate, or are the acts of heroism themselves valuable even if they go unnoticed? Is it essential that the heroes themselves be known for the heroic events or actions to have any meaning? Why or why not?

5. Why do you think these Navy SEALs are considered to be such large heroes in American culture? What is it about their actions that warrants the adoration of our culture at large? Do you agree that our praise of these men is warranted, or do you think too much has been made of this military action?

6.  Conduct interviews with members of your community about their response to the death of Osama bin Laden. What were their initial reactions to the news of his death? How have their views shifted or remained the same in the time since his death? Determine whether your interviewees consider these men to be heroes, and explain why they do or do not believe bin Laden's killing to be heroic. Accompany your essay with video or audio footage of your interviewees' responses.

7.  Research other famous and potentially heroic campaigns carried out by elite military forces such as the Navy SEALs or Delta Force. Describe the situation and the result of the raid or strike. How was it successful in accomplishing its goal? In what way did the public respond (if at all) to the news of the campaign in question? Were the military personnel considered heroes? Why or why not?

8.  Describe another national hero who has come to represent a heroic cause and explain who the person was and what his or her act of heroism was. How has the story that accompanies the heroic national figure shifted in the years since the action in question? In what way is the person identified as a national hero? Explain whether you agree that the person in question was more or less heroic than popular culture portrays him or her.

9.  Discuss the difference between the response to the killing of bin Laden in the public sphere versus within the military community. Research military publications, such as *Stars & Stripes* or the *Army Times*, to find stories that illustrate soldiers' reactions to bin Laden's death, and compare the responses to those featuring civilians in popular publications. How are the responses similar or different? What accounts for the similarities or differences? Which perspective do you agree with more, and why?

# "Miracle on the Hudson": All Safe in Jet Crash

MSNBC.com

**Let's Start Here•••▶**    Occasionally heroic events occur that capture the attention of the world at large simply because of their unlikelihood. One such event is the emergency landing of a passenger plane on New York's Hudson River in January of 2009. After take-off, the plane collided with a flock of birds, which resulted in the failure of the plane's engines. In the past, such events have usually resulted in the death of many, if not all, the passengers and employees aboard the plane. But in this particular event—which was almost immediately dubbed "Miracle on the Hudson"—the pilot managed to safely land the plane on the surface of the Hudson River, and everyone aboard the flight survived. The pilot was immediately lauded as a hero, and he was subsequently featured on countless TV shows as well as given a seat of honor at the president's State of the Union Address.

The following article was written in response to that event, and in it the miraculous and heroic nature of the river landing quickly becomes apparent. As you read through the account of the day's events, observe the manner in which the pilot, Chesley "Sully" Sullenberger, is described by MSNBC.com, as well as by the passengers whose lives were spared thanks to his actions.

MSNBC.com is the news website for the NBC News family, featuring interactivity and multimedia plus original stories and video which augment the content from NBC News and partners. This story originally appeared on the MSNBC.com website on January 15, 2009.

With both engines out, a cool-headed pilot maneuvered his crowded jetliner over New York City and ditched it in the frigid Hudson River on Thursday, and all 155 on board were pulled to safety as the plane slowly sank. It was, the governor said, "a miracle on the Hudson." One victim suffered two broken legs, a paramedic said, but there were no other reports of serious injuries.

The plane, a US Airways Airbus A320 bound for Charlotte, N.C., struck a flock of birds during takeoff minutes earlier at LaGuardia Airport and was submerged up to its windows in the river by the time rescuers arrived in Coast Guard vessels and ferries. Some passengers waded in water up to their knees, standing on the wing of the plane and waiting for help.

"He was phenomenal," passenger Joe Hart said. "He landed it—I tell you what—the impact wasn't a whole lot more than a rear-end (collision). It threw you into the seat ahead of you.

"Both engines cut out and he actually floated it into the river," he added.

In a city still wounded from the aerial attack on the World Trade Center, authorities were quick to assure the public that terrorism wasn't involved.

Police divers had to rescue some of the passengers from underwater, Mayor Michael Bloomberg said. Among those on board was one infant who appeared to be fine, the mayor said.

Helen Rodriguez, a paramedic who was among the first to arrive at the scene, said she saw one woman with two broken legs. Fire officials said others were evaluated for hypothermia, bruises, and other minor injuries.

"We had a miracle on 34th Street. I believe now we have had a miracle on the Hudson," Gov. David Paterson said.

The crash took place on a 20-degree day, one of the coldest of the season in New York. The water temperature was 36 degrees, Coast Guard Lt. Commander Moore said. He estimates that hypothermia can hit within five to eight minutes at that temperature.

## "Brace for Impact"

"The captain said, 'Brace for impact because we're going down,'" passenger Jeff Kolodjay said. He said passengers put their heads in their laps and started praying. He said the plane hit the water pretty hard, but he was fine.

The pilot was identified as Chesley "Sully" Sullenberger of Danville, Calif.

"It was intense. It was intense. You've got to give it to the pilot. He made a hell of a landing," Kolodjay said.

"He is the consummate pilot," his wife, Lorrie Sullenberger, told the *New York Post*. Sullenberger is an U.S. Air Force Academy grad who flew F-4 fighter planes while in the Air Force, she said. "He is about performing that airplane to the exact precision to which it is made."

> **consummate:**
> Perfect or complete in every way.

Sullenberger is an airline safety expert who has consulted with NASA and others, according to his résumé posted on the Internet. He has 40 years of experience, 29 with US Airways, and holds masters' degrees in public administration and industrial psychology.

Another passenger, Fred Berretta, who was on his way home to Charlotte from a business trip, told CNN doors were opened on both sides of the plane "as soon as we hit the water."

Witnesses said the plane's pilot appeared to guide the plane down. Bob Read, a television producer who saw the crash from his office window, said it appeared to be a "controlled descent."

Paramedics treated at least 78 patients, fire officials said. Coast Guard boats rescued 35 people who were immersed in the frigid water and ferried them to shore. Some of the rescued were shivering and wrapped in white blankets, their feet and legs soaked.

One commuter ferry, the Thomas Jefferson of the company NY Waterway, arrived within minutes of the crash, and some of its own riders grabbed life vests and lines of rope and tossed them to plane passengers in the water.

## Panicked People

"They were cheering when we pulled up," ferry captain Vincent Lombardi. "We had to pull an elderly woman out of a raft in a sling. She was crying...People were panicking. They said, 'hurry up, hurry up.'"

Two police scuba divers said they pulled another woman from a lifeboat "frightened out of her mind" and lethargic from hypothermia. Another woman fell off a rescue raft, and the divers said they swam over and put her on a Coast Guard boat.

**lethargic:**
Lacking energy or lazy.

US Airways Flight 1549 took off at 3:26 p.m. It was less than a minute later when the pilot reported a "double bird strike" and said he needed to return to LaGuardia, said Doug Church, a spokesman for the National Air Traffic Controllers Association. He said the controller told the pilot to divert to an airport in nearby Teterboro, N.J.

It was not clear why the pilot did not land at Teterboro. Church said there was no mayday call from the plane's transponder. The plane splashed into the water off roughly 48th Street in midtown Manhattan—one of the busiest and most closely watched stretches of the river.

US Airways CEO Doug Parker confirmed that 150 passengers, three flight attendants and two pilots were on board the jetliner.

Bank of America and Wells Fargo said they had employees on the plane. Charlotte is a major banking center.

The plane remained afloat but sinking slowly as it drifted downriver. Gradually, the fuselage went under until about half of the tail fin and rudder was above water. Bloomberg said the aircraft finally wound up near Battery Park, at the lower tip of Manhattan and about four miles from where the pilot ditched it.

The Federal Aviation Administration says there were about 65,000 bird strikes to civil aircraft in the United States from 1990 to 2005, or about one for every 10,000 flights.

"They literally just choke out the engine and it quits," said Joe Mazzone, a retired Delta Air Lines pilot. He said air traffic control towers routinely alert pilots if there are birds in the area.

"The plane flew through a flock of birds and both engines were damaged. That's all we know right now," said Dave Steyer, a technician with the wildlife research office of the U.S. Department of Agriculture, which helps the FAA study what it calls bird strikes.

Worldwide since 1960, crashes of more than 25 large aircraft were caused by bird strikes, according to a published study by Richard Dolbeer, a retired ornithologist with the Department of Agriculture at the Wildlife Services in Sandusky, Ohio. In 23 of these incidents, the strike occurred below 400 feet.

**ornithologist:**
A scientist who studies birds.

In the U.S., the FAA tracked more than 38,000 bird strikes from 1990 to 2004, according to a study by Dolbeer. He used data from the FAA's National Wildlife Strike Database for Civil Aviation. He concluded that management of birds should focus on the airport environment.

The Hudson crash took place almost exactly 27 years after an Air Florida plane bound for Tampa crashed into the Potomac River just after takeoff from Washington National Airport, killing 78 people. Five people on that flight survived.

On Dec. 20, a Continental Airlines plane veered off a runway and slid into a snowy field at the Denver airport, injuring 38 people. That was the first major crash of a commercial airliner in the United States since Aug. 27, 2006, when 49 people were killed after a Comair jetliner mistakenly took off from the wrong runway in Lexington, Ky.

**Let's Pause Here•••▶** What is it about Sullenberger's actions that were so heroic? Why did his actions grab the attention of the international media? Do you feel the media reaction was appropriate? What was your response to the manner in which MSNBC.com portrays Sullenberger? How do you feel about the witnesses' and passengers' descriptions of the event? Is it understandable why the pilot is so widely considered to be a national hero?

**Let's Take It Further•••▼**

1. What, specifically, was heroic about Sullenberger's actions that grabbed the attention of the world and its media?

2. If you were aboard the flight described by MSNBC.com, what would your reaction have been, and why? How would you have described Sullenberger as a hero to the media, if asked?

3. Based on the portrayal and descriptions of Sullenberger in the MSNBC.com text, to whom do you think the article is attempting to appeal? What about the descriptions given throughout the piece—as well as writing strategies—reveals MSNBC.com's intended audience? How might this have been written differently if the audience were other pilots or people in aviation, for example?

4. Why do you think it was necessary for the text to point out that authorities in New York were "quick to assure the public that terrorism wasn't involved"?

5. Why do you think MSNBC.com found it relevant or necessary to include Sullenberger's background experience? In what ways does the information given about his background add to his heroic qualities? In what ways does it make him a more "legitimate" hero?

6. Research the whereabouts of Chesley "Sully" Sullenberger since his emergency landing on the Hudson River. Where is Sullenberger now? In what ways did he use his celebrity hero status to do further good deeds, if he did at all? How did his fame affect his life positively or negatively? Explain whether he is still widely regarded as a hero. Overall, what was the outcome of the emergency landing on Sullenberger's life? Was his celebrity status ultimately a positive or a negative occurrence in his life, and why?

7. Research other similar air traffic incidents (such as the ones mentioned in the article) and compare the differences in circumstances and outcomes. What heroic actions, if any, were taken in the other incidents, and how were they praised and described by the media? How was the Hudson incident significantly different than the others? What do you think accounts for the media response to the different incidents. and why?

8. Research and describe a heroic incident in your own community that resulted in saved lives. What were the circumstances of the incident you have chosen to describe? How was the event portrayed in your local media? What was the community response to the hero or heroes involved in the event? How has the event continued to be remembered in your community, if it has?

## The Tillman Story: The Surprising Saga of a Football Star at War
Andrew O'Hehir

**Let's Start Here•••▶** In the aftermath of the 9/11 attacks on the United States, many people rushed to join the military in what they saw as their sense of obligation to the country and its safety. Stories of people who enlisted because of 9/11 abound. The surge in military personnel was unlike anything seen in previous conflicts. In the midst of the horrors and the fallout of that day, our media and culture at large seemed to be in desperate need of heroes. This is how the image in this chapter's introduction became an iconic portrayal of the heroism of members of New York City's fire and police departments.

One of the most famous 9/11 war heroes is a young man named Patrick Tillman, who turned down a lucrative NFL contract in order to serve in the military. Tillman quickly became a celebrity for his decision, and the narrative that grew around him was followed closely by the

media. The following essay addresses the story of Tillman, as well as the controversial mythology that the military and the media created in order to make him an icon of the Afghanistan war effort. As you read the essay, observe the manner in which competing narratives about Tillman were created and how it is that his family is trying to set the record straight about the young man, his sacrifices, and who he really was.

---

Andrew O'Hehir is a senior writer for *Salon* who has written about movies, books, and culture for *Salon* since 1996 and has covered the independent film world in *Salon*'s *Beyond the Multiplex* column since 2003. He has written for many national and international publications, including the *New York Times*, the *Washington Post*, *US Weekly*, the *Times of London*, *Sight and Sound*, and others. He was editor-in-chief of San Francisco's *SF Weekly* in the mid-Nineties and later a senior editor at *SPIN* magazine. He is the author of two produced plays and a novel-in-progress. The following essay first appeared in *Salon* on October 20, 2010.

The death of Pat Tillman, the National Football League star turned Army Ranger who was killed by friendly fire—or "fratricide," as the military puts it—in Afghanistan in April 2004, was a strange event in recent American history. On one hand, Tillman's death was covered far more extensively than those of any of the other 4,700 or so United States troops killed in the Iraqi and Afghan combat zones. To put it bluntly, he was the only celebrity among them.

> **fratricide:**
> The act of killing a brother or a countryman who is in a brother-like role, as in a fellow soldier.

On the other hand, Tillman's story remains poorly understood and has little social resonance. As a colleague of mine recently put it, Tillman didn't fit, either as a living human being or a posthumous symbol into the governing political narratives of our polarized national conversation. That's true whether you're on the right or the left. If he struck many people at first as a macho, hyper-patriotic caricature—the small-town football hero who went to war without asking questions—it eventually became clear that was nowhere near accurate. Yet Tillman was also more idiosyncratic than the equally stereotypical '60s-style combat vet turned long-hair peacenik.

> **posthumous:**
> Following the person's death.

> **polarized:**
> Broken into opposing groups.

> **idiosyncratic:**
> Peculiar in character.

Mind you, Tillman might well have become a left-wing activist, had he lived longer. He had read Noam Chomsky's critiques of U.S. foreign policy, and hoped to meet Chomsky in person. But as Amir Bar-Lev's haunting and addictive documentary *The Tillman Story* demonstrates, Tillman was such an unusual blend of personal ingredients that he could have become almost anything. It's a fascinating film, full of drama, intrigue, tragedy and righteous indignation, but maybe its greatest accomplishment is to make you feel the death of one young man—a truly independent thinker who hewed his own way through the world, in the finest American tradition—as a great loss.

> **hewed:**
> Cut with heavy blows.

*The Tillman Story* was made with the close cooperation of Tillman's parents and siblings, who have worked tirelessly over the past six years to expose the circumstances of Tillman's death and the extensive military coverup that followed it. The film is also meant, to some extent, as an antidote to journalist Jon Krakauer's 2009 book *Where Men Win Glory: The Odyssey of Pat Tillman*, which the family strongly disliked. (Tillman's widow, Marie, allowed Krakauer to read Tillman's journals, a decision other family members apparently regret.) Bar-Lev's dual goals are to document the family's long crusade to pry the grisly truth about Tillman's death and the ensuing campaign of lies from the military bureaucracy, and, perhaps more important, to capture the unconventional background that produced someone as unusual as Pat Tillman in the first place.

To use the Shakespearean cliché, Tillman was a man of many parts, and that goes back to his childhood in a rural California valley south of San Jose, where his parents, Pat Sr. and Mary, encouraged an almost libertarian blend of self-reliance and free thinking in their sons. (The Tillmans are now divorced, but have worked closely together on the campaign to unpack the military's deceitful behavior.) He emerged as a mixture of qualities that seem simultaneously liberal and conservative, all-American and heterodox. He was a football star and avid outdoorsman who read Emerson; an agnostic or atheist who read the Bible, the Quran and the Book of Mormon out of intellectual curiosity; a man who relished the high-testosterone simulated combat of sports, and excelled at it, while also maintaining an introspective personal journal he allowed no one to read.

**heterodox:** Contrary to established standards or beliefs.

As a friend of mine recently observed, many of Tillman's characteristics would seem completely normal among the metropolitan educated classes: He never went anywhere without a book, and typically rode his bike rather than driving a car. But Tillman wasn't a bearded, chai-drinking grad student riding that bike to yoga class in Brooklyn or Silverlake or Ann Arbor. He was the starting strong safety for the Arizona Cardinals, and parked his bike next to his teammates' Porsches and tricked-out Escalades. Bar-Lev's film is a bit light on Tillman's football career, and doesn't include any interviews with teammates. You have to wonder how much they liked or understood him.

Now you're asking the obvious question: If Pat Tillman was such a smart and interesting fellow, why did he walk away from an easy life of fame and money and volunteer for combat on the other side of the world, where he wound up standing on an Afghan hillside and shouting, "I'm Pat fucking Tillman!" at somebody who was shooting him in the head with a machine gun? There's no easy answer, and in making his film with the Tillmans, Bar-Lev has agreed not to go too far in trying to answer it directly. The Tillman brothers and parents want to respect Pat's refusal to discuss his reasons in public, so the film never quotes from the journals that Krakauer read.

Nonetheless I think *The Tillman Story* and Krakauer's book paint roughly the same picture, in that Tillman's decision to go to war was more personal and philosophical than ideological. He believed that the U.S. was at war after 9/11—with Osama bin Laden and al-Qaida, not Iraq or Afghanistan or Muslims in general, Krakauer says—and decided he had a moral responsibility to take part. He believed in an old-fashioned code of masculine honor and valor, but he had also begun wondering whether his life as a professional athlete was shallow and meaningless. You could almost say he joined the Army in a search for personal meaning and moral purpose.

After serving a tour of duty in Iraq, Tillman returned home with grave doubts about the morality and efficacy of that conflict, and began to make contact with people who opposed the war. (This is the Chomsky-reading period.) Bar-Lev makes clear that Tillman could have asked for a discharge at that point to resume his football career; the owner of the Seattle Seahawks was eager to sign him, and the NFL would no doubt have made a big show of welcoming a returning hero. Again that old-fashioned moral code intervened: Tillman disliked military life and thought the war was wrong, but he wouldn't use his fame to avoid fulfilling his three-year commitment. (He had joined up as an ordinary enlisted man, although he would almost certainly have been given an officer's commission had he requested one.)

I'm only guessing here, but one of the things the Tillman family hated about Jon Krakauer's book was probably the author's tendency to view Pat Tillman's death as a case study in the evils of war and the limits of idealism. I might incline toward that view myself, but the Tillmans don't. Right-wing propagandists quickly learned that the Tillman family wasn't going to stick to the pious, patriotic script. (Pat's drunken younger brother, Rich, at the nationally televised funeral: "Pat isn't with God. He's fucking dead.") But the Tillmans aren't interested in starring in an anti-war morality play either. As they see it, Pat Tillman died as he lived, as an American who thought for himself, hewed to his own course and kept his word. It's the rest of us who have betrayed him.

**Let's Pause Here•••▶** Prior to reading this essay, how familiar were you with the story of Pat Tillman? Why do you think he was chosen to stand as a national symbol of pride in the aftermath of 9/11? In what ways were his decisions related to serving his country heroic? Is it understandable why he would be chosen as an icon of American self-sacrifice? Why or why not?

**Let's Take It Further•••▼**

1. Why do you believe Pat Tillman was chosen from hundreds of thousands of troops as an example of heroism? What is it in particular about his history that so easily lends itself to his heroic narrative? How would this help our popular culture in terms of coping with 9/11? How might it have benefitted the military?

2. To whom is the author speaking within his essay? What elements of his essay prove his intended audience? Which choices in language, descriptions, and quotes reveal his intentions as a writer? What, ultimately, is the author trying to accomplish with this essay?

3. Research the conflicting causes of death as described by the military and Tillman's family. Also, research both biographical stories put forth by the military and the Tillman family, as well as the cover up that the Tillman family accuses the U.S. military of creating. Do you believe the military was justified in covering up the true cause of Tillman's death? Why or why not?

4. Why do you think O'Hehir makes a point of illustrating the contradictions in Tillman's personality? How is it that these traits explain the nature of Tillman as a man? Are these details relevant to better understanding him or not?

5. Do you think it was heroic of Tillman not to discuss his true reasons for turning down millions of dollars from the NFL to serve in the military? Why or why not?

6. O'Hehir ends his essay by stating, "It's the rest of us who have betrayed [Tillman]." What do you think this statement means? How have we, as a nation, betrayed Tillman and his legacy? If we have, how can we make amends for doing so?

7. Watch the movie mentioned in this essay, called *The Tillman Story*, and compare it to any of the many stories that were told about Tillman around the time of his death. (*Sports Illustrated*, *TIME* magazine, and many other major publications ran long stories about Tillman both before and after his death.) How do the stories differ about him, and why? What purpose did the narratives created about Tillman serve to those who told his story? How does the movie attempt to set the record straight?

8. Search online for the correspondence between Tillman's father, Patrick Tillman, Sr., and the military. In what way does Tillman, Sr., attempt to unearth the true story behind his son's death? Who do you feel is more in the right regarding the Pat Tillman narrative? How, if at all, has the issue of competing narratives been resolved? What is the final outcome of the Tillman saga?

9. Research the writings of Noam Chomsky and explain why it is a relevant detail for O'Hehir to include when speaking about the many contradictions that make up Tillman's identity. In other words, why would it matter that Tillman was a fan of Chomsky's writing but also decided it was his duty to serve in the military? Include examples or quotes from Chomsky's own writing to back your opinion on why his work is relevant to the discussion of Tillman's life.

10. Research another hero narrative that has been inaccurately portrayed by the government or the media and compare it to the Tillman narrative. Describe the story behind the hero, including what he or she was famous for and why the person gained national attention. What purpose did the misleading narrative of the hero serve? How did the person get misrepresented in the media? How did the real story emerge, and who was responsible for it? What is the purpose behind creating mythologies behind our national heroes? Why is this a bad or a good thing?

11. Compare the Jon Krakauer book, *Where Men Win Glory: The Odyssey of Pat Tillman*, to the movie *The Tillman Story*. How do the two differ? Which one makes the more convincing argument, and how? Why do you think the Tillman family would "strongly dislike" the Krakauer version of Pat's life? How is he portrayed differently in the film about him? Which one is a more convenient narrative for a nation looking for heroes in response to 9/11?

# Superhero Worship

Virginia Postrel

**Let's Start Here•••** ▶ Many of us are in awe of heroes for their ability to be larger than life. In many ways these people have achieved what so many Americans wish to achieve but most likely never will—fame and honor. In addition to the real-life heroes, there are fictional heroes with whom many Americans are just as obsessed.

Superheroes—near-humans who often have supernatural powers—in many ways represent the powers we wish we could have ourselves. They fight crime and evil. They are indestructible. And, according to Virginia Postrel, they have become thoroughly engrained in our popular culture. Beyond the Star Wars conventions and the annual ComicCon gathering of comic and sci-fi fans, our national obsession with superheroes is both meaningful and strange. In her essay, Postrel attempts to get to the bottom of what she calls "superhero worship" by dissecting the role these fictional characters play in our larger popular culture.

As you read the essay, pay attention to the ways that Postrel describes the various superheroes and their powers. If you have a favorite superhero, see whether you agree with what Postrel explains as that particular character's appeal. Also, note the ways in which she shows how these various characters have evolved over the years, as well as her explanation for their evolution.

---

Virginia Postrel is a political and cultural writer who is a contributing editor for *The Atlantic Monthly*, editor-in-chief of DeepGlamour.net, and the author of *The Substance of Style* and *The Future and Its Enemies*. She is currently writing a book on glamour for *The Free Press*. She previously wrote an economics column in the *New York Times* for six years, served as editor of *Reason*, and has worked as a reporter for *Inc.* magazine and the *Wall Street Journal*. She serves on the Board of Directors of the Foundation for Individual Rights and is a popular blogger and speaker. The following essay first appeared in *The Atlantic Monthly* in October 2006.

When *Superman* debuted in 1978, it invented a whole new movie genre—and a new kind of cinematic magic. Today, hundreds of millions of dollars depend on the heroic box-office performances of costumed crusaders whom Hollywood once thought worthy only of kiddie serials or campy parodies. The two *Spider-Man* movies rank among the top ten of all time for gross domestic receipts, and *X-Men: The Last Stand* and *Superman Returns* are among this year's biggest hits.

Superhero comics have been around since Irving Thalberg and Louis B. Mayer ruled the back lot, but only recently has Hollywood realized the natural connection between superhero comics and movies. It's not just that both are simultaneously visual and verbal media; that formal connection would apply equally to the "serious" graphic novels and sequential art that want nothing to do with crime fighters in form-fitting outfits. Cinema isn't just a good medium for translating graphic novels. It's specifically a good medium for *superheroes*. On a fundamental, emotional level, super-heroes, whether in print or on film, serve the same function for their audience as Golden Age movie stars did for theirs: they create glamour.

If that sounds crazy, it's because we tend to forget what glamour is really about. Glamour isn't beauty or luxury; those are only specific manifestations for specific audiences. Glamour is an imaginative process that creates a specific, emotional response: a sharp mixture of projection, longing, admiration, and aspiration. It evokes an audience's hopes and dreams and makes them seem attainable, all the while maintaining enough distance to sustain the fantasy. The elements that create glamour are not specific styles—bias-cut gowns or lacquered furniture—but more general qualities: grace, mystery, transcendence. To the right audience, Halle Berry is more glamorous commanding the elements as Storm in the *X-Men* movies than she is walking the red carpet in a designer gown.

> **manifestations:**
> An expression of something that is able to be visibly or outwardly perceived.

> **transcendence:**
> The state of being transcendent or rising above.

"You'll believe a man can fly," promised *Superman*'s trailers. Brian Chase, a forty-year-old Los Angeles lawyer and comic-book enthusiast, recalls, "They *did* make you believe it." He says that after seeing the movie for the first time, when he was thirteen, he "ran back from the theater jumping over things. I was embarrassingly convinced. I projected myself into it, and I was not going to let it go for the world." That is the emotional effect of glamour, and it's something superhero comics have delivered since Superman hit print in 1938. The *Superman* movie's marketing slogan was thus more than a promise of convincing special effects. It was a pledge to engage the audience's dreams without ridicule. In *Superman*, only the villains were silly. A decade later, Tim Burton's operatic *Batman* made even the clown-faced Joker seem genuinely scary. Influenced by Frank Miller's reinvention of Batman as the Dark Knight, Burton's *Batman* movies portrayed a dangerous world in desperate need of a masked hero. Instead of the campy straight man of the 1960s television series or the tame Mister Rogers of the 1950s comic books, Batman was again a glamorous creature of the night, powerful and mysterious.

The superhero movies that have followed, like the comics from which they were derived, have engaged their subjects without emotional reservation. They may have humor (Marvel comics like *Spider-Man* and *The Fantastic Four* are famous for it), but they lack the kind of irony that punctures glamour and makes the audience feel foolish for its suspension of disbelief, the sort of campy mockery exemplified by the *Batman* television show or Joel Schumacher's disastrous *Batman & Robin*, featuring a smirking George Clooney in the lead.

> **exemplified:**
> To serve as an example of something.

The superhero fans who wear costumes to comics conventions, buy miniatures of their favorite characters, or line up for artists' autographs aren't themselves glamorous. But neither were the Depression-era housewives who bought knockoffs of Joan Crawford's gowns or wrote fan letters to Gary Cooper. And neither are the *InStyle* readers who copy Natalie Portman's latest haircut or wear a version of Halle Berry's Oscar dress to the prom. But all are acting on glamour's promise. Glamour is, to quote a fashion blurb, "all about transcending the everyday." The whole point of movie glamour was—and is—escape. "What the adult American female chiefly asks of the movies is the opportunity to escape by reverie from an existence which she finds insufficiently interesting," wrote Margaret Farrand Thorp in *America at the Movies* (1939). Movies are "the quickest release from a drab, monotonous, unsatisfying environment in dreaming of an existence which is rich, romantic, glamorous."

**monotonous:** Tedious, boring, or unvarying.

Superheroes appeal to a different sort of romanticism. Brian Chase draws a distinction between himself and other members of a hip e-mail list called Glamour: "Their idea of glamour would be to get invited to the right party. To me growing up, the idea of glamour was to be the guy who could save the right party from a meteor." Says Richard Neal, owner of Zeus Comics, an upscale comics store in Dallas, "It's not just superpowers but dashing good looks, villains you can fight, getting aggression out." (Buff and business-savvy, Neal bears no resemblance to the classic comics-store proprietor, represented so memorably on *The Simpsons*.)

Superheroes are masters of their bodies and their physical environment. They often work in teams, providing an ideal of friendship based on competence, shared goals, and complementary talents. They're special, and they know it. "Their *true* identities, the men in colorful tights, were so elemental, so universal, so transcendent of the worlds that made them wear masks that they carried with them an unprecedented optimism about the value of one's inner reality," writes Gerard Jones in *Men of Tomorrow: Geeks, Gangsters and the Birth of the Comic Book*. "We all knew that Clark Kent was just a game played by Superman and that the only guy who mattered was that alien who showed up in Metropolis with no history and no parents."

Comic-book heroes, like all glamorous icons, cater to "dreams of flight and transformation and escape." Those words are from one of the best books ever written on glamour: Michael Chabon's 2000 novel, *The Amazing Adventures of Kavalier and Clay*. Like many a Hollywood story, *Kavalier and Clay* is wise to the perils of trying to live out glamorous dreams in the real world, again and again showing the tragicomic effects of such attempts. Early on, for instance, young Joe Kavalier almost drowns while attempting a Houdini-like escape designed to gain entrance to what he imagines is a glamorous private club for magicians. (It is, in fact, a rather run-down place whose dining room "smelled of liver and onions.") On the eve of

World War II, Joe and his cousin Sammy create a successful comic-book hero called the Escapist, whose villainous foes include Hitler himself. Their glamorous illusion is that such fights are easy to win.

Chabon explicitly defends the escapism of comics. After the war, his Kavalier reflects:

> Having lost his mother, father, brother, and grandfather, the friends and foes of his youth, his beloved teacher Bernard Kornblum, his city, his history— his home—the usual charge leveled against comic books, that they offered *merely an easy escape from reality*, seemed to Joe actually to be a powerful argument on their behalf...It was a mark of how fucked-up and broken was the world—the reality—that had swallowed his home and his family that such a feat of escape, by no means easy to pull off, should remain so universally despised.

Still, glamour is always vulnerable to those who love it. The more we're drawn to a glamorous person, place, or thing, the more we scrutinize it, seeking to fill in the details—which ultimately destroys the mystery and grace. Someone will always look for the hidden flaws, the seamy side of the story. Hence the demand for gossip about Princess Diana's bulimia or Jennifer Lopez's romantic problems. These *Behind the Music*–style revelations replace the transcendence of glamour with the mundane problems of mere celebrity. Beyond these grubby details is a more mythic kind of debunking: the artistic revisionism that warns of glamour's dangers and disappointments. The power of such revisionism, however, depends on the emotional pull of the original. Someone who knows little and cares even less about Hollywood dreams will miss the pity and terror of *Sunset Boulevard*. Someone who scorns superheroes as infantile won't understand the scary wonder of *Watchmen*, the brilliant 1987 graphic novel in which Alan Moore and Dave Gibbons deconstruct superheroes. To the wrong audience, glamour, even revisionist glamour, will seem like camp.

**infantile:**

Characteristic of an infant.

**revisionism:**

The advocating of revision (most commonly history or philosophy).

One way to balance the real and ideal while preserving glamour is to give the audience an insider's view. So superhero comics now tend to situate their stories in a world like our own, with ubiquitous, sensationalist media and inescapable trade-offs between personal and professional life. To their audience inside the comics, the superheroes are powerful and mysterious celebrities subject to public adulation and tabloid attacks. The real-world audience, by contrast, gets a

**ubiquitous:**

Being ever-present or everywhere at the same time.

glimpse behind the mask, a chance to identify with the character and to experience glamour once removed—to imagine *what it would be like to be glamorous*, and how much hard work, sacrifice, and attention to detail that seemingly effortless power requires. This double vision acknowledges the art behind the illusion. Glamour may look easy, but it never is.

**Let's Pause Here•••▷** What is your initial reaction to Postrel's explanation of the importance of superheroes in our culture? Do you agree with her assessment of their value and importance in our culture? Why or why not? Has she convinced you that superheroes provide a particular type of glamour that we cannot get from real-life heroes? How has she failed or succeeded at achieving this particular goal in her essay?

**Let's Take It Further•••▼**

1. In what way do superheroes provide our culture with glamour that cannot be achieved by actual human heroes?

2. To whom is Postrel addressing her essay, based on the manner in which she defines superheroes, as well as the examples and explanations she gives? Which writing strategies prove who Postrel's primary audience is supposed to be?

3. Why is it important that fans of comics and superhero movies buy into the fact that these people and their powers are real? Have you had a similar experience to Brian Chase's experience with superhero films when he was a boy?

4. Postrel quotes a blurb that states, "Glamour is…'all about transcending the everyday.'" How does a person use glamour to transcend the ordinary day-to-day existence that so many of us lead?

5. How might superheroes appeal to us because of their ability to control and master "their bodies and physical environment" in ways that ordinary people cannot?

6. In what other ways might comics and superhero movies provide an escape, besides providing readers/viewers with an alternative form of glamour?

7. Describe other genres of celebrities or heroes, beyond superheroes and Hollywood celebrities, who also provide their fans with a sense of glamour and escape. How would you justify classifying this particular group of people as celebrities or heroes, and in what way do they provide glamour and escape to their fans? Locate specific fan groups who see the celebrities in question as heroes of some sort, and describe the ways in which the fan bases glorify the celebrities in question. Finally, explain whether worshiping these particular types of celebrities is good or bad for their fans, and why.

8. Postrel refers to a number of now-classic superheroes, such as Batman and Superman, in order to make her case about the importance of superheroes in our popular culture. Locate and describe a newer superhero (from within the last five to ten years) and explain who the character is, what his or her powers are, and what sort of environment the character lives in. What is the character's appeal? And what types of national worries does the character respond to? In other words, why might the character have an appeal to a large audience?

9. Find a superhero who has undergone an evolution since he or she was first introduced and explain the ways the character has changed over time. How is the character different from earlier versions? What sorts of cultural events might account for the ways in which the character and the accompanying story line have shifted over the years?

**10.** While Postrel's essay focuses primarily on superheroes that provide an escape from ordinary existence to their fans, there are many other ways that people "escape" their lives. Describe one way in which you escape from your daily existence and what this form of escape provides for you. In other words, what is the thing with which you are obsessed, and how does it enable you to escape life temporarily?

# SpongeBob Squarepants and the Terminator Are Modern Heroes  Martin Miller

**Let's Start Here••• ▶**  One element of popular culture that lends itself to a deeper observation is the way in which fictional characters can represent something larger and more meaningful to us. Virginia Postrel discusses this in the previous essay when she explains what superheroes mean to us and why we need them in our popular culture. The interesting thing about fictional heroes is that they can be just as important as real-life heroes.

This is precisely the case in the following essay, in which Martin Miller dissects the ways that SpongeBob Squarepants and the Terminator are both heroic in their own right. What at first might appear to be an unorthodox essay giving undue importance to two meaningless fictional characters quickly becomes a case study in the ways a cartoon and a sci-fi character can actually be role models for their fans and stand in for heroes we wish we had.

As you read the following essay, observe the manner in which Miller attaches meaning to both of these characters, as well as how he makes the case for their value to American culture.

---

Martin Miller is a staff writer for the *Los Angeles Times* whose work focuses on TV, feature films, and popular culture. Miller, who was a reporter and an editor in the *Los Angeles Times*'s Calendar section from 2004 to 2009, oversees a TV team that includes two critics, four reporters, a slew of freelance contributors, and such popular blogs as *Show Tracker* and *Idol Tracker*. Through *A1, Calendar,* and *Sunday* cover stories, essays and critical reviews, blog posts, and photo galleries, Miller's multimedia team chronicles television's impact on society and examines the changing nature of news, the comings and goings of TV shows and personalities, and the national fascination with such reality shows as *Jon & Kate Plus 8* and *The Real Housewives of Atlanta*. Martin works with Web editors to break news on the Web and expand communities of interest online. The following essay originally appeared in the *Los Angeles Times* on July 12, 2009.

**metes:**
Gives out in a measured manner.

**gregarious:**
One who is fond of companionship.

One serves up the glorious Krabby Patty; the other metes out pitiless death. You might think that a gregarious sponge who is fond of red ties and speaks crystal clear English underwater has little in common with a time-traveling, red-eyed killing machine whose default language setting comes with a heavy Germanic accent.

And that's where you would be wrong. Spongy, dead wrong.

Despite their obvious differences, like for instance, a backbone and a penchant for murder, SpongeBob Squarepants and the Terminator are actually brothers from different mothers, as the kids might say. The two are alike in surprising ways that has everything to do with why there are SpongeBob ceiling fans at Target and a newly opened roller coaster called Terminator Salvation: The Ride at Six Flags Magic Mountain.

Although the two-dimensional characters share a host of traits— ferocious dedication to work, extreme mood swings, a distinct fashion style and an ambiguous sexuality—it is their mutual ability to emerge unbreakable from nearly all circumstances that helps explain their colossal worldwide appeal to three-dimensional humans. What mortal among us, subject to the blings and arrows of our consumerist, post-9/11 world, wouldn't like to plow through the day with the relative ease of either of these two fine fellows?

SpongeBob, who heartily soaks up the juice of life, feels everything. The Terminator (I'm talking strictly about the 800 Series, Model 101 here; subsequent portrayals in sequels are all mere commentary on the 1984 original) feels nothing. But whether it's a spotlight moment of acute social shame or a torrent of shotgun blasts, you can't bring this pair down, at least not for long.

Both mega-merchandised figures are marking notable cultural milestones this summer on television and at the movies. SpongeBob is a still vibrant 10 years old, a birthday Nickelodeon is celebrating with a weekend-long marathon that begins on Friday and culminates on Sunday, the actual anniversary of the pilot episode's first airing.

Meanwhile, the Terminator franchise chalked up its fourth major motion picture in May, a few months before its official 25th anniversary in October. The film has performed well internationally but only lukewarm domestically, foreshadowing perhaps that the unit may be nearing the end of its life span. Still, no matter how the future may look for either one, they haven't done too badly for an invertebrate with a name tag and a cyborg that looks a lot like California's governor.

The world crushes us all. No one more than children. Don't get me wrong, I have children, and with 6.7 billion inhabitants on the planet, everybody needs a little crushing now and then for society to function. (No, you cannot throw your spaghetti in the waiter's face.)

And yet SpongeBob and the Terminator are not cowed by the world's huge pile of petty conventions. SpongeBob laughs at the tsunami of rigid societal rules, while the Terminator fills them full of blazing hot lead— two coping techniques more than a few of us may have fantasized about.

Time and again, SpongeBob defies the established custom and instead of being punished is rewarded. In "Idiot Box," one of the television series' more memorable episodes—and that's saying something—the Stephen Hillenburg creation and his dimwitted sidekick Patrick Star excitedly open a giant box, which contains a television. The two promptly discard the device and hop into the big box, where they use their imaginations to create a new and more entertaining world of avalanche rescues and pirate adventures. (The friends are promptly ridiculed by Squidward, a sarcastic and naysaying octopus and stand-in for parents, who later tries to join in the box fun but can't.)

"We don't need television. Not as long as we have … our imagination," explains SpongeBob, who summons a tiny rainbow in his hands. The message is clear—don't be bound by the narrow vision of others and revel in the power of your own mind. Like the person who dreamed up the SpongeBob ceiling fan.

Another classic episode, which requires no imagination to understand its larger appeal, is called "The Bully." It sounds more like Terminator territory, but bullying is a theme frequently explored in the undersea world of Bikini Bottom. (Imagine television writers who were picked on as children and then working through their issues as adults—and getting paid for it!)

SpongeBob gets a new classmate named Flatts the Flounder, who despite earnest attempts at friendship is interested in only one thing—pulverizing the sponge. SpongeBob runs, hides, even tries to form alliances, but all to no avail. Finally, SpongeBob surrenders to his fate and Flatts pounds away.

Suddenly, SpongeBob realizes something everyone in a similar situation wishes they could—"I'm absorbing his blows like I was made of some kind of spongy material." It doesn't hurt, and eventually the bully is utterly exhausted and defeated by the rope-a-dope.

Even if your soul isn't ground to dust by the hectoring of the world, it's still hard not to get your feelings hurt along the way. Enter the Terminator, eyes cloaked by mirror sunglasses, a metaphor for death itself, with no feelings to get in the way of getting what he wants.

The James Cameron creation is the strong, silent type—even when he gets shot repeatedly, dragged underneath a speeding 18-wheeler or set on fire in a tanker explosion. (Even the more evolved—namely, more namby-pamby—"protector" Terminator in the second film admits he would never be able to cry. Oh, boohoo!)

Of course, he is still a character animated by his own decisive actions, which he directs more than a few times at one of the most confounding and enraging sources of modern life—the bureaucracy.

So we perversely love him because he's powerful and because he concentrates his rage at objects with which we can sympathize.

In the early scenes of the original film the Terminator goes into a gun store and we witness his distaste for the regulations. He's told there's a waiting period for the handguns, and when he begins loading a weapon, the store clerk abruptly tells him he can't do that. Blam! That's what the Terminator thinks about your stinking rules!

But the scene that made the Terminator an icon comes at a police station. He walks into its quiet lobby and asks if he can see Sarah Connor, the woman we all know he wants to murder. The police officer dismissively tells him that he can't see her and that he'll just have to wait. And then he utters what is still his most famous catchphrase: "I'll be back."

Then, in an act quietly cheered by those beaten down by the machinations of the state, he crashes his car through the station's front window and proceeds to shoot up the entire police station. Sure, he takes a few dozen bullets to the chest, which clearly stagger him, but that's a small price to pay for refusing to be dehumanized and brushed off by the system.

That's a sentiment even an eternally optimistic sponge could applaud.

> **machinations:**
> Scheming with the intention to accomplish something wrong or evil.

**Let's Pause Here•••▶** How well do you feel Miller makes the case for the value of these two fictional characters to our society? Were you surprised to see the manner in which Miller attached meaning to the characters' actions? Ultimately, do you agree with his assessment of SpongeBob Squarepants and the Terminator, or do you think there is not as much value to these characters as Miller would like his readers to believe? Why or why not?

**Let's Take It Further•••▼**

1. Were you able to take Miller's discussion of these two characters seriously, or was there some reason that you thought that the case for fictional heroes and how they can be meaningful was problematic? How, for example, does Miller manage—or not manage—to construct an argument that proves these characters can serve as potential role models to real people?

2. Based on Miller's choice of characters, as well as the language he uses and the examples he gives from each character's actions, whom do you think he is attempting to engage as a primary audience? What writing strategies does he employ that allow you to understand his intended readership?

3. Do you agree with Miller's assertion that these characters both have qualities that all people wish we could exhibit (such as the ability to emerge unscathed from potentially devastating events, or the ability to laugh off or destroy our adversaries)? Why or why not?

4. What other reasons are there for the "universal appeal" that Miller attributes to both franchises featured in his essay beyond those mentioned? Are there other ways in which these characters exhibit traits that humans wish they could have?

5. Make the case for the value of another fictional character by modeling the techniques employed by Miller in his essay. For example, who is the fictional character you have chosen? Describe the way he or she is presented and in what form of media. What sorts of actions does the character commit that you consider to be heroic, and why? How might this fictional character be meaningful to its audience by providing positive examples of responding to obstacles or dilemmas?

6. Using the compare-contrast writing strategy utilized by Miller in his essay, compare and contrast two other fictional characters that you believe to be heroic and valuable to viewers. Be sure to explain who the characters are and how they might not appear to be similar at first glance. Also, provide specific examples, as Miller does, to justify your choices and prove the similarities and value of the two characters.

7. Miller states in the essay that "subsequent portrayals [of Terminators] in sequels are all mere commentary on the 1984 original," which implies that they are all watered down versions less heroic than the original Terminator. View all four versions of the Terminator series of films and compare the various versions of Terminators to one another. Which is the most heroic or valuable? How does the character of the Terminator (and actors' portrayals of it) shift and change throughout the franchise? How are they represented the same as the original version, and how are they different? If the subsequent Terminators are all commentary on the original character, what is the comment being made?

8. Find a real person who actually does exhibit the traits that Miller claims most humans do not and explain how he or she fights against adversity. Detail the types of adversity this person has overcome and how. In what way do people emulate the person or comment on the person's abilities? Is the person seen as heroic, or is the person negatively portrayed in the media? Do you see him or her as heroic? Describe why or why not.

# mashitUP

Here is a series of essay and discussion topics that draw connections between multiple selections within the chapter. They also suggest outside texts to include in your essay or discussion. Feel free to bring in further outside texts, remembering the variety of texts (beyond articles) available to you.

1. Locate stories about normal, everyday heroes who help needy people within their own communities. Compare the situations you located to the situations of working class people featured in Barbara Ehrenreich's essay "Nickel-and-Dimed: On (Not) Getting By in America" in the Work and Careers chapter. How are the people featured in the Ehrenreich essay similar to the needy people being helped by the everyday heroes you chose? Based on Ehrenreich's descriptions of her fellow workers, how might the community program you are describing be valuable and have a positive impact on the lives of these people?

2. Compare a superhero, as defined by Postrel in her essay "Superhero Worship," to a real-life hero and discuss which is more valuable to our culture and why. Explain the real-life hero and the circumstance surrounding his or her heroism. Then describe the superhero, what traits he or she has, and the ways in which the superhero has value to popular culture. Make the case for why one is of more value than the other by citing examples from the narratives surrounding the character or person.

3. Compare the stories of the two real-life military heroes featured in this textbook ("*The Tillman Story*: The Surprising Saga of a Football Star at War" in this chapter and "Private Dwyer's Last Breath" in the Alcohol and Drugs chapter) and discuss the manner in which each man was represented in the media. How were their acts of heroism similar or different? How were their deaths similar or different? Why did their stories appeal to our popular culture? How much, if at all, did their celebrity status as military heroes factor into their lives and/or deaths?

4. Create a photo or video collage that illustrates comparisons between real-life heroes and fictional ones. For example, people have compared Donald Trump to the Terminator before because of his lack of concern for the public's opinion and the brutal nature of his show *The Apprentice*. Draw similar comparisons between fictional characters and real-life people, explaining whether you feel they are heroic and why. Also, explain how the two—the real and the fictional—warrant comparisons.

5. Using popular media (such as movies, TV shows, or websites), explain the ways in which real-life heroes are portrayed in the media and how the portrayals may have negative consequences. Choose a real-life hero who was made a celebrity and discuss the details of how the fame may have attributed to the hero's decline. How did our popular media respond once the hero declined or failed to live up to the standards set for the person by our popular culture?

6. Create a cartoon or drawing of a well-known hero accompanied by an essay that explains how you have chosen to represent the person in cartoon form and why. What acts of heroism are you attempting to include, and how do you intend to include them? What specific details do you include, and how do you hope they accurately portray the hero in question? Look to J.D. Crowe's cartoon at the beginning of the chapter for ideas or examples.

## Self-Destructing Celebrities    Dave Granlund

Dave Granlund has been an editorial cartoonist published in daily newspapers since 1977. Syndicated in 1978 with NEA-United Media, his work has appeared in over 700 newspapers, including the *New York Times, Chicago Tribune, Christian Science Monitor, GateHouse Media*, and the *Cape Cod Times*, plus magazines such as *Newsweek*, and have also been shown nationally on FoxNews.com, MSNBC.com, HBO, PBS, NPR, CNN, and NBC's *Today Show*. Granlund began drawing cartoons in grade school, and at the age of 16 he was published on the editorial pages of local weekly newspapers. While attending college, he drew editorial cartoons for the *Greenfield Recorder.* Granlund's newspaper honors include awards from UPI, New England Press Association, International Association of Business Communicators, Bronze Quill Award IABC, Associated Press, Massachusetts Press Association, and New England Press Award. His work has been nominated numerous times for the Pulitzer Prize. The following cartoon was first posted to PoliticalCartoons.com on October 27, 2010.

## Thinking About Celebrities

Take a moment to look at the accompanying cartoon. The artist, Dave Granlund, is illustrating our culture's strange obsession with watching celebrities fall from great heights. While we have focused so far on the manner in which heroes sometimes become celebrities, we will now delve more deeply into the larger role celebrities play in popular American culture, as well as what it means to be a celebrity and how celebrities are created.

In terms of celebrities and their fame, many Americans harbor some sort of celebrity obsession. In fact, people commonly long for celebrity status themselves, though by definition celebrities are a rare breed. After all, if everyone were famous, then fame would be meaningless. For the few people who reach the status of celebrity, their relationship with our larger popular culture is a strange and sometimes problematic one. American fans can turn on their celebrities at the drop of a hat. While some celebrities can literally get away with murder, others can be cast down from the peak of their fame for minor infractions such as simply uttering a phrase that disagrees with the American public, or by committing an act that we deem to be in strong opposition to who we believe the person really was. Oddly, one celebrity's drunken YouTube video (David Hasselhoff) might catapult him back from obscurity to the public stage, while another's alcohol-induced ramblings (Mel Gibson) might push him further into obscurity. Nevertheless, it appears as though when a celebrity stumbles in one form or another, the American public is quick to judge, despite our own shortcomings. It is this phenomenon that Granlund is addressing in his cartoon.

As a society, we have certain expectations about our celebrities. We want to worship them, on the one hand, for achieving something that most of us will never achieve: fame. On the other hand, we seem to relish their failures when they come to light, as though we are pleased to see that just because someone is famous does not necessarily make the person any better than us. They are just as prone to mistakes and bad habits. To be sure, many of us have made mistakes that we hope will go unnoticed, but we seem to expect more from our celebrities. If this is what our expectations are, if we expect our celebrities to behave differently than we do ourselves, then we will continue to be disappointed when they fail to meet the unrealistically high standards that we set for them. Where does Granlund appear to stand on the issue of celebrity obsession, based on his drawing, and which details lead you to believe what his opinion is?

Now, revisit the cartoon for a moment to see some of the drawing's finer details. For example, what do you think of the fact that the cartoon is titled "Self-Destructing Celebrities," and how do you feel about Granlund's assertion that "America's favorite spectator sport" is watching celebrities self-destruct? Why do you believe that he chooses to depict vultures watching TV, rather than human beings? How does it change the meaning of the cartoon that he uses vultures instead of humans? Does it matter who or what is sitting on the couch, or is it simply a matter of the words that the vultures are saying?

Finally, Granlund's drawing specifically states, "Watching Hollywood celebrities self-destruct," and yet there are many other types of people who achieve celebrity status with little or no connection to Hollywood (politicians, athletes, businessmen and women). Still, despite the fact that these types of celebrities sometimes have no Hollywood affiliation, we seem to derive just as much pleasure from watching these people fall from glory as the actors and actresses who reach the highest pinnacles of fame. If you were to create a cartoon about your own celebrity obsessions, what types of people would you choose? Would you be able to articulate a reason *why* you might enjoy watching these people self-destruct, even though you admire them? What accounts for this strange love-hate relationship that most Americans have with celebrities? Were you to become a celebrity, would you expect to be treated the same as any other, or would you hope to escape the critical eye of our popular culture? Why or why not?

# mash**UP** essay

The following essay is this chapter's Mashup selection. Keeping in mind our definition of a Mashup essay in Chapter 2 (an essay that includes multimedia texts, as well as multiple writing strategies), observe the way the following essay's author, Jason Kersten, utilizes multimedia texts. For example, the central theme of Kersten's essay is our cultural obsession with celebrity outlaws, which he illustrates by describing the various Facebook fan pages and fan websites that have appeared in the wake of the media spotlight focusing on Colton Harris-Moore's outlaw activities. Kersten also uses fan T-shirts—those emblazoned with Colton Harris-Moore's face and the words "Momma Tried"—as a text that to show the level of fame to which Colton has risen, as well as his new "folk hero" status. Additionally, in keeping with the idea of the multimedia celebrity that Colton has achieved, Kersten also uses Colton's MySpace page as a text, and the most famous image of Colton yet—which originally was posted to his MySpace page but has come to stand as a symbol of Colton's carefree outlaw attitude so admired by his fans—is described in great detail throughout the course of the essay.

Rather than simply showcasing Colton's criminal exploits, Kersten interviews Colton's mother and best friend, as well as the law enforcement officials who are working Colton's case. He also allows Colton to speak for himself by using and reading Colton's childhood photographs, artwork, and even cards the young man made for his mom. By using Colton's childhood mementos in tandem with the interview of Colton's mother, Kersten is able to reconstruct the circumstances surrounding the young man's journey from poverty to outlaw celebrity, all without glorifying the crimes themselves. Kersten also quotes from a *Popular Science* magazine article (featuring a similar story of an airplane thief) in an effort to show the danger Colton faced by flying and landing stolen aircraft without proper guidance and instruction. But Kersten makes a concerted effort to repeatedly, and frequently, allow Colton to speak for himself through the notes he left at crime scenes and the conversations he had with his own mother, in order to avoid appearing too sympathetic to Colton's case. The result is a well-rounded essay that dissects the very nature of celebrity as well as our cultural obsession with outlaws.

One of the most intriguing elements of the essay is that Kersten employs more than just the illustrative approach in his writing. The major thrust of the essay is, indeed, that Kersten wants to inform his readers about Colton's rise from obscurity to celebrity outlaw status, but this approach is combined with several other writing strategies. In addition

**Mashup Essay Flowchart**

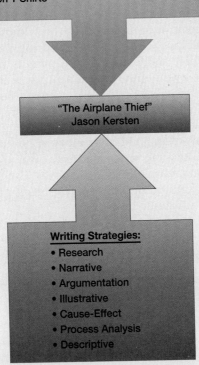

**Types of Media:**
• Interviews with Family, Friends, and Law Enforcement
• Colton's Childhood Drawings
• Colton's MySpace Page
• Colton's Juvenile Detention Center Artwork
• *Popular Science* Article
• Facebook Fan Page
• Colton T-Shirts

"The Airplane Thief"
Jason Kersten

**Writing Strategies:**
• Research
• Narrative
• Argumentation
• Illustrative
• Cause-Effect
• Process Analysis
• Descriptive

to the illustrative writing strategy, Kersten employs many others, which he simultaneously utilizes in order to show the human side of a young criminal, as well as the way Colton progresses from dreams of flying to action. One such strategy Kersten employs throughout is the narrative writing method, which allows him to tell the story of Colton as though he were right alongside him witnessing his crime spree. However, Kersten also employs the process analysis writing strategy to show the ways in which Colton taught himself to fly, as well as how he pulled off many of his acts of thievery. Kersten also uses the descriptive writing strategy to paint vivid pictures of Colton's artwork for his readers, as well as to show the poor and neglectful environment in which young Colton was raised.

In terms of using research in his writing (the research writing strategy), Kersten not only delves deep into Colton's troubled past by seeking out artifacts from the young man's childhood, but he also interviews Colton's mother, childhood friends, fellow young outlaw (Harley Davidson Ironwing), and the law enforcement officials whose job it was to capture Colton and end his crime spree. Kersten also includes articles from local newspapers, as well as the online social networking sites Facebook and MySpace, where fan pages have popped up in response to Colton's daring streak of airplane heists. In doing his research, Kersten also employs the argumentation writing strategy as he tries to put a human face on Colton and explain what may have driven the young man to become a rogue celebrity best known for committing crimes. He also employs the cause-effect writing strategy by showing how Colton's alcohol- and drug-abusing parents neglected him and sometimes failed to provide the bare essentials of life to their son. To Kersten, it seems almost inevitable that a young boy who was raised with nothing would become obsessed with acquiring material objects such as iPods and flat-screen TVs.

When you begin writing a Mashup essay of your own in response to the selections in this chapter, revisit Kersten's essay to generate ideas for multimedia texts and multiple writing strategies. Use the flowchart to see the ways in which Kersten employs the various writing strategies and multimedia texts he utilizes in his writing.

# The Airplane Thief

**Jason Kersten**

**Let's Start Here•••** ▶ One reason for the wild success of reality television shows can easily be traced back to our very American obsession with fame and celebrity. The average person is willing to do just about anything to get on television in the hopes of becoming the next Kim Kardashian or Snooki, even if it means potentially humiliating herself by allowing the nation and the media to poke fun at her. As long as people know who she is, then it ends up being a positive thing. All of this is what Andy Warhol famously referred to as the quest for the "15 minutes of fame" that he was convinced every person would achieve at some point in his or her life.

However, despite our frequent obsession with movie and TV stars, musicians, athletes, and politicians, there is another type of celebrity who holds a special place in our collective popular imagination: the outlaw. One such example of an outlaw celebrity is the subject of the following essay by Jason Kersten. In "The Airplane Thief," Kersten tracks a boy's troubled rise from poverty to fame. Instead of merely telling the facts of the case, Kersten shows how the young man, Colton Harris-Moore, went from small-time burglar to media sensation. A classic underdog-turned-outlaw, the cult of Colton grew rapidly when his stories of burglarizing the wealthy broke in the Pacific Northwest. In some ways, it is a modern twist on the Robin Hood story, and for that reason the appeal of Colton to average people fits wonderfully into our national obsession with celebrity, as well as our cultural passion for outlaws who skirt the law and take what they want.

As you read Kersten's essay, observe the way he patiently delves into Colton's depressing childhood to show how he evolved into the young man featured in the essay. Also, note the tone Kersten uses to describe Colton and his crimes in order to determine whether Kersten is a fan of Colton himself.

---

An author and journalist since 1998, Jason Kersten has written features for numerous national magazines, including *Rolling Stone*, *Men's Journal*, and *Maxim*. His first book, *Journal of the Dead*, was selected as a *New York Times* Notable Book of 2003. He has appeared as a guest and commentator on CNN, Fox News, TruTv, NPR, and numerous regional TV and radio shows. His works have been optioned for both film and television. The following essay first appeared in *Rolling Stone* issue 1104, from May 13, 2010.

> Using the narrative writing strategy Kersten explains Colton's long and complicated boyhood history to show how it led to him finally becoming an actual airplane thief and outlaw pilot.

He had talked about it plenty, dreamed about it even more and, during the endless days he spent holed up alone in the empty vacation homes of the strangers he robbed, he had learned everything he could about flying planes. He had studied flight manuals, taken online quizzes about flight procedures under false names, and logged hours on simulator programs he found on the Internet. He had even created a MySpace page listing his profession as pilot, but the lie was toneless and unsatisfying, a place marker for an act unfulfilled.

> Here Kersten incorporates Colton's MySpace page into his essay as a text to help explain the young man's lifelong obsession with flying.

The reality of his life was far more grim. He grew up without a father. His mother drank too much. At 17, he was a fugitive from the boys' home he had run away from a few months earlier, wanted in a string of more than 100 burglaries and other felonies. Now, it seemed, there was literally nowhere to go but up. He was finally going to show them who he really was, all the classmates and cops who had treated him like shit, told him he was worthless. *I'm going to steal an airplane*, he decided. *No more waiting.*

He knew just the place: Orcas Island Airport, a lonely landing strip on the Puget Sound some 80 miles from Seattle: surrounded by the towering green woods of the Pacific Northwest, no security, quiet as a graveyard at night. The aircraft, most of them single-engine prop planes used as island hoppers, were lined up on the tarmac like a row of shiny, expensive toys. That's where police suspect that Colton Harris-Moore was camped out on November 11th, 2008, hiding among the trees, watching and waiting for the right plane.

Toward late afternoon, a Cessna 182 buzzed in from the south. As a kid, Colton had a poster of a small plane's instrument panel on the wall of his room, and he'd spent hours staring up at the constellation of gauges and switches, marveling at their intricacy and the almost limitless possibilities of purpose and control. Now, as he watched the pilot land and taxi to a hangar on the airport's east side, it was easy to picture himself in the cockpit, to see himself guiding it down the runway, then climbing up and out of a life that had been claustrophobic with disappointment, poverty and uncertainty. He had never set foot in a plane before. He didn't mean to turn himself into a folk hero, a winged outlaw with thousands of fans who cheered his every move. But he was about to become the most legendary airplane thief in the history of aviation.

"The shortest distance to Far Away," proclaims the official slogan of Camano and Whidbey islands, which nest together like a pair of crescents at the north end of Puget Sound. Camano's south end features some of the most coveted getaway real estate in the Pacific Northwest. For well-heeled Seattleites, it's like the Hamptons for New Yorkers or Cape Cod for Bostonians. Million-dollar beachfront homes abound, and each summer the local population of 18,000 swells by nearly half, as doctors and dot-com executives from Seattle come to sit on the decks of their cabins at sunset and watch bald eagles wheel and dive into the waters of Tulalip Bay and Possession Sound.

Colton Harris-Moore—or Colt, as everyone called him—grew up only six miles from the southern tip of the island, but it might as well have been another planet. He was raised in a decaying mobile home on a five-acre patch in Camano's rural central woods. His father, Gordon "Gordy" Moore, was a journeyman concrete finisher; his mother, Pam, was a once-divorced city girl from the Seattle suburb of Lynnwood. She had bought the land with money she'd saved from working as an accountant for the National Park Service. Their dream was to build a house on the property, but Gordy kept getting in trouble with the law, busted more than two dozen times for drunk driving and other offenses. He abandoned the family before Colton was two, leaving his son with a single, mostly unemployed mom in her early 40s who drank too much herself.

In spite of the conditions, little Colt was a happy kid. He put on so much weight that Pam nicknamed him Tubby— almost as if his body knew he'd one day explode into a six-foot-five, 200-pound teenager. When he was four, Pam met and married Bill Kohler, a gentle, heavyset man who had once served in the Army and worked as a milker at a nearby dairy. The family kept chickens out back, and when Colt and Bill walked out to feed them, Bill would pretend he was a chicken, jerking his head and strutting. Colt adored him, but Bill turned out to be almost as unreliable as his father had been—an on-and-off junkie whom Pam threw out of the house when he was using.

Most of the time it was just Colt and his mom. He collected James Bond movies, watching them over and over. He loved animals, taking care of a blind duck that wandered onto the property, and playing with his dog, a Great Pyrenees named Cody. But he devoted most of his time to exploring an obsession he'd had since he was a toddler: airplanes. A love of planes is not unusual among boys, but where most move on to sports and girls, Colt got only more and more entranced with the intricacies of aviation, filling the pages of sketch pads with meticulously drawn aircraft. In the margins he listed detailed technical specifications that would have impressed a flight engineer: *"Dassault Falcon 2000EX—France, Max speed—603mph, Range—3,800 nm, Power Plant—two garrett ATF 4-7A-4C turbofans."* At the top of each image he included a pedigree: "my own free hand." When a plane passed overhead, he could look up and tell you what company made it, the type of engine, how many passengers it held. "He was looking up at a plane every time I went outside," Pam recalls. "I got tired of looking at planes."

---

*Kersten repeatedly describes Colton's home as a text—contrasting the level of fame that Colton has achieved with the humble and even impoverished reality of how his mother lives.*

*Moments such as these show that beneath the surface Kersten is using a subtle argumentation strategy (part sympathy and part admiration) to get his readers to side with Colton.*

**entranced:** Carried away with wonder or awe.

*Kersten uses these sketches to provide insight into Colton's obsession with flying, as well as to illustrate how thorough and meaningful young Colton's obsession was.*

*Kersten, using research, uses Colton's mother, Pam—and many other interviewees—as a source (outside text) for the complicated story of Colton's boyhood and his lifelong obsession with flying.*

Kersten employs the illustrative writing strategy repeatedly to paint a vivid and detailed picture of how young Colton became a cult hero and a legend among his fans.

Before the crime spree that made him a legend, Colt had never actually been in a plane. But right across the water was Whidbey Island, home to a naval air station, and A-6E Intruders and EA-6B Prowlers tore through the skies above him on a regular basis. The Blue Angels were a top attraction at the base's annual air show, and just 15 miles east was the main Boeing plant in Everett, the largest airplane factory in the world. "He had this book of all the Boeing airplanes that they had made, and he always told me he wanted to become a pilot," says Jessica Wesson, a childhood friend of Colt's since the second grade. "He even told me that his dad was a pilot. I'm pretty sure he was lying about that, though."

Colt was determined to become a pilot himself, but social gravity seemed to have other plans for him. On his eighth birthday, his mother bought him a $300 bike. A sheriff's deputy, unable to believe that a poor kid who lived in a mobile home could have such an expensive toy, accused him of stealing it and escorted him home in the back of his cruiser, embarrassing Colt in front of his mother. When Colt was eight or nine, his dog was run over and killed by the wife of a local cop. The worst blow came a year later, when his stepfather, Bill, was found dead in an Oklahoma motel room of a likely drug overdose. In a rage, Pam smashed every piece of glass in the house. "I went insane," she recalls. She hit the bottle hard after that, sometimes sinking into two-week binges in which she failed to stock the house with enough food.

Colt became depressed, unable to fall asleep until three in the morning, then waking up the next day feeling groggy and irritable. "I am not happy," he confided to a social worker at the time. "I could stay in bed all day. I need help. I am tired of this stuff." He felt trapped in his own home, at the mercy of his mother's addiction. He wanted her to quit drinking and go back to work, to provide him with what other kids had: cellphones, nice shoes, stability. He fought to project normality by keeping his hair short and his clothes clean, but he had trouble relating to other kids at school, eating by himself and rarely talking. When he did speak up, his mouth got him in trouble: In the sixth grade, he picked a fight with two kids who beat him up, and he teased another student so mercilessly that the kid began to choke him. "The older we got, the better Colton got at getting into trouble and getting out of it," recalls Wesson. "He was very sly and a good liar. I remember when he would get in trouble he always had this smirk on his face that said, 'You have no idea who you're dealing with.'"

One day when he was 12, Colt saw a cellphone sitting in an empty delivery truck in the nearby town of Stanwood. He had always wanted a phone, so he took it. After he made a few calls with it, the cops quickly tracked him down. More theft cases followed, mostly kid stuff, but it was enough to draw the attention of the authorities, who routed him into the system. A psychiatrist Pam consulted put Colt on Strattera, a failed antidepressant that was repackaged as a medication for kids with attention-deficit disorder. He began sleeping better, but Pam, claiming the drug made him depressed and moody, never renewed the prescription.

The two of them fought constantly. "He was like the Tasmanian Devil," Pam says. Social workers who visited the home reported that Colt experienced "constant meltdowns pretty much every day." Once, when he was 12, his mother pressed assault charges against him. During one epic battle, Colt later recounted, Pam screamed, "I wish you would die!" Although she denies she has a drinking problem, a report by mental-health experts put the blame squarely on her: "This conflict seems largely due to mom's drinking of alcohol." Social workers recommended that Pam put Colt in counseling and seek treatment for her alcoholism, but she refused both. In a case file that petered out with no resolution, a social worker would write, "Parent states her drinking helps her deal with Colton and helps her stand up to him."

> Kersten goes beyond simply interviewing Colton's mother and includes quotes from reports filed by social workers regarding Colton's case.

Colt tried to encourage her. He presented her with an AA handbook, but she burned it. Seething at the destruction that drugs and alcohol had wrought on his family, he resolved he would never do either. It would become his single greatest point of pride, a way to set himself apart from the adults who had failed him.

Stealing was another matter. He fell into a routine of petty theft—the cash box from the local public library, sodas from the teachers lounge at school, even two small boats. All he needed to take his criminal record to the next level was a mentor, who came along soon enough.

When he was 14, Colt made friends with a boy whose name sounded like something straight out of the annals of Wild West sidekicks: Harley Davidson Ironwing. Like Colt, Harley was fatherless. He'd lost his dad, an avid biker, to leukemia when Harley was four, leaving him with a mother he considered a junkie. The state placed him with a Native American foster family, and he adopted their last name. By the time he met Colt, at age 16, he was already supporting himself as a burglar, knocking over homes in and around Stanwood.

A blond, curly-haired kid with a hobbit's build, Harley was a foot shorter than Colton, but the younger boy looked up to him. "Colt wanted to be like I am, have a reputation where nobody messed with him," says Ironwing, who just finished serving two years for burglary at Airway Heights Corrections Center, near Spokane. "He'd been bullied, and I don't like bullies. I took him under my wing."

Interviewing Ironwing enabled Kersten to tell Colton's story from the perspective of a young man who was not only a fellow criminal, but also Colton's mentor in many ways.

To Colt, Harley was living life on his own terms, free from parental supervision, taking what he needed to get by without hurting anyone. "He knew I wouldn't go into a house if somebody's home," says Harley. "I'm not trying to get hit with kidnapping or anything like that." Colt realized that the key to winning the older boy's trust—and the material trappings he wanted—were right in his backyard: the vacation homes on Camano's south end. So he hid in the woods, staked out a vacant spread, then called Harley for help.

"You give me $300 upfront, and I keep whatever I find," Harley told him—and that was how the longest-running burglary spree in the island's history began. Ironwing taught him how to slip through the forests between homes, pick locks and stay invisible to neighbors. Soon the two friends were pulling off jobs every few weeks, stealing jewelry, cellphones, iPods, credit cards, laptops, a telescope, TVs and food. They'd often steal a car to ferry the goods, but after "borrowing" it, they'd fill it up with gas, drive it back to where they found it and wipe away the prints.

Just being inside the houses was a rush for Colton. They were clean and well-stocked with all the semblances of the normal, prosperous life he'd never had. If he was confident the owners were away, he'd kick off his shoes, pour himself a juice from the fridge and watch TV. Colton enjoyed it so much that soon he was logging on to peoples' computers and going online to learn new skills as a criminal. He taught himself how to rig a stolen credit card to a homemade reader, pull its PIN number and draw cash off it from an ATM. Later he began using the cards to shop online for commercial credit-card readers and specially crafted "bump" keys, capable of opening common household locks.

The computers and the Internet also allowed him to explore his deeper obsession. "He talked about stealing a plane," says Ironwing. An even better plan, the friends agreed, would be to steal a helicopter, which they could use to rob a Costco. "Me and him talked about landing it on the roof," says Ironwing. "There's a lot of things you can get at Costco."

For all their big talk, the two friends seemed more like teenagers playing at being crooks. They rarely left messes at the houses they robbed, careful to clean up after themselves, and Colton didn't even sell most of the goods he stole, hoarding them in a tent on his mother's property. That proved to be a mistake. One day in September 2006, police arrived at Pam's house to serve a warrant for Colton, who had missed a court date on charges that he bought $3,700 worth of computer equipment with a stolen credit card. Discovering the cache of stolen goods, they linked Colton to the string of burglaries.

Rather than get locked up for the credit-card charges, Colton decided to go on the lam. It was the beginning of his life as a fugitive: Aside from a stint in juvenile detention, he would spend the next four years on the run. Some speculated that he was living in the woods like an old-time outlaw, but Ironwing scoffs at the idea. "He had a place to stay," he says, but refuses to elaborate. What seems clear is that Colton supported himself by robbing homes and stores: Police suspect his haul may total as much as $1.5 million. Angered by the thefts, residents began to clamor for the cops to do something. "At one point I hated my house, which is really quite beautiful," one of the victims wrote to a judge. Another claimed that her "ability to live comfortable and safe within my own house was shattered. I didn't get a good night's sleep for weeks."

Mark Brown, the sheriff of Island County, printed up "Wanted" posters of Colton and Harley, and vowed to the media that he would capture them—an act he now says he almost regrets. "I did it to catch him," Brown says. "But the thing I agonize about is that I brought him to the media's attention in the first place."

Kersten describes the "wanted" posters as a text that actually had the opposite effect than the sheriff intended: adding to Colton's outlaw mystique and gaining him a larger following.

The chase was on. To Colton, the challenge was personal, a continuation of the conflict with Camano cops that went all the way back to the bike incident when he was eight. Deputies further stoked his ire when they temporarily confiscated his new dog, a beagle mix named Melanie, that they found tied up next to his cache of stolen goods. "Cops wanna play huh!?" Colton wrote in a note to his mom. "Well it's no lil game . . . . It's war! & tell them that."

Deputies came close to arresting Colton twice, when they caught him in the midst of a burglary, but both times he simply outran them, disappearing into the woods. Then, in February 2007, Sheriff Brown's campaign paid off when neighbors noticed a light on in a summer home and called the police. His men surrounded the residence and shouted out Colton's name. Terrified, he phoned his mom. She drove to the house, stood outside and talked to him for close to an hour by cellphone, finally persuading him to surrender.

Colton, then 16, pleaded guilty to three counts of burglary and was shipped off to Green Hill School, a maximum-security facility for juvenile offenders. After a psychologist determined that he was at heart a good, intelligent kid who didn't do drugs, he was sent to Griffin Home, a minimum-security group residence in the Seattle suburb of Renton. With only about 30 residents, the quiet, low-key setting made it feel more like a summer camp than a detention facility. He would be confined to Griffin for three to four years, depending on how quickly he straightened up his act.

**stultifying:**

Causing something or someone to appear to be stupid, foolish, or absurdly illogical.

Colton found the home stultifying. The fluorescent lights burned his eyes, and the counselors forced him to take a class on drug and alcohol abuse, lumping him in with the dopers and tweakers. For him, it was the ultimate humiliation, and he began teasing other boys during therapy sessions, playing the clown. But his wiseass routine failed to win him friends, and he felt isolated, misunderstood. "I wish I was home," he wrote on an elaborately designed card he sent to his mother, "but since I'm not, this is the best I can do. I hope you like it." He drew a sylvan scene evoking the best of home: a butterfly, a chicken, flowers, fir trees and a flaming barbecue.

Kersten dissects Colton's card to his mother—both the drawings and the actual writing—in order to unearth more details about Colton's psychology.

**sylvan:**

Relating to the woods or a forest.

Kersten illustrates how this artwork speaks volumes about Colton's frame of mind, the material goods Colton valued, and the feelings of greatness he expresses by labeling himself a "professional pilot."

Art was one of the only classes he enjoyed at Griffin. One collage he created, on the theme of what he wanted out of life, displays the crisp, orderly focus of someone who knows exactly what he wants to accomplish. It consists of 106 images, most of which are text, in a precise and careful arrangement. The word "money" appears four times, along with "wealth" and "dollars" and a dozen designer labels, from DKNY to Hugo Boss. Most of the images are high-end gadgets—Rolex watches, cellphones, PDAs—but there is also a strawberry cheesecake, and tourism logos from Mexico and Argentina. At the top of the collage, dead center, is a passenger jet, framed by prophetic words: "May I have another" and "Profession: Pilot."

But the life he wanted would never come to him as long as he was confined to Griffin Home. The place had no fence, and from his bunkhouse, the freeway leading back to Camano was only a thousand feet away. At 8:40 p.m. on April 29th, 2008, Colton waited until the first bed check of the evening was complete, then slipped out of his bunk and into the night.

There was no turning back for Colton once he left Griffin Home. He had violated the terms of his sentence, which would only add to the time he would be locked up. If they were going to catch him again, he decided, they would have to do it while he was pursuing his dream. He knew he wasn't going to win his wings by conventional routes: the military, college, flight school. He'd have to train himself, which would take time and resources.

What he did after fleeing Griffin can't be confirmed, but police suspect he resorted to his old habits. Two weeks after escaping from the home, they say, Colton was back on Camano, hitting the weekend homes hard. He applied for credit cards with info stolen from burglary victims, and had one sent to him at a mailbox he installed by his mother's property. (While he was at it, his mother insisted on cooking him a big breakfast—hash browns and eggs and sausage and bacon. Then he took off so she wouldn't get in trouble for harboring him.) He allegedly used the stolen cards to withdraw $300 in cash, and he went online and ordered card scanners and two iPods. He managed to stay off the police's radar for three months, until a deputy spotted him driving a stolen Mercedes. When the deputy gave chase, Colton jumped from the car and escaped into the woods.

Colton was clearly enjoying himself: Police recovered a backpack from the Mercedes containing a digital camera with photos he had taken of himself. In one, he's lying on his back among the trees and ferns, wearing a Mercedes polo shirt and smirking as he listens to one of his stolen iPods. The photo would become the iconic image of Colton, emblematic of his outlaw mystique: a cocky, resourceful thief, comfortable on the lam, doing his own thing.

Based on the photo, it was easy to assume that Colton was a survivalist, living in the forests of the Pacific Northwest like a boy Rambo or a "feral child," as one Camano detective called him. To track him down, the police sent out dog teams and helicopters equipped with infrared radar, but they never found a trace. That's because Colton was most likely staying in vacant homes or with friends: He wanted to fly, and he needed to be close to the Internet to prepare himself. He could download training programs like *Microsoft Flight Simulator* or *X-Plane*, fire them up on a stolen laptop or desktop and practice for hours. Both programs

---

Kersten dissects the photo—the most popular multimedia text, or representation of Colton—to shed light on how Colton evolves as both a criminal and a young man.

**emblematic:**
Symbolic of something, or representative of something.

This is one of few places Kersten employs the process-analysis writing strategy. The process Colton undertakes to learn how to fly shows his commitment to his goal, despite its difficulty.

offered dozens of planes to choose from, with realistic terrain and cockpit displays, weather settings and thousands of airports. By early November, seven months after leaving Griffin Home, his secondhand knowledge had reached its limit. He needed to fly solo, and the only way to do it was to steal a plane.

Airplane theft is a rare crime. In 2009, only seven airplanes were stolen in the United States; the suspects are almost invariably members of drug cartels, who use the planes to transport their products. Almost unheard of are thieves like Colton, who take to the sky with no practical experience and no greater motivation than to simply be airborne. An article in a 1929 edition of *Popular Science* tells the tale of a British mechanic who, responding to a dare, took off in a bomber. "He was gone for four hours and Royal Air Force planes went out to look for him or the wreckage," reads the account. "When he was sighted on his way back, they rushed fire apparatus to the landing field, expecting him to crash. But he made a safe landing, even if it was obviously inexpert." More recently, in March of last year, a Texan named Joshua Paul Calhoun commandeered a Bonanza 836 from a municipal airport and crashed it in a stand of trees five miles after taking off, walking away with only minor injuries. Later, in a jailhouse interview, Calhoun explained his motivation to a reporter in terms that Colton could relate to: a life-long fascination with flying.

Once Colton reached the hangar at Orcas Island Airport on the night of November 11th, his burglary experience came in handy. The door was locked, but he had no trouble forcing it open.

> This text shows how dangerous (and rare) Colton's plane thievery is, and also how good (or lucky) Colton had to be to not kill himself in his flight attempts.

There in front of him was the Cessna 182 that police say he had scoped out earlier that day. He rummaged around the hangar until he found a key to the Cessna, then climbed into the cockpit.

Colton browsed the manual, which owners are required to keep in the plane. Then, at first light, he switched both fuel tanks to the "on" position, pushed the mixture-control rod to "full-in" so that plenty of fuel would reach the engine, and flipped on the fuel pump to prime the aircraft. Moments later, after turning the key and pushing in the throttle, he found himself racing down the runway at 80 miles per hour, with nothing but the cold, unwelcoming waters of Puget Sound beyond. As the Cessna's nose wheel tipped off the tarmac, he pulled back on the yoke, and the plane popped gently off the earth.

> Once again, Kersten explains the process of flying to give his readers a better understanding of the complexities and potential dangers of flight, by using the process-analysis writing strategy.

After nearly 18 years of dreaming, he was flying.

Whether or not Colton had a destination in mind is known only to him, but his options were surprisingly limited. Unless he wanted to draw attention by crossing into Canadian airspace, his best bet was to stay far enough east, which is precisely what he did. He banked southeast, toward the Cascades. Heavy rain was pounding the mountains that morning, but to avoid the weather all he had to do was climb to 10,000 feet. There, he could soar between blue sky and a cottony sea of white, with Mount Rainier peaking through the clouds to his right like a sugar castle. Except for the occasional glint and contrail of an airliner, it was a world completely unmarred by humans, a bright, serene dreamscape that felt like it belonged entirely to him.

"In soloing—as in other activities—it is far easier to start something than it is to finish it," Amelia Earhart once said. She was referring to the art of safely landing an aircraft, a task that Colton faced three and a half hours after takeoff. He couldn't put down in a small airport without drawing the attention of authorities, so his only choice was an open, level field. He found one just on the east side of the Cascades, on the high plains of the Yakama Indian Reservation. He circled around, lined up for an approach and reduced speed, entering into a controlled fall that he had to precisely time and align. Bearing in to the field at more than 80 miles per hour, he was attempting a feat that had gotten pilots with far more experience killed.

Tribal police from the Yakama Reservation found the Cessna later that day. Its landing gear and propeller were mangled, its undercarriage crumpled. Where Colton disappeared to was anyone's guess. He was miles from the nearest town and 250 miles from home. The only trace he left behind was dried vomit in the cockpit. Whether it was brought on by airsickness or fear, it was a small price to pay. Flying had been everything Colton had imagined it would be—and better. He wanted more.

It would take almost a year for the authorities to accuse Colton of the Cessna theft. By then, he had already gained notoriety as the "Barefoot Burglar"—an alias bestowed on him after a security camera captured him stalking through a store he had allegedly robbed, sans shoes and socks. It was part of a frenetic string of suspected burglaries last summer, which not only included more homes but a boat, a bank, five stores, a rifle from a police cruiser, and another plane. According to the local sheriff, Colton stole his second aircraft, a Cirrus SR22, from the airport in a sleepy town called Friday Harbor, on September 11th of last year. He flew it only about 10 miles, back to the airport on Orcas Island where he had stolen his first plane—but what's remarkable is that he did it at night.

**frenetic:**
Frenzied or frantic.

Night flying requires far more focus than daylight flight. Unless there's a good moon, physical reference comes down almost exclusively to points of light. The FAA requires pilots to be "instrument rated" to fly in low visibility, an entirely different license that means you can go from takeoff to landing based on the readings from your instrument panel alone. John F. Kennedy Jr., who was not instrument rated, died along with his wife and sister-in-law while attempting to fly on a hazy night. Colton came close to nailing it on his first try.

"He broke one of my $300 runway lights," Beatrice von Tobel, the airport manager at Orcas, says with a laugh. "But the plane was actually still flyable."

The next night, a deputy spotted the fugitive in the town of Eastsound and gave chase. Colton easily outran the cop, laughing as he disappeared into the woods. The deputy said that Colton had "vaporized."

He was on a tear, suspected of linking together crimes so quickly and unexpectedly that the police could do little more than tabulate the toll. After outrunning the deputy, he worked his way to a nearby marina, where he stole a small yacht and navigated 15 miles north to the town of Point Roberts, right on the Canadian border. Based on subsequent burglaries there, the Royal Canadian Mounted Police believe that Colton crossed into Canada, then made his way to the British Columbia town of Creston, where he broke into two airplane hangars at the local airstrip. Unable to find a plane to his liking, he seems to have crossed back into the U.S. on foot, stolen a car, and driven it straight to another small airport in Bonners Ferry, Idaho. There, on September 29th, he is suspected of stealing the plane that would make him famous.

This time he took a Cessna 182 belonging to a local cattle rancher who used it to fly to auctions. "He broke open the passenger door with a crowbar or a screwdriver and got in the plane," says the rancher, Pat Gardiner. "He must have spent time in there reading manuals, because they figured he got in the night before, stayed in there and then opened up the door at first light, pulled the plane out."

Colton couldn't find any keys for the Cessna, but most single-engine planes are as simple to boost as a 1974 Pinto; he apparently started it up by jamming a screwdriver into the keyhole and twisting. An airport worker who saw the plane take off reported that its engine was "firewalled"—running at full bore—but even then Colton had trouble getting off the ground. Gardiner's Cessna was equipped with a variable propeller, which is kind of like a gearshift for propellers. He was taking off in low and barely cleared the tops of the trees.

After takeoff he turned southwest, following the Kootenai Valley to Spokane, then on to Walla Walla, where he swung northwest and crossed central Washington. He was heading home—but just after crossing the Cascades, his fuel reserves ran low. A few miles outside the town of Granite Falls, he dropped down beneath a thick cloud cover to search for a place to land. That's when he found himself in serious weather—and trouble.

Gardiner was stunned when he was briefed on an FAA reconstruction of the next few minutes, during which wind gusts in excess of 30 miles per hour tossed the small plane around like a toy. Colton nearly lost control of the aircraft. "He was going 90 degrees up and every which way," Gardiner says. As he finally leveled off, Colton spotted a timber clear-cut and bore down for a landing. Eager to get out of the rough weather, he approached the stump-strewn clearing at a suicidal 110 knots—a good 40 miles per hour faster than it's safe to land. It was the equivalent of jumping a pickup off a hill at 130 miles per hour and trying to put it down safely in a field of fire hydrants.

Upon contact with the ground, the plane immediately began careening into tree stumps, which ripped away its wheels and buckled the undercarriage. "When he hit the ground there were only 90 feet of marks," says Gardiner. "He had about a six- or seven-G stop." In pilot parlance: He went from almost 130 miles per hour to a dead standstill in less than three seconds.

**parlance:**
Speech, slang, or way of speaking.

The air bags in Gardiner's plane deployed, probably saving Colton's life. Investigators later determined that Colton was so scared the airplane would explode that he kicked open the passenger-side door and ran from the crash still wearing his headphones. When no flames erupted, he returned and diligently rubbed a quart of oil over the interior, successfully eliminating his fingerprints.

A logger discovered Gardiner's plane two days later; three days after that a family in Granite Falls reported a burglary, and the local police quickly mobilized a search team. As they scoured the woods behind the house, one deputy reportedly heard a gunshot. "It was close, and they felt threatened," a police spokeswoman later reported—but deputies found neither Colton nor proof that he had fired a weapon.

Harley Ironwing, who had turned himself in not long after Colton, saw the story on TV in prison and instantly recognized his friend. "I said, 'That's my little partner,'" he says. "I was actually expecting him to steal a helicopter." He has a firm opinion when it comes to the gunshot. "I know there's no way Colton fired that shot. Colt may be big, but he wouldn't hurt a fly. Everybody knows the hills around Granite Falls are filled with tweakers. It was probably somebody worried about their meth lab."

It was the Idaho plane theft, and a 26-year-old writer from Seattle named Zack Sestak, that turned Colton into a modern-day legend. Sestak had read about Colton back in September and decided to start a fan page on Facebook. "I read the article and thought, 'Wow, this kid is nuts,'" he says. "I started it kind of as a joke. For the longest time there were like seven members." After an Associated Press article about the Idaho plane theft mentioned the fan page, Sestak was surprised to find that it had gained more than 1,000 members in less than a day.

Kersten uses the Facebook fan page as a text to show the reaction people had to Colton and his growing legend, as well as how quickly the Colton legend spread.

"Fly, Colton, Fly!" "Colton is a true hero" and "You're a modern day Jesse James" were among the messages his fans wrote. Girls wanted to date him. Dozens offered to hide him from the police. A Seattle entrepreneur hawked Colton T-shirts emblazoned with his face and a slogan cribbed from the title of Merle Haggard's song: "Momma Tried." The boy whom hardly anyone had given a shit about when he needed help suddenly had friends everywhere.

These fan artifacts, such as tee shirts with slogans, can be read as texts in response to the Colton legend and subsequent cult of followers.

"You got people reading headlines about billion-dollar bailouts and executives getting million-dollar bonuses with taxpayer dollars," Sestak says. "People feel disillusioned, and they see Colton wearing the hat of somebody who's taking on the system by himself, and it looks like he's winning. It captures the imagination."

Colt was baffled by the celebrity. He called his mom and read her the Facebook messages. They had some good laughs, especially over newspaper articles that portrayed him as a barefoot renegade living in the woods, stealing food for survival. "He doesn't live in the woods and he never has," Pam says. "He lives in a house, with a lady and a couple of guys. The woman is a chef." She claims not to know the woman's name, but adds that Colton earns his keep by doing some sort of "computer work." The residence, she believes, is behind a gate and "heavily guarded." Colton drives a brand-new car, she boasts, and even goes out in public, albeit disguised. There are also rumors that he now has a girlfriend.

"The way I look at it is, he's living his life his way, and to hell with everybody else," she says. "I'm proud of that."

**Let's Pause Here••• ▶** What was your overall impression of Jason Kersten's essay on Colton Harris-Moore? Do you think he admires Colton, or is he simply reporting the facts of the case? How does his tone affect the way in which you felt about Colton as you read the essay? Do you believe that Colton is deserving of his fame, or do you think his actions warrant some other reaction? By the end of the essay, how did you feel about Colton as a person, given his upbringing, his boyhood dreams, and the nature of his crimes?

**Let's Take It Further••• ▼**

1. Why do you think it wasn't good enough for Colton merely to lie about being a pilot? Why would he need to actually steal planes to fulfill his dream?

2. Based on the language, writing strategies, and examples that Kersten employs, whom do you believe to be the audience that he is primarily targeting with his essay? How might the essay have been different if it were featured in a publication other than *Rolling Stone*? What do readers of this magazine expect from "celebrity" profiles that Kersten does and does not deliver?

3. Why do you believe that our culture in America constantly roots for the underdog, which is part of what's at the heart of our obsession with outlaws? What do these people do for us and our imagination?

4. Based on the information given in Kersten's article, do you consider Colton to be a hero or a criminal? Explain your reasons for considering him a hero or a criminal.

5. Why do you think it was such a point of pride for Colton that he refused to do drugs or alcohol? How is this a response on his part to his troubled upbringing?

6. What do you think about the fact that the sheriff, who printed up "wanted" posters of Colton, actually drew the media attention to Colton's actions, which resulted in the young man's fame? Is there another way he could have gone about it that wouldn't have given Colton so much media exposure? How did the sheriff contribute to the "text" that Colton ultimately became?

7. Compare Colton's outlaw fame to that of another popular American outlaw in recent years. Describe what elements of Colton's story are similar to the other outlaw you have chosen, and explain what about the two is different. How did the person whom you've chosen to describe become famous, and who are his or her biggest fans? What about his or her actions appeals to a large swath of the American population?

8. Research the Colton story further to see the ways in which Colton both responded to and bought into his own celebrity status. How did he "become" the outlaw hero that people so urgently wanted him to be, and how did it affect the types of crimes he committed and the manner in which he committed them? Did Colton's crimes that he committed after the publication of Kersten's article stay consistent with his previous crimes, or did they change in any noticeable way? Give evidence that shows how his celebrity status did or did not affect him.

9. Visit the site www.coltonharrismoorefanclub.com to see firsthand the types of fan media that have been generated thanks to Colton and his crime spree. After watching videos, reading posts, and browsing the merchandise for sale on the website, see if you can determine the appeal that Colton specifically has for his fan base. What, for instance, do people say is the reason they admire him? What kinds of responses have been generated in response to the young man's fame, and how do his fans interact with one another? Do you agree or disagree with their Colt obsession, or do you see him as a criminal instead of an outlaw hero? Explain your reasons why.

10. Research Colton Harris-Moore to see how the story of the "Barefoot Bandit" has continued since the publication of Kersten's essay in *Rolling Stone*. How has his legend evolved since the essay was published, and how has his fan base grown? How does the outcome of the Colton legend depend on whether he remains at large or gets apprehended by law enforcement officers? Has he been captured since the original publication of the article, and, if so, what was the outcome of the case against him?

11. Locate the Merle Haggard song "Momma Tried," which has become the unofficial theme song for Colton Harris-Moore's fan base. How is the story told in the Haggard song similar to and different from Colton's own story? Why do you believe his fans want to apply the classic country song to Colton and his story?

12. Research the types of crimes Colton has committed besides airplane theft and describe some of these crimes. Explain why you think people regularly make comparisons between Colton and the legend of Robin Hood. How can the crimes that Colton commits be aligned with the crimes of the English folk hero Robin Hood, or are the two unrelated? Whether or not you agree that his crimes and actions can be likened to Robin Hood's, be sure to explain your reasoning.

# 10 Celebrities Caught on Tape with Drugs

**LiquidGenerationTube**

**Let's Start Here•••** ▶ As we have already discussed in this chapter, Americans have a certain obsession with watching celebrities self-destruct. Of course, there are many ways in which celebrities occasionally manage to do this. Some get in trouble with the law, while others are simply taped or filmed while they say some off-color remark or go into a tirade against some person or group of people.

But for many celebrities, drugs and alcohol seem to play a major role in their downfall. The list of celebrities who have ruined their careers (and often their lives) is tragically long, and it continues to grow as years pass. From Marilyn Monroe to Elvis Presley, and from Michael Jackson to Anna Nicole Smith, celebrities from all walks of life and backgrounds seem to get caught up in the world of drugs and alcohol. Speculation abounds as to the reasons why celebrities appear to struggle more with drug addiction than the average person. Perhaps they are merely trying to cope with the downside of fame (being forever in front of the judgmental eye of American popular culture and its media), or perhaps they simply have more money and access than the average drug user and so they seem to crash faster and harder. Either way, when celebrities crash, we watch, and we judge them. Sometimes celebrities are revered for their drug use (Bob Marley or Amy Winehouse), and sometimes they are detested for how sad they become as they succumbed to their addictions (Whitney Houston or Lindsay Lohan). Occasionally, celebrities are even given another chance (Robert Downey, Jr., or Mickey Rourke), and we celebrate their comeback.

The following video is a compilation of ten celebrities who have been filmed while on drugs. As you watch the video, see how many of the celebrities you recognize. Also, make a note of which ones succumbed to their addictions completely and which ones have continued to have careers, as well as the ones that you continue to admire and those who you do not like.

---

LiquidGenerationTube is the YouTube channel for the company Liquid Generation, based out of Chicago, Illinois. The company describes itself on its website with the following statement: "Liquid Generation has been corrupting the Internet since 2000. We make funny, irreverent entertainment for Web junkies and procrastinators of all types. From cartoons to videos, from games to online pranks, we do it all and we do it awesome. Whenever you're alone. Whenever you want to avoid work. Whenever you have no one to hug. Liquid Generation is here to serve you." The following video was originally uploaded on April 26, 2009.

**Search on YouTube: "10 Celebrities Caught on Tape with Drugs"**
http://www.youtube.com/watch?v=anqbpL_BN5Y

**Let's Pause Here•••▶** What was your overall impression of the video? Did you find it to be disturbing or entertaining? Regardless of the response you had, explain the experience you had while watching the video. Were there any celebrities whom you failed to recognize? Were there any celebrities whose presence in the video surprised you? If so, why were you surprised?

**Let's Take It Further•••▼**

1. Based on the comments beneath the video, would you say that people who watched these wasted celebrities were entertained or disturbed by the images displayed by the YouTube user, "LiquidGenerationTube"?

2. Do you expect celebrities to be better role models than the people featured in this video, or have you come to expect that celebrities and addiction sometimes go hand in hand? What has led you to believe this?

3. Were you surprised by any of the behaviors of the celebrities featured in the video, or was the behavior here what you've come to expect from celebrities? Why or why not?

4. Choose any of the celebrities shown in the video whom you admire (or once admired) and describe who they are and what their career is that made them famous. Then, describe whether the footage of them in this video disappointed you or reaffirmed your interest in them. What reasons do you have for responding to these particular celebrities' video footage in the way you did?

5. Choose any celebrity featured in this video (or another celebrity with a history of drug or and/or alcohol abuse) who has damaged his or her reputation or career, only to be given another chance. Who is the person, and how did he or she do damage to his or her reputation? Has the celebrity managed to revive his or her career? If so, how? If not, why not?

6. Throughout the video, there are several celebrities who are so well known for their drug use that it has become a part of their image. Choose any of these celebrities known for drug abuse and explain how it plays into the image of themselves that they put forward. Explain

why it might be relevant (or even important) to the celebrity's career that he or she purposely uses drugs or alcohol to lend credibility to the career for which the person has gained celebrity status. How might the person's career be different if he or she were to "clean up" and stop using drugs or alcohol regularly?

7. Locate other videos of celebrities caught on tape doing something that turned out to be damaging to their career. Describe the video and the media reaction to the event. How did it negatively affect the person's career and why? What, if anything, did the person do to counter the video's release? How has the person's behavior changed or stayed the same since the video was released?

8. Create your own video or image collage featuring the self-destruction of celebrities. How are these celebrities perceived in light of their self-destruction? Whose careers have been harmed by their actions, and whose careers have been helped? Which of these celebrities decided to "clean up," and which of them allowed their self-destruction to become a part of their celebrity "text" or narrative?

# Here We Are Now...
**Jeff Gordinier**

**Let's Start Here •••▶** When it comes to musical celebrities, each decade has its musical icons who seem to bubble to the top of the heap of performers. While certain genres of music have their own icons as well, often there are one or two musicians who later are determined to represent an entire era because of the impact they made beyond their musical careers. For example, Michael Jackson and Madonna are widely touted as the most iconic performers of the Eighties, by most pop culture gurus' accounts. And while many might say that Lady Gaga could be the most iconic performer of the Aughts, only time will tell.

For many music buffs, one of the most iconic figures of the Nineties was Kurt Cobain, the lead singer of the wildly popular band Nirvana that is often credited with ushering in the "Grunge" movement of the Nineties. Cobain, who killed himself in 1994, is the central figure of the following essay, where author Jeff Gordinier explains how Cobain heavily influenced both fashion and popular culture when his band came onto the scene in the early Nineties. Moreover, Gordinier discusses the slippery concept of "selling out," and how Cobain might feel about the legacy that he left behind and what has been done with it.

As you read Gordinier's essay, observe the way in which he explains Cobain's relevance to popular culture both in his lifetime and in the years since his death. Also, pay attention to the ways in which Gordinier shows how popular culture has changed since 1994, and the ways in which Cobain's most rabid fans have themselves evolved since the height of Nirvana's fame.

Jeff Gordinier is the editor-at-large of *Details* magazine. His work has appeared in *Esquire, GQ, Fortune, Entertainment Weekly,* and the *Los Angeles Times*, as well as in the *Best American Nonrequired Reading* and *Best Creative Nonfiction* anthologies. He is the author of the best-selling book *X Saves the World: How Generation X Got the Shaft but Can Still Keep Everything from Sucking* (2009). The following essay originally appeared in *Details* magazine's March 2009 issue.

The place in Seattle where Kurt Cobain died is hidden in the pines. It's not easy to see from the street, and the pilgrims who are determined to get a better view walk down toward Lake Washington and rubberneck from a patch of grass that's known as Viretta Park. There they find two benches marked up with the inevitable rock-shrine greetings and invocations: "We miss you!" "R.I.P." "Kurt would have helped impeach Bush!" The messages have overlapped each other through the years, but early in 2009 this lyric was scrawled among them: "I'm not like them, but I can pretend."

**invocations:**
The act of calling on an authority (or god-like) figure.

It's a line from "Dumb," a melancholy tune from Nirvana's *In Utero* album, and to come across it now is to revisit the brief, bizarre moment when Kurt Cobain was the biggest rock star in the world. That moment seems like a long time ago. This year brings the 15th anniversary of his suicide—the Nirvana frontman slipped the barrel of a shotgun into his mouth in a spare room above the garage of his house at 171 Lake Washington Boulevard on April 5, 1994, at the age of 27, and his body was found three days later—and to some degree the city that catapulted Cobain to conflicted fame, along with the generation that he spoke for, has grown up and moved on.

In media shorthand Cobain is often referred to as the voice of his generation, but it's more accurate to say that he is the voice of what his generation used to be. A lot has happened since 1994. The slacker era has passed, and Generation X has filled the ranks of business, culture, and politics with a phalanx of strivers— the Google guys and Jeff Bezos, Jon Stewart and Stephen Colbert, Rachel Maddow and Anderson Cooper, Newark mayor Cory Booker and Louisiana governor Bobby Jindal and (if we're willing to stretch the demographic a bit) President Barack Obama and his wife, Michelle. Meanwhile, Cobain's identity remains stuck in the bong-water amber of the early nineties. For better or worse, he died before we got to see him go bald, grow a pony-tail, embrace Kabbalah, record an album of Broadway show tunes, and sip Bellinis by the pool with Sting.

**phalanx:**
A large, organized body or group of people.

Cobain's trapped-in-time twentysomething stance—sullen, angry, anti-everything—doesn't necessarily click with the issues that preoccupy his generational comrades in 2009. If Gen X has succumbed to the big sellout since then, well, it's not as though Cobain escaped the same fate. You might say he's the victim of posthumous gentrification: Memorializing Kurt has turned into its own industrious wing of the media business. In 2006, *Forbes* crowned Cobain No. 1 on its list of the most lucrative dead celebrities—higher than Elvis Presley and John Lennon. Cobain earned the rank in part because his

**gentrification:**
The process of wealthy people moving into a poor area to renew it, which often results in the displacement of poorer people.

widow, Courtney Love, had sold one quarter of the spoils from his back catalog to Primary Wave, a company that places songs in TV shows and commercials and builds associations with various products. Its most visible deal was with Converse, which created a line of Kurt sneakers decorated with Cobain's signature and chicken-scratch musings. (Scrawled on the sole of one version: PUNK ROCK MEANS FREEDOM.) "Kurt wore those shoes," Primary Wave's Devin Lasker says. "It wasn't like it was, like, some artist who never wore Converse before."

But Cobain didn't just stage-dive in Chucks. "He *died* in the things," points out *Ad Age* blogger Charlie Moran. "I mean, that's disturbing." Nevertheless, Cobain's gruesome finale hasn't proved much of an obstacle to the marketing machine. "He still represents the last bit of real mainstream rebellion, and I think that's really attractive to marketers, because he straddles a line by being this really incorrigible anti-authoritarian figure who, at the same time, was commercially very successful," Moran says. As with Che Guevara, Marilyn Monroe, James Dean, or Bob Marley, Cobain's narrative can be shorn of its complexity and contradictions and boiled down to an image on a T-shirt. "He's an easily identifiable figure," says Ted Royer, the executive creative director at the Droga5 ad agency. "It's easy to poster-ize him, to break him down to basic elements." Late last year a taped-together Fender Mustang that Cobain had played and demolished sold for $100,000. "When I was a teenager, the idea of Kurt Cobain having his own sneaker—that would've been like sacrilege," says Ben Gibbard, 32, of Death Cab for Cutie, a Washington State band that formed three years after Cobain's death. These days, the deal-making doesn't irk Gibbard as much. "If they were making 'Heart-Shaped Box' into 'Eight-Piece Box' for, like, Kentucky Fried Chicken, yeah, that would offend me," Gibbard says. "But if it takes a Kurt Cobain Converse to remind people to go buy Nirvana records, that's fine with me."

> **incorrigible:**
> Not able to be managed or ruled.

In other words, *well, whatever, nevermind.* Seattle's the city of Amazon.com and Starbucks now. Local legend maintains that Cobain was last seen alive at Linda's Tavern, a Capitol Hill jukebox-and-burgers joint, although the man in the moth-eaten cardigan might not recognize the area these days. Thanks to a building boom and the heady influx of Pacific Rim tech cash, the neighborhood that once signified the apex of the alternative is flush with yuppie condominiums. In the same way, the disaffected youth who rallied around Nirvana in the early nineties have become affected adults. Many of them now live in those yuppie condos, and if they could afford it, they wouldn't mind buying a comfortable waterside house like the one at 171 Lake Washington Boulevard. "I'm not like them," Cobain sang back in 1993, and yet we'll never know for sure. He stopped trying to pretend, while over the years we've become less and less like him.

> **apex:**
> The highest point of something.

**Let's Pause Here•••▶** How well does Gordinier make the case for Cobain's influence on both fashion and popular culture in his essay? Do you agree with his assessment of Cobain's importance, or do you think he's overstating the singer's relevance? How, if at all, has this essay changed your opinion of Cobain or his band Nirvana? What, in particular, led you to change your impression of Cobain or his band?

**Let's Take It Further•••▼**

1. If you agree with Gordinier's assessment of Cobain's importance to Nineties popular culture and fashion, explain why you think Cobain had such a huge impact. If you disagree, explain why you believe Cobain was not as relevant as Gordinier would have you believe.

2. Based on the discussion of Cobain and his impact on the Nineties (according to Gordinier), whom do you think Gordinier most wants to engage with his essay? Is he speaking to people who grew up in the Nineties, the so-called Gen Xers, or is he informing people who came of age prior to or after the Nineties? What, in particular, in his usage of language and writing strategies proves the identity of Gordinier's target audience?

3. Whether or not you are familiar with either Nirvana or Kurt Cobain, explain why you believe musicians are held in such high esteem in our culture. Why and how do they speak for their time in such an important way that they often gain a cult-like following of fans?

4. Consider other celebrities who had a large impact on popular culture in a particular decade. Who, if anyone, do you think had the largest impact on the decade that you have chosen to discuss? How did that person impact culture in such a way that he or she has become a symbol of that decade? Have there been "copycat" celebrities who have borrowed from the styles of the celebrity you chose?

5. What do you think about the statement Gordinier makes that Generation X (Cobain's generation) has "grown up and moved on"? In your opinion, is that a bad or a good thing? Why or why not?

6. Why do you believe that celebrities who die young, like Cobain, play such an important role in their generation's identity, even as that generation grows up?

7. Gordinier makes the point that Cobain is the voice of "what his generation used to be," and then he points out several Gen Xers who have gone on to achieve success and even fame. Describe another member of Generation X (which was widely referred to as the "slacker generation"), besides those mentioned in Gordinier's essay, who has "grown up" and become successful. Who is the person you have chosen, and how has he or she succeeded in the business, entertainment, or political world? How has the person exceeded the expectations that popular culture had for this particular generation?

8. Gordinier describes how the business of "memorializing" a dead celebrity is often at odds with the real person who they are memorializing. For example, he mentions how ironic it seems that Cobain—who despised fashion, materialism, and popular culture—has become a fashion and popular culture industry himself. Locate and research another deceased celebrity who has since turned into an industry of his or her own. Who is the celebrity, and in what way has he or she been "sold" and turned into an industry in the years since death? What does the celebrity symbolize for the people who buy products related to the person? In

what way is the person marketed to appeal to his or her particular niche group of fans? Do you think this is a good or a bad thing, and why?

9. Explain the concept of "selling out" and why it is such a big deal to fans of a celebrity when they capitalize on his or her fame. When celebrities sell out, does it matter to you at all? Why or why not? Find a celebrity who has "sold out" and explain both how he or she sold out and how it has affected the person's career, for better or for worse. What do you believe accounts for the success or failure of the person since the celebrity sold out?

10. In addition to cultural icons, every generation also has places that are seen as a "cultural mecca" for their time, such as Seattle in the Nineties. These locations often represent significant popular culture movements, usually because some type of popular fashion or music trend (or both) stemmed from the place. Locate one such place that is a "cultural mecca" of our time or any other era before now, and explain what popular culture movement emerged from there, as well as the impact it has had on our larger culture in the days since. If it is a location that was important for an earlier time, explain what has become of the place in the years since its cultural relevance.

# mash it UP

Here is a series of essay and discussion topics that draw connections between multiple selections within the chapter. They also suggest outside texts to include in your essay or discussion. Feel free to bring in further outside texts, remembering the variety of texts (beyond articles) available to you.

1. Using a similar approach as Jason Kersten uses in his essay "The Airplane Thief," research and describe the life of another real-life outlaw who has managed to capture the public's attention by becoming a hero to a group of people. Explain the nature of the person's crimes, as well as the explanation given by fans for why they find the person (and their crimes) to be not only acceptable, but also appealing.

2. Compare the decline of a celebrity as reported by supermarket tabloids versus websites such as TMZ.com or PerezHilton.com. What is the difference in the types of stories that are reported in print tabloids versus online celebrity gossip blogs? How do the various media utilize sources as "proof" of celebrities' shortcomings? Ultimately, which of the formats (print or online) has more credibility, and why?

3. Sites such as YouTube and Twitter have spawned many celebrities in recent years, as videos go viral and a person is catapulted from obscurity to fame overnight. Find a current YouTube/Twitter celebrity and describe what has made the person famous. Describe the manner in which the person's fans have responded to him or her (via comments or Tweets),

and explain how the person's celebrity status has risen or dwindled since the person first achieved fame online. Was the person's fame short-lived, or has he or she managed to turn it into a career that is meaningful?

4. How have the roles of celebrities in our society changed in recent decades? Seek out older tabloid magazines archived online or in a library and describe the types of people (and their lines of work) who achieved fame in earlier eras. Also, describe how the gossip has changed (or stayed the same) in terms of the types of stories reported, the sources used by tabloids, and the responses of the celebrities themselves.

5. The tone of the essays "The Airplane Thief" and "Here We Are Now . . ." are similar in the way that both authors have some sense of admiration toward the troubled subjects in each. Locate one further article about a troubled person whose actions you believe might not warrant admiration, and explain the way in which the author exposes his or her bias toward the subject of his or her essay. Then locate another essay on the same person where the tone of the writer is one of judgment instead of praise. Which makes the better case for or against the essay's subject, and how does each piece of writing achieve this?

6. Using modern popular media (such as movies, TV shows, or websites), explain the depictions of celebrities versus "everyday people" in America. Which of the two are better portrayed? What do you think accounts for the way in which one is portrayed as more "real" or desirable, and how has the line between real people and celebrities become blurred in recent years?

7. Choose a reality show within the last five years and describe the lengths to which its contestants are willing to go in order to achieve fame. What sorts of activities are they willing to take part in so that they might beat out other contestants? Do you find anything humiliating or degrading about these activities? If so, how can you explain people's willingness to humiliate themselves publicly?

8. Compare a show that glamorizes celebrities (such as MTV's *Cribs*) to a show that criticizes them (see James Parker's "Retching with the Stars" in the "Mass Media" chapter). Which of the two provide more entertainment, and why? Are you more attracted to celebrity self-destruction, as illustrated in Dave Granlund's cartoon? Or do you prefer to see celebrities glamorized and worshiped, as Virginia Postrel argues in her essay "Superhero Worship"?

# Work and Careers

# Chapter 11

## Making the Cultural Connection

One very pivotal aspect of the American identity is our nation's relationship with work and the very idea of working. We pride ourselves on being a country that has built itself up from virtually nothing in an amazingly brief period of time, at least compared to other civilizations that were around hundreds or even thousands of years before the United States existed as an entity. Hard work, in America, is synonymous with virtue. The very phrase "hardworking man" or "hardworking woman" is among the most flattering things one person can say about another. Conversely, there is little that Americans abhor more than a lazy person, at least as an idea. We speak negatively about people who are on welfare or those who are

### SELECTIONS IN THIS CHAPTER

able-bodied and choose not to work. Indeed, *not working* is almost as foreign a concept to our larger culture as the idea of not loving freedom.

By virtue of being enrolled in college, by taking these first important steps toward entering the workforce as a productive and active member of society (though many of you have probably held jobs for several years now), you prove your adherence to this time-honored virtue of our larger American culture. But if meaningful work is one of the ultimate goals of our lives, and if our nation's identity and culture are inextricably bound to how we work, where we work, what our work is, and whether we succeed at our chosen field, then it is necessary to dissect this concept of work more thoroughly in this chapter. After all, America has a very specific (though often troubled) history between its workers and bosses, its corporations and its general public. So, then, we will touch on these relationships and give students the chance to explore them more deeply.

First, however, it is important to note that although our nation has a tumultuous history of workers fighting their bosses for better treatment, we still consider our work, our jobs, and our careers to be an important part of our personal identity, just as much as it is a part of our national identity. Consider, for a moment, the first question two strangers almost always pose to one another after exchanging names: "What do you do?" This serves to illustrate just how deeply our identities are interlinked with the work that we do. We identify ourselves in a number of ways—as a particular race, or gender, or sexual orientation, for example—but few elements of our identity stand out as much as our jobs. We judge each other by our jobs as well. For example, if you were interested in dating two different people, one of whom was a lawyer and one of whom was a manager of a fast-food restaurant, which of them would you immediately see as the better "catch"? There is no shame in either job, to be sure, but certainly one outshines the other in terms of respectability on the hierarchy of careers.

Additionally, we carve out our identity in relation to our work, our jobs, and our careers into a variety of subcategories. In America, for instance, there are union and nonunion employees. There are blue-collar and white-collar jobs. We have vocations and trades, which we call "skilled" labor (carpentry, roofing, and welding, to name a few), and we have "unskilled" labor (the service, hospitality, and retail industries), which makes up a larger portion of the available jobs with each passing generation.

So important are work and labor to our national identity that from our earliest moments of a national popular culture (that is to say, around the time of mass print, radio, and film), our media has been deeply engaged in illustrating work and working lives in America. We have books, television shows, songs, and movies about doctors, lawyers, factory workers, servers, office workers, nannies, nurses, soldiers, police officers, politicians, bartenders, race car drivers, and just about every other possible type of job a person can aspire (or dread) to have. In one of his earliest and most famous films, called *Modern Times*, silent movie icon Charlie Chaplin won fans throughout the nation as he critiqued the plight of the American factory worker in the face of a rapidly expanding industrial workforce. The famous image (pictured here) of Chaplin caught in the cogs of machinery came to symbolize the era of industrialism and the occasional sense of powerlessness factory workers felt in the face of both the literal factory machinery, as well as the metaphorical machinery of sprawling corporations that rose to power at an amazingly rapid pace in the late 1800s and early 1900s.

There is, of course, a difference between a job (or merely working) and a career (work to which a person is willing to devote her life), which is one of the aspects of working life in America that this chapter will address. What we find, often, is that careers are the long-term work that we hope will actually mean something to us, while a job is something often understood to be a means to an end—or "working for a paycheck," as it's so often called. We will discuss the difference between "good" and "bad" jobs, or, more appropriately, desirable and undesirable jobs. And we will discuss the difference in work ethics and standards from one generation to the next, with a special focus on the generation of workers currently entering (or about to enter) the workforce.

Still, the question is, how do we form our identity as a nation of workers, especially when our country's success is tied directly to how many people are working? During the hard times, we gauge our nation's health by how many people who want jobs cannot find them. Likewise, during the good times, we judge the extent of our economic content based on the percentage of working-aged adults who are gainfully employed. Of course, the very definition of what it means to be "gainfully employed" will come up in this chapter as well, since many still debate whether that term means a job with livable wages and benefits, or whether employment is any sort of work that pays, even if that work is more service or industry related.

The most important thing to keep in mind as you proceed through this chapter is that even though we might be living in a time when good jobs are hard to come by, there are still ways to find careers that bring meaning to our lives. There is more to work than simply earning a paycheck. All the selections in this chapter address work and working, jobs and careers, and the relationships between employees and their employers from various angles in an attempt to understand the importance of these sometimes clashing pairs of concepts. We will discuss what it means to be a young worker and what it means to be an older worker, as well as the differences between management and "regular" employees. We will ask the questions. What do American workers deserve? To what are we entitled? Is a steady job with benefits still a part of the American Dream, or is it a withering concept to which future generations should cease to aspire? Are we as a country divided between rich and poor workers, between the "haves" and the "have nots," or do we still tend to divide ourselves primarily according to the work we do? Is there such a thing as a brotherhood or sisterhood of workers anymore? And what does the future hold in store for you, your siblings, and your own children? These, among other topics, are what we will address as we explore the concept of work and how it fits into our national and personal identity.

# Recession
                                                              **Paul Zanetti**

Paul Zanetti is a political cartoonist who works for the *Sydney Daily Telegraph* and is world-renowned for pioneering cartoon syndication in 1991. Currently he is the most widely circulated Australian political cartoonist, internationally syndicated with *New York Times* syndication and Cagle Cartoons. This cartoon originally appeared in the *Sydney Daily Telegraph* on July 6, 2009.

# Thinking About Working

Take a moment to look at the accompanying cartoon. Like most political cartoons, this drawing is attempting to make a statement about a topic that is popular in our culture. This cartoon's subject matter, which can be discerned at a glance, is the issue of finding work. Note that the cartoon is titled "Recession," which also shows that it is addressing America's most recent recession that began in the summer of 2008 and continues to affect the job outlook of Americans from all walks of life. Naturally, one of the most devastating factors for people during a recession is that unemployment numbers grow and jobs become harder (sometimes impossible) to find, as evidenced by the newspaper headline held by a businessman at the right of the cartoon: "Job Ads Down." Some out-of-work Americans feel as though they are being reduced to little more than street beggars, like the young man pictured carrying a sign with the clichéd panhandling phrase, "Will Work for [insert desired outcome here]."

Of course, there are many more elements of a recession that make life difficult for most Americans, but this cartoon is purposely addressing a specific slice of our population: Generation Y workers, who are generally agreed on as the people born between 1980 and 2000. Notice the way that the cartoonist, Paul Zanetti, illustrates the "Gen Y" worker who is unemployed. How does he differentiate the man holding the unemployment sign from the two men who are talking about him and his plight? Why would the younger, out-of-work man want "martinis" instead of food, clothing, housing, or something else more meaningful? What does it say about the artist's impression (as well as the impression of people older than Generation Y, in general) of younger workers and what their level of maturity is? What does it say about the perceptions in our larger American culture about young people and their work ethic?

Whether or not you are familiar with the actual or perceived differences between the various generations of American population booms (the Lost Generation, the Greatest Generation, the Baby Boomers, Generation X, and now, Generations Y and Z), it is still important to realize that there are defining characteristics of each generation's politics, work ethics, family values, and other key traits that become a sort of catchall for Americans born to a certain time period. And so, the fact that the older men are still employed and the young man is looking for work (but only wants martinis in return for his labor) speaks to the differences between the two. Of course, if you revisit such simple details as the clothing all three men wear, then it becomes apparent that they are from different generations: the older men wear more traditional, plain, no-nonsense business attire, while the younger man has on sunglasses, a "cool" hairstyle, and a more modern and trendy suit. These are some of the more obvious differences between generations of workers—the simple outer look that provides textual clues about the differences between the two generations.

Now, take a closer look at Zanetti's drawing. Notice some of the finer details. What do you suppose he is attempting to say about the older men—who are obviously still employed because they have their briefcases and are standing outside an office building—and their attitude toward the recession? Is one generation more worried than the other? Are they both worried, but about different things? What other differences do you notice between the two generations of men? What does it say about our society that recessions are to be expected occasionally, but that some people are better prepared for them (or less surprised) than others? What do you think Zanetti is saying about our nation's current state of unemployment and how this particular recession affects various generations in different ways? For example, why do you think the older men say, "It's Generation Y's *first* recession" (my emphasis)? Is the implication that Generation Y is clueless, or that they're in for many more recessions like the current one? Conversely, do younger generations of workers look to older ones for advice or wisdom for how to navigate a tough job market? Or, as the cartoon implies, are they clueless that help might be just a few feet away, as in the case of the young unemployed man who is oblivious to the older men who have obviously managed to keep their jobs?

# Factory Worker Management, 1955
### The Industry Film Archive

**Let's Start Here•••** ▶ There was a time in America when people could graduate high school and find a somewhat decent trade, or something like factory work, and keep a steady and stable income. People often refer to this period in American manufacturing as our "Golden Era" in industrial America. After the Industrial Revolution of the late 1800s, after the battles between laborers and bosses, and after basic workers' rights were made law, things settled into a somewhat steady routine of Americans working to produce products, receiving a fair amount of pay for their labor, and spending their money on homes, cars, clothing, and generally improving their positions in life. So began the massive growth of the American middle class.

But, as is most likely no secret to many students, the days when a factory job provided a living wage with steady raises and vacation time, not to mention job security, are all but gone. Hence the massive college enrollment numbers and the increasingly difficult market for unskilled workers.

There are many culprits who are to blame for the lack of American manufacturing jobs that are too various and complicated to address here, but the important thing to note as you watch the following video is how different the jobs being described are from the jobs currently available in our country. The video, called "Factory Worker Management, 1955," provides insight into the relationship between workers and their employers. It shows how companies get the most from their employees, while still keeping their workers fairly compensated and their businesses open to creativity and ingenuity. As you watch the video, pay close attention to the narrator as he explains the world of factory work from the perspectives of the workers as well as the managers and company heads. Make note of details that stand out as strikingly different from our own times.

---

The Industry Film Archive is a collection of industrial films, also known as sponsored films, made by companies and trade associations between the 1920s and the 1960s to promote a new product, industrial process, or even an entire industry. Footage from the Industry Film Archive is transferred from film originals. Learn more about the project at www.industryfilmarchive.com. This video was originally posted to YouTube on April 30, 2008.

**Search on YouTube:** "Factory Worker Management, 1955."
http://www.youtube.com/watch?v=gtZVtANG924

**Let's Pause Here•••▶**  What are your initial impressions of the video? How did the tone of the film's narrator affect the way you interpreted the video? How about the music? Did the video seem at all relevant to our current time? If so, how? If not, what made it seem so outdated, other than the obvious fact that the video was made in 1955?

**Let's Take It Further•••▼**

1. What elements of the video were the most surprising to you as you watched the film, and why?

2. Based on the narration of the video, as well as the music, the images shown, and the management techniques discussed throughout, who do you think the target audience of the video is meant to be? Which elements of the video prove to whom the organization that produced this video is trying to appeal? How well do they achieve their goal?

3. It seems that this video can be viewed as a celebration of both American ingenuity and productivity. If that is the case, what, in particular, deserves to be celebrated in this short film?

4. In what ways does the narrator show how factory managers strive to keep their workers both productive and happy? Would you be happy to work for a company such as this one? Why or why not?

5. In what manner does this company provide job security for their employees? Do you think that they have an effective strategy? What is so effective or ineffective about their strategy, in your opinion?

6. View other YouTube videos posted by Industry Film Archive and compare two or more types of management styles as explained in the films. What sorts of management techniques are stated in the film, and what do these techniques hope to accomplish with their employees? Which of the two management styles would you prefer to work under, and why?

7. Locate other management videos on YouTube and see how more current management styles are reflected in videos from the last 10 to 15 years. How do they differ from the videos of earlier years (such as the ones posted by Industry Film Archive)? What are the most notable shifts in attitude that management holds toward employees? Do managers seem more concerned with productivity, for example, or employee retention? What do you think accounts for this shift in attitude, and why?

8. Interview someone who works in a factory and compare his or her impressions of the modern-day factory work experience with the experiences of the workers in the video. How pleased is the person with the management techniques used by the company for whom he or she works? What are the particular management techniques used by the company? What, if anything, would the person change?

9. Create your own video or image collage of the work conditions wherever you work. Interview co-workers and management to get a sense of how the company attempts to appeal both to its customers and its employees. Are there some management techniques that work better than others? Are there suggestions you could give to either improve customer or employee relations? What is the overall impression of the company that people will take away after viewing your video?

# The Most Praised Generation Goes to Work

**Jeffrey Zaslow**

**Let's Start Here••• ▶** While some companies and managers scramble to identify the positive and negative traits of the incoming workforce, others feel as though they're way ahead of the curve. The solution (according to them): praise the workers. Make them feel special. Then, these Generation X and Y workers will do whatever jobs you want them to do.

At least, that's the theory behind Zaslow's essay, which believes that the root of younger workers' lack of productivity, loyalty, trust, and job satisfaction stems from the idea that the current generation of incoming workers is "the most praised generation" of employees to ever enter the workforce. To him, there are dangers in over-praising people, and the ways in which employers attempt to both please and manage the incoming generation of workers just might prove his point.

There is a general consensus among older generations that their childhoods were harder, and therefore they are better able to handle hardship, not to mention hard work, with little or no complaining. And this may or may not be true. But the important thing to note as you read the following essay is the impression older generations have of younger generations' upbringing and how that will affect future employer/employee relations.

As you read Zaslow's essay, try to determine whether you agree with his premise, as well as the solutions that companies and managers are concocting to "deal" with the "most praised generation."

---

Jeffrey Zaslow is an American journalist and a columnist for the *Wall Street Journal*. He is also the author or coauthor of three best-selling books: *The Last Lecture* (2008), *Highest Duty* (2009), and *The Girls from Ames* (2009). Zaslow's *Wall Street Journal* column, *Moving On*, focuses on life transitions and often attracts wide media interest. While working at the *Chicago Sun-Times*, from 1987 to 2001, Zaslow received the Will Rogers Humanitarian Award. He worked at the *Wall Street Journal* from 1981 to 1987, then returned in 2001. The following article first appeared in the *Wall Street Journal* on April 20, 2007.

You, You, You—you really are special, you are! You've got everything going for you. You're attractive, witty, brilliant. "Gifted" is the word that comes to mind.

Childhood in recent decades has been defined by such stroking—by parents who see their job as building self-esteem, by soccer coaches who give every player a trophy, by schools that used to name one "student of the month" and these days name 40.

Now, as this greatest generation grows up, the culture of praise is reaching deeply into the adult world. Bosses, professors and mates are feeling the need to lavish praise on young adults, particularly twenty-somethings, or else see them wither under an unfamiliar compliment deficit.

Employers are dishing out kudos to workers for little more than showing up. Corporations including Lands' End and Bank of America are hiring consultants to teach managers how to compliment employees using email, prize packages and public displays of appreciation. The 1,000-employee Scooter Store Inc., a power-wheelchair and scooter firm in New Braunfels, Texas, has a staff "celebrations assistant" whose job it is to throw confetti—25 pounds a week—at employees. She also passes out 100 to 500 celebratory helium balloons a week. The Container Store Inc. estimates that one of its 4,000 employees receives praise every 20 seconds, through such efforts as its "Celebration Voice Mailboxes."

**narcissistic:**
Having an extreme love of oneself.

Certainly, there are benefits to building confidence and showing attention. But some researchers suggest that inappropriate kudos are turning too many adults into narcissistic praise-junkies. The upshot: A lot of today's young adults feel insecure if they're not regularly complimented.

America's praise fixation has economic, labor, and social ramifications. Adults who were overpraised as children are apt to be narcissistic at work and in personal relationships, says Jean Twenge, a psychology professor at San Diego State University. Narcissists aren't good at basking in other people's glory, which makes for problematic marriages and work relationships, she says.

Her research suggests that young adults today are more self-centered than previous generations. For a multi-university study released this year, 16,475 college students took the standardized narcissistic personality inventory, responding to such statements as "I think I am a special person." Students' scores have risen steadily since the test was first offered in 1982. The average college student in 2006 was 30% more narcissistic than the average student in 1982.

## Praise Inflation

Employers say the praise culture can help them with job retention, and marriage counselors say couples often benefit by keeping praise a constant part of their interactions. But in the process, people's positive traits can be exaggerated until the words feel meaningless. "There's a runaway inflation of everyday speech," warns Linda Sapadin, a psychologist in Valley Stream, N.Y. These days, she says, it's an insult unless you describe a pretty girl as "drop-dead gorgeous" or a smart person as "a genius." "And no one wants to be told they live in a nice house," says Dr. Sapadin. " 'Nice' was once sufficient. That was a good word. Now it's a put-down."

The Gottman Institute, a relationship-research and training firm in Seattle, tells clients that a key to marital happiness is if couples make at least five times as many positive statements to and about each other as negative ones. Meanwhile, products are being marketed to help families make praise a part of their daily routines. For $32.95, families can buy the "You Are Special Today Red Plate," and then select one worthy person each meal to eat off the dish.

But many young married people today, who grew up being told regularly that they were special, can end up distrusting compliments from their spouses. Judy Neary, a relationship therapist in Alexandria, Va., says it's common for her clients to say things like: "I tell her she's beautiful all the time, and she doesn't believe it." Ms. Neary suspects: "There's a lot of insecurity, with people wondering, 'Is it really true?'"

"Young married people who've been very praised in their childhoods, particularly, need praise to both their child side and their adult side," adds Dolores Walker, a psychotherapist and attorney specializing in divorce mediation in New York.

> **mediation:**
> The act of promoting a settlement or reconciliation between two opposing people or parties.

Employers are finding ways to adjust. Sure, there are still plenty of surly managers who offer little or no positive feedback, but many withholders are now joining America's praise parade to hold on to young workers. They're being taught by employee-retention consultants such as Mark Holmes, who encourages employers to give away baseball bats with engravings ("Thanks for a home-run job") or to write notes to employees' kids ("Thanks for letting dad work here. He's terrific!").

Bob Nelson, billed as "the Guru of Thank You," counsels 80 to 100 companies a year on praise issues. He has done presentations for managers of companies such as Walt Disney Co. and Hallmark Cards Inc., explaining how different generations have different expectations. As he sees it, those over age 60 tend to like formal awards, presented publicly. But they're more laid back about needing praise, and more apt to say: "Yes, I get recognition every week. It's called a paycheck." Baby boomers, Mr. Nelson finds, often prefer being praised with more self-indulgent treats such as free massages for women and high-tech gadgets for men.

Workers under 40, he says, require far more stroking. They often like "trendy, name-brand merchandise" as rewards, but they also want near-constant feedback. "It's not enough to give praise only when they're exceptional, because for years they've been getting praise just for showing up," he says.

Mr. Nelson advises bosses: If a young worker has been chronically late for work and then starts arriving on time, commend him. "You need to recognize improvement. That might seem silly to older generations, but today, you have to do these things to get the performances you want," he says. Casey Priest, marketing vice president for Container Store, agrees. "When you set an expectation and an employee starts to meet it, absolutely praise them for it," she says.

Sixty-year-old David Foster, a partner at Washington, D.C., law firm Miller & Chevalier, is making greater efforts to compliment young associates—to tell them they're talented, hard-working and valued. It's not a natural impulse for him. When he was a young lawyer, he says, "If you weren't getting yelled at, you felt like that was praise."

But at a retreat a couple of years ago, the firm's 120 lawyers reached an understanding. Younger associates complained that they were frustrated;

**intergenerational:**
A blending of
more than one
generation.

after working hard on a brief and handing it in, they'd receive no praise. The partners promised to improve "intergenerational communication." Mr. Foster says he feels for younger associates, given their upbringings. "When they're not getting feedback, it makes them very nervous."

## Modern Pressures

Some younger lawyers are able to articulate the dynamics behind this. "When we were young, we were motivated by being told we could do anything if we believed in ourselves. So we respond well to positive feedback," explains 34-year-old Karin Crump, president of the 25,000-member Texas Young Lawyers Association.

Scott Atwood, president-elect of the Young Lawyers Division of the Florida Bar, argues that the yearning for positive input from superiors is more likely due to heightened pressure to perform in today's demanding firms. "It has created a culture where you have to have instant feedback or you'll fail," he says.

In fact, throughout history, younger generations have wanted praise from their elders. As Napoleon said: "A soldier will fight long and hard for a bit of colored ribbon." But when it comes to praise today, "Gen Xers and Gen Yers don't just say they want it. They are also saying they require it," says Chip Toth, an executive coach based in Denver. How do young workers say they're not getting enough? "They leave," says Mr. Toth.

Many companies are proud of their creative praise programs. Since 2004, the 4,100-employee Bronson Healthcare Group in Kalamazoo, Mich., has required all of its managers to write at least 48 thank-you or praise notes to underlings every year.

Universal Studios Orlando, with 13,000 employees, has a program in which managers give out "Applause Notes," praising employees for work well done. Universal workers can also give each other peer-to-peer "S.A.Y. It!" cards, which stand for "Someone Appreciates You!" The notes are redeemed for free movie tickets or other gifts.

Bank of America has several formal rewards programs for its 200,000 employees, allowing those who receive praise to select from 2,000 gifts. "We also encourage managers to start every meeting with informal recognition," says Kevin Cronin, senior vice president of recognition and rewards. The company strives to be sensitive. When new employees are hired, managers are instructed to get a sense of how they like to be praised. "Some prefer it in public, some like it one-on-one in an office," says Mr. Cronin.

**calibrating:**
Precisely adjusting
to a specific
function.

## No More Red Pens

Some young adults are consciously calibrating their dependence on praise. In New York, Web-developer Mia Eaton, 32, admits that she loves being complimented. But she feels like she's living on the border between a twentysomething generation that requires over-praise and a thirtysomething generation that is less addicted to it. She recalls the pre-Paris Hilton, pre-reality-TV era, when people were famous—and applauded—for their achievements, she says. When she tries to explain this to younger colleagues, "they don't get it. I feel like I'm hurting their feelings because they don't understand the difference."

Young adults aren't always eager for clear-eyed feedback after getting mostly "atta-boys" and "atta-girls" all their lives, says John Sloop, a professor of rhetorical and cultural studies at Vanderbilt University. Another issue: To win tenure, professors often need to receive positive evaluations from students. So if professors want students to like them, "to a large extent, critical comments [of students] have to be couched in praise," Prof. Sloop says. He has attended seminars designed to help professors learn techniques of supportive criticism. "We were told to throw away our red pens so we don't intimidate students."

At the Wharton School of the University of Pennsylvania, marketing consultant Steve Smolinsky teaches students in their late 20s who've left the corporate world to get M.B.A. degrees. He and his colleagues feel handcuffed by the language of self-esteem, he says. "You have to tell students, 'It's not as good as you can do. You're really smart, and can do better.'"

Mr. Smolinsky enjoys giving praise when it's warranted, he says, "but there needs to be a flip side. When people are lousy, they need to be told that." He notices that his students often disregard his harsher comments. "They'll say, 'Yeah, well . . .' I don't believe they really hear it."

In the end, ego-stroking may feel good, but it doesn't lead to happiness, says Prof. Twenge, the narcissism researcher, who has written a book titled *Generation Me: Why Today's Young Americans Are More Confident, Assertive, Entitled—and More Miserable than Ever Before.* She would like to declare a *moratorium* on "meaningless, *baseless* praise," which often starts in nursery school. She is unimpressed with self-esteem preschool ditties, such as the one set to the tune of "Frère Jacques": "I am special/ I am special/ Look at me . . ."

**entitled:**
Feeling as though they have a claim to something (usually unearned).

**moratorium:**
Calling for a suspension or an end to an activity.

**baseless:**
Unsupported or unwarranted.

For now, companies like the Scooter Store continue handing out the helium balloons. Katie Lynch, 22, is the firm's "celebrations assistant," charged with throwing confetti, filling balloons and showing up at employees' desks to offer high-fives. "They all love it," she says, especially younger workers who "seem to need that pat on the back. They don't want to go unnoticed."

Ms. Lynch also has an urge to be praised. At the end of a long, hard day of celebrating others, she says she appreciates when her manager,

Burton De La Garza, gives her a high-five or compliments her with a cell-phone text message.

"I'll just text her a quick note—'you were phenomenal today,'" says Mr. De La Garza, "She thrives on that. We wanted to find what works for her, because she's completely averse to confetti."

**Let's Pause Here•••▶** As you read Zaslow's essay, did you find yourself agreeing with his assessment of the current incoming generation of young workers? In other words, *is* this generation of workers the most praised generation, and are the examples he gives of how this generation became the most praised generation accurate or way off the mark? Why or why not? Even if you are not a member of Generation X or Y, discuss what you believe to be the defining traits of these two generations based on your own experience, especially in relation to the concept of work ethic.

**Let's Take It Further•••▼**

1. Whom do you believe to be Zaslow's primary audience in this essay? Is he speaking to the people of these particular two generations, or is he speaking to older generations? Is he speaking to future employers of Generations X and Y, or is he speaking to the future employees within these two generations? What about his language, writing strategies, and examples that he gives proves the identity of his intended audience?

2. If Zaslow's assessment of Generations X and Y is correct, do you think that the methods he describes companies using to appease incoming young workers are appropriate ways of dealing with the need for praise? Why or why not?

3. Zaslow points out a number of specific methods that employers use to heap praise on their employees. Which, if any, of these methods do you feel are excessive, and why?

4. Is the idea of a "celebrations assistant" (a person whose entire job is devoted to praising employees for their accomplishments) upsetting, logical, or humorous to you? Why or why not? How might a company justify such a position, especially during a time of low employment?

5. Do you agree with the assessment of professionals who warn in Zaslow's article of the dangers of excessive praise on future personal relationships? Why might this be a problem? Do you have any personal experience with this idea that you can draw on to back your claim? In other words, have you or someone you know been praised so often that you "distrust compliments" from the person giving them to you?

6. Undoubtedly, the idea of praising a person "for little more than showing up" might seem unnecessary and even counterproductive to some students. If that is the case, construct a list of accomplishments for which an employee might be praised, as well as the types of praise that are appropriate, to illustrate what you see as a better way to handle rewarding employees of these two generations. Explain and describe the process of how a manager might notice these accomplishments and what he or she might do specifically in order to praise employees without unrealistically raising expectations.

7. Zaslow gives a list of childhood examples (i.e., every child athlete receiving a trophy just for competing) that contribute to the "problem" of an overpraised generation of employees entering the workforce. Give other examples, in addition to Zaslow's, of the type of childhood praise that might be unnecessary and might also contribute to the later adult expectation of praise for minor achievements. Be sure to describe the scenario, as well as the type of praise generally given for such an achievement. Then discuss whether you believe the achievement or the praise itself is appropriate and how it might affect the recipients as they grow older.

8. Interview several people in this age group to test Zaslow's claim that "a lot of today's young adults feel insecure if they're not regularly complimented." Explain the list of questions you constructed to determine whether Zaslow's claim is true, as well as the responses that you received. Also, based on the responses and your observations, describe how your findings prove or disprove Zaslow's claim about young people. How does he get it right, and how does he get it wrong?

9. In the midst of all this talk of praise, there is one dissenting voice in the essay—Professor Twenge, a narcissism researcher—who "would like to 'declare a moratorium on meaningless, baseless praise.'" In light of the content of Zaslow's entire essay, explain why you agree or disagree with Prof. Twenge's conclusions that praise should only be given if earned. Be sure to thoroughly explain the dangers (or the value) you see in meaningless (or warranted) praise, depending on your opinion, and to provide real-life examples to back your opinion.

10. Create visual examples of awards (such as the types described in Zaslow's essay) that you feel accomplish the job of praising workers without going overboard. What types of awards have you designed, and what are they supposed to reward? Explain how these awards accomplish the goal of rewarding good work while not raising employee expectations for praise or cheapening the value of being rewarded at work.

# Yes, I'm 26. And Yes, I Do the Hiring
**Jamie Pritscher**

**Let's Start Here•••▶** When older generations of workers imagine the generations that follow them, usually each successive generation is seen as lazier and more demanding than those who came before them. These are just some of the assumptions that older generations make. Understandably, most people might even take issue with working under someone who is younger than them. It is in our nature to respect those older than us and to be more critical of those who are younger. So you can imagine the difficulty that Jamie Pritscher—a young hiring manager for a Chicago-based events company—might face on a frequent basis when she is faced with applicants and employees who are older than her.

In the following essay, Pritscher discusses the pros and cons of her age in terms of her interactions with employees. She also, in a roundabout manner, addresses some of the differences between her generation of workers and those who are older. As you read the following essay, see whether you can determine the methods Ms. Pritscher uses to combat the potential problems of hiring and managing older workers. Additionally, see if you can note the ways that she is similar to or different from the generational attributes that have been identified for Generation Y (of which Ms. Pritscher is a member, according to the dates outlined in this chapter). Does she go out of her way to be unlike the stereotypes, or does she fit them?

---

Jamie Pritscher is the director of logistics for a Chicago-based company called Tasty Catering, and an entrepreneur who created "That's Caring" (www.thatscaring.com), a website that offers "a greener way to give," with eco-friendly gift baskets. She was invited to be a guest columnist for the Jobs section of the *New York Times*, where this piece was originally published on May 1, 2010.

**logistics:**
Handling of operational details.

I'm director of logistics at Tasty Catering, a corporate catering and event planning services company outside Chicago. Our clients include McDonald's, Google, and Microsoft, which have offices here. My job is to assign staff members to events and to coordinate schedules for everyone, including event supervisors, crew leads, servers and delivery drivers, many of whom are older than me. I'm 26.

When I was promoted to this position, I was concerned about whether my age might be a problem for some people, so I talked to Larry Walter, one of the company owners, about it. I managed older women when I worked for a high-end salon several years ago, but I was worried whether our older male employees would respect my authority. Larry said I should hold my own and earn their respect. I spoke to my dad about it, too; he said the same thing.

I do the hiring, so new employees find out right away that I'm young. They get over the initial shock that way, and it sets the tone. I'm in charge of orientation for new employees, but their peers help with training, too. That builds camaraderie. Older employees have made comments occasionally, like, "How did you get to be the one that hires us?" But they say it in a joking tone, and I don't take offense.

I don't just sit in the office. I've gone on deliveries with some of the drivers, which has surprised them. Once people see that I'm capable of doing what they do, I think any uneasiness about my being their boss disappears.

I've heard it said that my generation feels entitled, or that we think everything should be given to us. I have seen people my age who fit that description, but it's a generalization. I come from a family of entrepreneurs who have worked hard for what they have. I know I have to do the same. I'm careful to be polite to everyone and treat everyone the same. I do see differences between the age groups, however.

Two years ago, we installed global positioning systems in our delivery trucks. The young employees thought that the devices were cool and fun to play with. Sometimes, the older ones wouldn't even log in, saying that, "The darn thing wasn't working." The systems are so important for customer service that we really needed everyone to use them. We drop off orders at 40 to 100 locations a day, and need to be able to reroute trucks and keep customers informed about where their orders are.

The younger workers showed the older drivers how to use the systems, but some of the older ones still weren't coming around. They just weren't used to jumping in when it came to technology. I thought of my dad, and it dawned on me that he always needs an instruction manual for the TV and other products. I asked some of the older workers whether they'd like the manual for the GPS and made copies for the ones who did. It made a big difference.

If a customer calls at 6 p.m. and places a breakfast order for the next day, I have to contact crew members at home. I can send text messages to most of the younger employees, but haven't always been able to get the older employees to use that form of communication. Some of them don't have cellphones. Occasionally, I'm reduced to leaving a message on an answering machine, if they have one, ending with, "Please let me know if you got this message." Slowly but surely, however, they're coming around to cellphones and text messaging.

Last year, we asked employees to come up with slogans for a marketing campaign. We planned to put the winning phrases on the sides of our trucks. One that we chose, which a younger employee suggested, was: "Eat something. You're all skin and BlackBerry." The point was that people work too much and need nourishment. Younger employees thought the slogan was funny, but some of the older drivers didn't recognize the wireless device's name.

Another we chose was: "Ask not what you can do for your company, ask what is for lunch." Some of the younger people knew they had heard something similar before but couldn't recall who said it. The older workers had them there.

Our oldest driver, Tom Campe, who's 75, is one of our most personable workers. Customers love him. Employees with years of work experience have so much to teach others, and they're great to work with. They can relate valuable lessons from previous jobs, and they've been to more places than most of us. They're more cultured

In January, our employees completed a survey, and we learned that they wanted more feedback about their performance. We realized that and have instituted monthly recognition programs. We also started calling customers for feedback and posting the responses around the company.

Sometimes being recognized for your efforts is more important than money. Employees want to feel appreciated, no matter what their age. A simple "thank you" goes a long way.

**Let's Pause Here•••▶** What do you think about the manner in which Ms. Pritscher describes her dilemma as a manager? Do you feel as though she has a legitimate worry because of her age? How might her age make her job more difficult, based on her descriptions of the company's other employees? Do you feel sorry for her, or are you impressed with how she handles the various difficulties with which she is met in her position? Would you work beneath her as an employee, based on her managing style? Why or why not?

**Let's Take It Further•••▼**

1. It is apparent that Ms. Pritscher is extremely aware of the perceptions her employees (both older and younger) have of her. However, do you think that she is speaking to other young managers in her essay, or is she speaking to the potential employees of a young manager? What in particular about her usage of language and her discussion of managerial crises reveals who she intends her audience to be? To whom is her essay most helpful?

2. Why do you think that she worries whether the company's "older *male* employees" (my emphasis) will respect her authority? Do you think she has cause for concern? Why or why not?

3. Why do you think that Pritscher spoke to her father and one of the company owners (also a man) about her managerial dilemmas, rather than to a woman in a similar position? How might this have helped or hurt her cause?

4. Based on Pritscher's descriptions of her management methods (doing work with her employees, incorporating new technologies, having contests, and so on), describe whether you think she is doing an effective job of fighting back against preconceived notions of her generation (Gen Y), as well as the potential negative elements of being a young *and* female manager. Use specific methods that she describes to explain how these might help her cause as a manager who wants to be respected, as well as one who runs a business successfully.

5. In what ways do you believe that Pritscher conforms to the traits of Generation Y workers? In what ways is she different? Using her own explanations of her managing methods, explain how she does and does not conform to the work and identity habits of her generation, as explained in earlier chapter selections on generational differences between workers.

6. Interview a manager at your own place of employment to learn what he or she views as the traits of Generation Y workers. Describe what the manager sees as the positive elements to this generation's work ethic, as well as the negatives. Then do the same for the person's impression of the generation of workers who came before Generation Y and compare the two.

How does the manager address these differences in his or her own managing style? Do you believe he or she is more or less effective than Pritscher in addressing managerial issues?

7. Based on your own work experience, what have you noticed about the different work habits you have that differ from your coworkers of different generations? Who do you feel would be the better group of people to employ, and why? Give a specific example of each group's work style (or work ethic) based on your own observations.

# mash it UP

Here is a series of essay and discussion topics that draw connections between multiple selections within the chapter. They also suggest outside texts to include in your essay or discussion. Feel free to bring in further outside texts, remembering the variety of texts (beyond articles) available to you.

1. One of the most common conceits in contemporary media (particularly TV and film) is that there is a divide between managers and the workers whom they manage. In other words, there is management theory, such as that laid out in Pritscher's and Zaslow's articles, and then there is the reality of managing employees effectively. Choose a film or TV show (such as *Office Space* or *The Office*) whose main theme is the difference between workers and management, and discuss the ways in which the show or film depicts the divide between the two classes of worker. How do these depictions differ from those of the two aforementioned articles?

2. Compare Pritscher's essay "Yes, I'm 26 . . ." and her management style to the Zaslow article. How does Pritscher adhere to the definitions of Generation Y (of which she is a member) outlined in the two articles, and how is she different? How aware of these definitions does Pritscher appear to be (based on her discussion of management difficulties), and how does she appear to be fighting against these preconceived notions of Gen Y workers?

3. Compare the attitude of management toward its employees in the "Factory Worker Management, 1955" video versus the management's view toward their employees in the subsequent essays (Zaslow and Pritscher). How do the attitudes differ between 1950s-style management and modern-day management? Which do you prefer, and why? Finally, find a modern management video on YouTube and compare the style of worker management to that of any of Industry Film Archives' various old-fashioned management films.

4. What are some of the other differences between Generations X and Y and previous generations that go beyond work ethic and style? If excessive praise helps to define the current generations (according to Zaslow), then what defining attributes can be attached to previous generations and how they maintain relationships, work, and live their lives? Use Zaslow's article as a template, making sure to discuss how the defining characteristics of the generations you choose to discuss affect several different aspects of their lives.

5. Compare Zaslow's impressions and depictions of Generations X and Y to Coach Michael Kinahan's critique of Generation Z in his email "Losing Is for Losers," featured in the "Violence" chapter. Which of the two writers' depictions of Generations X, Y, and Z, as well the causes at the root of what they see as these generations' shortcomings, do you more agree with? Research the causes both men give, and see which of them are the most prevalent in American popular culture and society in order to support your viewpoint.

6. One of the most famous work-related writers of the past 50 years was a writer named Studs Terkel, whose writing celebrated the lives of the working class, as well as depicted the hardships suffered by everyday people during hard times. Locate one of Terkel's works and discuss the ways in which Americans' attitudes toward work and its purpose has shifted since the days in which Terkel was writing. What might account for these shifts in attitude, based on how our media depict work, workers, and our relationship with our jobs, bosses, and coworkers?

7. Create a cartoon or visual collage that depicts the differences between generations in regard to work ethic, job availability, and similar concepts that address working and careers in America. How does the cartoon address the differences between the generations being illustrated? Explain and describe what sources you used (interviews, depictions in popular culture, etc.) in order to define one generation against the other. Which of the two generations has better opportunities? Which of them has a better reputation?

# Happy to Be Laboring Day

John Cole

John Cole has been *The* (Scranton, Pennsylvania) *Times-Tribune*'s editorial cartoonist since April 2005. He draws five to seven full-color cartoons weekly. Cole first began drawing for his junior high newspaper, continuing into high school and at Washington and Lee University, where he doodled comic strips and cartoons for the student newspaper. In 1985, he was hired as news artist and sometime cartoonist for the *Durham Morning Herald* (later *The Herald-Sun*) in Durham, North Carolina, and was named the paper's first full-time political cartoonist. He received honorable mention (1994) and first place (2004) in the John Fischetti Editorial Cartoon Competition. His work has been published in various newspapers and magazines worldwide and featured on the Web and national television. He is nationally syndicated with Cagle Cartoons. A collection of his cartoons, *Politics, barbecue & balderdash*, was published in 1995. This cartoon originally appeared in *The Times-Tribune* on September 2, 2010.

## Thinking About Careers

Take a moment to look at the accompanying cartoon. It is apparent that the artist, John Cole, is engaging the concept of our national holiday Labor Day, which is a celebration of American workers and their contribution to society. While we have focused so far on the manner in which employees and their employers interact, we will now delve more deeply into the specific types of jobs that working-class Americans hold, as well as how the job landscape has shifted through the last few decades.

In terms of working, most Americans aspire to white-collar careers, which is the topic of Cole's cartoon. For those students who work to obtain a college degree, the vast majority hope to obtain a well-paying white-collar job of some sort, which often is seen as a type of office work or labor that is less physically taxing than blue-collar, labor-intensive jobs. Of course, it goes without saying that a growing number of jobs available to American workers are blue-collar jobs, such as working in the retail, service, or hospitality industries, as well as working a trade. Nevertheless, there are still white-collar jobs, or office jobs, that remain, and these are the types of workers that Cole addresses in his cartoon.

There are two opposing ideas in this cartoon. One is the idea of an employee who—because of the stacks of work literally piled on his desk—is overwhelmed and most likely feeling quite overworked. But there is a second idea—that this worker is grateful, despite being overworked, because he has a job. Hence the cartoon's title, "Happy to Be Laboring Day." Judging by the title, as well as the artist's depiction of the worker in the drawing, what do you think Cole feels about the current state of jobs in the United States? Is he pro-worker or anti-worker, and what details lead you to believe which of the two he is advocating for?

Another element of Cole's cartoon worth noting is the way he uses two different fonts to make his point. In the midst of the office worker's speech bubble are the most immediate and obvious words, "Happy Labor Day," which is something that laborers might say to one another as a token of appreciation or even camaraderie—a pleasantry shared between working people on a holiday. However, the smaller type surrounding those words significantly changes the meaning of the man's words. How, for example, are the messages "Happy Labor Day" and "I'm Just Happy to Be Laboring Today" at odds with one another? How is one a celebration of employees and their contribution to society, while the other is a somewhat sarcastic statement about the current state of the job market? Which of the two messages do you think more closely mirrors Cole's intentions with his cartoon?

As a society, we have certain expectations when it comes to our careers. To be sure, many of us have "dream jobs" that we hope to obtain after we graduate from college. Still, we understand that these jobs are often referred to as "dream" jobs for a reason. We are trained from a very young age to believe that we can accomplish anything if we try, and so we set out to earn college degrees and land a career with a company that treats us well, that gives us security and benefits and fair pay, and where we will have opportunities to excel and to move up the ladder of success. If this is what our expectations are, if this is the implied promise of the American Dream, then how might the current job market and the wide divide in pay, benefits, and bonuses between average workers and corporate executives and management upset our expectations? Where does Cole stand on this issue, based on his drawing, and which details lead you to believe what Cole's opinion is?

Now, revisit the cartoon for a moment to see some of the drawing's finer details. For example, what do you believe is the purpose behind the words on the worker's screen? How do these words change your initial impressions of the cartoon? Why do you think that the clock above his desk shows the time that it does? Is the man working really *late*, or has he arrived really *early*? Does it matter which of these is true? What is your general impression of the state and attitude of the American worker based on these details?

Finally, it is worth noting that many Americans feel a sense of discontentment as our economy falters and job growth remains stagnant. Still, even during the good times, everyday American workers often feel underappreciated and underpaid. If you were to create a cartoon about your impressions of the current job market, as well as the ways workers and managers differ in attitude and compensation, what might you include in your drawing? Do you think that the career you desire to obtain will be easy or hard to land? What options are you considering when it comes to your career and the type of work to which you want to dedicate your life? Would you continue your career because you love the work you are doing, even if you felt—as the man in the cartoon appears to feel—overworked and underappreciated? Why or why not?

# mash**UP** essay

The following essay is this chapter's Mashup selection. Keeping in mind our definition of a Mashup essay in Chapter 2 (an essay that includes multimedia texts, as well as multiple writing strategies), observe the way the following essay's author, Daniel Brook, utilizes multimedia texts. For example, the central concern of Brook's essay is the idea of how payday lending is predatory, which he illustrates by describing the specific loan applications used in payday lending establishments such as those he visits in the course of researching his essay. Brook also uses the American flag, and the iconic idea that it stands for (particularly in regard to the irony of how one's American Dream might very well be built on the back of another fellow American), as a symbolic text that appears many times throughout his essay. Additionally, in keeping with the idea of the American Dream and how it strongly influences the working class, Brook begins his essay by referring to specific passages of Martin Luther King, Jr.'s, famous "I Have a Dream" speech, and then using King's metaphor about "cashing a check . . . a check marked insufficient funds" to transition to the larger point of the essay: check-cashing businesses as usurious.

Rather than simply critiquing the payday lending business, Brook allows the men who founded the nation's three largest payday lending corporations to tell their own stories through interviews, as well as documenting their daily interactions with customers and fellow citizens about the town. He also discusses several different studies (some funded by the payday lending industry itself, and some funded by the government) that illustrate the dismally low repayment rates of payday loans, as well as how these loans are purposefully set up to "trap" the borrower in a perpetual cycle of reborrowing and repaying the minimum fees. But Brook makes a concerted effort to repeatedly, and frequently, turn back to the origins of the payday lending business, as well as the legalization of payday lending in 17 states (with specific citations of payday lending laws) in order to show how he perceives this practice to be a dire threat to America's middle class. The result is a well-rounded essay that allows all Americans, regardless of class or work background, to see the potentially devastating effects that payday lending could have on all of us.

The strength in Brook's essay is not only his willingness to seek out a wide variety of sources to back his argument that payday lending—though it is legal in many states—still has the potential to oppress entire swaths of America's working class by virtue of the purposefully written terms that are designed to keep borrowers perpetually returning to lenders. Instead of simply pointing out that payday lending is "bad," Brook patiently pieces together an essay that primarily employs the illustrative writing strategy. What he illustrates, in a sophisticated but easy-to-follow string of interviews and research, is the rise of payday lending, as well as its history, its questionable legality, and the vast empires that have been built by a few entrepreneurial men. This makes for a more engaging and thought-provoking article, a more complicated and important essay, because it is hard to argue with the evidence Brook provides throughout his essay—whether it is an observation of a business transaction or the proud words of the lender explaining the history of payday lending and how he built an empire. And so Brook simultaneously informs his audience of payday lending's history and relevance to our lives, while also pointing out the dangers of a largely unregulated industry that has so far mostly flown beneath the average American's radar.

One of the most intriguing elements of the essay is that Brook employs more than just the argumentative and illustrative approaches in his writing. The major thrust of the essay is, indeed, that Brook wants to persuade his readers to see the dangers of payday lending and how it preys on the middle-class worker, but these approaches are combined with several other writing strategies that he employs. In addition to argumentation and illustrative writing strategies, Brook uses many others, which he simultaneously utilizes in order to show the wide-reaching effects payday lending practices can have on millions of Americans. One such strategy Brook employs early on is the compare-contrast writing method, which allows him to explore the irony of King's dream of a Poor People's Coalition (of all races) rising together out of poverty, which partially came true in that payday lending does not discriminate against color, but still renders working people in a permanent cycle of borrowing and repayment. However, Brook also employs the descriptive writing strategy to show the many different types of people who use payday lending services to make it from one paycheck to the next. Brook also uses the descriptive writing strategy to illustrate the ways in which people fall victim to the "trap" of payday

**Mashup Essay Flowchart**

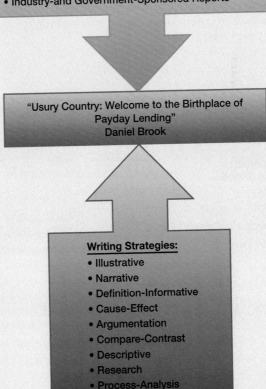

**Types of Media:**
- Martin Luther King's "I Have a Dream" Speech
- Interviews with Payday Lending Moguls
- American Flag as Iconic Text
- Payday Loan Applications
- Poor People's Campaign Document
- Payday Lending Laws
- Industry-and Government-Sponsored Reports

"Usury Country: Welcome to the Birthplace of Payday Lending"
Daniel Brook

**Writing Strategies:**
- Illustrative
- Narrative
- Definition-Informative
- Cause-Effect
- Argumentation
- Compare-Contrast
- Descriptive
- Research
- Process-Analysis

lending and how, despite our various backgrounds, more and more working-class Americans find themselves in need of these easy-to-obtain loans.

In terms of using research in his writing (the research writing strategy), Brook not only mines the history of racial inequality for comparisons to today's income inequality, but he also digs into the history of the practice, interviewing multiple payday lending corporation owners, as well as the people who take out the loans. He also chooses to include the Civil Rights movements of the 1960s, the laws that have been made to legalize payday lending, and the studies (both by the industry and the government) that prove the dangers of this practice in order to convince his readers of the threat. In doing his research, Brook also employs the definition-informative writing strategy as he explains how the industry works, and the process-analysis strategy when he explains the process of taking out and repaying a payday loan. He also employs the cause-effect writing strategy by showing the communities where payday loans have been around the longest, as well as the people who take advantage of this service and how their finances never seem to improve.

When you begin writing a Mashup essay of your own in response to the selections in this chapter, revisit Brook's essay to generate ideas for multimedia texts and multiple writing strategies. Use the flowchart to see the ways in which Brook employs the various writing strategies and multimedia texts he utilizes in his writing.

# Usury Country: Welcome to the Birthplace of Payday Lending
**Daniel Brook**

**Let's Start Here•••▶**

It is widely known that most people see work as the ticket to achieving the American Dream. But for some people, working is not always enough. If a person's wages are not sufficient to cover his life expenses, he sometimes turns to creditors for temporary financial assistance. Until the early 1990s, most people simply turned to stores for credit or to credit card companies. Sometimes people even approached banks for small loans to tide them over. But, in 1991, the concept of payday lending was invented, and it opened up an entirely new source (and method) of short-term credit for people struggling to make ends meet.

**Usury:**

Lending of money with exorbitant, unrealistic, or grossly unfair interest rates.

The following essay explores the history of payday lending, as well as the potential dangers it poses to working-class American people. In his essay, Brook makes the case for how these sorts of loans have taken the country by storm, as well as explaining who the lenders and the borrowers are. Most likely, many students have heard commercials for or seen the advertisements of these lending companies. You may very well have a few in your own neighborhood. But, unless you've taken out a payday loan, chances are you haven't given a second thought to those storefront lending businesses that seem to be popping up everywhere.

As you read Brook's essay, observe the way he patiently shows the history of payday lending and how he makes the case for how it might be a grave danger for working Americans. Also, note the way in which he depicts the inventors of payday lending, especially in the presence of their fellow townspeople, and consider the message he is trying to send to his readers about these men.

---

Daniel Brook is the author of *The Trap: Selling Out to Stay Afloat in Winner-Take-All America* and a journalist whose work has appeared in publications including *Harper's, The Nation,* and *Slate.* He has received fellowships from the Library of Congress, the Century Foundation, the Pulitzer Center on Crisis Reporting, and the Black Mountain Institute and was recently awarded the 2010 Winterhouse Award for Design Criticism and Writing. Brook was born in Brooklyn, raised on Long Island, and educated at Yale, and is currently based in Washington, D.C., where he is at work on a book on the architecture of globalization, to be published by W. W. Norton in 2012. The following essay originally appeared in *Harper's* magazine's April 2009 issue.

On a whitewashed church pew in Johnson City, I sat alone as James Eaton stood over me delivering a sermon. It was a Monday, and this was Eaton's office. One of the inventors of payday lending—the business of making small, short-term loans from retail locations at steep rates—Eaton operates out of a converted service station, with a tarp sign in red and white: here's where it all started. East Tennessee's first, oldest & finest. He had suggested we conduct our interview in his reception area, on the pew he brought up years ago from his wife's childhood church in Alabama. I balanced my coffee cup perilously on the green-felt pew pad as I listened to him enumerate his own good works—his donations to a Bible college, his support for a rural congregation of evangelical Harley-Davidson enthusiasts. Eaton's homily was heartfelt, if meandering and peppered with such biblical malapropisms as Jesus having "healed those leopards." As he preached, customers kept trudging in past us to the counter, where they wrote postdated bad checks and walked away with twenties at several hundred percent interest, all transacted above a vast American flag dangling from the countertop.

"Good to see y'all!" Eaton greeted each customer, his chirpy voice cracking with enthusiasm. "Good to see you too," generally came the more muted reply.

*Sidebar annotations:*

Here is the key concept that Brook will outline throughout the entire essay, using the illustrative writing strategy.

This interview with Eaton is one of the key pieces of research to Brook's entire essay.

**enumerate:**
List, or count out.

**malapropism:**
The incorrect usage of a word that sounds similar to the original, sometimes humorous (though not intended by the speaker).

This is one of the key objects that Brook uses as a symbolic text throughout the entire essay.

In his sermon, Eaton recounted a real-life *Christmas Carol*. "We opened up just before Christmas," he said. "A grandmother brought a little girl in here, holding her hand. And I cashed her a hundred-dollar check, and I looked down at the little girl. I said, 'Now what's Santa Claus going to bring you for Christmas? What's he going to put under your tree?' And the grandmother looked at me and said, 'Mr. Eaton, we had to decide whether we would put up a tree this year or the little girl would get a present.' And I said, 'I understand, I grew up that way.' But I felt sorry. I took money out of my pocket and I said, 'Go get that little girl a Christmas tree. Every little girl deserves a Christmas tree.' They go off. The very next day here's the woman pulling up with a Christmas tree sticking out of the back end of her car. The funniest thing, she comes in here, 'Mr. Eaton, I don't have anything to decorate the Christmas tree.' So back in my pocket, handed her some more money, she goes on her way. That little granddaughter is cashing checks with me today."

> Brook employs the narrative writing strategy to tell the story of how he researched the payday lending industry, as well as the story of Eaton, the "inventor" of this particular lending practice.

"She manages one of your stores?" I asked.

"She comes in and cashes checks," he clarified.

It was to be a two-hour oration. As I sat on the pew, sipping my coffee and taking notes halfheartedly, my eyes wandered from the American flag behind Eaton to the poster over his left shoulder: Martin Luther King, preaching to the masses at the March on Washington. The best-known trope of King's address that day was, of course, his famous "dream." But King began his speech with a very different metaphor. "In a sense," he said,

> **trope:**
> Figure of speech, or symbolic theme.

We've come to our nation's capital to cash a check. . . . A bad check, a check which has come back marked "insufficient funds." But we refuse to believe that the bank of justice is bankrupt. We refuse to believe that there are insufficient funds in the great vaults of opportunity of this nation. And so we've come to cash this check, a check that will give us upon demand the riches of freedom and the security of justice.

> This is an example of another symbolic text that Brook will utilize throughout his essay to construct his overall argument against the practice of payday lending.

In King's broader vision, the creditors were not simply the descendants of slaves but all Americans living in poverty, whose nation had made them promises long past due. Months before his death in 1968, King began planning a second march on Washington that would serve as culmination of a Poor People's Campaign, an inter racial movement of blacks, Latinos, and Native Americans, as well as Appalachian whites. "When we come to Washington in this

> Brook uses the actual words of the famous "I Have a Dream" speech as both a text and a way to further construct his essay's central point.

> Brook also uses this particular Civil Rights movement as a text that he incorporates into his overall argument.

campaign," King declared, "we are coming to get our check." Rallying striking sanitation workers in Memphis just a few days before his assassination, King declared that "it is criminal to have people working on a full-time basis and a full-time job getting part-time income." But in the decades since King's speech, working full time for a part-time income has become the fate of greater and greater numbers of Americans. In fact, the U.S. minimum wage, adjusted for inflation, has never regained its 1968 value. The average income of a full-time worker at Walmart, today the nation's largest private employer, is only slightly more than $17,000 a year. Fully 47 percent of Americans now report living paycheck to paycheck.

> Brook regularly cites statistical research such as this to further back his arguments.

During the Gilded Age of the late nineteenth century, the race-based legal oppression of slavery was replaced with the economic bondage of sharecropping—a race-neutral system that ensnared blacks and whites alike. In his short lifetime, King helped lay waste to more legal barriers, those of racial segregation, but in the past twenty years a new, race-neutral form of economic exploitation has arisen in their place. This twenty-first-century sharecropping is called payday lending; and each indentureship under it begins, fittingly enough, with a bad check.

> Using the argumentative writing strategy, Brook makes this his central argument of the entire essay.

> **indentureship:** Forced service to someone or something.

Like many payday-lending pioneers, Eaton came out of the credit-bureau business, back when credit bureaus would keep tabs with the local department store on who had fallen behind on bills. When that industry was consolidated nationally, Eaton began looking for another line of work. He settled on short-term loans—cash today to tide a worker over until payday, offered at triple-digit annual interest rates. Eaton took out a second mortgage on his house and opened up Check Cashing, Inc. on December 2, 1991.

> Brook employs the cause-effect writing strategy to show how Eaton originally came up with the concept of payday lending.

"I ran a little bitty ad in the paper in the personals section," he told me. *"We will hold your check till payday."*

A few weeks later, the son of an old colleague from the credit-bureau business flew into town to offer him a job. "He flew up here on that little private plane right then to try and hire me," Eaton explained. Between customers he chatted with the well-heeled visitor, but Eaton, with his promising new business venture, wasn't looking for work.

"Three or four weeks later he called. 'James, I want to come up there and find out what you were doing again. I have been thinking about that and I'm interested in it.' I said, 'Allan, you come on up.' So he flew back in. And we was opening up our office in Kingsport. He spent the day with us up there."

W. Allan Jones, the jet-setting visitor, went on to found Check Into Cash, the first of the national payday-lending chains. With a knack for marketing, Jones rechristened the transaction Eaton called "check cashing" as "the payday advance." It was Jones who saw the potential to expand someone else's business concept into a coast-to-coast empire. Jones saw how payday lending could be to finance what McDonald's is to food.

In the early 1990s, there were fewer than 200 payday lending stores in America; today, there are over 22,000, serving 10 million households each year—a $40 billion industry with more U.S. locations, in fact, than McDonald's. Today, Jones's company, based in his hometown of Cleveland, Tennessee, is the second or third largest of its kind. With 1,200 stores in thirty-two states, it is roughly equal in size to Virginia-based Check 'n Go but smaller than South Carolina's Advance America, founded by the director of scheduling and advance in the Clinton Administration, William Webster.

> Here's an example of Brook using the compare-contrast writing strategy to show the wide-reaching spread of the payday lending industry compared to one of the world's largest corporations, McDonald's.

Getting a payday loan is, in Check Into Cash's trademarked phrase, "Quick, Easy, and Confidential." The only paperwork required is a two-sided form with blanks soliciting contact information about the customer, her spouse, her landlord or mortgage holder, and three acquaintances in the area. An applicant need only fill out the sheet, show proof of employment and a bank account, and then write a bad check, dated her next payday, for the loan amount plus the fee. (In Tennessee, typical advances range from $50 in cash for a $58.82 check, to $200 for a $230 check.) On that next payday, the customer cashes her paycheck and buys back the check in cash for its face value.

> Brook employs the process-analysis writing strategy to show how simple (and complicated) it is to obtain a payday loan.

Such is the process in principle, but seldom does it work out that way. When the next payday arrives, most borrowers can't afford to repay, so they extend the loan until the following payday by paying another finance charge. (In Tennessee and many other states, a borrower technically cannot "extend" the transaction, but lenders make it a trivial process to pay back the loan and immediately take out a new one, adding another finance charge on top.) Like a sharecropping contract, a payday loan essentially becomes a lien against your life, entitling the creditor to a share of your future earnings indefinitely. Even the industry-sponsored research cited on the Check Into Cash website shows that only 25.1 percent of

> Brook employs the definition-informative writing strategy to show how a payday loan actually works.

customers use their loans as intended, paying each one off at the end of their next pay period for an entire year. Government studies show even lower rates of customer payoff. North Carolina regulators found that 87 percent of borrowers roll over their loans; Indiana found that approximately 77 percent of its payday loans were rollovers. This is hardly surprising, of course: if your finances are so busted that a doctor visit or car repair puts you in the red, chances are slim that you'll be able to pay back an entire loan plus interest a few days after taking it out. "On average," Jeremy Tobacman, a Wharton professor who studies the industry, drily put it, "payday borrowers seem to be over-optimistic about the future."

> The industry- and government-sponsored studies are valuable texts that Brook researches and incorporates into his essay. Brook also uses the compare-contrast writing strategy to show similarities and differences between them.

Once caught in the cycle, the borrower faces a choice each payday—pay Check Into Cash $30 or pay Check Into Cash $230. Unlike conventional loans, in which the creditor issues the debtor a lump sum to be repaid with interest in installments over time, the largest single transfer in a payday loan goes from debtor to creditor. With payday lending, the "debt trap" is not a figure of speech: the loan is actually structured as a trap.

> This is another of the many interviews Brook conducts throughout the course of his essay to allow both sides of the payday lending debate to speak for themselves.

In 1997, Tennessee became the nineteenth state in the union to explicitly legalize payday lending, which before then had operated in a legal gray area. Allan Jones and his family donated more than $29,000 to state legislators during the run-up to the vote. As in other states, the industry used a clever rhetorical strategy to cast interest-rate caps, or usury laws, as a form of government paternalism. Legislators, they argued, should grant their constituents the autonomy to make their own financial decisions. The idea that certain constituents needed their representatives to take care of them for their own good so clearly echoed themes from the state's past that no one had to explicitly connect the dots. Industry representatives highlighted the race-neutrality of payday lending to corral votes. "They hired a Noah's Ark of lobbyists," Steve Cohen, a state senator, memorably remarked to the Associated Press. "They hired a black lobbyist to get black votes. If we'd have had a transsexual, they would have hired a transsexual lobbyist." By creating the appearance of a multiracial coalition against government overreach, they presented the deregulation of usury as a latter-day civil rights issue.

> This is another example of Brook using the process-analysis writing strategy to show how payday lending "traps" customers.

**paternalism:**
Making decisions for citizens as though the government were a parent who knows what's best for its children.

**autonomy:**
Being independent and in control of oneself and one's decisions.

**peroration:**
The concluding parts of a speech.

Yet another example of Brook using an object as a symbolic text that relates to his overall argument.

This is one of the many places where Brook employs the descriptive writing strategy in order to illustrate the types of people who take advantage of this particular lending service.

This paragraph is another example of the narrative writing strategy, wherein Brook tells Jolliff's story in relation to how she became a payday lending customer.

In the peroration of the "I Have a Dream" speech, King lists a series of improbable places where freedom one day will ring, among them "the Lookout Mountain of Tennessee." Today, under Chattanooga's Lookout Mountain sits a strip mall whose tenants include a Check Into Cash. On Friday, October 31, 2008—the ultimate payday, the end of both a week and a month—I loitered in the parking lot and watched customers file in on their lunch hours to extend their loans. Since payments are due on the customer's actual payday, and branches are rarely open before 9:00 a.m. or after 6:00 p.m., there is inevitably a crush at lunchtime. A mix of black and white, young and old, the customers drove everything from a dented sedan with a Chattanooga Housing Authority parking permit to a spotless Nissan SUV. When I asked the African-American woman in the SUV about her loan, she politely brushed me off: "I don't want to talk about that. It's personal." Jack Atkins, a pockmarked white man driving a minivan, told me he'd been a customer for about a month. "It's been working out for me," he said.

Susan Jolliff was on her lunch break from her $8.96-an-hour job in quality control at Intersign, which manufactures vinyl signs for motel-room doors. As she left Check Into Cash, she stuffed a stack of twenties into her wallet, rattled off her phone number to me, and rushed into the supermarket. We spoke the following week. Jolliff had taken out her $175 loan three months earlier, after her wallet was stolen with the remainder of her stimulus-package tax-rebate cash in it. The company by now had more than recouped its principal in finance fees, but still she was unable to pay it off. "I figured it would take maybe a month," she said. "Maybe rewrite it once and then pay it back. But no. We get a bonus at work every month, and the last couple of months it's been kind of low, but hopefully next month . . ."

But she harbored no malice toward Check Into Cash's employees. "As far as the people who work in there, they're nice as can be," she said. So nice, in fact, that a few weeks ago when an employee accidentally re-loaned Jolliff the full $205 instead of the $175 principal, Jolliff courteously corrected her. " 'Oh no, I'm supposed to get one seventy-five and you're supposed to get thirty,' I said. 'You better watch that or you're going to be in trouble.' "

Steven Winslow, who worked for a year as a store manager for Check 'n Go after dropping out of a clinical-psychology graduate program, explained that these chummy customer relationships are carefully cultivated by the payday-lending chains. We met at a Check Into Cash store near the Knoxville private school where he teaches, appropriately, drama and personal finance. At store-manager training, he told me, the mantra was "Your repeat customer is your lifeblood." Managers were encouraged to be on a first-name basis with their customers, to ask after their families.

> In the following paragraphs, Brook uses the definition-informative writing strategy to explain the value of producing and maintaining strong personal customer relationships, as well as the desired outcomes for lenders.

The first few times a customer came in, Winslow said, he'd make small talk about their kids. Soon they wouldn't even look him in the eye. "It's a person in desperation crossing their fingers that they can pretend this will work," Winslow said. And when it invariably doesn't, the borrower feels tremendous shame and guilt. But the store manager feels anger, too. "It was *my* money. You take it personally in that you're responsible for taking this company's money and giving it to somebody, [and then] your job is on the line on the basis of Joe Blow's pay history—their habits, their character, their integrity, their decision, their choice, their difficulty, their crisis, their tragedy."

> Brook employs process-analysis one final time to illustrate the ways in which the lender/borrower relationship complicates the payday lending experience in favor of the lender.

What Winslow described was lives disintegrating in time-lapse, with a new shot snapped every two weeks. Maybe the customer started bringing in a family member or a friend, who would spot the cash to pay the loan and then get it back after the re-loan transaction. If a customer fell behind on payments, Winslow's staff would start making up to twenty collection calls a day to the debtor's home and workplace, as well as to her friends, landlord, boss—anyone who got listed on that first innocuous form. Other customers, to save face, would take out a loan from another payday lender to pay the first. "Once you're borrowing from Check Into Cash to pay Advance America to pay Check 'n Go, it's just a matter of time," he said. "You go to the second lender, it's game over. It's game over."

> **innocuous:** Harmless or inoffensive.

**Let's Pause Here•••▶** What was your overall impression of Daniel Brook's essay on payday lending? Prior to reading this essay, were you familiar with any of the companies featured in the essay? How familiar were you with the practice of payday lending? Do you agree with Brook that it is a dangerous practice and that all working people could potentially fall into the "trap" of this form of lending? Why or why not?

## Let's Take It Further•••▼

1. Why do you think that Brook begins and ends his essay by describing the "birthplace" of payday lending? How does it help or hurt his argument that payday lending is bad?

2. To whom is Brook most obviously appealing with his argument about the negative consequences of payday lending? Government regulators? Payday lenders? Payday lending customers? Potential customers? How does one of these groups, more so than the others, become the primary target throughout the entirety of Brook's essay? What writing strategies, word choices, statistics, and examples does Brook use that prove who his intended audience is supposed to be?

3. At the beginning of Brook's essay, James Eaton—one of the founders of payday lending—makes a point of discussing his various charitable gifts to his community. How does this change your opinion of the man, if it does at all? Why do you think Eaton wants to make his charitable gifts known? In what ways does Brook's portrayal of Eaton affect your impression of the "godfather" of payday lending?

4. Why do you think that Brook repeatedly points out American flag imagery? What effect might it have on a potential customer to walk into a business that has a huge flag draped behind the counter? How might it affect a person's willingness to question the ethics of the business that displays the flag? Or does it not make a difference?

5. What effect does Eaton's "*Christmas Carol*" story have on you? In other words, were you pleased or offended by the fact that Eaton helped out a grandmother whose granddaughter has since become a lifetime customer of his? How did or didn't it offend you?

6. Why do you think Brook took the time to quote from Martin Luther King, Jr.'s, "I Have a Dream" speech, particularly the "check cashing" metaphor that he uses? How does this help Brook build his case? Or do you think it is irrelevant to his essay?

7. Does the figure that Brook quotes—"Fully 47 percent of Americans now report living paycheck to paycheck"—bother you? If so, what is so bothersome about this number? What are the implications for your own life if this number stays the same or continues to rise?

8. During his Poor People's Campaign, King observed that "it is criminal to have people working on a full-time basis and a full-time job getting part-time income." In the more than 40 years since the Poor Person's Campaign, how much of King's claim is still true? How much of it is untrue? In other words, if there are still people who work in the United States full-time for part-time wages, compare and contrast the sorts of jobs are they working and who their employers are. Why do you think things have or have not changed since the late 1960s campaign for the working poor?

9. Research the terms of various payday loans and compare them by visiting two or more payday lending businesses in your community. As you read the terms, explain whether you feel they are fair, and whether you feel that Brook's claim of "usurious rates" is true or false. Explain why you agree or disagree, and use the actual payday lending applications to back your claim. What terms do they offer borrowers, and how are they fair or unfair?

10. Brook illustrates many "dirty jobs" in his essay (including the payday lending managers who are trained in "drama and personal finance"). What other sorts of jobs can you think of

whose tasks involve manipulating or performing for people in order to win their business? Research the job requirements, and explain why this particular job is good or bad for the people who are pinpointed as the prime customers of this particular line of work.

11. Brook points out that payday lending actually preys on the working class, rather than the lower-class, often out-of-work poor, as proven by the fact that a customer must have a job and a bank account to do business with a payday lender. Explain how this goes against popular conceptions of payday lending's customer base by interviewing people from two or more generations about the stereotypes they have of payday lending and its customers. Next, research the customers of a local payday lender by observing (as Brook does) the cars, clothing, and other external identifiers of the people who frequent the business you're observing. Do your observations prove or disprove Brook's claims? Why or why not? Ultimately, do you believe the threat that Brook is attempting to reveal is real or imagined?

# Nickel-and-Dimed: On (Not) Getting By in America
**Barbara Ehrenreich**

**Let's Start Here•••▶**  In the late 1990s, journalist Barbara Ehrenreich set out on a social experiment to discover just how difficult or easy it would be to survive on a low-wage job (which millions of Americans attempt to do). Her experiment was in response to the welfare reforms passed by the Clinton administration, which sought to get able-bodied people back into the workforce. Of course, the vast majority of the jobs to which these welfare recipients would turn were jobs in the retail, service, and hospitality industries. Because of this, Ehrenreich decided it was necessary to honestly depict how easily a man or woman would be able to find work, as well as the types of jobs available to them and how well they could subsist on these types of jobs.

The result of this research is an in-depth and honest look at the low-wage workforce and the plight of low-wage workers. While Ehrenreich embarks on her experiment to gauge the likelihood of a single mother surviving through low-wage jobs (which is her focus because the vast majority of the people who were on welfare at the time and would be returning to work were single mothers), the essay illustrates the plight of all those who work in the low-wage industries of retail, service, and hospitality. In fact, so moved was Ehrenreich by the experience of reporting for this essay that she ended up returning to low-wage work once more and penned a best-selling book with the same title as this essay.

While you read Ehrenreich's essay, make note of specific ways in which she outlines the realities of the low-wage working-class American. Also, see whether you agree with her ultimate assessment about the possibility of a person surviving or not surviving on these types of jobs.

Furthermore, make note of the rights these workers do or do not have, as well as the manner in which she documents the ways in which workers are treated. Finally, jot down details from this essay that shock or surprise you, as well as those that come as no surprise, based on your own experiences in any of these particular low-wage jobs.

---

Barbara Ehrenreich is a political activist and a widely published columnist and essayist. She is also the author of one book of fiction and 20 books of nonfiction. From 1991 to 1997, Ehrenreich was a regular columnist for *TIME* magazine. Currently, she contributes regularly to *The Progressive* and has also written for the *New York Times, Mother Jones, The Atlantic Monthly, Ms, The New Republic, Z Magazine, In These Times, Salon,* and other publications. In 1998, the American Humanist Association named her the Humanist of the Year. In 1998 and 2000, she taught essay writing at the Graduate School of Journalism at the University of California, Berkeley. The following essay (which later became the best-selling book of the same name, released in 2001), originally appeared in *Harper's* magazine's January 1999 issue.

At the beginning of June 1998, I leave behind everything that normally soothes the ego and sustains the body—home, career, companion, reputation, ATM card—for a plunge into the low-wage workforce. There, I become another, occupationally much diminished "Barbara Ehrenreich"—depicted on job-application forms as a divorced homemaker whose sole work experience consists of housekeeping in a few private homes. I am terrified, at the beginning, of being unmasked for what I am: a middle-class journalist setting out to explore the world that welfare mothers are entering, at the rate of approximately 50,000 a month, as welfare reform kicks in. Happily, though, my fears turn out to be entirely unwarranted: during a month of poverty and toil, my name goes unnoticed and for the most part unuttered. In this parallel universe where my father never got out of the mines and I never got through college, I am "baby," "honey," "blondie," and, most commonly, "girl."

My first task is to find a place to live. I figure that if I can earn $7 an hour—which, from the want ads, seems doable—I can afford to spend $500 on rent, or maybe, with severe economies, $600. In the Key West area, where I live, this pretty much confines me to flophouses and trailer homes—like the one, a pleasing fifteen-minute drive from town, that has no air-conditioning, no screens, no fans, no television, and, by way of diversion, only the challenge of evading the landlord's Doberman pinscher. The big problem with this place, though, is the rent, which at $675 a month, is well beyond my reach. All right, Key West is expensive. But, so is New York City, or the Bay Area, or Jackson Hole, or Telluride, or Boston, or any other place where tourists and the wealthy compete for living space with the people who clean their toilets and fry their hash browns.[1] Still, it is a shock to realize that "trailer trash" has become, for me, a demographic category to aspire to.

So I decide to make the common trade-off between affordability and convenience, and go for a $500-a-month efficiency thirty miles up a two-lane highway from the employment opportunities of Key West, meaning forty-five minutes if there's no road construction and I don't get caught behind some sun-dazed Canadian tourists. I hate the drive, along a roadside studded with white crosses commemorating the more effective head-on collisions, but it's a sweet little place—a cabin, more or less, set in the swampy back yard of the converted mobile home where my landlord, an affable TV repairman, lives with his bartender girlfriend. Anthropologically speaking, a bustling trailer park would be preferable, but here I have a gleaming white floor and a firm mattress, and the few resident bugs are easily vanquished.

> **vanquished:**
> Defeated in battle.

Besides, I am not doing this for the anthropology. My aim is nothing so mistily subjective as to "experience poverty" or find out how it "really feels" to be a long-term low-wage worker. I've had enough unchosen encounters with poverty and the world of low-wage work to know it's not a place you want to visit for touristic purposes; it just smells too much like fear. And with all my real-life assets—bank account, IRA, health insurance, multiroom home—waiting indulgently in the background, I am, of course, thoroughly insulated from the terrors that afflict the genuinely poor.

No, this is a purely objective, scientific sort of mission. The humanitarian rationale for welfare reform—as opposed to the more punitive and stingy impulses that may actually have motivated it—is that work will lift poor women out of poverty while simultaneously inflating their self-esteem and

> **punitive:**
> Inflicting harm or punishment.

hence their future value in the labor market. Thus, whatever the hassles involved in finding childcare, transportation, etc., the transition from welfare to work will end happily, in greater prosperity for all. Now there are many problems with this comforting prediction, such as the fact that the economy will inevitably undergo a downturn, eliminating many jobs. Even without a downturn, the influx of a million former welfare recipients into the low-wage labor market could depress wages by as much as 11.9 percent, according to the Economic Policy Institute (EPI) in Washington, D.C.

---

[1] According to the Department of Housing and Urban Development, the "fair-market rent" for an efficiency is $551 here in Monroe County, Florida. A comparable rent in the five boroughs of New York City is $704; in San Francisco, $713; and in the heart of Silicon Valley, $808. The fair-market rent for an area is defined as the amount that would be needed to pay rent plus utilities for "privately owned, decent, safe, and sanitary rental housing of a modest (non-luxury) nature with suitable amenities."

But is it really possible to make a living on the kinds of jobs currently available to unskilled people? Mathematically, the answer is no, as can be shown by taking $6 to $7 an hour, perhaps subtracting a dollar or two an hour for child care, multiplying by 160 hours a month, and comparing the result to the prevailing rents. According to the National Coalition for the Homeless, for example, in 1998 it took, on average nationwide, an hourly wage of $8.89 to afford a one-bedroom apartment, and the Preamble Center for Public Policy estimates that the odds against a typical welfare recipient's landing a job at such a "living wage" are about 97 to 1. If these numbers are right, low-wage work is not a solution to poverty and possibly not even to homelessness.

It may seem excessive to put this proposition to an experimental test. As certain family members keep unhelpfully reminding me, the viability of low-wage work could be tested, after a fashion, without ever leaving my study. I could just pay myself $7 an hour for eight hours a day, charge myself for room and board, and total up the numbers after a month. Why leave the people and work that I love? But I am an experimental scientist by training. In that business, you don't just sit at a desk and theo-rize; you plunge into the everyday chaos of nature, where surprises lurk in the most mundane measurements. Maybe, when I got into it, I would discover some hidden economies in the world of the low-wage worker. After all, if 30 percent of the workforce toils for less than $8 an hour, according to the EPI, they may have found some tricks as yet unknown to me. Maybe—who knows?—I would even be able to detect in myself the bracing psychological effects of getting out of the house, as promised by the welfare wonks at places like the Heritage Foundation. Or, on the other hand, maybe there would be un-expected costs—physical, mental, or financial—to throw off all my calcula-tions. Ideally, I should do this with two small children in tow, that being the welfare average, but mine are grown and no one is willing to lend me theirs for a month-long vacation in penury. So this is not the perfect experiment, just a test of the best possible case: an unencumbered woman, smart and even strong, attempting to live more or less off the land.

**mundane:**
Ordinary or commonplace.

**penury:**
Severe poverty.

**unencumbered:**
Free of burden or responsibility.

**auspiciously:**
Implying prosperity or a strong possibility of future success.

On the morning of my first full day of job searching, I take a red pen to the want ads, which are auspiciously numerous. Everyone in Key West's booming "hospitality industry" seems to be looking for someone like me—trainable, flexible, and with suitably humble expectations as to pay. I know I possess certain traits that might be advantageous—I'm white and, I like to think, well-spoken and poised—but I decide on two rules: One, I cannot use any skills derived from my education or usual work—not that there are a lot of want ads for satirical essayists anyway.

Two, I have to take the best-paid job that is offered me and of course do my best to hold it; no Marxist rants or sneaking off to read novels in the ladies' room. In addition, I rule out various occupations for one reason or another. Hotel front-desk clerk, for example, which to my surprise is regarded as unskilled and pays around $7 an hour, gets eliminated because it involves standing in one spot for eight hours a day. Waitressing is similarly something I'd like to avoid, because I remember it leaving me bone tired when I was eighteen, and I'm decades of varicosities and back pain beyond that now. Telemarketing, one of the first refuges of the suddenly indigent, can be dismissed on grounds of personality. This leaves certain supermarket jobs, such as deli clerk, or housekeeping in Key West's thousands of hotel and guest rooms. Housekeeping is especially appealing, for reasons both atavistic and practical: it's what my mother did before I came along, and it can't be too different from what I've been doing part-time, in my own home, all my life.

> **indigent:**
> Unable to afford basic life needs or in severe poverty.

> **atavistic:**
> Reverting to something in the past.

So I put on what I take to be a respectful-looking outfit of ironed Bermuda shorts and scooped-neck T-shirt and set out for a tour of the local hotels and supermarkets. Best Western, Econo Lodge, and Hojo's all let me fill out application f.orms, and these are, to my relief, interested in little more than whether I am a legal resident of the United States and have committed any felonies. My next stop is Winn-Dixie, the supermarket, which turns out to have a particularly onerous application process, featuring a fifteen-minute "interview" by computer since, apparently, no human on the premises is deemed capable of representing the corporate point of view. I am conducted to a large room

> **onerous:**
> Troublesome and unnecessarily complicated.

decorated with posters illustrating how to look "professional" (it helps to be white and, if female, permed) and warning of the slick promises that union organizers might try to tempt me with. The interview is multiple choice: Do I have anything, such as child-care problems, that might make it hard for me to get to work on time? Do I think safety on the job is the responsibility of management? Then, popping up cunningly out of the blue: How many dollars' worth of stolen goods have I purchased in the last year? Would I turn in a fellow employee if I caught him stealing? Finally, "Are you an honest person?"

Apparently, I ace the interview, because I am told that all I have to do is show up in some doctor's office tomorrow for a urine test. This seems to be a fairly general rule: if you want to stack Cheerio boxes or vacuum hotel rooms in chemically fascist America, you have to be willing to squat down and pee in front of some health worker (who has no doubt had to do the same thing herself). The wages Winn-Dixie is offering—$6 and a couple of dimes to start with—are not enough, I decide, to compensate for this indignity.[2]

I lunch at Wendy's, where $4.99 gets you unlimited refills at the Mexican part of the Super-bar, a comforting surfeit of refried

> **surfeit:**
>
> An overabundant supply or excessive amount of something.

beans and "cheese sauce." A teenage employee, seeing me studying the want ads, kindly offers me an application form, which I fill out, though here, too, the pay is just $6 and change an hour. Then it's off for a round of the locally owned inns and guesthouses. At "The Palms," let's call it, a bouncy manager actually takes me around to see the rooms and meet the existing housekeepers, who, I note with satisfaction, look pretty much like me—faded ex-hippie types in shorts with long hair pulled back in braids. Mostly, though, no one speaks to me or even looks at me except to proffer an application form. At my last stop, a palatial B&B, I wait twenty minutes to meet "Max," only to be told that there are no jobs now but there should be one soon, since "nobody lasts more than a couple weeks." (Because none of the people I talked to knew I was a reporter, I have changed their names to protect their privacy and, in some cases perhaps, their jobs.)

Three days go by like this, and, to my chagrin, no one out of the approximately twenty places I've applied calls me for an interview. I had been vain enough to worry about coming across as too educated for the jobs I sought, but no one even seems interested in finding out how overqualified I am. Only later will I realize that the want ads are not a reliable measure of the actual jobs available at any particular time. They are, as I should have guessed from Max's comment, the employers' insurance policy against the relentless turnover of the low-wage workforce. Most of the big hotels run ads almost continually, just to build a supply of applicants to replace the current workers as they drift away or are fired, so finding a job is just a matter of being at the right place at the right time and flexible enough to take whatever is being offered that day. This finally happens to me at one of the big discount hotel chains, where I go, as usual, for housekeeping and am sent, instead, to try out as a waitress at

---

[2]According to the *Monthly Labor Review* (November 1996), 28 percent of work sites surveyed in the service industry conduct drug tests (corporate workplaces have much higher rates), and the incidence of testing has risen markedly since the Eighties. The rate of testing is highest in the South (56 percent of work sites polled), with the Midwest in second place (50 percent). The drug most likely to be detected—marijuana, which can be detected in urine for weeks—is also the most innocuous, while heroin and cocaine are generally undetectable three days after use. Prospective employees sometimes try to cheat the tests by consuming excessive amounts of liquids and taking diuretics, and even using masking substances available through the Internet.

the attached "family restaurant," a dismal spot with a counter and about thirty tables that looks out on a parking garage and features such tempting fare as "Pollish [sic] sausage and BBQ sauce" on 95-degree days. Phillip, the dapper young West Indian who introduces himself as the manager, interviews me with about as much enthusiasm as if he were a clerk processing me for Medicare, the principal questions being what shifts can I work and when can I start. I mutter something about being woefully out of practice as a waitress, but he's already on to the uniform: I'm to show up tomorrow wearing black slacks and black shoes; he'll provide the rust-colored polo shirt with HEARTHSIDE embroidered on it, though I might want to wear my own shirt to get to work, ha ha. At the word "tomorrow," something between fear and indignation rises in my chest. I want to say, "Thank you for your time, sir, but this is just an experiment, you know, not my actual life."

> **sic:**
> Indicates that the word coming before this one was reprinted exactly as it originally appeared (often because of an error in the original).

> **indignation:**
> Anger caused by something unfair, cruel, or undeserved.

So begins my career at the Hearthside, I shall call it, one small profit center within a global discount hotel chain, where for two weeks I work from 2:00 till 10:00 P.M. for $2.43 an hour plus tips.[3] In some futile bid for gentility, the management has barred employees from using the front door, so my first day I enter through the kitchen, where a red-faced man with shoulder-length blond hair is throwing frozen steaks against the wall and yelling, "Fuck this shit!" "That's just Jack," explains Gail, the wiry middle-aged waitress who is assigned to train me. "He's on the rag again"—a condition occasioned, in this instance, by the fact that the cook on the morning shift had forgotten to thaw out the steaks. For the next eight hours, I run after the agile Gail, absorbing bits of instruction along with fragments of personal tragedy. All food must be trayed, and the reason she's so tired today is that she woke up in a cold sweat thinking of her boyfriend, who killed himself recently in an upstate prison. No refills on lemonade. And the reason he was in prison is that a few DUIs caught up with him, that's all, could have happened to anyone. Carry the creamers to the table in a monkey bowl, never in your hand. And after he was gone she spent several months living in her truck, peeing in a plastic pee bottle

> **futile:**
> Ineffective or serving no purpose.

> **gentility:**
> Manners or social conduct that implies a higher social standing over a person or group of people.

---

[3]According to the Fair Labor Standards Act, employers are not required to pay "tipped employees," such as restaurant servers, more than $2.13 an hour in direct wages. However, if the sum of tips plus $2.13 an hour falls below the minimum wage, or $5.15 an hour, the employer is required to make up the difference. This fact was not mentioned by managers or otherwise publicized at either of the restaurants where I worked.

and reading by candlelight at night, but you can't live in a truck in the summer, since you need to have the windows down, which means anything can get in, from mosquitoes on up.

At least Gail puts to rest any fears I had of appearing overqualified. From the first day on, I find that of all the things I have left behind, such as home and identity, what I miss the most is competence. Not that I have ever felt utterly competent in the writing business, in which one day's success augurs nothing at all for the next. But in my writing life, I at least have some notion of procedure: do the research, make the outline, rough out a draft, etc. As a server, though, I am beset by requests like bees: more iced tea here, ketchup over there, a to-go box for table fourteen, and where are the high chairs, anyway? Of the twenty-seven tables, up to six are usually mine at any time, though on slow afternoons or if Gail is off, I sometimes have the whole place to myself. There is the touch-screen computer-ordering system to master, which is, I suppose, meant to minimize server-cook contact, but in practice requires constant verbal fine-timing: "That's gravy on the mashed, okay? None on the meatloaf," and so forth—while the cook scowls as if I were inventing these refinements just to torment him. Plus, something I had forgotten in the years since I was eighteen: about a third of a server's job is "side work" that's invisible to customers—sweeping, scrubbing, slicing, refilling, and restocking. If it isn't all done, every little bit of it, you're going to face the 6:00 P.M. dinner rush defenseless and probably go down in flames. I screw up dozens of times at the beginning, sustained in my shame entirely by Gail's support—"It's okay, baby, everyone does that sometime."—because, to my total surprise and despite the scientific detachment, I am doing my best to maintain I care.

> **augurs:**
> Predicts the future.

The whole thing would be a lot easier if I could just skate through it as Lily Tomlin in one of her waitress skits, but I was raised by the absurd Booker T. Washingtonian precept that says: If you're going to do something, do it well. In fact, "well" isn't good enough by half. Do it better than anyone has ever done it before. Or so said my father, who must have known what he was talking about because he managed to pull himself, and us with him, up from the mile-deep copper mines of Butte to the leafy suburbs of the Northeast, ascending from boilermakers to martinis before booze beat out ambition. As in most endeavors I have encountered in my life, doing it "better than anyone" is not a reasonable goal. Still, when I wake up at 4:00 A.M. in my own cold sweat, I am not thinking about the writing deadlines I'm neglecting; I'm thinking about the table whose order I screwed up so that one of the boys didn't get his kiddie meal until the rest of the family had moved on to their Key Lime pies. That's the other powerful motivation I hadn't expected—the customers, or "patients," as I can't help thinking of them on account of the mysterious

> **precept:**
> A command intended to be understood as a rule of action and produce the action described.

vulnerability that seems to have left them temporarily unable to feed themselves. After a few days at the Hearthside, I feel the service ethic kick in like a shot of oxytocin, the nurturance hormone. The plurality of my customers are hard-working locals—truck drivers, construction workers, even housekeepers from the attached hotel—and I want them to have the closest to a "fine dining" experience that the grubby circumstances will allow. No "you guys" for me; everyone over twelve is "sir" or "ma'am." I ply them with iced tea and coffee refills; I return, mid-meal, to inquire how everything is; I doll up their salads with chopped raw mushrooms, summer squash slices, or whatever bits of produce I can find that have survived their sojourn in the cold-storage room mold-free.

> **plurality:** Numerous amount and type.

Sometimes I play with the fantasy that I am a princess who, in penance for some tiny transgression, has undertaken to feed each of her subjects by hand. But the non-princesses working with me are just as indulgent, even when this means flouting management rules—concerning, for example, the number of croutons that can go on a salad (six). "Put on all you want," Gail whispers, "as long as Stu isn't looking." She dips into her own tip money to buy biscuits and gravy for an out-of-work mechanic who's used up all his money on dental surgery, inspiring me to pick up the tab for his milk and pie. Maybe the same high levels of agape can be found throughout the "hospitality industry." I remember the poster decorating one of the apartments I looked at, which said "If you seek happiness for yourself you will never find it. Only when you seek happiness for others will it come to you," or words to that effect—an odd sentiment, it seemed to me at the time, to find in the dank one-room basement apartment of a bellhop at the Best Western. At the Hearthside, we utilize whatever bits of autonomy we have to ply our customers with the illicit calories that signal our love. It is our job as servers to assemble the salads and desserts, pouring the dressings and squirting the whipped cream. We also control the number of butter patties our customers get and the amount of sour cream on their baked potatoes. So if you wonder why Americans are so obese, consider the fact that waitresses both express their humanity and earn their tips through the covert distribution of fats.

> **penance:** Act of repentance for sin or wrongdoing.
>
> **transgression:** Sin or wrongdoing.
>
> **agape:** Brotherly or spiritual love.
>
> **autonomy:** Being independent and in control of oneself and one's decisions.

Ten days into it, this is beginning to look like a livable lifestyle. I like Gail, who is "looking at fifty" but moves so fast she can alight in one place and then another without apparently being any where between them. I clown around with Lionel, the teenage Haitian busboy, and catch a few fragments of conversation with Joan, the svelte fortyish hostess and militant feminist who is the

> **svelte:** Slender.

only one of us who dares to tell Jack to shut the fuck up. I even warm up to Jack when, on a slow night and to make up for a particularly unwarranted attack on my abilities, or so I imagine, he tells me about his glory days as a young man at "coronary school"—or do you say "culinary"?—in Brooklyn, where he dated a knock-out Puerto Rican chick and learned everything there is to know about food. I finish up at 10:00 or 10:30, depending on how much side work I've been able to get done during the shift, and cruise home to the tapes I snatched up at random when I left my real home—Marianne Faithfull, Tracy Chapman, Enigma, King Sunny Ade, the Violent Femmes—just drained enough for the music to set my cranium resonating but hardly dead. Midnight snack is Wheat Thins and Monterey Jack, accompanied by cheap white wine on ice and whatever AMC has to offer. To bed by 1:30 or 2:00, up at 9:00 or 10:00; read for an hour while my uniform whirls around in the landlord's washing machine, and then it's another eight hours spent following Mao's central instruction, as laid out in the Little Red Book, which was: Serve the people.

**proletarian:**
A member of the working class.

**idyll:**
Poem that romanticizes nature, and the beauty and pleasure of a simple life coexisting with nature.

**sloth:**
Laziness.

I could drift along like this, in some dreamy proletarian idyll, except for two things. One is management. If I have kept this subject on the margins thus far it is because I still flinch to think that I spent all those weeks under the surveillance of men (and later women) whose job it was to monitor my behavior for signs of sloth, theft, drug abuse, or worse. Not that managers and especially "assistant managers" in low-wage settings like this are exactly the class enemy. In the restaurant business, they are mostly former cooks or servers, still capable of pinch-hitting in the kitchen or on the floor, just as in hotels they are likely to be former clerks, and paid a salary of only about $400 a week. But everyone knows they have crossed over to the other side, which is, crudely put, corporate as opposed to human. Cooks want to prepare tasty meals; servers want to serve them graciously; but managers are there for only one reason—to make sure that money is made for some theoretical entity that exists far away in Chicago or New York, if a corporation can be said to have a physical existence at all. Reflecting on her career, Gail tells me ruefully that she had sworn, years ago, never to work for a corporation again. "They don't cut you no slack. You give and you give, and they take."

Managers can sit—for hours at a time if they want—but it's their job to see that no one else ever does, even when there's nothing to do, and this is why, for servers, slow times can be as exhausting as rushes. You start dragging out each little chore, because if the manager on duty catches you in an idle moment, he will give you something far nastier to do. So I wipe, I clean, I consolidate ketchup bottles and recheck the cheesecake supply, even tour the tables to make sure the customer evaluation forms are all standing perkily in their places—wondering all the time how many calories I bum in these strictly theatrical exercises. When, on a particularly dead afternoon, Stu finds me glancing at a *USA Today* a customer has left behind, he assigns me to vacuum the entire floor with the broken vacuum cleaner that has a handle only two feet long, and the only way to do that without incurring orthopedic damage is to proceed from spot to spot on your knees.

On my first Friday at the Hearthside there is a "mandatory meeting for all restaurant employees," which I attend, eager for insight into our overall marketing strategy and the niche (your basic Ohio cuisine with a tropical twist?) we aim to inhabit. But there is no "we" at this meeting. Phillip, our top manager except for an occasional "consultant" sent out by corporate headquarters, opens it with a sneer: "The break room—it's disgusting. Butts in the ashtrays, newspapers lying around, crumbs." This windowless little room, which also houses the time clock for the entire hotel, is where we stash our bags and civilian clothes and take our half-hour meal breaks. But a break room is not a right, he tells us. It can be taken away.[4] We should also know that the lockers in the break room and whatever is in them can be searched at any time. Then comes gossip; there has been gossip; gossip (which seems to mean employees talking among themselves) must stop. Off-duty employees are henceforth barred from eating at the restaurant, because "other servers gather around them and gossip." When Phillip has exhausted his agenda of rebukes, Joan complains about the condition of the ladies' room, and I throw in my two bits about the vacuum cleaner. But I don't see any backup coming from my fellow servers, each of whom has subsided into her own personal funk; Gail, my role model, stares sorrowfully at a point six inches from her nose. The meeting ends when Andy, one of the cooks, gets up, muttering about breaking up his day off for this almighty bullshit.

---

[4]Until April 1998, there was no federally mandated right to bathroom breaks. According to Marc Linder and Ingrid Nygaard, authors of *Void Where Prohibited: Rest Breaks and the Right to Urinate on Company Time* (Cornell University Press, 1997), "The right to rest and void at work is not high on the list of social or political causes supported by professional or executive employees, who enjoy personal workplace liberties that millions of factory workers can only daydream about...While we were dismayed to discover that workers lacked an acknowledged legal right to void at work, [the workers] were amazed by outsiders' naive belief that their employers would permit them to perform this basic bodily function when necessary . . . A factory worker, not allowed a break for six-hour stretches, voided into pads worn inside her uniform; and a kindergarten teacher in a school without aides had to take all twenty children with her to the bathroom and line them up outside the stall door when she voided."

Just four days later we are suddenly summoned into the kitchen at 3:30 P.M., even though there are live tables on the floor. We all—about ten of us—stand around Phillip, who announces grimly that there has been a report of some "drug activity" on the night shift and that, as a result, we are now to be a "drug-free" workplace, meaning that all new hires will be tested, as will possibly current employees on a random basis. I am glad that this part of the kitchen is so dark, because I find myself blushing as hard as if I had been caught toking up in the ladies' room myself: I haven't been treated this way—lined up in the corridor, threatened with locker searches, peppered with carelessly aimed accusations—since junior high school. Back on the floor, Joan cracks, "Next they'll be telling us we can't have sex on the job." When I ask Stu what happened to inspire

**upbraid:**
Severely criticize or scold.

the crackdown, he just mutters about "management decisions" and takes the opportunity to upbraid Gail and me for being too generous with the rolls. From now on there's to be only one per customer, and it goes out with the dinner, not with the salad. He's also been riding the cooks, prompting Andy to come out of the kitchen and observe—with the serenity of a man whose customary implement is a butcher knife—that "Stu has a death wish today."

Later in the evening, the gossip crystallizes around the theory that Stu is himself the drug culprit, that he uses the restaurant phone to order up marijuana and sends one of the late servers out to fetch it for him. The server was caught, and she may have ratted Stu out or at least said enough to cast some suspicion on him, thus accounting for his pissy behavior. Who knows? Lionel, the busboy, entertains us for the rest of the shift by standing just behind Stu's back and sucking deliriously on an imaginary joint.

The other problem, in addition to the less-than-nurturing management style, is that this job shows no sign of being financially viable. You

**stratagems:**
A clever series of tricks or schemes for achieving a desired goal or outcome.

might imagine, from a comfortable distance, that people who live, year in and year out, on $6 to $10 an hour have discovered some survival stratagems unknown to the middle class. But no. It's not hard to get my co-workers to talk about their living situations, because housing, in almost every case, is the principal source of disruption in their lives, the first thing they fill you in on when they arrive for their shifts. After a week, I have compiled the following survey:

- Gail is sharing a room in a well-known downtown flophouse for which she and a roommate pay about $250 a week. Her roommate, a male friend, has begun hitting on her, driving her nuts, but the rent would be impossible alone.

- Claude, the Haitian cook, is desperate to get out of the two-room apartment he shares with his girlfriend and two other, unrelated, people. As far as I can determine, the other Haitian men (most of whom only speak Creole) live in similarly crowded situations.

- Annette, a twenty-year-old server who is six months pregnant and has been abandoned by her boyfriend, lives with her mother, a postal clerk.

- Marianne and her boyfriend are paying $170 a week for a one-person trailer.

- Jack, who is, at $10 an hour, the wealthiest of us, lives in the trailer he owns, paying only the $400-a-month lot fee.

- The other white cook, Andy, lives on his dry-docked boat, which, as far as I can tell from his loving descriptions, can't be more than twenty feet long. He offers to take me out on it, once it's repaired, but the offer comes with inquiries as to my marital status, so I do not follow up on it.

- Tina and her husband are paying $60 a night for a double room in a Days Inn. This is because they have no car and the Days Inn is within walking distance of the Hearthside. When Marianne, one of the breakfast servers, is tossed out of her trailer for subletting (which is against the trailer-park rules), she leaves her boyfriend and moves in with Tina and her husband.

- Joan, who had fooled me with her numerous and tasteful outfits (hostesses wear their own clothes), lives in a van she parks behind a shopping center at night and showers in Tina's motel room. The clothes are from thrift shops.[5]

It strikes me, in my middle-class solipsism, that there is gross improvidence in some of these arrangements. When Gail and I are wrapping silverware in napkins—the only task for which we are permitted to sit—she tells me she is thinking of escaping from her roommate by moving into the Days Inn herself. I am astounded; How can she even think of paying between $40 and $60 a day? But if I was afraid of sounding like a social worker, I come out just sounding like a fool. She squints at me in disbelief, "And where am I supposed to get a month's rent and a month's deposit for an apartment?" I'd been feeling pretty smug about my $500 efficiency, but of course it was made possible only by the $1,300 I had allotted myself for start-up costs when I began my low-wage life:

> **solipsism:**
> The theory that a person (or self) can only know his or her own experiences, existence, or changes, and that the self is the only thing that truly exists.
>
> **improvidence:**
> The state of not being able to perceive or prepare for the future.

---

[5]I could find no statistics on the number of employed people living in cars or vans, but according to the National Coalition for the Homeless's 1997 report, "Myths and Facts About Homelessness," nearly one in five homeless people (in twenty-nine cities across the nation) is employed in a full- or part-time job.

$1,000 for the first month's rent and deposit, $100 for initial groceries and cash in my pocket, $200 stuffed away for emergencies. In poverty, as in certain propositions in physics, starting conditions are everything.

There are no secret economies that nourish the poor; on the contrary, there are a host of special costs. If you can't put up the two months' rent you need to secure an apartment, you end up paying through the nose for a room by the week. If you have only a room, with a hot plate at best, you can't save by cooking up huge lentil stews that can be frozen for the week ahead. You eat fast food, or the hot dogs and styrofoam cups of soup, that can be microwaved in a convenience store.

**niggardly:**

Extremely cheap, or grudgingly mean about spending or granting money.

If you have no money for health insurance—and the Hearthside's niggardly plan kicks in only after three months— you go without routine care or prescription drugs and end up paying the price. Gail, for example, was fine until she ran out of money for estrogen pills. She is supposed to be on the company plan by now, but they claim to have lost her application form and need to begin the paperwork all over again. So she spends $9 per migraine pill to control the headaches she wouldn't have, she insists, if her estrogen supplements were covered. Similarly, Marianne's boyfriend lost his job as a roofer because he missed so much time after getting a cut on his foot for which he couldn't afford the prescribed antibiotic.

My own situation, when I sit down to assess it after two weeks of work, would not be much better if this were my actual life. The seductive thing about waitressing is that you don't have to wait for payday to feel a few bills in your pocket, and my tips usually cover meals and gas, plus something left over to stuff into the kitchen drawer I use as a bank. But as the tourist business slows in the summer heat, I sometimes leave work with only $20 in tips (the gross is higher, but servers share about 15 percent of their tips with the busboys and bartenders). With wages included, this amounts to about the minimum wage of $5.15 an hour. Although the sum in the drawer is piling up, at the present rate of accumulation it will be more than a hundred dollars short of my rent when the end of the month comes around. Nor can I see any expenses to cut. True, I haven't gone the lentil-stew route yet, but that's because I don't have a large cooking pot, pot holders, or a ladle to stir with (which cost about $30 at Kmart, less at thrift stores), not to mention onions, carrots, and the indispensable bay leaf. I do make my lunch almost every day—usually some slow-burning, high-protein combo like frozen chicken patties with melted cheese on top and canned pinto beans on the side. Dinner is at the Hearthside, which offers its employees a choice of BLT, fish sandwich, or hamburger for only $2. The burger lasts longest, especially if it's heaped with gut-puckering jalapenos, but by midnight my stomach is growling again.

So unless I want to start using my car as a residence, I have to find a second, or alternative, job. I call all the hotels where I filled out housekeeping applications weeks ago—the Hyatt, Holiday Inn, Econo

Lodge, Hojo's, Best Western, plus a half dozen or so locally run guesthouses. Nothing. Then I start making the rounds again, wasting whole mornings waiting for some assistant manager to show up, even dipping into places so creepy that the front-desk clerk greets you from behind bulletproof glass and sells pints of liquor over the counter. But either someone has exposed my real-life housekeeping habits—which are, shall we say, mellow—or I am at the wrong end of some infallible ethnic equation: most, but by no means all, of the working housekeepers I see on my job searches are African Americans, Spanish-speaking, immigrants from the Central European post-Communist world, whereas servers are almost invariably white and monolingually English-speaking. When I finally get a positive response, I have been identified once again as server material.

How former welfare recipients and single mothers will (and do) survive in the low-wage workforce, I cannot imagine. Maybe they will figure out how to condense their lives—including child-raising, laundry, romance, and meals—into the couple of hours between full-time jobs. Maybe they will take up residence in their vehicles, if they have one. All I know is that I couldn't hold two jobs and I couldn't make enough money to live on with one. And I had advantages unthinkable to many of the long-term poor—health, stamina, a working car, and no children to care for and support. Certainly nothing in my experience contradicts the conclusion of Kathryn Edin and Laura Lein, in their recent book *Making Ends Meet: How Single Mothers Survive Welfare and Low-Wage Work*, that low-wage work actually involves more hardship and deprivation than life at the mercy of the welfare state. In the coming months and year, economic conditions for the working poor are bound to worsen, even without the almost inevitable recession. As mentioned earlier, the influx of former welfare recipients into the low-skilled workforce will have a depressing effect on both wages and the number of jobs available. A general economic downturn will only enhance these effects, and the working poor will of course be facing it without the slight, but nonetheless often saving, protection of welfare as backup.

    The thinking behind welfare reform was that even the humblest jobs are morally uplifting and psychologically buoying. In reality they are likely to be fraught with insult and stress. But I did discover one redeeming feature of the most abject low-wage work—the camaraderie of people who are, in almost all cases, far too smart and funny and caring for the work they do and the wages they're paid. The hope, of course, is that someday these people will come to know what they're worth, and take appropriate action.

**Let's Pause Here···** ▶ What was your overall impression of Barbara Ehrenreich's essay? Were there elements of the essay that surprised you? Were there elements of the essay that either offended or bothered you? Why or why not? Do you believe her professional and personal background might have influenced her essay and experiment? If so, in what ways? Overall, do you think that Ehrenreich's essay was a necessary exploration of the world of low-wage workers, or does it do little for the real issues these workers might actually face?

## Let's Take It Further•••▼

1. How—if at all—is Ehrenreich's credibility affected as a journalist attempting to experience the difficulties of low wage work when she is, by her own admission, "thoroughly insulated from the terrors that afflict the genuinely poor"? Does it matter that she is not genuinely poor, or is it enough that she consistently points this fact out as a weakness of her experiment?

2. Based on Ehrenreich's language choices, as well as her examples and writing strategies, identify who you believe to be her intended audience. How does the manner in which she addresses (and includes) the reader in her essay prove the primary group of people she hopes to engage in her essay? How well does she achieve this goal?

3. Ehrenreich explains that she is—by training—an "experimental scientist." How effective do you feel her experiment ultimately was? Did she accomplish what she set out to do, as explained in the beginning of her essay?

4. Prior to seeking low-wage employment, Ehrenreich sets up a few ground rules for herself. Do you believe the rules she has set for herself are fair and reasonable for her experiment? Why or why not? What rules would you delete or add to her list?

5. Based on your own experiences with low-wage work (or those described in the essay, if you haven't had low-wage work experience), what can account for the high rate of employee turnover that Ehrenreich is told by a manager is the norm? What specific reasons might lead to people frequently leaving?

6. Were you surprised by any of the revelations made by Ehrenreich over the course of her experiment, specifically in regard to the working conditions of her coworkers? Which surprises that she encountered were already known to you? Which were not?

7. Using the same approach and methodology as Ehrenreich does in her essay, document the current state of low-wage work and the people who hold these jobs. If you already work in the retail, service, or hospitality industry, interview (and/or observe) a coworker who has been there longer than you. If you do not work in one of these industries, interview a minimum of two people who work in a low-wage industry and describe the process of the interview as well as how they describe their own working conditions. How are the conditions different than they were during the time in which Ehrenreich wrote her essay (1999)? How are conditions the same? How do you feel about the differences and similarities, in light of Ehrenreich's experiment?

8. The entire "nickel-and-dimed" experiment began with Ehrenreich pondering what the effect of newly passed "welfare reforms" would be, specifically on single mothers. Locate the original welfare reforms as they were laid out in the late 1990s, and see how many of Ehrenreich's predictions about the potentially devastating outcomes of these laws either did or did not come to pass. In other words, compare the figures before and after these welfare reforms and describe whether there are more or fewer single mothers on welfare as there

were at the time of her essay. Are there more or fewer welfare recipients, in general, than there were in 1999? What might account for the differences in numbers?

**9.** Determine the amount of money that would be required to live without the aid of any government programs in the town or city where you live. Keep an accounting of the same costs Ehrenreich tracks for the basic needs of life. Then, determine what types of work can be found in your community that would enable a person to meet these basic minimum costs. How easily could a person survive in your community with a low-wage job, and why? What sorts of costs make it difficult (or easy) to get by on the types of jobs discussed by Ehrenreich?

**10.** It is no secret that there are stereotypes nationally for how many people view welfare recipients, both in terms of who the people are and why they are on welfare. Describe what you understand the stereotype of a welfare recipient to be, and then contrast these traits with the traits of the people described by Ehrenreich in her essay. How are the two different and how are they the same? Are the stereotypes at all accurate, or do Americans have misconceptions when it comes to the people who receive government aid?

**11.** Throughout Ehrenreich's essay, there are several mentions of employee mistreatment and lack of basic human rights that are raised for the reader. Choose any of the other texts that Ehrenreich cites, and see which, if any, of the issues that these texts address (employee rights to bathroom breaks, for example) have been legally addressed in the years since this essay's publication. Explain the circumstances of the particular issue, how it has been addressed (in scholarly publications as well as in law changes), if it has, and what about the issue surprises or offends you.

# The Tao of Plumbing: No Pipes, No Civilization
**John Richardson**

**Let's Start Here•••** ▶ Among the many types of jobs and vocations that are available to workers embarking on lifetime careers, there appears to be a preference for "white-collar" jobs (i.e., professional, clean) over "blue-collar" jobs. Nevertheless, as appealing as white-collar jobs might appear to be, our country was built by what today would be deemed blue-collar workers: factory workers, construction workers, firemen, plumbers, electricians, and the like. Of course, were many of us to have the choice, we would pick the jobs that earn us the most money and the most prestige, and blue-collar jobs are widely perceived to gain neither for the worker.

That is, until John Richardson decided to interview a master plumber, Tom McMahon, who makes the art of plumbing stand out for what it is: the backbone of civilization as we know it. In his essay, Richardson illustrates one of the many jobs we sometimes overlook as mindless labor, in order to show us how these are not just important jobs, but also that those who work them are often as wise and relevant as our culture's most celebrated minds. To Richardson and McMahon alike, the science of plumbing is a noble and complicated field.

As you read the essay, pay attention to the ways that Richardson describes both the plumber in question and the art of plumbing. Note your opinion of plumbing before the essay, and see if it shifts over the course of reading Richardson's piece. Also, see if you agree with the way in which Richardson depicts McMahon. Is he justified in his assessment of the man, or is he exaggerating?

---

John H. Richardson is a writer-at-large for *Esquire* and the author of *My Father the Spy* (2006), *In the Little World* (2002), and *The Viper's Club* (1996). His fiction has appeared in the *Atlantic Monthly* and the *O. Henry Prize Stories* collection. The following essay first appeared in *Esquire*'s July 2009 special issue on working.

You ask yourself, "What is a pipe? What purpose does it serve?" So muses Tom McMahon, master plumber of Croton-on-Hudson, New York, instructing a new disciple at the dawn of a new day. His beard is white, his head smooth as an egg, his face sweet and mournful as an old dog. He's sixty years old, and he's been fixing things all his life. He fixed cars in high school and the Army decorated him for fixing things in Korea, then he came home and got a job fixing forklifts at the GM plant down in Tarrytown and ended up as night-shift maintenance supervisor at the paint shop, striking out on his own back in 1988. He's the kind of master craftsman—if you're lucky, there's one in your town—who gets hired for the tough jobs, like replumbing an old hotel into dozens of independent heat zones or re-creating the giant pipes of the steam era for a local millionaire's private steam museum. So he's been thinking about this question his entire life.

"The pipe makes civilization possible," he says.

By separating the waste from the potable water, he explains, the pipe allows people to live together in large groups without dying of dysentery. And the Latin word for lead, which is what the Romans used for pipes, is *plumbum*. So the plumber, when you think about it, is the foundation for a whole host of miracles. "Put it this way, my daughter, working for ten dollars or twelve dollars an hour in a nursing home, working on her associate's degree, she can walk through the door of her apartment and command it to be light and dark. She can command it to be hot or cold. She can go into the kitchen and command sanitary water to come forth at whatever temperature she likes and dismiss it at her pleasure. She can go into this unit and you can keep food cold for days. You go to this unit and you can command your food to be hot. A *king!* with all his *troops!* a hundred years ago couldn't do that."

This is how McMahon's mind works. He's a born Irish philosopher whose field of study happens to be underneath our floorboards, his attentiveness and meticulous perfectionism infused with genuine reverence for the minutiae of God's creation—qualities that make him a very popular plumber indeed. "He's expensive, but you deal with it because he actually does better work," one of his clients told me. "I mean, he removed a massive oil burner from my house that had been burning coal and then oil since 1935 and he didn't smudge a wall or carpet. It was amazing."

| | |
|---|---|
| **reverence:** | Appreciation and respect, as if on a spiritual level. |

At eight sharp, his phone rings. He reaches down to unclip it from his belt. "K-Mac," he says. "Yeah, something's going on with that thermostat. Let me come up—no, no, it's important. You don't want to be without heat."

My job will be to fetch and carry, listen and learn. If I show any aptitude, he'll teach me to cut threads.

| | |
|---|---|
| **aptitude:** | Natural ability or talent. |

But first he has to get suited up. He still lives on the last four acres of his grandfather's farm, raising a harvest of trucks and vans that are all painted red and bearing the logo "K-Mac Corp., Tom McMahon, Master Plumber, Glory to God Thru Christ Jesus." He built this house—didn't sign a paper with a contractor, built it. Poured those footings with his father.

That gray house next door is the old farmhouse. It's empty now. Someday he's going to clean it out and do something with it.

Inside the basement there are rows and rows of gray metal shelves stocked with multiple copies of every elbow and flange and gasket a plumber could possibly need. In a small dingy office, dozens of books like *Primary-Secondary Pumping Made Easy!* and *We Got Steam Heat!* share space with pamphlets like "Prayer for the Closing of an Abortion Mill" and "Understanding the Times of Christ." On one wall, there's a reticulated Jesus that turns into the Shroud of Turin.

He comes out of the bathroom in the self-invented uniform he wears every day: insulated tan Carhartt overalls with quick-release snaps, a tan Carhartt jacket, and a tan Carhartt watchman's cap. Then he stuffs the pockets of the overall chest flap with a small red-handled screwdriver, pressure gauges, pens, and reading glasses, wraps a leather belt around his overalls, and starts clipping on Okay Key Safes that hold two huge clumps of keys plus a flashlight and a Swiss-army knife. With all that dangling at his waist, he looks like the eccentric mechanical genius in one of those Australian post-apocalyptic movies. "You don't say, Gee, I wish I had a screwdriver," he explains. "You learn to wear it all the time."

As we leave, the lessons begin. Steam is a volume of gas, so if you throw water on it, the steam collapses, reducing itself by 1,600 to 1, so the water at the bottom of the pipe jumps up and crashes into itself and goes *bang bang bang*—that's water hammer. For radiant heating you need putrid water, because fresh water brings in oxygen and minerals and causes leaks. The life cycle of the bald-faced hornet, which can be a pain when you're putting in a gas line. To make a building cooler, you put a set of coils in the building and a set of coils outside the building and you fill those coils with a liquid sponge called a refrigerant, then you bring the sponge into the house and let it absorb heat and take it outside and squeeze the heat out, and you do that over and over real fast—that's basic refrigeration theory.

And did you know the true meaning of sin? It's an old English term from archery—you sin to the left, sin to the right, sin short, or sin long. It means to miss your mark. "That's what humans do, they miss their mark. And that's why training is continuous at Camp K-Mac."

I need more pockets.

On arrival we check out the boiler, a spotless yellow box in the garage. It's the System 2000 from Energy Kinetics out in Jersey, one McMahon installed a few years ago. All the pipes are sheathed in black plastic insulation perfectly mitered at the corners. A line of zone meters tells the exact heat in each room in red digital numbers. Compared with my boiler, it's Swedish furniture. Then he lets himself in the house with one of the keys dangling from his belt. "Rita? It's Tom."

She hobbles to the door of her bedroom, releasing a big bounding dog. Her leg is in a padded splint.

"This is John, my new assistant," he says.

After she goes back to bed, he takes his little red screwdriver out and opens the thermostat cover. It's one of the new electronic thermostats, he explains. The old mercury thermostats are bad for the environment, but they work better—instead of doing a logic thing to figure out when to come on like the electronic ones, they're marvelously mechanical: "The temperature drops, the little thermostatic spring here cools and changes shape and hits the switch—in this case, the mercury bulb—and turns on the boiler."

But that raises another problem. Because it takes a while for the freshly generated heat to reach the thermostat, it will overshoot and make the house too hot. So what do you think the dead men did?

The dead men?

They put in something called an anticipator, which is a little electric heater that has to match the current draw of the unit, so as soon as this thermostat turns on the boiler, it also turns on this heater and this heater starts to heat the thermostat, and the thermostat shuts off the heat before the heat reaches here. "The dead men, they came up with this stuff."

Like Honeywell. He came up with gizmos for making heat, for making comfort. Like this mercury thermostat with the familiar round casing. We stand on the shoulders of those men.

Another call comes in, a pipe leaking water in the garage. "That's not good," he says. "I'll be there as soon as I finish here."

While connecting the last thin wires, he also connects, for my benefit, the long march of plumbing history to the holy minutiae arrayed before us. You read the heating books, for example, steam boilers used to explode all the time. The steam would condense back into water and flow back into the boiler and *boom,* you'd have body parts all over the street. Then a Connecticut tinkerer figured out that instead of running a pipe from the boiler straight to the radiator, you had to put a loop in it to lift it above the waterline—and today the Hartford Loop is used on every steam boiler in the world.

He snaps on the round cap. "Rita? Rita? I'm going to go. I changed the thermostat. Let's see if it behaves itself."

For some men, the truth reveals itself through things. Consider, for example, an unhappy marriage of thirty years' duration, three kids raised and sent off into the world. A divorce and a phone call out of the blue from an old customer he hadn't seen in years, a Jewish lawyer with the curly beehive and kindly face of a character in an Edward Koren cartoon. She had a water leak. He asked for a date.

They were an odd match, for sure. "At the beginning, I guess I kind of felt funny," she told me. "He'd pick me up at the train station, and here I am, the professional with my briefcase and suit, and he's got 'Jesus Christ Is Our Lord' on his truck." Within weeks, she sat him down for dinner and said she was never going to believe that Jesus Christ was her Lord and Savior and if he thought he was going to convert her, that was not going to happen. She found herself pulling out her Bible to dispute him on Scripture. His response was unfailingly kind, loving, and respectful. "One day I sat down and said, He's a really good person, and it's because of his beliefs. Why am I trying to change him?"

They got married last year.

But he says little about all that. What he says is this:

Water is tough stuff. It comes from the heavens, hits the ground, some of it runs off, and some of it percolates down through the ground. And because the rain around here is acid rain—the clouds pick up the western gases as they come east—it hits the ground with a pH that's 4 out of 14. You put that in your house, it's going to chew on your pipes. If it passes through ground that has limestone in it, or calcium or magnesium, it will give up some of its acidity, but it will pick up hardness. Perfect water is two to four grains of hardness. If it's too soft, your hair stays slimy no matter how much you rinse and rinse. But if the rainwater passes through iron, that can cause a lot of grief—iron causes staining at 0.3 parts per million. Around here you also have hydrogen-sulfide odor. So you put in a treatment tank, limestone to cut the acidity, ion exchange or an oxidizing agent for iron, pumped air for hydrogen sulfide.

It's half science and half art, and the jobs can run big. At one house, he put in a whole room to fight iron, a $20,000 job.

The pipe leaking water in the garage turns out to be completely minor, a loose joint on the drain for a washing machine. But the minute he gets back in his red truck, his phone rings again. "Hello Denise. What's up?"

"I noticed I was getting a lot of water from the melting snow."

"And where was the water going?"

"Under the garage door."

"You don't think it's anything underneath, like piping?"

"No. The asphalt is heaved up, so it may be making a little bit of a dam."

"Okay, I'll come look at it."

You can't live without water.

We swing by a stone shop to pick up a slab of marble, then roll up the hill to the grand golf course that overlooks the Hudson River. The men's showers have giant brass showerheads the size of a car wheel that need to be replaced, so McMahon had to cut some holes and now he has to cover those holes, a problem that led to a long train of considerations. Brass plate would take too long, regular tile was too thin. There were deadline issues. It had to have a certain look. That's another thing you learn as a plumber. It's never just simple plumbing. You have to know what you're getting into but you also have to use your imagination. Like this time, he ended up getting the stone shop to custom-cut a slab of marble that was going to cost $250 times five for each shower, not cheap. But it's an exclusive place and the fixtures need to reflect that.

At the country club, we pick up the new valves. These will show us how big a hole to cut in the new slab of marble. Then the caretaker asks us to check out the ugly new noise in the boiler room. It's coming from a small booster pump on the hot-water line, the sound of electric bees buzzing.

McMahon unscrews the control box. "If you watch, when I push one of these contacts, that should spin. Just don't stay in line in case it throws something in your face. Ready?"

A job! Yes, boss! He throws the switch.

"I can't tell, let me see the flashlight."

"Now?"

"Yeah, it's spinning."

He's puzzled. He pokes at the booster pump with his screwdriver. "Interesting." The pause stretches on. Then he nods. "It's motoring."

Other pumps in the system send water through this booster pump at just enough oomph to make it spin at a particular speed, he explains. It's starting and stopping so fast, it creates a frequency, like playing an instrument. So it makes an ugly noise. But there's nothing wrong.

What do you do? Replace the pump, which is worth a couple grand? "We could try the old standby."

"Squirting it with oil?"

Yes, mosquito. But the WD-40 doesn't work. So he puzzles some more, going into the same staring-at-the-wall focus I've seen from famous scientists, movie directors, and Buddhist monks. Maybe it's the starter motor, he says. That's a centrifugal device. You got your shaft and a plastic gizmo with a couple of weights and when it gets up to speed, the weights centrifuge out and pull this gizmo back and the column moves this starting switch, which opens these contacts and makes the green spark you see. "The thing is, when it closes down, the starting switch comes back in, and it's not unusual that they squeak a little bit because they're slowing down."

He tinkers with his little red screwdriver and the sound stops.

Now, in his workshop, the real job begins. He puts the piece of marble on the plywood bench and studies it for a long time. "You've got to look at things," he says.

"What for?"

"Whatever it wants to tell you."

It's off-white, polished. The back is rough and notched to fit into the wall. Outside of that, it doesn't seem to be saying much.

He digs a new valve out of its box and starts eyeballing huge drill bits, actually pieces of pipe with diamond teeth. The five-inch seems a little too small, so he tries a six-inch. It's perfect. Maybe too perfect. But he doesn't have a five-and-a-half-inch bit.

Problem is, the valve is set very deep and the screws don't quite reach. He could put in spacers here and here. Or maybe Kohler has a longer piece.

This is the time and place to figure it out, on the bench. Then you put it in nice and quick and they say, Gee, it only took you fifteen minutes! We paid too much!

He considers the five-inch again.

"I think I'll take a shot," he says.

Setting up the drill and a water trap takes another twenty minutes. I'm able to contribute a little lifting and pushing. Then he trusts me with a job even more important than my previous glorious task of watching for the spinning thing—turning on the drill. While he pulls the handle that cranks the bit down into the slab, he uses his other hand to pour water onto the marble to keep it from overheating. Every so often, he gives a nod and I shut off the power. Then he nods again and I turn it on again.

When the cut is done, the piece fits perfectly. "It's nice and tight, solid, nothing's floating around."

And now, finally, he tells me to pull a piece of that rusted four-inch pipe off the shelf and leads me over to the thread-cutting machine. It's green, about waist high, filled with oily silver pincurls. First he puts in a larger die head to match the pipe, explaining the machine to me. "Notice how that's inclined on an angle? You look at a pipe thread, it's tapered. It's sealed by wedging. You have to be careful. If you go past there when you're cutting the thread, you'll proceed to destroy the machine."

He shows me how to spin the handle to lock the pipe down and points out the speed shift, which ranges between turtle and rabbit. He steps on the go pedal and oil starts to flow over the pipe. "Now we push on it and it has to engage itself. If you look at the other end, you can see the teeth coming up."

Then it's my turn. I load in a fine fat piece of rusted pipe.

"Back up a little bit. Now you straighten this out. Wonderful. Now you're going to lift up the cutter. Bump that pedal a little bit. Keep tightening it. Squeeze the bejesus out of it. Kind of like castrating the testicles off of a steel bull."

Next we must ream it. We do this by spinning a fat diamond-shaped die head in the pipe's steaming wet hole. "So this is reaming," I say.

"All your expressions come from somewhere. Watch the pinch points. Make it spin. You have to do it with great vigor."

It makes a howling noise.

Now it's time to cut the threads. "All right, you have oil. Bring it right down, make contact. You have to give it sufficient force so it can self-feed."

It cuts fast.

"At one time," he says, "the world was put together this way."

The new silver threads gleam in my humble piece of pipe, the foundation of human civilization. Now it can connect to everything.

**Let's Pause Here•••▶** What is your initial reaction to the descriptions of plumbing in Richardson's essay, and how did it go against assumptions that you previously had about the work involved in plumbing? Do you appreciate Richardson's appraisal of McMahon? How does Richardson represent McMahon to us, and do you think it is an objective (nonbiased) representation? What questions would you ask McMahon if given the opportunity?

**Let's Take It Further•••▼**

1. Do you feel that it is appropriate for Richardson to paint McMahon as a prophet of sorts? In what ways is McMahon a prophet, and how does he instill his knowledge in his disciples?

2. What is your favorite tidbit of McMahon wisdom, and why?

3. To whom is Richardson appealing with his article, taking into account where it was originally published, as well as the descriptions and writing strategies he employs? How effective is he at reaching his target audience, and how might he make the piece more accessible? Is this only of interest to working-class people, or is there a message here that can be taken

away by someone who does not work in a trade or belong to the working class? What might that message be?

4. Based on Richardson's essay title and the explanation he gives over the course of his piece, do you understand how pipes "make civilization possible"? In what way do they make civilization possible? And how does this change your understanding of the importance of plumbing to our everyday lives?

5. McMahon argues that plumbing is responsible for a "whole host of miracles" and then lists several examples from our daily lives. Do you agree that plumbing provides us with many modern miracles, and can you think of other examples that show the importance of plumbing?

6. Why do you think that Richardson repeatedly points out McMahon's other accomplishments (such as the idea that McMahon built his house, "didn't sign a paper with a contractor, built it") throughout the article? How do you think he's trying to influence his readers with these sorts of comments? Would you say that he is successful in what he seeks to accomplish?

7. Locate and interview a person who practices a vocation or trade often ignored, misunderstood, or underappreciated. With the person's permission, accompany him or her on a day of work as he or she goes about his or her job and profile the person in the same manner in which Richardson profiles McMahon. Be sure to have a prepared set of questions and to take notes throughout the process. In the end, describe the experience, explaining the ways in which it was different from or similar to what you expected. Why is this particular line of work important to our daily lives? What else about life can be learned from working in this field?

8. Research some other trade or vocation and give the history of the particular trade you have chosen. Next, explain how it has helped to advance civilization, and list examples of everyday conveniences for which we have your chosen vocation to thank. Finally, describe the current state of the trade you have chosen. Is the number of practitioners dwindling or growing? Is it a field that you would consider working in yourself (or recommend to a peer)? Why or why not?

9. Do you believe that Richardson's respect for McMahon is earned? What, in particular, does McMahon do over the course of the interview that warrants Richardson's respect and awe? Would you have reacted in a similar way, or would you have reacted differently? Based on your knowledge of a particular trade, do you think Richardson does justice to McMahon and the types of men he represents? Why or why not?

10. Compose an essay, accompanied by a video or image presentation, that illustrates a vocation often overlooked or misunderstood by popular culture at large. How has the vocation that you've chosen been misrepresented in popular culture and mass media? In what ways has it been shown to be simpler or less meaningful (or important) than it actually is? Include in your essay and presentation an accurate representation of the vocation in a similar manner as Richardson employs in his essay.

# mash it UP

Here is a series of essay and discussion topics that draw connections between multiple selections within the chapter. They also suggest outside texts to include in your essay or discussion. Feel free to bring in further outside texts, remembering the variety of texts (beyond articles) available to you.

1. Compare Ehrenreich's essay (or book) "Nickel-and-Dimed" to the best-selling book *Waiter Rant*. Which of the two better captures the plight of waiting tables for low-wage work? Which of the two makes a better case for how waiters are mistreated by customers and/or managers?

2. How do the essays "Usury Country" and "Nickel-and-Dimed" work together to shed light on the growing low-wage working class? Which of the two provides realistic alternatives for low-wage work? What solutions can you construct as an answer to the dilemma of working-class people featured in both articles?

3. Much of "The Tao of Plumbing" seeks to shed light on the realities of a job that most people perceive as simply "dirty." This is also the premise behind the show *Dirty Jobs* on the Discovery Channel. Watch an episode of *Dirty Jobs* and compare your preconceived notions of the job being featured to the realities of the job, as illustrated on the TV show. Was the job better or worse than you expected? Did you manage to find something valuable for society about the job that you hadn't realized prior to being exposed to it?

4. How have the roles of the working class and those who manage them changed in recent years? One commonly mentioned difference is the "income equality gap" that continues to grow between the common worker and those in upper-management positions. Research the current income gap, or some other aspect of worker/boss relations, and explain whether the difference between the two jobs (in terms of pay, number of available positions, qualifications necessary, etc.) has grown more or less significant.

5. The tone of the articles "Usury Country" and "Nickel-and-Dimed" are similar in their negativity—and rightfully so. However, the last selection, "The Tao of Plumbing," has a more reverent (or appreciative) attitude toward the job it is describing. Locate one further article that depicts the negative elements of an undesirable career, and locate one that depicts the positive elements of a career that most people might not consider desirable. Which makes the better case for or against a job, and how does each article achieve this?

6. Using modern popular media (such as movies, TV shows, or websites), explain the depictions of working-class versus upper-class careers in America. Which of the two are better portrayed? What do you think accounts for the way in which one is portrayed as more "real" or desirable?

7. If you had to draw a cartoon (or compose a film or video) that depicts the positive elements of working, what might the piece include? How, specifically, would you show a particular job in order to make it seem appealing to people? Conversely, if you have to depict the downside of a particular job or career, in what way would you illustrate its negatives? Which of the two would you hope your audience would appreciate more?

8. Locate and dissect payday lending ads online (both print and video). In what ways do payday lending advertisements compare to other forms of advertisement discussed in the chapter on "Advertising and Shopping"? How, for instance, do payday lenders address particular marketing niches, or subpopulations in the United States? Judging from payday lending ads, who is the target audience, and how do the ads appeal to the primary customer base? Do you find that the ads misrepresent the reality of payday lending, as outlined in "Usury Country," or do you think the ads accurately represent the companies who commissioned them? Why or why not?

**Let's Connect •••▶**   "Like" our Facebook page for free, up-to-date, additional readings, discussions, and writing ideas on the topics of work and careers. Join other students and teachers across the country sharing in an online discussion of popular culture events. *American Mashup* is on Facebook at www.facebook.com/americanmashup.

# Credits

## Text Credits

## Photo Credits

# Index

**607**